ALL THE
PRESIDENTS'
BANKERS

Also by

NOMI PRINS

*Other People's Money: The Corporate
Mugging of America* (**2004**)

*Jacked: How "Conservatives" Are Picking Your Pocket
(Whether You Voted for Them or Not)* (**2006**)

*It Takes a Pillage: An Epic Tale of Power, Deceit,
and Untold Trillions* (**2009**)

Black Tuesday: A Novel (**2011**)

ALL THE PRESIDENTS' BANKERS

THE HIDDEN ALLIANCES
THAT DRIVE AMERICAN POWER

— NOMI PRINS —

NATION
BOOKS
New York

Published by Nation Books, A Member of the Perseus Books Group
116 East 16th Street, 8th Floor
New York, NY, 10003

Nation Books is a co-publishing venture of the Nation Institute and the Perseus
Books Group.

Books published by Nation Books are available at special discounts for
bulk purchases in the United States by corporations, institutions, and other
organizations. For more information, please contact the Special Markets
Department at the Perseus Books Group, 2300 Chestnut Street, Suite 200,
Philadelphia, PA, 19103, or call (800) 810-4145, ext. 5000, or e-mail special
.markets@perseusbooks.com.

Designed by Pauline Brown
Typeset in 11 point Minion Pro by the Perseus Books Group

Library of Congress Cataloging-in-Publication Data

Prins, Nomi.
    All the presidents' bankers : the hidden alliances that drive American power
/ Nomi Prins.
        pages   cm
    Includes bibliographical references and index.
    ISBN 978-1-56858-749-3 (hardback)—ISBN 978-1-56858-491-1 (electronic)
    1.   United States—Politics and government—20th century.   2.   United
States—Politics and government—2001–2009.   3.   United States—Politics
and government—2009–   4.   Bankers—Political activity—United States—
History—20th century.   5.   Bankers—Political activity—United States—
History—21st century.   6.   Presidents—United States—History—20th
century. 7.   Presidents—United States—History—21st century.   8.   Power
(Social sciences)—United States—History. 9. Alliances—Political aspects—
United States—History.   10.   United States—Economic policy.   I.   Title.
E743.P74 2013
332.10973'0904—dc23

                                                                        2013036297

10   9   8   7   6   5   4   3   2

CONTENTS

Cast of Main Characters   *ix*

Preface   *xv*

INTRODUCTION   When the President Needed the Bankers   1

CHAPTER 1   The Early 1910s: Post-Panic Creature
            and Party Posturing   17

CHAPTER 2   The Mid-1910s: Bankers Go to War   40

CHAPTER 3   The Late 1910s: Peace Treaties and
            Domestic Politics   57

CHAPTER 4   The 1920s: Political Isolationism,
            Financial Internationalism   69

CHAPTER 5   1929: The Room at 23 Wall, Crash,
            and Big-Six Take   96

CHAPTER 6   The Early 1930s: Tenuous Times,
            Tax-Evading Titans   105

CHAPTER 7   The Mid- to Late 1930s: Policing
            Wall Street, World War II   135

CHAPTER 8   The Early to Mid-1940s: World War II,
            Bankers, and War Bucks   158

CHAPTER 9   The Late 1940s: World Reconstruction
            and Private Bankers   180

CHAPTER 10   The 1950s: Eisenhower's Buds,
Cold War, Hot Money   196

CHAPTER 11   The Early 1960s: "Go-Go" Youth,
Murders, and Global Finance   229

CHAPTER 12   The Mid- to Late 1960s: Progressive
Policies and Bankers' Economy   251

CHAPTER 13   The Early to Mid-1970s: Corruption,
Gold, Oil, and Bankruptcies   274

CHAPTER 14   The Late 1970s: Inflation, Hostages,
and Bankers   301

CHAPTER 15   The Early to Mid-1980s: Free-Market
Rules, Bankers Compete   319

CHAPTER 16   The Late 1980s: Third World Staggers,
S&Ls Implode   340

CHAPTER 17   The Early to Mid-1990s: Killer Instinct,
Bank Wars, and the Rise of Goldman Sachs   357

CHAPTER 18   The Late 1990s: Currency Crises and
Glass-Steagall Demise   377

CHAPTER 19   The 2000s: Multiple Crises, the New
Big Six, and Global Catastrophe   393

Glossary of Financial Terms   425
Acknowledgments   431
Notes   433
Index   503

ON THE MORNING OF MARCH 4, 1933, SECRETARY *Hyde produced an account of two bankers involved in the Depression. He recounted that one of them, unshaven, hungry, his shirt gone, approached a circus manager for a job, saying he would do anything just for something to eat. The manager told him that he was not even able to feed his present employees, and that he had already killed the lion to feed the tigers. Just then an employee approached and said the gorilla had died of starvation, upon which the manager exclaimed in desperation, "This is the finish." Thereupon, the unquenchable, enterprising spirit of the banker came into action, and he proposed they skin the gorilla; he would get into the skin and perform provided he had a square meal and a cut in on the receipts. While he was performing in his cage, the lion in the next compartment pulled open the bars between them and made for him ferociously. The gorilla cried desperately for help. Whereupon the lion whispered in his ear, "Shut up, you fool, you are not the only banker out of a job."*[1]

CAST OF MAIN CHARACTERS

Bankers

Winthrop Aldrich: President of Chase, 1930–1934. Chairman of Chase, 1934–1953. Banker most publicly supportive of Glass-Steagall Act. Allied with FDR and Truman. Ambassador to Britain under Eisenhower.

Henry Alexander: Chairman of the Morgan Guaranty Trust Company Bank, 1959–1967. Chairman of J. P. Morgan Bank, 1950–1959. Allied with Eisenhower.

Samuel Armacost: Chairman of Bank of America, 1981–1986. Allied with Reagan.

George Baker Sr.: Cofounder and leader of the First National Bank, 1863–1931 (though after 1913, his son George Baker Jr. was more involved running the bank).

Lloyd Blankfein: Chairman and CEO of Goldman Sachs, 2006–present.

W. Randolph Burgess: Vice chairman of National City Bank, 1938–1952. Roles up through vice president at Federal Reserve Bank of New York (New York Fed), 1919–1938. Head of NATO, 1956–1962.

Willard Butcher: Chairman of Chase, 1980–1991.

George Champion: Chairman of Chase, 1961–1969.

A. W. Clausen: President and CEO of BankAmerica Corporation, 1970–1981. Chairman of Bank of America, 1986–1990. President of the World Bank, 1981–1986. Allied with Carter and Reagan.

Jamie Dimon: Chairman of JPMorgan Chase, 2004–present. Class A director of New York Fed, 2007–2012. Received $23 million package in 2011, more than any other bank CEO.

Thomas Gates: Chairman and CEO of Morgan Guaranty Trust Company, 1965–1976. Secretary of defense under Eisenhower.

A. P. Giannini: West Coast–based founder of Bank of America. Allied with Truman's Treasury secretary, John Snyder.

Gabriel Hauge: Chairman of Manufacturers Hanover, 1970–1979. Eisenhower's lead economic adviser.

Thomas Labrecque: Chairman and CEO of Chase Manhattan Bank, 1990–1996.

Thomas Lamont: Partner, then acting head of J. P. Morgan Bank, 1911–1943. Chairman of J. P. Morgan & Company, 1943–1948. Worked closely with Wilson on the Treaty of Versailles and promoted the League of Nations. Also allied with Hoover and FDR.

Russell Leffingwell: Chairman of the J. P. Morgan Bank, 1948–1955. Assistant secretary of the Treasury under Wilson. Also allied with FDR and Truman.

Ken Lewis: Chairman and CEO of Bank of America, 2001–2009.

John McCloy: Chairman of Chase, 1953–1960. Chairman of Council on Foreign Relations, 1953–1970. President of the World Bank, 1947–1949. Assistant secretary of war during FDR years. US high commissioner to Germany, 1949–1952. Served on Warren Commission after JFK assassination. Involved with "Seven Sisters" oil companies.

Hugh McColl: Chairman and CEO of Bank of America (having engineered its merger with NationsBank and many others), 1983–2001. Allied with Clinton.

Charles Mitchell: Chairman of National City Bank, 1929–1933. Allied with Coolidge.

George Moore: President of First National City Bank, 1959–1967. Chairman of National City Bank, 1967–1970. Mentor to Walter Wriston.

Jack "J. P." Morgan (J. P. Morgan Jr.): Head of the Morgan Bank, 1913–1943. Allied with Wilson for war financing effort in World War I. Supported FDR.

John Pierpont "J. P." Morgan: Head of the Morgan Bank, 1893–1913. Sponsored Jekyll Island meeting in 1910. Butted heads with Theodore Roosevelt over trustbusting.

James "Jim" Perkins: Chairman of National City Bank, 1933–1940. Ally of FDR and proponent of Glass-Steagall Act.

Rudolph Peterson: President and CEO of Bank of America, 1963–1969.

John Reed: Chairman of Citicorp and postmerger Citigroup, 1984–2000. Protégé of Walter Wriston. Allied with Carter, George H. W. Bush, and Clinton.

Gordon Rentschler: Chairman of National City Bank, 1940–1948. Allied with Truman.

David Rockefeller: Chairman of Chase, 1969–1981. Chairman of Council on Foreign Relations, 1970–1985. Allied with (and adversary of) JFK. Also allied with LBJ, Nixon, and Ford. Allied and clashed with Carter on Iran hostage situation after pushing for the Shah to enter the United States.

James Stillman Rockefeller: Chairman of National City Bank, 1959–1967 (joined the bank in 1930). Allied with Eisenhower.

John D. Rockefeller: Founder with his brother, William Rockefeller, and head of the Standard Oil Company (1870–1897). With William, also formed a financial alliance with National City Bank.

James Stillman: President of National City Bank, 1891–1908. Remained chairman of the bank until 1918. Early proponent of international banking expansion. Allied with the Rockefeller brothers and Wilson.

John Thain: Goldman Sachs copresident, 1999–2004. President of the New York Stock Exchange, 2004–2007. Head of Merrill Lynch, 2007–2009.

Frank Vanderlip: Vice president, then president, of National City Bank, 1909–1919. Assistant secretary of the Treasury under McKinley. Worked with Nelson Aldrich on Aldrich plan. Early friend of Wilson, later distant.

Dennis Weatherstone III: Chairman of J. P. Morgan (and knighted by Queen Elizabeth in 1990), 1990–1994. Advocate for dialing back Glass-Steagall.

Sandy Weill: Chairman of Citigroup, 2000–2006. Orchestrated final push to repeal Glass-Steagall after career of acquisitions that pushed its boundaries.

Sidney Weinberg: Leader of Goldman Sachs, 1930–1969. Helped finance FDR's election. Close to FDR, Truman, Eisenhower, JFK, LBJ, and Nixon.

George Whitney: Chairman of the Morgan Bank, 1950–1955. Joined Morgan in 1915. Progressive banker, allied with Eisenhower.

Albert "Al" Wiggin: Chairman of Chase, 1917–1933. Helped establish the Bank for International Settlements in 1930.

Walter Wriston: Chairman of National City Bank (which was renamed Citicorp/Citibank in 1974), 1970–1984. Allied with LBJ, Nixon, and Ford.

Attendees at the Jekyll Island meeting in 1910 where the Aldrich plan (Federal Reserve core) was created:

Nelson Aldrich: Rhode Island senator. Allied with J. P. Morgan, the Rockefellers, and President Taft.

Abraham Piatt Andrew: Assistant secretary of the Treasury.

Henry Davison: Senior partner at J. P. Morgan.

Benjamin Strong: Head of J. P. Morgan Bankers Trust Company. Later served as first head of New York Fed.

Frank Vanderlip: (Noted earlier, in Bankers.)

Paul Warburg: Partner in Kuhn, Loeb & Company. Representative of Rothschild banking dynasty in England and France. Later appointed by Wilson to Federal Reserve Board.

The Original 1929 "Big Six"

George Baker Jr.: Vice chairman, First National Bank

Thomas Lamont: Acting head of the Morgan Bank

Charles Mitchell: Chairman, National City Bank

William Potter: President, Guaranty Trust Company

Seward Prosser: Chairman, Bankers Trust Company

Albert Wiggin: Chairman, Chase National Bank

Key Political Officials

Nelson Aldrich: Rhode Island senator, 1881–1911. Head of National Monetary Commission, 1908–1911. Integrated with Rockefeller family through progeny.

Ben Bernanke: Chairman of the Federal Reserve, 2006–2013.

C. Douglas Dillon: Treasury secretary, 1961–1965. Chairman of the Rockefeller Foundation, 1972–1975.

Henry "Joe" Fowler: Treasury secretary, 1965–1968. Partner at Goldman Sachs, 1969–1999.

Timothy Geithner: President of the New York Fed, 2003–2009. Treasury secretary, 2009–2013.

Carter Glass: US representative from Virginia, 1902–1919. Senator, 1920–1946. Led Senate committee to adopt plan that became the Federal Reserve Act. Treasury secretary, 1918–1920, coauthor Glass-Steagall Act.

Alan Greenspan: Chairman of the Federal Reserve, 1987–2006. Major proponent and enabler of banking deregulation.

Colonel Edward House: Friend, confidant, and unofficial adviser to Wilson.

George Humphrey: Treasury secretary, 1953–1957. Honorary board chairman of the McHanna Company, 1957–1969.

Jack Lew: Director of the Office of Management and Budget, 1998–2001, 2010–2012. Citigroup banker, 2006–2008. Treasury secretary, 2013–present.

William Gibbs McAdoo: Son-in-law of Wilson. Treasury secretary, 1913–1918.

Gates McGarrah: First chairman of New York Fed, 1925–1930. Executive Committee chairman of Chase, 1926–1930. First head of Bank for International Settlements, 1930–1933.

Andrew William Mellon: Treasury secretary, 1921–1932. Prominent banker, industrialist, philanthropist, and art collector.

Henry Morgenthau: Treasury secretary, 1934–1945.

Henry "Hank" Paulson: CEO and chairman of Goldman Sachs, 1999–2006. Treasury secretary, 2006–2009.

Donald Regan: Treasury secretary, 1981–1985. Chief of staff, 1985–1987. Chairman of Merrill Lynch, 1971–1980.

Robert Rubin: Cochairman of Goldman Sachs, 1990–1992. Treasury secretary, 1995–1999. First director of National Economic Council, 1993–1995. Often appeared before Congress on behalf of banking deregulation. Joined Citigroup in October 1999, after Glass-Steagall repeal was passed by the Senate. Chairman of Citigroup, November 4–December 11, 2007. Chairman of Council of Foreign Relations, 2007–present.

John Snyder: Longtime friend to Truman. Treasury secretary, 1946–1953. First president of the National Advisory Council to International Monetary Fund (IMF) and World Bank, 1946–1953.

George Shultz: Treasury secretary, 1982–1989. Executive vice president, then president, at Bechtel, 1974–1982. Rejoined as adviser in 1989.

Larry Summers: Treasury secretary, 1999–2001. Present at signing of Gramm-Leach-Bliley Act, which killed Glass-Steagall.

Paul Volcker: Chairman of the Federal Reserve, 1979–1987. Vice president at Chase, 1957–1962, 1965–1969. Undersecretary of monetary affairs in Treasury Department, 1963–1965, 1969–1974.

PREFACE

THE IDEA FOR *ALL THE PRESIDENTS' BANKERS* CAME TO ME WHILE I WAS WRITING A historical novel called *Black Tuesday,* which follows the events leading up to the Crash of 1929 through the eyes of an immigrant girl who crosses paths with the bankers of the House of Morgan.

The book contains a scene based on a real meeting of the period's most powerful bankers that took place on Black Thursday. With the markets in chaos, Thomas Lamont, acting head of the Morgan Bank while Jack Morgan was in Britain, summoned the leaders of the five other major banks, most of which were intricately linked to Morgan through social and business connections. Collectively the "Big Six," as they were dubbed, took less than half an hour to decide to pool their banks' money to save the markets—and themselves—from their own recklessness and fraudulent behavior.

Fast-forward to the financial crisis of 2008. The prelude to the global debacle was similar, as the chapters on the 1920s and 1930s reveal. The men and their instruments of financial destruction were different only in certain specifics paralleling the complexity and technology of the times. More recently, though, it was the federal government and Federal Reserve that bailed out these top bankers in epic ways. Again, six main bankers steered the process. Most of them represented the corporate lineage of the bankers from that earlier meeting in October 1929. I became fascinated with their evolution.

But the impact of those Big Six on America stretched back even further.

These men also had ties to bankers from the late 1880s, especially J. P. Morgan, who expanded his fortune then. They participated in the Panic of 1907; they or their representatives met at Jekyll Island to create the Federal Reserve, which would back them in future panics; and they financed, and profited from, World War I.

Between the Crash of 1929 and 2008, these bankers reigned over America as monarchical rather than democratically elected leaders. Through the Great Depression, World War II, the establishment of the World Bank and IMF, the Cold War, and the financial and military expansion of the United States, Wall Street and the White House collaborated to shape national policy. To this day these elite bankers drive our financial systems, even if the men who rise to the top of their firms and dominate politics in any given period are largely interchangeable.

The political and financial alliances between bankers and presidents and their cabinets defined, and continue to define, the policies and laws that drive the economy. My research shows that the revolving doors between public and private service weren't created in the 1980s, as many more recent works claim. They were always present.

I approached this project from two angles. For each president and Treasury secretary, I noted the six biggest bankers of the time (for the most part the number of significant political ties trailed off after that point) and cross-referenced them with the six banks whose legacies snaked through that Morgan Bank meeting in October 1929. In most cases, the top six bankers of the time were related to the men in that room and possessed broad alliances with the presidents and their teams. I examined archival connections and correspondence to determine the nature of their alliances. In some periods, only one or two bankers dominated the alliances and had the most influence, just as some firms seemed to corner the market at certain times.

All the Presidents' Bankers is a story of relationships between powerful men; it is the financial political history of America, and it reveals not only how these alliances shaped America's domestic and foreign policy but also, by extension, how America's bankers shaped the world, and America's position as a superpower.

Between the 1930s and 1960s, the bankers who most influenced presidents were on close personal terms with them. They influenced policy to suit themselves, to be sure; but in the postwar world, that worked well for the population.

In the 1970s, the nature of these alliances changed. Bankers now had a fresh source of power: the ability to "recycle" Middle East petrodollars and expand into Latin America. The memories of the war and the Depression, and the sense of public spirit, had receded. By the 1970s, bankers like David Rockefeller and Walter Wriston were pushing presidents Nixon and Carter to do their bidding absent the kind of authentic personal ties that bound former bankers to former presidents.

This more selfish stance solidified through the 1980s and 1990s, when the notion of US banks being "competitive" with strengthening European and Japanese banks paved the way for a spate of banking deregulation and enhanced banker power that extends through today. Personal connections became merely opportunistic ones. Democratic president Bill Clinton and Republican president George W. Bush selected Goldman CEOs (in the form of Robert Rubin and Hank Paulson, respectively) to run the Treasury Department and network with the private bankers. Lobbyists and lawyers interacted more frequently with administration staff. Campaign donations took the place of discourse about issues (though results of policy decisions might have been the same anyway).

As for the archival records, all of the National Archives and Records Administration libraries for FDR through Carter have exceedingly accessible and well-organized information with consistent classifications. They were a pleasure to peruse, and I lost myself for days in all of them. After Reagan took office, records became less available. At the Clinton library in Little Rock, Arkansas, I learned that some records may never be uncovered without the benefit of Freedom of Information Act (FOIA) requests, not merely for "national security reasons" (as years go on, the number of redactions in documents rise anyway) but because the commitment to organize such a vast amount of material is not what it was before the 1980s. As such, the bulk of information that might be revealed by the FOIA requests that I filed at the Reagan, George H. W. Bush, and Clinton libraries is not available yet.

What remains to be examined by some curious person years from now is the nature of George W. Bush's and Barack Obama's relationships with the leading bankers of their day. We may never know the specifics of the discussions that were conducted; bankers don't put much in writing anymore, and there have been no tapes of White House conversations since Nixon. But we can be sure of one thing: those bankers and their firms are the financial descendants of the men at that Morgan meeting in 1929, and decades from now they still will be. On this, history is clear.

INTRODUCTION:
WHEN THE PRESIDENT
NEEDED THE BANKERS

"This country has nothing to fear
from the crooked man who fails. We put him in jail.
It is the crooked man who succeeds who is a threat to this country."
—President Theodore Roosevelt, 1905

BY THE END OF THE NINETEENTH CENTURY, THE TITANS OF BANKING WERE replacing the barons of industry as the beacons of economic supremacy in the United States. Some of the men who epitomized this transformation straddled both industry and banking. Others relied exclusively on their position within the financial arena. The shift would have a profound and irrevocable impact on America's future. New lines of power would be drawn, both within the country and beyond its borders. The modern age of financial capitalism had begun.

In this new paradigm, the White House would find itself operating in a more integrated manner with the most powerful bankers. On the way to that eventuality, President Theodore Roosevelt and the nation's top financier, John Pierpont (J. P.) Morgan, would engage in a battle of wills and egos to stake their respective claims.

Though the twentieth century would be dubbed "The American Century"—reflecting the nation's political and economic dominance, marked by the two-decade-long Progressive Era of social reforms and constitutional amendments—its early years also unleashed an epoch of enhanced political-financial alliances between Washington and Wall Street. Codependencies and tensions between the two spheres of authority would define not only the nation's domestic agenda but also its identity as an emerging financial and global superpower.

The domestic power game emanated from the railways, an industry cultivated by the country's richest barons. Though railroad companies constituted the majority of issues on stock and bond markets, industrial companies like US Steel, International Harvester, and General Electric were gaining ground. Meanwhile, the banking sector was evolving from a business predicated on lending for production and expansion purposes to one predicated on the consolidation, distribution, and packaging of capital for its own sake. As making money became more important than making products, control of America's direction shifted to a smaller group of elite financiers.

These early twentieth-century bankers were not simply focused on creating wealth, either; they were also interested in manufacturing "influence capital." The manner in which they dictated the behavior of money rivaled the way the government directed the country. Late 1890s economic crises had revealed that the Morgan Bank (J. P. Morgan & Company) held more money and gold than the Treasury Department. As the need for money became more critical, the men who controlled that money became that much more powerful. (Today, the Morgan Bank is a component of JPMorgan Chase, the nation's largest bank.)

Morgan controlled nearly 70 percent of the steel industry—following the creation of US Steel in 1901—and at least one-fifth of all corporations trading on the New York Stock Exchange.[1] His power intensified when the railroad industry began to crumble under the weight of too much speculation at the turn of the twentieth century. Like a hawk to a kill, he swept in to break up and then reconstruct the industry. In the process, he extended loans to any participants left standing. Desperate businessmen eagerly accepted his harsh terms.

Another major financial player convert was billionaire John D. Rockefeller. From 1886 to 1899, annual profits in Rockefeller's Standard Oil Company, one of the world's preeminent industrial companies, tripled from $15 million to $45 million. Such a gush of cash now required a place from which to spawn greater wealth, and the very seeking of such capital catapulted its accumulators to greater levels of influence. As Matthew Joseph-son wrote in his classic book *The Robber Barons*, "It became inevitable that the Standard Oil men make reinvestments regularly and extensively in new enterprises, which were to be carried on under their absentee ownership . . . [as] John D. Rockefeller announced his 'retirement' from active business."[2]

In conjunction with James Stillman, the formidable president of the Na-tional City Bank of New York (the largest US bank in terms of assets, which referred to itself as "The American Bank" and which has since morphed into Citigroup),[3] Rockefeller began investing in banks, insurance companies, cop-per, steel, railroads, and public utilities.[4] His brother, William, had met Still-man while William was a director of the Chicago, Milwaukee & St. Paul Rail Company, and the two had become close.[5] The Rockefeller brothers saw the business of capital production as a means to enhance their status. Stillman's bank proved a more natural fit for their aspirations than the rival Morgan bank, though the Rockefellers would also dominate the evolution of another major bank, the Chase National Bank (which, in turn, would also morph into JPMorgan Chase).

The Stillman-Rockefeller alliance ensured that "the City Bank" became known as the "Standard Oil bank."[6] Solidifying the business union, William's son, William Goodsell Rockefeller, married Stillman's daughter, Elsie Still-man, in 1902. The couple produced future National City Bank chair James Stillman Rockefeller.[7] The social and matrimonial elements of family part-nerships in the early part of the twentieth century thus served to fortify the industrial families' evolution into the financial realm.

The Panic of 1893 had triggered the collapse of lesser railroads, enabling Stillman, William Rockefeller, Edward Henry (E. H.) Harriman, and finan-cier Jacob Schiff to take control of one of the largest railroad companies, Union Pacific. Whereas the notion of a railroad trust, or combination of companies, had already emerged, these men constituted one of the two bur-geoning Wall Street "money trusts." Their elite group consisted of the Rocke-feller family, Union Pacific, Standard Oil, and the Wall Street firm of Kuhn, Loeb & Company under Schiff.

The other group—or "inner group," as it would be known—was the dom-inant Wall Street alliance. It pivoted around Morgan and included empire builders like Great Northern Railway CEO James Hill and George Baker Sr., a prominent society man who served as head of the First National Bank (which later became part of Citigroup). Stillman wisely chose to belong to both groups.

In his pathbreaking study of financial oligarchy in America, *Other People's Money*, preeminent Boston lawyer and future Supreme Court Justice Louis

Brandeis[8] stated that "the power of the investment banker over other people's money is often more direct and effective than that exerted through controlled banks and trust companies. . . . This is accomplished by the simple device of becoming the bank of deposits of the controlled corporations."[9] In other words, the more money a bank controls, the more power it can wield.

Within the financial sector, Morgan acted as a welder, craftily merging the greatest banks, trusts, and insurance companies into a single construct, "a solid pyramid at whose apex he sat."[10] Through stock ownership and interlocking directorates, Morgan spread his control across the First National Bank, National City Bank, the Hanover Bank, the Liberty Bank and Trust, Chase National Bank, and the nation's major insurance companies.

The three main insurance companies in Morgan's orbit were the New York Life, the Equitable, and the Mutual. Connections ran both ways. George Perkins, head of New York Life, was concurrently a vice president and partner at the Morgan Bank.[11] Together, these firms owned approximately $1 billion of assets by 1900. Controlling the domains of investment banking and insurance, Morgan, Perkins, and Baker could easily increase their wealth. Their insurance companies bought the securities (such as stocks and bonds) that they created as investment bankers. This circle of fabricated demand enticed outside investors to purchase their securities at higher prices. The trio then reinvested the profits as deposits, providing their banks with additional capital for similar activity.[12]

To monopolize the capital markets, National City Bank, First National Bank, and the Morgan Bank had an agreement that "on any issue of securities originated by any one of the three, the originating house was to have 50 [percent] and each of the other two was to have 25 [percent]."[13] In addition, these three major banks underwrote and accepted the deposits for many other nonfinancial businesses.

Another aspect of the cozy union among various titans of the financial sector was their propensity for meeting beyond the geographical confines of New York City. Equitable Life Assurance Society of the United States head Henry Hyde and Morgan shared an apartment complex on Jekyll Island, Georgia, the retreat of the nation's ultra-elite, where the two men could carve up the financial world away from the fray, while basking in the luxury of ocean views.[14]

Additionally, in keeping with his distinction as the world's main global banker, Morgan's reputation in Europe helped elevate his position in America. (It would later help elevate America's position over Europe after World War I.) European investors were major buyers of American stocks and bonds and coveted anything with Morgan's name on it. That support dated back to 1890, when the venerable Barings banking house nearly folded after a disastrous gamble on Argentinian bonds. While most London firms ignored its calls of distress, the Bank of England turned to Morgan to rescue Barings.[15] The bailout fostered a lasting international relationship.

Four years later, Morgan was called upon to save the United States from bankruptcy. And in 1899, Treasury Secretary Lyman Gage was forced to borrow $50 million from Morgan Bank to purchase foreign gold to sustain the nation's financial well-being. Congress later attacked Morgan's egregious terms as being "extortionate and unpatriotic."[16] But at the time he was considered a hero for providing them. It was one of many examples of Morgan's skills at soliciting other people's money to bolster his stature. Even in that instance, according to James Stillman, Morgan had approached him for the money to loan, on the verge of tears, "greatly upset and over-charged." Stillman cabled Europe for $10 million worth of Standard Oil gold and $10 million more from other sources, which he delivered to Morgan. It was Morgan who took all the credit, and in doing so he consolidated his position of influence.[17]

Trustbusting, White House Power–Defining Teddy Roosevelt

When Roosevelt made the unprecedented decision to use executive authority to "bust" the powerful trusts, he positioned the action as one that would help the country at large. He was not against big business per se, but he possessed a certain defiance on behalf of the underdog and sought to cultivate what he called a "square deal" for all Americans. He believed in the power of competition, but he believed the playing field had to be fair. He knew that as the trusts grew more powerful and consolidated, the relative power of the government would decline.

This awareness formed an integral part of Roosevelt's legacy. His trust-busting initiative began in 1902, just months after he took office following the assassination of President William McKinley. Roosevelt proved himself to be a formidable politician, attracting support from the business and working classes by positioning himself as a fighter against the "tyranny of wealth" (and not wealth itself), as wielded by the grossly advantaged trust titans, many of whom were his former companions.

Raised in a New York mansion, well traveled, and schooled at an Ivy League university like his would-be adversary (and later ally) J. P. Morgan, Roosevelt held the pedigree of a consummate businessman. But he also possessed a rugged edge and a rebellious streak: he had worked as a rancher in the North Dakota Badlands, and some people said he had the characteristics of a lion.

Roosevelt's use of presidential power to take on the trusts asserted the might of Washington in this new financier-dominated era. Roosevelt directed the Justice Department to pursue an antitrust suit charging the Northern Securities Company with violating the 1890 Sherman Antitrust Act, which prohibits trusts from becoming monopolies. Northern Securities, one of the nation's largest railroad trusts, had been formed by Morgan, Harriman, and Hill in 1901. The president's power play might have been avoided if Morgan had less of an ego. But when Morgan approached Roosevelt privately to settle the matter, Roosevelt decided, "Mr. Morgan could not help regarding me as a big rival operator who either intended to ruin all his interests or could be induced to come to an agreement to ruin none."[18] Morgan ended up just fine with his other interests, though, even after he was directed to break up his key trust.

The Northern Securities case preceded more than forty such lawsuits. In the process, Roosevelt gained enough popular support to win the election of 1904 with 70 percent of the electoral vote. But by 1907, either because he believed he needed Morgan's help to salvage an economic catastrophe or because he wasn't so different philosophically from Morgan after all, Roosevelt wound up doing Morgan's bidding.

Muckrakers, Muck Senators, and Muck Bankers

Congress was also flexing its muscles. Its members were increasingly taking bribes from the leaders of big business in return for favorable legislation. (Today that practice is called campaign financing.) In March 1906, *Cosmopolitan* magazine shed a light on the situation by running a hard-hitting investigative series, "The Treason of the Senate," written by popular novelist David Graham Phillips. William Randolph Hearst, a US House member, had purchased the magazine in 1905 with the goal of enticing readers with juicy stories. Subscriptions doubled within two months of the articles' appearance.

Phillips exposed widespread corruption of the Senate, in particular, by the Standard Oil Company. He revealed that New York senator Chauncey Depew had received more than $50,000 from his "seventy-odd" directorships of companies that wanted him to do their bidding—particularly insurance and railroad companies. Such serious conflicts of interest, though legal, were distasteful to the public.[19] (Many New York senators would finance campaigns on the back of Wall Street money, particularly in the last part of the century.)

Though Roosevelt attacked Morgan's railroad trust and spoke disparagingly of the "tyranny of wealth" and its influence over America, he was less pleased about this skeptical glare placed on Washington. He endorsed "benefactors" to wage attacks against evil with "merciless severity," but he cautioned against "hysterical sensationalism."[20] Roosevelt coined the pejorative term "muckrakers" to describe the new breed of investigative journalists, including Phillips; Upton Sinclair, who exposed the literal rot of the meatpacking industry; and Ida Tarbell, who focused on Standard Oil.

Most illuminating of America's future political-financial path, Phillips's article slammed Rhode Island millionaire businessman turned senator Nelson Aldrich for his connections with the elite. As Phillips wrote, "In 1901, his [Aldrich's] daughter married the only son and destined successor of John D. Rockefeller. Thus, the chief exploiter of the American people is closely allied by marriage with the chief schemer in the service of the exploiters."[21] Aldrich would soon play a more significant role in America's financial capitalism era than Phillips could have imagined. Though Roosevelt had purposefully steered clear of trying to change the nation's currency or banking system, Aldrich would be intricately involved in transforming both.

Muckrakers aside, the liberal and conservative press continued to seek out the bankers' expertise. Though there remained widespread belief in Washington and in the press that after the Panic of 1893 and the subsequent depression, something had to be done to avoid a situation whereby Morgan was called in to save the country again, nothing happened for years in that regard. Roosevelt had no interest in rocking that boat, particularly before the 1904 election. As such, the elite bankers generally, and Morgan in particular, increased their control over the US economy. The results proved disastrous.

The Panic of 1907

By early 1907, the US economy had dipped back into a recession born of a sell-off in the railroad industry and pronounced outflow of gold to Europe. The situation was reminiscent of the brief 1903 market panic, which had been referred to as "the rich man's panic," but this one showed signs of getting much worse. In March 1907, cartoonist Louis Glackens crafted an illustration for *Puck* magazine captioned "He loves me." In it, a woman dressed like Little Bo Peep and labeled "Wall Street" plucks paper petals labeled "Tight Money" and "Easy Money" from a paper flower. Among the petals strewn upon the ground is a medallion stating "In Cortelyou We Trust." Roosevelt's Treasury secretary, George Cortelyou, dressed as an Elizabethan suitor, stands behind the lass brandishing a diamond ring labeled "Treasury Aid."[22] It wasn't too far off from what would transpire six months later, when that aid was funneled through Morgan's banks.

In the wake of what would be called "Roosevelt's Panic," the president left his trustbusting battles aside and approved side deals for Morgan because he believed that doing so would save the country from a "frightful and nation-wide calamity."[23]

The financial panic that struck in October had been brewing through-out the year, but the climax was precipitated by the failed attempt by "copper king" F. Augustus Heinze and notorious speculator Charles Morse to make a killing by cornering the copper market.

By Monday, October 14, 1907, the three Heinze brothers, Morse, and their associates had formed a copper pool to drive up the price of United Copper stock. They succeeded in dramatic fashion and ran the price up $25 in mere minutes. To capitalize on the pricing activity, they ordered all the area bro-kers to deliver any stock held for or owed to them. They assumed they could retrieve their stock certificates, push the price up even higher, and then sell their extra stock at an even greater profit.

But the plan backfired. On Tuesday, brokers turned in so much stock that the Heinze brokerage ran out of cash to pay for it. Brokers dumped all the additional stock on the market on Wednesday, crushing the price from above $60 to below $15 per share.[24]

It could have been an isolated incident, except for one thing. Heinze, Morse, and E. R. Thomas were also directors of the Mercantile National Bank. In fact, Heinze was its president. On Thursday and Friday, depositors started extracting their money. The bank appealed to the Clearing House Association for help. Heinze resigned. The New York Clearing House Asso-ciation insisted the men immediately repay the loans they had received from their various bank interests. But they didn't have the money. So they sold their other securities, causing the entire market to plummet.[25] Fear and sus-picion settled in. Depositors distrusted banks. Banks distrusted one another. The perfect ingredients for a crisis coalesced around those city streets.

Moreover, as in all times of financial uncertainty, money ceased flowing. Scared investors dumped more stock into the declining market to muster up cash. In desperation, the president of the exchange appealed to Morgan, the one man who could halt the financial bloodshed. In response, Morgan formed a pool to supply the needed money. In less than half an hour, the national banks offered up $20 million to increase market liquidity. Stock prices recovered. Catastrophe was averted. The pool made another $50 million available for stock exchange purposes against 50 percent collateral—a steep amount, as stipulated by Morgan, but those strapped for cash had no other choice.[26]

The world seemed momentarily at ease. But it was the calm before the storm. The collapse of confidence in Heinze's banks had unleashed a cancer of general distress. For Morse and Heinze had amassed control of at least eight banks and two trust companies. Though the men were forced to resign from their official banking positions, rumors of unsoundness abounded. Depositors scrambled to withdraw money from all of their affiliated institutions.[27]

The Knickerbocker Trust Company Collapse

By Monday, October 21, depositors were drawing money from the Knickerbocker Trust Company, the city's second-largest trust, with a vengeance. On Tuesday, its president, Charles Barney, was forced to resign due to his affiliations with Morse. But this time, despite assurances from more powerful bankers and another $10 million guarantee from Morgan, the run accelerated.

The type of neighborhood dictated the nature of the run. At Knickerbocker's main office on Fifth Avenue and Thirty-fourth Street, it was reported that "automobiles and carriages drove up to the great white marble building, and handsomely dressed women and prosperous looking men ran up the steps and besieged the payment tellers."[28] At other branches, hundreds of more shabby depositors waited in line to withdraw their money. Harry Hollins, a company director, assisted tellers at 66 Broadway as depositors stretched alongside its colored windows and spilled into the street.[29] Shortly before noon the crowd outside the Harlem branch numbered nearly four hundred. Tellers stacked tall bunches of money on the counters to show strength, but to no avail. Shortly after noon on Tuesday, October 22, the Knickerbocker Trust Company closed the doors of its main office.[30]

The big New York banks responded by protecting themselves and restricting funds for longer-term projects nationally. Banks like California Safe Deposits and Trust of San Francisco went bust. A bicoastal meltdown was developing. The situation degenerated quickly as panic engulfed other trusts. Barney was also a director in the Trust Company of America, whose deposits totaled $67 million. There, heavy withdrawals had already begun. The difference was that this firm had more substantive ties to the major bankers. It was *too big to fail.*

The Hotel Manhattan Meeting

During that tense day, Roosevelt and Cortelyou were "in hourly communication with New York."[31] At midnight, Morgan's secretary dashed into the lobby of the Hotel Manhattan. Only after meeting with the Knickerbocker Trust Company at its Fifth Avenue office did Morgan summon Cortelyou to the hotel at 12:30 A.M.

Minutes later, Morgan and Stillman entered the hotel. Reporters clamored for information as the two titans hurried to the elevator. Upstairs, Cortelyou waited. Morgan's partner, George Perkins, hurried in. Reporters were anxiously awaiting word from the super-bankers when National City vice president Frank Vanderlip appeared. Vanderlip was a former assistant secretary of the Treasury under President McKinley, and he had been a financial journalist in Chicago before that—where he found success doubling as a public relations officer for the banks.[32] Someone especially fit for the situation, he called the reporters together and delivered the verdict.

On behalf of the committee, he stated that the trust companies of New York had united to stand behind the Trust Company of America, "whose assets," he said, "had been examined and found good in every way."[33]

At 1 A.M., Cortelyou announced confidently to the press: "To pass safely through such a day as this one of most unnecessary excitement as it has been, is the best evidence of strength and support on the part of those who've undertaken the difficult task of reestablishing public confidence. . . . As evidence of the Treasury's disposition, I have directed deposits in the city to the extent of twenty-five million dollars."[34] Cortelyou deposited $25 million of public money with the national banks, with the understanding that it would be largely redeposited with the Trust Company of America to stabilize the company.

With renewed vigor, the president of the Trust Company of America declared it would open for business as usual Wednesday morning. Unlike the Knickerbocker Trust Company, which had not garnered similar banker support, the Trust Company of America had been blessed by the sponsorship of the Morgan team.

Depositors remained on edge past midnight. In downtown Manhattan, lines stretched from the front door of the Colonial Branch of the Trust Company of America half a block toward Nassau Street. Some people huddled in doorways at Wall Street and Broadway. Throughout the night, depositors hovered in the rotunda of the main office of the Trust Company of America. More than a hundred crowded inside the building. Larger crowds teemed outside. "Coffee and frankfurters were the only edible things that could be bought, and messenger boys and millionaires alike chased them from the vendors who've reaped the harvest," the *New York Times* reported.[35]

Braving fatigue and chill winds into the early morning hours, a swirl of depositors clamored before the doors of the Dollar Savings Bank and even the closed Knickerbocker Trust Company. When the doors of the Dollar Savings Bank opened, about a thousand people were standing in a line that circled the block. Some depositors were admitted through a rear door at Willis Avenue; a small riot started, and police used nightsticks to restore order.[36]

Many bankers and businessmen visited Morgan the following day, as he allocated some $4 million to the disposal of the Trust Company of America. Cortelyou, stationed at the subtreasury in New York, was kept informed of the happenings but was not present for the dispensations. Those, Morgan controlled.[37]

By Friday, the atmosphere was significantly more subdued. The lines before the Trust Company of America and its Colonial Branch were much shorter than on Thursday and far less than on Wednesday.[38] On Saturday morning, the *New York Times* blared, "The sagacious measures put into effect by the hearty cooperation of secretary Cortelyou and the foremost bankers of the city, headed by J.P. Morgan, brought sterling results again yesterday" and noted "the long stride to the return of public confidence in the city banking institutions."[39]

But Morgan was not finished. On Monday, October 28, he received a visit from the New York City mayor George McClellan Jr.[40] The city needed $30 million for its own survival, having delayed a bond issue that would have raised money while still struggling to find buyers. Swiftly, Morgan, Baker, and Stillman agreed to provide the money, underwriting the bond issue and guaranteeing its sale with the other big banks.

Then, on Tuesday night, a syndicate of bankers and trust presidents headed by Morgan agreed to assist the Trust Company of America, which was still ailing; the Lincoln Trust; and Moore & Schley, a brokerage house run by Baker's brother-in-law that was $25 million in debt.[41]

Morgan held court in the library of his Madison Avenue home to formulate the best course of action. He assembled an informal steering committee of himself, Stillman, and Baker. Benjamin Strong, the young head of the Morgan-owned Bankers Trust, acted as secretary to the committee.[42] Also present was Thomas Lamont, a friend of Strong's who would become the youngest Morgan partner in 1911; he would later rise to run the firm and have a substantive impact on foreign-financial policy during World War I and for decades afterward.

According to Lamont, Morgan demanded that another $25 million loan be made "to save the Trust Company of America."[43] It would come from the healthier trusts, their presidents browbeaten by Morgan. He instructed his lawyers to create a "simple subscription blank" that he waved at the group, saying, "There you are, gentlemen."[44] They all signed. Such was his influence over the banking contingent.

Part of the bailout included the purchase of a majority stake held by Moore & Schley in the Tennessee Coal and Iron Company by its main rival and Morgan creation US Steel. But the strategy would have to be cleared by President Roosevelt.

And so on Sunday night, Morgan's partners—US Steel magnates Henry Clay Frick and Judge Elbert Gary—boarded a train for Washington to meet with the chief trustbuster himself. Despite potential antitrust violations, Roosevelt acquiesced over breakfast, saying it was "no public duty of his to interpose any objections."[45] The market rallied at the news.

Roosevelt later wrote that during the panic the "Morgan interests were the only interests which retained a full hold on the confidence of the people of New York—not only the business people, but the immense mass of men and women who owned small investments or had small savings in the banks and trust companies." It was on this basis that he approved the side deals on behalf of Morgan.

As he stated, "The action was emphatically for the general good. . . . The panic was stopped. . . . The action itself, at the time when it was taken, was vitally necessary to the welfare of the people of the United States."[46] The lion might have taken on Morgan from a broader economic and rhetorical perspective, but he was in no mood to risk doing so when the stakes were so high—or when he needed Morgan to save his legacy a year before the next election.

Panic Aftermath

Within a few weeks the panic appeared to be over. A 1907 *New York Times* headline, echoing the widespread sentiment that Morgan and his crew had masterfully saved the economy, declared Morgan the "world's central bank." Morgan didn't leave headlines like these to chance any more than he did the chess game of banks. He not only assisted other banks (for a price); in 1896, he had helped the Ochs family buy the *New York Times*.

What the papers didn't report at the time was that Morgan had not saved the day with his money or even with the sum of his compatriots' money. He had parlayed the government's money. As was later divulged in congressional testimony during the Pujo Committee investigation of the money trusts in 1912, the Treasury Department had deposited $39 million in the National Bank of New York at the beginning of the panic week.[47]

That $39 million was deposited without the requirement that any interest be paid on it, and a large part of it was left in Morgan Banks, from where it was loaned to the less powerful banks at substantial rates of interest. Even though $10 million had been designated to directly aid the Trust Company of America, Morgan allocated just $4 million for that purpose. All the while, small businesses around the country were unable to get funds because the "governments' resources were being used to relieve stock gamblers and to assist that Morgan Banks."[48]

The scarcity of money and absence of credit had punishing effects on the country. Banks in small towns continued to limit the money that depositors could extract. Manufacturing centers such as Pittsburgh had difficulty paying employees, as their own banks were hoarding funds, which incensed workers. The West got hammered because of unmet demands for money to pay for crops. Across the country, manufacturing, wholesaling, and retailing were affected by the lack of money flow.[49] The bank panic and tightening of money by the major New York banks had precipitated a national economic depression.

Yet on November 10, 1907, the *New York Times* ran a spread on Morgan titled "John Pierpont Morgan, a Bank in Human Form," glowingly recapping all the tactics he had deployed to keep the financial system from crumbling.[50] But as Fed historian William Greider observed, "Morgan and his allies not only failed to contain the panic of 1907, but were compelled to seek help from Washington."[51]

Indeed, their actions didn't stop the chaos. To stabilize the financial situation, Roosevelt had to order the Treasury to issue another $150 million in low-interest bonds for banks to use as collateral for creating new currency.[52] In the end, the president had his position to think of, and though he chose not to run in the 1908 election, he did not want his party burdened with an economic calamity. In that way, he proved a new rule: the president would work with the bankers when it was politically expedient, as it would be many times in the unfolding century. The government would not, it turned out, risk trying to thwart the titans of finance in times deemed emergencies.

Post-Panic Political Ascension and Alliances

The panic and President Roosevelt's response to it gave rise to a shift in politics. On November 8, 1907, Princeton University president Woodrow

Wilson delivered an address to a packed house at the Goodwyn Institute in Memphis. The auditorium overflowed into the main and gallery lobbies for Wilson's marquee speech: "Ideals of Public Life." Wilson had rejected a potential bid to become New Jersey senator a year earlier, but he was an influential force shaping national discourse. This speech was a pivotal point in his trajectory to becoming president of the United States and helped define the platform of the Democratic Party that he would lead to victory in 1912. It was his gift of speech that would capture and articulate the public's outrage with the wealthy class.[53]

"We live in a very confused time," Wilson said. "The economic developments which have embarrassed our life are of comparably recent origin, and our chief trouble is that we do not exactly know what we are about."[54] Wilson believed that America was at a crossroads, searching for its identity—politically, domestically, and, by extension, internationally. Like Roosevelt, he was convinced that Washington had to change its approach to power. "We no longer know any remedy except to put things in the hands of the government," he said.

Though he conceded this meant turning away from "all the principles which have distinguished America and made her institutions the hope of all men who believe in liberty," the Wall Street upheaval reminded him that the unchecked power of certain individual bankers could hurt the country's overall strength. Something had to be done about it. The answer, Wilson felt, was for the government to take a more active role in shaping the nation's economy.

By that time, Wilson had already come into contact with many major bankers. Morgan's father, Junius Morgan, had served as a trustee at Princeton.[55] One of Wilson's fellow classmates at Princeton was Cleveland Dodge, president of the mining company Phelps Dodge, who had become a director at National City Bank in the 1900s. It was Dodge who introduced Wilson to that bank's leaders, Stillman and Vanderlip. Dodge also paid to keep Wilson at Princeton as president of the university. Reciprocally, the future US president regularly approached Morgan and Vanderlip to help raise funds for the school. In 1909, Morgan donated $5,000 to Princeton and pledged to do so every year for the next five years. Wilson was grateful for the grand financier's support.

Wilson and Vanderlip became friends. They would frequently exchange views on international and economic matters, as was then common in the realm of the elite sphere of intellectual men of opinion. In the fall of 1908, when Wilson was plagued with "as wretched, radical a cold" as he ever had, he wrote his friend Mary Allen Hulbert Peck that if it were not for the company of the Vanderlips he would not have gotten up.[56]

Both men served as trustees of the Carnegie Foundation for the Advancement of Teaching.[57] When it came time to fill two life membership vacancies on the Princeton Board of Trustees, in early November 1908, Wilson suggested the spots "be filled by some man who can be of very material assistance to the University, some man like Mr. George W. Perkins, for example, or Mr. Frank A. Vanderlip."[58] Ironically, despite his somewhat opportunistic behavior toward Vanderlip, as Wilson rose in the American political system he allied himself less and less with Vanderlip, though he would befriend other bankers when he had to.

Two years after the panic, on December 11, 1909, Vanderlip invited his friend Wilson to speak at the annual banquet of New York bankers, to be held at the Waldorf Astoria hotel.[59] In an effort to impress Wilson and bind him to two very prominent politicians with respect to banking issues, he told Wilson, "Senator [Nelson] Aldrich will speak and [Treasury] Secretary [Franklin] MacVeagh will also make a brief address. . . . The audience, I hardly need to tell you, is the most representative gathering of financial men of the year."[60]

To Vanderlip's surprise, Wilson rejected his request.[61] He explained, "No man in public life irritates me and repels me more than Senator Aldrich of Rhode Island, except Mr. Joseph G. Cannon, the Speaker of the House, and I am frankly afraid that I would not behave myself properly if I were to speak after I had heard Mr. Aldrich speak. Moreover, it would be distasteful to me to be on the same program with him."

Wilson was developing an astute sense of public opinion, which had turned against Aldrich following the *Cosmopolitan* articles and the Panic of 1907. Aligning with Aldrich would not be a smart tactical move. Additionally, in 1908, Congress had enacted the Aldrich-Vreeland Act, which authorized a coalition of national banks to issue emergency currency in times of distress (much as a European central bank would, but absent the same kind of government control over the process). Wilson, who had been warm to the idea of a US central bank, did not support giving such extreme power to the bankers—nor, he believed, would the country. Aldrich represented everything that Wilson would later campaign against, though their proposals for a central bank would not be too different.

Vanderlip was insistent and persuasive. He replied, "In times past I have shared your feeling. I believe, however, that the Senator has been doing very intelligent work in the present instance, and if we are to have any adequate financial legislation within the next few years, it has got to come largely through his efforts. . . . I want you to come."[62]

At this, Wilson relented, but with reservations as to his ability to "come anywhere near" Vanderlip's expectations.[63] Though he would distance himself in platform, he concluded that some banker support could be helpful.

The 1907 panic had revealed the weakness in the Morgan-dominated banking system, in that it relied too heavily on the maneuvers and money of an elite group of men who wielded increasing control over the country. For their part, the bankers knew that too many emergencies could put them in danger of losing their preeminent position over US finance. But they needed backing in times of panics, as well.

As it turned out, the office of the president stepped in to take a more active role in the economy. But in doing so, it found itself not more separate in power but more connected with the nation's bankers. The collaboration of bankers and politicians would define the early 1910s. Morgan and his professional and genetic progeny and other titans of finance would remain in their prominent positions for decades, outlasting and influencing presidential administrations regardless of party affiliation.

The matter of creating a central banking mechanism that the two camps agreed upon, and that would support America's rise to a position of global power, would assume center stage in political discourse. The related alliances between presidents and bankers would truly come to define not just America but its position in the world.

CHAPTER 1

THE EARLY 1910S: POST-PANIC CREATURE AND PARTY POSTURING

*"We must break the Money Trust
or the Money Trust will break us."*

—Louis B. Brandeis, *Other People's Money
and How the Bankers Use It*

WHEN AMERICA ENTERED THE 1910S, IT WAS NOT YET THE GLOBAL FINANCIAL superpower that it would become by decade's end. Two key elements would propel it to such a height. The first was the creation of the Federal Reserve System (the Fed), which provided bankers backup in case of financial emergencies and enabled the nation to produce a unified currency on par with the British pound or French franc. The second was the Great War, which reshaped the landscape of international business and political power.

The nation's economic foundation was already transforming irrevocably in that direction. The baron industrialists and their sons had reinvented themselves as financiers; making money would no longer occur in tandem with production but would be an end unto itself. The war would provide the perfect opportunity to expand the global influence of that excess capital.

Within the United States, there was a pronounced westward movement and sprouting of new banks to address finance demands on that coast. But despite this dispersion of capital, the New York bankers maintained their dominant position, largely through their closer ties to the White House. In Washington, the Republican Party remained in power. Roosevelt decided not to run for reelection in 1908, but he backed William Howard Taft, a man later described by Senator Nelson Aldrich's great-grandson as a "well-fed patrician."[1] Like the Aldrich family, the Tafts had come to America from England in the late 1600s and settled in a small town in Massachusetts named after the English town of Uxbridge. As president, Taft would support Aldrich in fashioning a new currency system for the United States: the precursor to the Federal Reserve System, which would become law under Woodrow Wilson. Despite arguments from Democrats and populists that Aldrich's plan gave bankers too much control, Taft endorsed the banker-friendly aspects from Aldrich's earlier drafts.

The Morgan Bank would emerge unscathed from congressional investigations. Morgan associates and other key bankers would drive America to establish the Federal Reserve System. They would lead World War I–related financings, both for America's armament efforts and for those of the Allied countries. New-generation financier Jack Morgan (son of J. P. Morgan) would dictate how credit was extended to battered nations during the war and through postwar peace. One Morgan partner in particular, Thomas Lamont, would become the unlikely and critical ally of President Wilson. The two men, both of whom had Ivy League educations and religious fathers, would combine efforts and whims to forge a postwar treaty that would fail because of domestic political power plays. Though that failure would crush Wilson and the Democrats, the bankers would find other ways to render Wall Street the global center of financial capitalism.

By the decade's end, under the tutelage of a new generation of voracious bankers led by the brash and ambitious Charles Mitchell, National City Bank would become the first American bank to reach $1 billion in assets. Mitchell would establish the postwar model of short-term profit-seeking—not by leveraging relationships, the prevailing Wall Street model, but by accumulating customer deposits to finance global endeavors of sheer opportunism and speculation.

Jekyll Island, 1910

After the Panic of 1907, bankers and politicians alike sought a more stable banking system, though for different reasons. Despite J. P. Morgan's ability to harness backing from the Treasury Department when he needed it (and vice versa), he desired a more permanent solution to financial emergencies. The rest of the big bankers concurred. But they wanted such a mechanism to be established on their terms.

In Washington, Republicans and Democrats both concluded that excessive reliance on bankers to stabilize the financial system in times of turbulence was too high a risk to their own influence over the country, and possibly damaging to America's status in the world. The axiom that the group that controlled the money controlled the country remained true. But with the nation struggling economically, such a condition had political implications and had to be navigated accordingly.

Taft knew this when he campaigned on a vow to continue Roosevelt's reform policies, including the trustbusting activities Roosevelt had set in motion. Though his own background was largely blue-blooded and warm toward the financiers, he knew the population blamed the bankers for their problems and that the Democrats would capitalize on those suspicions if he didn't balance his support for business interests with empathy for the public. The tactic worked. In the presidential election of 1908 Taft won handily over populist Democrat William Jennings Bryan, even as the country was experiencing a post-Panic recession.

Despite rhetorical speeches about the undue influence of the bankers, especially Morgan, nearly five years passed before Congress launched an investigation into the money trusts' influence. Meanwhile, to alleviate concerns of another panic (or simply to take advantage of the situation to press for an initiative whose time had come), Congress established the bipartisan National Monetary Commission to develop a banking reform proposal and study the problems underlying the panic and alternative foreign central banking systems, for analytical and competitive purposes.

The commission had no populist bent; it was headed by Aldrich and largely made up of men sympathetic to bankers and their lawyers. The Aldrich-Vreeland Act enabled an elite group of national banks to formulate a reserve association to create currency backed by their securities, or excess capital. In that way, the act gave the banks a way to alleviate their own credit concerns (and retain control) in times of emergency. It was the true precursor to the Federal Reserve System.

During the summer of 1908, Aldrich and some subcommittee members journeyed to Europe.[2] Their official mandate was to study the operations of European central banks for background information with which to fashion some sort of central bank for the United States. Unofficially, Aldrich and the bankers wanted to strengthen America's economic position relative to its European counterparts—that would require establishing a means to further consolidate or centralize a method of creating currency in downturns, or for other purposes, as the European central banks could.

Aldrich was expected to provide a summary of his findings and draft a currency bill that fall. Yet when he and his men returned, they did not bring home a fully formed strategy for a US equivalent to the English and French central banks that would both create a stronger national currency and support the desires of the bankers. Also, constructing the first central bank in the United States required a fair bit of maneuvering; the idea did not yet have broad bipartisan or popular support. With elections looming, it was risky to push for a system that might be deemed unacceptable or too bank-centric by voters who didn't understand that this was already the premise of the Aldrich-Vreeland Act. There was a recession going on, after all, and public opinion equated this matter as residue from the Panic of 1907.

Aldrich tapped his Wall Street friends to advise him further. The world stood at a financial crossroads: the most powerful and capital-rich US bankers could realistically consider the possibility of competing with European bankers for the first time, just as the United States itself could now consider competing with Europe. It would be advantageous for the US government and for Wall Street to establish a strong central bank that would strengthen the US currency to aid both factions in that quest for international power. The only question was: How would this central bank be fashioned? How would it be controlled, and who would have the most influence over it—actually or at least with respect to the public eye? The solution would require constructing an entity that worked for both the president and the bankers, politically and practically. Even before the panic, banker Jacob Schiff, head of Kuhn, Loeb & Company, had warned the New York Chamber of Commerce that "unless we have a central bank with adequate control of credit resources, this country is going to undergo the most severe and far reaching money panic in its history." Schiff's son-in-law's brother, Hamburg-born banker Paul Warburg, would play a key role in fashioning that bank.[3] Warburg would fortify his relationship to Kuhn, Loeb by marrying Nina Loeb, daughter of Solomon Loeb.

In March 1910, Aldrich tested the popular waters among friends by intimating at an Economic Club gathering that he leaned toward having a central bank. He hoped to see New York become the center of the financial world.[4] As he told the group of bankers to hearty applause, "It is a disgrace to this country, with its vast resources, that we are obliged to pay our bills in sterling drafts or in drafts drawn payable in marks or francs in London or Berlin or Paris. The time will come—and it ought to come soon, gentlemen—when the United States will take the place to which she is entitled as the leading financial power in the world."[5]

Through their travels, Aldrich and his fellow commissioners put together twenty-three volumes of analysis of foreign financial and central banking systems, hoping to provide enough information to assuage political critics who doubted that such a mechanism was needed while leaving room to adopt a system that would be more tightly connected to the main national banks than the European private banks were. The American system would accomplish three things: it would promote America's overall power in the world, support bankers with an excess money source in their quest for domestic and international financial control, and enable presidents to enhance their global political stature in the process.

In the summer of 1910 Aldrich selected National City Bank president James Stillman to accompany him on yet another fact-finding mission to Europe.[6] Stillman had ties to two of the most powerful families in the United States. His daughter was married to William Rockefeller's son, William Goodsell Rockefeller, and he worked in a banking alliance with both J. P. Morgan and William Rockefeller.

For Frank Vanderlip, a founding father of the original plan for the Federal Reserve System, who was serving as vice president of the National City Bank at the time, "the beginning of the adventure" came in the form of a letter from Stillman, his boss and mentor, while Stillman was traveling in Paris with Aldrich. Stillman said that he had "just had a long conference" with "Zivil" (their code name for Aldrich), who was "keen to get to work on banking and currency revision." Zivil was upset that Vanderlip and Henry Davison (a senior partner at J. P. Morgan) had not been able to join him and Stillman in Europe that summer, where he felt the group would have had "plenty of time for our discussions and been free from interruptions."[7] Stillman told Vanderlip to "make everything else subservient," to give his "whole time and thought to a thorough consideration of the subject."

Retaining secrecy was crucial for Aldrich and the bankers, not just because the plan would have to come across as free from banker input to get passed in Congress, but also because these men were in effect formulating a financial avenue to propel America's financiers to a more dominant global position. If the notion of private bankers influencing a central bank was un-palatable to the public, the idea of private bankers constructing America's path to achieve global power would be impossible to get approved.

The main conclusion of the commission's report was that the more effi-cient European central banks were a key to establishing national superpow-ers in world trade through the issuance of centralized bank notes and loans to banks. If the United States was going to compete on a global platform, it would need a unified currency backed by one centralized entity. This would render the dollar, and hence the United States, stronger politically and finan-cially. The challenge was convincing the political elite and the US population that a strong central bank and currency meant a strong America. Three years after a major banker-induced panic, this had to be traversed with caution.

As a former reporter, Vanderlip considered some degree of financial trans-parency to be beneficial; it could potentially reduce instances of rumor-incited panics.[8] But, he noted, "there was an occasion near the close of 1910, when I was as secretive—indeed, as furtive—as any conspirator. . . . I do not feel it is any exaggeration to speak of our secret expedition to Jekyll Island as the occasion of the actual conception of what eventually became the Federal Reserve System."[9]

Vanderlip characterized the secrecy surrounding deliberations over the creation of the Federal Reserve System as reflecting the manner in which the banking titans of the time operated. "None of the big men of Wall Street could tolerate the thought of publicity when I arrived there," he later wrote. "Baker, Morgan, Stillman, habitually avoided journalists."[10] As such, the Fed-eral Reserve plan would be penned clandestinely, and these men would not be present together when it was formulated.

Conception

Jekyll Island, the smallest of Georgia's barrier islands, lies midway between Savannah, Georgia, and Jacksonville, Florida. Endowed with majestic moss-coated oaks, marshes, and beaches cradled by windswept sand dunes, the Jekyll Island Club hosted aristocratic members including J. P. Morgan, William Rockefeller, Vincent Astor, Joseph Pulitzer, George Baker, and James Stillman.

It was a place where the unelected leaders of the country often convened to enjoy leisure time and discuss their business affairs in an isolated retreat with all the creature comforts of home. They built 6,500–12,000 square foot "cot-tages" near the main clubhouse, as well as the nation's first "condominium," a six-apartment compound in which Morgan, Rockefeller, and four others shared a common space. On Jekyll Island, the country's ultra-select luxuriated in a six-to-one servant-to-guest ratio and impeccable hospitality under the watchful direction of Edward Grobe, a Swiss man who ran the hotel like a European manor. They usually visited during the winter season, which began at Christmas and lasted through March.[11]

Jekyll Island was not the first choice for this secret rendezvous, however. Stillman had originally suggested transporting Davison and Vanderlip to Warwick, Aldrich's Rhode Island abode, to begin substantive strategy sessions. But on October 21, 1910, while in New York City, Aldrich was struck by a southbound Madison Avenue trolley car. He was hurled into the street and knocked unconscious.[12] Confined to bed in the Park Avenue home of his son, Winthrop (who would later become chairman of the Chase Bank), Aldrich reluctantly postponed work on the central bank plan.

As the deadlines for issuing a report and introducing a draft bill to Congress drew nearer, Aldrich's concern about the as-yet-unwritten report intensified. In the wake of growing antibanker sentiment and ascendant muckraking journalism, Aldrich was paranoid. He knew he couldn't conceivably get a plan passed through Congress if it were branded a ploy between Republicans and bankers, and if it became known that he was seeking help from Wall Street.

That's when the idea of meeting at "the richest, the most exclusive, the most inaccessible club in the world" came to being. Aldrich had close personal relationships with Morgan, Stillman, and Rockefeller, all of whom were members of the Jekyll Island Club. Yet these men decided they were too prominent to risk association with an expedition to bang out the central bank plan, so they sent their lieutenants. No one on the team accompanying Aldrich to Jekyll Island, including Aldrich, was a member of the club at the time. They could only enter the exclusive locale if a member sponsored them.[13]

That member, who had ties to each person in the group, was J. P. Morgan. He was thought to have made the arrangements for all of them to be his guests, or "strangers," as visitors were called in the Jekyll Island guest book.[14] In attendance were Aldrich; his personal secretary, Arthur Shelton; assistant secretary of the Treasury A. Piatt Andrew; Frank Vanderlip; Henry Davison; Benjamin Strong, head of J. P. Morgan Bankers Trust Company; and Paul Warburg, a partner at Kuhn, Loeb & Company and a representative of the Rothschild banking dynasty in England and France.[15] The men represented the Morgan and Rockefeller empires but possessed a stronger link to Morgan and National City Bank (which was related to Morgan via the Stillman connection).

Precautions were taken as if the men were spies. The club circulated notices on the Georgia mainland reminding locals that the island was "private," as it did before every winter season. But this time the notices were posted earlier. Aldrich instructed the members of his team to avoid dining together on the night of their departure and to go to the railroad terminal on the New Jersey side of the Hudson River as "unobtrusively as possible." There, his car would be attached to the rear end of a southbound train. If anyone asked, the men were duck hunters going on an expedition.

"When I came to that car, the blinds were down and only slender threads of amber light showed the shape of the windows," Vanderlip recalled. "Once aboard the private car we [would] address one another as 'Paul,' 'Ben,' 'Nelson.' . . . Davison and I inducted even deeper disguises abandoning even our first name . . . he became Wilbur and I became Orville after those two aviation pioneers, the Wright brothers."[16]

The men spent ten days in seclusion on Jekyll Island, hard at work though no doubt also enjoying leisure activities. (Aldrich and Davison were so taken with the island that they became club members two years later.)[17] Over a Thanksgiving dinner of wild turkey with oyster stuffing, they argued and debated. But the men knew they were hatching something bigger than themselves. They were formulating a blueprint for banking in America and for American banking power around the world.

As Vanderlip said, "I enjoyed it as I have never enjoyed anything else. I lived during those days on Jekyll Island at the highest picture of intellectual awareness that I have ever experienced. It was entirely thrilling."[18]

Their plan called for the establishment of a National Reserve Association. In keeping with the strategy to create a central bank without calling it such, the moniker omitted the word "bank." The men agreed upon a central structure, with fifteen quasi-independent branches whose policies would be coordinated through a central national committee. It would have the power to create one standard currency that would support the country and the big banks in times of emergency, ensuring their stability. The Treasury was in charge of creating coins and paper currency; its Bureau of Engraving and Printing had been producing all currency for the US government, including silver and gold certificates, since 1877.[19] A central bank would add another dimension to the US banking system. (On October 28, 1914, the bureau began printing paper Federal Reserve notes, as instructed by Federal Reserve members.)[20]

On its surface, the Aldrich plan seemed a fair idea for a country as geographically expansive as the United States. Congress would surely see the logic in such a structure. And the population would surely take comfort in what would be presented as a way to keep the economy protected from the money trusts' machinations. The fact that it really was a means to provide an easier money supply to the big banks would not be part of its publicized benefits.

Satisfied with the results, Aldrich set out to present the draft bill to the Senate. The men departed as covertly as they had arrived. Aldrich and Andrew exited the northbound train at Washington, DC. Warburg, Davison, Strong, and Vanderlip traveled onward toward New York.[21]

But on November 26, 1910, the New York contingent got word that Aldrich had fallen ill. The strain of the days so close to the accident had proved too taxing. Aldrich was too weak to write an appropriate document to accompany his plan. There was no time to waste.

In a pinch, Strong and Vanderlip traveled to Washington and prepared the summary report. "If what we have done then had been made known publicly, the effort would have been denounced as a piece of Wall Street chicanery, which it certainly was not," claimed Vanderlip.[22] Such was the thinking of one of the wealthiest bankers in the country.

President Taft Supports Aldrich's Plan

All that was left was to market the plan to Congress and the American people. On January 16, 1911, Aldrich formally delivered the "Suggested Plan for Monetary Legislation, Submitted to the National Monetary Commission," otherwise known as the Aldrich plan. It circulated around Congress and made its way to the press.[23]

The plan's creators endorsed it through various avenues. First out of the gate was Davison, who praised the "admirably effective and simple" plan (if he did say so himself) in a January 20 *New York Times* article.[24] In early February, at the annual dinner of the New York Chapter of the American Institute of Banking, A. Piatt Andrew assailed the "serious defects" of the current system and described how the Aldrich plan would solve them.[25] In late February, Vanderlip "warmly endorsed" it in an address at a Commercial Club banquet.[26]

One of the plan's most stalwart supporters was President Taft himself. Just as he had backed the Payne-Aldrich Act in 1909, which lowered tariff rates by 5 percent and increased coal and iron ore prices, Taft strongly advocated the Aldrich plan. He too was convinced that a powerful US required a powerful currency and that passing a solid plan for a US central bank under a Republican White House could give him leverage in the upcoming elections. He offered advice to ensure its passage in the Democratic-controlled Congress.

In a January 29, 1911, letter to Aldrich (who had returned to Jekyll Island as a guest), Taft was already providing a backup strategy in case there were problems. He wrote, "If you formulate your scheme into a definite bill backed by the Commission, I can recommend it and present it with the arguments in its behalf to a Democratic Congress and in this way perhaps prepare the way for its being adopted as a plank of the next Republican platform. So that if we are successful in the next election we can put it on its passage in a Republican Congress as the performance of a platform pledge and promise."[27] Taft wanted to pass the bill through the Democrats; but if it didn't pass, he wanted to retain the option to push it through during the next session, which he hoped would have a more favorable Republican balance. Both parties had an interest in addressing the nation's currency and financial challenges, and to be seen tackling the issue. The struggle was over which party would be the one to take ownership of the solution.

Five months later, at a meeting of 1,500 members of the New York State Bankers Association on June 23, 1911, Taft promoted the Aldrich plan to a hearty round of cheers and applause. In his speech, he stressed the "association" term in particular, as there was growing concern (or at least political posturing) among progressives that a singular central bank, or construct, would have too much power or be too influenced by the money trusts. Not that there was any particular reason why an "association" would be less influenced, but in the fight for political power, distinctions such as these were less important than controlling the outcome.

"It is true that the National Reserve Association is a central bank in a certain sense," Taft said, equivocating to assuage critics. But, he argued with bankers' logic, though a singular central bank wouldn't pass popular opinion muster, an association "will inure greatly to the benefit of the people of this country."[28] He was betting—or banking, as it were—on the fact that people would feel that a nonsingular bank would by its nature be more diffuse, less likely to fall prey to concentrated influence from the bankers. It was really a matter of spin and linguistics, for diffused influence is not the same as the absence of influence.

Such verbiage and the promise of an outwardly decentralized structure did prove more enticing to the population. This suited the big bankers just fine; they were less concerned with the details than ensuring that they would retain influence over the association and access to easily created currency. It would also be a victory for the president, as it would help expand the power of his office and of the country over the world. But Aldrich's plan would not become law—not yet, anyway.

The *Titanic* and the Pujo Hearings

J. P. Morgan was in France when word spread that the *Titanic* had sunk on April 15, 1912, and with it the investment money Morgan had contributed on behalf of the shipping trust that built it. He had attended the ship's launch at the Harland and Woolf shipyard in Belfast in 1911 and narrowly missed being a passenger in the suite that bore his name. If he had not been dealing with health issues in France, he might have gone down with the ship.[29]

As the world reeled from the loss of the "unsinkable ship," the congressional hearings that probed the money trusts and Morgan's labyrinth of influence kicked off in Washington on May 16.[30] Congressman Charles A. Lindbergh Sr. (father of the future flyer) had introduced a resolution to look into the money trusts after passage of the Aldrich-Vreeland Act, which he considered a coup for the banks and "the first precedent established for the people's guarantee of the rich man's watered securities, by making them a basis on which to issue currency."[31] Lindbergh's resolution led to the 1912 House Banking and Currency Committee hearings, in a subcommittee led by Louisiana Democrat Arsène Pujo.

The timing of these hearings was advantageous to the Democratic Party. New Jersey governor Woodrow Wilson wisely leveraged public outrage against the bankers and the Republican embrace of them during his presidential campaign (though he said little about the Pujo hearings specifically—after all, certain major bankers, notably Jacob Schiff, were financing his campaign). If he entered the White House with the people's mandate, he could create his own banking system, even if it turned out to be nearly the same one the Republicans were pushing.

Lead prosecutor Samuel Untermyer summoned Morgan and other Wall Street financiers, including George Baker, James Stillman, Paul Warburg, and Benjamin Strong. William Rockefeller's partial testimony was gleaned by investigators who journeyed to find him on Jekyll Island, where his doctor pronounced him too ill to say very much. The hearings cast some of these bankers into the public eye for the first time. Untermyer's investigation focused on bankers' manipulation of markets and stocks, and the negative implications on the entire country of such a concentration of power and influence within the inner group of bankers.

Though the hearings succeeded in drawing media attention to the bankers and their clandestine alliances and activities, the investigation was politically dogged at every step. The pro-banker *New York Times* jeered at Pujo, "When panics rage, resort is not made to gentlemen of Pujo's caliber, but to the leaders of the Money Trust, who are laughing in his face as he tries to hold them up to popular punishment."[32]

By June, bankers bristled at Untermyer's attempt to obtain more information on the names of stockholders and the nature of their holdings. The bankers appealed to the comptroller of the currency for relief.[33] Their efforts to keep their activities a secret had been supported by an executive order given by Roosevelt in his last term and reaffirmed by Taft. The order prevented agency heads from furnishing reports to congressional committees unless approved by the president. It was a loophole that the bankers could use to their advantage mostly because the president was on their side. Untermyer pleaded directly with Taft to compel the bankers to cooperate, but the president shrewdly decided not to respond until after the election, when he would refuse him the information avenue he desired.[34]

With political tensions rising and so much at stake for both parties, the hearings were suspended as the presidential race heated up. This was partially because the Democrats had lost some faith in the investigations despite public support for them, given the roadblocks befalling Untermyer. The official reason given by Taft, whose party was equally wary of what the election would bring, was that he wanted to avoid creating the impression that the purpose was to gain partisan advantage.[35]

Anxiety over which party would gain control of the White House was linked to how the money trusts were positioned. The issues of banking and currency reform were central to the 1912 election. Both parties had to tread carefully, balancing public opinion against the need to keep bankers and big business supporting their campaigns.

Wilson panned the Aldrich plan throughout his campaign. He told audiences that he believed control over the nation's finances should be held by the government and not the money trusts.[36] It was the exact kind of power-play articulation that Roosevelt had used against the other trusts. Wilson said he envisioned a semicentralized banking system where each district revolved around its own Federal Reserve Board. This wasn't very different from the Aldrich plan. But Aldrich was a Republican, and that was reason enough to disparage an idea with his name on it. Wilson knew this, even though one of his largest campaign contributors happened to be Jacob Schiff, a "money trust" banker who ran Kuhn, Loeb & Company, and whose protégé, Paul Warburg, would eventually be appointed to a position on the Federal Reserve Board by Wilson—who, as this tale will tell again, was good to his friends.

Vanderlip and Wilson

As previously mentioned, Wilson's alliances with the power brokers of Wall Street began before 1879, when he graduated from Princeton alongside Cleveland Dodge. According to Ferdinand Lundberg, author of the enthralling *America's Sixty Families,* "For more than twenty years before his nomination Woodrow Wilson moved in the shadow of Wall Street."[37] After law school, Wilson rose quickly through the Princeton ranks, from young conservative professor of political science to the head of the university. He could not have raised funds as its president or run for governor of New Jersey or later for the presidency without the elite-banking contingent.

In the early part of his career, Wilson befriended Vanderlip, then a shy, rising star at National City Bank. Their "long acquaintance" began in 1903 through Dodge's introduction. According to Vanderlip, the two had "many fine stimulating talks" about the nature of the US economy and other issues. It was Vanderlip who insisted that Wilson address the need to expand American business abroad as a way to secure the "industrial supremacy" of the United States in world trade. But they saw less of each other when Wilson left his post as Princeton's president in 1910 to become governor of New Jersey. Vanderlip established the National City Company as a subsidiary, to circumvent laws forbidding national banks to open foreign institutions. As Wilson moved further to the political forefront, contact between the men ceased. Wilson chose to limit the appearance of having a connection to the bankers he was disparaging in public, except for one final instance that stuck in Vanderlip's head.

During Wilson's presidential campaign, William Gibbs McAdoo, president of the Hudson and Manhattan Railroad Company (and later Wilson's Treasury secretary), approached Vanderlip several times on Wilson's behalf to discuss issues of banking and currency systems. Given his sense of hurt over Wilson's distant stance toward him, Vanderlip ignored many of these overtures. Finally, Wilson invited Vanderlip to meet him at McAdoo's home at Hastings-on-Hudson, New York, near Vanderlip's Scarborough estate. Perhaps this was an opportunity for Vanderlip to renew his friendship with Wilson, or so he thought.

"We had a long talk together alone and quite in the warm tone of our old friendship," Vanderlip recalled of their meeting. That warmth proved illusory. Vanderlip pressed Wilson on the need for a central bank mechanism along the lines of the Aldrich plan. He wanted Wilson to consider the broader necessity of their plan, and the success it could provide the United States on the international stage. For Wilson during that conversation, the issue wasn't the plan but the power to implement it, or something similar, in Washington. "You don't understand politics," Wilson told Vanderlip. "It does not make any difference what I thought ought to be done, I first need to get elected in order to do these things."[38]

Recalling that incident, Vanderlip came to believe that Wilson "was just moving my hair with one hand and keeping me at arm's length with the other." In other words, Wilson wanted input from Vanderlip, but he didn't want to appear to be associating with such a high-ranking banker. Though Vanderlip did "not feel that it was a crime to be the president of the National City Bank," he sensed Wilson felt "it would be a political crime if he were caught talking with me."[39] The nation's opinion of bankers had soured further since the Panic, the ensuing recession, and the press coverage of the Pujo hearings, a condition that Roosevelt, who decided to run on the Progressive "Bull Moose" Party ticket, used to his advantage in the 1912 election. Wilson would use it more successfully.

Perhaps because of spurned feelings or divergent interests, Vanderlip withdrew his financial support for his old friend. A chill settled between the two men that, combined with Vanderlip's sensitive and slightly eccentric personality, would have major repercussions for Wilson and the country in the years to come.

Wilson began campaigning in earnest in Buffalo, New York, on Labor Day, September 2.[40] He targeted the nexus between big business, Wall Street, and the Republican leadership. He vowed to "break up the little coterie that has determined what the government of the United States should do."[41] His rhetoric was designed to outflank Roosevelt, who had been a trustbuster of every trust except the money one during his presidency.

In particular, Wilson dubbed the Payne-Aldrich Tariff Act "the most conspicuous example ever afforded the country of the special favors and monopolistic advantages" given by the Republican Party to its campaign contributors.[42] He disparaged the concentration of control of credit in Wall Street and said he wanted that power to reside with Washington instead—as had Roosevelt, though Wilson had articulated the sentiment with much more finesse.

Capitalizing on his growing popularity during his October 11 campaign address before the Central Armory in Cleveland, Wilson claimed, "The whole situation in the United States might be summed up by saying that the Republican Party has put the intelligence of this country into the hands of receivers in Wall Street offices. Very able receivers they are, and they have received a great deal!"[43]

Wilson's anti–Wall Street proclamations matched the country's sentiments. On November 5, he won the election with 42 percent of the electoral vote. Roosevelt came in second with 27 percent of the electoral vote, while the incumbent President Taft got a mere 23 percent.[44] Wilson's read of the American public allowed him to out-Roosevelt Roosevelt. However, in practice, he would further empower the very banking class he disparaged. In doing so, he would propel America to the role of a financial superpower during and after World War I, though he would not get everything he wanted in that regard.

Wilson's victory ushered in an atmosphere of jubilance in Washington for the Democrats. On November 6, 1912, Samuel Untermyer, who had stumped for Wilson during the election,[45] promptly requested his input on the ongoing "Money Trust Inquiry," though Wilson had not discussed the specifics or mentioned any bankers by name during the campaign. "There are important questions of policy . . . requiring immediate decision before the hearings, which are fixed for the end of this month, are resumed," Untermyer wrote.[46] Wilson responded that he would deal with the matter once he got back from his upcoming vacation.[47]

Carter Glass, the Democratic chair of the House committee in charge of reviewing what had become the Aldrich Bill and the banking and currency system, also wasted no time addressing the matter of a system overhaul. Two days after the election, he not only congratulated Wilson on his victory but plunged straight to the issue over which he would now have jurisdiction. Glass informed Wilson that he and economics professor H. Parker Willis had formulated a substitution for the Aldrich bill, though he did not provide the president-elect with further details, perhaps shrewdly awaiting more guidance.[48] As he told Wilson, "I think the committee would not like to proceed without some suggestion from you . . . as to what you think should be done."[49]

Plagued with a raging cold once he returned to Princeton after Christmas, Wilson invited Glass and Willis to his home to discuss the reform bill.[50] The Glass-Willis draft bill called for a more decentralized reserve system than the one Aldrich had proposed. It would still be privately controlled, centered around a group of local reserve banks, with each having the full power of the reserve banking system.

Based on their conversation, Willis concluded that Wilson didn't think the plan provided the comptroller of the currency, the system's general supervisor, enough control. But other than that, he didn't feel as strongly as his campaigning had indicated about how the central bank would be constructed. Perhaps, now that he had won the election, Wilson was less inclined to upset the bankers who had quietly supported him—though he still wanted to ensure the presidency retained power over the new currency system.

Afterward, Glass pondered the political landscape. It made him uncomfortable, and he wanted to pass legislation as quickly as possible. He told Wilson that he was trying "to reduce the suggestions made to something tangible in order that the hearings . . . may be directed to a definite, even though tentative, plan of currency reform." Glass's main concern was a letter he had received from a New York banker who had attended his subcommittee hearings, which Glass interpreted as a veiled threat. It stated, "The American Bankers Association as a body . . . endorsed the Aldrich bill. It would seem, therefore, impossible for us as members of the Currency Commission of the American Bankers Association to take another position or do anything else before your committee than to endorse the bill, if we were to appear before you officially."

From this, Glass knew that the bankers would fight for the Aldrich plan as it was drafted, so he tried to find a way to capitulate but still leave his and the party's mark on it. He publicly suggested drafting a bill giving local reserve banks equal power, as opposed to one that would empower a strong centralized source, and placing the burden on the advocates of the Aldrich bill to show that a central superstructure would not possess "the evils of bank monopoly and the dangers of centralized power."[51]

Unofficially, though, Glass knew nothing would pass unless he preserved the elements of the Aldrich plan that the bankers supported. Though he wrote Wilson several letters about his centralization concerns, Wilson did not reply to his concerns until it was clear that Glass was leaning toward a better compromise with the bankers, and the bankers were indicating their approval of the Glass plan in return.

Morgan's Defiance

While those conversations were progressing, J. P. Morgan traveled from New York to Washington on December 17, 1912, with an entourage of fifteen men—including his son, Jack, and his partner, Thomas Lamont.

In his testimony before the Pujo Committee, Morgan was curt and defiant. In one exchange with Untermyer, he brushed aside both the idea that he could save the country's finances in a panic, as his admirers insisted he had done in 1907, and that he could control them for his advantage.

Q. Your power in any direction is entirely unconscious to you, is it not?

A. It is, sir; if that is the case.

Q. You do not think you have any power in any department of industry in this country, do you?

A. I do not.

Q. Not the slightest?

A. Not the slightest.

Thus the man who routinely convened with the heads of finance and industry in New York, London, and Jekyll Island yielded no information about his methods and presented no awareness of the power of their impact.

Ten days later, as a parting gift to the bankers, outgoing President Taft attempted to stonewall the final stages of the investigation. He informed Pujo that he would refuse to force the comptroller of the currency to gather any additional information from the national banks for use in the investigation.[52]

On February 26, 1913, the Pujo Committee issued its final report, a searing indictment of the dangers of high concentration of money and credit in the hands of a few elite "money trusts." The report outlined a list of their unsavory practices, such as "wash sales," which provided the appearance of demand for securities cultivated by the firms that created them to entice investors, and "short sales," which gave firms the ability to sell their securities to give the appearance of weaker demand and then profit by buying them back later at lower prices.[53]

The report revealed that J. P. Morgan & Company—"the acknowledged leaders of the allied forces," as Louis Brandeis put it—held seventy-two directorships in forty-seven of the largest American companies. More broadly, its members and the directors of its controlled trust companies, the First National Bank, and the National City bank held 341 directorships in 112 corporations with resources or capitalizations of $22.25 billion (including in banks, trusts, insurance companies, transportation systems, and public utilities).[54]

Brandeis considered this the tip of the iceberg. He believed that "wealth expressed in figures give[s] a wholly inadequate picture of the allies' power. . . . Their wealth is dynamic. It is wielded by geniuses in combination. It finds its proper expression in means of control."[55]

Morgan had a different perspective. His firm had declared in its letter to the Pujo Committee that "practically all the railroads and institutional development of this country has taken place initially through the medium of the great banking houses." Conversely, Brandeis argued, "nearly every contribution to our comfort and prosperity was 'initiated' *without* their aid." Banks entered the picture once success had been established.[56]

Once the spectacle was over, the committee came up empty-handed. Wall Street rallied around Morgan's performance.[57] The *New York Times* praised the accompanying letter from the firm as a "sermon" to the unconverted.[58]

It was to be Morgan's last mortal triumph, capping off the short-lived and shallow decline of the money trust, which would soon be resurrected in a broader, global form as the Great War provided the firm with more opportunities for influence and placed Wilson's government in a greater position of financial dependence than ever.

Six weeks after the report was issued and just past midnight on March 31, 1913, Morgan died at the Grand Hotel in Rome. His partners attributed the death of the great titan to the stress of the Pujo investigations. There may have been some truth to that, but as Morgan's biographer Ron Chernow wrote, "Pierpont was seventy-five . . . smoked dozens of cigars daily, stowed away huge breakfasts, drank heavily and refused to exercise."[59]

Leaders from Pope Pius to the German emperor to fellow bankers publicly mourned his death. Jack Morgan took over the firm and gained control of its political alliances at the age of forty-six. Though he never led the firm with as controlling or exacting a command as his father, or possessed the ability to gather its collaborators in the same way, Jack would shepherd the bank through the ratification of the Federal Reserve Act, which his father had championed behind the scenes, and navigate the bank through the war.

Passing the Federal Reserve Act

It turned out that 1913 was a busy year for legislation. On February 3, the Sixteenth Amendment was ratified, allowing the Treasury Department to impose an income tax. Two months later, the Seventeenth Amendment, requiring direct popular election of US senators, was passed. But Washington's main debate concerned the Glass-Owen bill, the reformation of the Aldrich bill. That legislation would define financial power in the United States and, by extension, US private banking power globally.

Despite concerns over the structure of the board and who would be in charge of appointing its officials, the bankers adopted a more conciliatory tone toward this version of the Glass-Owen bill, which, after all, granted them the ability to access currency when they needed it and to expand their branches overseas. Glass was encouraged by the changed attitude of some of the influential bankers.

"These gentlemen," as Glass informed Wilson on January 27, "concluded that they could not carry out Mr. Warburg's purpose of 'battering the committee into a repudiation of the Democratic platform.'" Glass continued, "They were now willing to cooperate with the committee in trying to secure the 'best remedial legislation that is possible to obtain.'" Having the bankers on board ironically placed a potential bull's-eye mark on Glass, who realized "too pronounced activity by the organized bankers might arouse suspicion and hostility among those who regard banks as essentially evil." He decided, therefore, "to proceed discreetly."[60]

Work on the bill thus progressed through the spring. Based on advice from his confidant Colonel Edward House, Wilson appointed William McAdoo—who had worked on Wilson's campaign and had been his interlocutor with Vanderlip—as his Treasury secretary.[61] On April 11, House and McAdoo dined at the White House at Wilson's invitation. After dinner, the three men adjourned to the library to discuss New York appointments, currency reform, and the Glass bill. They agreed that McAdoo, Glass, Owen, and House should meet Monday evening and "whip it in shape."[62] It could represent an early and strong political victory for Wilson.

Two months later, as the Glass bill adopted more of what the big bankers wanted, Brandeis voiced his concern to Wilson over the pending legislation in an attempt to swing the pendulum away from Wall Street. "The power to issue currency should be vested exclusively in Government officials," he wrote. "The American people will not be content . . . in a Board composed wholly or in part of bankers; for their judgment may be biased by private interest or affiliation."[63]

But Glass was now leaning toward giving the bankers precisely that power. On June 18, 1913, he asked Wilson to allow bank representation on the proposed Federal Reserve Board.[64] Glass had been up past one o'clock the night before discussing the matter with Representative Robert Bulkley, a member of the subcommittee on banking and currency and "a strong man of the committee with whom we must reckon," as he told Wilson.[65]

Bulkley, a millionaire Democrat from Ohio, was popular in the Washington society circuit; he counted as his friends bankers and Republicans alike.[66] He didn't want the banking business exposed to undue government controls. As such, he proposed an alteration to the current draft of the plan to allow bankers to sit on the main Federal Reserve Board. He confirmed Glass's new belief that it would prove "an almost irretrievable mistake to leave the banks without representation on the Central Board."[67]

Five days later, Wilson addressed the issue of banking and currency reform before a joint session of Congress. He again stressed that control of the banking system "must be vested in the Government itself, so that the banks may be the instruments, not the masters, of business and of individual enterprise and initiative."[68] But he shied away from specifics about how the board should be comprised.

Signing the Federal Reserve Act

Wilson had privately agreed to incorporate Bulkley's suggestions. He intended to allow bankers on the Board of the New York Federal Reserve, one of a dozen reserve banks that would comprise the Federal Reserve System—the most powerful one by virtue of its location in the heart of the banking community and the size of its assets. It was a compromise that gave the bankers the power they wanted but preserved the president's power to appoint the main board in Washington, DC. By doing so, Wilson got the Republican votes needed to pass the bill.

After six more months of haggling over minor details, Wilson signed the Federal Reserve Act into law on December 23, 1913, establishing the twelve-bank Federal Reserve System and its powerful Wall Street–centric arm, the New York Fed (the part that complied with the bankers' demands).[69] The name sounded "public" and "of the government," and indeed the act delineated the Fed's ability to balance credit, monitor inflation, and help cultivate employment. (Though that aspect was absent from the private conversations that preceded the act, the addition played well publicly.) And yet its members were the private banks that wanted it to exist. It was Aldrich's plan in essence, if not in each particular detail.

Wilson painted the act's passage as a political victory for the power of the presidency and his party, coated in populist terms. At the signing he effused, "This bill furnishes the machinery for free and elastic and uncontrolled credit, put at the disposal of the merchants and the manufacturers of this country for the first time in fifty years." (The National Banking Act was passed in 1863—with revisions in 1864 and 1865—to help fund the Civil War by creating currency notes issued by the larger nationally chartered banks rather than state-chartered ones. The Union government established many more nationalistic institutions, as opposed to the more fractious and weaker brand of federalism that existed beforehand.[70] The National Banking Act also formed the Office of the Comptroller of the Currency, which issued national banking charters, ensured these banks adhered to strict capital requirements, and required them to back currency notes via holding US government securities.)

At the signing ceremony, in the spirit of bipartisanship and the influence it bestowed upon him politically, Wilson said, "We rejoice together."[71] In a quiet moment afterward, he wrote Glass of his admiration for the way he had carried the fight for the currency bill so successfully.[72] He presented his partners Glass, McAdoo, and Owen with gold signing pens.

Though it was largely devised with bankers' input, the act was presented to the American public as in their best interests domestically. Like the European powers, the United States would now have a centralized entity that operated on the principle of "discount" rates, whereby large national banks would receive loans stemming from reserve funds for a certain interest charge, which would supposedly be used to lend onward to businesses and citizens as needed.

The Federal Reserve System was similar to a European central bank from a monetary policy perspective in that it was able to set rates, but some of its members were more powerful than others. Though all twelve member banks theoretically decided matters with equal influence, the most powerful components of the system characterized the power-sharing arrangement of the president and the bankers. The Board of Governors would be selected by the president, and the Board of the New York Fed would be closest to the Wall Street bankers, who would hold the most sway over the Federal Reserve System because they controlled the largest portion of reserves.

The Bankers' Bank

Officially the Federal Reserve was created in response to the Panic of 1907 and earlier ones. But its main purpose was to elevate the stature of the United States in global financial activities relative to European central banks, and as a result to strengthen American bankers' dominance domestically and internationally. It served the dual role of perpetuating the power of the president and that of the bankers, and as such, despite publicized differences of opinion on the matter, it served the alliance of the two.

Though the Fed's decisions were technically "independent," the body would serve the bankers first, by keeping them flush with money and by acting as their lender of last resort. National banks were automatically members of the system, as are more than one-third of all US banks, including the biggest ones, today.

The role of running the New York Fed fell to one of the original Jekyll Island authors of the Aldrich plan, Bankers Trust head Benjamin Strong.[73] As Ron Chernow wrote, "The New York Fed and the [Morgan] bank would share a sense of purpose such that the House of Morgan would be known on Wall Street as the Fed bank."[74]

Though Morgan was dead, his spirit, will, and legacy would live on. The Fed would not prove able to stop subsequent crashes or crises, but it would always provide financing to the big banks and their closest friends in times of need. Satisfying bankers' international aspirations, the Federal Reserve Act removed the prohibition keeping US banks from opening overseas branches. It also allowed US banks to use the Fed to rediscount bills in order to raise money for financing foreign transactions, thereby removing the old reliance on London discount firms to provide this capital. For New York, this was a major step toward being able to rival London for global financial superiority.

Though publicly spun by Wilson and others as an "equalizing" measure that made credit available to banks of all sizes, the Fed's initial charter didn't even cover smaller savings banks. Additionally, state banks were disadvantaged by a requirement to maintain reserves of 32 percent, whereas the big national banks only had to hold 18 percent.[75]

As Fed historian William Greider observed, "the Fed may have actually preserved the financial power of those very bankers who the public thought were at last being brought under control."[76] Indeed, the mathematics of Fed operation was designed to serve the big bankers the most, and always would. The money trusts were happy.

Wilson, Morgan, and Compromises

Even so, after he signed the Federal Reserve Act, Wilson was perplexed by and somewhat suspicious about the uncharacteristically public acquiescence of Jack Morgan and the banking community to its rules forcing bankers to abandon any external directorships that could be construed as anticompetitive. (The rule was a concession to the smaller bankers, who thought the eastern establishment connections put them at a disadvantage.) Concerned he might have missed a power play, Wilson sent a telegram on January 6, 1914, to his private secretary, Joseph Patrick Tumulty, requesting his impression of Morgan's action and asking him what the "leading business men and the public mind generally expect."[77]

Tumulty examined the matter on behalf of his boss. It was simple, really. He replied, "The country accepts the Morgan announcement as an act of good faith on the part of 'big Business' . . . an indication of the willingness on the part of intelligent leaders in finance to put themselves in accord with the spirit of the times." In other words, the public accepted that by establishing the Federal Reserve, Wilson had taken power from the banks and put it in the White House, and the bankers felt it a small price to pay to relinquish the official trappings of interlocking directorships (with the men they saw socially anyway) in return for a guaranteed emergency source of money.

But there was a catch. In return for their acceptance, business leaders expected Wilson to "clear up the atmosphere of doubt surrounding the Sherman law" and cease any remaining Roosevelt-era trustbusting. They wanted him to provide "a gentle admonition" to Congress that such legislation must not be undertaken in a spirit of hostility to business, which is now showing itself "ready to meet the administration half way."[78]

As Congress debated strengthening this antitrust legislation, Wilson reflected the renewed camaraderie and expected reciprocity from the banking and business community by weakening the legislation.

As an additional olive branch to the banking community, and in gratitude for the financial support that Jacob Schiff had given him during the election, on April 30, 1914, Wilson requested that Kuhn, Loeb & Company banker Paul Warburg "provide the country the great service" of accepting his appointment to the Federal Reserve Board.[79] The bankers didn't have to clamber for a spot on the board after all. The president handed it to them. Now, two of the six Jekyll Island authors were part of the Federal Reserve System leadership: Warburg in Washington and Strong in New York. Moreover, America had the currency-creation ability necessary for any rising superpower to compete for world power. This ability would soon be tested on the global stage as the United States approached World War I.

CHAPTER 2

THE MID-1910S:
BANKERS GO TO WAR

"The war should be a tremendous opportunity for America."

—Jack Morgan, personal letter to
President Woodrow Wilson, September 4, 1914

BOTH FEDERAL RESERVE AND DOMESTIC ANTITRUST ISSUES WERE SOON overshadowed by more ominous events occurring overseas. On June 28, 1914, a Slavic nationalist in Sarajevo murdered Archduke Franz Ferdinand, heir to the Austrian throne. The battle lines were drawn. Austria positioned itself against Serbia. Russia announced support of Serbia against Austria, Germany backed Austria, and France backed Russia. Military mobilization orders traversed Europe. The national and private finances that had helped build up shipping and weapons arsenals in the last years of the nineteenth century and the early years of the twentieth would spill into deadly battle.

Wilson knew exactly whose help he needed. He invited Jack Morgan to a luncheon at the White House. The media erupted with rumors about the encounter. Was this a sign of tighter ties to the money trust titans? Was Wilson closer to the bankers than he had appeared? With whispers of such queries hanging in the hot summer air, at 12:30 in the afternoon of July 2, 1914, Morgan emerged from the meeting to face a flock of buzzing reporters. Genetically predisposed to shun attention, he merely explained that the meeting was "cordial" and suggested that further questions be directed to the president.[1]

At the follow-up press conference, Wilson was equally coy. "I have known Mr. Morgan for a good many years; and his visit was lengthened out chiefly by my provocation, I imagine. Just a general talk about things that were transpiring."[2] Though Wilson explained this did not signify the start of a series of talks with "men high in the world of finance," rumors of a closer alliance between the president and Wall Street financiers persisted.

Wilson's needs and Morgan's intentions would soon become clear. For on July 28, Austria formally declared war against Serbia.[3] The Central Powers (Germany, the Austro-Hungarian Empire, the Ottoman Empire, and Bulgaria) were at war with the Triple Entente (France, Britain, and Russia). While Wilson tried to juggle conveying America's position of neutrality with the tragic death of his wife, domestic and foreign exchange markets were gripped by fear and paralysis.[4] Another panic seemed a distinct possibility so soon after the Federal Reserve was established to prevent such outcomes in the midst of Wilson's first term. The president had to assuage the markets and prepare the country's finances for any outcome of the European battles.

Not wanting to leave war financing to chance, Wilson and Morgan kicked their power alliance into gear. At the request of high-ranking State Department officials, Morgan immediately immersed himself in war financing issues. On August 10, 1914, Secretary of State William Jennings Bryan wrote Wilson that Morgan had asked whether there would be any objection if his bank made loans to the French government and the Rothschilds' Bank (also intended for the French government).[5] Bryan was concerned that approving such an extension of capital might detract from the neutrality position that Wilson had adopted and, worse, invite other requests for loans from nations less allied with the United States than France, such as Germany or Austria. The Morgan Bank was only interested in assisting the Allies.

Bryan was due to speak with Morgan senior partner Henry Davison later that day. Though Morgan had made it clear that any money his firm lent would be spent in the United States, Bryan worried that "if foreign loans absorb *our* loanable money it might affect our getting government loans if we need."[6] Thus, private banks' lending decisions could affect not just the course of international governments' participation in the war but also that of the US government's financial health during the war. Not much had changed since the turn of the century, when government functions depended on the availability of private bank loans.

Wilson wasn't going to deny Morgan's request. He approved the $100 million loan to finance the French Republic's war needs. The decision reflected the past, but it also had implications for the future of political-financial alliances and their applications to wars. During the Franco-German war of 1870, Jack's grandfather, J. S. Morgan, had raised $50 million of French bonds through his London office after the French government failed to sell its securities to London bankers to raise funds. Not only was the transaction profitable; it also endeared Morgan and his firm to the French government.

Private banking notwithstanding, on August 19, 1914, President Wilson urged Americans to remain neutral regarding the combat.[7] But Morgan and his partners never embraced the policy of impartiality. As Morgan partner Thomas Lamont wrote later, "From the very start, we did everything we could to contribute to the cause of the Allies."[8]

Aside from Jack Morgan's personal views against Germany and the legacy of his grandfather's decisions, the Morgan Bank enjoyed close relations with the British and French governments by virtue of its sister firms—Morgan, Grenfell & Company, the prestigious merchant bank in London; and Morgan, Harjes & Company in Paris. The bank, like a country, followed the war along the lines of its past financial alliances, even to the point of antagonizing firms that desired to participate in French loans during periods of bitter fighting.

Two weeks after Wilson's August 19 speech, armed with more leverage because of the war, Jack Morgan took it upon himself to approach Wilson about his domestic concerns. "This war . . . has thrown a tremendous and sudden strain on American money markets," Morgan wrote. "It has increased the already pronounced tendency of European holders of American securities to sell them for whatever prices they could obtain for them, and the American investor has got to relieve the European investors of these securities by degrees and as he can."[9] Market tensions were exacerbated by the fact that European investors were selling securities to raise money. That was a problem whose only solution required the provision of more loans. But there was something else, with more lasting domestic repercussions echoing the trust-busting of the Morgan interest in US Steel.

Morgan argued that rather than encouraging investors to feel safe, the government's Interstate Commerce Commission, formed to regulate national industry in 1887, was doing the opposite by restricting eastern railroad freight rates and investigating railroad companies. In Morgan's mind, war was definitely not a time for enhanced regulations against business. And if railroad securities fell in value relative to the loans secured by them, banks would not be able to lend enough to make up the difference. The whole credit system could freeze.

As Morgan further warned, "Great depreciation in the value of these securities" would "throw back to the bank loans secured by them" and lead to a "great tieing up of bank funds, which will interfere with the starting of the new Federal Reserve System, and produce panic conditions." He concluded that the war "should be a tremendous opportunity for America," but not "as long as the business of the country is under the impression of fear in which it now labors."[10] Levying such serious threats, Morgan became the first banker to reveal that credit, the Federal Reserve, the big banks, the US economy, and the war were inextricably linked. Wilson knew this too.

Morgan was especially concerned about the Clayton Antitrust Act, which Congress was considering to strengthen the restrictions against monopolies and anticompetitive practices laid out in the 1890 Sherman Antitrust Act. Having passed the Senate, the bill was headed to a conference committee. Should it pass in its current form, libertarian Morgan believed, it would demonstrate that "the United States Government does not propose to allow enterprises to conduct normal business without interference."[11]

Wilson took Morgan's concerns seriously. He knew the last thing the United States needed was a credit meltdown. To avoid such a crisis and placate the bankers, he was already rewriting the Clayton Antitrust Act, but he didn't admit it to Morgan. Wilson calculated that there had to remain some areas of negotiation to better one's hand.[12] Though the two argued over interpretation of the bill, a white flag flew between Wall Street and Washington for the time being. Such periods of strife called for allied, not adversarial, relationships between the president and the bankers, and friendly relations would also promote the global power positioning of both parties.

In general, the war meant that the goodwill extended to bankers and business from the president continued, lending protocols included. An October 15, 1914, news report proclaimed, "American Bankers May Make Loans to War Nations."[13] It was a government decision pushed by the banking contingent that would reverberate throughout the war and afterward, drawing clearer lines of competition among the various Wall Street powerhouses. Though the pro-Allies Morgan Bank sought cooperation with the British, for instance, National City Bank set up international branches around Europe and Russia to compete for future financial power, causing a rift between two of the three biggest New York banks that financed the war.[14] Partly, that rift had to do with the change of leadership at these firms.

Jack Morgan's friend James Stillman, head of National City Bank, had ideas about the war that closely reflected Morgan's own: though the war presented numerous expansion opportunities, old ties to the British and French banks had to be respected in the process, their countries supported unequivocally. Stillman's number-two man—midwestern-born Frank Vanderlip, who harbored a grudge against the eastern banking establishment and Wilson for cold-shouldering him during his presidential campaign—didn't share the same loyalties. He was less concerned than his upper-crust boss and the Morgan partners about the war's outcome and openly opposed American intervention until 1916, by which point German-American relations were more obviously battered. Nor did he support British demands that National City Bank terminate dealings with German banks, to which Stillman had responded that in victory the British would remember the banks that helped them.

Thus, at the end of 1914, it was National City Bank that opened a $5 million credit line for Russia in return for the designation of Russian purchasing agent for war supplies in the United States. The Morgan Bank remained true to its pro-Allies position and chose not to be involved in such dealings, while Vanderlip was more detached and sought to strengthen National City's position for whatever the postwar world would bring.

Stillman was less interested in war-related financing than Vanderlip, who believed it would augment the bank's position as well as America's global status. To him, it was important to forge ahead in Latin America and other underdeveloped countries while the European financial powers were busy with their war. That Stillman took some of this advice to heart enabled National City Bank to cover much ground postwar, not just relative to the European banks but also to the Morgan Bank. As Vanderlip wrote Stillman in December 1915, "We are really becoming a world bank in a very broad sense, and I am perfectly confident that the way is open to us to become the most powerful, the most far-reaching world financial institution that there has ever been."[15] Vanderlip's views ruffled Stillman's feathers because of Stillman's past collaboration agreements with the Morgan Bank. But they also ruffled the feathers of Morgan and Lamont in a way that would have huge repercussion for postwar peace.

War Thickens

The situation in Europe was deteriorating quickly. On May 7, 1915, a German U-20 torpedoed the starboard side of the British luxury liner *Lusitania* off the Irish coast. Nearly 1,200 people, including 124 US citizens, were killed.

Though the Germans expressed regret for the loss of American lives, it was a reticent regret. Wilson opened secret talks with the German ambassador Count Johann von Bernstorff to mitigate the targeting of Americans.[16] But publicly, Wilson issued a harsh note to the German government on May 14, 1915. In response, Morgan conveyed to Wilson his "intense satisfaction of both the substance and the manner of the note to the German Government."[17]

Morgan's renowned support for the Allies led to an assassination attempt at his Glen Cove, Long Island, home on July 3, 1915. Shot twice in the groin, he returned to work a few weeks later, renewed in his vigor to defend the Allies.[18] The shooter—a German nationalist who bombed the US Senate reception room the day before—was sent to a local jail, where he committed suicide before being questioned. The incident left Morgan even more paranoid and reclusive than lore about him suggested he was.[19]

By late summer, the brutality had escalated. On August 19, a German submarine sank another British passenger ship, the *Arabic,* without warning and with more loss of American lives. In response, Wilson negotiated the Arabic pledge of September 1, in which the German government promised not to torpedo passenger lines without warning.

More money would be needed for the Allies to combat their enemies. On September 25, the Morgan partners formed a syndicate to underwrite a $500 million bond issue for the British and French governments. They agreed to forgo their usual managing fee to support the war effort.[20]

Wilson remained hesitant about taking the country to war. In early January 1916, he sent Colonel Edward House as foreign policy adviser to London on his third peace mission.[21] While there, House met with British foreign secretary Sir Edward Grey to assess the situation. He returned to the United States in early March with the intent to cooperate in an Anglo-American peace plan agreement.

But German-American relations reached a new crisis when a submarine torpedoed an unarmed Channel packet, *Sussex,* on March 24, 1916. Three weeks later, Wilson presented Berlin with an ultimatum: he would break all relations unless Germany abandoned its unrestricted submarine campaign. Though Germany agreed, the peace was tentative.[22]

Still, as a result of Wilson's attempt to maintain a better relationship with Germany, America's relations with the Allies, particularly with Britain, deteriorated. Stateside, Wilson focused on his upcoming presidential campaign. Before the election, he reappointed Paul Warburg, a man considered sympathetic to his birth country, Germany, as vice president at the Federal Reserve.[23]

Whereas the last election hinged on policies toward bankers, this one was a referendum on the war. Republican presidential candidate Charles Evans Hughes, along with Theodore Roosevelt and other Republicans, criticized Wilson and his administration for alleged inefficiency and spinelessness toward Germany and Mexico, which was in the midst of a revolution. Wilson accused the Republicans of wanting to take the country into an unnecessary war.

On September 30, 1916, Wilson campaigned before a gathering of the Young Men's League of Democratic Clubs, with many Tammany men among them, at Wilson's grand summer residence, Shadow Lawn mansion (now Woodrow Wilson Hall), in West Long Branch, New Jersey.[24] He stressed his domestic achievements, most notably the establishment of the Federal Reserve System, "the great banking system by which the credits of this country, hitherto locked up, the credits of the average man, have been released and put into action." Contextualizing the establishment of the Federal Reserve System as a marquee Democrat accomplishment, Wilson played up the ineffectiveness of the original plan put forth by Republican Senator Nelson Aldrich.

"The heart of the Aldrich plan was a single central bank," Wilson told the audience of hopeful politicians, "which was susceptible of being controlled by the very men who have always dictated the financial policy of the Republican Party, whereas the heart of our system is not a great central bank, but a body appointed by and responsible to the government and, by the same token, responsible to the people of the United States."[25]

But control of financial policy was not as partisan as Wilson claimed. In fact, the bankers were largely unconcerned with the party in power, as long as they could influence it. The larger truth that Wilson hid from his prospective voters was that without Wall Street's help, war financing would have been impossible. The war could not be fully funded publicly; it needed the support of private bankers. Still, Wilson's general appeals for greater economic and social justice garnered widespread support from organized labor, Socialists, female voters in suffrage states, and farmers in plains states. Despite early returns indicating a victory for Supreme Court Justice Charles Evans Hughes, California handed the Electoral College majority to Wilson in a narrow victory.[26]

In the afterglow of his 1916 reelection, Wilson attempted to flex his power in a way he thought could help end the war. He persuaded the Federal Reserve Board to warn American bankers of the dangers to peace posed by continuing to purchase renewable short-term Allied notes and extending the

Allies credit in return—he thought if he could cut off the money supply for the warring nations, he could coax them into peace. The British had virtually exhausted their dollar reserves, and Wilson believed he could force the British and French to the peace table more quickly if he cut off their supply of private bank loans. This was no small request of the bankers, and they did not agree to it. There was too much money to be made from their international clients and too much financial ground to corner while their competitors were getting crippled in the war.

In addition to lending money, American banks were stockpiling foreign securities as a result of the war. Foreign countries decided it was safer to keep their wealth in America than risk losing funds because of military activities.

Before the outbreak of the war, the total amount of foreign securities held by national banks was $15.6 million. By May 1, 1916, it had increased tenfold to $158.5 million. And between May 1 and September 12, 1916, the national banks increased foreign securities holdings so that the total amount of foreign government and other foreign securities was nearly $240 million.[27] This influx of capital greatly enhanced Wall Street's position as the preeminent global lender and enhanced its ability to reloan funds to other countries and to war-related manufacturers domestically.

Marching Toward War

After another year of bitter trench warfare, Wilson was still convinced that the Allied war effort depended upon supplies from the United States, and he still believed he could use that leverage to force the British and French governments to negotiate peace. The Germans continued with their U-boat campaign, the consequences of which manifested throughout the United States. American ship owners began refusing to send their vessels into the war zone. As goods for Europe piled high on wharves in the United States, growing cries for war rippled across America. It was one thing to remain neutral for moral reasons, but quite another when the war began to hamper the US economy.

Wilson remained skeptical. Still, in his second inaugural address, he declared that the United States would adopt an armed neutrality to protect American commerce without resorting to full-fledged war.[28]

Morgan remained the key player in funding the war and handling all government matters of loans and bonds for the Allies. Congress had authorized the Federal Reserve Board and the comptroller of the currency to encourage the national banks to participate in a $250 million issue of British Exchequer bonds, the proceeds of which would be used to finance the export of materials to Britain. In addition, on March 25, 1917, Colonel House informed Wilson and McAdoo that efforts "will probably be made" to put the Morgan Bank at the "fore in the event [that] any large international financing is to be done in conjunction with this country."[29]

Raising money and waging war continued in lockstep as conditions worsened. A week after Morgan became the government's de facto wartime bank, German U-boats sank the *Algonquin* and four other US merchant ships.[30] It was the final straw for Wilson. On April 2, 1917, speaking before a joint session of Congress at 8:32 P.M., Wilson presented his decision to declare war. The Senate approved the war resolution on April 4, and the House followed on April 6. At 12:14 on Good Friday, the United States was at war on European soil for the first time in its history.[31]

The outpouring of approval from around the country was immense. Thousands of letters and telegrams offering services and support poured into the White House. They hit Wilson's desk mixed with hundreds of other papers awaiting his review and signature.[32] Wilson's private secretary, Thomas Brahany, singled out just one for the president's immediate attention: a handwritten note from Morgan dated April 4. It read:

> We are most heartily in accord with you as to the necessity of the United States assisting the allies in the matter of the supplies of materials and of credits. To those matters we have been devoting our whole time and thought for the past two years. I write to assure you again that the knowledge we have gained in those two years of close association with the allies in these matters are entirely at the disposal of the United States Government at any time or in any way you may wish to use it.[33]

The Allies had already disbursed more than $2 billion in the United States since the war began. The amount comprised 75 percent of the total amount of the Allies' purchase of munitions and raw materials in America.[34] The Morgan Bank, which was guiding these purchases, controlled war financing to an unprecedented extent.

There was no doubt about the necessity of the president-banker alliance. Each needed the other in this time of uncertainty and to secure their rise in the hierarchy of global power during and after the war. Wilson answered Morgan personally, "I am sure I can count upon you and your associations in this emergency."[35]

Three days later, the House Ways and Means Committee met to consider the bond bill.[36] The administration had asked Congress for authority to issue $5 billion of government bonds to fund the war with Germany. The request included $2 billion to finance part of the organization and operation of the Army and Navy and the conduct of the war generally, and $3 billion to supply credit to Allied governments, which would help them secure supplies in the United States.

In addition, McAdoo sought assistance from the Federal Reserve banks, national banks, state banks, savings banks, insurance companies, private bankers, and investment bankers to help raise money directly from the population.[37] The leaders of the financial community extended the use of their services to place government bonds with the public free of charge; they would find other profitable ways to make use of the new customers who streamed through their doors later.

The United States wound up selling nearly $17 billion in Liberty bonds.[38] McAdoo wanted to reach the broadest population of bond buyers possible—from small farmers to businessmen to workers. By doing so, he inadvertently created a new generation of American investors who would later participate in the 1920s stock bubble. McAdoo appointed Wall Street lawyer Russell Leffingwell, his old neighbor in Yonkers, New York, as counsel on the effort—and later made him assistant Treasury secretary in charge of the Liberty bond drives.[39] Leffingwell went on to become head of the Morgan Bank in the 1940s during World War II.

In addition to Liberty bonds, big banks went into overdrive to lend money to the Allies. By July 13, 1917, there were fifty-one private banks providing Britain with another batch of loans totaling $234 million. Morgan led the pack with nearly $70 million. Other top lenders included Chase National Bank with $12.5 million, First National Bank with $45 million, Guaranty Trust Bank with $20 million, and the National City Bank with $30 million.[40]

National City Bank's Charles Mitchell and *Forbes Magazine*

The war had another distinctly financial dimension that helped the bankers. It served to push memories of the Panic of 1907 and the Pujo hearings into a receding spot in the national consciousness. Citizens began to view the bankers not as crooks but as patriots in the war effort. Thanks to this sentiment of unity, a space opened up for the rise of a new generation of independent bankers with few ties to the panics and trials of the past, who could use their real or alleged commitment to the cause as a way to bolster their reputations. Men who were not connected by blood to the Morgans or Rockefellers, and who were not members of the Jekyll Island Club or predisposed to side with any particular country, began to vie for spots at the country's major firms. These men would bring with them a fresh stance on the role of finance that was based more on opportunism than on prior relationships. The result would propagate two types of Wall Street bankers: the ones who worked on the basis of personal alliances and the ones who worked on the basis of profit alone.

One journalist was especially fascinated with documenting these shifts. In September 1917, Bertie Charles Forbes launched *Forbes Magazine* from offices at 120 Broadway, near Wall Street. With the war escalating, American financial titans stood to become definitive global leaders, and Forbes sought to lead the press in capturing their ascent.

The first issue paid homage to a rising financier from outside the usual family names or connections: Charles Mitchell, who later turned National City Bank into America's first supermarket financial services firm.

Forbes characterized Mitchell as a "human financial dynamo" and quoted Mitchell as saying of his early career as an investment banker, "I had more nerve than capital." Mitchell's first major deal with his firm Mitchell and Company had been selling a block of $300,000 of equipment notes secured by New York harbor scows. Mitchell, an exceedingly persuasive salesman, had the note presold to eager inside investors before it was officially available for sale in the market (not unlike the way shares of Facebook were sold to inside investors before others could buy them publicly in the stock market a century later).

"It was the big game that fascinated him," wrote Forbes. Fortunately for Mitchell's ego, National City asked him to join the firm in March 1916. There, he could play that game in a bigger arena. "This was exactly in line with my ambition," Mitchell said. "There was virtually no limit to what might be accomplished in the way of constructive financing."

As soon as Mitchell became vice president of National City Bank, he began to fashion the firm into something resembling a private investment bank. This was similar to what Morgan had done, but with a significant twist—unlike his elitist rival, who depended on large corporate clients, Mitchell sought to broaden the firm's capital base by also appealing to "the Everyman," as he called individual depositors.[41]

Mitchell's decision to open the doors to average citizens, many of whom were still banking at smaller local banks, ushered in the modern age of national banking. World War I helped secure these new customers because in addition to providing them with banking services, National City Bank also pushed the notion that opening an account was a way to support the war effort, peppering its advertising campaign with this notion.

Mitchell's brash philosophy propelled the firm to success in this new era, as it would grow to become the first bank in the United States to reach $1 billion in assets. Mitchell would become the bank's president and preside over its extensive postwar international speculation on the back of those new deposits. He would also be at the helm when the market crashed in 1929. In fact, Carter Glass would later say, Mitchell, more than any other banker, was responsible for the Crash. But all of this was years away. For now, Mitchell brought his new ideas to bear to make his bank into an international powerhouse, using the war as a means to that end.

Economic Entanglements of War

In the wake of the Austro-Hungarian and German attack in Northern Italy on October 24, 1917, President Wilson sent Colonel House for another round of negotiations with the British and French allies.[42] There, he would discuss matters of critical economic and financial importance. Wilson also sent Morgan partner Thomas Lamont, who was intimately involved in organizing Liberty and foreign loans, to serve unofficially as a private adviser. Lamont had been working closely with McAdoo and Leffingwell, and he would broker meetings between US Lieutenant Colonel William Boyce-Thomson, stationed in Petrograd, and British officials on the situation in Russia.[43] The war would continue for more than a year, and a treaty would take nearly two years to gain acceptance by most of the countries involved, but Wilson's negotiating team already had a key representative from America's most powerful bank on it.

Serving in a dual capacity (helping the president while protecting the Morgan Bank's postwar position), Lamont spent the next ten days working with his colleagues at Morgan, Grenfell & Company in London and meeting with members of the House mission. Not to leave money on the table, he also negotiated Morgan's 0.125 percent compensation from the British treasury for acting as its paying agent for all the British government's US purchases now being handled by the US government. The sum offset all the expenses Morgan had agreed to forgo as the British government's purchasing agent.[44]

By December 7, 1917, the United States was also at war with Austria-Hungary. A week later, just as Morgan had predicted, the financial markets quickly sank into disarray. The upheaval and the anxiety surrounding the drop threatened the very survival of the war effort, and thus America's ability to navigate the war from a solid economic stance. But the main problem the markets had wasn't a military one; it was a regulatory concern.

Responding to the bankers' pressure to do something about railroad industry regulation, a nervous McAdoo informed Wilson that New York security markets were "demoralized." He said there were rumors swirling around Wall Street that "if the Government took over the railroads, the rights of bondholders and stockholders would not be protected." The exaggeration linked the government's domestic policy to its foreign war policy. Fears that undue regulations would strain credit and subdue the markets, which Morgan had warned about since the war's start, were being realized at the worst time for the nation.

At the bankers' insistence, McAdoo warned Wilson that declines "might reach a point where a panic would set in, grave injury would result and the financial operations of the Government would be seriously imperiled."[45] He encouraged Wilson to issue a soothing statement to the public. Instead, Wilson exercised his presidential authority to effectively nationalize the railroads for war purposes. Rather than dampen the markets, this news sent them rallying into the year's end. Investors saw the government's financial support as a positive, even if bankers considered it overly intrusive.

Wilson was more concerned about solidifying public support for the war and congressional support for his strategy to end it. The peace he sought would increase US power in a world in which European power was diminishing, a strategy the bankers were happy to support. On January 8, 1918, Wilson delivered his "Fourteen Points" address to Congress. Among other things, he proposed freedom of the seas, a reduction of armaments to establish a route to a more equitable peace, and an end to secret diplomacy and economic trade barriers among nations. The latter comforted Germany, which feared financial repercussions, and delighted international bankers.

The final point paved the way for the League of Nations, a world parliament containing members from all nations, with a central council controlled by the greater powers, including the United States. From a diplomatic perspective, the idea seemed to have everything one could want. From a banker's standpoint, a united set of trading partners, with a central US influence, was full of opportunity.

National City Bank Transitions

By early spring 1918, a prominent change occurred at the nation's largest commercial bank that would have important ramifications for its postwar position as an international superbank. On March 15, after battling illness for a month, National City Bank chairman James Stillman died in his home. Stillman had handled all the bank's business ever since president Frank Vanderlip took a leave of absence in September 1917 to chair the national War Savings Committee. A few weeks before he died, Stillman called Vanderlip back to New York because the bank's Russian positions, engineered by Vanderlip, were a disaster. They had already cost $10 million, but the losses stood poised to rise to $33 million, or 40 percent of the bank's capital. The meeting never came to pass because of Stillman's death, but internal rumors had Vanderlip on his way out the door.

While the Morgan Bank focused on war efforts mostly on behalf of Allied European countries, Stillman (following an agreement with Vanderlip) had concentrated on extending National City Bank's international influence— particularly in South America, where it was challenging British banks for market share. Shortly after the war began, Stillman established branches in Buenos Aires and Rio de Janeiro, and later expanded to all the major cities in South America and Cuba, as well as in Europe.

Following Stillman's death, Vanderlip met with National City's attorney John Sterling before returning to Washington.[46] Vanderlip had become obsessed with a grand plan to expand National City's international presence by infusing the European recovery (not just that of the Allies) with US capital. This tested the patience of the Morgan Bank, which was supporting only the Allies. Stillman had been caught between Vanderlip's urging and the alliances he had forged at the turn of the century with the Morgan Bank and J. P. Morgan.

National City directors appointed Stillman's son, James A. Stillman, as chairman. The younger Stillman was at odds with Vanderlip personally and regarding the Allies.[47] That slight propelled Vanderlip, still eager to make his mark on the bank, to undertake a three-month, seven-country tour of Europe while his banker rival Tom Lamont and former friend President Wilson were there involved in treaty negotiations. Perhaps eager to retain his corner of influence after being passed over for the chairman position, Vanderlip made a speech following his trip that fueled the fire regarding a congressional rejection of Wilson's treaty and League of Nations proposal. This was his last major move before he faded into obscurity.

By June 1919, Vanderlip had been kicked out of National City.[48] Charles Mitchell, the brash outsider, rose within the bank embracing the notion of short-term profit ahead of long-term relationships or strategies. His doctrine would drive the bank to attain the broadest international presence of any US bank at the time. Mitchell cared less about the moral implications of which country he sided with after the war and more about the opportunities to make money. In that opinion, he concurred with Vanderlip, but his style was far more aggressive.

Approaching Armistice

By the time the Allied armies pushed their formidable counteroffensive on the Western front in the summer of 1918, Wilson had amassed much world support as a voice of morality.[49] He wanted to use his global popularity as a backdrop upon which to deliver his party the majority in Congress in the fall elections. He also knew that the more support he could garner in Washington, the stronger his position would be in postwar negotiations with other superpowers.

Aligned with Wilson's global intentions and methods, Lamont offered the services of his recently acquired newspaper, the *Evening Post*, to help the president clarify his position on postwar peace. Late in the afternoon on October 4, 1918, Lamont stopped by the White House to discuss how the two men could help each other.[50]

The *Evening Post* was a personal venture for Lamont, a former reporter. Morgan had consented to the purchase as long as Lamont agreed to keep its editorial stance separate from the private affairs of the Morgan Bank. In order to maintain the paper's independence, Lamont selected *Atlantic Monthly* editor Ellery Sedgwick as trustee.[51] Lamont had no daily managerial responsibilities. Still, he wanted to eliminate a "certain fault-finding, or carping, attitude" that had led the paper, as he told Wilson, "at times to make criticisms without due consideration or compel study of the fact." Wilson agreed: "I always used to call the *Evening Post* the 'whipping post.'"

Lamont believed his paper could show the American people the war from Wilson's perspective. He too believed that a "fair" peace would hold great promise for the country and its financiers. But first he had to discuss his reservations with some of Wilson's globalist views, as he sensed they were not in sync with the nation's predisposition. He played devil's advo-cate. "The country is in a mood just now for war," he told Wilson, "and that mood is what is making the work of our soldiers in France so effective. We are necessarily intolerant and not ready as a whole to listen to such senti-ments as you express."

"Yes, not only intolerant," said Wilson, "but we are growing revengeful . . . a very dangerous attitude and not one calculated to have us conclude the wis-est sort of a peace."

"Exactly!" said Lamont. "Now, the *Evening Post* has considerable influ-ence throughout the country. . . . I want to know how the *Post* can help you in educating the country properly."

Wilson astutely replied that the *Evening Post* should point out that "if we conclude a peace that is not wholly just to every one of the large nations, then each one of those powerful nations will not rest contented until it has righted what it deems to be its wrongs. That of course means more wars."

Lamont asked, "About your League of Nations, just how is it to be made effective? I am one of those who believe that economic force is about the only instrument which can serve to make a League of Nations effective."

"You mean," said Wilson, "to use economic force in the way of penalties?"

Lamont replied, "Not only that [but] it seems to me that the League of Na-tions will not work if it is to be made dependent purely upon written rules."

At the time, Wilson wasn't considering a rigid written constitution; he en-visioned producing a written plan at peacetime that could evolve naturally. To some extent, Lamont's prodding made him begin to think about formal-izing such a plan even sooner—not to appease Lamont, or necessarily the public, but to take control of the process.

Near the end of their conversation, Lamont offered his endorsement and that of his newspaper. This was no small matter, as he was spurring his po-litical party affiliations to side with Wilson. He said, "I am a Republican . . . and I do not wish to give you the impression that my support will be given to you thick and thin, for all time to come, but I want to have you know that you have that support to the very limit throughout the war."[52]

Thus the two began a transformative relationship that would solidify through postwar collaboration. Lamont, a Republican Morgan banker who personified all the attributes Wilson denigrated in his political speeches, threw his support behind Wilson. He would become the president's most loyal banker supporter.

On November 2, 1918, US food administrator Herbert Hoover reported dire circumstances in Belgium, which portended an epic European economic crisis. Domestic economic conditions across the continent were deteriorating rapidly, a factor contributing more than combat developments to the war's end. The Germans in Belgium had given notice to the coal mines that all workers would have to be furloughed for lack of funds, which meant a lack of fuel through the winter. As Hoover wrote, "It will result in enormous loss of human life" and impose "a greater burden upon the German people at the hands of the allies."[53] It was one of many desperate actions that would complicate future reparations negotiations.

Against that horrific backdrop, on the eve of November 11, 1918, a few hours before the armistice agreement was signed at Compiègne, Wilson read the military and naval terms to Congress and announced, "The war thus comes to an end."[54]

CHAPTER 3

THE LATE 1910S:
PEACE TREATIES AND DOMESTIC
POLITICS

*"The masters of the government of the United States are the
combined capitalists and manufacturers of the United States."*

—Woodrow Wilson, 1913[1]

THE 1918 MIDTERM ELECTIONS TRANSFERRED CONTROL OF THE SENATE FROM THE
Democrats to the Republicans. In the process, Henry Cabot Lodge, a twenty-
five-year veteran power politician, became the Senate majority leader and
chair of the Foreign Relations Committee. In both roles, Wilson would need
the support of this longtime nemesis but was unable to garner it. Following
his party's defeat, a disgruntled Wilson thought he could do more outside the
confines of Washington to establish a new world paradigm than by dealing
with party maneuvering at home.

A week after the elections, contrary to the advice of his inner circle to
remain in Washington, Wilson declared he would head the American peace

delegation in Paris. He was the first sitting American president to travel to Europe. His other chief peace commissioners were Secretary of State Robert Lansing; Republican diplomat Henry White, one of the few Republicans who supported Wilson's goals; Colonel House; and General Tasker H. Bliss. Wilson did not take Lodge, but he drafted Thomas Lamont, with whom he had discussed his ambitions for the League of Nations so candidly, as a representative of the Treasury Department, now headed by Carter Glass, alongside the other Treasury Department representative, Albert Strauss. As American delegation chair, Wilson appointed Vance Criswell McCormick.

Wilson and his group set sail for Europe aboard the *George Washington* on December 4. He returned to the United States on February 24, 1919, but traveled back to Europe on March 5, where he remained until July 8.[2] It was and would remain the longest period of time a sitting president was off American soil.

In all, thirty-two nations were involved in the Paris Peace Conference, which began in January 1919 (Germany was not included). But the Big Four—President Wilson, British prime minister David Lloyd George, French prime minister Georges Clemenceau, and Italian prime minister Vittorio Orlando—began meeting privately to negotiate the treaty. The European leaders were concerned about geographical victories and, more critically, the amount of war reparations they would receive from Germany.

The Big Four were reluctant supporters of Wilson's League covenant, and they weren't particularly interested in Wilson's "just peace." They wanted optimal financial retribution. That meant gutting Wilson's Fourteen Points as much as possible. In the end, the treaty contained no provisions to end secret diplomacy or preserve freedom of the seas. Still, after many concessions, Wilson gained approval for the League of Nations and sailed to the United States to present the Treaty of Versailles to the Senate.

While Wilson returned to the United States to address the Senate Foreign Relations Committee about the importance of a League of Nations in conjunction with a peace treaty, Lamont remained in Paris to address reparations matters. The desires of Wilson and Lamont were aligned, for both believed the League would give the United States greater power in the new international order politically and from a financial standpoint. The Anglo-French obsession with German reparations was a thorn in their side. The other thorn came from an increasingly isolationist Republican Senate.

Thus Wilson returned to Paris on March 14 without the support he sought from Congress. Republican reticence weakened his negotiating position in Europe, ultimately by forcing him to request changes to the peace covenant that would appease his congressional opponents and to succumb to more of the Allies' demands in return. At the heart of the covenant was Article X, by which each member guaranteed the "territorial integrity" and political independence of the other members "against external aggression."[3]

Leading the mostly Republican opposition to that was a confirmed isolationist, Senator William Borah, who didn't believe that the path to America's strength lay in working with other countries. While Wilson was in Paris, Borah embarked on a nationwide tour, drumming up opposition to the League in speeches before packed audiences. (On November 19, 1919, Borah delivered an epic two-hour speech against the Treaty of Versailles and the League of Nations on the floor of the Senate, which helped secure its defeat.)

Most bankers, however, preferred to do business with European countries that were confident in their own futures—ones that could seek and repay loans during the reconstruction period and beyond. American banks' opportunity to grow globally relied on a field of counterparts that was as open and healthy as possible. Isolationism would thwart their opportunities. In that regard, most bankers were, and would always be, more internationalist than many factions of the government.

Lamont had asked his partners Jack Morgan and Dwight Morrow to solicit the views of Senator Elihu Root, a former secretary of state under Teddy Roosevelt who had won the Nobel Peace Prize in 1912. If anyone could see the logic of international peace, it would be him. But Root's response was disappointing. He told the men that he felt it was proper for the United States to have an interest in world affairs, but that American force should enter European disputes "only when required to protect world order."[4] The sticking point of obligating the military to protect friendly nations in the League was beginning to look like an insurmountable problem. But Wilson remained optimistic. He believed that with some clarification and amendment, Congress would come around. This would turn out to be a major, and eventually tragic, political mistake.

The British and French, noting the tension in the United States, were cooling on the notion of a League of Nations—or at least they believed they could squeeze Wilson for more demands. Reparations were more important to them than the League covenant. In meetings Lloyd George was throwing up numbers with wide and illogical variations. He thought that the most Germany could pay was $25 billion, but his financial advisers wanted to request $55 billion. House advised Davis, Lamont, and Strauss not to go above $35 billion unless the amount could be reduced easily if necessary.[5]

A few days later, Lamont, McCormick, and Davis again visited Wilson's house in Paris. There they found Wilson, Lloyd George, Clemenceau, and

Orlando arguing about reparations amounts. At that point, Lloyd George and Clemenceau wanted to leave the decision to a future commission report. For political reasons, they said they didn't want to be seen agreeing to too small an amount, which the United States was pressing for.[6] Their countries were so battered economically that they didn't feel they would retain their mandate to lead if they were seen to capitulate on reparations.

The next day, McCormick met with Lamont, Davis, American financier Bernard Baruch, and John Foster Dulles (grandson of former secretary of state John W. Dulles, and nephew of Wilson's secretary of state, Robert Lansing) to consider Lloyd George's latest ultimatum: the inclusion of British servicemen pensions as a category of claims to be paid by Germany.[7] The group reluctantly agreed to Lloyd George's proposal, but patience was wearing thin. A month later, and three days after Clemenceau presented the "preliminary conditions of peace" to the German delegates at the Grand Trianon Palace at Versailles, the Paris Peace Conference began in earnest. A severe virus and neurological illness temporarily prevented Wilson from serving as "commanding actor on the grand stage," and allowed Lloyd George to emerge as the key force in the Supreme Council leveraging Wilson's absence and physical weakness.[8]

Lamont, meanwhile, had been touring Europe assessing conditions and considering the reparations claims of the various countries he toured.[9] Europe was plagued by severe hyperinflation and food shortages, and was facing an acute recession caused by the end of wartime production and an influx of labor from returning troops. As a result of his findings, Lamont requested credits for the newly constituted, "lesser" nations such as Poland, Czechoslovakia, Yugoslavia, Romania, and the Baltic states. He also requested credits to France, Belgium, and Italy for raw materials; credits to France and possibly Belgium for reconstruction; and even working capital for enemy states like Austria.

True to his feelings on global finance, Lamont wanted those credits to come from "the normal channels of private enterprise and commercial banking credits," not from the government. But he conceded "while the situation is still unsettled . . . further government aid on a limited scale may be necessary."[10] Wilson agreed with Lamont's credit suggestions but remained reticent about his proposals on addressing the American public, which was increasingly antagonistic toward the idea of a League of Nations.

Wilson's alliance with Lamont had evolved into more than a reform experiment; it had become a bond of deep mutual trust, respect, and necessity. One evening, Wilson and his physician, Dr. Grayson, were walking along the Avenue du Bois de Boulogne. They sat and watched the pedestrians, equestrians, and motorcars pass by. Wilson used this time to gather his thoughts on Lamont and bankers in general. He said, "I have given representation to Wall Street which may be misunderstood at home, especially by Democrats and Progressives. I chose, purposely, for instance, Tom Lamont of Morgan & Company, because I wanted him to see at first hand exactly the plans and purposes and manner of the administration's way of doing business. I wanted him to be a partner of reform for the country. If Wall Street continues to try to turn the finances and economic conditions of the country a revolution is inevitable. And I do not want to see a revolution."[11]

Vanderlip's Negative Intervention

Frank Vanderlip had also been touring Europe on behalf of National City and in an effort to secure his own place in history. Once he returned to the United States, he began stirring the pot. On May 27, 1919, he addressed the Economic Club at the Hotel Astor in New York City.[12] Vanderlip claimed that since the war, England's premier position in the international industrial markets had been maintained "by underpaying labor," yet now the British government was "undertaking to build a million houses for workingmen." Vanderlip didn't believe the United States should be financially responsible for such a sudden socialistic shift in British domestic policy, nor any reconstruction efforts that didn't directly benefit American banks and business.

"I was in Europe from the first of February to the ninth of May," Vanderlip told his audience. "I met every finance minister . . . many of the prime ministers [and] the leading financiers and bankers. . . . However black a background I paint . . . I believe Americans must know it, must comprehend it, must get it in to heart and mind, because we must act; and if we do act, we can save Europe from catastrophe, a chapter that will involve us."[13]

Unlike his former boss, James Stillman, who had used a softer tongue in discussing the British—not least because of his long-standing business arrangements with the staunch Anglo supporters at the Morgan Bank—Vanderlip blamed the British government for the impaired economic and social conditions in England, France, and Spain. "Let us pause, therefore, and put our own house in order lest the fires that are now burning in Europe shall spread and destroy our own country," he said.[14] It was not so much that Vanderlip was against helping Britain or Europe. It was that he didn't want to support Britain's mistakes or provide it undue economic collaboration. He was against the idea of the League of Nations for the same isolationist reasons as that faction in Congress.

As he later said at a speech to the Radcliffe Club, "We must all be guided by intelligent self-interest—that is, interest for our people and an eagerness to progress, and a League of Nations or a similar document would not encourage such progress. We must have an incentive for progress, and competition with other nations is the greatest, and in fact, the only incentive in trade relations."[15] (At the same speech, Vanderlip also claimed that building a railroad in China was more important than trying to save the lives of the ten million people perishing there because of famine.)

Senate critics used Vanderlip's speech to fuel their growing antagonism toward the League of Nations.[16] Their reliance on Vanderlip's words did not go unnoticed by the Morgan bankers. As Morgan partner Dwight Morrow wrote Lamont, "Senate opposition to the League of Nations will be very formidable. . . . For instance, the speech of Vanderlip . . . incited the feeling among business men that perhaps after all the European situation is in such a mess that cooperation at the present is impractical."

Meanwhile, in an underhanded effort to further malign Wilson and his team, Lodge's Senate Foreign Relations Committee subpoenaed Lamont for effective treason, though the charge was not called anything quite so dire. Lodge wanted to determine how copies of the peace treaty had been leaked to the international bankers before being made public. Lamont had furnished a copy of the treaty to his former associate Henry Davison, who had been at the Red Cross since 1917.[17] Lamont believed the League of Nations covenant could apply to many facets of Red Cross work. But before long, the newspapers had obtained a copy and printed it for the public to see. Whether Lamont intended to shape public opinion before Washington voted on the treaty was not clear. But even so, the intent was not malicious.

Lamont was unhinged by the senseless antagonism of his fellow Republicans; he was being assailed by the people he had supported for years. The sabotage had apparently emanated from Wall Street and been exacerbated by elements in Washington, though an exact source was never determined. It rattled Wilson, who couldn't understand why some people didn't seem to realize what was going on in the world and focused on such petty items.

Jack Morgan and Henry Davison were subpoenaed. Lamont instructed them to be truthful and to share with the Senate every aspect of his communications. He wrote them that when he returned to the United States he would be very glad to come to Washington and "supplement his written statement with any further information that the Senate might desire." Wilson considered his action commendable and informed Lamont as much.[18]

On June 11, 1919, Baruch, Lamont, Davis, and McCormick discussed the more pressing issue of Wilson's final proposed answer to Germany on reparations. Lamont remained touched by Wilson's faith. He told McCormick he "was considerably worried about the leak issue, but greatly pleased by a letter from the President showing his confidence in him."

McCormick replied, "The Chief stood by his friends."[19]

That same day, the Senate Foreign Relations Committee testimony noted that Davison had secured a copy of the treaty from Lamont before the secrecy injunction had been imposed—just as Lamont had explained in writing. Davison had brought the copy to the United States and given it to Root, who showed it to Lodge. Root finally came to Lamont's rescue and testified, "he has had it several weeks, that it was no longer secret, and every American citizen was entitled to see copy of the paper after it was made public by German Government."[20]

Morgan denied having seen a copy and heard of none in circulation in the financial district. Even Vanderlip testified that he had never seen the treaty.[21] The witch hunt was over. But the incident revealed an unease and distrust of the treaty situation and of Lamont, a Republican who was breaking ranks with the party to support the League of Nations. It also appeared politically motivated to weaken Wilson's hand before the final approvals took place in Europe.

Negotiations hit yet another snag in Paris. The British were now attempting to control the purchase of raw materials and foodstuffs throughout the world. With Lloyd George's irrational demands lingering in the air, Lamont expressed further worries over Senate passage of the League covenant. He urged Wilson to "play up a speech-making tour" and explain why the covenant and the rest of the treaty could not be separated. "I do not have to assure you of my intense interest in the prompt ratification of the Treaty and of the Covenant," he wrote. "I consider it a crisis for the world."[22]

Eugene Meyer, of the War Finance Corporation, had arrived in Paris to work with Lamont on proposed legislation to enlarge the powers of the American corporation to operate internationally.[23] If the League didn't work, there had to be a structure to facilitate private business and extend private credit to Europe.

As the US government and population grew increasingly reluctant to help Europe financially, even the Treasury Department refused to approve additional credit extensions to cover European purchases, even of American goods. The isolationist stance was one of the main reasons private American banks were able to step into the arena of credit extension and greatly enhance their global financial position.

Based on Lamont's earlier disposition toward private assistance, Senator Walter Evans Edge introduced Senate Bill 2472 (which became the Edge Act of 1919), authorizing American corporations to deal in any foreign banking that met the approval of the Federal Reserve Board (which had been given permission to consider foreign banking under the Federal Reserve Act) and the secretary of the Treasury.[24] The private banks would officially take up the slack for the government on this account. The Edge Act allowed for a substantial expansion of American corporate and banking power abroad. The legislation would catalyze a dispersion of US banks into Europe, and around the world, for the next century.

The Treaty of Versailles and Sailing Home

On June 28, 1919, the peace treaty with Germany was signed in the Galerie des Glaces in the Palace of Versailles. At promptly three o'clock, Clemenceau opened the great assembly. Within less than an hour, as Secretary of State Robert Lansing wrote in his diary, "the last delegate had affixed his name to this greatest of treaties."[25]

Herbert Hoover remained behind to take account of Europe's "demoralized productivity."[26] Fifteen million families were receiving some form of unemployment allowance. Hoover estimated that "the population of Europe is at least 100 million greater than can be supported without imports and must live by the production and distribution of exports, and their situation is aggravated not only by lack of raw material imports but by low production of European raw materials."[27] Not only was production far below the level it was at when the armistice was signed, he informed Wilson; it was "far below the maintenance of life and health."[28]

The treaty was signed with many grumblings, especially from the Germans, who preferred the Fourteen Points as Wilson had initially presented them to the watered-down version they became. Two orders of business remained: the United States had to ratify the treaty, and Europe required massive funds for reconstruction.

On July 10, Wilson addressed the Senate about the Treaty of Versailles and the League of Nations. The Senate was divided, particularly over Article X, which required all members "to respect and preserve as against external aggression the territorial integrity and existing political independence of all Members of the League." At least six Republican senators, or "irreconcilables," remained steadfastly opposed to the treaty and US intervention in any more "European wars." Nine others, the "mild reservationists," would consider approving the treaty but only if they could ensure that America would not necessarily have to enter wars on behalf of other nations. That left nearly three dozen undecided Republicans. As for the Democrats, though many sided with Wilson, some supported the mild reservationists and irreconcilables.

At the end of the Paris Peace Conference Lamont had promised Wilson that he would fight for the League of Nations after returning to the United States. On July 11, he sent Wilson resolutions adopted by the League of Free Nations Association, a countrywide organization he had chaired. The association called for the progressive reduction of armaments by all nations. It also resolved to "call upon all forward-looking citizens to urge the United States Senate: to ratify without reservation the Treaty with Germany, including the League of Nations Covenant . . . and for the full participation of both Germany and Russia on equal footing in all economic intercourse as the best insurance against any reversion to the old scheme of balance of power, economic privilege and war."

This was the crux of Wilson's proposed covenant, but it also dovetailed with bankers' interests for a more open financial playing field. Both the president and the bankers wanted to realign the Old European balance of power and put an end to secret side treaties and imperial economics. Breaking these barriers would leave a broader platform on which America could position itself as a dominant political and financial force.

Lamont had submitted his association's resolutions to Republican Senate majority leader Lodge, hoping that his intervention would help break through the political deadlock and assuage long-held philosophical hostilities between Wilson and Lodge.[29] Lodge's reply was immediate. He responded that "the difficulty with the resolutions covered by his reservations" was that of "amending the League of Nations after its ratification."[30] He didn't want to take the chance of letting the League of Nations slide until his reservations against it were addressed. Of course, doing so would undermine the agreement that the European nations had signed, with the understanding that the United States would be a military presence if needed in any future European upheavals.

Upon Lamont's renewed and persistent suggestions that Wilson take the matter to the people, Wilson agreed to tour the country to drum up support for the League of Nations and the treaty ratification, but Dr. Grayson, his physician, warned him that his health would not likely survive the intense campaign. Indeed, on July 19, Wilson suffered a "small" stroke that affected his mood, leadership, and memory.[31]

His condition led him to refuse to negotiate with the Republicans. Four days later, a news report stated, "An unyielding attitude against reservation to the treaty of peace was taken by President Wilson in talks today with four Republican Senators at the White House. . . . President Wilson was reported by the Senators to have explicitly stated that he would accept no compromise with the opposition forces."[32]

Lamont soldiered on. Unaware of his friend's waning health, he urged Wilson to "go direct to the Senate" and explain the chief points of controversy. Such a direct course, he believed, "would rivet the public attention."[33]

But by early August, Europe's economic crises had spilled into the United States. Increased costs of living due to global shortages became an absorbing domestic problem making Washington and the population even less interested in helping Europe.[34] The economic turmoil rendered the environment even less malleable to helping external nations and added vigor to the isolationists in Congress.

In the emotional haze of his mini-stroke, Wilson was deflated. He wrote Lamont, "I thank you sincerely for every ray of light you shed on the present perplexed and somewhat distressing situation, and you do shed many that help me to see the path."[35]

Mounting tensions between Japan and China threw another wrench in the works. Concerns grew that Japan's grip on China would ripple through US financial, industrial, and economic systems.[36] Lansing suggested that to mitigate the situation, Lamont become US minister in China, given his unique skills and "force of character."[37]

On August 19, 1919, Wilson made an unprecedented presidential appearance before the Senate Foreign Relations Committee to argue for ratification of the Treaty of Versailles. Four days later, the committee responded by deciding to approve its first weakening of Wilson's agreements—returning the Shantung Peninsula, which had been given to Japan, to Chinese control.

Lamont remained focused on the League upon hearing the news. During his late August vacation in Maine, he sent Wilson his draft statement on the matter for approval. He had previously refrained from making any public statement for fear of its potential adverse effects. "People, for instance like Senator Root, with whom, of course, I have been in disagreement, as he has been still hanging out for firm reservations, told me that if I made a statement, praising your course in Paris, I might get Borah, et al, so angry it would get their backs up still worse against the Treaty. . . . To tell you the truth, I am getting a little tired of being shut up all the time, just because I might get somebody 'mad.'"[38]

Fortified by Lamont's support, Wilson muscled up the strength to travel to Columbus, Ohio, where on September 4 he made his first stop on a national tour to rally public opinion.[39] But his failing health inhibited his oratorical skills. Wilson's talent for memorizing and delivering speeches was faltering. His sentences came out incomplete, disconnected, and rambling.

Still, Lamont remained tireless. This had become his and Wilson's cause, and for a moment that cause loomed larger than what either had to gain separately. On September 10, he tried to bolster Wilson's confidence over the impact of his statement, noting that "The New York Tribune . . . is beginning to hedge very strongly in its support of the Lodge types." In other words, the press was beginning to lean away from Wilson's detractors. Lamont praised Wilson on his recent speeches and told him that "they must have their effect upon the country & thus upon the Senate."[40]

The shifting sentiment in the press appeared to be doing the trick, for critics in Washington looked like they might budge. Lodge and the mild reservationists finally agreed to the critical Article X, on the condition that Congress would approve any use of US forces.

But it was not to be. Wilson declared the compromise "a rejection of the Covenant." Three days later, as his train reached Colorado, he suffered such a severe stroke warning that Dr. Grayson canceled the rest of his tour. In wavering health and frustrated with the Republicans' suggestions, which he believed would gut the entire point of the treaty and the League of Nations, Wilson returned to Washington on September 28. At about 8:30 A.M. on October 2, a major stroke paralyzed the left side of his body.[41] The next day, the White House issued a statement that Wilson had been working on, saying that the coming election will be a "genuine national referendum" on the issue of American membership in the League of Nations.

Toward the 1920 Election

Lamont defended and advised Wilson during the campaign period through the following year. But Wilson's ideals and Lamont's push would go unappreciated. On Election Day, November 2, 1920, voters rejected Wilson and his League, as represented by Democratic presidential candidate James A. Cox and vice presidential candidate Franklin Delano Roosevelt (FDR). Republican Party presidential candidate Warren Harding and vice presidential candidate Calvin Coolidge, catering to an increasingly isolationist citizenry, won in a landslide victory.[42]

Two and a half weeks later, on November 19, 1920, the Senate rejected a peace treaty for the first time in history, by a vote of thirty-nine to fifty-five. A group of Democrats helped Lodge's mild reservationists and the irreconcilables defeat the proposal. The United States never ratified the Treaty of Versailles, nor did it join the League of Nations.[43]

On March 1, 1921, Wilson said farewell to his cabinet at their last meeting. A few minutes later, "leaning on his cane and limping slightly," he "passed slowly out of the executive offices."[44] The Progressive Era was officially over.[45]

In the coming decade, the bankers would extend their power by expanding their franchises globally and by consolidating the deposits of the more insular-focused US population. The result would be extreme speculation within and beyond America's borders that would bring about great highs and subsequent economic collapse. The presidency would be weakened in the process. And the absence of America's presence in the League of Nations, coupled with the overcompromised, tension-laden Treaty of Versailles, would set the stage for a deadlier second world war.

To be sure, America was destined to become a financial, military, and political superpower. But it would do so by way of the conservative Republicans (with support from a war-weary public), who believed that global power would be amassed by focusing on domestic fortification rather than by helping other countries. Adopting a stance of nationalistic elitism, they weren't willing to risk contamination by socialistic doctrines or accept the labor rights Wilson supported through the League (which more liberal Democrats wanted strengthened). Even though the bankers constantly sought ways to rise above isolationism in the direction of financial and trade internationalism, the victorious politicians wanted a more self-centered, laissez-faire style of government, and that in turn fueled a more mercenary breed of financial capitalism. The prevailing stance would have an economic impact worldwide and helped pave the way to a war that would claim millions of lives.

CHAPTER 4

THE 1920S: POLITICAL ISOLATIONISM, FINANCIAL INTERNATIONALISM

*"Human nature cannot be changed by an act of the legislature.
It is too much assumed that because an abuse exists
it is the business of the national government to remedy it."*[1]

—President Calvin Coolidge, 1926

THE NOTION OF AMERICAN ISOLATIONISM AFFECTED THE WAY THE 1920S PRESIDENTS conceived of the role of chief executive domestically as well. They didn't attempt to shape their authority or that of the White House relative to the bankers in the way that Teddy Roosevelt and Woodrow Wilson had. As such, financiers stepped in to enhance their power, primarily by expanding on the influence they already had but also by doing what they wanted to do without any Washington-imposed restrictions.

President Warren G. Harding was an uninspiring politician who saw his job as calming a nation, balancing a postwar budget, and leaving bankers and businessmen alone. President Calvin Coolidge represented more of the same, though with an even more reticent personal style. Coolidge even kept most of Harding's cabinet, including Treasury Secretary Andrew Mellon and Secretary of Commerce Herbert Hoover. Given his international experience under Wilson, Hoover might have done more to mold the power of the presidency and adopt a more internationalist doctrine when he assumed the presidency. But his time as president was marred by an epic financial disaster and all that the bankers had done to instigate it.

For the most part, the philosophy of these three Republican presidents was simple. They believed the role of government should be to facilitate, rather than regulate, the growth of business and finance, and that such an approach would strengthen America. They embodied the "laissez-faire" (in English, "Let them do") doctrine, and they were determined not to leave a distinctive mark on the post of the presidency. Isolationism became a form of denial, leaving room for the bankers to expand their control over the country's economy—and to take greater financial risks domestically and globally.

Harding shunned Wilson's foreign policy ambitions during his campaign, reflecting the country's disenchantment with internationalism, peace treaties, and debate over whether America should join the League of Nations. The population and politicians became increasingly disengaged from the preceding Progressive Era and cultivated a strident sense of individualism, particularly as it pertained to personal economics. Relegated to the back pages of newspapers were strikes, riots, and the growing vilification of immigrant "radicals." Promising a "return to normalcy," of which this insularity was indicative, Harding grabbed the presidency by a landslide (404 to 127 electoral votes).

Political isolationism was fine for some bankers, as long as it did not interfere with their global expansion goals. Charles Mitchell, president of National City Bank—as mentioned earlier, it was the largest bank in terms of assets in the United States, with the most extensive network of overseas branches—solidified his position by standing outside the fray of postwar financial diplomacy as much as possible, even as he dumped loans into countries that couldn't pay for them and sold the related shabby and fraudulent bonds to the American public.

Meanwhile, the Morgan Bank, under the daily direction of Thomas Lamont (with oversight from Jack Morgan), continued to influence foreign policy by collaborating with the New York Federal Reserve Bank to assist in the European recovery through more targeted loan extensions, particularly to the Bank of England. The firm maintained its role of indispensability to the presidents regarding war debt and reparations discussions. However, unstable economic conditions in Europe—and, to a lesser extent, in Latin America—contributed significantly to the more subtle power plays between the White House and major bankers. Lamont believed that a stronger Europe would catapult American dominance forward faster, expanding the Morgan Bank's footprint in the process. But he and the presidents had differing opinions on the degree and nature of US participation in European reconstruction and debt forgiveness.

The chess game between the main financiers for supremacy on Wall Street intensified significantly during the 1920s. The isolationist foreign policy position spurred fractious relationships among the key bankers, who had once been bound by side agreements similar to those that the European powers had made with each other before the war. (The Morgan Bank, National City Bank, and the First National Bank, for example, shared whatever business each upended at the turn of the century.) Relationships among the former heads of these banks were born of decades of intimate collaboration and Jekyll Island–type gatherings. Now it was becoming every man for himself—until the next crisis.

It was as if the war had provided a damper on the latent whims of the hungriest financiers; the fighting had invoked a spirit of cooperating on behalf of the combined good of the country, the world, and their firms. That was gone now. The fact that the government itself deployed a hands-off policy relative to the bankers meant that aggressive speculative ventures and big bank mergers would forge ahead unhindered. A war for sovereignty, of sorts, had moved into the financial realm.

As for President Harding, the reserved yet calculated method with which he came to power was indicative of his relaxed governing approach, particularly as it applied to big business and Wall Street. Hailing from Ohio, Harding had little opportunity to cultivate relationships with New York bankers in his earlier years, but he still aligned with them during his presidency.

Copying his Democratic predecessor, Harding turned to Lamont in that regard, though the two would never develop the same close relationship. Lamont's concentration still revolved around European debt repayments. The Treaty of Versailles didn't help the countries struggling from debt overhang (to the US government and its banks). The United States had become the world's biggest creditor, while its private bankers relentlessly scoured the world in search of more borrowers. The postwar recession that engulfed the globe in the early 1920s made war debt repayment, and thus the ability of banks to extend even more credit, extremely difficult.

Britain, the former power center of European and global business and finance, was staggering under its huge war debt and the costs of maintaining its overseas empire. Once fighting came to an end, it abandoned the gold standard and stopped inflating its currency to help finance the war. As a result, the US dollar began to surpass the British pound in international transactions and emerged as the global reserve currency.[2]

After the war, the Morgan Bank solidified its status as the leading world bank by organizing huge loans to foreign governments for reconstruction and development. Precious little financing activity during the war or afterward hadn't somehow passed through Morgan's doors. The firm wanted to keep this position.

Like most bankers, Lamont saw the world as a potential client base; the wake of the war provided—if not intentionally, then coincidentally—a means to an end. Thus, he remained a staunch supporter of the League of Nations throughout the 1920s. It would behoove American bankers, he believed, to have open trade and financial ties with the rest of the globe, particularly with Europe, in order to enhance their international presence and growth opportunities abroad.

Lamont Presses Harding for League

On August 23, 1920, at the height of campaign season, Lamont urged Senator Harding to support the League of Nations. "As a life-long Republican I am bound to tell you that you are making it exceedingly difficult for papers like the *Evening Post* and for hundreds of thousands of loyal Republicans to come strongly to your support. There is only one way out . . . the ratification of the Treaty and League with proper reservations."[3]

When Harding refused to change his stance, Lamont broke from his party and his banking friends. In a letter in the *New York Evening Post,* he endorsed the Democratic ticket of Cox and Roosevelt. His reasoning was simple. "Cox is for the League of Nations and Harding is against it . . . this is why I vote for Cox."[4] Lamont's support for the ticket was based on the issue of internationalism: he knew many foreign problems lingered, and he was wary about Harding's ability or desire to deal with them properly.

Before leaving office, Wilson had attempted to alleviate the growing European debt problems by submitting a proposal to the Senate to substitute German government war reparation bonds for the Belgium war debt owed to England, France, and the United States. Harding was "shocked" at Wilson's motion and what he deemed its secrecy. His pointed reaction would have driven a wedge between the incoming probusiness president and the Morgan Bank executive if Lamont had not traveled to Florida to meet with Harding and deny reports that a mysterious agreement to cancel Germany's war debt had been made.[5]

The *Telegraph* reported that particular press attention was paid to Lamont's dramatic trip because of Lamont's "intimate knowledge of the Versailles negotiations and because his firm is the principal fiscal agent in this country for the debtor powers." The paper further surmised, "Mr. Harding is understood to have discussed with him his own proposal for converting the debts into negotiable paper, but neither could comment afterward on that feature of the discussion."[6]

The next day, at an end-of-term luncheon at the White House with President Wilson and the First Lady, Lamont saw that Harding's victory had squashed Wilson's spirit and lingering hopes for renewed political support for the League.[7] The Senate had also rejected Wilson's debt-swapping proposal, meaning the subject of war debt and reparations agreements would linger on. That financial problem had the potential to turn the postwar peace into another war.

Harding may not have understood all these ramifications, but he knew he needed someone on his side who could assess the issues and work with him on a solution that reflected his political doctrine yet helped avert a disaster. That someone was Lamont.

Thus, in April 1921, a month after Harding took office, Lamont set sail on the *Adriatic* for a six-week trip to England, France, Holland, and Belgium. Though it was described in the papers as a "pleasure" trip, Lamont had a bevy of credit matters to attend to on behalf of Morgan, Harding, and the US government.[8]

He wanted to meet his London and Paris partners in person, to determine the true loan propensity of the countries in which they operated. J. P. Morgan & Company had propelled itself to the center of postwar financing to foreign governments. The advance of postwar American bank loans to Europe began with a $250 million convertible gold bond issue to Britain constructed by J. P. Morgan & Company in October 1919, followed by a $100 million loan to the French government in September 1920.[9]

As a result of his trip, in May 1921, Lamont secured another $100 million French government issue. He worked out the details with his French colleagues while his wife, Florence, shopped for furnishing for their new home.[10] A tipping point was brewing: private banks wanted to extend more loans to Europe, though Europe was staggering under the weight of current debt.

Lamont knew very well how unstable these postwar economies were, but his inner banker drove him to find ways to postpone their pain—or inevitably inflict more pain with more loans, depending on how one looked at it.

Harding's Real Legacy

Harding's brief presidency would be forever tainted with a scandal perpetrated by his inner circle: the infamous Teapot Dome incident, in which Secretary of the Interior Albert Fall leased petroleum reserves owned by the Navy in Wyoming and California without competitive bidding to two private oil companies, and received millions of dollars in kickbacks. The scandal shadowed Harding's administration from 1921 to 1923. In his 1928 report on the incident, North Dakota Republican senator Gerald Prentice Nye wrote, "The investigation has uncovered the slimiest of slimy trails beaten by privilege."[11]

Harding's two enduring contributions to the course of American political-financial history were choosing Herbert Hoover as secretary of commerce (and putting him in play to become president) and appointing Andrew Mellon as Treasury secretary.[12] Mellon was a Pittsburgh industrialist-financier, head of the Mellon National Bank. He had founded the Aluminum Company of America (Alcoa) and the Gulf Oil Company. With Henry Clay Frick, he founded the Union Steel Company, which he later sold to J. P. Morgan's consortium for an obscene price, reflecting a short-term speculative gambit that was very bold for its time.[13] Mellon was an "operator." He owned numerous trusts, insurance, railroad and utility companies, and the Pittsburgh Coal Company, the largest of its kind in the world.

In 1911, *Munsey's Magazine* described Mellon as the "J.P. Morgan of the Steel City."[14] On issues of economics and foreign trade, Mellon was more conservative than Harding. He also believed in low taxes. Harding promoted Mellon's efforts to extend huge tax cuts for the rich and corporations. (By 1926, a person making $1 million a year paid less than a third of the taxes paid in 1920.) To further remove the Roosevelt-era legacy of government intrusion into business, Harding encouraged the Federal Trade Commission, the Justice Department, and the International Commerce Commission to cooperate, rather than regulate or engage in antimonopoly actions against business.[15]

One of Mellon's initial acts as Treasury secretary was to push through the 1921 Budget and Accounting Act.[16] The act was the first to require the president to draft an annual budget.[17] It also created the General Accounting Office (renamed the Government Accountability Office in 2004) to get a better handle on the debt and increasingly complex federal financial transactions that followed World War I.

Harding gave his secretary of state, Charles Evans Hughes, free rein over foreign affairs.[18] Hughes collaborated with Hoover and Mellon on foreign policy, which philosophically supported American bankers' drive to replace the British ones at the top of the pile of global financiers as a way to enhance American power. Hoover and Hughes also encouraged seven US oil companies to form a consortium led by Rockefeller's Standard Oil and seek participation in Iraqi oil concessions, initiating the "open door" policy in the Middle East—and the tight relationship of Chase ("the Rockefeller bank") to the region, which will be explored later in this book.[19]

Presidents and Bankers and Foreign Loans

As Hoover put it later, Harding "was not a man with either the experience or the intellectual quality that the position needed. But he was neither a 'reactionary' nor a 'radical.'" Though his style of governing vis-à-vis the bankers was primarily "hands off," Harding did briefly stand up to them by demanding government supervision of their foreign loans. But this was mostly to assert the power of his office rather than to assert his jurisdiction over their practices.[20]

For the most part, it was Hoover who kept a sharp eye on lending and the general finances of Europe. In February 1922, Harding appointed Hoover to the new World War Foreign Debt Commission, designed to settle the Allies' debts based on "their capacity to pay." The total debt owed the US government was about $11 billion, 40 percent of which had been lent after the armistice. Debt payments totaled only $250 million annually, whereas the interest the United States owed on the bonds issued to finance the debt was $450 million.[21] Harding was not at all impressed with that disparity. Nor was Mellon.

Unable or unwilling to define the amount of reparations Germany would pay going into the Treaty of Versailles, the Allies and the United States had instead established a reparation commission to consider the amount later. In May 1921, the commission set Germany's payment amount at $31.5 billion, plus interest, starting with annual payments of $500 million. But within a year Germany was in default.[22]

Lamont began to think that neither the Germans nor the Allies could *ever* make good on their debts. The situation required a drastic remedy. A year later, at the annual meeting of the American Bankers Association on

October 2, 1922, Lamont shocked the banking community and the president with his declaration that European debt should be canceled.

Echoing Wilson, he argued that America, the "greatest economic power in the world," should assume a "more constructive and responsible role in world affairs." The trouble, he claimed passionately, using but rejecting the words that ardent isolationist Borah had used on the Senate floor to help defeat the League of Nations, was that "we have been timid and fearful of petty entanglement."[23]

Lamont did what he had urged Wilson to do in Paris in mid-1919. He strived to appeal to a latent sense of American altruism. He knew his speech would reach beyond the bankers and urged citizens to consider the Allies' heavy burden of repaying war debt. Britain and France owed three-quarters of the debt. If France agreed to reduce its reparations demands on Germany, Lamont argued, it was only fair that the US government reduce its demands on France and other countries.

Though Congress had recently agreed to stretch loans up to twenty-five years and reduce interest rates, Lamont claimed the amount owed still greatly exceeded what Europe could pay. There was also the question of morality. Half the debt had been issued between April 4, 1917, when the United States declared war against Germany, and a year later, when large numbers of American soldiers first entered the French trenches. During that year, Britain and France gave up more blood and the United States more money. Lamont felt that this inequity deserved consideration relative to debt repayments. It was only just.

Lamont was the first prominent figure to stress debt forgiveness, even though when Harding asked him about the matter after the election, he had vigorously denied that he, the bankers, or Wilson had ever entertained debt cancellation. Now the three thousand bankers he spoke to in New York supported him on the notion, but for more selfish than altruistic reasons. (After all, if the US government forgave debts, the bankers could more easily extend credit to those same nations, a shift of the burden to the government and away from the bankers.) The press waxed skeptical. Some papers pointed out that the Morgan Bank would benefit financially from a public debt cancellation because it had arranged $2 billion in loans to begin with. Cancellation of debt owed to the US government would strengthen the ability of European nations to repay their private debt and to borrow more from Morgan.

Four days later, as a result of the fallout from Lamont's speech and the public outcry it stirred on both sides of the issue, Secretary of State Hughes summoned Lamont to the State Department. He argued that while Lamont saw a direct link between the war debt and reparations issues (which there was), the administration preferred to consider the two as separate matters (which they weren't). The World War Foreign Debt Commission was negotiating revised reparations agreements, but beyond that, congressional authority was needed to modify the war debt.[24] He wanted Lamont to back off and let the US government deal with the debt its own way.

Breaking Point

American banks hadn't improved the financial health of the European countries laboring under war debt repayments. Under the Treaty of Versailles, the idea was that Germany would pay reparations to the Allies, who would use that money to pay off their war debts to the United States and its bankers. The Morgan Bank and others kept lending to European countries through private bond issues on that basis.

The Allies were hard-pressed to make payments, though. Those difficulties were exacerbated when, in January 1923, Germany defaulted on its reparations payments to France.[25] In response, France and Belgium moved to occupy the German industrial area of the Ruhr in an effort to collect their monies. These developments had the real possibility of escalating into renewed conflict.

True to his austere form and isolationist stance, Mellon resisted efforts to forgive European debt. Lamont retained his position on debt cancellation even while he was actively involved in raising more debt. By the summer of 1923 he completed work on a $25 million Austrian bond issue (a decade later, under those and other loans, Austrian banks would descend into widespread depression.) In mid-May, Lamont and his wife had traveled to Rome. There, he cautioned Prime Minister Benito Mussolini about hurrying to borrow abroad, urging the newly appointed National Fascist Party leader to support the League of Nations and participate in its councils first and then borrow. Lamont believed Mussolini would lead Italy from postwar economic chaos and had the potential to become a prime Morgan client.

Over the next decade Lamont solidified his ties with Mussolini and promoted the strength of Italy in his statements. On April 25, 1925, Lamont was the guest of honor at a Roman dinner with fifty of Italy's most prominent banking and political officials, and he took two US senators with him on the trip (Mussolini had to cancel at the last minute but sent a warm letter in support of Lamont). The Italian government and the Morgan Bank had to reinforce each other; in the process, Italy felt well represented to America and the world, and Lamont felt he was securing a major client for the firm.[26]

The following year, Lamont found himself defending Mussolini against growing charges that fascism was a doctrine of "force and fear," most publicly from Harvard professor William Elliott. In response, Lamont stated, "Since Minister of Finance Di Stefani, not himself a fascist," was summoned by Mussolini to fix fiscal policy, the country had reduced labor disputes "and unemployment is at an end." (Lamont didn't consider how the smashing of Italian unions played a part in reducing those disputes.) He said that with respect to budget deficits, no European country has approached Italy's financial record.[27]

No other bank established such strong ties to Italy in those years as the Morgan Bank did. Mussolini would continue to be available to Lamont for private meetings in Rome through the late 1930s. But as Italy moved toward an alliance with Nazi Germany, Lamont would find that the relationship he believed he had with Mussolini was not nearly as strong as he thought it was.

Shift of Power

On the domestic front, the postwar recession was turning around. US businesses and individuals weren't hampered by war debt matters, even if the government was. From this perspective, isolationism was working. On August 2, 1923, Harding died suddenly of an alleged heart attack. The nation buzzed with conspiracy theories over the suspicious circumstances surrounding his death. Was it suicide? Murder?

The ever-placid Calvin Coolidge assumed the presidency. He was sworn in while on vacation in his hometown of Plymouth Notch, Vermont, by his father, a local judge.[28] Dubbed "Silent Cal" by the press, Coolidge had few close friends. The prevailing description of him when he served as Harding's vice president was of a man who "packed his lunch in a tin box and ate alone."[29] A beacon of power he was not, yet he now occupied the most powerful political office in the world.

As vice president, Coolidge was so shunned by the power players of Washington that, according to Ferdinand Lundberg, when he was elected president "he made Senator Frank B. Kellogg, the only man in Washington who had spoken a kind word to him, his Secretary of State."[30] Records of his meetings while president indicate extreme brevity, though that might also have been indicative of his reserved Northeastern upbringing. Later, John F. Kennedy (JFK) kept many of his White House meetings succinct as well.[31]

Having entered politics in Massachusetts and given his introverted style, Coolidge was not very close to the New York bankers. His only major Wall

Street relationship was with Morgan partner and Lamont protégé Dwight Morrow.[32] Coolidge and Morrow had been Amherst classmates and friends for years.[33]

The rise of influential Amherst alumni in Washington and on Wall Street was extensive during the Coolidge period. The list also included top financiers such as National City Bank chairman Charles Mitchell and future Chase Bank chairman John McCloy, who would serve several presidents in a variety of capacities, including as assistant secretary of war during World War II and as president of the World Bank in the late 1940s. In minting the powerful, Amherst gave that "other" venerable Massachusetts institution, Harvard, a run for its money.

Lamont and the Morgan partners harbored high hopes that Coolidge would adopt a more liberal approach to government debt forgiveness. Yet Coolidge was bitterly opposed to forgiving the European debt. Domestically as well, he was upset that "the whole country from the national government down had been living on borrowed money."[34]

His views on money developed early on. Of his homestead town in Plymouth Notch, Vermont, he later wrote reverently, "If any debts were contracted they were promptly paid."[35] Later, as governor of Massachusetts from 1919 to 1920, he oversaw appropriations and expenditures with great parsimony. His ideas of private and public business came from his father, who had the "strong New England trait of great repugnance at seeing anything wasted."[36]

Though Coolidge was an isolationist at heart, he was aware of the need to maintain American power. He certainly didn't want to preside over another world war. So in late 1923, at the suggestion of Secretary of State Hughes, he appointed a committee of experts headed by Harding's old budget director, Charles Dawes, to propose a plan to settle reparations questions once and for all. Dawes had been instrumental in facilitating the $500 million Anglo-French loan that the Morgan Bank managed during World War I; he was a man the bankers cherished and Coolidge trusted.

By April 1924, with assistance from Lamont and other bankers, Dawes crafted a resolution: the Allies would restructure Germany's debt to help reorganize the German central bank. Meanwhile, US banks would provide Germany the capital to repay its loans.[37] The Dawes plan proposed internationally supervised controls over German government expenditures and allowed for the new central bank, the Reichsbank, to issue currency backed by gold reserves. Reparations payments would start at $250 million a year and rise to $600 million in five years.

A key ingredient was necessary to get the plan off the ground: a $200 million international loan to Germany to cover its initial payment. This extension of private debt was intended to give the appearance of paying off public debt; it was essentially a bait-and-switch strategy. There was no question that the Morgan Bank would head the American loan syndicate. Though Jack Morgan still didn't want to help Germany, Lamont believed that the Dawes plan would open avenues of private lending everywhere.

All that remained were the details. Before Jack Morgan set sail to join the world's political and financial leaders in London, where they were gathering to discuss the specifics of the Dawes plan and German loans, he described the bankers' attitude as "very simple": it "merely consisted of making sure that the bankers would get bonds which they could hope to sell."[38] This wasn't an issue of diplomacy or benevolence; it was about finance and cultivating the appetite of international investors. President Coolidge didn't journey to the conference, but Treasury Secretary Mellon did. The press ate it up: the Washington–Wall Street alliance would not just resolve an American market crisis, as it had during the Panic of 1907; now it would save the world. This loan took on a political and financial significance far beyond its size.

As the *New York Times* reported in late July 1924, the "three outstanding figures in the discussion of a German loan upon whom the American investing public will depend for reasonably safe security" were Mellon, Morgan, and Lamont. The paper praised Mellon's mind as "razor-sharp," able to cut "through the technicalities and complications of problems that ordinarily have average men floundering." It was equally admiring of Lamont. For it was Lamont (and not Mellon or Federal Reserve chair Daniel Richard Crissinger, who has been forgotten by history) who worked on the crucial loan details with his British counterpart, Montagu Norman, governor of the Bank of England, because the United States and Britain would assume the largest portion of the German loans.

Over two weeks of arguments vaguely reminiscent of those preceding the Treaty of Versailles, the conference of delegates deliberated on the terms. There were problems. Notably, France wasn't interested in helping its former foe in any financial way, and particularly not via a strategy that would entail devising one large international bond that American banks could sell a year later to avoid what they considered too heavy a burden on the US bond market.

Lamont was dispatched from the midst of meetings in Switzerland to attend the London negotiations, and from there, he traveled to discuss the matter in Paris with Étienne Clémentel, the French minister of finance. He managed to obtain agreement for France's participation in the loan to Germany.[39]

The London *Daily Telegraph* reported that Lamont presented an ultimatum to the arguing Allies and that the bankers threatened to abort the $200 million loan if their conditions were not met. Lamont had saved Europe, according to the press. The byproduct was positioning the US government and its currency as savior, too. A *New York Tribune* story concluded that "in the final analysis the dollar really talks."[40] As it turned out, there was no need for the waiting period that so bothered France; it was a bankers' ploy to drum up demand for the bond.

In August, Germany and the Allies agreed to back the Dawes plan and accepted the bankers' terms for the German loan. Coolidge added his support. But there was another catch: though Lamont and Morgan supported the loan terms, Morrow had doubts about Germany's intentions (as it would turn out, he had good reason to be concerned). Morrow sought a stronger expression of support from the State Department in case matters went awry, and the State Department complied.[41] The loan was on.

The bond, offered in nine countries simultaneously, would be the most complex in history. Dollar bonds would be issued in the United States, sterling bonds would be issued in Britain and Continental Europe, and lira and krona bonds would be issued in Italy and Sweden. The Morgan name would appear on a line by itself above the names of other syndicate members. It was the precursor of huge global syndicates of issuers that would rise after the 1940s, and that would profit from a combination of debt issuance and currency fluctuations. It was genius for its time.

The offering, which took place in most countries on October 14, 1924, was an unmitigated success. In New York subscriptions of more than $500 million for the $110 million US allotment poured in: According to J. P. Morgan & Company, it was "the largest oversubscription" the bank had ever received.[42] It was heavily oversubscribed in London, where it was managed by Morgan, Grenfell & Company.

As a result of the Dawes plan, an extra $2 billion of capital from the private bankers gushed into Germany over the next five years. The German economy entered a boom period. European nations would use the German reparations payments—which were funded by private bank loans—to fund their debts (which had also been reduced by the Dawes plan) to the US government (and its banks). The result of this shell game, for which Dawes won a Nobel Prize, was that the actual total debt paid to the United States was a fraction of the original debt and interest owed.[43]

A Voice of Reason?

On October 20, 1923, Secretary of Commerce Herbert Hoover, already expressing concern about excessive private loans, had addressed a bankers' convention about bankers' risky behavior in extending more debt. "There are responsibilities which come to you . . . to develop an understanding of the difference between speculation and investment at home, but of even more importance, to safeguard our country in the investments abroad. In the case of loans . . . to foreign countries our people are even less able to judge of the security than they are in the case of domestic issues. Thus where foreign loans are involved even more depends upon the character of the bankers."[44]

But by late 1924, the bankers didn't care about a possible collapse of international loans. Such lending expanded their power to finance and thus to direct development of the world. The combination of isolationism at home and internationalism abroad had rendered bankers more reckless, competitive, and hungry. They embraced Coolidge's leadership, unencumbered as it was by notions of regulation or oversight. Coolidge and Mellon were spectators, cheerleaders, and enablers, infatuated with what appeared to be substantial growth in the nation's wealth—which is, of course, always good for politics.

Moreover, Coolidge and Mellon wanted to ensure the private domestic economy retained more of its profits. In 1924, Mellon published his collected writings on lowering federal income taxes in *Taxation: The People's Business*. Organizations like the American Bankers Association rushed to promote his views by sending thousands of copies to members and clients. In the book, Mellon explained, "The Government is just a business, and can and should be run on business principles."[45] Coolidge agreed, famously quipping, "The chief business of the American people is business."[46] In that vein, reduced taxation was a means to generate revenue to run that business.[47]

When Chase National Bank chairman Albert "Al" Wiggin received his advance copy of *Taxation*, he promptly praised Mellon: "We were so enthusiastic over [the book] we could not resist the impulse to distribute quite a large number of copies to customers and friends of the Chase National Bank."[48]

The Revenue Acts of 1924, 1926, and 1928 put Mellon's ideas into motion. Though the basic income tax rate had remained low into the 1920s, the surtaxes imposed by Wilson during World War I on citizens with incomes greater than $6,000, in addition to the income tax, meant that the topmost incomes were taxed at 70 percent. The Coolidge-Mellon tax plans ultimately cut rates for the rich to 25 percent and raised the surtax threshold.

Not to be left out of his own tax reduction policies, during his first four years in office, Mellon gave himself a tax refund of $404,000, the second biggest rebate after John D. Rockefeller's refund of $457,000 (around $6 million today).[49] Mellon also cut taxes for the middle class, exempting the first $4,000 of income for each citizen.[50] By 1928, most Americans paid no federal income tax at all.[51]

Americans were grateful, and a heady "buy now, pay later" consumer society emerged. Earnest Elmo Calkins, author of the 1928 bestseller *Business, the Civilizer,* credited a combination of business and advertising for this phenomenon: "We have seen the evolution of shaving creams, safety razors, and tooth pastes, as well as soap powders, laundry chips, washing machines, vegetable shortenings, self-rising flours, electric irons, vacuum cleaners, hot-water taps, aluminum cooking utensils, refrigerators, kitchen cabinets—everything, in short, that constitutes the difference between our mothers' kitchens and our wives."[52] All that desire and all those products upon which to spend money made the appeal of betting in the stock market that much more potent during the 1920s.

The Diplomatic Era of Banking

Lamont wasn't the only banker in the mix of postwar debt negotiations. By early fall 1924, Charles Mitchell of National City Bank was working on a settlement of his own—for French debt.[53] He chose to work more independently.

Mitchell's interest in acting as a debt-structuring ambassador was also stoked by the benefit it could have for his lending business. Otherwise, he said, it would have been "difficult to measure the credit status of France for private loans."[54] In this capacity he brokered loans between the governments of France, Germany, Belgium, Italy, Japan, and Austria to help reduce reliance on foreign government debt.[55] It was in his interest to limit that debt, in order to extend the private bank loan business and to try to overtake the Morgan Bank as the top credit provider to Europe.

His financial diplomacy spawned another foreign policy initiative: the 1925 Locarno agreements, which resolved territorial disputes outstanding since World War I and helped restructure war debt. That was the year Dawes shared the Nobel Peace Prize with British Foreign Secretary Austen Chamberlain for his plans. Dawes and Chamberlain had done more for the big banks than they had for Europe. Coolidge biographer David Greenberg described the financial mirage as "something absurd," with "American funds going to

Germany, through the allies, and back to the United States—which was contrived partly to satisfy each country's sense of a more prosperous period."[56]

Mitchell had the instincts to hedge his exposure to Europe. He had been pushing National City to expand its Latin America presence, in part to offset potential losses in Europe but also to stake its own territory in the field of world finance. In late January 1922, after a ten-day tour of Cuba he took with Percy Rockefeller and a bevy of other bankers, culminating in a luncheon in Havana given in his honor by two hundred of Cuba's top businessmen, he had proclaimed, "You businessmen must find a way to carry Cuba's story before our country."[57] But his real intent was to soak Cuba in debt and get US investors to fund it through National City Bank–arranged bonds.

Mitchell correctly predicted that the $5 million loan made to Cuba during that last week of January would be the "forerunner of a larger loan." He told reporters that Cuba's future lay in merging its companies. By "putting some of these properties together into one large company, whose shares could be taken by investors in all parts of the United States, some of the financial burden at least is lifted," he said.[58] As such, he laid the path for future investment banking business in the country. By the late 1920s, many of the loans to Cuba, including to sugar and other interests, were in default.

Domestically, Mitchell remained the nation's steadfast economic cheerleader throughout the mid-1920s. National City remained the country's largest bank, if not the most prestigious, and he retained the status of a rising pillar of the Wall Street banking fraternity—not by birth but by sheer ambition (and, as he later admitted, a bit of luck).

In January 1925, the *New York Times* reported that the prior year had been a "banner year for New York banks," the most profitable in history.[59] That summer, Mitchell issued a statement proclaiming, "The country is enjoying a prosperity at present. . . . There is every promise for better business than this country has had since 1920." He added, "While there is more bank credit in use than ever before, bank resources are greater than ever before."[60] Those "resources" were largely the deposits National City was amassing from citizens.

Coolidge's Kid Gloves and Mitchell's Pronouncement

Early in his second term, on February 26, 1926, Coolidge signed the Mellon Bill, which further cut income taxes, deleted the gift tax, halved the estate tax, and reduced taxes on the wealthy to 25 percent.[61] Solidifying his stance in the face of rising public criticism of favoritism to the elite throughout the year, Coolidge argued that "human nature cannot be changed by an act of the legislature. It is too much assumed that because an abuse exists it is the business of the national government to remedy it."[62]

Coolidge's belief that government should yield no overbearing presence in people's lives coincided with Mellon's plans to cut taxes and tighten budgets—a tactic that might have worked had it not left the financial world to its own devices in the process. But increasingly, prosperity was measured by bankers' ability to inflate the values of paper representations (stocks and bonds) of production and goods, not the goods themselves. Money in people's pockets, realized or illusory, needed an outlet. That was the stock market, which billowed on extensive domestic borrowing to fund investment.

The overzealous international lending was not going unnoticed. Addressing the Pan-American Commercial Conference in 1927, an even more worried Hoover stated, "One essential principle dominates the character of these transactions. That is, that no nation as a government should borrow or no government lend and nations should discourage their citizens from borrowing or lending unless this money is to be devoted to productive enterprise."[63] It was increasingly unclear to him that this was the case.

Still, Mitchell maintained his exuberance. On December 10, 1927, at a Detroit Athletic Club luncheon, he claimed that American prosperity was growing, largely on the back of automobile production, and predicted that "every country and community on the face of the globe would buy the Model A Ford and General Motors cars."[64]

"The year 1928 will be one of unparalleled prosperity," Mitchell proclaimed. "The powerful influence of a sound credit situation, a return of Mr. Ford and other manufacturers to a normal output and continuance of large-scale buildings will swing business back into its stride."[65] His heady words cascaded across the nation even as cracks were beginning to show in the armor of American prosperity.

Earlier Signs of Impending Problems

Even before the bubble of the mid-1920s, there existed signs of trouble brewing in the land of plentiful credit extensions. In November 1923, the Federal Reserve began increasing its holdings in government securities (such as Treasury bonds) by a factor of six, from $73 million to $477 million, in what could be considered the first instance of "quantitative easing." This keeps rates low, not by setting them explicitly but by forcing the price of bonds up, which has the net effect of driving rates down.

The Fed's move made money cheaper for the banks to borrow at the beginning of the 1920s and paved the way for speculative excess. The prevailing mentality was that prices would rise forever—a classic bubble mentality. But by the mid-1920s, the amount of deposits backing loans or shaky investments declined significantly as leverage increased, such that any losses would reverberate more than during any prior crisis.

By August 1924, Chase's chief economist, Benjamin Anderson, expressed concern about a dangerous speculative bubble caused by: "the present glut in the money markets, with excessively cheap money and its attendant evils and dangers to the credit structure of the country. . . . Both incoming gold and Federal Reserve Bank investments are reflected almost entirely in an increase of member bank balances with immediate and even violent effect upon the money market. The situation is abnormal and dangerous."[66]

But the bankers weren't thinking about these dangers. They remained focused on seemingly limitless expansion. On the evening of January 12, 1925, Mitchell and Mellon sat among six hundred of the banking elite at a tribute event for George Baker Sr., one of J. P. Morgan's inner circle and founder of the First National Bank of New York (which later became part of Citigroup), in the glittering ballroom of the Waldorf Astoria hotel.

It was a grand occasion, not least because it was where Jack Morgan, a notoriously private man, gave his first public speech—calling for a code of ethics for bankers. "There is, and must be, in every profession, a code of ethics, the result of years of experience," he said. "Where I am required to state an ethical code for our profession, I think that I would say the first rule should be: never do something that you do not approve of in order to more quickly accomplish something that you do approve of."

At the event, Mitchell proposed a toast to President Coolidge, his fellow Amherst alum, after which his fellow bankers downed what the Prohibition-era press referred to as "pellucid ice water."[67]

Money poured just as freely. Mitchell and the other bankers collected it to lend for market speculation and related lending from two sources. First, as with all banks, money came from deposits—the bigger and more spread out the bank, the more channels for receiving new deposits. Mitchell saw opportunity in extending banking to "smaller individuals." *The Nation* later called this an example of the "socialization of banking," though the magazine concluded that this was not likely Mitchell's intent.[68] With extra deposits, Mitchell could increase his power to provide loans for speculative purposes using other people's money.

Second, funds came from the Fed, which kept rates relatively low on loans to banks during the speculative period and required little in the way of reserves, or collateral, to be set aside for stormy days.

As a result of both methods, ordinary individuals weren't really engaged in collective prosperity. They were, rather, engaged in collective debt creation, and would suffer most acutely in the aftermath of its destruction.

For now, crisis was still far in the distance, and bankers raked in cash. In 1927, the Morgan Bank was the leading syndicate manager of bond issues, with just over $500 million. Postwar foreign bond issues comprised a third of the Morgan managed offerings. National City Bank and Kuhn, Loeb followed close behind.

The rush to extend foreign loans and sell foreign bonds to American investors would prove disastrous. In a talk before the International Chamber of Commerce in Washington on May 2, 1927, Mitchell's rival Lamont warned investors of what he saw as a potentially ugly situation, though he was probably also concerned that Morgan was losing its standing as the leading international bond house: "American bankers and firms [are] competing on an almost violent scale for the purpose of obtaining loans in various foreign money markets overseas. . . . That sort of competition tends to insecurity and unsound practice."

The bankers' reckless underwriting of loans (without any useful regulation from Washington to curtail it) would implode at the public's expense. Losses on the Latin American bonds sold to investors to raise money for loans would come from the pockets of investors and take a toll on the American economy, as would the stock market crash.

Hoover's Prep for
President and Bankers' Support

Coolidge shocked the nation when he announced in early August 1927, while on summer break in South Dakota, that he would not seek reelection.[69] As the country digested the news, Mellon snuck in one more round of tax cuts. The US economy stood on the precipice of a six-year run of stock market growth and record high Wall Street profits, which masked underlying problems: home prices had softened in 1926, car sales dropped in 1927, and construction would level off in 1928.[70] Inequality had increased dramatically, threatening economic stability. The whole system was buckling.

But such signs of weakness were not the stuff of great political rhetoric, so when Herbert Hoover won the 1928 presidential election, he declared, "We in America are today nearer to the final triumph over poverty than ever before in the history of any land."[71] Americans might have been somewhat skeptical, given their growing difficulties in finding jobs and small business loans, but the financial leaders were pleased at the vote of confidence. It buoyed the market, and all of their plans and fortunes along with it.

Hoover proceeded to select a cabinet reflective of his status as the "first millionaire to reach the White House." Other millionaires in his inner circle included Henry Stimson, Andrew Mellon, James Good, Charles Francis Adams III, Robert Patterson Lamont, and James Davis. They filled six of his top ten posts.[72]

That Mellon, "one of the four richest men on this continent," according to *The Nation,* remained in the Treasury secretary post showed the growing strength of those with money in Washington, despite obvious conflicts of interests. As *The Nation* wrote of Mellon, "During eight years he has so administered that office that $3.5 million in refunds, credits, and abatements of income taxes has gone to wealthy individuals and corporations." The magazine further pointed out, "On the eve of the coming in of the new Administration, the Senate has voted an inquiry into his eligibility to hold his post—from which a person interested in commerce or trade or in the liquor industry, is barred. His own Aluminum Company of America has escaped the prosecution proposed for it by the Federal Trade Commission, and has received large refunds of taxes."[73] In his public post, Mellon took care of his own interests.

The bankers were happy with Hoover. He offered a sense of continuity with the Harding and Coolidge policies, which had lined so many bankers' and brokers' pockets with so much cash. The stock market roared the first six months of Hoover's term, from a slump in March 1929 to record highs that fall.

Gathering Clouds

As for the Morgan Bank, while foreign loans and financial diplomacy were near to de facto chief executive officer Lamont's heart, domestic business, including industrial financing, was also a staple of income. As such, after his winter holiday in late 1928, Lamont began working on a new kind of domestic business: a large loan to the Van Sweringen brothers' holding company.

A decade earlier, the "unprepossessing, reclusive and hard-working bachelors" had begun building a major railway system through the acquisition of the New York, Chicago, and St. Louis lines. Using a pyramid structure of holding companies, they borrowed heavily from banks to speed up the process. They shared their forthcoming aggressive acquisition plans with the Morgan Bank, which believed the secured loan of $25 million to them represented the first step in a growing and profitable relationship.

Russell Leffingwell, a Morgan partner and former assistant Treasury secretary to President Wilson, and his Morgan partner associate George Whitney harbored strong reservations about the bubbling market. While traveling abroad in March 1928, Lamont received a cable from the Morgan offices: "the market is boiling." Leffingwell was increasingly troubled, while Lamont remained an optimist.[74] Perhaps it was all his time abroad that blinded him to the machinations of the domestic stock market, or the more shady practices of his competitors, but he decided to get more involved with the market nonetheless.

For years, J. P. Morgan & Company had limited the underwriting of securities it offered the public (or for "public offering") to high-grade, less risky bonds, for governments and large corporations. Its policy was not to underwrite what it perceived as riskier stock issues for public distribution. The company wasn't interested in acting as a securities broker for little people.

But the frenzied stock speculation and profits had affected Lamont and many of the other Morgan partners who became millionaires trading stocks for their own account. They decided to pursue a risky holding company strategy for clients: combining several companies into a single holding company against which they could then sell new securities—to the public, no matter what the condition of that web of firms.

In January 1929, Lamont oversaw the planning of two large domestic financings based on this new strategy. One of them was a large package for the Van Sweringen brothers: a $35 million bond issue combined with $25 million in preferred stock and $25 million in common stock. Funds would be used to back the newly formed Alleghany Corporation. The Morgan Bank purchased $25 million in common stock at $20 a share, part of which it sold to the public at $24 a share. The Morgan name, which had been so profitable with loans and bonds, would now "bank" on the stock market, following on the heels of National City Bank, which had issued its first stocks in 1927. This thirst for Wall Street domination would provoke market collapse, as no firm wanted to be left out of the speculative festivities.

It wasn't until the spring of 1929, when the market suffered a sharp break, that Lamont turned more cautious. In May, after liquidating seven substantial holdings (including Chase National Bank, General Foods, and Humble Oil), he raised about $4 million in cash from the sale of securities—for himself. But then his own isolationism took hold; he didn't make these sales public to the rest of the nation buying Morgan-backed securities. He didn't have to legally, but still he chose to protect the information; it would do the market no good if word got out that bankers were cashing in their chips.

Besides, there was still money available in case something went wrong thanks to the safety net that the Morgan Bank and others had pushed for after the Panic of 1907: the Federal Reserve. The primary tool of the Federal Reserve to influence credit conditions was the discount rate that each regional Federal Reserve bank charged the other banks for loans. Because this rate was generally kept below market rates, banks had an incentive to borrow the reserves they needed to finance their rapidly expanding activities. Throughout much of the 1920s, discount window borrowings represented more than half of total Federal Reserve assets.[75]

In practice, that meant banks used their "membership" with the Fed to suck up money for speculative and risky lending purposes. They could lend that "easy" money at a profit to client companies or encourage investors to buy bonds of Latin American countries or stock of budding American companies that were packaged by National City Bank or Chase, while also lending to investors to buy into the pooled trusts they created from blocks of shares in those same companies. The more shares in the trusts bought with borrowed money, the more the prices of those shares and trusts rose, and the more new investors borrowed to invest in them.

The bigger the banks were, the more they were aware of looming problems with the shares of various trusts and companies because they had more information about them given their involvement in underlying loans and bond payments. It was always the case that banks knew more about the quality of loans and the bonds that financed them than investors. Missed payments to banks, whether on international or corporate bonds, meant an unhealthy situation was arising. To provide extra capital in the face of common disaster, the New York banks would increase loans and investments to their own accounts from October 2 to October 30 (mostly in the last week of October) by $1 billion and increased their reserves by nearly $250 million. Loans from smaller banks dropped by $800 million.[76]

The banks would attempt to keep ordinary investors from extracting their cash (often their life savings), even as values plummeted. The trusts might have been engineered and marketed "for the public" to buy securities alongside the big players, but when push came to shove, the masters were there to garner fees for their trusts and inflate stocks in their portfolios.

None of the starry-eyed free-market types, who promised that trusts were safe, ever mentioned the extent to which they were propped up by borrowed money and debt. That wouldn't matter as long as the stock bubble remained inflated. But the trusts and stocks began trading up to 150 times earnings, puffed up by leverage debt and smarmy hype, not inherent value. That meant, as Bertie Charles Forbes would write in mid-November 1929, that "when things popped, they would pop badly."[77]

As bankers and other citizens returned from their summer vacations on Labor Day 1929, New York City was a sweltering cauldron of putrid smells and record heat. The Dow's temperature had also risen—to an all-time high of 381. The protracted bull market in stocks had enabled corporations to finance cheaply by issuing stocks rather than bonds or finding the cash with which to pay old debts or expand.

Merging to Power

Every chief financier had his preferred method of amassing influence and power during the 1920s. Mitchell chose to grow National City Bank's "Everyman" deposits and disperse them in epic global speculation. Lamont's position was more closely aligned with the US and other governments, as it had been during and after World War I. Chase's chairman, Al Wiggin, executed his own buying spree—of other banks.

Wiggin's pedigree was grittier than that of some of his upper-crust compatriots. He began his career in 1885 as a bank clerk in Boston.[78] He joined Chase as a vice president in 1904 and rose to the post of president in January 1911; by 1917, he had become chairman of the board.[79] Wall Street legend had it that Wiggin was the "only man who ever refused a Morgan partnership."[80] According to *Time* magazine, he was an intense poker player and was known around Wall Street as "the man with a million friends."[81] "Tall, heavy, slightly pop-eyed," Wiggin created his own alliances in banking and business by joining all the clubs he could. An avid golfer like Lamont, he was known to be "never more dangerous to his opponent than when behind."[82]

Relative to the Morgan clique, Wiggin was an outsider to Washington power-elite alliances. He focused on growing his power through acquisitions of banks and club memberships. He collected banks like he collected etchings. His reign at Chase was one big buying spree, capped by merging two of the oldest banks in the financial district; Chase National and the Mechanics and Metals National Bank. The marriage was announced on February 12, 1926.[83] The newly combined Chase National possessed just over $1 billion in assets, ranking second only to National City Bank's $1.25 billion. Wiggin maintained his position as chairman of the board of directors over the combined company.

The well-connected Gates McGarrah, chairman of the board of the Mechanics and Metals National Bank, became chairman of the executive committee of Chase. In addition to his many prominent local positions, McGarrah was also a member of the general board of the German Reichsbank, the American director under the Dawes plan, a post from which his international influence would blossom in the early 1930s. In February 1927, McGarrah was appointed chairman of the New York Fed.

Unlike Mitchell, Wiggin cautioned against excess in the mid-1920s, even while engaging in its spoils. Like Mellon and Coolidge, Wiggin was opposed to excessive debt, public or otherwise. In January 1927, he publicly praised the government's policy of steadily reducing the public debt since 1920, calling it "one of the most wholesome financial developments of the period" in his annual report to stockholders, where he urged "the use of the present Government surpluses in further scaling down the debt."[84]

He foresaw something potentially dangerous about the speculative boom and believed that while surpluses existed in banking and other businesses, they should be utilized to pay down federal debt. In early 1927, he had warned that the "revenues of 1926 are probably abnormally great, reflecting, as they do, the incomes of 1925. A great expansion of bank credit was being expended in capital uses and when business activity and speculative enthusiasm were very high. Bank expansion of this kind cannot safely continue and in its absence . . . it is well to use the present surplus . . . in reducing public debt."[85]

By the fall of 1929 Chase had acquired six major New York banks, making it the second largest private bank in the world, next to Mitchell's National City. The rivalry that would reverberate for decades—different men, same pursuit—characterized the relationship of Wiggin and Mitchell, the two outsiders who would fight for their spot in history, on Wall Street, and in the world—and for whom it would all turn out very wrong.

Charles Mitchell, Salesman and Mega-Banker

In 1921, when Mitchell became president of National City, the bank had four offices. Within three years it had fifty, and by 1929 it was the largest distributor of securities in the world, with one hundred branches in twenty-three countries. Its motto was: "When it comes to investing your money, solid facts outweigh whispered rumors."[86] In other words, bank with us—*trust us.*

Personifying the modern banker-titan, Mitchell aggressively pursued investors as if they were prey. Behind his desk at National City Bank's headquarters hung a portrait of George Washington, reflecting one of his favorite maxims—that "the typical US system is the concentration of responsibility in the hands of one accountable individual."[87]

As competitive in his private life as in business, he believed himself to be just such an individual—intoxicated with the game of banking and his prowess at it. Enjoying "exercise and combat," he kept fit and alert by "frequently walk[ing] from his home at 933 Fifth Avenue to his office at 55 Wall Street," according to *Time*.[88] Navigating that five-and-a-half-mile walk, Mitchell revealed himself as a precursor to the Wall Street "masters of the universe" portrayed in the 1980s by Tom Wolfe in *Bonfire of the Vanities*. For a time, he believed himself to be, and was, invincible.

Mitchell sold corporate bonds to a growing investor class at far more than they turned out to be worth.[89] In doing so, he made National City a financial supermarket. During the 1920s, its securities arm underwrote more than 150 bond issues, raising nearly $11 billion, or 21 percent of total US issuance.[90]

In 1928 and 1929, Mitchell (who became chairman in 1929) earned $1.2 million in total compensation, two hundred times the average American's salary of $6,000.[91] His family resided in a six-story townhouse in Manhattan with sixteen live-in servants, plus chauffeurs. He had another mansion in Southampton, Long Island. He earned about $1 million more than Wiggin did at Chase, or Lamont did at Morgan.

In early 1929, Mitchell, a consummate salesman, pushed his employees to sell nearly 2 million shares of National City stock to the public for $650 million. According to *Time*, "National City through its security affiliate National City Co. had put on the most flamboyant high-pressure bank stock selling campaign in all history."[92]

But when the market wobbled in early March 1929, the great bamboozler got scared. All of a sudden, he needed backup to keep his stock price up. But he failed to convince the New York Fed to dump funds into the market to save, among other things, his shares, so he took matters into his own hands. On March 26 he announced, over the Fed's objections, that he would provide $25 million from his bank, and an additional $5 million if necessary, to keep the escalating call money rate that banks charge on loans to brokers—who, in turn, lend the money to their clients to help them purchase stock—stable at 15 percent, amid fears that it would reach 20 percent. His move suggested he had more information about the true condition of the capital markets than the public.

"So far as this institution is concerned," Mitchell said, "we feel that we have an obligation which is paramount to any Federal Reserve warning, or anything else, to avert, so far as lies within our power, and [*sic*] dangerous crisis in the money market."[93] Though not with personal money, Mitchell nearly single-handedly kept the party raging. Many leading bankers and industrialists were grateful that his move saved the market and possibly the country's financial systems.[94] A banker had trumped the Federal Reserve.

Mitchell's tactics didn't ingratiate him with certain congressmen belaboring under the illusion that the Fed didn't normally act to the bankers' benefit. George Norris, a Republican senator from Nebraska, pronounced the obvious: Mitchell was on the side of "the gamblers in Wall Street [and] has shown no sympathy with the Federal Reserve Act. . . . Such defiance of the principles of the act ought not to be countenanced by the board."[95]

Senator Carter Glass of Virginia called for Mitchell's resignation from the New York Fed Board.[96] But Mitchell remained.[97] The day after his heroics, Mitchell quixotically warned, "I feel that with the immediate pressure passed, the people will do well to bear the credit condition in mind, and in stock activities to see that their margins are maintained and that they lean less heavily upon the credit structure."[98] He knew he had propped up a system that was teetering, if not on the brink of toppling completely.

Mitchell's solo maneuver worked, temporarily—like the collective efforts of Morgan in 1907. National City shares and the Dow Jones skyrocketed through the spring, summer, and early fall. Mitchell had other motives for his macho antics. He was trying to protect what would have been his coup d'état deal, a page right out of the Wiggin book of major acquisitions, and in pursuit of his rival. He sought to merge National City Bank with the Corn Exchange Bank Trust Company and establish the world's largest bank. In the deal, National City shares would be used to buy Corn Exchange shares, for which Mitchell had to maintain a price of $450 per share.

This was no small deal. On September 29, 1929, the *New York Times* prematurely blared the headline "The Ruler of the World's Largest Bank," dramatizing the moment that Mitchell discovered he would be the leader of the world's biggest bank, overseeing what would be $1.73 billion in deposits and 201 branches, 103 of them in New York City.

Mitchell's proposed consolidation, the fifth major merger in three years, was the culmination of a three-year trend that spawned fifty bank mergers in New York City alone, from which seventeen corporate entities had emerged, cutting competition by 65 percent. Smaller banks would succumb to the big New York banks' dominance, as would the nation.[99] History was clear on this:

the big banks won. With consolidation, there would come more deposits, influence, and control. Mitchell knew this. He counted on it.

But when the Corn Exchange price took a dive during the jitters that ultimately led to the main crash, the deal was off. Not even Mitchell's furious buying through his securities affiliate could sustain it.[100] As National City stock plunged and his dreams of becoming a global banking superpower crumbled, Mitchell had other headaches. He couldn't sell enough shares in his company to meet his personal loan payment to the Morgan Bank. As a result, the House of Morgan temporarily became the second largest stockholder in National City.[101] (Mitchell was not alone in owing money to Morgan; even Charles Dawes, the Nobel Peace Prize winner, did, but his ego was prepared to handle it.)

With so much at stake, Mitchell had no choice but to remain the market's public cheerleader, to try to turn things around by sheer will and showmanship. Despite substantial wobbling, even in early October 1929, Mitchell proclaimed to the *New York Times*, "The industrial condition of the United States is absolutely sound and our credit situation is in no way critical."[102] It was classic Mitchell salesmanship, the kind for which he earned the nickname Sunshine Charley. And yet the pending market crash was intrinsically connected to the public's dumping of bonds, stocks, confidence, and trust in the shady securities that Mitchell and voracious bankers had created.

In an October 19, 1929, letter to Hoover on the situation, Lamont tried to both calm him and blame random forces for the market tremors, an excuse that would come up during the investigations and would continue to be used by many bankers and economists whenever meltdowns occurred. Lamont wrote that "every protracted market on either the up or down side of the stock market (or of commodity markets, for that matter) has its excesses." As a postscript, he noted, "The developments of the last few days in the stock market would seem to indicate that nature is already operating pretty vigorously."[103] In fact, nature had nothing to do with it. This crisis was all about the exploits of man.

All hell broke loose anyway.

CHAPTER 5

1929: THE ROOM AT 23 WALL, CRASH, AND BIG-SIX TAKE

"There is a panic now—among stock gamblers."

—Senator Carter Glass, October 1929

THE BELLS OF TRINITY CHURCH IN LOWER MANHATTAN CHIMED NOON ON THAT cool, overcast Thursday, October 24, 1929. Their clangs were reminiscent of those that had marked the decade's start. At the same hour, on September 16, 1920, a wagonload of explosives erupted in front of the Morgan Bank, presumably destined to kill Jack Morgan. Jack survived. Less lucky were the thirty-three civilians killed and more than one hundred wounded.[1]

Now, as the decade approached its climactic close, Morgan was across the Atlantic in Britain, far from the chaos engulfing the population. It would be Thomas Lamont who would act on behalf of the firm and in shades of its former patriarch to try to save the markets.

Black Thursday, as it would be called, was a day of reckoning: for the stock market, as share prices of companies plummeted in a frenzy of trading; for former President Calvin Coolidge, who had presided over much of the 1920s boom; and for recently elected President Herbert Hoover, who had emphasized in campaign advertisements that "the slogan of progress is changing from the full dinner pail to the full garage."[2]

More critically, it was a day of reckoning for the "Big Six" bankers, who represented the collision of old and new money, speculative versus productive capital use, and the preservation of power and influence at the epicenter of civilized society. Four of them strode from their nearby offices through teeming crowds toward a spartan yet stately three-story building at 23 Wall Street—the heart and soul of the House of Morgan. Charles Mitchell was the first man to enter the building, the sighting of which set Wall Street abuzz with conjecture. (He had the most to lose.) Just afterward, Al Wiggin walked over from the Chase bank, one block north. He was followed by William Potter, president of the Guaranty Trust Company, and Seward Prosser, chairman of the Bankers Trust Company.[3]

A day earlier, the stock market had experienced its largest single-day drop ever. Not only shares fell; so did the country's spirits. The ideal of shared prosperity was shattered. As John Kenneth Galbraith later put it, "By the summer of 1929 the market not only dominated the news. It also dominated the culture."[4] Its subsequent plunge was thus a decline of greater than financial ramifications. Not everyone was *in* the market, but the mood of those speculating in stocks (fewer than 1 percent of the population) dictated the story of the economy's endless possibility. The media did their part to stoke the enthusiasm, which in turn fueled their most active manipulators: the bankers, or "operators." Plus, when stocks fell, so did bonds, and so did people's ability to borrow money to hire, pay, or sustain businesses.

The legendary action that J. P. Morgan had undertaken to "save the markets" more than two decades earlier with a similar group of bankers was foremost in everyone's mind. Expectations and hopes ran high for a repeat performance.

These 1920s bankers weren't deer caught in the headlights of market mayhem. They knew much more about why the market was tumbling than the unsuspecting public. They were aware that the margins (or collateral backing loans) they had tried to collect from customers would put many out of business. They understood that inflated stock and bond prices were the result of their words and strategies and how flimsy that kind of support was. Lamont and Wiggin had taken profits on their personal trades. They also knew that international bonds were poorly constructed and backed by shaky collateral.

These men took comfort in knowing that the institutions they represented were deeply interlocked with board memberships and stock ownerships. They might as well have been one big bank, and a bank that contained so much potential for future American financial glory couldn't—wouldn't—fail. All they needed was a plan to convince the average American that this "panic" selling was temporary and unfounded. Or so the thinking went.

The Morgan Bank headquarters stood like a fortress, a monolith with nary a signpost to draw attention. The building's demeanor reflected that of its forefathers: J. P. Morgan and his son, Jack, both of whom were notoriously private. Yet everyone knew the building. It was positioned catty-corner from the New York Stock Exchange, an architectural homage to the Greek Empire and its gods. On that day the exchange was a scene of hysteria; behind its marble pillars an avalanche of stocks was crashing faster than sweaty floor runners could repost prices on the big board.

The nervous financiers marched through Morgan's entrance, beneath the lobby's 1,900-piece crystal Louis Quinze chandelier. They rushed to the second floor, where the partners' enclave was located. There, they assembled before the mahogany rolltop desk of Morgan senior partner Lamont. Usually they were competitors, but today Mitchell, Wiggin, Potter, and Prosser were collaborators. George Baker Jr., vice chairman of the First National Bank, joined the second meeting the group had later that day.

The men formed the core of a powerful Wall Street fraternity named the "Big Six" by *Forbes Magazine* founder B. C. Forbes.[5] They had been schooled at the finest institutions (with the exception of Wiggin, who had entered banking straight from high school); they were members of the most elite clubs, possessors of the most exclusive relationships, and intermarried into the bluest lines of American aristocracy. They represented the heart of finance; their client companies, the arteries. If the heart ceased beating, the arteries would shrivel and die.

Lost in the immediate retelling of the chaos was the notion that the financial havoc, impacting everyone from welders to seamstresses, clerks to drivers, electricians to grocery store owners, was fueled, if not completely then in large part, by these men and the institutions they ran. Such was the glowing aura in which newspapers bathed their actions that day amid banners of "Bankers Halt Stock Debacle,"[6] "Business Is Sound, Bankers Declare,"[7] and "Banks Restore Stability to Raging Stocks."[8]

These men personified the phrase "too big to fail." Indeed, none of their banks would fail. Instead, they would retain their status and morph into the biggest banks of the twentieth and twenty-first centuries. Their hierarchy would slightly shift through mergers, deaths, and changes in leadership, but their overall influence would remain intact.

It didn't take long for the Big Six to reach an agreement. This was simple, and it had precedent from the collaborations between the Morgan-led bankers and the Roosevelt government during the Panic of 1907. This time, the bankers tried it without presidential aid first. Money had to be poured into the market. A united front was crucial. Each man would use his customers' deposit money to bolster the stocks the group was most concerned about. In such times of strife, the best solution was socialistic in nature.

At the end of the meeting, which lasted a mere twenty minutes, reporters crowded the doorway and rushed at the ashen-faced bankers.[9] Lamont calmly assured reporters that the situation was under control.[10] Though he denied outright stock purchasing, brokerage circles reported that "large orders emanating from these banking interests had been executed on the floor of the exchange shortly after the conference ended."[11]

Sure enough, during the afternoon trading session, order appeared to be restored. Ticker machines across the land showed stocks like US Steel rally from 190.5 to 206.[12] Disaster had been averted. It seemed that all would be okay. The manifestation of gushes of capital—in whatever form, and under whatever circumstance—was the grease that would keep the wheels of the market turning. Or so it seemed.

Following Lamont's instructions, the team dispatched financier Richard Whitney, also known as the "Morgan broker" because his brother George was a Morgan partner who pushed business toward his brokerage firm (Whitney, who ran the New York Stock Exchange from 1930 to 1935, later spent three years in jail for embezzlement).[13] In what would become one of the most infamous moments in stock market history, Whitney, his Harvard Porcellian Club gold pig's head dangling from his watch chain,[14] descended to the stock exchange floor on a mission to buy massively, beginning with the exchange's Number Two post, where US Steel was traded.[15] "I bid $205 for 25,000 shares of steel!" he yelled, as he started snatching up huge stock blocks to bolster the market. Word traversed Wall Street and the nation that the House of Morgan had come to the rescue.[16] Again.

Lamont, Wall Street's Spokesperson

Substantiating this tone of optimism, the *New York Times* continued to lionize the top bankers. It was all so 1907. As the paper put it, "Wall Street gave credit yesterday to its banking leaders for arresting the decline on the New York

Stock Exchange at a time when the stock market was being overwhelmed by selling orders. . . . The five bankers who met at . . . noon yesterday and again at 4:30 PM following the meeting of the board of the Federal Reserve Bank of New York . . . represented more than $6 billion of banking resources [$80 billion in today's dollars]."[17]

Separately, bond prices rose on the rumor that "the Federal Reserve Bank would be forced to purchase government securities instead of bankers' acceptances." With the Fed swooping in to buy Treasury bonds in high volume, the prices in the bond market "would turn upward sharply."[18]

The next day, conditions appeared even better, as word got out that Baker had joined the five bankers at an afternoon meeting.

But as Forbes later wrote, the Big Six weren't exactly serene about the situation (which was the only valid explanation for such a quick vote to dump so much money into a plummeting market). "Conditions actually were more precarious at times than the public realized." Having been taken into the confidence by the Big Six, Forbes reported "there were moments when they were on tenterhooks, fearful that something would happen the next instance to precipitate a total deadlock." Forbes also claimed that had no concerted action been taken, "the panic unquestionably would have been infinitely worse."[19] Lost in this analysis was the notion that the bankers were coordinating to save the markets they had overinflated to begin with. The Federal Reserve's actions in buying securities to boost prices also helped promote the illusion of financial health.

If anything, the very public actions of the bankers and the more private (or less widely understood) actions of the Fed served to suck more people into an unstable market. True, if no concerted action had been taken, the loss would have been more *immediately* shocking; but the slow burn that devastated the population over the following decade was no better.

Black Tuesday

The market dove massively beginning the following week. Mitchell had frantically, and secretly, borrowed millions of dollars from his own bank to support its share price. But National City stock still lost 50 percent of its value on October 29, 1929, as the market crashed amidst frenzied selling, before stabilizing somewhat over the next six months.

The bankers took that stabilization as a sign that the 1907-type moves had worked. In early November, the *New York Times* ran the headline "Record Christmas Bonuses Are Expected as Rewards in Brokerage Houses This

Year."[20] This was but a week after the stock market had plunged by its largest margin amount ever.[21]

Congress vowed to look into the Crash and the bankers' role in it. Utah Democratic senator William Henry King declared that when Congress reconvened in December, "it will make a searching investigation into our financial system, including the question of credit, the operations of the Federal Reserve System, the field in which investment trusts are operating, the conduct of the New York Stock Exchange and generally those matters which so vitally affect the welfare and prosperity of the people."[22] It would take three years for that investigation to begin.

Meanwhile, Charles Mitchell—not a man to leave the "recovery" of the market to chance—sprang into action. In November 1929, at his urging, the New York Fed eased rates further by purchasing more US Treasury bonds. The action, the second instance of a maneuver later referred to as "quantitative easing," had the effect of keeping all rates down without the Fed having to lower the discount rate explicitly—which it also did. On October 31, the Fed reduced the discount rate from 6 percent to 5 percent. (Federal Reserve chairman Ben Bernanke did the same thing after the 2008 financial crisis, but he lowered rates further and bought far more Treasury bonds and other securities to keep rates down. In his mind, the post-Crash Fed had not acted aggressively enough. And in the minds of Presidents George W. Bush and Barack Obama, along with many journalists and economists who supported him, Bernanke's approach to so-called quantitative easing saved America from a second Great Depression—though one could reasonably argue that providing artificial support is not the same as stabilizing conditions.)

By keeping a lid on rates, the Fed rendered money cheap, particularly for the big banks, which had more collateral to pledge than smaller banks did, and thus more access to that money. But even though a pronounced credit crunch emerged, the banks didn't lend what they borrowed cheaply to the public for productive uses. They held onto it in desperate self-preservation mode. (This action was also repeated during the 2007–2008 financial crisis, which precipitated five years—as of the writing of this book—of the Fed's 0 percent interest rate policy for the big banks, which would restrict lending it forward to the population.)

By November 1929, the New York Fed had increased its discounts for member banks by $150 million and purchased $150 million of government securities in the open market to further reduce rates.[23] It remained selective in deciding who to help more explicitly. Relationships and positioning mattered. The amount of money lent to member banks—like the Big Six—was increased, but nonmembers were left to fail. The Fed's policies may not have been deliberately constructed to cause thousands of nonmember firms to fail, but they nonetheless had the *consequence* of benefiting the member banks the most—with the largest member banks gaining the most favor.

In the process, the larger banks ate up the smaller ones like crows at a kill: taking them over and using their deposits as additional survival fuel. The Fed commended their strategies of taking over the loans of their smaller brethren. During the week ending October 30, the loans and investments of New York City member banks had increased by $1.4 billion, largely because they had taken over a large part of the loans in the call loan market, which had previously been made by out-of-town banks and nonbanking lenders, who withdrew funds from the market.[24]

That small local and state (nonmember) banks were left to die while larger ones enjoyed the benefits of the Fed's benevolence is a major overlooked reason for the length of the Great Depression. People saw their deposits shut off to them at the smaller banks that collapsed, which hurt rural communities disproportionately. Even during recovery times, their trust in the system remained shattered.

By mid-November 1929, Lamont and other financial leaders had declared the crisis fully behind them. After they met on November 15 at the Morgan Bank for a follow-up conference, the *New York Times* claimed, "The bankers disclosed no reports of any serious difficulties or of any weak situations." The paper went on to say that Lamont, acting as spokesman for the financiers, "gave the impression that the efforts to stabilize the market were industry-wide, not limited to the banks represented by the group of six," and that "the other banking institutions of the city have rendered most effective cooperation throughout the emergency and have been in constant touch with the group."[25]

President Hoover was personally uncomfortable with the power that the bankers had displayed and been praised for. But he was hard-pressed to determine the best course of action. He decided to assemble his own group of industry and financial leaders to discuss strategies for stabilizing the economy. Though hesitant at first, Hoover soon decided that he needed a stronger alliance with the bankers to secure future calm. Four bankers were selected to participate in a conference held in Washington on December 5: Al Wiggin; Arthur Reynolds, chairman of Continental Illinois Bank and Trust of Chicago; John Scott, president of the National Bank of Houston; and Herbert Fleishhacker, president of Anglo & London Paris National Bank of San Francisco.[26]

Hoover's meeting with the bankers was later described by Galbraith as a "no-business business meeting." Galbraith wrote that President Hoover "was also conducting one of the oldest, most important and unhappily, one of the least understood rights in American life. This is the right of the meeting which is called not to do business, but to do no business . . . to create the impression that business is being done . . . to provide . . . the illusion of importance."[27]

Wiggin, Acquirer and Deceiver

The top bankers found ways to make their personal losses work for them. One strategy was tax evasion (even in the Mellon era of lax tax policy, evasion was a useful ploy). Wiggin made the most money from this maneuver. His secret was the creation of shell companies; he established six private corporations, three in the United States and three in Canada (which would be discovered during the Pecora hearings) to hide his wealth before the Crash.[28] During the bull market, he had organized investment pools that bet on shares of Chase Securities and Chase National Bank to inflate their values. He also cut some of his friends in on the action, and made sure that everyone borrowed from Chase to pay for their holdings. His family extracted $8 million of loans from Chase, even though they could have afforded to buy stock without the loans.[29] They used those loans to purchase more stock to inflate its values further.

Wiggin knew he was covered no matter what happened. Shortly before the Crash, he shorted shares in his own bank by borrowing shares from various brokers at prices he anticipated would fall, at which time he would buy the shares in the market at lower prices and return them to the brokers, making money on the difference. When the Dow stood at 359 on September 23, 1929 (the market had topped out twenty days earlier at 381), he placed what would be a hugely profitable bet that Chase's stock would fall.[30] He might have united with the rest of the Big Six to save the markets after the meeting with Lamont, but his short would net him a tidy fortune.

Before shorting those shares, Wiggin executed another profitable and shady strategy, using his bank's funds to plump the shares up. He placed $200 million of his depositors' money into trusts that speculated in Chase stock, thus participating in the very pool operations that artificially boosted its price during the run-up to the Crash. He pocketed $10.4 million from these trades, including $4 million from shorting the shares he drove up (after he drove them up) during the two-week period preceding the Crash.[31] His justification for selling his own shares while Chase Securities was pushing customers to buy them was that the price was "ridiculously high."[32] He had, in effect, bet against all the other Chase shareholders who had trusted in his hype about the firm.

As the decade counted down its final minutes, the New Year's Eve parties held in the midst of the glittering business and banker community flowed with prohibited elixirs, lavish gaiety, and sumptuous feasts. In the Grill Room at the Roosevelt Hotel in New York City, known as "the Grand Dame of Madison Avenue," the wealthy clanked their champagne flutes at midnight to the strains of Guy Lombardo's first live rendition of "Auld Lang Syne" (which became an annual tradition).[33]

The ditty blared on radios across the land. Relief mixed with exhaustion and a tepid, manufactured optimism punctuated the close of the 1920s. On December 5, 1929, speaking at a Chamber of Commerce conference, President Hoover had said, "The cure for such storms is action; the cure for unemployment is to find jobs."[34] A defiant President Hoover, a nonintrospective Treasury Secretary Mellon, and the Big Six allowed themselves to imagine they had dodged a bullet.

But the worst was yet to come. The country would plunge into a Great Depression, a third of the nation's banks would close, and unemployment would rise to capture one of every four employable citizens.

CHAPTER 6

THE EARLY 1930S:
TENUOUS TIMES,
TAX-EVADING TITANS

"We are thoroughly justified in saying, 'Business as usual.'"

—Albert Wiggin, chairman of
Chase National Bank, January 13, 1930

THE 1930S BEGAN ON THE FALSE NOTE OF ECONOMIC SECURITY WITH WHICH the political-financial alliance had capped off the 1920s. After the hysteria around the Crash subsided, President Hoover caught his breath. He could briefly push away doubts about his ability to extend his party's leadership into his second term. Most of the Big Six were equally relieved that their collaboration to save the markets, buoyed by the staunch support of the White House and Treasury Department and abetted by the Federal Reserve, had turned the tide back to one of unbridled opportunity.

The man who had the most on the line was characteristically enthusiastic about the economic fallout. "The recession will not last long," proclaimed

National City Bank head Charles Mitchell on January 15, 1930.[1] If one simply considered the invigorated behavior of the stock market, that conclusion was almost believable. For it was enjoying a brief resurgence from its Black Tuesday depths. Dipping to a low of 199 on November 13, 1929, the market was on its way up to 294, a 50 percent increase, by April 17, 1930.[2] Bankers, politicians, and a Wall Street–infatuated media gushed optimism at every point along the way. After a few threatening comments by some senators right after the Crash, there didn't seem to be much lingering concern about investigating how the financial system could bounce up and down so quickly—or who was responsible. The rebound was all that mattered.

But those delusional days were short-lived. The economy had suffered a severe blow not just because of the Crash but because of the preceding years of excess and borrowing to support that excess, yet its weakness was masked by the vibrant stock market. Bankers had been fortified by the Fed to "try again," but the injection of post-Crash speculative money in the market simply couldn't negate systemic problems for very long. There were too many bonds defaulting, too many businesses closing, and too many people losing their jobs and their hope of a more secure future. The money that was being funneled into the market to fuel financial speculation (rather than productive or social capitalism) provided the illusion of stability and prosperity, but it was not the kind of long-term capital upon which true economic growth could be sustained. Paper profits had shriveled faster than they had once increased. This could, and would, happen again.

Yet President Hoover, either because he wasn't fully informed about the inner workings of the markets by his banker friends or because he didn't want to admit that the bottom could still fall out of the economy on his watch, found himself pulling a Mitchell. On May Day 1930, he declared to the nation, "We have now passed the worst and with continued unity of effort we shall rapidly recover."[3] His statement wound up foreshadowing a nearly two-year market dive to a low of 41 on July 8, 1932, and a Great Depression that brought the American economy to its knees.

Were it not for parallel crises unfolding globally, the Depression would have dampened America's international power. But since the rest of the world would suffer in tandem, America would retain and even extend its dominant position throughout the 1930s. By the decade's end, the Depression would become the backdrop for another world war, and a war effort that would unite most of the same banks as the first one.

The Fed-Bank Shuffle

The first wave of deepening Depression, in the fall of 1930, coincided with the first of three major episodes of bank closings and mini panics. It began in the Midwest, where banks had been starved for credit since the Crash. The Fed stayed out of the fray. In general, it showed little empathy for the general credit condition of the country, focusing instead on how the big banks were faring. The Fed governors were pleased that the level of indebtedness at the bigger member banks hadn't changed much since the Crash, a sign they deemed as a positive indicator of a recovery.

But the population wasn't experiencing a recovery at all, especially not in the poorest areas. As the Fed reported, "The growth of deposits . . . has not been felt by rural communities. . . . At the present time their level is lower than at any time in recent years."[4]

It wasn't surprising that there was no growth in deposits; the public couldn't manufacture money out of thin air. Yet the Fed board remained blissfully unaware of the broader hardship and focused instead on its elite members. Thus it concluded in October 1930, "The exceptionally strong position of commercial banks and of the reserve banks, the prevailing ease in credit conditions, the low level of money rates, and the attitude of the federal reserve system" meant "the country's credit resources will be available to facilitate in every possible way the orderly movement of agricultural commodities from the producer through the channels of trade to the ultimate consumer."[5] (The Fed's obliviousness about broad economic malaise would resurface after the 2008 crisis.)

It didn't work out that way. By the end of 1930, it was clear that a new group on Wall Street, comprising most of the same banks as in the early 1900s but with new faces at their helms, was selecting which companies would live or die based on the relationships of their leaders to the likes of the Morgan Bank, National City Bank, and Chase. As such, the New York–based Bank of United States collapsed on December 11, 1930, eviscerating $200 million in deposits and wiping out the accounts of about four hundred thousand people (or two hundred thousand families).[6]

The Bank of United States was the largest bank in New York and the first major financial firm to close, and it had catered mostly to ordinary citizens. The average account there contained about $200, some families' total savings. The impact of the closing was that much sharper for the mostly Jewish and immigrant customers.

The bank wasn't innocent in its downfall. It had employed a plethora of shady schemes before its demise, such as selling shares of its stock to depositors at $200 a pop, assuring them they could sell the stock at the same price at any time (which turned out not to be the case). By early December shares were trading at 20 percent of their original value. And that was just the beginning.

The Big Three, a subset of the Big Six that included Thomas Lamont, Albert Wiggin, and Charles Mitchell, convened to consider bailing out the Bank of United States. But as Liaquat Ahamed chronicled, "after an all-night meeting that spilled into the next day, not even pleas from New York superintendent of banks Joseph Broderick could convince these major players to save this bank."[7]

Instead, the trio pushed the matter onto the New York State Banking Department, which took over the Bank of United States and concocted a plan with the Clearing House Association of banks whereby the bank's customers could borrow up to half of their deposit values from a fund created by the Clearing House and the New York State Banking Department. No promises were made about returning the deposits.

Lamont was quick to distance the good banks (such as his) from the "bad" ones. At a meeting of the members of the New York Stock Exchange, he said that the problems leading to the closing of the Bank of United States were "not symptomatic" of the general New York banking community, which he characterized as being "founded on a rock."[8]

The Bank of United States became the poster child for a bank that collapsed because of its "ill" practices; it was the Enron of its time. The philosophical cordoning off of such an errant bank shielded the big bankers from certain elements of investigation, as would later be shown during congressional hearings. They may have conducted similar activities, but they would not suffer the same consequences.

The Bank for International Settlements Is Born

President Hoover had reintroduced the term "Depression" in late 1929 to replace the more commonly used "Panic."[9] He thought it was more placating. The term stuck. Now, with domestic conditions faltering and people extracting their deposits, bankers turned to international markets to seek business and increase global influence.

Though the US economy was staggering, conditions were worse in Europe. Neither the Treaty of Versailles nor the Dawes plan had solved the war debt or German reparations problems, so US bankers needed another plan to keep the financial system percolating.

The first entity to be designed for that purpose, with a global name but a decidedly American bent, was the Bank for International Settlements—or, as it was fondly called among international bankers, the "cash register of German reparations."

The BIS was officially established in Basel, Switzerland, on May 17, 1930. It would continue the ideas of the failed Dawes plan, which had been extended into the Young plan (fashioned by Owen Young). The charter for the BIS was adopted at a conference in The Hague on January 20, 1930; the BIS would deal with ongoing German reparations matters in conjunction with the bankers. It would act as the new central body for the collection and distribution of payments, and as a trustee for the Dawes and Young loans that helped finance those reparations. The Young plan reduced German reparations payments further than the Dawes plan did and likewise allowed for the financing of those payments to come from private banks. It was another game of shuffle, but it allowed the American bankers to once again extend loans.

The seed money for the BIS (five hundred million Swiss francs) came from the same collection of banks that supplied loans to Europe: J. P. Morgan & Company, along with several central banks.[10] That money would be fused with capital from the New York Fed, despite the lack of a mandate or precedent for such an action—other than the fact that its former chairman, Gates McGarrah, was appointed as the first head of the BIS.

Six months into McGarrah's appointment, he and Chase chairman Al Wiggin were working hard to turn the global Depression into something financially and politically expedient for the United States and its financiers. The international focus provided both men a shield of sorts—it protected McGarrah from culpability in his banker-friendly role at the helm of the New York Fed during the lead-up to the Crash and diverted attention from the fraud Wiggin had committed against his own bank, which no one knew about yet.

The Wiggin Committee

On a frigid afternoon in January 1931, Wiggin issued a report to his shareholders. He blamed Europe's precarious debt position, rather than banks' speculative and credit-overextension actions, for the dire economic situation. (This was not too different from the blame placed on ransacked European countries following the US crisis in 2008.) His solution was not too different from the one Lamont had proposed during the mid-1920s: to effectively make it easier for Europe to borrow from US banks by reducing their current debt.

As he said, "Cancellation or reduction of the international debts has been increasingly discussed throughout the world. . . . I am firmly convinced it would be good business to initiate a reduction of these debts at this time."[11]

This was code for wanting to keep the bank's biggest borrowers coming back for more. President Hoover would have to find a way to do as Wiggin was suggesting while balancing the move with the political ramifications of helping Europe financially at a time when the public was primarily concerned with its own economic survival (even more so than it had been during the recent isolationist wave).

A few years earlier, President Coolidge had selected a fairly passive Federal Reserve head in Roy Young. Neither man believed that the Fed should have undue influence over economic policy. In 1928, Coolidge had stated that stock market speculation should not cause alarm, which dovetailed with Young's policies of leaving the banks alone. Under Young the Fed had not interfered with banks borrowing at the discount window at rates near 6 percent and lending those funds at rates near 12 percent in 1929, providing lots of incentive for them to make speculative loans.

The New York Fed had acted on Charles Mitchell's wishes.[12] He had pushed harder than anyone for rates to remain low and borrowing to remain cheap before the Crash. Indeed, when the New York Fed's board of directors voted to increase rates between February and May 1929, Mitchell objected.[13]

McGarrah supported Mitchell, and on May 31 he upped the ante. He told the Federal Reserve Board that "it may soon be necessary to establish a *less* restricted discount policy in order that the member banks may more freely borrow for the proper conduct of their business." The board kept the discount rate at 5 percent.

A week later, emboldened by the support, Mitchell urged a more liberal discount policy *and* an easing of credit conditions through a Fed purchase of bills and government securities. (The Fed did the same thing after the 2008 crisis.) Mitchell knew well the first law of banking—cheap money is better than expensive money—and used that mantra to force the Fed to keep him afloat for as long as possible.

With McGarrah at the BIS, it was Roy Young (who had left his post as Fed chairman on August 31, 1930) who came under fire setting those terms. According to the Senate Banking and Currency Committee subcommittee hearings held in January and February 1931, it was Young, not the bankers, who had been ineffectual in thwarting the speculation that led to the Crash.

Instead of raising the discount rate sooner, the consensus was that Young merely issued verbal warnings to the public to curb speculation in the late 1920s. Arguably, warning the public rather than clamping down on banks was wrong for more reasons than the committee discussed. The public wasn't responsible for shady trusts, speculative stock pools, or bank-engineered fraud. But blame doesn't need to be logical if it serves the political purpose of alleviating culpability for those levying it.

During the hearings, according to *Time*, witnesses placed fault largely with Young's "foggy-headed uncertainties."[14] That was rather unfair, though. Domestic and international speculation had been brewing for half a decade, pooled trusts had been sprouting for years, and tremendous fraud had been perpetrated to manipulate prices, as was later presented at the Pecora hearings. Quibbling about a six-month period of hiking rates seemed ridiculous then, and seems even more so with the benefit of hindsight. But nonetheless it proved politically useful at the time by shielding the president and the bankers.

A few months later, in the summer of 1931, Wiggin took a team of Chase bankers with him to Europe.[15] On a balmy August afternoon, Wiggin played master of ceremonies to representatives from twelve countries who had gathered in a swanky hotel room in Basel. Reporters referred to them as the Wiggin Committee.[16]

The point of the meetings was to investigate Germany's ongoing credit problems. In 1930 Germany owed more than twenty-five billion reichsmarks to foreign lenders (about $65 billion after adjusting for inflation), predominantly as a result of World War I reparations.[17] Yet with unemployment above 33 percent and facing a massive collapse in industrial production, Germany was having trouble making payments. The crisis was made worse by a divided government challenged by growing political extremism inside and outside the Reichstag.[18] Just three months before the Wiggin Committee met, the Austrian lender Credit-Anstalt—the biggest bank east of Germany—had gone bankrupt, unleashing a knock-on effect on German banks and leaving the German economy teetering on the precipice of disaster.[19]

The Wiggin Committee pressed for a six-month debt moratorium for Germany's foreign creditors. Wiggin cared deeply about the issue; Chase had issued more short-term debt to Germany than any other US bank, and since the Crash it had been unable to collect the money it was owed.[20] Wiggin was less concerned about the long-term loans his bank and others had sold to the public, but he cared a lot about those short-term notes because his bank had lent its own cash against them. (Chase eventually got paid after Wiggin and John Foster Dulles sailed to Europe in May 1933 to meet with German authorities.[21] But all $1.2 billion of the public-financed long-term loans went bust.[22])

In Basel, Wiggin not only represented Chase but all New York banks. He had taken a group of Chase men with him, though the international community had expected Jack Morgan or Tom Lamont to lead such a gathering, as had been the custom since the World War I days.[23] But that might have been awkward. First, Chase was one of the largest US holders of German bonds.[24] Second, Morgan had served primarily as France's banker.[25] It would have been odd for a Morgan partner to oppose France's wishes regarding Germany in such an open forum, and France was against any sort of help for Germany's debt problems; it had enough economic concerns of its own.

Wiggin was happy to play the power broker role that J. P. Morgan had played when the two men first crossed paths during the 1907 panic, only now in a more international realm. His famous rejection of a Morgan partnership back then had stemmed from his desire to make his own mark in the world. This was his opportunity.

Germany had already appealed to President Hoover for a debt moratorium. Unlike the isolationist mid-1920s when such an official stance would have been unthinkable, this time the world economy, including the United States, was in danger. On June 20, 1931, Hoover had proposed a one-year moratorium on "all payments on intergovernmental debts, reparations, and relief debts."[26] Debts to private banks were excluded from his proposal.

Hoover explained to the American public, "The worldwide depression has affected the countries of Europe more severely than our own." He said this situation could hurt the United States: "The fabric of intergovernmental debts, supportable in normal times, weighs heavily in the midst of this depression."[27] The proposed moratorium was not about taking sides regarding European countries or internationalism per se; it was a matter of global and American economic stability.

Finally, on July 6, France had agreed to Hoover's moratorium, raising the number of nations supporting it to fifteen. But it was too late. The damage to Germany's economy, which would lead to a seismic economic breakdown and sow the seeds of the next world war, had been done. By the time the National Socialist government consolidated its power in 1933, German payments had stopped; only about one-eighth of the original amount from the Treaty of Versailles was paid. Contributing heavily to Germany's economic problems and the rise of the Third Reich were the additional piles of loans extended by the private banks to "help" Germany abide with the Treaty of Versailles, Dawes plan, and Young plan stipulations. Those private loans didn't get repaid either.

The Great Depression's Global Reach

The banking system failures throughout Austria and Germany, and the Wiggin and Hoover moratoriums, were followed by Britain's abandoning the gold standard on September 21, 1931. The global Depression was in full swing.

In the United States, hundreds of other banks were closing their doors. City landlords were throwing out more and more tenants for not making rent. Home foreclosures spiked. People couldn't afford heating fuel during the harsh winter months. Construction and other jobs disappeared. Smaller businesses weren't making enough money to pay operating costs, let alone the interest on their loans. They didn't get debt moratoriums; they just defaulted. Meanwhile, banks were steeped in self-preservation mode. By mid-1931, mass layoffs were the ugly norm. Even Henry Ford shut down many of his car factories in Detroit, throwing seventy-five thousand men out of work.[28]

The combination of strained lending for productive uses and bankruptcies of small establishments coalesced in widespread financial degradation. Meanwhile, big banks ceased lending to agriculture, industry, and local businesses in order to repay "a substantial amount of their borrowings at the reserve banks."[29] Their first allegiance was to the Fed, which ensured their survival with cheap funds. This strategy would become a time-honored way for the most powerful banks to survive at the expense of their clients.

A few weeks after Britain went off the gold standard, a panicked Hoover held a secret meeting with thirty prominent American financiers at the Massachusetts Avenue apartment of Treasury Secretary Andrew Mellon. As Irving Bernstein wrote in *The Lean Years*, "The president was overwhelmed with gloom and the fear of impending disaster." He now saw "imminent danger to the American banking system as a consequence of the events in Europe."[30] Blaming Europe for the woes of the US economy, however, was not looking at the full picture; it indicated a lack of understanding of the US bankers' culpability in the crisis.

In his memoirs, Hoover remained detached and similarly unreflective of his or the bankers' role, blaming the Fed and European bankers instead. "To be sure, we were due for some economic readjustment as a result of the orgy of stock speculation in 1928–1929," he wrote. "This orgy was not a consequence of my administrative policies. In the main it was the result of the Federal Reserve Board's pre-1928 enormous inflation of credit at the request of European bankers, which, as this narrative shows, I persistently tried to stop, but I was overruled."[31]

To be fair, much of the laissez-faire attitude that had festered during the 1920s occurred during the Coolidge administration. Hoover had attempted to steer bankers toward lending restraint, particularly internationally, and tried measures to bolster the economy after the Crash, but by failing to examine the role of the financial community in providing the debt and fabricating the enthusiasm that stoked the speculation—not just in the market but throughout the economy—he failed to hold himself accountable for the frenzy of risky banking activity. There were political opportunities lost in his denials, such as examining whether it was appropriate to have the chairmen of the largest banks in the country seated on the board of the New York Fed, as National City Bank chairman Charles Mitchell was, and had been before the Crash, and as Chase chairman Al Wiggin would be from January 1932 to March 1933. (The alliance between the New York Fed and the financiers remains recklessly codependent to this day.)

Hoover did establish the Reconstruction Finance Corporation in 1932. The government bailout program was tasked with lending $1.5 billion to ailing banks and industries, but its funds were channeled disproportionately to the bigger banks.[32] One of those banks was the First National City Bank, whose chairman, New York Fed Class A director Charles Mitchell, had aggressively pushed the Fed to keep rates low after he realized that his bank and the entire financial landscape were in trouble.

The massive bond-buying program that the Fed initiated in May 1932, in which it agreed to buy $26 million worth of bonds a week from its member banks, reached a total of $1.82 billion in Treasury securities holdings.[33] The idea was that banks would sell their Treasuries and use the money to pay off their debts. After that, they would use the remaining cash to lend out or buy corporate bonds to help the greater economy. This was in addition to getting the benefit of low rates on their loans from the Fed's discount window.

But only half of that plan happened. The banks did sell the Fed their government bonds to raise more capital. But they did not lend the money back out. (This tactic would be repeated after the 2008 crisis.) As The Nation put it, "You can lead a horse to water but you can not make him drink, and you can offer the banks limitless Federal Reserve credit, but you cannot make them lend."[34]

Discount rates were eventually lowered to 2.5 percent in 1934, 2 percent in 1935, and 1.5 percent in September 1937. But this lowering of rates didn't inspire an outpouring of lending either. The largest banks sat on their money.

Mellon's Tax Problems

While presiding over a collapsing economy, President Hoover was faced with another political conundrum that eroded confidence in his leadership abilities. Not only was his power to stop the Depression diminishing, but his Treasury secretary was under attack in Congress. The Democrats were gearing up to return to power; the economy was a mess; and Mellon, who represented the excesses of the wealthy, was an easy target.

On January 6, 1932, Texas Democratic representative Wright Patman told the Speaker of the House that he wanted to impeach Mellon on the charge of "high crimes and misdemeanors." His claims were based on an old 1789 statute that forbade a Treasury Department head from engaging in trade of commerce while holding that position. Patman noted that Mellon owned voting stock in three hundred corporations with combined assets of $3 billion.[35] To Patman, this was clearly an engagement in commerce and a violation of US law.

Since becoming secretary, Mellon had remained "owner in whole or part of many sea vessels competing with other sea vessels in commerce, and was thus personally interested in the importation of goods, wares, and merchandise in large amounts," Patman alleged.[36] Sea vessels, he submitted, were explicitly forbidden in those laws.

In addition, Patman pointed out that Mellon received tax refunds from his ownership in various bank and trust companies, including his Pittsburgh-based Mellon National Bank. He had also been profiting personally from decisions made in his public position, such as appropriation for multimillion-dollar construction projects utilizing aluminum while Mellon was principal owner of the Aluminum Company of America. In Patman's eyes, these types of conflicts were highly unethical and borderline illegal under the statute.

Patman went on to present evidence that Mellon had spent $7 million in 1930 on artwork from the Hermitage Museum in Leningrad. Not only did Mellon deny purchasing those paintings; on his 1931 tax return he deducted the purchase price as a charitable donation.[37]

With those commerce and tax evasion charges in the hands of a Senate subcommittee, Hoover accepted Mellon's resignation from his Treasury post on February 12, 1932. President Hoover appointed him ambassador to Great Britain instead.[38] Ogden Mills, undersecretary of the Treasury, took over Mellon's post for the rest of the Hoover administration.

Mellon's tax problems didn't end there. On March 19, 1934, Attorney General Homer Cummings launched a federal income tax evasion suit against him, Thomas S. Lamont (Thomas Lamont's son, also an executive at Morgan), and several others.

In response, Mellon commented, "For many months now a campaign of character wrecking and abuse has been conducted against me. . . . I know there has been no evasion of taxes on my part."[39] Cummings didn't get very far. He launched his investigation in Pittsburgh, where Mellon, a generous philanthropist, was popular among the political elite. The grand jury denied the government's request to prosecute.[40] The matter was dropped.

Still, the administration that followed Hoover's was determined to make an example of Mellon, an old-money titan who represented the perceived excesses of the 1920s. The extent of Mellon's tax "creativity" would be tried in front of the US Board of Tax Appeals in early 1935. Though Mellon avoided the fraud charges, he was found to be on the hook for some $800,000 in unpaid taxes.[41]

The First Glass Bill

On February 27, 1932, Hoover signed into law the first banking bill championed by Virginia Democratic senator Carter Glass and Alabama Democratic representative Henry Steagall.[42] The primary purpose of the Glass-Steagall Act of 1932 was to protect the country's depleting gold reserves by permitting government securities to be used to back Federal Reserve notes in excess of the prevailing 40 percent minimum threshold.[43] The act reduced the collateral required for Fed member banks to post at its discount window. It was a godsend for the bankers, giving them easier money in a tight credit market.

Thanks to the bill, banks no longer had to set aside gold to use as collateral for Federal Reserve notes. With the extra money, they could reduce their own debt burdens rather than liquidate investments and loans, or sell them at bargain basement prices, to raise money. Bankers could also place more Treasuries on reserve at the Fed, so in a way the Fed was funding itself. But actually, bankers, the Fed, and the Treasury (which issued the government securities instead of depleting gold) were all benefiting.

By the second week of May 1932 (when the act went into effect), member banks had pledged more than $98 million in new reserves to the Fed, more than half of which came from New York banks. (In 2009, long after gold ceased being necessary as collateral for banks to raise cash at the Fed's discount window, the same process of buying Treasury bonds to pledge to the Fed as bank collateral came back into play, but to a far more extensive degree than Depression-era bankers could have imagined.)

Franklin Delano Roosevelt and the Man from Goldman

President Hoover was increasingly overwhelmed by the Depression, and the population was increasingly tired of him. Conversely, New York governor Franklin Delano Roosevelt saw the situation as a second opportunity for him to become president (he had missed the first opening when he ran unsuccessfully as James Cox's vice presidential running mate in 1920).

Roosevelt won the 1932 election by a margin of seven million votes, coincidentally the same number by which Harding had beaten Cox twelve years earlier. He secured the White House on the strength of his promises to a beleaguered nation and with help from a bevy of rich supporters. One of his main campaign money raisers was Sidney Weinberg, head of a relatively small, boutique investment bank named Goldman Sachs, which had launched the Goldman Sachs Trading Corporation in December 1928. That fund had subsequently invested in a host of shady enterprises, pumping its shares to a high of $326 before the Crash, collapsing to $1 in 1932, and bankrupting many of its investors in the process. At the time, Goldman Sachs didn't have anywhere near the clout of the elite Wall Street banking firms. It couldn't touch the Big Six, let alone the Big Three. That would come later, in spades.

Weinberg positioned himself behind FDR as a key member of the Democratic National Campaign Executive Committee.[44] This helped divert attention from the negative feelings toward his firm. For FDR, it was the beginning of a close alliance, not just with Weinberg but with all the business leaders Weinberg would make accessible to the president over the coming years.

Weinberg excelled at building relationships with people at all levels of wealth and position. He began his career the year of the bank panic of 1907, working as a janitor's assistant at Goldman at the tender age of sixteen. By 1930, he had risen to become head of the firm.

FDR, himself a master politician, used the moniker "The Politician" to describe Weinberg.[45] In return for Weinberg's help financing the election,

FDR later appointed him to the Business Advisory Council of the Department of Commerce on June 26, 1933. The council was created to enable corporate executives to get their views heard in Washington.[46] In that position, Weinberg was able to meet with key business heads and leverage those relationships into business for Goldman. He could simultaneously grow his influence in Washington and on Wall Street: two birds, one stone. The council remained one of the main channels of communication between business and FDR during the New Deal period. The alliance with FDR provided Weinberg with a position of influence in Washington for decades, and also thrust Goldman Sachs into the political-financial power sphere.

One month before his inauguration, FDR survived an assassination attempt in Miami by an unemployed bricklayer named Giuseppe Zangara. The bullets missed FDR thanks to the quick thinking of a nearby woman, who grabbed Zangara and "tried to strangle him."[47] But the assassin's bullet struck Chicago mayor Anton Cermak, who died from his wounds.

The incident further galvanized the nation in support of FDR. It also brought forth an expression of relief from, among others, Morgan partner Russell Leffingwell, a Democrat who would engage in respectful policy arguments with FDR for the duration of his presidency. Leffingwell's relationship with FDR snaked back to the Wilson years, when he had served under Wilson's Treasury secretary, William McAdoo, and his successor, Carter Glass, during World War I, while Roosevelt was assistant secretary of the Navy. It was Leffingwell's work on postwar policies and war-debt management with Lamont that led to his eventual recruitment into the Morgan Bank in 1923.[48]

After the assassination attempt Leffingwell wrote to FDR that he was "filled with relief" that his old buddy had survived.[49] And how different the trajectory of American history might have been had he not escaped the assassin's bullet.

The Pecora Hearings, Part I

While FDR waited to begin his first term, a congressional investigation into bankers' practices initiated by the Republicans was under way that would pave the way for a major reconstruction of the very landscape of US banking and restrain the type of speculation that had led to the Crash and Great Depression.

Though the hearings officially began in April 1932, not much happened during the first eleven months. There was no cooperation from the bankers, no help from Hoover, and criticism from the Democrats, who thought it was all a Republican sideshow anyway.

Just as the Pujo hearings hadn't gotten much attention until Wilson took office, and even then had little lasting impact, neither did these hearings gain momentum until FDR was set to take office. But in early 1933, with FDR about to take the presidential oath and a Democratic majority coming into the Senate, outgoing Senate Banking and Currency Committee chairman Peter Norbeck, a Republican from South Dakota, hired the brash and ambitious former New York deputy district attorney, Ferdinand Pecora, to lead a set of new investigations.

The Pecora hearings provided America with an awareness of *how* bankers operated for the first time in twenty years. They also provided solid reasoning for the legislation that would curtail those activities. The public again saw the bankers as predatory, creating the illusion of value through fraudulent information and parceling out shares to their inner circle at lower prices than were available to the public. The hearings shed light on the financial manipulations that led to the Depression. As they uncovered these unsavory practices, the hearings provided Roosevelt with the political capital to enact some of the most sweeping financial reforms in the history of the country. What the public did not know was that he was collaborating with the bankers who were closest to him in the process.

As Pecora called financiers before Congress, he ripped the lid off the unethical and fraudulent activities of the Big Three. Two of the financiers would resign as a result, but their banks would thrive under new leadership more aligned with FDR and his policies, which would also benefit those incoming leaders.

In February 1933 Charles Mitchell was the first to undergo examination for his role in the multimillion-dollar losses that took place during the Crash. He strode into the hearings indignant, a man with no remorse and nothing to hide. But after a grilling from Pecora that covered everything from shady Cuban sugar deals to shaming customers into keeping plummeting stocks, he left with a pending indictment. The indictment was not for stuffing bum Latin American bonds down investors' throats or financially strangling small investors, but for tax evasion. Mitchell had sold National City stock to members of his family at a loss in order to avoid paying income tax.

Humiliated before Congress; the press, which had once adored him for his vision; and the public, Mitchell resigned as chairman of National City Bank on February 26, 1933. James Perkins, a Harvard alum and friend of FDR, replaced the disgraced banker. Perkins heralded a new era for National

City Bank, in which a more prudent, socially minded banker aligned strongly with a progressive and politically aggressive president.

FDR Takes Office

On March 4, 1933, a cold, bleak, and cloudy Saturday, Hoover rode with Roosevelt to the Capitol. In his final moments as president, he said wearily to FDR, "We are at the end of our strength, there's nothing more we can do."[50]

For FDR, the challenge was just beginning. During his inaugural address, he famously pronounced, "The only thing we have to fear is fear itself." There were fourteen million people out of work; nine million had lost their savings. Fear didn't begin to describe the hopelessness. Yet FDR spoke with the confidence of a man who would figure it out. To the millions of unemployed Americans he vowed, "Our greatest primary task is to put people to work." And speaking to the growing antibanker sentiment, he promised, "The money changers have fled from their high seats in the temple of our civilization. We may now restore that temple to the ancient truths."

Toward the end of his speech Roosevelt vowed to install "two safeguards against a return of the evils of the old order." The first would be "a strict supervision of all banking and credits and investments" in order to end speculation with other people's money. The second would be "an adequate but sound currency." FDR was no isolationist; like the bankers, he realized that a strong dollar would promote American power in the world and help fix problems at home.

It had been a rough few years. In 1930, 1,350 banks had failed, followed by 2,293 in 1931 and 1,453 in 1932. The smaller banks fared the worst. Even the great Morgan Bank had seen its assets decline from $118.7 million in 1929 to $53.2 million by 1933, though in general the big New York banks did much better than others. Things got worse as 1933 opened, with 273 banks closing in January alone, bringing about another rush of citizens extracting whatever deposits they had left, fearing the worst. On February 14, the state of Michigan declared a bank holiday to stop the drainage; another twenty-one states had followed suit by March. By the time FDR took office, the situation had reached its lowest point.

FDR's banking-oriented ideas were tinged with Wilsonian sentiment. But rather than rely on the Federal Reserve to decentralize control of the banks, he harnessed the power of Congress and the president, and gained support from the people and even most of the bankers, to foster a more stable banking system.

Lamont's Landlord

FDR was a quintessential "Eastern Establishment" man, a Harvard graduate with solid blue-blood family connections, two townhouses in New York, and a mansion overlooking the magnificent Hudson River. He was able to speak the language of the bankers, and he had their respect—even if some of them occasionally criticized him and his party in public.

What mattered, though, was what happened behind closed doors, in letters, in meetings, on boats. Roosevelt socialized with the bankers. He yachted with them. His presidency broke the chain of leaders from the Midwest and New England who did not grow up in the same social circles as the nation's most powerful financiers. Even if FDR rebelled against his heritage at times— and though he and his wife, Eleanor, were instrumental in advancing major progressive causes, and he would be called a traitor to his class—his roots were inalterable.

The presidency had returned to the hands of a New Yorker: a Democrat, yes, but a man more like most financiers than the former three presidents. There would be differences of opinion, but they would come from an origin of similar upbringing. And as such, they would be negotiated to satisfy everyone's desire to retain their own piece of power.

FDR's father, James Roosevelt, had been a successful banker who traveled in the circles of J. P. Morgan and his ilk. The Roosevelts owned a home on the majestic banks of the Hudson River, in Hyde Park, New York, near where many elite industrialist-financiers spent their autumns amid the colorful foliage. The Morgans, Rockefellers, Astors, and Vanderbilts were all friends or neighbors of FDR.

Then there was Thomas Lamont. His relationship with Roosevelt went back years. In 1915, Lamont had rented the Roosevelts' New York City home. Lamont and Roosevelt participated in Harvard alumni events together (along with Jack Morgan).[51] They had both been editors of the *Harvard Crimson*: Roosevelt in the early 1900s, Lamont a decade or so earlier. And they had both served and admired Wilson during World War I.

Once FDR was in the White House, Lamont wasted no time in contacting him about his concerns, writing, "I believe in all seriousness that the emergency could not be greater."[52] He offered a five-page memorandum of initiatives including the Federal Reserve banks' unlimited purchasing of government securities, which could be used as reserves against Fed loans instead of gold. The more government securities the Fed could take, the more banks could borrow against those securities. Lamont also suggested authorizing the

Reconstruction Finance Corporation to deposit money in state and national banks without requiring additional security, and recommended that the government raise $1 billion to fund "urgent necessities."[53] His proposals were all about increasing liquidity to the banks.

FDR's Republican Treasury Secretary and Morgan's Favors

Roosevelt cleverly harnessed the public's anger at the bankers, stoked by the unfolding congressional investigations, to promote a progressive agenda. But many of his reforms were designed to help most of the bankers as well as the population.

FDR appointed Republican William Woodin, president of the American Car and Foundry Company, a leading maker of railway wheels and cars, as his first Treasury secretary.[54] Woodin was FDR's point man for the seven-day national bank holiday that began on March 5, 1933, the day after his inauguration.[55] During that time banks were closed for examination by regulators while replenishing their reserves and stabilizing their conditions.

The appointment presented problems when the Pecora Commission discovered that Woodin's name was on the Morgan Bank's "preferred customer list." The exclusive list represented clients to whom shares of "hot" issues—the most desirable stocks, whose prices would escalate once they hit the public market—were allocated first.[56] These high fliers got an early chance to acquire new stock at a cheaper price and with the certainty of a greater profit relative to the public. Charles Mitchell and Al Wiggin were also on the list.[57]

In itself, there was nothing illegal about the list, but the disclosure stoked the public's wrath. Woodin resigned in December 1933, citing poor health.

FDR's Secret Meeting with Banker James Perkins

Just two days after FDR's inauguration, Roosevelt invited National City Bank chairman James Perkins to the White House for a secret meeting. In a slick preemptive move that history has long overlooked, the men put into action a plan that would lead to the Glass-Steagall Act of 1933.

FDR reasoned that the population would support any bill that looked like bank regulation, especially if it protected their deposits, and the Democratic Congress would support the president when it came time for a vote. But first Roosevelt secured Perkins's backing. Perkins was convinced it was better to focus on deposit taking and lending than speculative trading or securities creation. He and FDR were on the same page regarding separating the banks. Both men would win if such legislation was passed: Perkins would retain the support of FDR (or "Frank," as he called him) and control of the stronger arm of his bank, and FDR would receive policy approval from the nation's largest holder of customer deposits.

It was fortuitous for FDR that Perkins had nabbed the helm of National City Bank after Mitchell brought such scandal to the firm. The management shift represented turning over a new leaf, something FDR could exploit by blaming a few bad apples for the overzealous speculation and reckless moves that precipitated the Crash. Perkins, one of the good apples, would support the Glass-Steagall Act as it weaved through Congress.

The next day, under Perkins's direction and in anticipation of the bill's passage, the National City Bank board passed a resolution to split the trading and deposit-taking elements of the bank. The split was publicly announced the following day. Afterward, FDR thanked Perkins for his actions, adding, "It was fine to see you the other day."[58]

The Second Alliance: FDR and Chase's Winthrop Aldrich

For FDR, Perkins was just the appetizer. The main course was another Harvard alum and friend, Chase chairman Winthrop Aldrich, who would be a major power player in the political-financial sphere for the next two decades.[59]

Following the 1930 merger of Chase National, Equitable Trust Company, and the Interstate Trust Company to create the largest bank in the world, Aldrich ascended to president of the new entity, Chase National, while Wiggin retained his title of chairman.[60] But when Wiggin resigned as chairman on January 11, 1933, the board of directors selected forty-seven-year-old Aldrich to take over.[61] Aldrich was far more practical, conservative, and globally savvy than Wiggin, who in addition to his personal shenanigans had built a web of bad speculative debt through Chase's trading subsidiary, racking up losses Aldrich wanted to reduce.

Aldrich was a man of high class and pedigree: he was John D. Rockefeller's brother-in-law and the son of Fed architect Nelson Aldrich.[62] He was also an avid sailor and a member of the exclusive Seawanhaka Corinthian Yacht Club, which held its monthly meetings at the J. P. Morgan and James A. Roosevelt–founded Metropolitan Club in Manhattan.[63]

Aldrich's ascent at Chase was as much about family connections as it was about his financial and legal acumen. In 1929 he became president of Equitable Trust, which had grown through the 1920s via a series of strategic mergers to become one of the largest firms in America. Winthrop persuaded Wiggin to merge Chase with Equitable at the suggestion of Rockefeller, Equitable's main shareholder. As president of the conglomerate, Aldrich eventually ousted Wiggin as chairman and took over the helm. (Wiggin's suspiciously high pension of $100,000 per year would be attacked during the Pecora hearings.)

Aldrich's rise had broad ramifications for the banking industry and political relationships; up to that point, it had been the Morgan Bank whose partners had the closest ties to the presidents. Now a wider array of president-banker alliances was forming that included the heads of Chase and National City. Even the West Coast–based Bank of America would soon be involved.

As New Deal scholar Thomas Ferguson noted in his much lauded paper "From Normalcy to the New Deal," "With workers, farmers, and many industrialists up in arms against finance in general and its most famous symbol, the House of Morgan, in particular, virtually all the major non-Morgan investment banks in America lined up behind Roosevelt."[64]

This was not to say that Roosevelt didn't have support among the Morgan bankers. Indeed, many of them were men he had known for decades. But banking reform presented particular opportunities for Chase and National City, especially, to rise above the Morgan Bank in terms of political-financial power and to raise their banks' status domestically and globally.

To achieve this goal, Aldrich and Perkins joined forces to support the Glass-Steagall bill, which they thought would diminish the strength of the Morgan Bank. The bill would force banks to decide between keeping deposits and lending, and maintaining the issuance of new securities. The latter was the means by which Morgan, in particular, had raised money for domestic and foreign lending, which was how it had become so influential. The Morgan Bank had never tried to gather deposits from ordinary investors to back its lending practices to the extent that Chase and National City had.

Three days after Roosevelt called Perkins to the White House, Aldrich's views on splitting up banks hit the front page of the *New York Times*. Vying for the position of the most powerful banker in the country, he vehemently backed the proposed Glass-Steagall Act of 1933, which would force a separation of commercial and investment banking activities. (The idea had been batted around Congress for more than a year; Wiggin had strongly opposed it because he was more interested in the trading side of the bank, where he had made most of his money.)

In conjunction, Aldrich announced that Chase National Bank and Chase Securities Corporation would become separate entities, effectively enforcing the bill within his own company even before it became law, as Perkins had done. This wasn't a simple restructuring—the Chase Securities Corporation was the biggest of its kind in the world.[65] From an initial financial seedling of $2.5 million in May 1917 it had grown to $37 million in capital by the end of 1932, with $18 million in surplus and profits.[66] The securities arm was so powerful that in July 1929 it bought 98 percent of the American Express Company.

Nor were Aldrich's moves altruistic. He forced a restructuring of the banking landscape knowing it would be comparatively beneficial for his bank. It would also help restore consumer confidence, which was a critical requirement for raising capital and expansion. As Ferguson later noted, "By separating investment from commercial banking, [Glass-Steagall] destroyed the unity of the two functions whose combination had been the basis of Morgan hegemony in American finance."[67] Aldrich deftly went one step further than even Glass had envisioned. By pushing for the separation of commercial and securities activities for private banks (the original bill had considered merely public ones), Aldrich would make life very difficult for the Morgan Bank.

The banking community went up in arms over Aldrich's actions, taking sides depending on allegiance to Morgan or Aldrich. William Potter of the Guaranty Trust Company, which closely collaborated with the Morgan Bank, called Aldrich's ideas "quite the most disastrous . . . ever heard from a member of the financial community."[68]

Roosevelt was delighted. Not only did he want this split but his foot soldiers, the bankers, were making his job easier. He wrote Perkins and Aldrich letters of effusive appreciation for their preemptive moves.[69] Aldrich replied somewhat adoringly: "I find myself lost in admiration of the courage and wisdom you have shown in dealing with the problems created by the immediate banking crisis."[70]

It was useful to FDR that Wiggin and Mitchell, with their speculative natures and thirst for power relative to the presidency, were out of his way. He wasn't really close to them anyway. The bankers who were left knew how to gain power: by supporting his.

Fireside Chat on Banking

On March 12, 1933, eight days after he took office, FDR gave his first "fireside chat" radio address to the nation. The topic was the banking crisis. Millions of nervous Americans—a quarter of whom were unemployed—gathered around their radios to hear his address. These listeners, many of whom had seen their savings go with the closure of their banks, had a faint hope that there was light at the end of the tunnel.[71]

FDR truly understood banking. He explained to his listeners that when people deposit money, banks invest it "in many different forms of credit— bonds, commercial paper, mortgages, and many other kinds of loans," and that the "total amount of all the currency in the country is only a small fraction of the total deposits in all of the banks." In other words, banks don't keep a lot of peoples' deposits in storage for stability.

At the end of February and beginning of March, he explained, "there was a general rush . . . to turn bank deposits into currency or gold . . . so great that the soundest banks could not get enough currency to meet the demand." By the afternoon of March 3, many state and local banks had to close to protect themselves, which is why a "nationwide bank holiday" was required: the banks needed time to breathe.

FDR took care not to blame *all* the bankers for the country's economic and credit problems. He knew it was important for Americans to regain trust in the bankers. Instead he said, "Some of our bankers had shown themselves either incompetent or dishonest in their handling of the people's funds. They had used the money entrusted to them in speculations and unwise loans. This was, of course, not true in the vast majority of our banks."[72]

A skilled tactician, FDR would strengthen the banking system with the help of his friends, the "good" bankers. For he understood something very important: his power and influence would be greater if he had the bankers on his side *and* solved the banking crisis for the population. The bankers, in turn, realized that collaborating with FDR would help elevate their own financial power later.

On March 16, Bank of America head A. P. Giannini, who had recently visited with FDR in New York, enthused, "The President is certainly doing great work and I don't think that even Teddy, in his palmiest days, gripped the imagination of the people as has he in the past few days."[73]

Teddy Roosevelt had taken on the nonfinancial trusts in his day, but he had supported the "money trusts" during the Panic of 1907. Woodrow Wilson had bashed the money trusts in public (never by name), but established a Federal Reserve from which they could be assured support during emergencies. Hoover had tried unsuccessfully to work with the money trusts and secure the financial system at the same time. FDR had figured out how to effect real structural change with support from both parties: key commercial bankers and citizens.

The Pecora Hearings, Part II

The Pecora hearings were more probing and public than the Pujo hearings had been, but they became more of a show than a political necessity once FDR got the significant bankers' endorsement for reforms on the legislative agenda—though they did serve to vanquish, if not jail, the tainted leaders.

A few weeks after Charles Mitchell testified that he sold his stock "frankly, for tax purposes," FDR was informed that the former head of National City Bank had been indicted for tax evasion.[74] Mitchell was arrested at his Fifth Avenue home on March 21, 1933. As the Pecora hearings continued in the background, the New York papers splashed sensational headlines about his tax evasion trial in May and June 1933.

On June 22, after twenty-five hours of jury deliberation, Mitchell was acquitted of all charges. The jury agreed with Mitchell's defense attorney, who claimed that Mitchell's "intent" was to "abide by the law" and that, technically, he had done that.[75] Mitchell wept when the verdict was read. The press had readied bulletin copy announcing Mitchell's conviction. The atmosphere was supercharged, as crowds milled in the corridors of the federal building.

(The government entered a civil claim for the taxes and an adjustment of $1.1 million in back taxes and penalties. Mitchell appealed that case up to the Supreme Court and lost, rendering a final settlement on December 27, 1938.[76] Roosevelt wrote the lead prosecutor in the case to congratulate him, saying "the amounts involved are not important. The Government's successful challenge of the practices to which Mr. Mitchell resorted in this case has served largely to end those practices."[77])

With that bad apple out of the way, FDR and Aldrich began a series of private conversations and meetings at the White House about the pending banking legislation. Washington insiders knew what was going on, and Aldrich's political position elevated quickly in the eyes of Congress.

As Aldrich wrote FDR on March 23, 1933, "Since writing you on March 20th two Senators, members of the Banking and Currency Committee of the Senate, have approached me indicating that they would like to talk with me about . . . banking reform. . . . I have felt myself that it might be more useful to you if I talked with you fully with regard to this matter before talking to anyone else." Four days later, FDR invited Aldrich to the White House to discuss the matter.[78]

Aldrich didn't just call for the divorce of commercial and speculative banking, a tactical blow for the Morgan Bank. He also demanded reforms regarding interlocking directorships, which were at the heart of Morgan's business policies. "No officer or director nor any member of any partnership dealing in securities should be permitted to be an officer or director of any commercial bank or bank taking deposits, and no officer or director of any commercial bank or bank taking deposits should be permitted to be an officer or director of any corporation, or a partner in any partnership, engaged in the business of dealing in securities," he wrote.[79]

FDR decided to include Aldrich in his conversation with Senators Carter Glass and Robert Bulkley.[80] FDR's aides concluded that Aldrich should be sent to convince Glass of the necessity for incorporating his view in the Glass legislation.[81]

The Morgan Testimony and Fed Blaming

Pecora's roasting of Mitchell was second in terms of public fascination only to that of Jack Morgan. And as the Pecora hearings heated up, Thomas Lamont learned that his relationship with FDR wasn't going to provide him many privileges.

In April 1933, a politely frustrated Lamont wrote to Roosevelt to complain about the mistreatment he and Morgan counsel John Davis received at the hands of Pecora, who had interviewed the men as part of his preliminary research for the hearings (Davis had been US solicitor general under Wilson and the Democratic presidential nominee in 1924). Lamont was incensed at Pecora's accusations that his bank had "absolutely refused to answer" any of his inquiries. "In fact," Lamont wrote, "there is not one single item in our whole business that we are not quite willing to show to anybody who is entitled to see it."[82]

This was perhaps not the best tack for Lamont to take. His hands were dirty from his son's tax plays and the tax-dodging securities deal involving his wife. When later asked by Pecora why that transaction had been performed without an intermediary, Lamont responded that it "didn't occur to me to do it in any other manner."[83]

Morgan was better prepared for Pecora's relentless questions, and he maintained a composure that gave away nothing. Even the charge of tax evasion bounced like a rubber ball off his steely demeanor. As he declared in his opening statement on May 23, 1933, "If I may be permitted to speak of the firm, of which I have the honor to be the senior partner, I should state that at all times the idea of doing only first-class business, and that in a first-class way, has been before our minds."[84]

On May 27, days after Morgan was grilled by the Pecora Commission[85] and before Lamont was sworn in to testify on June 2,[86] Lamont wrote Adolph Ochs, publisher of the *New York Times,* to challenge the paper's uncharacteristically negative editorial comment regarding Morgan's use of preferred lists to distribute stock. Lamont condemned Pecora's handling of the investigation, describing his preferred clients as "men who are prepared to take a chance with their money."[87]

The Nation took a different view, charging that Pecora's commission only scratched the service of deceit and condemning Morgan generally: "Morgan and Company, and their fellow private investment bankers, may declare and believe that even in these transactions they render important services. Actually, their services are not only useless but definitely anti-social and obstructive."[88]

During the Pecora hearings, *The Nation* proclaimed Morgan "one of the greatest enemies our society ever had," characterizing "most of the devious and damaging corporate strategies which have brought us into our present hole" as "developed and perfected and varnished with respectability by him. He was no rescuer. He lived on wrecks. He thrived on depression. He built nothing. He pounced upon what other people built."[89]

Pecora's investigation focused in particular on three of the 1929 issues made available to clients on the preferred stock list—United Corporation, Allegheny Corporation, and Standard Brands—which subsequently dove in value, with citizen investors taking the biggest losses.

The Allegheny Corporation, the Van Sweringen brothers' web of railroad companies, which had once been the cornerstone of Morgan's foray into the stock issuance business, incensed the public the most. Allegheny shares were parceled out to 227 clients and close friends at $20 a share at a time when the market price for them was $35–$37. Not only were other financiers in on the deal; some of the men were now holding public office. These included former Treasury Secretary William McAdoo (Leffingwell's former boss during the Wilson administration, now a California senator on the Senate Banking Committee), Norman Davis (FDR's ambassador at-large in Europe), and, most tellingly, current Treasury Secretary William Woodin.

Morgan said these men "were selected because of established business and personal relations, and not because of any actual or potential political relations," adding that "we conduct our business through no means or measures of 'influence.'"[90] In a sense, what he said was true: given the position of power and substantial relationships that the Morgan firm enjoyed, it was not necessary to give away stock to gain influence.

As a sort of denouement to the Morgan hearings, the final man of the Big Three bankers to be called before Pecora was Wiggin. His crimes were the most intricately executed, it turned out. Through a collection of shell companies listed under various family member names, Wiggin had bagged $4 million in profits while his clients lost money during the Crash. He was ultimately fined $2 million in a civil suit but escaped any federal or criminal repercussions.

Compared to Mitchell's actions, Wiggin's schemes were more shocking to the Wall Street community. Wiggin was considered a "reserved," "rather scholarly man" whereas Mitchell was a "genial extrovert with a talent for headlines."[91] Wiggin had not only been Chase chairman, for which he officially made $275,000 per year ($3.8 million in today's dollars). He also served on the boards of fifty-nine other corporations that paid him a salary, and he used his position to troll for business, which was not against the law but gave him an unfair advantage in financial-corporate dealings. In the hearings he also defended a series of loans his banks made to their own officers (which enabled them to speculate on their own stock) on the grounds that such moves helped them develop "an interest in their institution." Again, this was not illegal, but it was certainly unsavory.

Federal Deposit Insurance

The Federal Deposit Insurance Corporation, established by the second Glass-Steagall Act (also called the Banking Act of 1933), was supposed to be an emollient for bankers that chose to keep the commercial banking business. It would back depositors by insuring their deposits in case of a bank failure. As such, it provided banks with a safety net, too, as it mitigated the possibility of bank runs by scared citizens trying to extract their money in times of panic.

Though he supported the Banking Act, Aldrich criticized the premise of having a federal guarantee on deposits. "The unlimited guarantee puts a premium on bad banking. . . . [It is] very dangerous from every point of view," he later asserted.[92] Roosevelt, too, was concerned that the FDIC would enable banks to take too many risks, knowing the government would back their customers' deposits if necessary. Aldrich warned FDR that "unfortunate circumstances would ensue if the bank deposit insurance provisions contained in the Glass Bill were enacted into law."

Much of Aldrich's concern centered on the industry's confusion over its liability. Though he conceded that a temporary guarantee was useful, he said, "My suggestion is that if it is necessary to have a permanent form of deposit guarantee system, the temporary system in the Banking Act of 1933, with its limited guarantee and limited contributions, should be adopted. But I earnestly believe we should seek by every practical means to make any kind of permanent deposit guarantee unnecessary."[93]

His point was both valid *and* self-serving. On the one hand, banks that knew they had an implicit government guarantee and could use that assurance to explore new methods of taking risk would be bad for the system. On the other hand, banks that thought they were "better" at risk management than others didn't want to be held liable for others' foibles. Aldrich was in the latter camp.

Aldrich shrewdly saw the direction of the political winds and positioned his company accordingly. Beyond sticking it to a rival, he believed the future of banking resided on the commercial side of the business, and that Chase would be best positioned to capitalize on it after the Banking Act passed. Indeed, without Aldrich and Perkins's support for FDR and vice versa, it's possible that the act never would have passed. The powerful bankers' backing pushed it through in an even stricter form than Glass had envisioned. The Banking Act of 1933 was approved by the House on May 23, as the Pecora hearings were ongoing.[94]

Morgan joined the chorus of bankers and politicians blaming the Fed for the financial chaos of the past few years. In his final statement to the Pecora Commission on June 9, 1933, he characterized the crash as "the great inflation":

> It is true that the failure of the then Federal Reserve Board to take the necessary measures to control the inflation in time encouraged the speculative frenzy, which carried the market quotation out of bounds. . . . The great inflation. The cheap money policy of the last half of 1927, the indecisive policy of 1928, and the Board's veto of a dear money policy in the first half of 1929—these are the cause of the great super inflation of that period and of all the disastrous consequences.

By the time those words entered the public record, Morgan was yesterday's news. Aldrich and Perkins had outmaneuvered him. Morgan's political power on the national stage, along with the praise and criticism it attracted, would become subordinate to these rising bank titans and the new regulations they promoted.

A week after the Morgan testimony was completed, on June 16, 1933, FDR signed the second Glass-Steagall Act. He was surrounded by a group of men that included Senator Glass, Representative Steagall, Senator McAdoo, and others. The bankers were not present in body, but Aldrich and Perkins were there in spirit that day, as was their alliance on the matter with FDR.

The deposit guarantee aspect of the act, the creation of the Federal Deposit Insurance Corporation, went into effect on January 1, 1934.

The Glass-Steagall Act and the New Deal

With the force of a man who would lift the power of the presidency to a new level, FDR signed fifteen major bills into law within his first hundred days in office, including the Banking Act, and created a slew of new agencies. Tens of thousands of people returned to work. FDR pledged billions to save homes and farms from foreclosure, provide relief for the unemployed, guarantee savings, and support the banks.

Though the substance of the first part of FDR's New Deal centered around fortifying the banking system (the cornerstone of financial capitalism) and US financial power (through the Glass-Steagall—or Banking—Act and the Truth in Securities Act of 1933, which required better disclosure from the financial community), FDR moved quickly to other initiatives.

He backed the Agricultural Adjustment Act of 1933, a sweeping farm-relief bill designed to subsidize farmers for the sharp drops in prices of their crops; for the first time, the government paid farmers not to plant, so supply could be capped until demand and prices increased.

FDR also established the Federal Emergency Relief Administration in May 1933, which ran until December 1935. The $3.3 billion public works program provided unemployed people with various government jobs. In 1935, the plan divided into the Works Progress and Social Security administrations.

Toward the end of his first hundred days, FDR signed the National Industrial Recovery Act, which created the National Recovery Administration to regulate industry pricing, hours, and wages, and to stimulate the economy. The act also included a provision for collective bargaining by unions.

Many critics, at the time and more recently, fixed on the notion that the government should not bear so much responsibility for the public welfare. But in the context of the power play between the president and the bankers, it can be viewed another way: FDR sought to preserve presidential power, and hence the country's preeminence relative to other nations, by taking more control over the economy. He did not get rid of the market, capitalism, or banking; he merely rearranged it, or regulated aspects of it, in a way that empowered the federal government.

FDR's legacy would lead Democratic and Republican presidents alike to invoke the power of the federal government to preserve economic stability in ways they deemed necessary for the overall population, though few presidents would be able to do so while balancing such a tight alliance with the nation's key financiers.

FDR restored public confidence in banking. He propped up capitalism and saved the bankers from themselves, with their blessings. In addition, his actions instigated a changing of the guard in the banking industry, which saw a new generation of less risk-taking, more public-minded (though still exceptionally powerful) internationalist bankers take their positions at the top of the American and global banking hierarchy.

There were no hard feelings levied at FDR from the Morgan contingent, but there were remaining issues to iron out. On October 2, 1933, Leffingwell wrote FDR: "I want to congratulate you upon what you have accomplished in the seven months since you took office. The country today is scarcely recognizable as the country it was on March 4th, when all the banks were closed."

Leffingwell had a number of qualms regarding FDR's bank reforms, but it was a regulation (referred to as Regulation Q in the Banking Act) prohibiting interest payments on demand deposits that he claimed as "being reductive to bank deposits and therefore deflationary." By restricting bankers from raising interest rates to entice customers to provide them with their deposits, especially in times when inflation might cause rates to rise, Regulation Q was restricting their access to capital, their lifeblood. Of all the stipulations of the Banking Act, it was Regulation Q that evoked the greatest condemnation from the bankers, and it would be the first part of the act to be obliterated several decades later.

Jack Morgan kept in touch with FDR on a friendly basis, but he decided to let Leffingwell do the legal arguing. The two bankers remained, Leffingwell said, at the service of FDR and Treasury Secretary Henry Morgenthau, and would publicly support their monetary policy objectives.[95]

As a pivotal year in the rising power of the presidency and the next generation of commercial bankers came to a close, Aldrich was summoned by FDR for a private wrap-up meeting at the White House.[96]

The two men had forged an important political-financial alliance. The Big Three retained enough liquidity and funds to summarily outperform their weakened competitors, who didn't have the same access to capital. The public felt safer. And though Aldrich would disagree with some banking legislation to come, he and FDR were satisfied that a year that had begun in the malaise of a panic-stricken nation and credit-frozen financial system had worked out quite well for them both.

Decades later, Aldrich's and Morgan's banks combined to become JPMorgan Chase, regaining all the commercial and investment banking abilities that Aldrich had separated, after the Clinton administration repealed the Glass-Steagall Act in 1999.

CHAPTER 7

THE MID- TO LATE 1930S: POLICING WALL STREET, WORLD WAR II

*"We cannot afford to accumulate
a deficit in the books of human fortitude."*

—Franklin Delano Roosevelt, June 27, 1936[1]

BY 1934, THE COUNTRY APPEARED TO BE SLOWLY EMERGING FROM THE GREAT Depression. Though unemployment was still near 22 percent, the national mood was lifting thanks to confidence in FDR's New Deal programs coupled with the rising trust in the banking system that the president had carefully engineered.

A. P. Giannini, head of San Francisco–based Bank of America, was a veteran banker yet new to the game of political and financial alliance. He saw the Banking Act of 1933 as a way to broaden his bank's geographical and influence reach, and he was as delighted as his New York counterparts that some power would be diffused from the Morgan Bank. In addition, deposit insurance was a godsend for Giannini; it was hard enough to engender trust for a West Coast bank nationally, but the addition of insurance helped level the playing field. Even Regulation Q, which prohibited banks from paying interest on demand deposits (i.e., checking accounts) and capped the interest rates they could pay on savings accounts, helped him comparatively.[2]

During the mid-1930s, the financiers who were focused on commercial banking pushed the FDR administration forward with additional regulations, while the private bankers remained sidelined. This internal power struggle in the industry coincided with a recession that shook up some of FDR's banker alliances, as financiers began to think that it was time to reduce government intervention in the economy. All those domestic fights would fade, however, as it became increasingly clear that the country was headed to war, much to the chagrin of the isolationists in Congress. During that progression, FDR would find himself returning to all of his banker friends for support. As they had during World War I, the bankers would rally behind their "chief" regardless of their personal grievances, though this time they would be insistent about their requirements for a less constrained policy on the flow of capital. The Morgan bankers were well equipped to navigate wartime economics, and they knew the value of aligning with the president. Other bankers, like Aldrich and Perkins, would quickly find their way.

Policing Wall Street

The very structure of the US banking system had been dramatically altered under the Glass-Steagall Act of 1933. But there remained a need for a federal body to enforce the laws that would ostensibly keep the stock and bond markets from being manipulated by the financiers. To deal with this matter, the Fletcher-Rayburn bill, which would become known as the Securities Exchange Act, was introduced on February 10, 1934. It met with an intense and immediate opposition campaign chiefly engineered by Morgan confidant Richard Whitney, now president of the New York Stock Exchange. Many grievances remained in the Morgan realm over the Glass-Steagall Act, but establishing an entity to police the stock exchange was adding fuel to the fire. Plus, Whitney wasn't exactly the cleanest of operators, as 1938 indictments and time in Sing Sing would reveal.

The bill was proposed to deal with the kind of securities fraud and violations that had been amply demonstrated in the Pecora hearings. It was designed to give the Federal Trade Commission power to regulate all aspects of organized exchanges, and to outlaw an array of shady market practices including excessive margin buying, wash sales (fake sales initiated by banks solely to lure the public with the illusion of true demand), and pool operations (where prices could be rigged by the larger financial firms that gathered together to push prices up and then sell their shares before the public knew what was happening).[3]

Whitney was having none of it. As a stunt, he invited members of the House Committee on Interstate Commerce, who were deliberating over the bill, and the press to visit the floor of the New York Stock Exchange on February 23. "We have nothing to hide, gentlemen," Whitney said.[4]

Senator Duncan Fletcher, the chairman of the Senate Banking and Currency Committee and sponsor of the bill, called Whitney's efforts "countrywide propaganda."[5] Whitney's antics riled FDR. In a letter to Congress he noted that this kind of public opposition bore "all the earmarks of origin at some common source" and demanded that Congress pass legislation "with teeth in it."[6]

Whitney advocated creating a commission with representation from the exchange, so as to exercise control over its decision-making. Instead, Senator Carter Glass passed an amendment establishing the Securities and Exchange Commission and prohibiting its administrators from having any personal business with the exchange.[7]

Russell Leffingwell's Plea for Deposits

At the start of 1934 Morgan partner Russell Leffingwell was enjoying a Caribbean cruise. The prior year had been a tough one, and he was regrouping under the warmth of the equatorial sun. But that didn't mean he wasn't considering how to undo the damage to the firm that his old friend FDR and his competitors had inflicted. The matter weighed on his mind. On January 4, he wrote to ask FDR if he would "be so kind as to let me come down and see you after I get back?"

Along with his request Leffingwell sent his concerns about the Banking Act of 1933. He argued that the ban on taking deposits would push legitimate incorporated banks and private bankers out of the business. He implored FDR to permit national banks to underwrite securities under whatever regulations were deemed necessary. That would allow a loophole through which private bankers could engage in the securities business as national banks could.[8]

While FDR deferred his reply, Leffingwell persisted. On February 20, he took another tack, asking FDR, "What would you think of extending for a year the time limit on securities dealings by banks and bankers [to] June 1935 instead of June 1934?" He reiterated, "I do think it is a vital necessity of your administration to find some way to keep the banks and private bankers in the underwriting business."[9]

FDR stuck to his guns. He held more power over the industry than any other president before him had. Plus he had the people's support, as well as that of Congress and some key bankers. So he postponed the meeting with Leffingwell, citing the fact that there was "too much press" around, and instead replied on February 24 that "a very large proportion of the bankers themselves do not want the present law changed." (He was referring, of course, to Aldrich and Perkins, but keeping *all* of his banker friends close at the same time was part of his brilliant divide-and-conquer strategy, while using them against each other as necessary.) "Secondly," wrote FDR, "Senators and Members of Congress are very loath even to consider amendments which would restore commercial banks to the investment business, even in a remote degree."[10]

In truth, the day Leffingwell sent his second letter, FDR met with Aldrich at the White House to discuss the Securities Exchange Act.[11] Still, FDR wanted to keep Leffingwell in his corner, so he rescheduled to have a "quiet" talk over dinner on March 5.[12] The day before their dinner, Leffingwell made clear that he wouldn't let the desires of private bankers go. In a letter to FDR, he wrote, "I accept your decision against letting the banks underwrite—partly because I must! and partly because you have been so amazingly right in your political and economic judgments. But—forgive me one question in which I have a special interest—what about the private bankers? The Banking Act of 1933 put them too out of the underwriting business on June 16th. Who is to underwrite new issues then?"[13] It was a question Leffingwell would never relinquish, and the dinner between the two men didn't resolve it.

FDR continued his plans for reforming the financial system with the help of his banker allies. On April 19, when it looked like the proposed legislation was weakening, he called another private meeting with Aldrich and Perkins.[14] Fletcher was considering a new bill to postpone the time that bank affiliates, or securities arms, would have before being cut off from their banks—the Morgan partners had gotten to him. Making matters worse, the new measure would allow private bankers to take deposits for one year longer. Aldrich was irate about the extension when the bill was introduced officially. On April 30, he informed Roosevelt's assistant secretary, M. H. McIntyre, he was coming to Washington the next day to see Fletcher and talk to FDR about it.[15] The extension that the Morgan bankers had sought was denied.

On May 10, Aldrich announced that the official separation of Chase's securities unit, Chase Harris Forbes Corporation, would be completed by June 14, in accordance with the Banking Act. The unit would merge with the similar offspring of the First National Bank of Boston, the First of Boston Corporation, and would drop the Chase name for clarity.[16]

Perkins followed suit less than a month later and announced to shareholders that National City Bank's securities affiliate, the City Company of New York, would go into liquidation.[17] The *fait accompli* that began when the two men announced that their securities arms would split from their commercial banking business was official. The separated units were now completely different companies. Solidifying the New Deal banking regulation initiative, the Securities Exchange Act was finally passed on June 6, creating a federal regulator to police the securities industry.[18]

For his part, Jack Morgan had chosen to stay above the fray of legislation, letting his more able legal mind, Leffingwell, deal with the lobbying effort. Yet Morgan would maintain the social relationship with FDR he had enjoyed for decades. On June 8, upon discovering that FDR was attending the sailing races in New London, Connecticut, and that his son was rowing on the freshman crew, Morgan said he looked forward to the "privilege of entertaining [FDR's son] along with the rest of the squad" on his yacht, the *Corsair*.[19] He invited FDR to join them for lunch, but the president declined. "Unfortunately, I must go back on board the little "Sequoia" after the morning races," he said. "Perhaps I shall see you on the Referee's boat—I hope so."[20] Both men wanted to resurrect their friendship.

The Kennedy Connection

Three weeks later, to the dismay of New Dealers and big business alike, FDR selected the first man who would run the Securities and Exchange Commission. He did not choose just any old banker but a notorious one, Joseph Patrick Kennedy, to lead the new unit.[21] It was a good time to be a Harvard graduate; they now ran the six spots with the most control over the financial industry: the presidency, the New York Stock Exchange, the three largest banks, and the body that watched over them.

Ironically, while the battle over the Fletcher-Rayburn bill was raging, Ferdinand Pecora was grilling banker Henry Mason Day over his role in creating a pool to speculate in the stock of the Libbey-Owens Ford Glass Company, in which Kennedy was included and from which he profited $68,800.[22] Thus, Pecora had implicated Kennedy in the same shady practices he would be tasked with policing.

But Roosevelt had a more personal reason for installing Kennedy into the prime national regulator's slot: he owed him one. They were old friends who had first encountered each other when Roosevelt was assistant secretary of the Navy and Kennedy was running the Bethlehem Shipbuilding Company.[23]

Kennedy had been instrumental behind the scenes during Roosevelt's 1932 presidential campaign. Not unlike Sidney Weinberg, he had donated $25,000 directly and raised another $100,000 from others. At the time, Kennedy was in California—beginning a highly lucrative foray into the film industry and serving as one of Roosevelt's "silent six," traveling ahead of the candidate during his West Coast tour and acting as a financial adviser.[24] Kennedy convinced William Randolph Hearst to support Roosevelt in California, and as a result Roosevelt captured the nomination after the state swung his way.[25] Once in office, as part of his expression of gratitude, FDR invited Kennedy to come over to his place for a weekend and sail on the *Sequoia*.[26]

Kennedy took measures early on to reassure the banking community that he'd be working for them. At the National Press Club in early August 1934, he proclaimed that his job was to give bankers the opportunity "to live, make profits, and grow." He added, "We of the SEC do not regard ourselves as coroners sitting on the corpse of financial enterprise. . . . [We] are not working on the theory that all men and all women connected with finance . . . are to be regarded as guilty of some undefined crime."[27]

Bankers, initially skeptical, were elated. In response to his speech, the *New York Times* reported, "Nowhere on Wall Street was any disapproval or unfriendly criticism of the speech heard." Even Richard Whitney commented approvingly, "I think Mr. Kennedy has shown that he is approaching his job carefully and from a sane and sound point of view."[28]

On September 2, not wishing to be outgunned by the big New York commercial bankers, Bank of America head Giannini informed the White House, "I am one hundred percent with the President and his New Deal and I hope he will not let any one block him in his efforts to put it over."[29]

On October 1, Thomas Lamont decided it was time to resurrect the most congenial aspects of his relationship with FDR. So he sent FDR his notes from an intimate mid-September business dinner he had attended given by Perkins, who had initiated the gathering to ensure ongoing support for FDR.

Not to be shafted by Perkins, who had boasted about all of his "talks" with FDR at the dinner, Lamont wanted to regain the ear—and the confidence—of the president. He conveyed his approval for the New Deal stimulus objectives and reminded FDR of his international experience and progressive leanings: "When people complain to me of the amount of money that the Government has been borrowing, I always answer it by saying: 'Well, if that country was willing to spend thirty billion dollars in a year's time to try to lick the Germans, I don't see why people should complain about its spending five or six billion dollars to keep people from starving.'"

As to the "general attitude of the banking community," wrote Lamont, retaking ownership for their combined thinking, "the attitude is generally the same as it is in this [the Morgan Bank] office, namely one of backing up the Administration to the limit." This support, he believed, was exemplified by the vast amount of US government bonds the New York banks were holding. In closing, he informed Roosevelt, "I may be a Republican but you can bear witness from my association with President Wilson that I do want to be loyal to any Democratic President with whom I happen to be working, especially one who is a friend and of many years' standing as F.D.R. is."[30] Somewhat upended by Glass-Steagall and related issues, Lamont was ready to join the president's side. In return, he hoped to maintain his position as the dominant domestic and global banker.

Under Kennedy's leadership, the SEC implemented some major reforms but took no further actions against the big banks.[31] What most concerned Kennedy, as it did the bankers, was the restoration of the capital markets to supply the nation's corporations with credit. Before February 1935, issues of new debt securities had nearly stopped. New Dealers called this "a strike of capital," with big business holding the economy hostage while demanding less stringent oversight.

The Morgan bankers attributed the credit crisis to the Glass-Steagall Act's separation of securities issuance from deposit-taking businesses. At any rate, all that changed when Swift and Company negotiated a $43 million bond issue with the SEC; soon afterward, the capital markets came roaring back.[32] This loosening of credit played a role in resurrecting the business economy.

Kennedy was appointed chairman of the SEC for one year, but he stayed nearly sixteen months. He remained a strong supporter of Roosevelt, though, lending his name to the book *I'm for Roosevelt!*, published during the election year of 1936. Roosevelt enthusiastically responded in a personal note, "I'M FOR KENNEDY!"[33] As a campaign surrogate, Kennedy strongly defended Roosevelt's record in front of hostile audiences.[34] After 1938, Kennedy and his family traveled to London, where he took up his FDR-appointed post as US ambassador to the Court of St. James's.

1935: The Morgan House Divided

Though the Banking Act of 1933 would garner the most attention for regulating the industry in later years, what has been nearly forgotten is how it was almost completely gutted by Washington and Wall Street during the debate over the Banking Act of 1935. Sharp clashes over the successor bill further accentuated the battle lines between the Morgan interests and those who advocated more restrictions on private banks.

Lending muscle to the Aldrich side was Bank of America chief A. P. Giannini. He was also a director of the National City Bank and its largest single stockholder, and he harbored a huge dislike for the "New York Banking fraternity."[35] Hence, he was for anything that could tamper with its power. He would be helped in this effort by the Federal Reserve. Marriner S. Eccles, whom FDR appointed governor of the Federal Reserve Board, was a western banker like Giannini. The proposed banking bill challenged the powerful New York Fed's control of the Federal Reserve. Giannini, like Eccles, wanted this influence curtailed.[36]

On February 5, 1935, Steagall introduced the three-part bill in the House.[37] For the remainder of the spring and into the summer the fight in Washington and on Wall Street was over the particular part of the bill known as Title II, which centralized control of the Federal Reserve system in Washington. It was something Wilson had not been able to do when the Federal Reserve was first established. FDR would accomplish it—for a while, anyway. Morgan Guaranty's William Potter publicly decried the act, stating it would make inflation "more inviting, more dangerous and more imminent."[38] Testifying in the Senate, even Aldrich said it would turn the Fed into "an instrument of despotic authority."[39]

Meanwhile, another front in the battle of the bankers was emerging. On June 28, Aldrich was forced to release a statement in response to claims (probably, but not conclusively, made on the Morgan side to discredit him) that he was getting "inside information" on the Senate subcommittee's deliberations.[40] Aldrich denied the charges but admitted that he had phoned Senators Carter Glass and John Townsend to discuss rumored changes to a part of the bill that had received little attention: Title III. He was vehemently opposed to those changes, which went against provisions he had persuaded Glass to include in the 1933 bill.

The next day, the *New York Times* published the details of a leaked version of the bill (again, probably but not conclusively engineered by the Morgan bankers) with the headline "New Bill Will Let Banks Underwrite Securities

Again."[41] Glass was furious about the leak but quickly moved on to defend his version of the bill.[42] Indeed, an amendment in Title III would restore the underwriting privileges to deposit-taking banks that had been taken away under the Glass-Steagall Act of 1933. In the opinion of the commercial bankers who sided with Aldrich, the proposed amendment to the Banking Act of 1935 marked "an almost complete reversal of the underlying philosophy of the Banking Act of 1933."

This represented a deeply personal blow to Aldrich's ego and tactical skills; the proposed measure would demolish the banking reform he had most ardently pushed for and allow the Morgan contingent the practice they sought most to regain.[43] FDR largely sat this one out, letting Aldrich and the Morgan bankers fight among themselves. Opponents of the proposed change were so blindsided by the Morgan move that it took them some time to regroup, particularly because the politician championing the change was Senator Glass himself (who had never intended the original act to apply to private banks like Morgan, anyway). Aldrich mistakenly believed that the matter had been settled, and that Glass would not relaunch a counterattack on his own act alongside the Morgan Bank, but that was exactly the situation unfolding.

When asked by the press if his proposed amendment meant that J. P. Morgan & Company could again underwrite securities, Glass's response was, "Well, why not?"[44]

Aldrich, livid, went straight to the administration. In a July 11 conversation with McIntyre, he pressed and augmented his case to encompass all the activities that Morgan could possibly want resurrected. McIntyre recorded the following conversation:

> ALDRICH: [We] are absolutely against this amendment in its present form. What we did say six months ago was that we would be willing to have commercial banks agree to *purchase* [emphasis added] securities, but that is not origination, and we don't want them to originate and we don't want interlocking directors.
>
> McINTYRE: Are you active or just passive?
>
> ALDRICH: We are actively opposed to the power to originate.
>
> McINTYRE: I appreciate that.
>
> ALDRICH: I am actively opposed to interlocking directorates between two banks. I haven't changed my views at all at any time.
>
> McINTYRE: Are you actively supporting that latter phase?

ALDRICH: We would be in favor of permitting a commercial bank to agree to *purchase* [emphasis added] securities from investing bankers—not originating them.

McINTYRE: You would be agreeable to it but not forcing the issue?

ALDRICH: We are agreeable to it but not forcing the issue. I am awfully anxious for the President to know that I haven't changed my views.[45]

Roosevelt now supported Aldrich. He wanted to keep underwriting and deposit-taking activities separate to contain the risk of one infecting the other. He had, however, wanted to see the debate between the bankers play out—and during the past two years, the Morgan bankers, having adopted a strategy of friendliness mixed with lobbying, had given FDR some pause. Around the time Aldrich was meeting with McIntyre, and perhaps as a result of it, FDR wrote Senator Glass concerning the amendment, "I have seen more rotten practices among banks in New York City than you have. Regulations and penalties will not stop them if they want to resume speculation."[46] The chief had spoken.

The Banking Act of 1935

In August 1935, the deregulatory amendment was withdrawn, and the Banking Act of 1935 was finally passed. When he signed, Roosevelt asked jokingly if anyone had even read the bill, perhaps referencing the leak a little over a month earlier. Glass responded that he was the only one who had.[47] The chess game was over. FDR and Aldrich had won, Morgan and Glass had lost. The defeated group succumbed to the inevitability of the law, and to the more influential political and financial leaders.

Two weeks later, J. P. Morgan & Company invited the business press to 23 Wall Street to give an official statement. The bankers were dignified in their defeat, though they had a workaround that would enable them to retain much of their way of doing business. Thomas Lamont, standing beside George Whitney and Harold Stanley, announced the resignation of five partners. Upon leaving the Morgan Bank, they would assume the job of setting up Morgan Stanley and Company—a separate securities underwriting entity that would be run by men with long-term blood and professional ties to the Morgan Bank.[48] "We believe that the members of the new organization will be able, with the ample experience which they have heretofore had, to serve usefully the investment interests of the community," Lamont said.

On September 16, 1935, the new investment bank opened its doors on the nineteenth floor of 2 Wall Street, overlooking Trinity Church at the head position on Wall Street. Jack Morgan's son, Henry, one of the firm's founding partners, was aboard a transatlantic liner returning home. In a sign of changing times, the firm's president, Harold Stanley, chose to advertise its opening rather than issue an official press release.[49]

The Morgan Bank had won a small battle in the war for Wall Street supremacy by creating a securities firm populated by Morgan partners and progeny that would act in concert with its parent firm. But Aldrich had won the war.

The New Deal: Phase II

Though the first phase of the New Deal had improved economic conditions somewhat, the country hadn't returned to prosperity. In fact, it was faltering. Broad despair turned to anger. Violent protests and strikes swept the country. This was the era of militant industrial unionism, sit-down strikes, factory occupations, and the rise of the Congress of Industrial Organizations. Industrial businesses were barely hiring, or not paying enough when they were. The far left called for greater reforms than Roosevelt had passed. The right attacked government and regulatory bodies and agencies as being too large and intrusive. People demanded a living wage and nationalization of the banks, if only to make ends meet and have better access to credit.

In the second phase of the New Deal, FDR introduced a safety net for retirees and the disabled through the Social Security Act, which also created the unemployment insurance program as a partnership between the federal government and the states.

In addition, FDR instituted aggressive tax hikes on the wealthy. Under Hoover's Revenue Act of 1932, the marginal tax rate for the top bracket had jumped by one of the highest amounts in US history, from 25 percent to 63 percent. But tax rates across the board had risen as well, as Hoover attempted to thwart the effects of the Great Depression on the government's budget without being seen as disproportionately taking from the upper class. His attempt failed. The widespread economic devastation didn't allow for even the marginal contributions of the wealthiest Americas to properly fund the ailing country's budget, and the wealthy were consuming less because their investments had soured. The middle and poorer classes suffered because of a more acute lack of jobs and income.

FDR raised this top bracket rate to 75 percent in the Revenue Act of 1935. The more progressive tax initiative was dubbed the "wealth tax" or "class tax," and passed in August after bitter congressional battles. (The Revenue Act of 1942 would raise this tax rate on income above $200,000 to 82 percent and increase the top rate of corporate taxes from 31 percent to 40 percent to help fund the war. The Individual Income Tax Act of 1944 went further, raising the top-bracket tax rate to 94 percent.)

It wasn't so much the income tax elements of the Revenue Act of 1935 that riled bankers; it was the higher undistributed profits tax rates from the second phase of the New Deal that served to convert friends of FDR to enemies. By late 1935, FDR's popularity among even his business class advocates was fading. Businessmen accused him of interfering with free enterprise. With the 1936 election in the wings, anti–New Deal groups sprouted up everywhere. The people FDR had grown up with, and who had supported him in his last election against Hoover, and for the most part in his quest to stabilize the banking system and US capitalism, were now accusing him of going too far, of being too radical, of being—now that his policies no longer suited their needs for banking stability—a "traitor to his class."

The Mid-1930s Economy: 1934–1936

The jobs crisis was one of the most dire and deeply entrenched problems of the Great Depression. The unemployment rate leapt to 15.9 percent in 1931 and to 23.6 percent in 1932. Despite the New Deal's efforts, it averaged approximately 20 percent between 1934 and 1936. Average family income in the mid-1930s stood virtually unchanged from the World War I period. Though wages for trade, finance, and services had risen around 30 percent, as had wages for government jobs (with public utility wages up 41 percent due to FDR's programs), these were false signals that the economy was on the mend. It was finding steam thanks to a combination of more speculative activities and federal stimulus for federal jobs. This contributed to higher growth rates but not necessarily higher living standards or much of a budge in broader unemployment at first. Helping the population somewhat was low inflation. Food prices in the mid-1930s were approximately 30 percent lower than they were during World War I, and thus inflation policy was important to FDR and the bankers, who would disagree on how best to handle it.

But banks were still sitting on their money, and their reluctance to lend inhibited smaller businesses from hiring, let alone thriving. Beginning in 1934 the financiers used the more stable banking system that had been engineered by the New Deal as a platform upon which to drive up the volume of stock speculation, and with it stock prices. The confidence this exuded and the media attention paid to it combined with New Deal stimulus to make the country appear to be exiting the Depression. This rise proved unsustainable, and the market and the overall economy would dip again in 1937 and 1938, until it became more substantively elevated by war financing efforts and related employment opportunities for those not in combat overseas.[50]

Still, by early 1936, the second part of FDR's New Deal (particularly his jobs programs) seemed to be working to some extent, as the unemployment rate dropped to 16.9 percent. Even though that was still high, six million people had returned to work, corporate profits were rising again, and Detroit was rolling out almost as many cars as it had done before the Crash. A bulge in government jobs and the rising number of women in service jobs, combined with lower goods prices, appeared to be helping the economy for the time being.

Hitler Storms Through Europe

Since the end of World War I, public sentiment had staunchly favored an isolationist stance on foreign policy, not only because of the massive economic problems at home but also because of a growing perception that the war had been waged for profit. This was thanks in large part to North Dakota Republican senator Gerald Nye's work as head of the Special Committee on Investigation of the Munitions Industry, established in April 1934.

In January 1936 Lamont, George Whitney, and J. P. Morgan Jr. were hauled up to hearings of the committee. Politically motivated by isolationists to thwart FDR (and what was construed as the bankers' thirst for another war), the hearings ended up putting to rest the charge that adopting an internationalist policy toward financing the Allies had dragged the United States into World War I.

Nye's committee examined the relationships between firms like the Morgan Bank and King George V of England to determine whether their financial agreements had created World War I.[51] But when Nye claimed that President Wilson had lied to the Senate Foreign Relations Committee about secret Allied treaties during the war, the old guard in the Senate rallied to protect the former president's good name. Funding to Nye's investigation was cut off.[52]

Despite ninety-three hearings and more than two hundred witnesses, including Jack Morgan and Pierre du Pont, chairman of chemical company giant DuPont, the committee failed to nail down any hard evidence of a widespread conspiracy to enter World War I in order to profit off munitions sales.[53] Still, Nye's penchant for eyeball-grabbing headlines did its job. His antics helped sway public opinion against support for US involvement in another major conflict.

Across the ocean, Fascist armies were marching across Europe and Africa. On March 7, 1936, Hitler's Germany seized the Rhineland in violation of the Treaty of Versailles and the Locarno agreements. Benito Mussolini's Italy annexed Ethiopia on May 9, 1936.

FDR saw the signs for exactly what they were. On March 16, 1936, he wrote his German ambassador, William Dodd, "Everything seems to have broken loose again in your part of the world. All the experts here, there and the other place say 'There will be no war' . . . but as President I have to be ready."[54]

The Americans who still remembered World War I reverted to an even sharper isolationist stance regarding another war. Congress quickly passed neutrality laws to prohibit FDR from taking sides from a foreign policy or economic perspective. Wilson's initial reaction had been to declare neutrality without a congressional law, and shortly thereafter bankers and businesses got involved as they saw fit. The same thing would eventually happen with FDR, but it would take more time and maneuvering.

As the presidential election loomed, fresh aid for FDR's campaign came from A. P. Giannini, who continued to lavish public support on FDR. This time, FDR responded personally. On May 7, 1936, he wrote, "In the midst of so much misunderstanding and misinterpretation it was decidedly reassuring to hear your radio address."[55]

In late June 1936, Giannini's endorsements traversed the West Coast newspapers. The *San Francisco News* ran a glowing headline, "A. P. Giannini Gives Support to Roosevelt." The *Herald Express* of Los Angeles wrote, "A. P. Giannini favors Roosevelt Re-election." An editorial in the *Los Angeles Illustrated Daily News* noted, "Although Mr. Giannini has long been one of the few big bankers in the Roosevelt New Deal camp, this evidence that he intends to stay there despite pressure is considered of high political importance."

Giannini's alliance proved crucial to FDR, who needed the California vote. Something about the way that Giannini had grown his bank to be more citizen-oriented than the New York banks, combined with his support for the New Deal, gave his words weight and helped improve his stature as the people's banker. By late 1936, the Bank of America's profits were up 38 percent, showing that support for FDR could be lucrative as well.[56]

FDR's opponents remained focused on the negatives and labeled the pre-election economy a "Roosevelt recession" (it would become a full recession in 1937–1938). Leffingwell wrote Roosevelt to persuade him to reduce his antibanker rhetoric and interventionist policies. In a September 8 letter to

FDR, Leffingwell, a libertarian Democrat (back then they were called "liberal"), wrote, "It was natural at the moment of the crisis in 1933 for the people to demand scapegoats. . . . It hurts our feeling to have you go on calling us money changers and economic royalists. . . . What such liberal democrats as I would like to hear from you is that you do regard some of the measures of the last three years as transitional and emergency measures; and that you do mean to use your second term to strengthen by your own example the prestige—now sadly lowered through the world—of government by democratic methods."

Some bankers, including Aldrich, had acquiesced to the marginal tax rate hike on the wealthy as preferable to increasing the nation's debt to sustain the economy. But Leffingwell felt that "tax policies which are punitive or directed to some ulterior social objective rather than to revenue-producing should be avoided."[57]

FDR's Timely Victory

Despite Leffingwell's overtures FDR deployed the same strategy he used to win his first election: speaking out against big business and the elitist money types. "Government by organized money is just as dangerous as Government by organized mob," he said.[58] His political acumen proved impeccable. He won reelection by the biggest electoral margin victory since James Monroe ran unopposed in 1820, capturing 98.49 percent, or 523 electoral votes, the largest number of electoral votes ever recorded, and 60.8 percent of the popular vote. (Johnson would supplant this record in the 1964 election.)

Despite the victory and public support for the New Deal, FDR did lose some major fights with the Supreme Court about certain programs. The Court declared much of the National Industrial Recovery Act unconstitutional in May 1935, a month before the program was set to expire. Seven months later, it declared the Agricultural Adjustment Act unconstitutional through a narrow interpretation of the constitutional clause empowering Congress to regulate commerce.[59]

When the Supreme Court ruled against a New York law providing a minimum wage for women and children in June 1936, FDR retaliated by trying to pass a bill that would ostensibly force justices to retire at age seventy. After that point, and following FDR's landslide victory, Supreme Court Justice Owen Roberts began siding with the president, and the "court-packing" bill was dropped.[60]

FDR's win was well timed, for the end of 1936 gave way to a recession that would last through the next couple of years. The stock market dove considerably, the number of business failures and bankruptcies rose, and two million more people lost their jobs. As a result of the downturn, FDR's plans and policies would come under attack by the bankers for strangling the economy and by liberals for not going far enough.

FDR had an ally at the Morgan Bank with respect to the war, if not his domestic policies. An eager Thomas Lamont was thrust back into his dual role as international banker and diplomat. There was no way to deal with a potential war situation from a stance of isolationism, he believed. He took matters in his own hands, keeping FDR informed along the way.

Lamont traveled to Rome on April 17, 1937, as a step in his joint peace-keeping and client-keeping diplomacy. During this trip, he sought a private meeting with Mussolini to persuade him to stay on the side of Britain, France, and the United States. Mussolini saw Lamont the following week for a private "courtesy" meeting.[61] But the results of that rendezvous would transpire in manners far from what Lamont hoped.

The US Economy Wobbles

At home, news of an impending European war unleashed a bout of capital speculation. On November 10, 1936, the stock market hit a high of 144.44 before receding somewhat by the end of the year. Early in 1937, global rearmament programs and related private bank financings and reinvigorated speculation pushed up prices. Prices for steel and other metals commodities rose, as did shares of industrial companies on the stock market.

The bull market that lasted from 1932 to 1937 was the longest in US history at the time, belying a job-challenged, wage-challenged economy. Banks began to loosen their lending purses for corporations in 1936. The war would eventually boost employment, but there would be bumps along the way to recovery.

Soon after the stock market reached a high of 142.93 on March 8, 1937, FDR and Treasury Secretary Henry Morgenthau became worried about inflation. The word from Washington was that such a market boom was unwelcome. As the Federal Reserve increased bank reserve requirements in an attempt to tighten monetary policy, FDR issued a statement against speculators he believed were pushing up metals prices, indicating that the government might cease purchases from the capital goods industry unless prices were contained.[62] To him, the issue was less about interest rate policy, which the bankers wanted loosened, and more about the dangers to funding a possible war effort and to the population of speculators driving prices up.

Prices remained stable until August 1937, when Charles Gay, who had replaced Richard Whitney as head of the New York Stock Exchange, publicly denounced "over-regulation in the securities markets" and spoke against the federal government surtax on undistributed profits. His speech set in motion a major sell-off. By November 24 the market had dropped 43 percent for the year, falling to 82.07 (it had been climbing each year since hitting the Great Depression low of 33.98 on July 8, 1932).

By the winter of 1937, US bankers and businesses were struggling again, and the US economy was faltering. In his January 1938 address, National City Bank chairman James Perkins apologized to his shareholders for the weakening economic conditions. He said, "It is a disappointment to everyone to find that we come to the end of the year with our business activity as low as it was at the end of 1934." He blamed this on the fact that the government had stopped what he referred to as "pump priming," or stimulus, even though private industry wasn't able to take up the slack because the Fed was restricting funds to the banks.[63]

During the early Depression years, GDP had decreased significantly: by 8.5 percent in 1930, 6.4 percent in 1931, and 12.9 percent in 1932. The bottoming-out period ended in 1933, with GDP decreasing just 1.3. GDP rebounded over the middle part of the decade, showing a 10.8 percent increase in 1934, an 8.9 percent increase in 1935, and a 12.9 percent increase in 1936.[64] But by 1938, unemployment shot up again to 19 percent, not too far below the 1934 level of 21.7 percent.[65] GDP fell by 3.3 percent from 1937 to 1938.

Capital "Lockout"

As the recession set in, bankers found themselves back in the spotlight for restricting capital. On January 27, 1938, at an address at the University of Pennsylvania's bicentennial campaign, Lamont spoke out for his kind. He denied that capital had "gone on strike," thereby causing the current recession. Instead, he characterized it as being "locked out."

He might have been traveling to Europe on business-tinged diplomacy missions, but now Lamont publicly turned against FDR's domestic policies. He was one of a half-dozen leaders representing banking, industry, and labor who had met with FDR that week to discuss the matter. He had concluded that much of the recession resulted from five years of a "general attitude of distrust toward business" and "extreme legislation, which, in aiming to cure evils, had placed obstacles in the path of progress" and "crippled the natural interplay of economic forces." He called for a spirit of "good will" between government and business.

Lamont further blamed the capital "lockout" on the surplus profits tax and excessive government. "In America," he said, "we are all agreed that no individual must be allowed to go hungry," but "we must beware too much pampering, and of rendering potentially useful citizens useless, by allowing them to assume that it is government's function not only to meet pressing temporary emergency, but to look after all their needs."

In a thinly veiled threat disguised as a suggestion to reduce regulation and loosen credit, he said, "The entire business community has . . . made the most . . . determined effort to maintain the improvements that marked 1936 and early 1937 . . . but . . . if enterprise is to continue to advance, fresh capital must be made constantly available for it."[66]

On February 14, 1938, Lamont again met with FDR at the White House to discuss credit policies, capital markets, and public utilities. In a follow-up letter, he pressed the urgency of his ideas, noting that "my contacts with you date back twenty-five years: so I allow myself some latitude."[67] He lambasted, in his own courteous way, Federal Reserve chief Marriner Eccles for tightening monetary policy. He urged FDR to persuade Eccles to reverse his "deflationary policies," particularly because, as Lamont knew more than the public realized, FDR would have to get involved in a war for "the preservation of the European peace" and he would need capital and bankers to finance it.

Lamont was concerned that the economy was dipping again, and that a "long-continued depression here is bound to have similar effects abroad," which could devolve into a long, drawn-out war. An "early arrest of the depression" in the United States was critical, and a loose monetary policy would achieve that. Without such a policy, unemployment, which was already creeping up again, would skyrocket. Lamont stressed that the improvement of the past two years had a high degree of artificiality because "so much of it was based on Government spending which has recently been wisely curtailed. Any suggestion that the remedy should be the resumption of government spending, or another round of "pump-priming," seemed "almost incredible" to him.[68] Lamont wanted money to flow cheaply, but from the Fed to the banks, not from the government to industry or the population directly.

Lamont's instincts on war were sound. In March 1938, German troops swept in to occupy their former ally Austria without a single shot being fired. Czechoslovakia fell next. By the fall of that year, European war was imminent. In a September 28 note to FDR, Lamont—who had been following the movements in Europe and traveling back and forth quite a bit—wrote ominously, "I just finished talking over the phone with one of my London partners who says that whereas yesterday Noon there the chances seemed 1000 to 1 for war, now they feel they are about 10 to 1 against there being war."[69] Two days later, Britain, France, Italy, and Germany signed the Munich Agreement recognizing Hitler's annexation of the Sudetenland in western Czechoslovakia.

The United States could only avoid involvement for so long. In his December 5 speech to the University of North Carolina student forum, FDR reminded his audience that his policies hadn't changed. "Actually, I'm an exceedingly mild-mannered person, a practitioner of peace both domestic and foreign, a believer in the capitalist system and for my breakfast a devotee of scrambled eggs."[70] FDR wanted to cater to the pacifists and the isolationists' desires to avoid war, but he still wanted the United States to play a lead role in international politics, particularly if the global landscape would change as a result of war. The United States had come a long way, and he wanted to retain its hegemony.

A Final Plea for Peace

While FDR's hands were tied by Congress and a cautious public, on April 14, 1939, he was forced to broadcast a personal appeal in a telegram to Hitler and Mussolini to halt further aggression. After pointing out that the United States "is not involved in the immediate controversies which have arisen in Europe," FDR asked for assurances that the armies of Germany and Italy would not invade thirty-one independent countries in Europe and the Middle East, including Britain, France, the Netherlands, Poland, Greece, and Turkey.[71]

Two weeks later, on April 28, Hitler ridiculed FDR's overture to thunderous applause and laughter in a speech at the Reichstag.[72] "Long before an American continent had been discovered—not to say settled—by white people, this Reich existed, not merely with its present boundaries, but with the addition of many regions and provinces which have since been lost," Hitler told an enamored audience.[73] He blamed "Jewish parasites" for plundering the nation, and outlined his plan for the Third Reich to take over Europe. That same day, Lamont sent FDR his thoughts about Hitler's speech. "Of course, Hitler is saucy, as was expected," said Lamont, "and makes no direct answer to the suggestion [floated by FDR in his telegram] of a [peace] conference. That was also expected. Furthermore, his remarks are calculated to rally his own people behind him."[74]

(Actually, Hitler had been specific about FDR's conference request, saying "no statesmen, including those of the United States and especially her greatest, made the outstanding part of their countries' history at the conference table, but by reason of the strength of their people.")

Notwithstanding Lamont's naïveté, FDR would turn to him often for his opinion on Europe. The president called Lamont when he needed to speak with an internationalist who had experienced the last war as closely as he had, and who supported his views about the negatives of military and financial isolationism.

As war spread through Europe, Lamont continued his private diplomacy with Mussolini to try to keep him from aligning with Germany. He dispatched several letters to his colleague and friend in Rome Giovanni Fummi to pass on to Mussolini. Lamont had hired Fummi to work with the Morgan Bank in 1920, and Fummi had helped the firm gain Italian business, including with the Vatican. The letters warned Mussolini that Americans were angered by Hitler's aggression and persecution of Jews. American sentiment could turn to join the war against Germany, and Italy should remain on the side of the Allies.

Lamont informed FDR of his communications with Mussolini. A very interested FDR wrote him on May 23, 1939, "I appreciate the effort you have made to prevent misunderstanding in Italy of the point of view of the American government and people, and hope that your letter may have born[e] fruit."[75]

But it was too late. A day earlier, Hitler and Mussolini had signed the "Pact of Steel," establishing their military and political alliance and formally creating the Axis powers, which would later include Japan.

Mussolini's duplicity was soon revealed to Lamont. On September 20, 1940, Fummi was arrested and imprisoned by the Fascist police.[76]

Aldrich's Mistake

For his part, on May 23, 1939, Aldrich told the Bankers Club of New York that the immediate threat of war had been greatly diminished in recent weeks, and that it was "far more important for business and political leaders in this country to concentrate upon domestic problems than to go on worrying about what is taking place in Europe."

In his opinion, continued high government spending and debt would lead to a situation of "containment" in which "economic nationalism will become inevitable." He disagreed with FDR's undistributed profits taxes, claiming that the solvency of the national government and the balancing of the budget ought "not to be on such a high level of expenditure" that it weighs too "heavily on industrial activities."

Aldrich's belief that a European war would be avoided was based on his recent trip through Europe, where he said that he found most of the people he met in Britain and France opposed to war. He also thought that the "vulnerable economic situation" in Germany and Italy diminished the possibility of a long-term war.

Aldrich declared that "it is of the highest importance that, as rapidly as possible, positive moves be taken for conciliation and compromise looking to reduction of armaments, to diplomatic settlements issues which might otherwise be the cause of war, and . . . to international economic cooperation" with the nations short on war materials so they could buy the goods and raw materials they needed.

As did all of the major bankers, Aldrich believed the lowering of trade barriers and elimination of exchange controls (in which the FDR administration was engaged) would be "recognized by the responsible German and Italian financiers, to be to the advantage of both Italy and Germany, along with the rest of the world."[77]

But if he was talking up the role that the US bankers could have in open trade to end the war, he was wrong on the war. On September 3, 1939, following Hitler's invasion of Poland, British prime minister Neville Chamberlain announced that Britain was at war with Germany. Over on Wall Street, the New York Stock Exchange experienced an inexplicable buying spree, recording a 7 percent gain in the Dow[78] and the heaviest one-day bond market volume in history.[79] The last war had proven an economic boon (after a short-lived recession) for the United States, and this one had that same potential in the eyes of investors. As it turned out, another prolonged and vicious conflict fought on foreign soil would benefit the American economy for the same reasons. The war would hurt the European competition, placing US banks' funds and financial services firmly at the top of the global financial pile.

More than FDR's New Deal stimulus or the war requirements of hiring people to produce weaponry, it would be the propelling of the US bankers into the epicenter of global war financing that would catalyze the US markets. The war would enhance economic confidence in business lending and unleash the flow of US capital through its bankers, even during what would be a treacherous and deadly time.

As the reality of another European war dawned on Wall Street, bankers put their own quibbling about financial regulations and government stimulus on hold. The Morgan Bank supported the British and French again, and stood solidly behind FDR. On September 2, 1939, Leffingwell confirmed the backing: "I do say, with the authority of my partners, on behalf of the J. P. Morgan & Co. and all of us, that if there is any service great or small which we can render to you and to our country we shall be proud and happy to render it. And it is for you to command us."[80]

A grateful FDR responded, "That is a mighty nice note of yours and I appreciate it. I talked with Tom [Lamont] the other morning. These are bad days for all of us but we have got to see to it that civilization wins through."

The country remained reticent about entering another European war. On September 15, 1939, famed aviator Charles Lindbergh gave a national radio broadcast against getting involved. He characterized the war as "an age-old struggle between the nations of Europe," one in which "we cannot count on victory." He went on to say, "We could lose a million men, possibly several million of the best of American youth."

Lamont believed Lindbergh's broadcast strengthened public support for the isolationists. As far as he was concerned, the war would require bankers' financing of the Allies. "I and many others are convinced that there is no certainty of our being able to avoid war, but the greatest tangible hope lies in our making it possible immediately for the allies to get . . . material supplies . . . [so that they] will stand a much better chance of holding off the Germans."[81]

For his part, Aldrich shifted from criticizing Roosevelt to wholeheartedly backing the war cause. He gave a radio address in support of mobilizing the country's manpower and industry. He even turned down an invitation to speak at an American Bankers Association meeting to avoid having to publicly admonish the administration's monetary policy while Roosevelt prepared for war.[82]

Lamont and Aldrich joined forces, forgetting their differences surrounding the Banking Act. Together, they lobbied the Senate on behalf of FDR to repeal the 1937 Neutrality Act, which had been passed to prevent the big banks from reprising their role of taking a central position in the financing of World War I and to prevent the United States from adopting a position that favored any one country in the supply of funds or supplies. On November 4, 1939, the amended Neutrality Act was passed by Congress and signed into law by FDR. FDR thanked Lamont for his assistance in helping to get the more restrictive act repealed. The bankers could now focus on a renewed war financing effort.

That same month Lamont addressed a thousand bankers at the Academy of Political Science, where he conveyed the same anti-German stance that had characterized the Morgan Bank during World War I: "There is nothing that businessmen the world over fear and detest quite so much as war. . . . It is against the nature of things that the Fuhrer should be able to continue to overrun one sturdy and independent nation after another; declare it to be German whether it is or not, and expect it to remain a vassal State. . . . [British sea power] and France's wonderful army . . . [will] bring victory."[83]

Just before the New Year, Lamont phoned FDR to say that no matter what would transpire, he would be there for the president. And FDR would need him, as Wilson had. In fact, he would need all the bankers in his corner for the war to come.[84]

Debate continues over whether the Great Depression ended because of FDR's New Deal federal stimulus policies or because the war provided economic stimulation with its need for weaponry and supplies and the employees to create them. The argument would filter through discussions of Keynesian vs. free market politicians and economists and writers for years. But such discourse would rarely examine the significant role of the US bankers seeking to retain the power they had won, at great costs to the world, in the global arena after World War I.

Throughout the World War II years, these bankers spurred the US economic and financial boom. The flow of US capital through the US banks, and the subsequent expansion of financial capitalism within the United States and around the world to sustain war operations, would resurrect the US economy relative to the rest of the world. US bankers would become busily involved in the war financing effort, and they would profit more this time, as the funding drive was greater.

There had been a shift in banking leadership during the Great Depression and into World War II. The men who emerged to run the country's main banks, such as Aldrich and Perkins, were more risk-averse and public-spirited, outwardly anyway. They had their own thoughts on consolidating power, but they would act more in concert with the country's and the world's needs than some of their predecessors and successors had and would. They would realize, as Jack Morgan told Wilson during World War I, that this war was a tremendous financial opportunity for them, their business clients, and America.

CHAPTER 8

The Early to Mid-1940s: World War II, Bankers, and War Bucks

"The sale of bonds is the banks' great opportunity."

—W. Randolph Burgess, vice chairman, National City Bank,
and chairman, American Bankers Association, February 18, 1943[1]

DURING THE WAR YEARS, WALL STREET AND WASHINGTON COLLABORATED closely. Several of the men running America's largest banks were appointed by Presidents Roosevelt and Harry S. Truman to prominent positions on various government committees designed to facilitate war financing and foreign trade. These financiers slipped more seamlessly through the doors between public and private service than they had during World War I, as they recalibrated their strategies to fund war-related endeavors and to participate in the global expansion that would follow the war.

American bankers had begun preparing for World War II well before FDR officially declared war. Patriotism and the importance of public service once again became equated. The bankers facilitated the sale of war bonds to support the effort, financed war production alongside the government, and toured European cities to ascertain foreign borrowing needs. They also supported FDR publicly and lobbied Congress to provide him more power to navigate America's increasingly internationalist position as it entered the war.

From a business standpoint, the war was an excellent opportunity to reestablish a more benevolent domestic image and expand internationally. It was a time to promote the idea of unity between the bankers and the White House. All the relationships that had been established with FDR over the years would coalesce to aid the president and enable the bankers to influence war from a position of financial strength.

Key 1940s bankers wielded their power while retaining an exterior style of personal reserve, self-sacrifice, and modesty. In many respects, that was a response to the post-Depression prudency that trickled into the war days. But it was also a sign of reverence for public service; the bankers' role in supporting the war effort bestowed upon them an additional element of gravitas, a marked shift from the mistrust that engulfed bankers after the Crash and during the Pecora hearings.

The goals of nonisolationist Democrats, Republicans, and bankers were reflected by the financiers who operated with FDR and Truman. They remained on the same philosophical page, particularly after the war. Both groups endorsed open foreign financial policy and noninflationary domestic economic policy, two doctrines particularly well disposed to growing financial monoliths against a backdrop of political supremacy.

In fact, the global framework of finance and economics that would dictate the next century of world policy was fashioned by these elite 1940s bankers within domestic constructs like the Council on Foreign Relations, and new international ones like the World Bank (officially the International Bank for Reconstruction and Development) and the International Monetary Fund.

Financing the War

During World War I, the US government had raised $5 billion to fund military operations through the sale of Liberty bonds. The drive to finance World War II would eclipse that amount by a factor of thirty; Americans purchased $150 billion in war bonds during those years. More than half the US population (eighty-five million people) bought them—many through branches of the biggest banks in the country. This time, thanks to Treasury Secretary Henry Morgenthau Jr. (who had particular input from National City Bank), the commercial bankers were far more involved in the distribution and initial design of the bonds.

Commercial banks sold and redeemed war bonds for their customers directly through deposit accounts. Bankers proposed ways to structure the bonds so that they would be most appealing to American citizens. The government subsidized the banks in the process, paying banks' servicing fees on the bonds at an average of twelve to thirteen cents on the dollar.[2]

As a result of National City Bank's dual capacity of distributing bonds and retaining deposits for domestic and foreign clients, its new chairman, Gordon Rentschler, had a sense of financial maneuvers that could portend military ones in Europe before even the Fed or the White House did.

Rentschler succeeded James Perkins at the helm of National City Bank in July 1940 after Perkins died of a heart attack following dinner with US Steel magnate Arthur Anderson. Perkins had run the bank during the Depression in the wake of the scandals of his predecessor, Charles Mitchell. He had been instrumental in helping FDR push through sweeping banking reforms.[3]

Another Eastern Establishment fixture, Rentschler was a Princeton graduate who used the escalating war to steer his bank toward the epicenter of America's money-raising effort, coordinating his efforts with Morgenthau. Like his contemporaries, he served as a director at multiple companies that benefited from the reorientation of the war economy, including Union Pacific, Anaconda Copper, National Cash Register, and Consolidated Edison.[4] (His brother, Fred, was the head of United Aircraft, which made planes for the French and British.)

Another National City man would insert himself into the war bond and postwar financial reconstruction efforts with even more vigor. Two years before he died, Perkins enlisted his close friend Warren Randolph Burgess to become a vice chairman at National City Bank.[5] The fiscally conservative Burgess, former vice president of the Federal Reserve Bank of New York and head of the American Bankers Association, did much to tailor the symbiotic relationship between the government and big private banks during the war effort. Burgess's position as one of the top three men at National City Bank provided him access to private capital as well as a public role in overseeing domestic policies and foreign practices.[6]

When Burgess started at National City Bank, Treasury Secretary Morgenthau, an old friend, opened an account there with a $5,000 deposit as a vote of confidence. In July 1940, Burgess approached Morgenthau to discuss the government securities market, which was behaving quite well under the circumstances but which he feared could falter if the government raised too much debt too quickly. He told Morgenthau he'd been giving "a good deal of thought to what may occur if we get worse news from abroad and what might be done about it." He was especially concerned about repealing the president's power to devalue the dollar through raising more debt, though he realized that Morgenthau's allegiance would be with FDR on that score. Still, he suggested that "if the authorization to raise the debt limit were accompanied by a proposal to limit other expenditures," then the government security market would fare better.[7]

Lamont, Leffingwell, FDR, and War

After FDR won the presidency for the third time on November 5, 1940 (though with a lower popular and electoral percentage than the prior election), Morgan partner Russell Leffingwell was quick to congratulate him. But like many bankers, he had not supported Roosevelt during this election. "I was not for a third term," he wrote FDR in the spirit of directness that underscored their relationship. Pushing his candor, he added, "I know that no man can really want to carry the burden another four years in these hard times." But as a matter of civic duty, he promised to do anything he could to help FDR.[8]

A wise FDR saw beyond the less tactful elements of Leffingwell's intentions. Knowing that Leffingwell and his bank's help would be crucial in the coming years, he replied, "I appreciate the spirit of helpfulness in which you write."

Augmenting his colleague's positive sentiments, Lamont got down to the business of offering FDR unequivocal support. On December 18, 1940, he phoned FDR to say he was "immensely pleased with the president's' approach to helping the British, and getting away from the dollar mark."[9] The tensions that had accompanied the banking reforms were over for now. Just before Christmas, Lamont visited FDR and confirmed, "Whatever differences there may have been about domestic affairs, I and my colleagues are heart and soul with you for unlimited material aid to Britain and for national defense."

The old articulate diplomat in Lamont, who had advised Wilson on how to garner the public's backing for the League of Nations two decades earlier, suggested similar tactics to FDR before the president's December 29 radio address. Speaking on behalf of his British compatriots, who he believed could stop the contagion of the war with enough support from the United States,

Lamont said Americans needed to be told "that you will not go to war, but you cannot promise that Hitler will not make war upon us . . . that the first step in national defense is to give unlimited material aid to England."[10] The Morgan bankers' and FDR's strategies were identical.

National City and War Bond Bucks

For this war, the Morgan Bank would not be operating alone, controlling other banks' involvement from atop the American banking hierarchy. FDR had changed that game. When the National City Bank and Chase backed the Glass-Steagall Act in 1933, they also severed themselves from the old Morgan "inner group" mentality, which had prevailed for the first third of the century. All the major firms would unite behind FDR and on behalf of America's position in the war, but they would also be competing more aggressively for war-related business behind the scenes. They would choose different paths; the Morgan Bank would pursue the old path of leveraging government relationships to secure financing. The commercial banks would favor working through deposits and war bond distribution. Both types of banks would retain government securities equal to one-third of their overall assets by the war's end.

At noon on January 17, 1941, Rentschler addressed an august gathering at National City Bank's 129th annual stockholders meeting. There, he proclaimed to a roomful of pensive, silk-suited men that the bank was actively participating in the financing of the national defense program—not just by distributing war bonds but also through enhanced lending to private industry.[11]

As he told the crowd, the war's "implications for this country have become our primary national concern." He too was committed to support his president and his country. His bank had two major roles: "to safeguard the funds entrusted to us" and "to give our utmost aid to the national defense program." Gone was the recklessness and heady talk of prosperity linked to the stock market that had characterized 1920s banking; the 1940s were about prudency and patriotism.

Nevertheless, expansion remained a key strategy for National City Bank. The bank was now operating branches in Spain, the Far East, Belgium, France, and England. And as Rentschler stressed, "in no case have we as yet incurred any losses of consequence." He informed the group that his bank had cooperated with the government to design a new form of bankable contract for emergency plant facilities, and that the bank was among the first to make loans on such contracts. Those contracts made it possible for private banks to finance a greater portion of the defense effort.[12]

The war was already proving a boon to National City's global business. The bank's deposits had risen 25 percent to $2.9 billion in 1940, representing nearly half a million domestic accounts, as people rushed to open new accounts through which to purchase war bonds as a means to support the war without spilling American blood. National City had also extended $1 billion of new loans in the past year, partly for war-related manufacturing plants.

The firm's South American branches were showing a substantive increase in activity, too. This was largely, Rentschler explained, "due to diversion of business from Europe." This war-related shift made way for a new core strategy; for decades to come, the bank would continue to press for "more extensive economic relations between the two continents."[13] Rentschler's promise on that accord came to fruition; National City became the most active US bank in the region during and after the war.[14] In the wake of the war, it extended its global presence more quickly than any other American bank.

Three days after his colleague addressed the shareholders, on FDR's third inauguration day, W. Randolph Burgess introduced Allan Sproul as the new president of the Federal Reserve Bank of New York at the midwinter dinner of the New York Bankers Association in the Hotel Astor. It was a solemn occasion, given the circumstances. He said, "On one major objective the people of the nation are united as seldom before. It is the defense of our democracy. In that task the president can count upon the loyal support and cooperation of the bankers of this state." At the same dinner, Sir Louis Beal of the British Purchasing Commission warned, "The longer the war . . . the more will Britain be in need of reconstruction. . . . How much we shall then be able to buy from you . . . [depends] on the extent we retain our position as creditor nation."[15]

Wartime financing provided banks a boost in less obvious ways. First, the Federal Reserve made bank reserves readily available to banks at low rates, which enabled them to increase their assets by as much as 50 percent throughout the war. Additionally, holding a mix of securities heavily weighted in Treasury bonds (with 35 percent of US government debt issued remaining on their books) gave them the appearance of better health.

With such strong federal backing, investors and banks could borrow against their Treasury securities holdings to purchase new issues or more Treasuries. The Federal Reserve encouraged the practice because it helped bolster the price of government securities. Both the government and the banks benefited. As John Wilson wrote in *The Chase,* this "pyramiding of security purchases produced the major increase in Chase's loans, as it did with loans of all major banks."[16]

The ability to hold and use extra Treasury bonds as collateral upon which to extend lending more brought America and its major banks back to life. Bankers stood ready to resume their international expansionary goals, picking up the slack that would be created as European banks succumbed to chaotic war conditions.

Infamy

Bankers like Lamont, Morgan, and Aldrich continued to back FDR as he considered whether to join the war, while the American population and press waffled between isolationism and horror at the Nazi atrocities.

On October 2, 1941, Aldrich found a way to put his weight, and that of the Chase bank, behind US intervention. Speaking as head of the British War Relief Society in America, he requested and received immediate approval from the White House for his organization and similar ones to receive the same status as the Red Cross, "which is not hindered from giving aid to any organization of the country affected."[17] The provision would allow private banks like Chase to profit from extending aid.

By late October 1941, as talk of a British invasion of the continent escalated, Lamont was pressing foreign policy ideas on FDR. "I can't help wondering," mused Lamont, "whether Mr. Churchill might not welcome a letter from you which he could make public, to the general effect that American industry was rushing ahead in the Defense Program and was turning out in large quantities munitions, tanks, airplanes etc . . . especially allocated for British defense purposes all over the world (and for Russia and China)."[18]

The Neutrality Act forbade US manufacturers from selling war munitions to any belligerent country in any war, and an amendment in 1937 prohibited loans to warring nations. But after World War II began, Congress began to ease up on the restrictions, which allowed munitions be sold to countries being attacked by Nazi Germany. On November 13, 1941, after the US destroyer *Reuben James* was sunk by a German sub, remaining restrictions were lifted. Merchant ships would be allowed to arm themselves in self-defense and could enter European waters with the appropriate financings and munitions in place.

The Japanese bombed Pearl Harbor on December 7, "a date which will live in infamy," said FDR famously, as he signed the official declaration of US war on Japan the following day. Four days later, Germany and Italy declared war on the United States, and the United States responded by declaring war on them. The European and Southeast Asian wars had become a global conflict. The United States was officially in World War II.

Postwar Finance Before the War Ends

Just after the United States entered the war, two simultaneous initiatives unfolded that would dictate elements of financing after the war, through the joint initiatives of foreign policy measures and private banking whims. Plans were already being formulated to navigate the postwar peace, especially its international power implications for finance and politics, in the background. American political leaders and scholars began considering the concept of "one world" from an economic perspective, void of divisions and imbalances. Or so the theory went.

The original plans to create a set of multinational entities that would finance one-world reconstruction and development (and ostensibly balance the world's various economies) were conceived by two academics: John Maynard Keynes, an adviser for the British Treasury, and Harry Dexter White, an economist in the Division of Monetary Research of the US Treasury under Treasury Secretary Henry Morgenthau.

By the spring of 1942, White had drafted plans for a "stabilization fund" and a "Bank for Reconstruction and Development." His concept for the fund became the seed for the International Monetary Fund. The other idea became the World Bank.[19] But before those entities would come to life through the Bretton Woods conferences, many arguments about their makeup would take place, and millions of lives would be lost.

Taxes, Inflation, and Recovery

Inflation became a central concern to bankers, the population, and the FDR administration as the European battles intensified. With the stimulation of war effort requirements domestically and European war-related demand, the United States was truly recovering from the Great Depression. Adopting Aldrich's view, tax policy would play a dual role in continued recovery, as FDR saw it, by raising money to fund the war and containing consumer purchasing power to curb inflation of nonmilitary goods.[20]

In that regard, the Revenue Act of 1942 called for tax revenues to be raised by $18 billion, and brought millions of new middle-class taxpayers into the income tax system. It also included an added "victory tax" of 5 percent on all income over $624 until the war's end, which was lowered to 3 percent in a subsequent act.

As the war effort gained momentum, the federal budget and the need for funds escalated. In 1942 FDR had presented the country with a budget that included a $30 billion increase over the previous year; it was nearly six times as large as the budget had been at its peak during World War I. "Victory," said FDR in his budget message to Congress for the fiscal year beginning July 1, 1943, "cannot be bought with any amount of money however large; victory is achieved with the blood of soldiers, the sweat of working men and women and the sacrifice of all people." By this point the budget exceeded $100 billion.

Though blood, sweat, and sacrifice would be the horrific ingredients of victory, money still had to be found to fund the war in as many ways as possible. The White House used the bankers to enhance the process. In mid-November 1942, FDR was informed by his staff that plans were growing in cities across the country to centralize and convert the "war drives" into "war chests." The best man they could think of to run the effort properly was Winthrop Aldrich.[21]

The leaders of Chase and National City Bank rose to the occasion. The December 1942 Victory Bond Drive was a huge success; $13 billion in bonds were sold, exceeding a goal of $9 billon. Money that wasn't raised via the population was minted by the government, and on both accounts bankers would play a pivotal role. The average US bank bought and held government securities equal to *nearly half* of its total deposits to support the prices of that Treasury debt on behalf of the US government. But more was needed.

Despite their support, the bankers had mixed views about the increase in debt and the potential for inflation that could result from it. Some of them believed it was better for the country (and for their business) to target the public as investors in war bonds than to raise money by issuing more Treasury bonds. FDR couldn't afford to neglect the bankers' inflation concerns; he needed their private fundraising avenues as much as he needed to raise money through public channels, including through tax increases.

Aldrich Seeks Alternatives to National Debt Increases

In a speech on January 21, 1943, at a Connecticut Bankers Association dinner, Aldrich wielded his influence on domestic policy, suggesting Treasury debt be augmented by taxes during the war, so as to limit national debt increases. He urged an at-the-source income tax and adoption of a federal retail sales tax "to check the increases of public debt," even though "they are not a good form of taxation . . . in times of peace."

With federal debt at $143 billion, and set to hit $180 billion that year, he was concerned that the United States had relied "too little upon taxation and too much upon borrowings" as the war progressed. In 1941, about 50 percent of total federal expenditures were covered by taxes (the figure dropped to 31 percent in 1942). Aldrich believed that "investors had purchased too little and commercial bankers too large" a portion of debt, which had caused "an inflationary expansion of bank deposits" and "carries with it serious implications for the banking system." He had rising concerns as to whether banks should bear as much of the costs of war debt as they were, and about inflation in general.

In 1942, commercial banks bought $19 billion of government securities (38 percent of the increase in total debt). Through 1943, he estimated, commercial banks might have to absorb $40 billion (60 percent of the estimated increase in federal debt). Though commercial banks stood ready to do their part in the war effort, they didn't want to shoulder all the debt burden; it would be less profitable than using their capital to fund war supplies during the war and reparations afterward.

Aldrich praised the "notable success" of the Victory Fund Committees in placing 60 percent of the related securities sold with noncommercial buyers. He believed this would prevent the need for another such large offering until April, concluding "the wider the ownership distribution of the debt, the greater is the amount of debt that a nation can stand."[22]

After the German Sixth Army admitted its first defeat at the Battle of Stalingrad, the Treasury Department announced plans for another $13 billion fund drive.

FDR summoned Aldrich to the White House in April 1943 to offer him the position of chairman of the National War Fund, which would coordinate local fund drives throughout the country. Aldrich was honored to accept the post. As he had written FDR beforehand, the National War Fund was "more important than the unification of the raising of money nationally [by] the private war relief agencies."[23] The fund centralized the bankers' roles in the war effort and elevated their ability to control the flow of funds relative to the private relief agencies they would circumvent.

On May 21, FDR endorsed Aldrich and the fund publicly: "As Commander in Chief, I ask all our people to remember this—that a share in the National War Fund is a share in winning the war." Two weeks later, Aldrich set the goal of the National War Fund drive at $250 million. He and Treasury

Secretary Morgenthau planned to start their coordinated drive in late September to avoid interfering with the Red Cross drive the following spring.[24]

Aldrich's compatriot National City Bank chairman Gordon Rentschler was selected to be treasurer of the National War Fund. As the next wave of the drive swung into high gear in the fall of 1943 all the individual checks started flowing to him—such as a $5 check from Mac Grossman, a member of the US Army who tried to send it to his field officer and was told there'd be no organized drive in the field. Over the next year, other personal gestures of financial support flowed through Rentschler, such as $724.68—one day's salary for the employees of A. Steinam Company—and $1 from Mrs. Grace Fox of Philadelphia.[25]

Burgess and Inflation

In keeping with his ideas about placing more of the financing burden on the citizenry, W. Randolph Burgess campaigned for the second bond drive to reach more individuals. "Coverage must be broader if inflation price advances are to be checked," he wrote Federal Reserve chairman Eccles.[26]

Burgess was motivated by more than a lifelong concern about inflation; the broader the national coverage of bond buyers, the more customers would be performing their financial activities through the banks selling those bonds. It was a customer drive as much as a war bond drive. Patriotism could be linked to opening an account at National City Bank. Amassing savings in that account was akin to providing the public service of frugality in the face of mounting international bloodshed and the military operations that would be needed to fight Hitler.

By extension, National City Bank was opening new branches around the world, in countries with governments sympathetic to America and its allies. The growth was spun as a patriotic deed. The bank's ads depicted international locales where battles were being fought and new branches were opening. After victories, National City Bank would be on hand to facilitate funds for reconstructing those countries on behalf of America and itself. From that local vantage point, the bank's power over future development would be acute.

In addition, with national income expected to reach new levels as the nation entered high-production and full-employment mode, Burgess believed people should save their money voluntarily or make bond purchases to contain inflation. The bankers were thus abetting the process to align the people with the government. "With the inspiring achievements of the Armed Forces, with miracles and production by American industry," he wrote Eccles, "the bankers of the country can be counted on to do their share."

On April 8, 1943, FDR had frozen prices, wages, and salaries in further efforts to stem inflation. The Current Tax Payment Act took effect on June 9. The act allowed the government to raise money in advance of the end of the tax year by collecting people's income taxes the year the money was earned, not the following year. At the time, most bankers recognized the need to raise money through taxes. The Revenue Act of 1943 also provided for the distribution of the payment of taxes through the population. It carried a small concession to the wealthy, alleviating some of the elite's negative feelings around the idea that prior incarnations were simply "class taxes."[27] It also increased excise taxes and raised the excess profits tax to 95 percent from 90 percent. Though FDR vetoed the act, claiming it was too business-friendly, the House overrode the veto to pass the Individual Income Tax Act of 1944.

With respect to the bond drives, everything went full steam ahead. On September 27, 1943, Burgess, who had been conferring regularly with Morgenthau on the matter, informed the Treasury secretary that "New York City went over the top today and I think the State will be tomorrow night. We are driving ahead on individual subscriptions."[28]

While Aldrich and Rentschler focused on bond drives, which also fit into the framework of their banks' strategies for opening accounts, Lamont concentrated on his area of political expertise: lobbying for passage of one of FDR's major foreign policy initiatives, which dovetailed with his internationalist stance on trade matters. The Republicans had opposed the first incarnation of the measure, the Reciprocal Tariff Act of 1934, through which FDR extended the power of the presidency to establish foreign trade agreements with other countries (particularly with Latin America) and reduce tariffs (which the Republicans preferred to keep higher) to spur greater global trade liberalization. The bill had passed despite their opposition.

FDR expressed his gratitude to Lamont for his efforts in convincing the Republican opposition to pass the Reciprocal Trade Agreements Act of 1943, an expansion of the president's tariff and trade negotiation powers. John Franklin Carter of the National Press Club informed FDR that "Lamont went to great personal trouble" to do so, fighting against a number of "recalcitrant Republican Senators and Congressmen." It was a repeat of 1919, when Lamont wrestled the more isolationist components of his party on behalf of the president and a global banking and trade framework. Carter told FDR, off the record, that "word went out from the House of Morgan to support renewal of the Trade Agreements Act."[29] Both the Morgan Bank and FDR emerged victorious.

The Postwar Power Play During the War

There was more to the notion of war funding than ending the war; capital considerations became a battle for political and economic supremacy. Both America and the British wanted to control the postwar financial system. Britain had conceded ground to the United States and its bankers after World War I. This was a second chance, perhaps. But the United States didn't want to forfeit the spot it had won as a new superpower.

The American and British Treasuries had published the White and Keynes plans for the creation of multinational finance entities in April 1943. Treasury Secretary Morgenthau presented the American plan to the relevant subcommittees of Congress. Both Congress and the British Parliament began debating both plans, but nothing was settled.[30]

White released an updated design in August 1943. That fall, Keynes visited Washington for the first time since the plans were announced to discuss the details. Neither plan was seen as sufficient by the American bankers or Congress. As John H. Williams wrote in *Foreign Affairs,* the flagship publication of the Council on Foreign Relations, "From the time of the publication of the revised White plan in August the American press and American banking and foreign trade opinion have been almost uniformly unsympathetic to both plans."[31]

The reason had less to do with the optics of using economic equality as a means to alleviate wars or elevate the status of struggling national populations, and more with maintaining influence. US bankers wanted the dollar to be the world's singular reserve currency. So did the Federal Reserve, the Treasury Department, and FDR. Gold could be involved from a pegging perspective, but no American banker wanted a global currency that could not be controllable by the Federal Reserve. This war presented the opportunity to assert not just American domination from a foreign policy perspective but American banker domination over global economic and financing decisions.

White's plans went through several drafts—though none turned out dramatically different from his initial proposal.[32] In the end, they reflected the bankers' requirements that the dollar and their private institutions would play a significant role in whatever multinational entity and doctrine arose from the ashes of the war. This suited the FDR administration perfectly well. The government had raised much debt to fund the war, as the bankers frequently pointed out, and that had the potential to weaken the dollar as a global currency. But if the multinational entities required use of the dollar, that would ensure a stronger dollar—something FDR was keen to preserve as an indicator of American hegemony.

Keynes, White, and Power Transfer
to the United States

By early 1944, nearly two-thirds of the European GNP had been devoted to war; millions of people had been slaughtered. But six months after the complete liberation of Leningrad, it was the international financial aspects of the coming peace that exercised the imagination of the policy elites. In July 1944, 730 delegates representing the forty-four Allied nations convened at the Mount Washington Hotel in Bretton Woods, New Hampshire. Amid picturesque mountains, hiking trails, and oppressive heat, they sat to determine the postwar economic system.

For three weeks, they debated the charter for the International Monetary Fund and discussed how the International Bank for Reconstruction and Development, or the "World Bank," would operate.

White and Keynes had competed for influence over this final result for the past two years. To a large extent, the personal vehemence of each man aside, they did so as an extension of the jockeying for position between the United States and Britain as the incoming and outgoing financial superpowers. At first, virtually every American banker and politician opposed the main aspects of Keynes's plans, particularly his idea about creating a new global currency—the unitas—that would supersede gold and the dollar.

Many subsequent histories of the Bretton Woods Conference consider the final doctrines for the IMF and World Bank as representing a clear compromise between White and Keynes. But they leaned far more toward White's model and vision.[33]

From the bankers' standpoint, White's model was more tolerable because it preserved the supremacy of the dollar. Former President James A. Garfield once said, "He who controls the money supply of a nation controls the nation." But in the negotiations surrounding those Bretton Woods meetings, the mantra was more "Those who control the banks backed by the currency that dominates the world control world finance."

While final drafts snaked through Congress after the July 1944 meetings, one key US banker maintained his public opposition to Bretton Woods. Even after it became clear that the multinational entities would be dollar-based, Chase chairman Winthrop Aldrich remained opposed to the idea. Mostly, he feared the slightest amount of competition from any uncontrollable source. Though Aldrich favored removing trade barriers, which would provide the US banks a wider field for cross-border financing, he didn't want some supranational entity getting in the way of private lending to facilitate that trade.

In his "Proposed Currency Plan" of September 16, 1944, Aldrich slammed the accords, which he saw as a distinct challenge to the power of private banks. "The IMF," he said, "would become a mechanism for instability rather than stability since it would encourage exchange-rate alterations."

Like most bankers, Aldrich was fine with the World Bank taking responsibility for exchange-stabilization lending.[34] That element would aid bankers; a supranational entity providing monies to struggling countries would bolster them sufficiently to be able to borrow more through private banks. But bankers didn't want a fund constructed as a competing lending mechanism that could possibly take business away from them, operating in the guise of economic security.

Aldrich warned, "We shall have the shadow of stability without the substance. . . . Perhaps the most dangerous aspect of the Bretton Woods proposals is that they serve as an obstacle to the immediate consideration and solution of these basic problems."[35]

Aldrich's public outcry was unsettling to FDR and Morgenthau, who knew that it was politically important to get all the main bankers' support. Not only did they hold a solid proportion of US Treasury debt; they had become the distribution mechanisms of that debt to more and more citizens and countries. There couldn't be an IMF without the support of private lenders, and if the US was going to be in command of such an entity from a global perspective, US bankers had to be on board. Concession to the bankers wasn't a matter of empty appeasement but of economic supremacy.

The American Bankers Association, on which Aldrich was a board member, also wanted to restrict the IMF's powers. Burgess, who served as chairman of the American Bankers Association and National City Bank vice chairman, was unwilling to back the Bretton Woods proposals unless White made more concessions to reinforce the supremacy of the US banks and the dollar. He would play hardball and get Morgenthau involved if he had to.

Though White refused to bow to Burgess's requests, Congress incorporated them into the final documents.[36] To make the bankers happy, a compromise was fashioned that restricted the IMF funds to loans offsetting *short-term* exchange rate fluctuations, such as when one country has a sharp and sudden shift in the value of its currency relative to another.[37] That loophole left plenty of room for banks to supply aggressive financing to developing nations over the loosely defined *longer-term*. It also meant that all nations receiving short-term assistance from the IMF would likely be on the hook for more expensive debt at the hands of the bankers in tandem, or later. But in the scheme of White's plan, this alteration was more cosmetic than substantial.

Truman Takes Office

On January 20, 1945, FDR took his fourth and final oath of office. Two days later he traveled to Yalta, a Soviet Black Sea resort town. There, he met with Soviet Premier Joseph Stalin and British prime minister Winston Churchill for the last time, to discuss how to carve up the postwar world from a superpower perspective.

The three men agreed that the Soviets would obtain a sphere of influence in Manchuria after Japan surrendered in exchange for its participation in the Pacific region. They also agreed to include France in the postwar governing of Germany as the fifth permanent member of the UN National Security Council (alongside the United States, the Soviet Union, Britain, and China), and for Germany to pay reparations after the war. In general, the Yalta Conference was perceived as successful regarding the potential for collaboration between the United States and the Soviet Union, but that would soon change.

On April 12, 1945, at the "Little White House" in Warm Springs, Georgia, FDR signed some papers, ate his lunch, and slumped into unconsciousness. With his death came the death of agreements with the Soviets over their influence in Eastern Europe and the UN and the collaborations in which FDR had engaged.[38]

When Vice President Truman received the call that FDR had died, his first reaction was fear. Though the war was winding down, it was clear that navigating its ending would be critical in avoiding future combat. But Truman assumed FDR's mantle without a battalion of his own to command and absent many close relationships to draw on in the White House. FDR hadn't shared much with him.

Truman was the former captain of the "Boys from Battery D" during World War I. As a small-town farm boy he had a hankering for politics, which he had spun into a stint as a Missouri senator before rising to the position of VP. His humble roots offered him few opportunities, and even less inclination, to engage with the Eastern Establishment bankers. The elite circles hadn't paid much attention to him, either.

Since his younger years, Truman had cultivated a midwestern "Jacksonian" suspicion of bankers, having altercated over a loan with one in Kansas City in the early 1920s during which his business partner was forced into bankruptcy. Truman escaped the same fate only because of his position as a public servant.[39] (The reason he believed he didn't owe on the loan was simple: the loan had been made in boom times, when a dollar was worth more, and came due in the early 1920s bust times.[40])

Truman tended to embrace people from his own class and background.[41] He was more comfortable with bankers who hailed from his part of the country, such as Frank Houston, president of the Chemical Bank & Trust Company. But even though Houston shared words of support at the start of his presidency ("As a former Missourian, I am very proud," he said[42]) and offered praise for Truman's speeches, but he didn't attempt to exert any political influence on the president.[43] That would come from the usual New York bankers, who leveraged Truman to carve out their power in the postwar world.

Aldrich and Truman

Aldrich decided not to waste any time in acquiring the role of most influential banker to Truman. Two months before World War II ended, in late June 1945, Aldrich made his first major gambit to incorporate Truman into his plans. Their relationship had begun on a touchy note. The two had first met at the Chase offices four years earlier, when Truman was heading a Senate committee investigating potential waste in the National Defense Program in the run-up to World War II. As Truman later recalled of their encounter, "I had to go to New York to see this fella Aldrich. Even though I had an appointment, he had me cool my heels for an hour and a half."[44]

Now Aldrich knew he had to bond with Truman on a foreign policy basis. He requested a meeting with Truman regarding his duties as president of the International Chamber of Commerce. He was planning to visit London in August for a meeting that would be attended by delegates from North America, Western Europe, and Asia. As he told Truman, "The International Chamber is desirous of throwing its entire influence in the direction of reducing trade barriers, so that international trade may again be resumed throughout the world and private enterprise be stimulated."[45]

As chairman of the nation's largest bank, Aldrich reminded Truman that he was already doing his part in financing postwar development, perhaps more quickly than the government was. Chase, Aldrich noted, had been approached by France, Italy, and the Netherlands, "all desirous of discussing with us elaborate operations looking toward the reestablishment of their national credit." He was going to continue European financial discussions during his trip abroad.[46]

Though Truman was unable to clear a meeting time before Aldrich's trip, he invited Aldrich to discuss the results after his return. To further solidify his alliance with Truman, and in the spirit of public-oriented service, Aldrich used his role as president of the National War Fund to bestow Truman with a citation for his service, stating in an October 30 letter that "his personal assistance and efforts have meant much toward the success of the final appeal of this important part of our war effort."[47]

Bretton Woods Agreement Approved

Congress approved the Bretton Woods agreement on July 20, 1945. Twenty-seven other countries joined as well. The Soviet Union did not. It was a portent of how rapidly the world was falling into the Cold War and how rapidly the United States was forging its own foreign alliances in the postwar economy.

By the time the Bretton Woods delegates reconvened to settle the final details of the agreement at Savannah, Georgia, in March 1946, Churchill had already coined the term "the Iron Curtain" to describe the line between Communist Soviet Union and the West in his famous "Sinews of Peace" speech at Westminster College.[48]

In addition to the growing Cold War mentality, or perhaps because of it, expectations that White would lead the IMF were squashed when the FBI alerted Truman that White and other senior civil servants had passed secret intelligence to the Soviet Union. It's doubtful that Truman believed the allegations; though he took White out of the bidding for the head position, White remained an executive director.

The incident served as a precedent for how the top positions at the World Bank and the IMF would be allocated along political-geographical lines. The post was offered instead to Belgian economist Camille Gutt, establishing the protocol whereby the IMF would be headed by a Western European and the World Bank by an American.

But while politics dictated the initial leadership choices, private bankers' behavior would soon overshadow the functions of both bodies. Despite their "international" monikers, the World Bank and the IMF disproportionately served the interests of the Western European nations that were most important to the United States from the get-go. The bankers could exert their influence over both entities to expand their own enterprises.

Later, another element that reinforced this dynamic was added. Thanks to a minor technicality introduced by Truman's Treasury secretary, John Snyder, "aid monies" to "friendly" (or large and friendly) countries would be considered "grants," which would not show up as national debt, thereby providing the illusion of better economic health.[49] Money granted for military operations for the friendly countries would not show up as debt either. This presented a foreign business opportunity whereby banks could provide loans at better terms to larger countries and make more money off higher interest loans to developing ones because of the disparity in their perceived debt loads.

In addition, as Martin Mayer observed in his classic book *The Bankers,* "the growing and unregulated Eurodollar market would become a cauldron of out-of-control debt and heady profits for US banks."[50] Through this market, many of the major midcentury postwar loans would be made.

The End of the War

The war in Europe had drawn to a close in April 1945, with the American sweep to the Elbe and the Russian drive into Berlin, followed by the announcement of Adolf Hitler's death on May 1. The first surrender agreement of World War II was signed at Reims, France, on May 7, and then countersigned in Berlin on May 8, requiring hostilities to end at midnight on May 9, when Nazi Germany surrendered to the Soviet Union.

According to *Foreign Affairs* writer William Hyland, "Two tremendous factors operated to bring about Germany's defeat: British courage in adversity . . . and Russian manpower and the vastness of Russian distances. But the cornerstone of victory was the American machine. The mass industrial output of America provided the sinews of conflict for all the Allies."[51]

On June 18, Truman canvassed his senior advisers for their view on invading Japan. Just before the meeting adjourned, Truman said, "We haven't heard from you, McCloy." Assistant Secretary of War John McCloy replied, "We ought to have our heads examined if we do not seek a political end to the war before an invasion." He suggested assuring the Japanese they could retain their emperor and warning them of the *existence* of the atomic bomb. Truman assigned McCloy and Secretary of War Henry Stimson to fashion a plan along those lines.[52]

Yet on August 6, Truman dropped a massive atomic bomb on Hiroshima, Japan, and followed a few days later with another one on Nagasaki. About seventy thousand people died immediately in the Hiroshima explosion, with seventy thousand more from radiation over the next five years.

Debate over why Truman decided to drop the bomb continues to this day: some argue that he felt he had something to prove stepping into FDR's shoes; others claim he believed it was necessary to secure US hegemony. In response to a February 12, 1965, letter from Alan Weiner, an American history major at Long Island University who wrote, "I . . . would appreciate it very much if you would take the time to write me a brief letter stating your basic reasons for dropping The Bomb," Truman said, "It was dropped to stop a war—and it did."[53]

US Political, Financial, and Military Dominance

The United States dominated the global economy in the late 1940s. With 7 percent of the global population, America controlled 42 percent of the world's income and half its manufacturing output. It produced 57 percent of the world's steel, 43 percent of its electricity, and 62 percent of its oil.

After the war, controlling global banking became easier for the US banks, because their competitors were mired in expensive reconstruction efforts (which the US bankers and government helped fund, as they had done after World War I). In addition, the American-influenced global agencies favored their largest trading partners with grants upon which US banks could lend more. US banks quickly opened a succession of overseas branches to accommodate the flow of money.

The domestic economy wasn't being as cooperative. After World War I, a mini recession had broken out; in 1946, the threat of inflation emerged as a critical issue for the Truman administration. War costs that had been financed through taxes and the sale of government bonds were now being replaced with bank credit, which fueled consumer appetites. A large volume of pent-up demand met by a new gush of bank loans had pushed prices up and stirred inflation.

The bankers remained concerned about inflation despite their role in exacerbating it. On April 24, 1946, the Philadelphia, New York, and San Francisco Federal Reserve Banks voted to roll back the discount rate of 0.5 percent for member banks using government securities as collateral, which had prevailed during the war years, in their own bid to curb inflation and speculation.[54] The preferential rate was designed to encourage banks to borrow to purchase additional government securities, or lend at low rates to others to buy them, to finance war efforts. In an address at the Annual Convention Dinner of the Illinois Bankers Association on May 2, 1946, Aldrich agreed with the new Fed strategy, and outlined his views on how to further combat this inflation threat. "To the extent that wars can be financed through taxes and the sale of bonds to non-commercial bank investors, postwar financial and economic distortions are diminished," Aldrich reasoned. "Only if we follow the course of action outlined, can we maintain the private enterprise system, which, in the economic field, is the counterpart of democratic action in the political field."

Aldrich's statement embodied the core assumption of the bankers regarding postwar governance: the pursuit of capitalism was akin to the pursuit of democracy. His recommendations included refinancing short-term debt with longer-term debt, stimulating production, and relieving the Federal Reserve of the need to maintain an artificial level of interest rates. In other words, it was time to let free markets dictate interest rates and bond prices, even if he conceded that certain federal stimulation was also needed.

But Aldrich had no wish to re-create the environment that led to the Great Depression. "As bankers," he concluded, "we, too, have a distinct responsibility. We must make sure that bank credit is extended on a sound basis . . . to facilitate production and not speculation. We must encourage our depositors to retain rather than to spend their savings."[55] This notion ran counter to the idea that spending would stimulate the economy, but it made sense in the framework of banking at the time. The more money depositors kept with banks, the more money banks would have to advance their postwar global lending and investment strategy.

On that accord, Aldrich remained very active. On June 24, 1946, he informed the French Ministry of Finance that the Morgan Bank and National City Bank were assisting the Dutch government in selling or liquidating American securities to raise money, and that Chase would happily do the same for them. US banks would provide credit for two to three years at low interest rates guaranteed by French-held American securities so that the French could obtain cash and not have to sell all those securities at once. This would keep the prices of American securities lifted and allow banks to increase their lending to this key US ally and borrower.

In the distance, the task of reconstructing Western Europe and the Far East loomed as an opportunity for the US government to exert massive political influence, and for private US banks to do so from a financial perspective. One man's war was another man's war loan.

Meanwhile, the American public resumed its isolationist stance. Just as the US population had turned insular after World War I, so it did again after World War II. A 1946 Bureau of the Budget report noted that foreign concerns were no longer at the forefront of Americans' minds. Concerns about domestic economic policies, such as the high cost of living and jobs, were the consuming issue.[56]

To make their mark on international trade while the domestic mentality turned inward, the bankers realized they had to get more involved in the postwar loan efforts, just as they had after World War I. Having spent so much time in Europe during and after the war, Aldrich concluded he was the best man to address these matters. Truman agreed and appointed him as chair of the Committee for Financing Foreign Trade, a group of twelve bankers and industrialists tasked with coordinating postwar US trade policy and private company endeavors. In that capacity, Aldrich would have Truman's ear, and he would facilitate communication from the rest of the committee regarding the role of American business and finance in foreign trade policy.

From the end of the war onward, the bankers would be in a position to drive federal monies, as well as dictate the rules of the supranational entities created at Bretton Woods. They would do so amid a remarkable shift in public perception. Having been held in utter contempt by the American population after the Crash and during the Great Depression, they had erased their aura of undue power through engagement in the war effort coupled with speeches of their own responsibilities to the country. And yet they stood to gain more global influence than ever before.

CHAPTER 9

THE LATE 1940S: WORLD RECONSTRUCTION AND PRIVATE BANKERS

"We must unite to win the peace with the same assurance and in the same businesslike manner as we organized to win the war."[1]

—Chase chairman Winthrop Aldrich, September 30, 1947

WORLD WAR II HAD NOT JUST REVITALIZED THE AMERICAN ECONOMY; IT HAD resuscitated the reputation of the banker as a public servant, a partner of the president, a defender of America. The bankers, through more unifying speeches and less ostentatious styles, had demonstrated their desire to support the war—and the peace—effort beyond simple financing. The result of this shift was their ability to influence global finance in a much broader way than their predecessors had, with less scrutiny.

On July 2, 1946, Truman told Chase chairman Winthrop Aldrich that he looked to him as chairman of the Committee for Financing Foreign Trade to organize the work of its members.[2] It was a critical component of the White

House agenda. Truman had written each member personally to say that "the conduct and financing of foreign trade should be handled by private industry with the cooperation and such assistance as is necessary from the proper Government agencies."

Truman had positioned himself as playing backup to private industry and the bankers as far as foreign economic policy was concerned. This was exactly what Aldrich had wanted; a supportive government that gave private bankers latitude. But Truman didn't leave matters fully up to Aldrich. Instead, he asked each committee member to draft a report on problems concerning foreign trade and to provide recommendations for handling them to the National Advisory Council, which would prepare a definite plan of procedure.[3]

Two and a half months later, the twelve-man committee (which included Bank of America head A. P. Giannini and National City Bank chairman Gordon Rentschler) gathered in Washington for their first official meeting with the president.[4] These would become frequent occurrences as America's global role was mapped out.

Truman grew to trust Aldrich, much as Wilson had grown to trust Morgan's Thomas Lamont after World War I. For his part, Aldrich became a leading figure in organizing financial relief to Europe during and after World War II, with great influence over the direction of the IMF. As Lamont had been extremely vocal about the need for Wilson's League of Nations, Aldrich was the banker most publicly supportive of the Marshall Plan, which spelled out how the United States would aid foreign nations. As it would turn out, he added ideas of his own to benefit private industry and banking.

During the postwar phase of the late 1940s, Aldrich traveled the world in a triple capacity: as chairman of the Chase bank, president of the International Chamber of Commerce, and chairman of the Committee for Financing Foreign Trade. The impact on the bank's bottom line was substantial. In 1946, Chase reported, "The volume of business handled in all divisions of the foreign department increased enormously."[5] Chase commercial loans in London doubled that year. Aldrich's dual work as public servant and private banker was reaping rewards for his firm, and for his status as a diplomat. His partnership with Truman assured him of both.

Truman's Treasury Secretary and Postwar Savings Bonds

Another aspect of the banking-government alliance was the makeup of public debt, which had quintupled during the war and totaled $270 billion on June 30, 1946. Between war defense and finance programs, government obligations represented 60 percent of all outstanding debts, public and private, compared to less than 25 percent in 1939. Commercial banks held $84.5 billion, or about one-third of the US debt securities, representing 71 percent of their total assets.[6] War financing replenished the banking system's assets and offered it a foundation of securities upon which to expand.

Though he was not of the eastern bankers' ilk, Truman's Treasury secretary, John Snyder, was still quite familiar with the world of banking. He had served as vice president at First National Bank of St. Louis, Missouri, for a couple of years before joining the Truman administration.[7] Snyder would take a lead role as the communication point between Truman and the bankers through the late 1940s.

As "one of Truman's closest advisors on not only financial matters, but also general domestic and foreign policy issues," according to the Treasury Department and Federal Reserve, Snyder was "often the last person to whom Truman spoke before he made final decisions."[8]

Snyder was a banker's perfect Treasury secretary, comfortable on both sides of the political aisle. As he later said, "I like many of the Democratic aims and objectives. I was brought up a Democrat. Of course, my private business associations have been largely with Republicans. The officers in the banks that I've associated with have been largely Republicans."[9]

Bankers eagerly advised Snyder on issues of postwar debt management, "selecting the right kind of securities to offer to the public," and various tax matters. But Snyder tended to rely more on bankers hailing from outside the New York area. Among his most trusted confidants in the banking industry were A. P. Giannini and his son, Mario.[10]

When it came time to reconsider the postwar savings bond program, Snyder enlisted the Gianninis' advice. He needed a new way to entice the population to buy bonds and realized that an appeal based on a patriotic act would no longer do. This was potentially a big problem: the government still had its own debt to pay down, and turning to citizens for financing needs had proven quite useful during the war. Snyder now needed the bankers to collaborate with him to "sell the idea that savings was good for the individual to prepare him to buy the things that he might otherwise miss buying: an education for his children, a new house, maybe an automobile in the future . . . an economic purpose, a standard of living purpose."[11] The more people saved, went his reasoning, the more they would consider investing in things like bonds.

Thus, Snyder played a key role in fashioning the acceptability of debt to fund the pent-up needs and desires of postwar America. The bankers did their share to provide the credit to support that way of life, appealing to the public to both save and borrow. The Federal Reserve played its part, too. The Fed had accommodated the war by maintaining the low interest rates that fueled private banks' ability to lend to manufacturing companies.[12] From 1937 to 1947, the Fed kept its "rediscount rate," enjoyed by commercial banks borrowing cash against Treasuries, at 1 percent.

During the war, there was widespread bipartisan support for rising deficits and taking on additional debt to fund the war. But afterward, the Truman administration continued to favor lower interest rates as a means of economic stimulus, while the Fed wanted to raise them to fight inflation.

Aldrich Supports the Marshall Plan

For Truman, navigating postwar peace less than a decade after the Great Depression without economic fallout would prove challenging.

The World Bank and the IMF had been shaped at Bretton Woods and then refined by Congress with input from the private banking community. Another pillar of global reconstructive and foreign policy efforts, the Marshall Plan, would provide further aide to "friendly" countries in the early years of the Cold War. The plan would also establish the bedrock upon which the nation's premier bankers would propel their international lending and other foreign businesses.

Truman carefully unveiled the Marshall Plan in the spring of 1947. To foster public support, he played it up as a way to counter the threat of Communism. He warned the nation that Europe was disintegrating economically, and said he feared that Greece and Turkey would come under Communist control. In addition, the Communist Party had become the biggest left-wing party in France and Italy. America's new perceived enemy was not Germany or the Nazis but the doctrine of Communism, which was manifesting itself more broadly in the postwar era. Recall Aldrich's speech associating capitalism with democracy, linking bankers' goals with American foreign policy ones. Communism was opposed to capitalism, and as such it stood in the way of American prosperity.

Truman's concerns directly led to the Truman Doctrine, a foreign policy initiative by which the United States agreed to support Greece and Turkey economically and militarily to keep them from falling prey to Soviet expansion. The Truman Doctrine became the cornerstone of the more expansive Marshall Plan, which divided the non-Communist and Communist allies for the purposes of apportioning economic aid.

In a speech at Harvard on June 5, 1947, Secretary of State George Marshall, a retired general, announced the US-led economic assistance program that the Europeans would administer on the western side of the Iron Curtain. Congress approved $13 billion to reconstruct Western Europe for two reasons: first, to aid Europe's fight against Communism; and second, to bolster trading partners for American industry and banks.

Additionally, as more currencies became readily available to be converted to the dollar, it would become easier to solve the problem of dollar scarcity without new restrictions, which would be "disastrous both for the United States and for the people of Europe." The more dollars in the world, the fewer barriers to foreign trade. The Marshall Plan wasn't just about helping allies; it was also about ensuring the domination of the dollar, a plan supported by President Truman and the bankers.[13] The theme of Communism vs. American democracy would be the selling point to the broader population.

Even before the Marshall Plan was approved, banks had begun negotiating private postwar loans to allied countries. In 1945, Chase became the first big bank to start the process with a loan to the Netherlands. The firm continued lending money to France alongside the Morgan Bank. Giannini flew to the country of his forebears, Italy, to extend credit to Italian banks. These divisions enabled banks to profit in postwar reconstruction efforts along nationalist lines. The White House took note. "The President [Truman] and I are pleased," John Snyder, then head of the Office of War Mobilization and Reconversion, wrote Giannini. "I regard this type of action as a positive contribution to worldwide recovery."[14]

Aldrich's support for the Marshall Plan was solid from the start. Arriving in New York from England on July 1, 1947, he declared that it provided "new hope for the people of Europe."[15] To further establish the supremacy of private business in global affairs, Aldrich also sought to establish "a [nonpartisan] Government Corporation . . . as the United States Corporation for European Reconstitution . . . to encourage direct investment by American firms and corporations in the plants and industrial equipment of Western Europe."

Hence, Aldrich would combine the notions of political stability (lending to developing nations and fighting Communism, which often amounted to the same thing) and private direct investment. Big banks would be engaged in both efforts.

The Marshall Plan wouldn't just help distribute financial aid; it would give each major US bank its own European country to play in. Chase would beat them. From 1948 to 1952, the bank amassed the biggest commitments to

Europe, at nearly $1 billion, followed closely by National City Bank. The Bank of America, with its focus on Italy, stood in sixth place, with $389 million.[16]

The Marshall Plan delivered a bevy of new opportunities for US banks in Europe. But it also enabled major European banks to spring back to life through incoming funds and associated US political relationships, though at first in the shadows of their American counterparts. Again, it was Aldrich who put the situation into perspective. President Coolidge had said that "the business of America is business," but to Aldrich the business of the world was business, and it was there for the American banker to take.

The mass-circulation *Life* magazine put its weight behind the Marshall Plan by underscoring the need to fight Communists:

> Last week in Paris, the 16 nations that responded to Secretary of State George C. Marshall's plea for a concrete European recovery plan put their reports in a green manila folder, bounded up with a ribbon of shocking pink and sent it to Washington. The Europeans said they needed $22.4 billion worth of goods and dollars in the next four years. . . . Whether the US Congress and the American people were prepared for the sacrifices such a program would entail was far from clear. . . . [But] Paris, LIFE correspondent Charles Wertenbaker cabled, "if no new credits are allowed, France will be virtually bankrupt in 3 weeks. No American aid would mean big communist gains."[17]

In late 1947, Chase extended its German and Japanese branches, becoming the first US bank invited to expand in postwar Germany. (National City and Bank of America made it to Japan first, mostly to service US military bases.)

The National Advisory Council and the Rise of John McCloy

As important as his Treasury secretary post was in shaping economic policy, Snyder held an even more critical position in foreign financial policy as the first chairman of the less-known but powerful National Advisory Council, the entity that called the shots for the World Bank and IMF.

Congress had established the council to be the "coordinating agency for United States international financial policy" and as a mechanism to direct that policy through the international financial organizations. In particular, the council dealt with the settlement of lend-lease and other wartime arrangements, including the terms of foreign loans, details of assistance programs, and the evolving policies of the IMF and World Bank.[18] Snyder carried a vast amount of influence over those entities, as many major decisions were discussed privately at the council meetings and decided upon there.

There was one ambitious lawyer who understood the significance of Snyder's role. That was John McCloy, an outspoken Republican whose career would traverse many public service and private roles (including the chairmanship of Chase in the 1950s), and who had just served as assistant secretary of war under FDR's war secretary, Henry Stimson. McCloy and Snyder would form an alliance that would alter the way the World Bank operated, and the influence that private bankers would have over it.

It was Snyder who made the final decision to appoint McCloy as head of the World Bank. McCloy, a stocky Irishman with steely eyes, had been raised by his mother in Philadelphia. He went on to become the most influential banker of the mid-twentieth century. He had been a partner at Cravath, Henderson, and de Gersdorff, a powerful Wall Street law firm, for a decade before he was tapped to enter FDR's advisory circle.

After the war, McCloy returned to his old law firm, but his public service didn't translate into the career trajectory that he had hoped for. Letting his impatience be known, he received many offers elsewhere, including an ambassadorship to Moscow; the presidency of his alma mater, Amherst College; and the presidency of Standard Oil. At that point, none other than Nelson Rockefeller swooped in with an enticing proposition that would allow McCloy to stay in New York and get paid well—as a partner at the family's law firm, Milbank, Tweed, Hope, and Hadley.[19]

The job brought McCloy the status he sought. He began a new stage of his private career at Milbank, Tweed on January 1, 1946. The firm's most important client was Chase, the Rockefeller's family bank. But McCloy would soon return to Washington.

Truman had appointed Eugene Meyer, the seventy-year-old veteran banker and publisher of the *Washington Post,* to be the first head of the World Bank. But after just six months, Meyer abruptly announced his resignation on December 4, 1946.[20] Officially, he explained he had only intended to be there for the kick-off. But privately, he admitted that his disagreements with the other directors' more liberal views about lending had made things untenable for him. His position remained vacant for three months.

When Snyder first approached McCloy for the role in January 1947, he rejected it. But Snyder was adamant. After inviting McCloy to Washington for several meetings and traveling to New York to discuss how to accommodate his stipulations about the job—conditions that included more control over the direction of the World Bank and the right to appoint two of his friends—Snyder agreed to his terms.

Not only did Snyder approve of McCloy's colleagues, but he also approved McCloy's condition that World Bank bonds would be sold through Wall Street banks. This seemingly minor acquiescence would forever transform the World Bank into a securities vending machine for private banks that would profit from distributing these bonds globally and augment World Bank loans with their private ones. McCloy had effectively privatized the World Bank. The bankers would decide which bonds they could sell, which meant they would have control over which countries the World Bank would support, and for what amounts.

With that deal made, McCloy officially became president of the World Bank on March 17, 1947.[21] His Wall Street supporters, who wanted the World Bank to lean away from the liberal views of the New Dealers, were a powerful lot. They included Harold Stanley of Morgan Stanley; Baxter Johnson of Chemical Bank; W. Randolph Burgess, vice chairman of National City Bank; and George Whitney, president of J. P. Morgan.[22] McCloy delivered for all of them.

A compelling but overlooked aspect of McCloy's appointment reflected the postwar elitism of the body itself. The bank's lending program was based on a supply of funds from the countries enjoying surpluses, particularly those holding dollars. It so happened that "the only countries [with] dollars to spare [were] the United States and Canada." As a result, all loans made would largely stem from money raised by selling the World Bank's securities in the United States.[23]

This gave the United States the ultimate power by providing the most initial capital, and thus obtaining control over the future direction of World Bank financial initiatives—all directives for which would, in turn, be predicated on how bankers could distribute the bonds backing those loans to investors. The World Bank would do more to expand US banking globally than any other treaty, agreement, or entity that came before it.

To solidify private banking control, McCloy continued to emphasize that "a large part of the Bank capital be raised by the sale of securities to the investment public." McCloy's like-minded colleagues at the World Bank—vice president Robert Garner, vice president of General Foods and former treasurer of Guaranty Trust; and Chase vice president Eugene Black, who replaced the "liberal" US director Emilio Collado—concurred with the plan that would make the World Bank an extension of Wall Street. McCloy stressed Garner and Black's wide experience in the "distribution of securities."[24] In other words, they were skilled in the art of the sale, which meant getting private investors to back the whole enterprise.

The World Bank triumvirate was supported by other powerful men as well. After expressing his delight over their appointments to Snyder on March 1, 1947,[25] Nelson Rockefeller offered the three American directors his Georgetown mansion, plus drinks, food, and servants, for a three-month period while they hammered out strategies. No wives were allowed.[26] Neither were the other directors.[27] This was to be an exclusive rendezvous.

It is important to note here that the original plan as agreed upon at Bretton Woods did not include handing the management and organization of the World Bank over to Wall Street. But the new World Bankers seemed almost contemptuous of the more idealistic aspects of the original intent behind Bretton Woods, that quaint old notion of balancing economic benefits across nations for the betterment of the world. Armed with a flourish of media fanfare from the main newspapers, they set about constructing a bond-manufacturing machine.

With the Cold War hanging heavily in the political atmosphere, the World Bank also became a political mechanism to thwart Communism, with funding provided only to non-Communist countries. Politics drove loan decisions: Western allies got the most money and on the best terms.

McCloy's Return to Wall Street via Germany

By early 1948, World Bank loans had spread to Asia, Latin America, and various African countries. Within ten months, the media were declaring McCloy's World Bank initiative and its bonds an utter success. It was McCloy's particular view that Latin America should be more open to private investment. This view was widely shared by the banking community, the 1929 Crash of the region's bonds notwithstanding.

In a letter to Snyder on January 7, 1949, McCloy pressed the opening of Latin America in this manner: "I believe that both of our institutions should be more and more devoted to the flow of private capital into that area." Snyder approved of the progress that McCloy's Latin American loaning program was making.[28] With Snyder and McCloy's coordinated efforts, the doors of Latin America were pried open to allow a rush of private investment, which reduced the ability of the region to control its own economic destiny. These developments significantly extended America's political control over the region, propping up the dictators that toed the US line and punishing the ones who didn't by means of might and money.

In the background, the man who had penned the initial plan for the IMF, Harry White, was forced to resign from the IMF and dragged before the House Un-American Activities Committee in August 1948. Congressman Richard Nixon and others pelted him with questions about his alleged Communist loyalties. Three days after testifying, he died. He was fifty-five. The extent of his involvement with Soviet spy rings and his motivations have been a subject of debate in the history profession since his death, overshadowing the means by which his plans were augmented by the banker contingent.

The Economic Cooperation Administration

The Marshall Plan easily passed through Congress on April 3, 1948. Also called the Foreign Assistance Act of 1948 and the Economic Cooperation Act of 1948, it was approved by the Senate by a vote of 69 to 17 and passed the House by a vote of 329 to 74.[29]

Truman set up the Economic Cooperation Administration to oversee the Marshall Plan. In practice, it controlled many foreign economic activities, including trading patterns and international finance initiatives. Aldrich made it a point to throw his backing behind the entity. As a result, the correspondent banks came to Chase to service a large chunk of their international financing needs. He had again successfully steered the fortunes of Chase and public foreign policy concurrently.

As he expanded the Chase empire to support the foreign policy goals of the US government, Aldrich thought it only fair to obtain federal assurances of safety for Chase's private endeavors in return. So he requested that the Treasury Department back the risk Chase was taking in setting up private offices in war-torn countries.

On July 27, 1948, Snyder obtained support for Aldrich's request from Secretary of the Army Kenneth Royall, to whom he wrote, "The American Express Company, Inc., and the Chase National Bank have requested that the agreements executed by them be amended to exclude any liability for the loss under certain specified circumstances of . . . foreign funds lost, stolen, captured or destroyed by or because of enemy action. . . . The Treasury Department feels that the requests . . . are not unreasonable and is willing to enter into agreement with these two banks, and other banks similarly."[30]

The United States ultimately approved approximately $13 billion in aid during the four years that the Marshall Plan was active. At first, Europe's economy slowly improved, though it was unclear if that was related to the US monies. As far as the American people were concerned, though, the Marshall Plan was an anti-Communism device as marketed by Truman, the bankers, and the popular press. It was fear rather than altruism at work.

Truman's Four Points Plan

Though Truman employed antibanker rhetoric in his 1948 presidential election campaign, as most Democratic presidential candidates tended to do for political reasons, he maintained a balance between appearing prolabor and hard on Communism. With the exception of throwing some political capital at the Wall Street Seventeen—a case involving investment bank price rigging, which went on for years and was dismissed under the Eisenhower administration—Truman didn't get much in the way of the New York bankers. In fact, he brought those he deemed trustworthy into his cabinet or appointed them to committees.

Truman unveiled his "Four Points" plan during his 1949 inaugural address. The first point was support for the United Nations. The second was reiterating US determination to work for world recovery by giving full measure to the Marshall Plan in promoting trade for all the world's markets. The third point centered on the North Atlantic Security plan. He said, "We will strengthen freedom-loving nations against the dangers of aggression . . . within the recognized framework of the United Nations charter and in the pattern of the Western Hemisphere arrangement." In his fourth point, Truman proposed a program for sharing American scientific and industrial progress with the rest of the world.

McCloy, still smarting because he believed Marshall Plan financing might upend financing for the World Bank, expressed his frustration with Point Four to the *New York Times,* where he pouted that the World Bank "would simply have to take a back seat to Point Four aid in the developing world."[31]

For Aldrich, however, the Point Four program to begin technical assistance to underdeveloped countries was a gold mine. As a result of increased federal support, 1949 would become the most active year Chase's foreign department had ever experienced.[32]

In 1950, Truman appointed Aldrich's nephew, Nelson Rockefeller, to chair the International Development Advisory Board, the main task of which was the implementation of the Point Four program. In turn, Aldrich advised Truman fairly extensively on the Point Four program in war-torn Europe.[33]

Russell Leffingwell and
Morgan's Waning Influence

Thomas Lamont, who had run the Morgan Bank through much of the war, passed away quietly in his sleep at age seventy-seven in early February 1948.[34] His death marked the end of an era during which the Morgan Bank partners held the tightest alliances with the White House, even when presidents attacked bankers in their speeches. Lamont had negotiated war-related financing with America's allies and foes for three decades, sailing back and forth across the Atlantic dozens of times. He had stood before many congressional investigations and crossed party lines to support Democratic presidents and the ideals of internationalism, which he believed benefited the country, the presidency, and the bankers. After he died, leadership of the firm passed to longtime partner Russell Leffingwell.

A Washington insider from his days as President Wilson's assistant secretary of the Treasury during World War I, Leffingwell reigned as chairman of the Morgan Bank from 1948 to 1950 (after which he retired to a directorship position).[35] He was also chairman of the Council on Foreign Relations from 1946 to 1953, at a time when it actively promoted the Marshall Plan.

Leffingwell engaged with Truman on an array of issues, including on the tension between postwar domestic security and individual liberties. Both men believed that the Cold War was no excuse for monitoring the nation's citizens, which was becoming an abrasive issue in Congress. The libertarian in Leffingwell found the notion of undue government oversight of people's lives off-putting. In general, his method of subtle sway over the Truman administration was effective, particularly regarding matters of interest rate and debt policy—though not as overwhelming as the methods of the Chase and National City Bank influencers.

Leffingwell periodically took to the press to publicize his views. In October 1948, he penned a *Fortune* article in which he argued the Federal Reserve should "drop the peg," meaning it should discontinue its artificial support of long-term government bonds (through purchasing them, which also kept rates down). The article provided Treasury Secretary Snyder, who agreed with Leffingwell, ammunition against the Fed.[36]

After the war, a battle brewed between the Treasury Department and the Federal Reserve over how to deal with rates, inflation, and reserves. Snyder's views were in lockstep with those of the bankers; excess reserve requirements would hamper banks from lending and expanding. In an August 9, 1948, statement before the House Banking and Currency Committee, Snyder said, "After careful and deliberate consideration of the proposed increase of reserves that commercial banks must carry in the Federal Reserve banks; we are firmly of the opinion that such a move will bring about a credit panic."[37]

Leffingwell agreed: "The Federal Reserve and commercial banks' reserve requirement should not be increased."[38] A true internationalist, he was also of the opinion that trade barriers should be eased as much as possible to enable international business and financial activities to thrive. This was the same view that had been held by his predecessor at Morgan for decades.

When Truman won the 1948 presidential election, the Belgrade press, reading the fusion of the bankers and the presidency correctly, dubbed the election a battle between the candidates of J. P. Morgan & Company and the Chase National Bank, giving the victory to Morgan. (Thomas Dewey, who lost to Truman, was a close friend of Chase chairman Winthrop Aldrich, though of course Aldrich was very supportive of Truman and his postwar foreign financial policies.) Truman considered the distinction a joke, writing Leffingwell on November 22, 1948: "I was very much interested in the attached report from Belgrade to the effect that the recent election was a battle between J.P. Morgan & Company and the Chase National Bank. This is merely to congratulate you on the election of your candidate."[39]

Leffingwell responded in his typical deferential manner: "Your letter of the 22nd reached me this morning. I read it promptly to our officers' meeting and we all enjoyed a good laugh. A President with so human a touch makes everybody feel good. Though you were not my candidate, you are my President, and I pledge you my support and help, and that of my colleagues, in your great task."[40] In turn, Leffingwell had made a contribution to the Democratic Campaign Fund.[41]

This would be the beginning of a friendly relationship between the two men.

McCloy Leaves the World Bank

By 1949, the postwar economic recovery was waning. World exchange rates reflected this. Britain devalued the pound from $4.03 (the 1946 rate) to $2.80. Other countries followed suit. The US economy experienced its first, albeit minor, postwar recession. Loan volume declined for the first time in three years, with business loans dropping by 19 percent.[42]

Around that time, McCloy's stint as president of the World Bank was coming to an end after two short years. Truman offered him the position of US high commissioner of Occupied Germany. (As assistant secretary of war,

McCloy had been situated in Germany in the spring of 1945, when Eisenhower's troops occupied 43 percent of the country.[43]) As he had done before accepting his World Bank post, McCloy gave Truman a list of requirements. Again, he asked for "a free hand in picking people" to assist him and an assurance that "no substantial decisions on Germany" would be made "without consultation with me."[44]

In addition, he demanded full authority over Economic Cooperation Administration monies dispensed in Germany and for Truman to name Eugene Black as his successor. The president agreed to his demands. Only then did McCloy send Truman a brief note accepting the job.[45]

When McCloy officially resigned from the World Bank on June 30, 1949, Snyder didn't miss a beat. He wrote Black, "I know that under your leadership the successful administration of the Bank will continue" and that "regarding matters relating to international financial programs you may be assured that at all times the Treasury will be glad to assist you in any way it can."[46]

In his new capacity, McCloy worked on the creation of the West German state from 1949 to 1952. In 1951, he controversially reduced the sentences on convicted Nazi war criminals (about which many in Europe and the United States were extremely upset).[47] McCloy retained a characteristically independent style in Germany, sending Truman reports rather than engaging in regular dialogue. Overseeing the development of Germany was one of McCloy's favorite roles, perhaps more interesting to him than running the Chase Bank, which he did afterward (though budding Middle East relationships would eventually fulfill his capacities for juxtaposing his public and private roles).

After four years in Germany, McCloy returned to New York City. In 1953, when Aldrich was nominated by Eisenhower to become ambassador to Britain, Aldrich chose McCloy to assume his slot as Chase chairman.

Old to New Guard

Three influential men stood in the wings of the 1940s. They wouldn't emerge into the national consciousness until the 1960s, but nonetheless they were beginning their political and financial ascent. The first was John F. Kennedy, who ran for Congress for the first time in 1946 and won.

The second was David Rockefeller, whom Aldrich recruited to join Chase in 1946. Rockefeller had spent the summer of 1937 with the Chase economics department, and as a student at the London School of Economics he had devoted half a day each week as a trainee at the London branch of Chase. While traveling through Europe in 1945, Aldrich met Rockefeller in Paris and suggested that he join the bank. Rockefeller started his Chase career as an assistant manager in the foreign department.[48]

The third man was Walter Wriston, son of Henry Wriston, a conservative former president of Brown University and a friend of W. Randolph Burgess. Burgess enticed Walter to work at National City Bank in 1946.

American power unfolds more like a monarchy than a meritocracy. There are no accidents in global influence, no surprise emergences. All three young men harnessed family connections on their way to leading the country and its two biggest banks, respectively. The views of these men at the time were more alike than they would be perceived to be in later years. Before he turned more liberal on the national stage, Kennedy was critical of Truman's "soft" policy on Communism. Wriston and Rockefeller were both free-market advocates who harbored international ambitions, positions passed on by family patriarchs.

All three believed in America's right to global expansion and the necessity of an offensive stance as a way to fight the Cold War. Likewise, the Cold War would prove a convenient excuse for making money, as well as for political posturing. The sort of patriotism that had been associated with World War II would become associated with the war against Communism and its threats, real or fabricated. This fight would allow them to consolidate their roles in the epicenter of global finance.

NSC 68

The Cold War also dictated foreign policy and budget appropriations in the White House. On April 14, 1950, a top-secret report on US objectives and programs for national security—compiled by Truman's executive secretary, James Lay Jr., and the secretaries of state and defense—was distributed to the National Security Council, the Treasury secretary, the Economic Cooperation Administration, the director of the Bureau of the Budget, and the chairman of the Council of Economic Advisers.[49]

The report, dubbed NSC 68, opened the door for future wars against Communism, and also for the funding and financing that would come from the private bankers along those foreign policy lines. It concluded that "the gravest threat to the security of the United States within the foreseeable future stems from [the] formidable power of the U.S.S.R.," and that "the risk of war with the U.S.S.R. is sufficient to warrant, in common prudence, timely and adequate preparation by the United States."[50]

The threat, it said, "is of the same character as that described in NSC 20/4 [approved by Truman on November 24, 1948] but is more immediate than had previously been estimated. In particular, the United States now faces the contingency that within the next four or five years the Soviet Union will possess the military capability of delivering a surprise atomic attack of [considerable] weight."[51]

To mitigate that threat, the report suggested developing "a level of military readiness . . . as a deterrent to Soviet aggression . . . should war prove unavoidable."[52] As it said further, "Our position as the center of power in the free world places a heavy responsibility upon the United States for leadership."[53] Also, "We must, by means of a rapid and sustained build-up of the political, economic, and military strength of the free world, and by means of an affirmative program intended to wrest the initiative from the Soviet Union, confront it with convincing evidence of the determination and ability of the free world to frustrate the Kremlin design of a world dominated by its will."[54]

Bankers had a propensity to capitalize on wars, but they were equally adept at profiting from peace, especially if it could be backed by US military power and foreign policy initiatives that would augment and protect their financial expansion policies by fortifying "democratic" countries that could be their clients.

During the previous three and a half decades, the world had witnessed two major global wars, revolutions in Russia and China, and "the collapse of five empires—the Ottoman, Austro-Hungarian, German, Italian and Japanese," according to the NSC 68.[55] The report concluded that "the defeat of Germany and Japan and the decline of the British and French Empires have interacted with the development of the United States and the Soviet Union in such a way that power has gravitated to these two centers. . . . The Soviet Union . . . is animated by a new fanatic faith, antithetical to our own, and seeks to impose its absolute authority over the rest of the world."

Six months after the report was distributed, the United States entered the Korean War. In late 1950, Truman signed a letter to Secretary of State Dean Acheson saying that recent developments required review and adjustment of certain policies and programs with respect to "international communist imperialist aggression." Truman wanted to enlist the cooperation and support of other nations in carrying this out. To the extent that US legislation, organization, and funds permitted, Truman wanted all "appropriate programs now to be adjusted and administrated in light of [those] determinations."[56]

The Korean War would find the US population less financially supportive than it had been during World War II. Thus, bankers would turn toward mergers and credit extension to grow their domestic power base, while keeping their eyes on international financial developments and their feet in the corridors of Washington.

CHAPTER 10

THE 1950S: EISENHOWER'S BUDS, COLD WAR, HOT MONEY

"Recognizing economic health as an indispensable basis of military strength, and the free world's peace, we shall strive to foster everywhere, and to practice ourselves, policies that encourage productivity and profitable trade."

—Dwight D. Eisenhower, inaugural address, January 20, 1953

ON THE SURFACE, THE 1950S EMBODIED THE FAIRY-TALE ASPECT OF THE American Dream. As society emerged financially stable from the clouds of the Great Depression and World War II, the model suburban family with perfectly coiffed hair beamed smiles from the pages of *Life* magazine. Oodles of must-have gadgets offered jolts to the economy while Elvis Presley's hips mesmerized a generation of teenage girls.

President Eisenhower, the moderate Republican war hero, hugged the country's traumas away like a political grandfather. President Truman's mantra of "unity" and collective responsibility for the world gave way to Eisenhower's use of the popular 1920s Coolidge and Hoover mantra "prosperity." To attain more widespread wealth, the US population would pursue a brand of isolationism similar to that which followed World War I, but the White House would be more primed to international intervention, and Wall Street to open trade. Indeed, the doctrine of interventionism against the threat of spreading Communism, which could hamper America's emergence as a world superpower and US bankers' standing as the world's superfinanciers, suited both the White House and Wall Street. The Cold War became the glue binding presidents' desires to accumulate non-Communist allies like pins on a map and the bankers' desire to open up shop in the same countries backed by American military and foreign policy.

The United States was no longer involved in one world war. However, the drive to battle the Soviet Union militarily and economically paved the way for a fresh set of regional wars for ideological and global control. The battle of capitalism vs. Communism manifested in the Korean War in the early 1950s and in other forms of aggression later in the decade, like Lebanon in 1958. Moreover, "containment" (as the Council on Foreign Relations dubbed it) of the "domino effect" (as Eisenhower dubbed it) of Communism provided the impetus to carve up the parts of the world that hadn't been involved in World War II, like the Middle East and Latin America, into American democratic capitalism and Soviet Communism camps.

From a domestic economic policy standpoint, Eisenhower supported many of the elements of FDR's New Deal, though his advisers held more conservative views on that score. When mild recessions surfaced in the United States intermittently in the 1950s, he thwarted them by utilizing government funding for initiatives like the construction of the nation's superhighways— the largest public works program in US history, which also helped the auto industry, stoked pent-up consumer demand, reaped bank loans to finance new car purchases, and provided profits to oil companies supplying gasoline.

During the 1950s, Americans enjoyed a decade of domestic tranquility and growing middle-class security, to an extent that has not been experienced since then. In tandem, the bankers' concentrations were split between branching out internationally to regions and nations supported by the Eisenhower administration and its anti-Communist doctrine and merging domestically to consolidate more customer deposits and lend credit to more of the population. The atmosphere for doing this was perfect. More financially stable citizens gave the bigger banks more deposits and required more loans from them, fueling their domestic operations with capital to expand internationally in tandem with the president's policy to enhance American power abroad.

Truman, and to a far greater extent Eisenhower, used the Cold War as a reason to supply non-Communist allies with US economic and military aid, which also meant prying these countries open to US banks for financial activities. Attaching the double carrot of aid and loans (from the US government, the IMF and World Bank, and the private banks) to countries that embraced US political ideologies enabled the United States to maintain the global power position it had cultivated through two world wars, and enabled its bankers to expand into countries that were on the "right" side of the Communist divide—mostly in Latin America, where the United States could exert additional power as a neighbor and trade partner, and the Middle East, which became a Cold War battlefield saturated with oil and blood.

While Eisenhower spoke eloquently of helping allies, bankers saw dollar signs emanating from South America and the Middle East. Again, US policy and the expansion goals of the main bankers were aligned. Whereas Europe was emerging slowly from the war, and the Far East was rife with conflict, those two other regions became increasingly attractive to US bankers. The Middle East had oil. Latin America had a bevy of natural resources that could be extracted cheaply and transformed into great profits for US companies through financings that doubled as foreign trade policy initiatives.

As the US bankers and government were repositioning themselves throughout the globe, Americans' fortunes continued rising. The wartime economies and postwar inflation had given birth to a new normal of stability; the middle and poorer classes were enjoying the beginning of nearly two decades of income growth relative to the wealthy.[1] As the entire pie of corporate profits increased, so did the size of workers' slices, an unprecedented historical experience for the US labor force.

Yet the country's solidity rested on a tenuous base. New enemies had to be concocted to keep postwar industry humming along. Three recessions, McCarthyism, the Korean War, and the Cold War darkened the cheerful buzz. But the Cold War also united Americans against a common enemy, and propelled them to purchase American goods as consumption became the new mode of patriotism.

US bankers leveraged the expansion opportunities unleashed by the World Bank, IMF, and Marshall Plan decisions to lend to reconstructing or developing countries. They opened branches throughout the world, staking their claim against a strengthening European banking system beyond Europe. The US bankers possessed something their competitors in Britain and France (and later Germany and Switzerland) did not: a larger domestic population and set of companies from which to draw deposits, lend money, and raise capital—

plus, a fully aligned president who would augment their expansionism with US military might. They also turned inward to consolidate their domestic power. Bank mergers hit all-time highs as bankers acquired competitors in a sort of domestic financial war. As banks grew, they enticed the growing middle class with perks and charge plans and mutual funds, precursors to the credit cards and personal debt and speculation that would define the 1960s.

The unofficial policy of Truman and Eisenhower (and all presidents since then) was to stay out of the big bankers' way, even while Congress fought battles against them here and there. Both 1950s presidents knew that bigger and stronger US banks were crucial to supporting a stronger US military and economic position in the Cold War superpower hierarchy. The two pillars of American hegemony needed each other more than ever; their power and influence would be forever intertwined, as the Cold War transitioned both into a new realm of global dominance.

And so, the most influential American bankers would spend the 1950s plowing a transitioning domestic and international financial terrain, where depositors were becoming borrowers, savers were becoming spenders, and consumerism and reborn speculation were rising from the shadows of the Great Depression and World War II.

Aldrich—Onward to the Middle East and Latin America

As his opening 1950s gambit to expand his banks' influence, Chase chairman Winthrop Aldrich embarked upon the first Chase executive trip to the Middle East in the spring of 1950. It was not just a move exclusive to Chase, but to several major US banks, who were salivating over the potential of providing oil-related financing and banking services. But Aldrich still enjoyed the tightest banker connection to the Truman administration, so his ability to mingle policy and banking initiatives was more prominent, particularly in the Middle East.

While in the Middle East, Aldrich engaged in a whirlwind relationship-building tour, as he had done when he traveled through Latin America in 1947, meeting with rulers in Cairo, Jeddah, Dhahran, Kuwait City, Abadan, Tehran, Beirut, and Istanbul. The trip was the harbinger of a strong regional presence.[2] He was well aware of the profit potential of infiltrating such an oil-rich region, both to finance infrastructure projects and to facilitate American oil companies' access, particularly since relationships with former financial power Britain were strained.

As a result, Aldrich made it a point of fostering a warm connection with the Saudi Arabian Monetary Agency, the country's central bank, while also securing a personal one with its ruler, Ibn Saud. Though Aldrich couldn't get a direct banking presence in the country approved at the time, he did much to sow the seeds for more substantive engagements later.

The Korean War

While Aldrich was performing political-financial reconnaissance, the first major battle of the Cold War was heating up. After World War II, Korea had been split into a Soviet-backed government in the north (the Democratic People's Republic of Korea) and an American-backed government in the south (the Republic of Korea). On June 25, 1950, war broke out along the dividing thirty-eighth parallel.

In a statement on June 30, 1950, the White House said, "The President announced that he had authorized the United States Air Force to conduct missions on specific military targets in Northern Korea wherever militarily necessary."[3]

Since there was little appetite among the American population to finance another war by purchasing war or savings bonds, bankers sought other ways to capitalize on the situation. Instead, Truman wound up finding funding by increasing income, corporate, and excess profits taxes through the Revenue Acts of 1950 and 1951 and the Excess Profits Act of 1950.[4]

On July 6, 1950, Aldrich returned from overseas and headed straight to Washington to convene with Truman. There, he told White House reporters that "the world at large is unsettled. I don't think that under the situation there will be much foreign investment at the present time."[5] What he meant was that with the Cold War escalating and the Korean War beginning, it might be difficult to ascertain which countries were ripe for expansion. Such opportunities would have to be seized more carefully and in tighter conjunction with government policy.

Aldrich and the rest of the bankers knew they would have to penetrate areas the United States could dominate from a political and military perspective, and along the lines of the Truman Doctrine and Marshall Plan. Equally, the US government would provide safe passage and support for its bankers to develop stronger financing and trading relationships in those countries, which in turn could be leveraged for political or military purposes.

The Korean War fueled an economic and banking system recovery in Western Europe, but to a lesser extent than the two prior world wars had done for the United States. The nature of US aid soon shifted from funding reconstruction efforts to financing new military ones. In 1950 and 1951 industrial production in Europe leapt to 30–40 percent above prewar levels.

Foreign trade blossomed for the United States as civilian and war-related demand rose. As a result, US banks witnessed a marked increase in commercial loans; Chase's business reached a new peak in 1950 and climbed another 40 percent by 1951. Foreign bank deposits in US banks also hit historic highs, and as a result Chase began to supplant the premier political-financial space formerly held by the Morgan Bank, supplying and comanaging loans to governments like France and the Netherlands.

Yet Chase's branch expansion in Europe was relatively subdued; its London offices were losing money, as were those of its main rival, National City Bank. In contrast, the Caribbean and Latin America, and then the Middle East regions, beckoned. While his boss was focused on the Middle East, Chase senior vice president David Rockefeller made it his mission to open branches across Latin America, competing with the bankers at National City Bank who had staked their claims on the area.

By early 1951 Rockefeller had opened four branches in the Caribbean. His motto was that Chase didn't just exist to serve US customers; it was also interested in developing local economies with particular regional strengths. The countries he selected matched the US government's policy of aiding its political friends.

As those local political-financial relationships grew, they exacted a steep price from the local economies: indebtedness to US banks, forced privatization, and access to multinational companies and international investors seeking raw materials. The opening of US bank branches underscored a trend that was less about aid and more about control and external appropriation of resources and profits.

As for its domestic position, in the early 1950s most of Chase's core deposit and loan business still came from major corporate clients, although it began to increase its individual customer business, à la National City Bank, as checking and savings accounts began bulging in tandem with rising incomes. The part of the bank that grew the most during the 1950s, though, remained Chase's trade-related and international business. It served lingering war-related reconstruction efforts and benefited from more stable currency and trade activities in formerly war-torn countries.

On May 15, 1951, Truman helped US bankers enhance that war-related business by signing a bill enabling the financing of defense contracts by private banks. He believed it was "important to encourage private financial institutions to make loans for defense production."[6] Bringing US banks into the fold, as they had been during World War II, would help fund the Cold War.

That was certainly sweet for the larger New York banks that were already active in defense, and whose 1950 profits had already eclipsed historic highs before this additional official gift. US commercial banks earned a record $937 million net profit in 1950, an increase of 13 percent over 1949, mostly because of income from Cold War–related lending.

1952: Eisenhower's Bankers

In 1952, General Eisenhower was commander of the North Atlantic Treaty Organization, a new military alliance established between the United States, Canada, and leading Western European powers to deter Soviet expansion, thwart the rise of nationalist militarism in Europe with a strong US military presence, and promote European political integration. For Eisenhower NATO was "a necessary mechanism." It was intended to blend military, political, and economic stability. According to the treaty's Article 5, "an armed attack against one or more of [the allied countries] shall be considered an attack against them all" and would beget an appropriate response. Even with the Soviet threat, Eisenhower believed, "the knowledge that a unified, progressive effort to mobilize and generate strength was under way had an almost electrifying effect on European thinking."[7]

Strong sentiment that Eisenhower had excellent presidential qualities was building back home. Truman apparently had made overtures to him in 1951, suggesting he would make a strong Democratic candidate in 1952. Eisenhower rebuffed him.

In the spring of 1952 Aldrich traveled to Europe with a small entourage of powerful business leaders to persuade Eisenhower to run for president on the Republican ticket. But Aldrich wasn't the only banker backing Eisenhower after Truman decided not to run. The self-described "Independent Democrat" and "practical liberal" Goldman Sachs chief Sidney Weinberg shifted his political allegiance and helped form the Citizens for Eisenhower Committee, which raised $1.7 million for Eisenhower's campaign. He endeared himself to Ike in the process.[8]

Weinberg's connections aside, Goldman did not approach its zenith of influence in the scheme of alliances between key bankers and presidents until the 1980s, when the firm lobbied behind the scenes for laxer commodities trading rules, and in the 1990s and beyond, when it stretched into the heights of political-financial influence in the Treasury secretary post on both sides of the aisle through Democrat Robert Rubin and Republican Henry Paulson. Revisionist history makes it seem as if the firm was always as influential as it came to be, but really Weinberg was an anomaly for decades, a true operator and connector. It wasn't until Lyndon Johnson's Treasury secretary, Henry Fowler, who was a friend of Weinberg's, left Washington to go to Goldman Sachs that this new chain of power relationships between the firm and DC truly began.

As William D. Cohan, author of *Money and Power,* put it, "Under Eisenhower, Weinberg could have been anyone in Washington."[9] But Weinberg preferred to influence Washington from the outside. (His only official public posts were as assistant director of the War Production Board during World War II and briefly as a special assistant in the Office of Defense Mobility during the Korean War.[10])

Still, Weinberg served as a significant point man offering endorsements to people who wanted to join Ike's administration. Letters came to him from everywhere asking for his blessings. On March 3, 1953, he endorsed Harry Dunn for chairmanship of the SEC.[11] On April 17, 1953, Weinberg recommended Paul Felix Warburg for "some position in a small Embassy." The following week, he endorsed Earl Jay Gratz for judge of the Eastern District of Pennsylvania. And so it went.

Occasionally, Weinberg would get involved in specific issues. In February 1954 he wired former New Hampshire governor Sherman Adams (Eisenhower's second chief of staff) to inform him that the Democrats were spreading the "fear deal" (as opposed to the New Deal), using Adams's coined phrase to Adams's delight. But usually, there was an element of political recruitment involved, as when Weinberg combined his support for the Road Committee (charged with carrying out the president's interstate highway system initiative) with suggestions as to how to populate it in mid-1954. More letters came to Weinberg soliciting his opinion than he ever answered.

Ike's Victory

Eisenhower handily won the 1952 election, backed by both Republican and Democratic bankers. His messages of peace interlaced with Cold War warnings also provided bankers the perfect angle from which to further engage the population in their services. This time, banks wouldn't have to count on wartime patriotism to sell bonds; they could extend credit to Americans for all the things they had been denied during war.

Most accounts of President Eisenhower, including his own ample collections, emphasize his status as a war hero, his farewell warning about the dangers of the military-industrial complex, and his superhighway initiative. There are poignant moments in his diaries where he feared growing older and less important. Perhaps he felt that the extensive advisers he surrounded himself with were calling more shots than he was.

A moderate conservative (in today's terms he might even be considered a conservative democrat with libertarian leanings), Eisenhower was opposed to US debt increases (many of his aides were debt hawks) and government intervention in the private lives of citizens, yet he acknowledged the periodic necessity of both.

On the foreign front, Eisenhower deposed the leaders of Iran and Guatemala, ended the Korean War by threatening an atomic bomb attack, and shunned the idea of too overt an association with Britain before, and after, the Suez Canal crisis.

From an alliance standpoint, Ike was a president who "belonged" to Wall Street in policy and personal ways. Truman's personality and background didn't lend itself as well to trust or interconnectivity with the wealthy elite. But Eisenhower, with his gregarious and commanding demeanor, coveted the counsel and company of bankers, as well as the leading industrialists upon whose boards they sat. Perusing hundreds of his letters and diary entries, it's clear that Ike really liked them. He relied on their opinions more directly for counsel on his economic and domestic policies than any other president had during the first half of the century.

In return, the bankers found in him a staunch buddy, a chief commander they golfed with and engaged in conversations about changing times, sharing war stories and discussing the bright horizons beckoning America as the world's sole superpower.

Eisenhower's Wall Street Ties

At the advice of Sidney Weinberg and General Lucius Clay, who had worked with Weinberg on German reconstruction plans, Eisenhower appointed George Humphrey, former president of the Cleveland-based steel company M. A. Hanna and an industrialist fan of free-market doctrine, as his Treasury secretary. (Humphrey would return to M. A. Hanna afterward.)

In December 1952, following discussions with Humphrey aboard the cruiser *Helena* during his return trip from Korea, Eisenhower named three other men to round out the Treasury Department.[12] W. Randolph Burgess, chairman of the executive committee at National City Bank, would be special deputy on monetary and debt management policies; Marion Folsom, treasurer of the Eastman Kodak company, would be undersecretary with a focus on tax policies; and H. Chapman Rose, counsel for M. A. Hanna, would be assistant Treasury secretary.

Both Folsom and Burgess, who considered a balanced national budget "the most sacred principle of sound money" and favored more independence for the Federal Reserve, supported the idea of a foreign policy centered on trade rather than aid. Trade was profitable; aid was too socialistic.

Burgess's responsibilities in public office were similar to the ones he had in the private sector, but in a more influential sphere: he oversaw Treasury financing and foreign operations, and made decisions about IMF activities.[13]

However, Eisenhower's most trusted economic adviser was not his Treasury secretary; it was Gabriel Hauge, a young economist who would shape US policy behind the scenes for six years before leaving to become a senior executive at the Manufacturers Trust Bank. (Established in 1905, it would later become one of the legacy banks that would comprise JPMorgan Chase.)

Ike's Right-Hand Economist-Banker

Hauge filled in the president's "uneven" knowledge of economics, as he called it. The two also got along well. "I remember he always used to refer to me as 'Dr. Hauge' or 'Hauge,'" he later recalled, "until one day he referred to me as 'Gabe' in a meeting. Then I knew we were all right."[14]

A slightly jowly man with slicked-back black hair and light rimmed glasses, Hauge was born in Hawley, Minnesota, in 1914, son of a pastor at the local Lutheran church. After receiving his MA and PhD at Harvard, he became a prominent economics professor at Harvard and Princeton. From there he (like Burgess) became a senior statistician at the Federal Reserve Bank of New York. He joined Citizens for Eisenhower in November 1951.

Hauge served as Ike's lead speechwriter during the 1952 campaign, and as his main economic adviser from 1953 to 1958. It was not just in economic policy but also in the perfect articulation of the messages behind it that Hauge's influence shone. He was dogmatic about crafting, and measuring responses to, Ike's statements: a skilled spinmaster.

For instance, in a June 22, 1953, memorandum to Eisenhower, he noted negative press reaction to Ike's informal remarks about "creeping socialism" regarding FDR's Tennessee Valley Authority. Hauge suggested the terms "creeping centralization" or "creeping big government" instead.[15] Though he technically served on the personal staff of the president and didn't hold an official public post, Hauge's free-market opinions would populate many of Eisenhower's domestic policy speeches.[16]

Ike's banker sphere also included his secretary of war, Thomas Gates, who would later chair the Morgan Guaranty Bank. The circle encompassed the globally minded Chase chairman Winthrop Aldrich, who would become Ike's ambassador to Britain, and the ubiquitous power broker John McCloy, who spent the Eisenhower years as chairman of Chase National Bank. McCloy had met Ike during World War II while serving as assistant secretary of war and as one of Secretary of War Henry Stimson's six "wise men." He and the president shared a fascination with puddle jumper planes.[17]

Ike's more domestically oriented Wall Street friends included Weinberg, who served as his behind-the-scenes headhunter but influenced little policy, and Morgan head George Whitney, who shared his populist opinions and golf club lifestyle. Rounding out the mix was Whitney's successor, Henry Alexander, who presided over a mega-merger in 1959, recapturing the wilted power of the House of Morgan.[18]

These men, by virtue of their positions and ambitions, were more a part of Ike's presidency and America's legacy than any other official cabinet member. All of them would use the Cold War backdrop to usher in a policy of American freedoms, which in the heart of America meant free markets and a free banking system. This would translate to initial campaigns to reduce regulations and enable mega-mergers that fostered greater consolidation and thus decreased competition. Whereas competition was the theoretical cornerstone of the notion of "free markets," these moves would foster the opposite: markets that were not free but that merely benefited the larger players.

George Whitney, Ike's Progressive Banker

George Whitney counterbalanced the more conservative approaches of Ike's Treasury Department and economic advisers. After nearly two decades at J. P. Morgan, he succeeded Leffingwell as chairman and served from 1955 to 1959. Like Weinberg and Aldrich, he played a major part in helping to finance Eisenhower's campaign. He also had a warm personal relationship with Ike and served as his close unofficial adviser on a variety of issues.

Whenever he requested one, Whitney received an appointment with Eisenhower. He helped balance Eisenhower's economic thinking relative to his more right-wing advisers. Whitney's opinions were unique; he was one of the few bankers advocating for policies to strengthen the middle class, even if the upper class was sacrificed in the process.

For example, while Hauge opposed cost-of-living increases for workers, Whitney advocated an equalization policy for the lower class. Whitney expressed as much to Ike in a private letter penned on January 19, 1954. At the time employment figures were dipping, and there were calls emanating from the business community to balance the budget and reduce corporate taxes. Whitney wanted to help the nonrich, ignore the deficit, keep corporate taxes where they were, and support the nation's workers. His thoughts reflected Eisenhower's, and Eisenhower was grateful for his perspective, which weaved its way back to the president's advisers.

"It is not now the time to balance the budget," wrote Whitney. "I couldn't agree more that the further reduction in corporate taxes and excise taxes are not proper in principle and certainly not unless something is done in the income taxes of those in the lower economic brackets. That is the greatest shot in the arm to the economy because it puts the spending money in the hands of those who spend it. $75 in the hands of a $4,000 a year man is a lot of money when multiplied by some 50 million families." He concluded, "The economic welfare of the whole country is still more important and the best way to stabilize it is to increase the spendable income of the lower tax brackets."[19]

Whitney appealed to Eisenhower's more public-spirited views. His brand of populist considerations also snaked its way into certain bankers' views during the administration of Lyndon B. Johnson in the 1960s, but afterward it became a relic of a bygone postwar, post-Depression era, as bulging paychecks trumped self-sacrifice.

The End of the Korean War

In a June 10, 1953, statement, Eisenhower made it clear that US military isolationism was not an option. This enabled him to invoke US military intervention against Communism while promoting free trade, which entailed international financing and helped the bankers' expansion plans. Two days later, in his role as British ambassador, Aldrich endorsed Eisenhower's two-way trade program at a dedication of the Aldrich (in honor of his father, Fed founder Nelson Aldrich) and Kresge Halls at his alma mater, Harvard University. He pressed for immediate support for Eisenhower's proposed program of "healthy two-way trade" with other nations, calling it vital to the political and security interests of the United States and the free world. He also stressed the importance of increasing US imports and admonished the "archaic" policy of purchasing goods abroad only in "exceptional cases." Absent extenuating circumstances, he recommended that the US make its public purchases "wherever goods of comparable quality can be found on competitive and advantageous terms."[20]

Thus, Aldrich also served as an ambassador for globalized "free trade," which in practice meant the removal of barriers around commodity-rich nations. His old colleagues at Chase were translating this into a business strategy that involved finding nations where cheap goods or raw commodities could be purchased and converted to products for external consumption and profit. These nations tended to be located in Latin America. The idea of prying open local markets into which new bank offices or branches could situate themselves dovetailed nicely with Eisenhower's doctrine of increasing foreign trade with allies and non-Communist countries. The more countries that remained faithful to the US notion of democracy (equated with free-market capitalism), the more countries in which US bankers could operate.

Aldrich went so far as to claim that failure to initiate more open trade would be a political failure as well, undermining the prosperity of the United States and its allies. "The US learned by painful experience that it can afford neither political nor military isolationism," he stressed. Americans "now must learn that we cannot afford economic isolationism."

In that manner, Aldrich summarized the Cold War president-banker doctrine of political, military, and economic internationalism; all three elements coalesced to promote the export of American financial capitalism wrapped in a package called "free nations" with an added flourish of "free markets." The doctrine would result in a world divide that wasn't just between capitalism and Communism but also between the countries that produced cheap goods, like in Latin America, and the ones, like America and its major European allies, that exploited them.

Two weeks later, on July 27, 1953, Eisenhower ended the Korean War with the threat to drop another atomic bomb. The way he accomplished this left lingering bad feelings with British prime minister Winston Churchill because Churchill felt he had not been sufficiently consulted in the process. In a December 10, 1953, diary entry, Eisenhower was irritated by the Brit's emotional response. "[Secretary of State John] Foster Dulles explained the position in Korea," he wrote. "The only part of the discussion that led to opposition (this from Winston) was the assertion that in the event of renewed attack, we would feel free to use the atomic bomb against military targets."[21]

In general, Eisenhower didn't believe that America and Britain should be joined at the hip.[22] He regarded this method of the "joint ultimatum" as "self-defeating."[23] That prevailing attitude would lead to the Suez Canal crisis. It would also help catapult the United States above its former superpower ally, politically and from an international banking perspective.

John McCloy, the World's Most Powerful Banker

As mentioned, when Eisenhower won the presidential election in 1952, ending twenty years of Democratic control of the White House, he sought advice from a panel of bankers who supported his domestic and foreign trade policies of tight budgets and open markets.

Nearly simultaneously, transitioning from his Truman-appointed post as US high commissioner to Germany, Aldrich chose John McCloy to succeed him as Chase chairman for $150,000 per year plus benefits ($1.3 million in today's terms). McCloy remained chairman of the Board of Trustees at the Ford Foundation and became chairman of the highly influential Council on Foreign Relations concurrently. Coupled with his tight relationship with Eisenhower and connection to the World Bank through his former friend and colleague Eugene Black, McCloy became the most influential banker in the world.

Most of McCloy's public service roles had been under Democratic presidents, though he considered himself a classic Republican. Generally, during Republican presidencies, he'd worked in the private sector. He modestly downplayed his influence on Eisenhower. As McCloy put it, "He had his own advisors."[24] But McCloy would not hesitate to get in touch with Eisenhower when he needed, or wanted, to.

When Eisenhower became president, he considered McCloy for the secretary of state position, but instead offered him the subordinate position of undersecretary of state under John Foster Dulles, a man McCloy held in low regard. Adding insult to ego, it was Dulles, not Eisenhower, who approached him about the role.

Describing the incident, McCloy later explained, "Eisenhower . . . indicated that there had been more to it than just the Under Secretaryship for State, that it was really the Secretary of State he had in mind . . . because Dulles wanted to be relieved of the job of Secretary of State. . . . [As] I understood the proposal, Mr. Dulles was to still be the general advisor on foreign affairs although no longer Secretary of State. If I was going to be Secretary of State I wanted to be responsible for foreign policy. At any rate I indicated to him that that wouldn't have made any difference. . . . It was a flattering offer but it did not appeal to me."[25] McCloy had no interest in subordinating his foreign policy views to Dulles, whatever the capacity.

David Rockefeller's name was batted around the White House in consideration for assistant secretary for economic affairs, but Rockefeller decided to remain at Chase as senior vice president, where he focused on growing the firm's Latin American businesses.[26] His and McCloy's public post rejections portended a major transition of power alliances: Wall Street was becoming an increasingly more appealing platform for influence than a public post in Washington.

It took McCloy five months after starting at Chase to call the White House for an "important" meeting with Eisenhower. On May 18, 1953, they met regarding word McCloy had received about pending testimony before the Senate. Later that day, Eisenhower wrote his thoughts on Senator Joe McCarthy to Harris Bullis of General Mills: "With respect to McCarthy, I continue to believe that the President of the United States cannot afford to name names in opposing procedures, practices, and methods in our government . . . but, whether a Presidential 'crackdown' would better, or would actually worsen the situation, is a moot question."[27]

The topic would soon rear itself in a very public way. For in July 1953, McCloy was called before a Senate subcommittee investigating the Internal Security Act. The inquiry was based on a Jenner Committee report that accused the Army of being too tolerant of Communists during World War II, implying that McCloy was responsible. In February 1954, McCloy was subject to more direct attacks by Senator McCarthy regarding commissioning Communists to Army positions and having ordered the destruction of Army Intelligence files when he worked in the War Department. Eisenhower, who had at first stayed on the sidelines regarding McCarthy, became irate. As White House Press Secretary James Hagerty wrote in his diary on February 24, "Pres very mad and getting fed up . . . it's his army and he doesn't like McCarthy's tactics at all." McCarthy was operating too close to home for Eisenhower, who said, "This guy McCarthy is going to get into trouble over this. I'm not going to take this one lying down. He's ambitious. He wants to be president. He's the last guy in the world who'll ever get there, if I have anything to say."[28] The charge was dropped two days later.[29]

These incidents might have rendered McCloy more inclined to focus on his private-sector responsibilities, but they didn't serve to alienate him from his involvement with the Eisenhower administration. Thus, when Congress wanted to slash Eisenhower's appropriation requests for the Mutual Security Program, McCloy came through and explained the necessity of the program to Congress and the public. In June 1954, Eisenhower told Congress, "Our Mutual Security Program is based upon the sound premise that there can be no safety for any of us except in cooperative efforts to build and sustain the strength of all free peoples. Above all else communist strategy seeks to divide, to isolate, to weaken. . . . We have chosen to help develop and expand world markets, because we believe that this course will strengthen the economies of all free nations, including our own."[30]

The bankers' efforts were successful. As Ike wrote McCloy and the other bankers who supported him, "I am most grateful for your vigorous help. . . . Since you and others have taken steps to avoid a crippling appropriations cut, the action of the Subcommittee on Foreign Operations of the House Appropriations Committee has been twice postponed."[31] The bankers supported the Mutual Security Program largely because it was also a mutual government-banking alliance program. The better funded Eisenhower's military program, the more financially successful it would prove for the bankers as they expanded into the related countries.

McCloy's Foreign Banking Legacy

By mid-1954, following a brief and mild recession, US newspapers were singing Eisenhower's praises for allowing his advisers to steer his domestic policy to one of deregulation with respect to businesses. "Their [businessmen's] attitude and that of investors throughout the country," wrote the *New York World Telegram*, "is best expressed by the action of the stock market, which is currently at the highest levels in a generation."[32] In addition, by the fall of 1954, the unemployment rate had dropped to 4.8 percent, from a postwar peak of 7.6 percent in February 1950.

By late 1954, Chase's foreign loan department was booming. Despite being known for his fiscal prudence, McCloy had taken the opportunity to increase the bank's risk by lowering the amount of cash reserves the bank held against the loans it extended. Combining this more speculative lending with his shaping of international private banking policy, McCloy led a precedent-setting deal. With the US Treasury and IMF as partners, Chase extended a $30 million loan to the Peruvian government. The twist was that there was no collateral from Peru; instead the deal forced Peru to adopt IMF-dictated austerity measures in return for loans.[33]

The Peru deal was the first of many instances since Bretton Woods where US banks, the US government, and the multinational agencies would cooperate to force developing countries into the American-dominated financial system in return for their economic and political concessions, through the extension of public or private loans, or a combination of both. The loan further cemented the role that Chase and other private banks would play in the supposed spirit of helping developing countries.

While at the World Bank, McCloy had consummated an agreement by which all loan proposals would require approval of the core "management" team, the elite American directors that he was friends with, as opposed to that of the broader board. This meant that he could more easily influence World Bank loans while at Chase. A stark example of that would occur when McCloy's friend and former colleague World Bank president Eugene Black enlisted McCloy's financial and advisory help with respect to the Aswan Dam in Egypt. Ultimately the incident had dire consequences beyond the control of either man.

The Inter-American Community

In April 1955, Eisenhower submitted another request for increased appropriations for the Mutual Security Program, including economic aid to "the free nations of South and East Asia." He considered US determination to fight Communism as "rooted in our own revolt against colonial status" and "exemplified by our encouragement of Cuba and the Philippines to assume full freedom and control of their own destiny as independent nations." He reiterated that America's foreign economic policy expresses the combined embrace of political, military, and economic security across all "free nations."[34] It was the conservative Republicans, in particular, who opposed the provision of foreign aid to other nations. Eisenhower's request unleashed another avalanche of banker moves to support him.

Three months later, his foreign policy initiatives were underscored by the Council on Foreign Relations's flagship journal, *Foreign Affairs*. In a July 1955 article, former assistant secretary of state Edward Miller Jr. wrote that "Latin America is changing with sensational rapidity." "As one country after another has become aware of the great progress and great wealth that the United States enjoys," he explained, "the people have come to demand for themselves, and for their countries as a whole, a greater share of the good things of life and a better place under the sun."[35]

Miller continued, "The economic contribution which we have made to the development of Latin America during the ten years following the end of World War II has been far greater than our prewar aid." But it was up to the United States to pick up the slack Britain, Germany, Italy, Japan, and France had left after World War II in terms of their critical economic roles as "suppliers and consumers of goods and as suppliers of capital."

The United States and Latin America had similar population sizes, yet the aggregate national income per year in the United States was "ten times as large as all 20 Latin American nations combined." He regarded the wealth disparity as a reason to strengthen economic ties to the region, an action that would be paired with anti-Communist rhetoric and US military support. The bankers and the White House embraced the notion of Latin America as a region desirous and needy of US support. Piling on debt and creating expensive financial arrangements between Latin American producers and US refiners of products was seen as beneficial to the region.

During the mid-1950s, US bankers were opening branches as fast as they could throughout Latin America. National City Bank had the edge over Chase in the region (except in Venezuela). In the Middle East, though, Chase was outpacing National City Bank, as we shall see.

McCloy's Merger Legacy

Domestically, the banking system was undergoing dramatic changes, having remained relatively static during the 1940s, when bankers put up a unified front to finance the war, and the 1930s, when speculative activity was restricted due to the Great Depression, the Glass-Steagall Act, and thousands of bank closures.

The growing trend of mergers and merger applications from the industry was not going unnoticed in Congress, where there was concern that the big banks (mostly in New York) would acquire smaller ones around the country for the sake of growing their deposit bases, which would hamper competition. According to a July 30, 1955, statement by North Dakota Republican senator Milton Young, the Federal Reserve reported that from 1953 to 1955, small and medium-sized locally owned banks were going out of existence through mergers and voluntary liquidations at an average rate of over two per week. At that rate, Young claimed, "50 [percent] of the 14,000 commercial banking corporations now in existence are doomed to disappear from the financial scene in the next two generations."[36]

Young's concerns were the antithesis of the conservative deregulatory doctrine that would prevail in later years. Rather than representing the free market at its best, he saw these mergers as a threat to smaller, more localized financial enterprises and regarded them as anticompetitive and monopolistic.

But it was McCloy's vision that prevailed in 1955 and dictated the framework for how the US banking industry would be structured going forward. His contribution to keeping banks outside antitrust laws came in the form of a relatively brief, heavily legalistic thirty-six-page document titled "A Statement on Bank Mergers," which he submitted to the antitrust subcommittee of the House Judiciary Committee on July 5 of that year.[37]

His submission was to oppose a bill introduced by Congressman Emanuel Celler, a Democrat from New York, to extend Section 7 of the Clayton Anti-Trust Act of 1914. Celler's bill would make commercial banks subject to the antitrust law, and more specifically would prohibit bank mergers that would substantially reduce competition or create a monopoly.

McCloy stressed that banks "provide a steady flow of lifeblood into America's growing economy, and it is essential to the well-being of the nation that they remain sound, vigorous, and strong."[38] He believed they should remain free to expand without the confines of antitrust entanglements. Big banks, he reasoned, weren't stifling the competitive opportunities of other banks because all banks were already subject to more regulation than other businesses.[39] His reasoning overlooked the fact that big banks, with more capital and larger deposit bases, could wage effective takeovers of smaller banks—not only thwarting competition but annihilating it. Big banks might be subject to regulations, but their unfair advantage was, and would continue to be, indicative of monopoly behavior. Of course, sitting on top of one of the biggest, most powerful banks in the world was a pretty comfortable spot from which to be spouting these views.

A seasoned lawyer and negotiator who knew more about banking than Congress, public-private citizen McCloy won the argument, as he usually did. Though the assistant attorney general and five other Justice Department officials lobbied for the more restrictive legislation, the Clayton Act was never amended.[40] The Justice Department remained impotent, legally and operationally, against banking power.

McCloy was irrevocably altering international and national banking. He had fashioned the World Bank into a mechanism whose financial cues came from the banking community's decisions, and now he had set the stage for mega-mergers that would consolidate power under the largest banks. It was not the first time he won a major battle against antitrust rules (he had already done that on behalf of John D. Rockefeller's Standard Oil Trust). But as a result of his more recent efforts, big banks engaged in a litany of mergers. Thanks to his quiet intervention, their financial power and influence scaled heights not seen since the 1920s.

When McCloy presented his case, the top 100 banks held 46.6 percent of the nation's deposits. Banks now rushed to engineer more powerful mergers. Neither legislators nor the Fed did anything about this. (By 2012 just the nation's new "Big Six" banks would control 40 percent of deposits, rendering them "too big to fail.")

McCloy's timing was perfect. In the early 1950s, all the major New York banks, Chase included, sought fresh sources of lendable funds to service their corporate customers' credit needs and expand internationally. Retail-focused banks like the Bank of Manhattan, which tended to service individual customers, were growing their deposit bases, while giant wholesale banks like Chase, Guaranty Trust, and to a lesser extent National City Bank, which focused more on corporate and government clients, were losing their deposits to other forms of financial firms and funds. Acquisitions were needed to grow, compete, and survive. Without deposits, speculative global lending would be severely restricted.

The thirst for wholesale commercial banks to acquire branches and commandeer their deposits was intense. Aldrich, who had been ahead of the curve, had already tried to merge the Bank of Manhattan and Chase in 1951, but the deal had fizzled because of a personality clash with the Bank of Manhattan's chairman, J. Stewart Baker.[41] Additionally, the Bank of Manhattan's 1799 charter required unanimous consent of its shareholders in order to be taken over, and they weren't budging.

McCloy was determined to complete what Aldrich had begun: to close Chase's acquisition of the Bank of Manhattan, which would be one of the biggest mergers in American banking. To get around the charter issues he simply structured the deal so that the Bank of Manhattan appeared to be taking over Chase, not the other way around.

Thus, in 1955, the Chase Manhattan Bank was born. The marriage opened the floodgates for a slew of similar mergers, all predicated on the same "Jonah eats the whale" technicality. Ordinary Americans didn't raise their eyebrows at any of this; at the time, much of the US population was enthusiastically investing in the stock market and oblivious to the old money-trust concerns that followed the Panic of 1907 or the role that the big banks had played in precipitating the Crash of 1929. On November 21, 1955, *Time* magazine ran a cover story titled "Wall Street: Every Man a Capitalist," about New York Stock Exchange president George Keith Funston. A professional marketer, Funston vowed, "I'll try to be a salesman of shares in America." And he was. During his reign, the number of American shareowners more than tripled, rising from 6.5 to 21.5 million.[42] The Dow tripled in value over the decade.

The markets had gathered steam after the Korean War, but the Cold War kept them going. Defense companies, flush with government contracts, represented 10 percent of GNP from 1954 to 1959. The Interstate Highway Act of 1956 would unleash a construction boom spurring cars, suburban homes, motels, fast food chains like McDonald's, and amusement parks like Disneyland.

All sorts of new mutual funds catering to small and midlevel investors sprouted, as did corporate pension and retirement funds. Huge open-plan trading floors were erected around Wall Street. People carted out the money they'd "stuffed under their mattresses" during the Great Depression and started buying stuff like crazy—on credit.

As a result, private debt nearly tripled during the 1950s, growing from $100 billion to $260 billion. The more accounts a big bank held, the more chances to spin deposits into debt for its customers. McCloy was not the only banker who saw that wave coming. They all did. He was just the man who battled Congress for the privilege.

The Bank Holding Company Act of 1956

Despite McCloy's 1955 victory over antitrust laws, Congress made other attempts to ensure that banks didn't expand too dangerously, especially across state lines. The lessons of the Great Depression weren't *that* far behind. Since the Banking Acts of 1933 and 1935 were passed, there had been considerable back and forth between the House and Senate over various versions of the Bank Holding Company Act. By early 1956, though, it appeared that a compromise bill would be approved.

On April 30, a worried McCloy telegrammed Eisenhower's chief of staff, Sherman Adams, urging him to tell Eisenhower to "make a careful examination of the Bank Holding Company Bill, before signing."[43] It wasn't the act he minded as much as the possibility that it might wrestle regulatory authority away from the banks' major regulatory friend, the Fed. As it turned out, the act would ultimately give the Fed even more authority. Eisenhower signed it into law on May 9.

The act did three things. First, it required bank holding companies to secure Fed approval before acquiring additional banks. Second, bank holding companies had to divest themselves of nonbanking investments and were prohibited from making them in the future. Third, it prohibited bank holding companies from acquiring banks across state lines, a concession to North Dakota Republican senator Milton Young, one of the longest-serving senators in US history.[44]

In practice, the act solidified the Fed's power within the banking industry. The requirement to divest nonbank holdings mostly hurt Bank of America, whose constellation included nonbank companies like fisheries. But the New York banks were dealing mostly in financial ventures anyway, so it didn't bother them—as long as the Fed could continue to approve their mergers.

Nonetheless, the definition of "nonbank" investments would be disputed by the banking sector for decades. Ike hadn't really restricted the big banks at all; he'd merely signed regulation that the elite New York banks had no reason to object to at the time. By the time the act was passed, most major mergers had already taken place.

The Chase Manhattan merger was the largest and served as the catalyst for the others that followed. All four of JPMorgan Chase's major ancestral firms grew significantly through 1950s mergers: J. P. Morgan & Company, the Chase Manhattan Bank, Manufacturers Hanover Trust Company, and Chemical Bank. Chase even came close to merging with J. P. Morgan when McCloy persuaded Morgan head George Whitney to strongly consider it. But other Morgan partners prevented it; that merger would wait until the year 2000.

Instead, J. P. Morgan merged with Guaranty Trust. Chemical Bank acquired Corn Exchange Bank in 1954 and took over New York Trust in 1959, becoming Chemical Bank New York Trust.[45] Not to be outdone, Chase's main rival merged when National City Bank of New York bought First National Bank of New York in 1955.[46]

The Justice Department occasionally paid lip service to possible antitrust violations in banking, but it did nothing to prevent them. Nearly every bank leader had an official or unofficial advisory role in the Eisenhower administration at the time, which didn't hurt.

A small group of powerful banks came to dominate Wall Street more substantively, cornering a larger share of the population's funds than they had in the earlier part of the century. Commercial banks utilized advances in technology to automate banking processes; ATMs were introduced in the late 1950s to expand customer service and attract deposits for more ambitious activities. Meanwhile, investment banks, which had been sidelined during World War II, reemerged. But it was still the international frontier that held the most promise for real power expansion.

The Aswan Dam and McCloy in the Middle East

In December 1955, after a series of private consultations, McCloy and World Bank president Eugene Black concluded it made sense to join the American and British governments in financing the Aswan Dam in Egypt. The idea was to keep Egypt from embracing Communism by providing it with development capital. Black pledged that the World Bank would lend $200 million at 5 percent interest to support the project.

In February 1956, McCloy embarked on the first of many trips to the Middle East, under the auspices of expanding Chase. As his biographer Kai Bird wrote, his "high-level conversations with foreign leaders constituted a special form of private diplomacy. . . . This was a man who on the basis of his own authority and contacts could provide material aid to a country desperate for Western investments."[47] McCloy was seeking relationships that would expand upon Chase's business of financing oil companies to help develop new oil fields and technologies in the Middle East.

His predecessor, Aldrich, had initiated cordial relations with Egypt six years earlier, and the firm had already established branches in the region. But McCloy cultivated his own relationship with Egyptian president Gamal Abdel Nasser.[48] He also spent three days in Beirut, accompanied by two of Chase's petroleum consultants and the chairman of Empire Trust.[49] His first visit to Beirut was hailed by the local press as validation of Lebanon's liberal financial policies, which had opened the country to foreign capital.

But when the British and Americans withdrew from the Aswan Dam deal after Egypt appeared to be embracing the Soviets, Black withdrew the World Bank's lending support—and revealed its true colors. As British author Anthony Sampson wrote of the incident, "For the first time the West had used aid openly as a policy weapon in the developing world. And the withdrawal soon precipitated Egypt's nationalization of the Suez Canal and the subsequent Suez War."[50]

But there was more to it than that. McCloy believed, as did Aldrich, that the event resulted from the diplomatic ineptitude of Secretary of State Dulles. The Egyptians were very anxious to get the British troops out of their country. But as Aldrich recounted, "up to the time when Dulles, without warning to anyone, suddenly canceled the agreement that had been negotiated between the British, the United States and the World Bank to build the high dam in Aswan . . . Nasser had had no excuse to act."[51]

A crisis brewed after Nasser responded by nationalizing the Suez Canal. Britain and France informed Washington they stood ready for battle. The US Treasury froze the assets of Egypt and the Suez Canal Company—which had sizable deposits with Chase in New York and London. By October 1956, tensions were rising. Rather than ask Aldrich about Britain's thoughts on the developments, Dulles asked McCloy if he'd seen a large extraction of British sterling by British clients that might indicate hostile positioning. But McCloy hadn't. Shortly thereafter, Israel launched a ground attack, and the British and French waged a bombing campaign. Later, Eisenhower obtained a cease-fire. UN Secretary-General Dag Hammarskjold and McCloy collaborated to calm the situation.

McCloy flew out to talk with Nasser, who insisted that he was not under undue Communist influence. Back in the United States, McCloy briefed two hundred Council on Foreign Relations members, assuring them that Nasser was following a policy of independence. Still, McCloy believed that "Nasser and other nonaligned leaders like him were the kind of men whom Washington had to work with if the United States was to conduct a sound foreign policy, grounded in the political realities of postcolonial nationals."[52] Though Dulles didn't exactly agree, McCloy's foreign policy views, which fit nicely with US bankers' international objectives, remained prevalent.

The incident further strained not just Aldrich and Eisenhower's relationship but also that of America and Britain. Aldrich blamed it on Dulles and, by extension, Eisenhower. As he commented later, "I say in one of these papers that I was very disappointed in him. . . . He just turned foreign affairs over to Dulles and he simply coasted along."[53] In the fall of 1956, just after the Israelis launched their ground assault on the Sinai Peninsula and British and French forces began bombing Egyptian airfields, Dulles phoned McCloy, pulling him out of a Ford Foundation meeting to discuss whether Israel should be "restrained."[54] McCloy felt that the United States should take a harder stance with Israel. Given his private ties and professional ambitions, he was more interested in maintaining a strong relationship with the oil-rich nations, a stance that would become eminently clear during the Iran hostage situation in 1979.

Arguably Eisenhower's major foreign policy crisis, the Suez crisis pitted the United States against its traditional allies, Britain and France. Eisenhower's public condemnation of the invasion further drove a wedge between the new and the old superpowers.

After the crisis subsided, Aldrich was "completely fed up at Dulles."[55] He wanted to return home, but Eisenhower demanded he remain in Britain until the crisis blew over. Afterward Aldrich expressed "a very unfavorable opinion of Eisenhower—publicly."[56] He was disappointed in the president for turning over his foreign affairs to Dulles.

But it was clear that McCloy's sphere of global influence and power was rising above that of his predecessor; he now led one of the largest US banks, with command over its assets and strategies, and was the man called in to deal with foreign policy crises.

Ike's Second Term: The 1956 Campaign

The Suez incident strengthened Eisenhower's reputation as a president who could deal forcefully with the threat of Communism and keep the United States on its path to perpetual superpower status. Entering his second campaign, he also kept his bankers' support. Sidney Weinberg's tactical expertise as a money raiser during the 1956 campaign so impressed Ike that he sent him a telegram stating that he'd like Weinberg to explain to him "the origin and intricacies of a blitz as applied to politics." Weinberg replied that he would be glad to oblige, and that the "techniques of a money-raising blitz, which is not unlike a military blitz, [have] the same characteristics of planning, strategy, fortitude and a noble cause."[57]

In general, Ike's correspondence revealed a warmth that transcended what Weinberg could do for him (which was more than he did for Weinberg). He simply wanted to remain in contact. "Dear Sidney," he wrote in May 1956, a few weeks after signing the Bank Holding Company Act, "This morning I spent a few minutes with the Citizens group . . . here in Washington. The occasion reminded me that you have neglected me shamefully of late, and that I have missed seeing you. . . . Next time you are in Washington, won't you give my office a ring? . . . There is nothing special on my mind—just an opportunity to chat with you for a little while."[58]

In addition to playing headhunter for the administration, Weinberg was friendly with the staff. Eisenhower's personal secretary, Ann Whitman, sent Weinberg a rare personal note saying she was sorry his appointment with the president had to be canceled, "and I was cheated out of seeing you, in addition to all my troubles!"[59]

When he could not be present for any of the various "honoring Weinberg" dinners, Ike sent along remarks. For a November 13, 1957, dinner honoring Weinberg after fifty years at Goldman Sachs, he wrote, "The story of your life is not only the exciting fulfillment of the dreams of many a small boy; it represents the very essence of America. . . . I salute you as one of the great leaders of our business community and I count myself most fortunate that I can call you my friend."[60]

The 1957 Economy and
Treasury Department Shift

From 1939 to 1953, the dollar lost nearly half of its purchasing power, even as it moved into global dominance as a currency in conjunction with greater

US political power.[61] The fear among Eisenhower's advisers was that this situation couldn't go on indefinitely; the dollar had to be strengthened to support a strong nation.

To remedy the problem, Gabriel Hauge pressed the importance of tight policy in increasingly public settings. In a 1957 speech before the Economic Club of Detroit, he proclaimed, "If history tells us anything—and history has been said to have more imagination than men—it is that a sound economy, a sound nation, a sound people travel the same road as a sound money."[62]

Without a strong currency, Hauge and other bankers thought, it would be more difficult to retain a controlling position over world affairs from a political or financial perspective—something that both the president and the bankers wanted.

Two months later, it appeared that Eisenhower acknowledged the need for a strong currency to prop up his foreign political-financial policy. The *New York Herald Tribune* reported that the "President Upholds Tight Monetary Policy."[63]

The Eisenhower Doctrine and the Middle East

When Nasser nationalized the Suez Canal on July 26, 1956, Syria destroyed its oil pipeline running from Iraq to the Mediterranean Sea, causing vast oil shortages that provoked a recession in Europe and, by extension, its trading partner, the United States.

On January 5, 1957, amid growing pan-Arab anti-American sentiment and still wary of containment issues in the Middle East, the president announced the Eisenhower Doctrine. Congress approved it two months later. It was really just another version of the Truman Doctrine and the US sliver of NATO, offering US military and economic support for countries under Communist attack.

In response, Egypt nationalized its banking system and required all foreign banks operating in the country to become Egyptian companies. As a first step, foreign banks were sold to private Egyptian banks; those banks became nationalized in 1961. It wasn't until 1974, under President Anwar el-Sadat, that Egypt liberalized its banking system and allowed American banks and then other foreign ones back in.

Latin America and the Fight for Regional Power

Thus Latin America became the capstone of the bankers' expansion efforts. Making the region more attractive was the fact that the accounting systems of US banks weren't too careful about where profits were made, especially if they were booked overseas; the more countries in which to exhibit profits, the more they could be embellished if necessary.

Though Europe was still a future focus, it wasn't as profitable yet. During World War II, National City Bank had closed all its European branches except the one in London. All of them remained closed in the mid-1950s except the ones in London and Paris.

On the other hand, in Latin America—a region relatively untouched by World War II—the bank had at least one branch in nearly every country. The bank was well positioned to handle the growing financial and trade demands of Latin American businessmen and American companies operating in the region. Puerto Rico, Cuba, Brazil, and Argentina accounted for the majority of National City Bank's overseas deposits.

In the 1920s former chairman Charles Mitchell had first claimed a position in Cuba issuing bonds for sugar companies and others that defaulted and fell subject to the Pecora investigations. Despite that debacle, eleven National City branches were blossoming under Fulgencio Batista's regime (until he was overthrown during the Cuban Revolution in 1959, which brought Fidel Castro to power). The bank had successfully resurrected its 1920s role in financing sugar interests and was the "principal US depository for American companies operating in Cuba during the heyday of the 50s."[64]

As for Argentina, National City had been there financing meatpacking customers since the 1900s. But when Juan Perón rose to power in 1946, he nationalized its deposits. After his overthrow in 1955, deposits were restored. By early 1956, First National and Chase had lent Argentina $15 million to finance imports, with more to come.

The nationalization of the Suez Canal in 1956 and Syria's destruction of the oil pipeline had triggered an oil boom in Venezuela. Chase had a trick up its sleeve to capture the financial attention of that nation and trump National City Bank in the race for regional supremacy. On April 17, 1957, Chase appointed the son of the president of Peru, Manuel Prado—a Harvard graduate, former Chase trainee, and Banco Popular banker—to run its operations in Venezuela.

Not wishing to be outdone by his rival on international expansion, First National City Bank chairman Howard Sheperd countered with some serious personnel shifts. Leo Shaw, the senior vice president who had run the bank's overseas division since 1946, had launched its Middle East presence after a visit there in the mid-1950s. The firm's branch in Jedda, Saudi Arabia, would be a source of vast oil-related profits. But given the instability in the region,

Shaw's moves were not enough. In the drive to compete with Chase for financial global power, Sheperd called his domestic division chief, Missouri-born George Moore, to his office in late 1956. There, he and National City president James Stillman Rockefeller offered Moore Shaw's position, which Moore officially assumed in March 1957.[65] Working with his number-two man, Walter Wriston (who had been promoted to vice president), Moore launched an aggressive overseas expansion.

On June 16, 1957, First National City Bank announced it would open its seventy-first overseas branch in Havana, Cuba, by the José Martí International Airport. This was the bank's sixth branch in Havana and its eleventh in Cuba. First National City Bank was on a Cuban roll. On August 23, 1957, the Freeport Sulphur Company announced that its wholly owned subsidiary, the Cuban American Nickel Company, had arranged to borrow just over $100 million from banks and large nickel firms. The funds would be invested in a nickel and cobalt mine at Moa Bay, Cuba, to build a nickel refinery near New Orleans and a special ship for transporting the nickel and cobalt ore concentrates.

The Moa project was scheduled to begin production in mid-1959. It was financed by a six-company banking group led by the First National City Bank and included four other New York banks and four New Orleans banks.[66] (Following the Cuban revolution, Fidel Castro's 1960 nationalization of foreign businesses would throw a wrench into those works.) The deal capped off a mid-1950s rush of speculative investing that followed US bankers into the region. The resultant bubble popped first in Brazil in 1958. The threat of an American recession caused bankers and investors to protect their money by quickly extracting it from Brazil, which was forced to devalue its currency as a result. The "contagion" spread to Argentina, Chile, and Paraguay. It was not the first instance of US bankers piling into the region, opening outposts, doing deals, enticing foreign capital, and then fleeing at the first sign of instability, leaving bond defaults and depression in their wake. Nor would it be the last.

The 1958 Recession

Toward the end of 1957, after thirteen years of relatively unfettered growth, the United States experienced its first major recession, partially because of its efforts to uphold the strength of the dollar for foreign policy purposes. From August 1957 to February 1958, more than five million people lost their jobs as domestic demand for extraneous goods and unnecessary appliances and gadgets shriveled. The banks that had just aggressively poured capital into developing regions slowed their lending due to the budding economic crises in Latin America, rather than reduce the rates of their prior loans. The economic pain spread east and north, to Europe and Canada, hitting the mining, agriculture, and oil sectors particularly hard. Car sales dropped 30 percent for the whole of 1957 versus the previous year, and car dealers took to having all-night sell-a-thons to spur waning consumer demand.[67]

Eisenhower's visions of permanent prosperity and the bankers' belief in unlimited deposit growth were hit hard, too. Debate in Washington centered on whether or not a tax cut proposal should be sent to Congress. But Gabriel Hauge joined Treasury Secretary Robert Anderson in opposing tax cuts. In the end, Eisenhower agreed with them. The thinking at the time was that tax cuts would increase the nation's debt burden (a notion lost on Republicans in the wake of the 2008 crisis) and thus were not a good remedy. As it turned out, the recession began dissipating by late spring.

In June 1958, as the markets were springing back to life, H. C. Flanagan, chairman of the Manufacturers Trust Company, asked Gabriel Hauge to become the firm's finance committee chairman and a board director. Hauge's resignation was as much a professional as a personal blow to Eisenhower, who had grown fond of Hauge over his six years in Washington.

The large New York City banks fared better than the rest of the population during the recession. National City Bank, J. P. Morgan, and Morgan Guaranty even posted increased annual profits in October 1958 compared to the year before. Wall Street was a perfect place for Hauge to go.

Banking in Beirut

Meanwhile, in July 1958, Lebanon's president, Camille Chamoun, had requested US assistance to help prevent attacks from his political rivals, some of whom leaned Communist and had ties with Syria and Egypt. In response, without directly invoking the Eisenhower Doctrine, Eisenhower sent thirty thousand US marines and soldiers into Lebanon. Some media commentators thought this was a response to a bloody revolution in Iraq that overthrew the pro-Western government in favor of the socialist Baath Party. But beyond the colder relations with Syria and Egypt and the threat of socialism in Iraq, there was another, more banking-related reason Eisenhower interpreted his own doctrine so loosely. Beirut had become the most active city in the Middle East from a financial services perspective, home to numerous branches of US banks that were using the city as a key outpost from which to do financing and trade business throughout the Middle East. Beirut was the region's major financial services center, offering foreign firms and investors a plethora of benefits such as unnumbered bank accounts and loose tax laws.

Chase, National City Bank, and Bank of America had opened branches in Beirut in 1955. Around the same time, American news outfits like *Newsweek, Time,* and the *New York Times* (which stated that Nasser's nationalism "has set his country back years economically") had relocated from Cairo to Beirut, as Beirut transformed itself into the western outpost in the area. Though without oil resources, Lebanon had the benefit of being a politically stable, western-oriented country that was attractive to foreign capital.

When Syria cut its pipelines during the Suez crisis, American banks saw their chances for profitability in the region diminished by the sheer possibility of such volatile actions. If the United States was going to maintain access to Middle East oil, not only its political and military but also its banking strategies needed a home base. That home base was Beirut. Those were powerful reasons for Eisenhower to send troops to preserve that status.

Henry Alexander and the Morgan Merger

Henry Alexander succeeded George Whitney as chairman of J. P. Morgan in 1959. Like Whitney, Alexander was a longtime "Morganer."

On Christmas Eve 1938, Jack Morgan, who had been impressed by Alexander's legal mind, personally invited him into the Morgan partnership. The son of a Tennessee grain merchant, Alexander worked his way up to Yale Law School and into the Eastern Establishment banker sect. Born to a Democratic family, Alexander registered himself as a Republican. At Eisenhower's request in 1952, he headed a $10 million drive for the Korean War relief effort. Six years later, Eisenhower appointed him to a committee to examine US foreign economic policy.[68] On November 1, 1955, Alexander received the Republic of Korea medal for his work in the American-Korean Foundation in 1953 and 1954.

By the late 1950s, his banking work was heralded by the press. In 1959, *Time* called Alexander "the nation's most prestigious banker." Eisenhower's archives didn't substantiate the pervasive press view that he was also Ike's most important banker, but Alexander certainly courted the press successfully.[69]

More important to the overall banking landscape, Alexander deployed McCloy's "Jonah swallowing a whale" strategy with his own mega-merger. Under Alexander, J. P. Morgan & Company, which had fallen to tenth place among New York commercial banks and twenty-eighth in the United States, merged with the much bigger Guaranty Trust Company to become the fifth largest bank in the country.

With his Tennessee drawl, outdoorsy demeanor, salt-and-pepper hair, and bushy dark eyebrows, Alexander ushered in a breed of salesmanship banking, reminiscent of the Mitchellian 1920s but with a wider scope. As would be more indicative of 1960s banker style, Alexander hired seventy young men, dubbed his "bird dogs," to hustle and spoil customers. As "chief bird dog," Alexander focused on the same groups that J. P. Morgan focused on at the turn of the century: the business, finance, and government elite.

At a time when middle-class wealth was growing and companies were decentralizing—more suburban relocations were spawning as cars and highways made them more accessible—many old-school New York banks began offering more retail services to their customers to keep hold of them and their deposits. But under Alexander, Morgan didn't follow suit, preferring to merge with the Guaranty Trust Company to get a larger capital base. That strategic difference allowed the firm to retain its elitist stature while other banks mucked about with the broader population.

For his part, Eisenhower, contrary to any concerns about antitrust violations, expressed a keen interest in the Morgan merger. On January 23, 1959, he complimented Alexander on the report that he and his associates on the Committee on World Economic Practices had put together on the mounting Sino-Soviet bloc economic offensive. Ike then added, "May I further add a personal note? I was much interested in the recently announced proposal to merge J. P. Morgan and Company with the Guaranty Trust Company; I trust that it will work out well for all of you."[70] The two banks merged on April 24, 1959. Alexander reigned as chairman of the Morgan Guaranty Trust from 1959 to 1966.

London Rising

Under the Marshall Plan, the US government had posted $13 billion to facilitate Europe's recovery. Given that extra backing for their client countries, American bankers were assured that this time, unlike after World War I, their loans would be repaid. That was one of the main reasons they were so keen on the Marshall Plan. Additionally, the Truman and Eisenhower Doctrines extended US economic support to nations that adopted US ideology and were military allies. This meant more potential customers who would require private bank loans in their own drives to grow.

By the late 1950s, the inevitable clash between rich and poor nations was intensifying, and international inequality was growing. Developing nations didn't want their prosperity dependent on western aid but on fair trade and prices and open markets for their raw materials (the pure definition of a "free market"). That was not what the Marshall Plan, the IMF, or the World Bank had accomplished for them. So many of these nations made the grave decision to secure private loans from the international banking community, from which they believed less policy strings would be attached. This action would generate its own problems—uncontrollable lending terms—that would prove devastating in other ways. Meanwhile, the number of National City Bank offices overseas tripled to 208, as the bank expanded from twenty-seven to sixty-one countries to accommodate the private loan demand. Other major banks followed suit.

Burgess had left his post in the Treasury Department when he was appointed US ambassador to NATO in 1956; he served in that role until 1963, noting that "the shine of postwar NATO was getting a little dull."[71] By the turn of the decade, the stronger European countries felt less threatened by Soviet aggression. This made them less pliable to US policies. As a result, their banks began spreading their wings globally again.

Burgess moved to take a position at the Organization for European Economic Cooperation (which he later renamed the Organization for Economic Cooperation and Development), with the aim of "maximizing its service to the Atlantic community."[72] From that vantage point, he was instrumental in developing the "common market" to bring in the British, under a common financial umbrella to augment NATO. This focus on a new world order common market platform was a boon to US banks and helped bring British and other European banks back into the global financial fold.

London hadn't yet become a major international financial center again, but Eurodollars (dollars outside America) were on their way to becoming a dominant global trading and lending currency. As a result, London was resuming its position as the epicenter of global finance, the trading hub of Eurodollar-backed loans.

In the late 1950s, the entrenchment of NATO and beginnings of the European Community encouraged Burgess's alma mater, National City Bank, to lead the big banks back to Europe alongside a host of enthusiastic American multinationals.

In 1958, most western countries (except Britain) had agreed to allow their currencies to be convertible into dollars for the first time since the war, which provided freer flow across borders. But because dollars were converted into gold at the fixed rate of $35 an ounce, foreigners began dumping dollars and extracting gold, causing a massive outflow of US gold reserves and raising US interest rates.[73]

As interest rates rose, they exceeded the rates banks could pay on demand deposits. Under the Depression-era Federal Reserve Regulation Q, interest rates on those savings accounts were capped. As a result New York banks lost more than $1 billion in deposits as depositors rushed to the Eurodollar market, where rates could be as high as the market dictated. The United States lurched into a deficit. Dollars flowed quickly into Europe, as Eurodollars could earn higher interest. That's what brought London back as a financial banking center.

Bankers who took up their business in the Square Mile of London's banking heart could smell the Eurodollars in the air. As Anthony Sampson wrote, "Young British bankers and their foreign counterparts began to earn higher salaries than other bankers. Skyscrapers shot up by the old classic architecture near St. Paul's Cathedral. Far Eastern and Arabic banks appeared, as did Mercedes and Cadillacs to cart bankers around the thin London streets."[74]

The US bankers still called the shots, not least because the US government did too. As Eisenhower approached his final year in office, the core power emanating from New York City remained backed by US foreign and military policy.

But the bankers would have to find new ways to compete with a strengthening European banking network by opening more offices there and by eliminating New Deal regulatory restrictions on their operations, so they could grow domestically and use their larger size as a global competitive weapon. Those campaigns would come.

By the end of the 1950s, the arc of the postwar 1920s, the 1929 Crash, the Great Depression, World War II, and the Cold War had been drawn. Legacy leaders of the Big Six banks that had gathered to save the markets in the late 1920s still dominated Wall Street and White House relationships. The current elite were largely based on that old set: First National City Bank of New York, Chase Manhattan Bank, and Morgan Guaranty Trust (encompassing J. P. Morgan Bank) were the old guard, while Chemical Bank New York Trust and Manufacturers Hanover Trust were the new guard, hovering just outside the Big Three. They would later be subsumed into the Chase Manhattan Bank and then into JPMorgan Chase. Added to the mix was the West Coast cousin, reluctantly accepted as a political "player" by the eastern bankers: Bank of America.

Many of the financiers who had been influential during Eisenhower's administration would retain power after he left office. With the next president, they would delve even further into the international realm.

CHAPTER 11

THE EARLY 1960s: "GO-GO" YOUTH, MURDERS, AND GLOBAL FINANCE

"The reduction of global tension must not be an excuse for the narrow pursuit of self-interest."

—John F. Kennedy, address before the Eighteenth
General Assembly of the United Nations, September 20, 1963

THROUGHOUT THE 1960s A SINGULAR FORCE DROVE THE SEEMINGLY DISPARATE realms of politics, pop culture, and banking: youth. Youth helped propel handsome, impeccably groomed, and pedigreed John F. Kennedy into the White House. Major papers oozed praise on rising young moguls like First National City's Walter Wriston and Chase's David Rockefeller. By the end of 1963, even Morgan Guaranty Trust was equating "the current round of business expansion" with "an impressive display of youthful pep."[1] By the mid-1960s, 65 percent of Wall Street bankers were under the age of thirty-five. They had no Great Depression memories and few World War II ones.

As younger men who lacked shared crisis experience put themselves into play for important positions, they catalyzed a widespread attitudinal shift toward privileging private gain over public spirit. There was no "national trial" to foster population-oriented feelings from the financier sect. Political themes of unity were increasingly absent from public discourse. The bankers' push to become international financial gods would increasingly sever them from an explicit alignment with the country's greater needs and blind them to the suffering of developing countries, many of which were losing their economic sovereignty to private US (and later European) bankers and their clients. Bankers were rapidly discarding the implicit mantra of "America first" in favor of, simply "Go where the money is."

The presidential and banker policy alliance was tighter at the start of the Cold War, when the feeling of US invincibility was more pronounced. Eisenhower's mutual security agreements, which provided non-Communist countries with US military and economic aid, had enabled bankers to set up shop in those countries. Now that feeling of strength was giving way to an emerging sense of global instability. The fresh crop of powerful financiers began to question whether the shield of the president and government was solid enough to protect their international interests. By the end of the 1960s, they would no longer rely on the White House for support but would begin to forge ahead with their own plans to secure global power.

Following a slow start to the decade, an air of financial immortality born of booming corporate profits, rising wages, and easy credit buoyed the stock market again. It was the dawn of spin: *Mad Men*–style advertisements about "trading up" abounded, beckoning Americans to "have more"—to upgrade from black-and-white to color TVs and from cars the size of a small living room to muscle cars that tested the limits of power. Consumerism became the new pastime, debt the designer drug. Total household debt hit more than $300 billion by 1964, more than double the figure from a decade earlier.[2]

On Wall Street, the term "go-go" underscored a surge of market participation last seen in the 1920s. Trading volumes ballooned as all-American companies like Howard Johnson[3] and Tyson Foods went public.[4] America's obsession with gas-guzzling cars and greasy fast food ignited shares in drive-thru restaurant chains like Kentucky Fried Chicken and McDonald's.[5] Budding mutual funds enticed individuals to invest their savings rather than keep it in banks, just as trusts had done in the 1920s. This forced banks to seek overseas profits more strategically to hedge their potential lack of deposit inflow. Nearly 120 million Americans directly or indirectly had a stake in the markets.[6]

Kennedy, the Economy, and the Bankers

On January 3, 1960, Senator John F. Kennedy of Massachusetts gave his first TV interview after announcing his intention to seek the Democratic nomination for president. He eerily alluded to the possibility of dying in office: "People presume that the presidential candidate will have a normal life expectancy."[7]

But Kennedy didn't mince words about the economy. Even though it had recently rebounded from a mild recession, he was not convinced the worst was over, and he warned the viewing public, "All the pigeons are coming home on the next president. . . . He'll have the most difficult time next to Mr. Hoover, because I think we're due to have a recession . . . more serious than the 1958 recession."[8]

As it turned out, JFK would preside over thirty-three months of economic growth.[9] But he would fail to execute many of his economic goals; perhaps because he didn't have enough time, but also because his more distant personal connections with certain influential bankers and businessmen hampered his ability to harness their support for his policies while helping them with theirs, as FDR had cleverly done for years.

Kennedy tried to limit foreign tax benefits on US subsidiaries abroad and impose other "equalization" taxes. This riled the American bankers, who advocated the free flow of everything finance-related. In his book *Battling Wall Street: The Kennedy Presidency*, historian Donald Gibson described the relationships between Kennedy and the bankers as tension-lined. "Not only did they not embrace each other," he wrote, but "the Establishment's rejection of Kennedy became increasingly intense during his time in office."[10]

The relationships were complex. Whereas Wriston and Rockefeller, the two bankers most primed to dominate Cold War–era financial power politics in the 1960s, disagreed with some of Kennedy's policies (notably ones that restrained their expansionary goals), others, like the elder John McCloy, were far more reverent toward the president. Yet despite philosophical disagreements on US economic supremacy in the global sphere, Kennedy's relationship with Rockefeller was solid enough that his choice for secretary of state was Dean Rusk, who was president of the Rockefeller Foundation from 1952 to 1961 after having served in various State Department roles during the Truman administration.

Kennedy had first met David Rockefeller in 1938 at the coming-out party for his sister Kathleen. The gala was thrown in London by their father, Joe Kennedy, the ambassador to Britain, after which Rockefeller briefly dated (or, as he put it, "enjoyed the company of") Kathleen. The two young men studied at the London School of Economics (both had attended Harvard). They hadn't kept in contact for more than two decades, possibly because both were busy pursuing their own agendas and hadn't quite figured out how to use each other in the process. Indeed, the frequency of their communication increased as both settled into their roles: Kennedy running the world's most powerful country and Rockefeller close to running the world's most politically powerful bank (and serving as a self-appointed ambassador at-large for US foreign policy).

One Chase Plaza

John McCloy was set to retire on March 31, 1960, his sixty-fifth birthday. But internal battles at Chase delayed his plans to return to his private legal practice. He remained at his post six months longer, while his potential successors—the internationalist Rockefeller and the older, more domestically focused George Champion—sparred over who would get his job.

Rockefeller thought McCloy's lack of support for him stemmed from a long-standing resentment of his family's wealth and stature. He believed McCloy began nursing a grudge in 1912, when he tried and failed to secure a tutoring job at the Rockefeller mansion in Mount Desert Island, Maine.[11]

Eleven years Rockefeller's senior, Champion had been an all-star football player at Dartmouth, from which he graduated in 1926. Afterward, he secured a job at the Equitable Trust Company. Like his then-boss Winthrop Aldrich, he joined Chase when the two firms merged in 1930. Champion rose as a lending officer through the 1930s and 1940s, courting high-profile corporate customers. An "ardent golfer," he was appointed head of the bank's marquee unit, the commercial banking department, in 1949.

Absent a sign either way from McCloy, the board ultimately decided to make both men co-CEOs. Rockefeller was named president and chairman of the executive committee. Champion, to Rockefeller's disdain, was elected chairman of the board. To Rockefeller, Champion was like the archaic office furniture he kept around, "wedded to the past" and to Chase's domestic preeminence. Rockefeller wanted to dominate the international arena. "Our joint tenure at the bank," he later wrote, "would be an extended open unpleasant struggle for primacy."[12] During that tenure, Rockefeller triumphed in the field of molding Washington and the world to his way of seeing things. Less than a decade later, he would do so from atop the Chase bank.

The Chase Manhattan Building at One Chase Plaza—a block from the Federal Reserve Bank of New York—was McCloy's lasting physical contribution to the firm. In May 1961, the sixty-story skyscraper opened to global fanfare.[13] Architecturally and symbolically, it was the tallest bank building in the world. The firm Skidmore, Owings, and Merrill, specialists in the international "glass-box" style, designed the monolith. SOM later built several "tallest buildings in the world," including the Sears Tower in Chicago and Burj Khalifa in Dubai. The austere style inspired its share of disapproval over the years; critics called it ugly and elitist. Mostly, the Chase Manhattan Building conveyed a cold and reserved power befitting the time, with its elite executive headquarters situated at the top, far away from the antlike humans scurrying about on the streets below.

From these headquarters, Champion set about expanding Chase's funding avenues. There were two main sources he could tap: the growing certificate of deposit market and the Eurodollar market. He did both. Chase's asset base tripled through the 1960s, as did its domestic loans and deposits.

Domestically, CDs provided huge pools of domestic money for banks. Introduced by First National City Bank of New York (now Citigroup) in 1961, CDs enabled banks to raise money from investors, thereby circumventing Regulation Q, the Federal Reserve's restriction on interest rate payments. Since the late 1950s, corporate and individual depositors had been transferring money from banks into higher-yielding investments, such as commercial paper (for business borrowing) and bankers' acceptances (used in international trade). Since banks were prohibited under Regulation Q from paying interest on checking and savings accounts held for less than thirty days and limited in their ability to pay interest on accounts held for more than thirty days, CDs provided a way to get money in the door at market interest rates and lend it to keep foreign expansion buzzing.

Companies didn't mind tying up their capital for the longer periods these forms of deposits required, provided they enjoyed higher interest rates. But there was a roadblock: new unrestricted money market funds could pay higher rates and drain deposits from commercial banks. This troubled Champion and all his banker compatriots.

There was a solution though. Across the Atlantic, the Eurodollar market was a more dependable source of funds. The Cold War provided an extra kick to US banks in London. The Soviet Union and other Eastern Bloc countries needed dollars for trade but wanted to avoid adverse US policy by not keeping or borrowing money in the United States. So they stuck funds in the London offices of British and American banks, causing the City of London to grow as a banking center and recoup some prewar financial glory.

Other offshore markets developed as well, as did "shadow banking," a secretive element of the global financial system that moved debt and profits around the world outside the purview of standard banking regulations.

Chase remained a leading participant in the dominant Eurodollar market. The firm also expanded its European loan services, including to big petroleum companies, a group that encompassed one-third of Chase's business loans and a large proportion of former chairman McCloy's law clients. US banker global positioning began to grow independently from domestic political posturing, largely through the Eurodollar market.

McCloy: Kennedy's Disarmament Adviser

For the most part, McCloy sat out the 1960 presidential election. He was ambivalent about Richard Nixon. Like other Republican bankers, he had a mild personal aversion to Nixon but didn't fully support Kennedy either. He was unimpressed by Kennedy's lack of engagement with establishment institutions like the Council on Foreign Relations, which McCloy chaired from 1953 to 1970.[14]

Conversely, Kennedy wanted McCloy in his corner. He admired his fellow Irishman. While vacationing in Palm Beach in November 1960, JFK remarked, "When one mentions the names of [David] Rockefeller and [Wall Street financier Douglas] Dillon and McCloy, one has exhausted the supply of good Republicans."[15]

Just after he won the election, with the tightest electoral victory margin since 1916, Kennedy summoned McCloy to his presidential suite at the Carlyle Hotel, where he often conducted meetings when he was in New York City. When McCloy arrived in the pouring rain, he was so scruffy in his dirty old raincoat that the gaggle of reporters camped out at the hotel didn't even notice him.[16]

Once the two men sat down, Kennedy offered McCloy the secretary of defense role, but McCloy demurred. He harbored a slight aspiration to be Treasury secretary, but Kennedy decided there might be a conflict, given McCloy's "contractual relationships" at his law firm.

After a second meeting, McCloy accepted a disarmament position, with one characteristic stipulation: he wanted autonomy. This meant reporting directly to Kennedy rather than to anyone else on the bureaucratic chain. Once Kennedy agreed, McCloy became chairman of the General Advisory Committee on Arms Control and Disarmament.[17]

Through the spring of 1961, and surrounding the March 1961 Geneva Conference at which disarmament positions were discussed, McCloy, JFK, and his national security advisers met biweekly to discuss disarmament plans and the process of unwinding weapons stockpiles. The Soviets wanted a more definitive solution, proposing complete disarmament of both sides within four years. McCloy was skeptical of their fervor and timeline. Without broad agreements for peace in tandem, these Russian promises seemed like mere public relations ploys to him.[18] After one of his meetings with Kennedy at the Oval Office, he complained that "this Geneva Conference constitutes the most discouraging exercise in disarmament negotiations since the close of the war."[19]

Still he soldiered on. Tasked with reinvigorating East-West disarmament talks, McCloy and Valerian Zorin, the Soviet delegate to the United Nations, met for two weeks in June 1961 to hash out principles for disarmament discussions set to begin August 1.[20] They submitted their agreement to the UN that September, but subsequent discussions got stymied in international politics.

McCloy's frustration with the process intensified. He and other disarmament advisers met with JFK on September 24, 1961, at Kennedy's Carlyle Hotel suite. In a photo of McCloy, Kennedy, Secretary of State Rusk, and Arthur Dean, chairman of the US delegation to the Geneva Conference on Disarmament, Kennedy is standing uncomfortably, his hands stuffed in his pockets.[21] The tension was palpable.

McCloy had drafted a bill to establish the US Arms Control and Disarmament Agency, which Kennedy signed on September 26, 1961.[22] But he was unnerved by the reaction of the Soviets to his earlier proposals for disarmament, since they had resumed nuclear testing on September 2, 1961. In April 1962, McCloy penned an eleven-page missive on the Soviet disarmament situation in *Foreign Affairs*. "Prior to the reconvening of negotiations at Geneva in March of 1961," he wrote, "I believed that the Soviet Union, in spite of its almost pathological abhorrence of any system of thorough inspection—or, perhaps better stated, its traditional attachment to secrecy and its distrust of our motives—did sincerely wish to reach an agreement." That belief was "practically destroyed on September 2, 1961, [with] the resumption of Soviet testing."[23]

Despite McCloy's frustration with the March 1961 Geneva episode, he continued working on a disarmament agreement that summer with Zorin. Kennedy met with Soviet premier Nikita Khrushchev in Vienna in June 1961, five weeks after the Bay of Pigs debacle in which CIA-aided Cuban exiles launched a botched invasion of Cuba. But absent a solid conclusion on the matter of disarmament between Kennedy and Khrushchev, tensions rose further: the Berlin Wall was erected in August 1961, and the Soviet Union announced it had resumed atmospheric testing.

Yet McCloy and Zorin had still reached an agreement on the *principles* of disarmament on September 20, 1961. Kennedy presented "The United States Program for General and Complete Disarmament in a Peaceful World" to the UN five days later. In that address, he challenged the Soviet Union "not to an arms race, but to a peace race," leaving the issue of arms basically unresolved despite the applause he received.

The superpower rivalry devolved into the October 1961 testing of the "Tsar Bomba," the largest nuclear bomb in history. The resumption of American testing began on April 25, 1962, the month McCloy published his *Foreign Affairs* article on the matter. These problems, according to McCloy, were the Soviets' fault. And, he believed, they were economically illogical to boot. As he wrote, "It would be advantageous to the Soviet Union, one would think, to be free of the economic burden of the arms race."[24]

David Rockefeller's Dream and Kennedy's Alliance for Progress

Kennedy officially announced the Alliance for Progress with Latin America during a reception for Latin American leaders at the White House in early 1961.[25] It was formally born through documents signed by twenty countries at Punta del Este, Uruguay, on August 17 of that year. But the idea for the initiative came from two earlier sources. The first was Kennedy's take on Eisenhower's Mutual Security Program, whereby the United States would provide economic and military aid to nations that were politically aligned. The second was the ideologies of Walt "W. W." Rostow, Kennedy's deputy assistant for national security affairs from 1961 to 1962 (who later served as special assistant for national security affairs to President Johnson, where he was actively involved in shaping US foreign policy). Rostow was staunchly anti-Communist and pro-free-market capitalism. (He was also a strong advocate for US involvement in the Vietnam War, and he won the Presidential Medal of Freedom in 1969.)

In 1960 Rostow wrote *The Stages of Economic Growth: A Non-Communist Manifesto*. The book was widely read, especially in the power circles of Washington and Wall Street. Besides being a rebuttal to Karl Marx and Communism, his explanation of historical economic development was almost biblical doctrine for bankers wishing to expand into developing nations, where they could buy up local banks and companies (in whole or in parts) and export the profits.

Rockefeller was a devout practitioner of Rostow's theories. He had been running Chase's Latin American business since the 1950s. Under his tutelage, Chase opened branches in Cuba, Panama, and Puerto Rico.[26] For the most part, his banking expansion strategy was in line with Kennedy's Alliance for Progress philosophy, which stressed that "each Latin nation must . . . establish the machinery for vital social change [and] stimulate private activity and initiative."[27] Rockefeller acted on the notion that this meant private *banking* activities and *financial* initiatives.

Yet there was a catch. No US bank could operate in countries that adhered to rigid protectionist notions that impeded the flow of free-market capitalism. Rockefeller was thus critical of "overly ambitious concepts of revolutionary change" in the region. He wanted the alliance to focus on private business interests, which would enable more US bank loans and privatization deals.[28] He was less interested in what the masses of the region might want, or whatever their political ideologies might be.

Practically, he set about prying open the region through meetings with leaders and local elites willing to part with their share of the countries' resources or profits. He also used Chase as a means to purchase pieces of local and national banks. The goal was to enable the flow of international private capital under the auspices of a program that ostensibly benefited Latin American populations from a cultural and intellectual perspective. In the spirit of providing these nonfinancial benefits, he helped organize the Council of the Americas and the Center for Inter-American Relations, which worked to "maximize private enterprise contributions and cultural and intellectual exchanges."[29] Chase loans to the region grew substantially in conjunction with these entities. The maximization of private enterprise would far surpass any cultural aid Rockefeller or any other US elite believed they could impart upon Latin America.

Rockefeller remained committed to "putting down roots" in all the major countries of the world.[30] A main focus was Brazil, the fastest-growing country in South America. In 1961, an associate of his brother Nelson informed him that Antonio Larragoiti, the chairman of Sul America, South America's largest insurance company, was prepared to sell Chase 51 percent of his stock in its banking subsidiary for $3 million and give Chase full management control. The deal was concluded in April 1962 and wound up being quite lucrative for Chase. Renamed Banco Chase Manhattan in 1987, that small subsidiary became one of the leading foreign banks in Brazil, with more than $1.1 billion of assets.

Rockefeller's style was akin to venture (or vulture) capitalism: he could swoop in and convert a local bank into an international vessel of financial services through which to lend and speculate in the host country, and make millions in the process. Thus, while his former boss, John McCloy, concentrated on worldwide peace and disarmament agreements, Rockefeller focused his attention on Kennedy's Alliance for Progress initiative and developed a strategy to use it to his advantage.

In his thirty-five years at Chase, Rockefeller visited 103 countries and took forty-one trips to France, thirty-seven to England, twenty-four to West Germany, fifteen to Japan, fifteen to Egypt and Brazil, three to Africa, as well as to forty-two of America's fifty states.[31] He logged five million air miles. He considered his presence essential to securing relationships, offices, and, of course, his own reputation among the global elite.

As Rockefeller blossomed into a full-scale international power broker who communicated regularly with Kennedy on the foreign impact of US economic policy, his dual identities—banker and self-anointed global "diplomat"— meshed so intricately that it proved impossible to tell them apart. Rostow's doctrine paralleled his own conviction that economic growth could occur only if national walls restricting the might of global finance were torn down. If it was "manifest destiny" that had propelled America westward, it was a kind of financial manifest destiny that propelled its bankers around the world.

US Steel, Taxes, and Bankers

In early 1962, Kennedy battled a foe close to home: the steel industry—and, by extension, its financial supporters, including the Morgan Guaranty Trust Company, the Ford Foundation, and First National City Bank. He accused these players of anticonsumer price-fixing.

On April 10, US Steel head Roger Blough appeared at the White House to tell Kennedy he would raise steel prices to $6 a ton despite the price-fixing charges.[32] Kennedy eventually persuaded Blough to deescalate steel prices, but at the cost of expending great political capital.[33]

Afterward, Kennedy explained his feelings about the incident in a handwritten scribble: "I shall be Pres.—come what may for the next 3 years. We can have disagreement between business and the government . . . there should however not be war or hostility between business & the govt. I can stand it . . . but the country cannot—we have too many common interests involving the welfare of our country."[34]

Kennedy's tax proposals were less well received by the business and banking community, especially those that tampered with overseas expansion. During the early 1960s, firms rapidly increased foreign investments. New terms snaked into the annals of corporate lingo to describe these corporations, including heady labels such as "multinational," "global," and "transnational." US banks facilitated and profited from the lending blitz corresponding to these foreign animals. Neither banks nor their client companies wanted the party stopped.

Yet Kennedy was considering putting restrictions on all of it. He proposed eliminating tax breaks for companies set up by US interests as foreign investment companies, and for wealthy individuals transferring wealth abroad. Most of his proposals, considered unattractive by the wealthy, died in congressional compromises.[35] They also may have been encumbered by the nature of Kennedy's relationships with the elite banking and business crowd. Earlier in his term, he didn't appear to *need* bankers to support his policies. He didn't stroke their egos or exchange bubbly pleasantries; he didn't go out of his way to embark upon lengthy meetings or calls with most of them; he didn't solicit their advice. This mutual feeling of uneasiness manifested even in Kennedy's physical stance; he often stood with his hands in his pockets in their presence. His attitude lay in stark contrast to Eisenhower's warm embraces to the banking crowd and those of his vice president, Lyndon Johnson.

To be sure, there were certain financial players who were more frequent guests of Kennedy than others, including Henry Alexander of Morgan Guaranty and David Rockefeller and George Champion of Chase. Plus, Goldman Sachs head Sidney Weinberg was a member of Kennedy's Business Council.[36]

But it wasn't until his second year in office that Kennedy opened more lines of official communication with bankers and businessmen.[37] It wound up hurting him, in more ways than one, that he hadn't done so right off the bat.

Blue Monday

Adding to Kennedy's troubles with the steel industry, the Dow took a dive on May 28, 1962, losing $20.8 billion in one day, the largest amount ever.[38] *Time* magazine plastered Kennedy's economic adviser, Walter Heller, on its cover, sporting slicked-back hair and brown-rimmed glasses over earnest eyes.[39] (In a memo to Kennedy on the economic situation before the story was published, Heller described himself as Time's "cover victim."[40])

According to Time, "The night of Blue Monday, 1962, was the grimmest evening on the New Frontier since the failure of the Bay of Pigs invasion. Measured by the Dow-Jones industrial average, the stock market was down 35 points in the deepest one-day plunge since the black year of 1929. . . . President Kennedy told staffers to prepare an agenda for a meeting next morning with his chief economic advisers."

In early May the outlook had appeared better. In a handwritten note to Kennedy, Heller explained, "Here's the best dope so far available on corporate profits in the first quarter—not bad, not as good as we had hoped, but still headed for well over $50 billion for the year (vs. a previous peak of $47 billion)."[41]

Yet the market kept trending downward. The Standard & Poor's Composite Index lost 22 percent of its value between March and May. The German stock market was down 26 percent from 1960, the Swiss was down 18 percent from 1962, the Japanese was down 29 percent from 1961, and the British index was down 21 percent from 1961.[42]

The economic situation had worsened psychologically because of the steel crisis (portrayed as evidence that the Kennedy administration was hostile toward business), an SEC investigation into brokerage firms, and a steady outflow of gold.

The president's economic brain trust decided to do nothing. Though the lack of response was publicly criticized, it proved wise. By May 30, the European markets and the Dow had rebounded.[43] Underlying what ended up being a market blip was the contentious relationship Kennedy had with the nation's top financiers. But by midsummer 1962 Kennedy had gone from resisting bankers' advances to finally extending the olive branch at the White House.

During a dinner with French minister of cultural affairs André Malraux at the White House on May 11, 1962, Kennedy took Rockefeller aside to discuss financial matters. He persuaded Rockefeller, who needed little arm-twisting, to write down his thoughts in a letter that made its way to the editor-in-chief of Life magazine.

While Rockefeller gathered his thoughts, Kennedy made it known to a recalcitrant Congress that he might consider loosening fiscal policy with regard to the US balance of payments deficit, a turnaround from his prior stance. In addition to weakness in domestic businesses and the stock markets, nations using their surplus dollars had drained America's gold reserves to a twenty-two-year low.[44] It was on this and related international elements upon which Rockefeller chose to focus. On July 6, 1962, *Life* featured the letters between Rockefeller and Kennedy in a piece titled "A Businessman's Letter to J.F.K. and His Reply." "I am confident," wrote Rockefeller, "that the thoughts I express are shared widely within the financial and business community, both here and abroad."[45] He went on to criticize Kennedy's proposed exchange controls over capital movements, which he said "would destroy the effective functioning of the dollar." He had definite opinions about the White House idea of requiring a "25 [percent] gold reserve against Federal Reserve notes and deposits." He believed that suspending the requirement briefly might be the best way to "handle the problem." But he was not averse "to seeing the law repealed altogether." Kennedy ignored the negatives, instead responding to Rockefeller with his appreciation: "I am gratified that we agree so widely on basic problems and goals."[46]

The exchange was dubbed a "landmark" by the media. It also helped elevate Kennedy in the eyes of the business community. On July 13, 1962, Rockefeller met for a financial policy meeting with Kennedy for nearly ninety minutes, one of the longest one-on-one meetings with a lead banker during Kennedy's presidency.[47] Yet Kennedy still wanted to contain the outflow of capital whereas the financiers wanted to set it free. Kennedy lost that battle. He wasn't able to push through any of his capital-restraining initiatives. But he did push through an important trade initiative that was right up the bankers' alley. The Trade Expansion Act of 1962 reduced tariffs and promoted free trade, particularly with the Atlantic community. At the signing speech, he said, "A vital expanding economy in the free world is a strong counter to the threat of the world Communist movement." These words served as a true bridge to the globalist financiers.

The *Life* incident and its aftermath had forced Kennedy to conclude that it would be better to publicly befriend more bankers. He followed up by inviting bankers like Weinberg (who, though a Democrat, had supported Nixon in the 1960 election) and Thomas S. Lamont (vice chairman of the Morgan Guaranty Trust Company and son of former Morgan head Thomas W. Lamont) to an intimate luncheon at the White House.[48] (Thomas Lamont, though a Republican, publicly supported Democratic presidents, like his father had—notably JFK and LBJ.)[49]

Yet JFK's efforts to push his economic policies through Congress remained encumbered. He had come to the realization that to push them through, he would need more active bankers' support. But this was a game they played better than he did.

David and *Time* Magazine, September 1962

The *Life* article elevated Rockefeller's stature more than Kennedy's. In its September 7, 1962, cover story, "Banker: The Man at the Top," *Time* magazine paid homage to Rockefeller through an interview that took place while he was navigating New York traffic. The article portrayed him as a multitasking god, driving, exposing his views to the reporter, and "dictating to the secretary at his side a highly technical memorandum on the need for U.S. banks to give long-term loans to foreign importers so that they might buy more U.S. goods."

The piece considered the mogul one of that "little group of men" located at "the financial hub of the world's wealthiest nation" who "by their nods give the stop or go sign to enterprises from Bonn to Bangkok." It aptly noted, "They wield vast powers." With Chase's twenty-eight foreign branches and fifty thousand correspondent banking offices circling the globe, *Time* noted, "Rockefeller frequently hops about the world cementing relationships and encouraging correspondents to be more openhanded with loans to good local risks." In a page from Rostow's book, Rockefeller advocated the "profit motive" for progress, telling *Time,* "Business leaders must point out forcefully and persuasively those government policies or actions that prevent the private economy from achieving its full potential."[50] US Cold War foreign policy saw a fine (or no) line between "forcefully" pointing out policies that prevented private capital from moving where it wanted to and creating such a situation through the use of military force.

McCloy and the Cuban Missile Crisis

After Fidel Castro rose to power following the 1959 Cuban Revolution, Cuba and the Soviet Union forged closer economic ties. As Nasser had done in Egypt, Castro also nationalized the foreign banks. This didn't sit well with the major US bankers who had considered Cuba a potential strategic financial services hub in the 1950s. The Soviet Union wasn't just supplanting American capitalist ideology with Communism by its tighter relationship with Cuba; it was keeping bankers from a major financial outpost. The situation grew worse when Kennedy issued an embargo against Cuba by an executive order announced on February 8, 1962.

Eight months later, on October 14, 1962, an American U-2 spy plane discovered medium-range ballistic Soviet missiles in Cuba.[51] Fearing that the Cold War could become a real war, Kennedy convened eighteen advisers, including John McCloy, to discuss his options. Eight days after that, Kennedy ordered a naval quarantine of Cuba to pressure Khrushchev to remove the missiles. Though McCloy was in Germany on other business, Kennedy urged him to return to the United States to negotiate the Cuba situation at the United Nations.[52]

Kennedy wasted no time in sending a US military plane to collect McCloy and bring him back. Two days later, Soviet vessels approached the quarantine line anyway. Then, they turned back. Three days after that, the Cubans downed a US reconnaissance plane. Diplomacy appeared to be failing. The whole crisis had begun because the Soviet Union was providing economic assistance and arms to Cuba, which was, as Khrushchev wrote JFK, "constantly under the continuous threat of an invasion." Now, with various US planes flying over Soviet territory, he declared that his government "could not remain indifferent." Further, he said that the Soviet government had supplied "defense against aggression" and not "offensive means," as JFK described it, to protect itself from possible invasions.[53]

The situation appeared dire. But after thirteen nailbiting days, on October 28, Kennedy accepted Khrushchev's offer to withdraw his missiles from Cuba in return for an end to the quarantine, a US pledge not to invade Cuba or violate Cuban airspace, and, more covertly, a US pledge to extract its arms from Turkey.[54] The unintended consequence of that official end to the Cuban missile crisis was a three-and-a-half-year bull market, and a renewed vigor of bankers to expand elsewhere into Latin America.

McCloy Returns to the Private Sector

On January 1, 1963, the White House received the official announcement that "John J. McCloy has again become a member of the firm." "The firm" went from being named Milbank, Tweed, Hope, and Hadley to Milbank, Tweed, Hadley, and McCloy.

Though detangled from Washington officially, McCloy continued his disarmament efforts through the Council on Foreign Relations and *Foreign Affairs*. He also remained an adviser to the group he had created within the Kennedy administration. He had come to the realization that the Cold War served no obvious business purpose for him or for US bankers or businessmen. Financial and business growth required an open global market. Whereas at one point war had been good for finance, and postwar US government support for its allies had been as well, now its threat was detrimental, restrictive, and would scare international speculators from forging into new territories.

McCloy's official time with Kennedy had proved personally profitable. The goodwill that Kennedy had for him enabled McCloy to retain a major piece of legal business: that of the "Seven Sisters," the seven largest international oil companies, controlling 85 percent of global oil reserves.

McCloy persuaded Kennedy that US oil companies, particularly, had to unite against the Organization of the Petroleum Exporting Countries (OPEC) countries for the sake of price stability. His argument was positioned as a matter of national security.[55] Kennedy responded by asking his brother Robert Kennedy, the attorney general, to provide McCloy whatever latitude he required. McCloy also benefited from one of RFK's earlier promises to help him whenever he needed it.[56] As a result, McCloy was allowed to represent all seven firms, despite the antitrust implications of doing so. The move would be extremely lucrative for his clients during the 1970s Middle East oil embargoes.

In early 1963, McCloy traveled to the Middle East as ambassador for his oil clients, not for Chase (though it amounted to the same thing). There, he struck up a relationship with Prince Abdullah bin Abdul-Rahman of Saudi Arabia, which would serve him, Rockefeller, and their respective companies (Milbank, Tweed was Chase's law firm) well, especially during the price spikes of the 1970s.[57]

As always, McCloy deftly mixed his private business dealings with US foreign policy goals: while traveling he leveraged his post as chairman of the Council on Foreign Relations to ensure that the appropriate power players in Washington and the private sector were aligned. In Saudi Arabia, he discussed the effect of OPEC's demands for increased oil revenues on his clients (years before what would be a full-blown oil crisis), and Chase's desire to handle Saudi Arabian and Aramco pension funds. All this while he was making diplomacy suggestions on Kennedy's behalf.[58]

Late Support and Criticism for Kennedy

On January 14, 1963, during what would be his final State of the Union address, Kennedy emphasized the need to keep the recovery going with high growth and full employment.[59] Again, he pushed for a balanced budget and tax reductions for individuals—which he had championed during his inaugural address. Six weeks later, at an American Bankers Association symposium at Washington's Mayflower Hotel cohosted by David Rockefeller, he attempted to rally business support for his proposals.

It was difficult. Neither the business community nor Congress wanted tax cuts without requisite spending cuts. In response to one loaded question,

Kennedy said briskly, "The alternative today is between keeping this econ-omy moving ahead and a recession, and in my judgment the best medicine for that recession is a tax reduction."[60]

On April 23, in a speech at the Economic Club of Chicago, Rockefeller proposed creating a private business advisory committee to work with gov-ernment organizations implementing the Alliance for Progress.[61] He endorsed Kennedy's support for broadening the government's investment-guarantee program, which encouraged a greater flow of private investment. He also indirectly admonished Communist-leaning governments, stating, "Latin-American governments cannot lure foreign capital by harassing companies already there." Three days later, Rockefeller had an off-the-record meeting alone with Kennedy to discuss these private business-government synergies.

On the one hand, Kennedy was learning their language. "I want to make it clear that, in solving its international payments problem, this nation will continue to adhere to its historic advocacy of freer trade and capital move-ments, and that it will continue to honor its obligation to carry a fair share of the defense and development of the free world," he said. "At the same time, we shall continue policies designed to reduce unemployment and stimulate growth here at home—for the well-being of all free peoples is inextricably en-twined with the progress achieved by our own people." He also made it clear that he would maintain the dollar "as good as gold," freely interchangeable with gold at $35 an ounce, "the foundation-stone of the free world's trade and payments system."

Yet Kennedy stubbornly targeted that balance of payments deficit, to the chagrin of bankers. It was largely because of their opportunistic expansion that the Eurodollar market had roughly tripled during the 1950s, and doubled again in the early 1960s amid the rapid expansion of American multinational corporations and the companion growth of US banking branches abroad.[62]

Kennedy feared that the outflow of funds into Eurodollar accounts was damaging the US balance of payments that tabulated the amount of physical and financial exports and imports. The declining balance meant that more money was flowing out, and that more American companies and individuals were investing their dollars outside the United States.

To combat this inequity, he announced a program on July 18 that in-cluded a temporary 15 percent tax on purchases by Americans of foreign se-curities and a tax on loans made by American banks to foreign borrowers, a quasi-regulation impinging on banks' global expansion activities. His action infuriated the bankers, who had positioned themselves above US balance of payments problems by opening foreign branches that could cater to foreign investors and borrowers, or sell foreign securities to America. The government concerns over where money was spent was less important to US banks.

But privately, Kennedy was worried about the value of the dollar and of gold. Certain US aid to developing countries wasn't pouring back into the US economy but going into gold purchases. During a July 31 phone conversation, Treasury Secretary C. Douglas Dillon told him Peru, for one, was "using our aid money to buy gold."

Kennedy commented, "It's an insane system to have all these dollars floating around [that] people can cash in for a very limited supply of gold."

Dillon agreed, saying they should tell Congress "we have a policy: if countries have so strong a balance of payments, we can't give these soft loans."[63]

But in terms of the gold standard, the banking sector, as per Rockefeller's *Life* article, considered it restrictive to their desired open policy of money and investment flow. To them, this transcended any national balance of payment issues. First National City Bank executive vice president Walter Wriston was especially livid. "Who is this upstart President interfering with the free flow of capital?" he demanded. "You can't damn capital."[64]

Born in Middletown, Connecticut, on August 3, 1919, Wriston was "an unbending proponent of laissez-faire capitalism," much like his father, Henry, who considered FDR's New Deal a folly and had served in various advisory capacities for the Eisenhower administration and as president of the Council on Foreign Relations from 1951 to 1964.

In 1942, with a master's degree from Harvard, Walter Wriston began a three-year stint as a junior Foreign Service officer. He intended to remain at the State Department. But his father had a powerful friend at National City Bank, Vice Chairman W. Randolph Burgess, who found a spot for him in the bank's credit department.[65]

By June 1960, at the age of forty, Wriston was running First National City Bank's international division. Under his direction, the firm opened banks in Puerto Rico, Cuba, Brazil, and Argentina. The resource-rich Latin American region soon accounted for the bulk of its overseas bank deposits.[66] There, its presence exceeded Chase's, to Rockefeller's chagrin.

Instead of fighting Wriston, on October 2, 1963, Kennedy appointed him to serve with other financiers on a task force to study ways to increase foreign investment in the securities of US private companies and survey the availability of foreign financing to US private companies operating abroad (the opposite of his proposals), as another possible way to balance payments.[67]

It was a clumsy, desperate notion on Kennedy's part; to ask Wriston to find ways for foreign banks to fund US companies abroad would be to ask him to detract business away from his overseas branches. He had no incentive to put the country's economic issues ahead of his own.[68] Nor did he try to. There was too much money to be made.

The bankers did support Kennedy's foreign aid budget—or at least the part that aligned with their goals. On October 11, Rockefeller and nine other prominent business leaders protested a cut in Latin aid from $600 million to $450 million that the House had just passed and urged the Senate Foreign Relations Committee to restore the $150 million to the Alliance for Progress. In a cover letter to Senator J. William Fulbright, Rockefeller wrote that the actions of the House were "deeply disturbing to many in the business community."[69]

Rockefeller, First National City president George Moore, and Kennedy got their wish. The Senate restored the $600 million in their November 7 budget vote, even as it voted to reduce Kennedy's foreign aid budget in general.

As one of his last personal requests to Kennedy, McCloy asked him to give a speech at his alma mater, Amherst College, for the groundbreaking of the Robert Frost Memorial Library. Kennedy flew to Massachusetts to address a crowd of ten thousand people and pay homage to the recently deceased poet. He also received an honorary law degree. At a time when 50 percent of the students at private universities came from the top 10 percent of the wealthiest Americans, Kennedy said, "Privilege is here, and with privilege goes responsibility."[70] He also said, "When power leads men towards arrogance, poetry reminds him of his limitations." But rather than taking Kennedy's words to heart, bankers were working hard to increase their power around the globe.

Bankers Forge Ahead

As the mid-1960s approached, private investments by Americans and companies abroad totaled $60 billion, exceeding foreign holdings in America by $25 billion.[71] The US banks that operated through their British arms were free of the constraints of the Glass-Steagall Act. In London, they could underwrite securities and perform other related deposit and lending activities, a combination off-limits to them in the United States.

This international loophole stoked First National City Bank's global profits. For instance, Shell Oil called First National City Bank requesting an immediate $100 million term loan to buy an international company. In a matter of days, Wriston put together the world's first Eurodollar syndicated loan.[72]

From that point onward, the amount of syndicated Eurodollar loans escalated. With their rise, the days of true relationship banking and individual banker culpability became numbered. A new era of anonymous banking was being born. Rather than one bank being predominantly responsible for a major loan, a whole syndicate would share the risk, which meant they could afford to care less about the risk and the client. That spelled the end of the illusion of personalized service, even for major corporate clients.

The "syndicate" was evangelized by "tombstone" advertisements that listed the participating banks on the pages of glossy financial publications, in order of their importance in the deal. Banks jockeyed for the top spot to attain bragging and selling rights. First National City and Chase topped many tombstones. Flashy young salesmen with little knowledge of finance itself infiltrated the banking business, pitching loan deals at lavish dinners, exclusive sports events, and upscale stripper joints.

With more capital finding its way over national borders, cracks began showing in the Bretton Woods system of fixed exchange rates. Wriston (like Rockefeller) considered attempts to control monetary flows detrimental to the US role as a preeminent financial center, but more so to free-market banking philosophy generally. Kennedy, on the other hand, didn't support that view. In October 1963, Congress considered doubling the price of gold, or freeing up $12 billion in gold, to counteract foreign governments and central banks that were calling in the gold that backed their US dollars.

Wriston later wrote, "In 1963, the United States began a futile bout with capital controls, triggering a further exodus of American capital. In this period, New York banks began to finance projects in America with dollars deposited in European banks."[73] This deregulatory argument would be used widely from that point onward.

First National City president George Moore also wanted the government to back off. He explained, "Any prolonged debate in Congress over the enactment of such legislation would further damage confidence in the dollar."[74]

As it turned out, further decisions as to what would have happened to the dollar and to gold under a Kennedy administration were cut tragically short. Shortly after noon on November 22, 1963, Kennedy was assassinated.

Country in Mourning, Bankers in Flux

Treasury Secretary Dillon immediately telegrammed his condolences to Vice President Lyndon B. Johnson upon hearing the news.[75] Similar wires, telegrams, and letters began streaming in from around the world. Every Wall Street titan quickly offered his sympathies to the Texan who would assume the Oval Office.[76]

Within an hour of the announcement, all major exchanges had ceased trading. The Federal Reserve moved to prevent a possible panic. Alfred Hayes, president of the New York Fed, signaled to investors that the Federal Reserve and European central banks would cooperate to thwart speculation against the dollar in the foreign exchange markets.[77] Bankers were summoned to the New York Fed headquarters for a damage-control meeting, where they were asked to buy dollars around the world.

New York governor Nelson Rockefeller declared November 25, 1963, a state holiday. Banks, securities exchanges, and commodity markets would be closed to mourn Kennedy and avoid the possibility of related losses.[78]

Along with the rest of the nation, Joseph P. Kennedy watched his son's funeral procession and his grandson's salute to the motorcade carrying the flag-draped coffin on television. He sat virtually speechless and crippled from a stroke two years earlier.[79] There had been much talk about frosty relations between father and president, not least because, as columnist Drew Pearson recalled, it was only once "Joe, Jr., was shot down by a Nazi pursuit plane off the coast of Portugal during the war" that "Joe, Sr., concentrated on his next son, Jack."[80] Joe had also lost his daughter Kathleen at the tender age of twenty-eight. Regardless of the status of their relationship at the time, in the days that followed the death of his son, Joe Sr. brimmed with personal, historical loss.

Young Bankers Rising

In the shadow of Kennedy's murder, his young adversary stood poised to grab a larger role influencing international financial policy. Wriston's international division opened its 100th and 101st foreign branches, in Durban, South Africa, and New Delhi, India, respectively.[81] First National City Bank now had more overseas branches than any other American bank, spanning thirty-four countries on five continents.

In a piece it decided to run just two days after Kennedy's death, the *New York Times* glowed, "Tall, lanky, youthful Walt Wriston looks, talks, and acts like anything but the 'typical banker' . . . whose fingers rest on the levers that make the big money flow."

The paper was oblivious to tension between Wriston and Kennedy before his death. According to the article, Wriston "knows the bankers who count from London to Tokyo, from Cape Town to Cairo," yet he never "served a pitch on foreign soil." Technological advances in banking and communications, the offering of more flight routes, and an eager set of bankers willing to jet anywhere to push a deal enabled Wriston to do much from his New York office.

Of the recent rush of American banks opening offices in Europe to take advantage of the Eurodollar market, Wriston quipped, "Europe is a pretty girl everyone has just discovered at the dance."[82] In truth, as Wriston knew well, the Eurodollar market was more than a fad. It was a means to circumvent US banking regulations and establish an international command station from which to dominate an increasingly globalized financial arena.

David Rockefeller's Unfolding Agenda

Under Johnson, the globe remained David Rockefeller's theater, and his connection to Washington would solidify. He became the banker with whom Johnson had the most frequent communication on policies. (Johnson had the closest personal contact with his banker friend Sidney Weinberg.)[83] Rockefeller was also the first banker to follow his condolences to Johnson with his agenda.

He saw Kennedy's Alliance for Progress program as a support mechanism for his expansionist economic policy, and he had no intention of letting Kennedy's death change the momentum. Less than a week after Kennedy was laid to rest, Rockefeller informed Johnson that Kennedy had sent him a letter two days before his death in which he said he "would welcome having the appropriate agencies of government" meet with Rockefeller's Business Group for Latin America.[84]

Rockefeller needed Johnson's approval for the plan to come to fruition. Johnson responded with unequivocal support for the Alliance for Progress, particularly the private enterprise component that Rockefeller so earnestly advocated. The initiative served both men. For Rockefeller it provided broader entry into a region rich with financial promise, and for Johnson it meant business-sector support for an area rich with political promise. Backing non-Communist countries in Latin America with a combination of private and public capital would provide another signal of Johnson's strength against the Soviets.

"I . . . want . . . to reaffirm the important role that private enterprise has to play in helping to achieve the goals of the Alliance for Progress," Johnson replied.[85] Over the next few years, several critical meetings took place between Johnson, Rockefeller, and the Business Group for Latin America. As a result of the alignment of Johnson and the financial sector, US banks more aggressively set up branches and bought ownership percentages in locally established banks in the region.[86] The financialization of foreign policy would continue to disperse globally with impunity.

CHAPTER 12

THE MID- TO LATE 1960S: PROGRESSIVE POLICIES AND BANKERS' ECONOMY

"We are willing to offer our free-world friends access to American markets,
but we expect and we must have access to their markets also."

—President Lyndon Johnson, April 21, 1964

THOUGH KENNEDY'S ASSASSINATION GAVE STOCKS AN INITIAL SHOCK, THE New York Stock Exchange scored its largest one-day percentage gain since 1940 the day after his funeral.[1] For much of Wall Street, Kennedy's death seemed like a minor obstacle to be discarded, not unlike the capital-flow restrictions he had supported as president. The country required a sense of continuity after the emotional trauma of his murder, and that was something Johnson could provide. The bankers, on the other hand, supported Johnson because they knew that he supported them—politically and personally. Their mutual power reinforcement would last through much of the Vietnam War, waning only as Johnson's own power faded in its dark shadows.

George Keith Funston, president of the New York Stock Exchange, equated the buoyancy of the market with the American spirit, concluding that "the emotional selloff of Friday did not reflect a real appraisal of the country's economy and its strength."[2]

It was also indicative of how little the nation's executive leadership meant to Wall Street, since its lead bankers now felt more firmly in command. If anything, Johnson would enable their influence over the US economy and international trade partners to grow. After congratulating Funston, Johnson shrewdly capitalized on the stock market's resilience to solidify his business credibility. He invited ninety top members of the Business Council to the White House Fish Room. There, he rallied their endorsement with his signature booming voice.

"We need the can-do spirit of the American businessman," he told them. "So I ask you: banish your fears, shed your doubts, renew your hopes. We have much work to do." His speech achieved its intended goal of strengthening his alliance with the financiers and their clients. "No one has ever made a more stirring address to businessmen," pronounced Goldman Sachs head Sidney Weinberg, "and in thirty years I've heard a lot of them."[3]

As Johnson assumed the presidency, the country was enjoying an economic boom that had begun under Kennedy and surged after the Cuban missile crisis. Industrial production hit new highs. Companies reached an unprecedented $51 billion in pretax profit.[4] Detroit's automakers enjoyed their best year ever. Steel attained its highest output level in six years. By the end of 1963, the economy was only a few months away from its longest sustained peacetime recovery since World War II.[5]

Consumers were setting new spending records. That "buy now, pay later" mentality cradled the nascent credit card business, which had experienced growing pains in the 1950s but stood poised for an upsurge. Racking up debt inevitably trumped saving. That was good for banks, which would make more money on interest payments for the new credit they extended while seeking out fresh capital sources, internationally and domestically. Bankers were also becoming less conservative about maintaining that capital in reserve against potential losses. The risks that bankers would soon take was commensurate with the invincibility they felt, as the pain of the Great Depression, and the prudency it fostered, gave way to a recklessness of accumulation.

During the pre-Depression era, consumer credit had more than doubled, from $1.4 billion in 1925 to $3 billion in 1929.[6] But that increase was nothing compared to what transpired in the early 1960s. Outstanding household consumer credit increased nearly $10 billion in 1963, from $69.3 billion to

$77.9 billion.[7] Appliance manufacturers were having their best years since the early 1950s. Abundant mortgage money fueled a housing boom. The stock market hit records.

"The little man is buying stocks again," noted *Time Magazine*.

That vote of confidence meant that the financiers could profit further from the little man's investments. In this quest, President Johnson would prove an able partner. If Eisenhower was a liberal Republican, Johnson was his doppelgänger: a conservative Democrat, friendly and respectful with bankers, progressive with the public. The banking community's embrace provided Johnson with an easier platform from which to pass economic proposals that Kennedy couldn't. For instance, Kennedy never managed to get his $11 billion tax cut bill through Congress, which wrangled obsessively over companion spending cuts and barely restrained antagonism toward the young president.

Johnson was determined to bulldog it through, Texas style. He privately enlisted bankers and businessmen to help him, and publicly assured the country of continuity with an adored Kennedy. In his November 27, 1963, speech before Congress, he said, "No act of ours could more fittingly continue the work of President Kennedy than the early passage of the tax bill for which he fought all this long year."[8] Johnson did not leave the result to chance. He utilized Wall Street's backing.

Bankers were now supporting the very policy they had rejected, citing inflation fears, under Kennedy, who didn't live to see his tax plans approved. For Johnson, the timing of Kennedy's death could not have been better. With an economy on the rise, he had the political capital (and skill) to pass progressive acts like Medicare and the various Great Society initiatives that enabled people to achieve greater economic equality. He passed the 1964 Civil Rights Act. He would preside over the biggest drop in national poverty of any president—from 22 percent to 13 percent during his five years in office. He increased the minimum benefit of Social Security, lifting 2.5 million seniors out of poverty. He established higher education grants and scholarships; the Elementary and Secondary Education Act, which provided federal aid for the first time to local public schools; and the food stamps program. He managed to do all this while remaining the bankers' ally. In short, he struck a perfect political-financial balance.

"So far, Pres. Johnson has won a reception from businessmen that is cordial beyond anything lately experienced by a Democratic president," noted a December 1963 *Time* article. "In homey speeches to them at White House meetings and in personal phone calls, Johnson has appeared a friendly, conservative chief executive who understands business."[9] And he would do everything to keep it that way.

Dillon and Wall Street

Given the circumstances, Kennedy's Treasury secretary, C. Douglas Dillon, remained in his post. But even if Kennedy hadn't picked a Republican banker to run the Treasury Department, Dillon suited Johnson's strategy of incorporating the business community in his policies in a bipartisan manner. Keeping Dillon in place further validated Johnson in the eyes of the Wall Street community.

Dillon had plenty of Wall Street ties from his banker days, along with the benefit of having been born the son of the founder of the prestigious US-based international investment bank Dillon, Read & Company.[10] He was also uniquely positioned to offer contrasting observations between Kennedy and Johnson with respect to their economic policies and personalities. Notably, he considered Kennedy to have been narrowly obsessed with the balance of payments and his "phobia about gold," whereas he considered Johnson's conceptual scope about domestic and foreign financial polices much broader.

With respect to the tax program, he felt both presidents were on the same page.[11] But regarding the budget cuts that accompanied the tax cut bill passed under Johnson, Dillon said that Johnson had more experience to negotiate them, having served on the Senate Appropriations Committee. In general, Dillon felt that Kennedy didn't have a "particular interest in budget details," and that he and Johnson were very "different kinds of men."[12]

The difference in their personal styles, among other things, was reflected in the length of their conversations and the extent of their written communication. Johnson, Dillon recalled, liked to talk (a lot!) when someone came in to see him, whereas Kennedy would "sit down and talk for three or four minutes about something" and then say, "Bye."[13]

The amount of time Johnson spent interacting with bankers and businessmen—talking to them on the phone, remembering details about their families, asking them for help directly and indirectly, writing them letters—greatly affected their support of him and his policies. The relationship was one of mutual use value.

Under Johnson, bankers didn't need to worry about regulatory impediments to their practices. And with bankers' support, Johnson could be assured a host of positives, from campaign funding to backing for his progressive policies to support for the Vietnam War. The nature of the symbiotic relationship Johnson had with the financiers was something that Kennedy either didn't fully understand until well into his second year or hadn't successfully entertained. Perhaps his ego or personal style rendered him uncomfortable asking for assistance from these men until later in his term. Or he didn't think he needed them until it was too late. But whatever his reasons, his behavior toward bankers made his policy progress harder to attain. Johnson was having none of that. Besides, he liked the bankers. They spoke the same "get it done my way" language.

In another contrast to Kennedy, Johnson was not a huge fan of John McCloy.[14] Johnson's friend J. Edgar Hoover, head of the FBI, didn't like McCloy at all, having clashed with him over alleged Communist tendencies during the Eisenhower presidency.

Yet Johnson needed a loyal legal mind to probe into Kennedy's murder—in order to move past it. So he appointed McCloy to the Warren Commission, established to circumvent a broader congressional investigation into the assassination.

Johnson wanted the investigation wrapped up by the November 1964 election. Lingering questions about Kennedy would detract from his power. But the commission got off to a slow start. McCloy expressed his doubts about this delay and lack of subpoena power at a January 8, 1964, dinner at CIA director John McCone's home.

The next day, McCone informed Johnson that McCloy was concerned "over the lack of action on the part of the Commission."[15] Despite that concern, McCloy attended just sixteen of fifty-one formal commission sessions. He had been hesitant from the start despite his past collaboration with Kennedy and was now focused on private concerns. He forewarned Warren he had "a terrific schedule" that was "just piled up at this time."[16] Despite his reservation on the matter, he ultimately inserted a key phrase into the summary of the commission's 50,000-page report indicating that "based on all available evidence" there had been no findings of any conspiracy.[17] It was a legalistic cop-out that served Johnson's goal of moving forward.

The exercise appeared to have left a bad taste in his mouth, though, for as soon as Johnson began his second term (first full term) as president, McCloy removed himself from Johnson's administration. He tendered his resignation as chairman of the General Advisory Committee on Disarmament on January 20, 1965.[18]

Rockefeller, Russia, and Johnson's Victory

Though the domestic economy was thriving, Cold War–related hostilities were hampering bankers' international growth ambitions. The financial globalists sought to realign US foreign policy with their expansion goals. They wanted the US government to open trade relations with more countries; Kennedy's Trade Expansion Act had not done enough to expand financial opportunities around the world.

As a result, on March 12, 1964, the Senate Foreign Relations Committee began hearings on the topic of East-West trade, specifically trade with Communist nations, which had been an almost forbidden topic since the Cold War began. But for the financiers, more than ideology or even military supremacy was at stake. US companies and bankers were starting to lose significant amounts of money to other countries that had emerged from the economic burdens of World War II and adopted more open trade policies than the United States was entertaining. They weren't, in other words, tying trade and market activities to political ideologies. During 1962, for example, the non-Communist countries had sold $4.5 billion of goods to the Soviet Bloc in Europe, whereas the United States had sold only $145 million. Both the US manufacturing and banking industries wanted a piece of that activity.

The Cold War atmosphere made the idea of publicly supporting trade with the Communist nations less than fashionable, even detrimental vis-à-vis the domestic customer base, and thus something to be discussed only off the record. But certain businessmen began expressing their discontent at prevailing foreign trade policy in caged tones, such as: *If* the government would only support selling US products to the Soviet Union, *then* they would be happy to oblige.[19]

One businessman, David Rockefeller, had no interest in such chicken-and-egg equivocations. Chase had recently opened a branch in Hong Kong, after all. He directly called for the US government to explore an arrangement whereby if China abandoned its "belligerence" and started trading openly with the United States, then the United States could do the same.

Rockefeller's political-financial diplomacy extended to the Soviet Union. During midsummer 1964, he and his daughter Neva arrived in Leningrad. They were subsequently collected from their hotel and transported to the Kremlin to meet with Premier Khrushchev.[20] When the conversation that transpired inevitably centered on Cuba, Khrushchev pointed out that the

Cuban Revolution had occurred well before the Soviet Union was even recognized diplomatically by Castro, and thus the Soviet Union was not to be blamed for it. The Cuban Revolution, and Castro's assent and subsequent nationalization of foreign banks, had placed a real damper on the affiliations that Chase and other banks had established in Cuba during the mid-1950s.

Rockefeller disagreed with Khrushchev, and the conversation became heated. The two men eventually reached an impasse. Khrushchev aptly summarized, "You are a capitalist and a Rockefeller. I am a Communist. You are a banker. I was a miner."[21]

Upon his return to the United States, Rockefeller sent his meeting notes to President Johnson and Secretary of State Rusk, who had previously served for eight years as president of the Rockefeller Foundation. Johnson was grateful that Rockefeller had "expressed most effectively the American viewpoint on the key issue" that he discussed. On a more personal note, as he always found, Johnson added, "I understand your daughter, Neva, was a genuine asset to the American delegation in Leningrad."[22]

Johnson subsequently invited Rockefeller to the White House to discuss Rockefeller's impressions further. Rockefeller conveyed that Khrushchev was open to peace but warned Johnson that he couldn't be seen as soft on Communism before the election against Barry Goldwater. Johnson had already been taking Rockefeller's advice. Following the Tonkin Gulf incident, in which North Vietnam and the US engaged in two instances of sea and air combat, Johnson declared in his August 5, 1964, speech to Congress that Vietnam was "not just a jungle war, but a struggle for freedom on every front of human activity."[23]

Channeling Eisenhower's policy of providing US military support to countries subject to Communist revolt, and JFK's decision to dramatically increase the number of troops Eisenhower had placed in Vietnam ("We also have to participate—we may not like it—in the defense of Asia," he declared in September 1963), Johnson recommended Congress pass a resolution expressing its support "for all necessary action to protect our Armed Forces and to assist nations covered by the SEATO Treaty."[24] Further, as per Rockefeller's advice, he stressed that "an additional reason for doing so at a time when we are entering on three months of political campaigning" is that "hostile nations must understand that in such a period the United States will continue to protect its national interests, and that in these matters there is no division among us." Johnson signed the Tonkin resolution on August 10, 1964.[25] He positioned the fighting in Vietnam as a matter of national security and political unification. The strategy worked for him.

Weinberg's Help

Johnson had Wall Street on his side. In particular, Sidney Weinberg gave him more than election or anti-Communism advice. He cofounded the 1964 National Independent Committee for Johnson to raise money for his campaign. Later, in mid-1965, he became a chief contributor to the American Friends of Vietnam, a nonprofit organization created "to support a free and democratic Vietnam." In this role he raised $22,500, including $10,000 from his client the Ford Motor Company Fund.[26]

Weinberg's relationship with Johnson spanned decades, going back to the FDR days. Under Johnson, he became a regular on the list of White House invitees for everything from sixty-person "businessmen luncheons" to intimate White House Family Dining Room dinners confined to Johnson's inner circle.[27]

On September 17, 1964, the *Washington Daily News* ran the fourth segment of its "Big 10 in Business" series. Highlighting Weinberg, the paper described him as "short (5 feet 4), effervescent, energetic, smartly-dressed, owl-eyes and brimming over with ego . . . a perky and pragmatic 72 year old [who] remains today the highly influential businessman he has been for the past four decades."[28]

The article captured Johnson's attention and appreciation. The next day, in a letter of gratitude, he recalled the days when the two were "Roosevelt men": "You don't know how good it is to have that Happy Warrior of FDR, Sidney Weinberg helping me out in the year 1964. Having you here the other day made me remember my days as a young Congressman when both of us were Roosevelt men. It makes me proud that you stand with me as you did with him."[29]

Weinberg worked tirelessly during the campaign, courting the press and raising money. At a White House dinner in October 1964, Johnson asked him if he would deliver a message to "Jock Whitney" (referring to John Hay Whitney, publisher of the *New York Herald Tribune*), thanking the paper for endorsing him. Weinberg happily did.[30]

With his media, business and banking, and popular support, Johnson decisively won the 1964 election with 61 percent of the popular vote, the highest of any president since 1820. His campaign deftly mixed his progressive initiatives with an attack on Goldwater's extremism while escalating war in Vietnam. He reserved enough goodwill to launch his Great Society plan.[31] And he never forgot his friends.

Weinberg continued to provide regular recruitment recommendations for the Johnson administration. For the next few years, he also regularly reported on the pulse of the business community.

As a matter of reciprocity for his assistance, Weinberg, like the other bankers, balanced supporting Johnson with pushing his own agenda. For instance, at congressional appearances, Weinberg would strike a perfect chord between endorsing Johnson and equating the ongoing health of the national economy with the need for more lenient and favorable investment and foreign expansion related legislation.[32]

Johnson and the Bankers' Economy

In his spirited inaugural speech on January 20, 1965, Johnson declared, "In a land of great wealth, families must not live in hopeless poverty. In a land rich in harvest, children just must not go hungry."[33] He made good on his word. When Johnson began his second term, 20 percent of people in America were living in poverty. Between 1965 and 1968 he raised federal expenditures addressing the War on Poverty from $6 billion to $12 billion (Nixon would double the figure again to $24.5 billion by 1974). That spending, in conjunction with a booming economy, made a big impact. When Johnson left office in 1969, the poverty rate in America had dropped to 14 percent.[34]

On February 18, 1965, Johnson increased his focus on his friends in finance. He invited Rockefeller, Weinberg, and other prominent bankers to an intimate White House dinner to discuss his voluntary program for an early reduction in the balance of payments deficit. His plan would require each of their firms to curtail their international transactions so as to limit dollar outflow, a request that brought the ire of Wriston when it came from Kennedy but solicited no such reprimand under Johnson.[35] Johnson also established a nine-member advisory committee on balance of payments, which included Weinberg, George Moore, and railroad mogul Stuart T. Saunders to keep the business community engaged, and on his side, on the issue.[36]

That same day, Rockefeller, in turn, invited Johnson to a Business Group for Latin America gathering the following month. Johnson informed Rockefeller that he would be pleased to meet with the group in Washington. Johnson knew how to swap favors.[37]

After the event, Johnson wrote Rockefeller a warm note: "I appreciate more than I can express every line of your fine and thoughtful letter. To put it in a Johnson City way, I got more than I gave from being with you and your associates on the Council."[38]

Even when the two were at odds, Johnson maintained a deferential tone with the financier. "Thank you for sending me your views, which I am always glad to have, even when we disagree," the president wrote on November 30, 1965, after Rockefeller described some of Johnson's Great Society policies as "handouts."[39]

The bankers acted against their own profit motives and for the economic strength of the United States, possibly for the last time in American history, when they responded to Johnson's request to streamline some of their international capital outflows. On March 3, 1965, Johnson thanked Morgan Guaranty Trust Company president Thomas Gates for "the response of Morgan Guaranty and other banks to my request to voluntarily limit their foreign lending." He assured Gates, "You can count on our willingness to work with you closely."[40] Everything was up for bargaining between Johnson and the bankers, and everyone would get something out of it, including the Main Street economy.

Like other key bankers, Gates, who was appointed to the Committee on Voluntary Overseas Activities in February 1967, earned Johnson's gratitude and supported his efforts over the years. His backing included a crucial press release in August 1967, in which he regarded "a war tax essential to the support of our effort in Vietnam and the conduct of vital domestic programs," hoping it would "be enacted without delay."[41]

Wall Street and Johnson's New Treasury Secretary: "Joe" Fowler

By early 1965, Dillon wanted to return to the private sector. There was speculation in Washington that the Treasury secretary post would go to Johnson's friend and unofficial adviser Don Cook. Congressional insiders wanted Rockefeller.[42] Dillon wanted Rockefeller too. He penned a fervent four-page letter to Johnson equating Rockefeller with US dollar strength on December 29, 1964. "I have given a great deal of thought to the Treasury position," he wrote. "The more I have thought the more certain I have become that David Rockefeller has unequalled qualifications for the job. . . . At 49 [he] is young, vigorous and at the very height of his capacities. . . . Another important consideration is David Rockefeller's unique, worldwide reputation. . . . His appointment would signify, as nothing else could, your own resolve to protect the value of the dollar."[43]

The *idea* of the value of the dollar and the value of the dollar itself represented two sides of a coin. One, the political ideological-narcissistic side, had the ring of global dominance to it (strong dollar equals strong country equals American "exceptionalism"). The other, the economic side, concerned the amount of dollars that were needed to pay for certain imports or would be received for exports. In practice, the two sides canceled each other out. The more dollars dispersed throughout the world, the more their economic value would be diminished. However, the more the United States supported the dollar through its monetary or trade policies, the more that value would be artificially buoyed. This paradoxical role would manifest through various banker, Federal Reserve, Treasury Department, and White House policy decisions for the next half-century.

Although Johnson respected Rockefeller, he trusted his loyal supporter Sidney Weinberg more. At Weinberg's suggestion, Johnson chose Democrat Henry "Joe" Fowler, Kennedy's undersecretary of the Treasury, for the position. Fowler had worked on Kennedy's $11 billion tax cut plan. (Weinberg later enlisted Fowler to join Goldman Sachs as a senior partner. Fowler would be the first major Goldman executive to move from that elite public to private office; in the future, the direction would go the other way.)

In true form, Johnson didn't announce his decision right away. He wanted to ensure all the bankers and the media were on his side. So he strategically built up a consensus in the banking community. On March 17, 1965, he held a select White House luncheon with half a dozen key bankers to broach the topic. Afterward, he made some follow-up calls to secure their approval.[44] Then Johnson called Fowler: "Henry, I talked to all these bankers we met with yesterday: [First National City Bank president] George Moore, George Murphy, William Moore—there's a Princeton meeting. I'll have a Jetstar so you can land there. Go up there, no newspaper reporters, just say I don't know if I want to be Secretary or not, but I want to work with you guys."[45]

Next, Johnson called Moore, saying, "I talked to Fowler and told him to go up there tomorrow . . . you take charge of him. I want some good statements coming out. He's going to be Secretary."[46]

Moore replied, "You can rest assured the bankers will support him and his program in every way."[47]

On March 25, 1965, the Senate unanimously confirmed Fowler. Johnson sent an effusive thank-you note to another advocate, Chase chairman George Champion, writing, "I do—and will always—appreciate your constructive support of him."[48]

Political mission accomplished, Johnson wrote Weinberg the next day: "I am sure that Joe Fowler is going to make an outstanding Secretary. One reason is his talent and experience. The other is the support of men like Sidney Weinberg."[49]

Wall Street embraced Fowler. Three months later, Johnson sent Champion a letter thanking him again, this time for a dinner he had hosted for Fowler, saying, "I agree with your observations that large corporate entities are essential for continued progress in this country, that business leaders have an awareness of the need for competition. . . . I asked Joe Fowler to explore your observations concerning the balance of payments, restrictions on bank credit and the effect on exports in detail."[50] A month after Johnson asked the bankers to curtail their operations on behalf of the balance of payments deficit, he was willing to have the matter renegotiated, having won the political victory of getting the bankers to embrace his Treasury secretary appointment.

Johnson and Mergers

Toward the middle of 1965, Johnson spoke widely of national economic growth, progress, and the Great Society. He presided over the enactment of the Medicare program, and when he signed the Medicare bill into law on July 30, 1965, at the Harry S. Truman Library in Independence, Missouri, he paid homage to a plan that "all started" with Truman.[51] A year later, Johnson presented Truman and his wife, Bess, with Medicare cards number one and two.

With respect to financial regulations, however, Johnson was nearly as laissez-faire as his banker friends. Both Johnson and the bankers felt the country had moved past the more prudent restrictions of the Great Depression (the bankers more publicly so). Neither Johnson nor the bankers saw any reason to entertain legislative restrictions on the bankers' desires to grow freely. Like Eisenhower, Johnson equated strong American banks with a strong America. He also equated the size of US companies with national strength.

The pace of US corporate mergers had already accelerated under Kennedy. In 1963, the number reached 1,311, the highest figure since the Federal Trade Commission began tracking mergers in 1951. The number of antitrust cases filed by the Justice Department had also risen—to twenty by the end of 1963.

This became a key concern for Johnson. As *U.S. News & World Report* noted, "For the first time . . . businessmen have sounded protest against this action in [Johnson's] administration."[52] The FTC was launching more complaints against big companies like US Steel, GM, and AT&T, as well. Fortunately for him, the major bank regulator, the comptroller of the currency, sided on behalf of bank mergers. This helped Johnson's and the bankers' cause.

Johnson was not above using his muscle to support mergers that would increase political power. The *Houston Chronicle*, for instance, had been critical of him and endorsed Richard Nixon in 1960.[53] But John Jones Jr., the *Chronicle*'s president, was also the president of Houston's National Bank of Commerce and was attempting to merge with Texas National.

The merger had been agreed upon by both boards of directors but was stalling at the Federal Reserve, which tended to approve eastern mergers more quickly than other ones. But Johnson intervened; he made Jones guarantee him the *Chronicle*'s support as long as he held the presidency. Following an off-radar meeting at Johnson's ranch, the president got his guarantee and Jones got his merger.[54]

Manufacturers Hanover president Gabriel Hauge was fighting his own merger battle against Donald Turner, the assistant attorney general in charge of the Justice Department's antitrust division, who had filed several suits against bank mergers on the grounds that they violated Section 7 of the Clayton Act and Section 1 of the Sherman Act, which prohibited anticompetitive or monopolistic mergers (though not generally for banks).

On August 24, 1965, Hauge sent an eleven-page letter defending his bank's 1961 merger to Congressman Richard Bolling. He deemed Turner's August 6 letter to him "such an extraordinary amalgam that I cannot let it pass without comment."

Turner had contended in that letter, "there is no room for the argument that the antitrust laws were displaced in whole or in part by the Bank Merger Act [of 1960], and if Mr. Hauge's materials are intended to assert to the contrary, they are plainly wrong."[55]

Hauge argued that his merger occurred "in good faith" and was "legal under then existing law." Further, he had never received notice from the Justice Department that it intended to sue either of the banks involved in the merger. Turner eventually dropped his charges, and Manufacturers Hanover, the merged entity, remained intact.

A few months later, the bank merger bill finished its route around Washington. When the House, Senate, and Johnson passed the subsequent Bank Merger Act of 1966, it gave the appearance that more mergers would be rejected for "monopoly" reasons under Section 7 of the Clayton Act and Section 1 of the Sherman Act. But in practice, the bill left major bank mergers open to approval by the comptroller of the currency and the Federal Reserve, both of which supported the consolidation of the financial arena.

Eight months later, an antitrust suit was filed to block a proposed merger of First City National and Southern National Bank in Houston on the grounds it would substantially reduce competition and increase "concentration in commercial banking in the Houston area."[56] The merger had been approved by the comptroller of the currency. With Johnson's intervention, it remained so.

A month afterward, Special Assistant Joe Califano told President Johnson that "Stuart Saunders has been calling me about the Penn-Central merger. He claims that you told him if he ran into any problems delaying the merger, to get in touch with you and that you would move things along."[57]

In response, Johnson signaled his support directly: "You can be certain that I will be watching your merger developments, and wishing you all success."[58] Penn Central would become America's biggest bankruptcy in the 1970s.

The Latin American Alliance

On the foreign policy front, Johnson and the bankers remained in agreement over where America should wield power: both wanted to infuse more US private enterprise into Latin and Central America. Not much had changed in that regard since Eisenhower, despite a diversion by Kennedy to be more willing to provide aid based on economic need rather than strict ideological assurances.

Johnson had stated, "We are embarked on a great adventure with the Latin Americans. It is nothing less than to transform the life of an entire continent." In a letter to Rockefeller, Johnson noted, "I share your view that the private sector throughout the hemispheres has played a creative role in the life of the Alliance [for Progress]." Johnson was "especially grateful" for the "leadership" of Rockefeller and his colleagues in this "great undertaking."[59]

Johnson aligned solidly with Rockefeller, and changed or reversed certain Kennedy policies. Kennedy had been sympathetic to leaders of Latin America and its people, but under Johnson, the Alliance for Progress once again served neocolonialist goals, encouraging bankers to infiltrate the region for their own private gain.[60]

As the White House concluded in an internal note to Walt Rostow in June 1966, "Our modest security assistance to Latin America ($80 million annual) is small enough an investment to protect our major investment ($1 billion annual) in the economic, social and political development of the area."[61] Thus, as with many foreign policy ventures, US military and financial goals meshed.

Robert Kennedy made this a bone of contention with LBJ early on in his campaign to wrest the Democratic nomination for president from him. He wanted to carry on his late brother's wishes for a more peaceful, economically just Latin America. An October 31, 1966, *Washington Post* article, "RFK Would Cut Latin Aid," noted that he proposed a reduction of economic aid to Latin American nations engaged in military buildups at the expense of social reform.

RFK's position was a swipe at Johnson's policies. "This proliferation of arms," he warned, referring to sales of fighter planes to Peru and twenty-five Skyhawk jets to Argentina, "threatens to cause conflict and instability between nations and to obstruct the great objectives of the Alliance [for Progress.]"[62]

RFK was right about the more idealistic aspects of the Alliance for Progress as his brother had conceived it. The region had only seen the beginning of future abuses at the hands of US corporate and banking interests. These would blossom in the 1970s and implode catastrophically in the 1980s.

Arguably, if JFK or RFK had lived and retained the mantra of economic equality or self-sufficiency in Latin America rather than a free-for-all profit grab accompanied by military alignments, the third world debt crisis, which enabled bankers to use the federal government to support private speculation (the harbinger of more such maneuvers to follow), might never have occurred. But because the third world remained a bastion of opportunity for private bankers, and there was no political doctrine to tone down their zeal for such activity, there were no barriers to stop US bankers and their business clients from going off a speculative cliff. Once they did, the US government backed their losses, while the developing countries suffered extreme economic hardship when they were forced to default on their debts.

Bankers and Vietnam

At first, bankers were supportive of the Vietnam War. They recognized that war in general had buoyed the US economy as well as their domestic and international businesses. Indeed, by early 1965, Chase and other banks had experienced skyrocketing demand for credit, particularly from their subsidiaries abroad, as demand for war-related funding had increased.

The balance of payments had even gravitated toward the United States during the buildup to the war. Following Johnson's efforts to engage the bankers on the issue, the balance of payments showed a whopping surplus of $259 million by the week ending March 3, 1965.

Johnson expressed gratitude to the bankers for standing firmly behind him on Vietnam. On April 12, 1965, his aide Jack Valenti—who would go on to be Hollywood's supreme lobbyist for several decades—wrote First National City Bank president George Moore to say, "We are deeply grateful for your articulate analysis of the President's Vietnam address and your sound, patriotic response to the business luncheon. The knowledge that the President's policies stand your penetrating examination is both comforting and encouraging."

But two months later, Moore saw causes for financial concern. He warned that the balance of payments increase might be short-lived, and predicted another $100 billion of gold would be pulled out of the United States that year. He was aware that "certain people overseas" were growing nervous. "Banks in Asia and Europe and individuals are doing the buying."

As quickly as it had boosted the balance of payment a few months earlier, the war began to take a toll on foreign investment in the United States. On August 25, 1965, following a dinner at the White House, Moore gave Johnson suggestions on how to reverse the process. "For example," he said, "it is important to promptly enact H.R. 5916 [for] the removal of tax barriers which have served to discourage foreigners from making investments in the United States." He stressed, "This would also help to restrain inflation influences which may be heightened by the Vietnam War."[63]

War had other economic costs too. On January 14, 1966, Treasury Secretary Fowler transmitted to Congress details of the tax program that Johnson announced in his State of the Union address, intended to raise billions of dollars to help pay for the war. The program was signed into law in mid-March 1966.[64] By then, half a million troops were fighting in Vietnam and the population was openly protesting it.

The Dow, however, was inspired by war. It hit a record 1,000 on February 6, 1966, and it kept rising through April 1968. Additionally, the US housing market was booming. In five years, George Champion quintupled the size of Chase's real estate credit portfolio; it reached $1 billion in 1966, outpacing the growth of all other Wall Street commercial banks. First National City ratcheted up its personal credit and auto loans. The Vietnam War was proving great for banks.

Rockefeller used the war to expand into Asia. In 1966, he raised the ire of peace protesters by opening a Chase branch in Saigon. He also engaged two former Chase men, John McCloy and Eugene Black, to drum up financial support from the banking community for the war.

But Rockefeller rarely operated without a quid pro quo, and the war boom was now revealing a troubling side for him. On January 25, 1966, he sent his concerns to Johnson that Vietnam was draining focus from Latin America. "Latin Americans are concerned that the harsh exigencies of the war in Vietnam may again make Latin America a low-priority area in U.S. policy," he wrote. "We ourselves are well aware that your Administration gives Latin America a high priority indeed, but we are equally well aware that Latin Americans need constantly to be reassured of that fact."[65]

Support Wavers

Rockefeller's worries were soon shared by many bankers who had originally supported Johnson. Though they saw the war's early benefits, they now feared it could be detrimental to their global expansion goals, particularly if it escalated into full-scale multiregional battles. From a domestic standpoint, Vietnam wasn't going to be a war of national unity that would open channels for them; it was becoming a nuisance.

Construction companies that were engaged in war material production were fine with US intervention and military escalation into Southeast Asia because it brought them more contracts and profits.[66] But in general, elite support was fading. As University of Houston professor Robert Buzzanco put it,

> The bankers and other corporate elite who had global visions for American investment and commerce came to believe that the war in Vietnam was damaging their interest because it focused resources on Indochina and undermined their larger goals by running up huge deficits and providing resistance from traditional European allies. And so, significant elements in the ruling class opposed the war in Vietnam . . . not because they believed the war was wrong, but because it was, in their estimation, breaking doctrinal ligature that defined foreign relations since Wilson: free-trade imperialism and non-intervention.[67]

Regarding the Great Society, bankers were also becoming lukewarm. In truth, the success of those policies mattered less to bankers than overseas growth did. As long as bankers were making money and increasing their global influence, what happened domestically was of secondary importance; providing support to Johnson was no hardship. But now they were growing wary of backing Johnson's efforts.

In 1966 Johnson signed the Participation Sales Act, which encouraged substitution of public credit with private credit. The initiative, started by Eisenhower and extended by President Kennedy's 1962 Committee on Federal Credit programs, was meant to be a favor to the bankers.[68] By replacing $3.3 billion in outstanding public debt (through government-issued bonds) with private debt (or bank-issued bonds), the government effectively converted public loans into private loans for the banks, giving them $3.3 billion of business guaranteed by the US government.

Soon after the bill was signed, Johnson's aide Robert Kintner suggested that Johnson form a confidential program to determine how "important business, financial, and industrial leaders feel toward the job being done by the President and particularly how they feel in relation to the Vietnam operation, the President's European and Latin American policies, the character and duration of prosperity, and the President's economic, financial and social policies."

The survey would be based on off-the-record interviews with prominent figures including David Rockefeller, Sidney Weinberg, Roger Blough, and Bobby Lehman.[69] But Johnson preferred the route of his private soirées at the White House, which increased in frequency as public opinion turned against the war. As long as the finance and business community could be swayed to support the war, he figured, funding would continue unabated.

War and Taxes

By mid-1967, war and inflation and antiwar demonstrations were escalating, and Johnson was getting increasingly nervous. In August, he held one of his regular off-the-record, no publicity luncheons with the usual crew to gain validation for his domestic and war-related strategies. The "old warrior" Sidney Weinberg came through. He submitted a statement to the House Ways and Means Committee on September 13 in which he urged Congress to give "prompt and favorable consideration" to Johnson's request for the 10 percent surtax to protect the credit and capital market and "to help finance the war in Vietnam and to prevent an inflationary boom." Weinberg closed his statement by stressing the importance to the health of the economy that "nothing be done in this legislation to impair the incentives offered to business in the foreign tax credit and the investment tax credit."[70]

New First National City Bank president Walter Wriston also supported the war surtax bill, not because of any opinions about the war but primarily because he wanted lower rates to fund expansion. He said that the rising interest rates caused by the union of greater private and government borrowing would worsen in the absence of the surtax.

Wall Street had just undergone an inevitable power shift that placed Wriston in a more influential position in such political-financial matters. In June 1967, *Time* ran a story titled "Banking: The Plum at First National City," in which it observed, "Command changes at major banks are usually about as suspenseful as tomorrow's office hours. But not at Manhattan's aggressive First National City Bank," where "President George S. Moore, 62, was a cinch to succeed Chairman James Stillman Rockefeller" (David Rockefeller's second cousin), who would be retiring in July. But the "plum" president's slot went to Wriston, the forty-seven-year-old executive vice president for overseas operations. With Moore three years from retirement, Wriston "would lose no time getting into 'the maximum possible responsibilities.'"

Surging Borrowing and War Expenditures

By the late 1960s, the US balance of payments was falling again as expenditures for Vietnam abroad grew. Johnson reluctantly asked banks to reduce foreign credits once more to compensate for the imbalance. This time, they were less supportive.

In London, borrowings by the overseas branches of US banks were surging in the Eurodollar market. First National City Bank had developed the first multicurrency loan agreement, which gave corporate treasurers flexibility to borrow in different currencies (and introduced a greater element of currency risk into the global financial system).

By the time Wriston was appointed president and CEO of First National City Bank, his name had already been circulating in the Washington influence sphere for two years. He was nominated to the Business Council on July 5, 1967, and was seen as a possibility for assistant secretary of the Treasury for international affairs and various other foreign affairs positions.[71]

When Johnson announced he would escalate his war against the mounting balance of payments deficit by attempting to control international capital flows (as Kennedy had attempted), the increasingly confident Wriston now publicly attacked the policy. "Foreign-exchange controls in peacetime never have operated effectively, and man being what he is, they never will," he said.[72]

His words did the trick. Johnson eventually capitulated to the bankers, announcing that dollar loans in US overseas branches would be excluded from the interest equalization tax. Wriston had won. As a result, even more Eurodollar transactions occurred abroad, away from US regulators.

Domestically, consumer demand for credit cards escalated. To feed the demand and build up fee income from credit card operations, Wriston created First National City Bank's own credit card, the Everything Card, in August 1967.[73] To promote it, he initiated mass credit card mailings, sending more than twenty million cards across America.

But First National City Bank realized $1 billion in losses before turning a profit in its credit card division.[74] Between 1967 and 1970, twenty-six million people held the bank's credit cards. An astounding five million of them defaulted. The Everything Card eventually became too costly to maintain as an independent brand, and Wriston subsequently partnered with MasterCard. Under Wriston's successor, John Reed, Citibank (as the bank would later be called) became the largest issuer of credit cards in the world. In 1968, though, Bank of America led the credit card industry, with eight million cardholders across thirty-three states.

Vietnam Escalates, Johnson Exits

On January 30, 1968, the Tet offensive began. Vietnamese Revolutionary Forces attacked South Vietnamese cities and towns. Suicide squads from the National Liberation Front (Vietcong) hit the US embassy on January 31, while the former capital of Hue was captured by Communist forces and retaken by US forces. As Johnson increased the war effort, protests in the United States grew.

Later, Fowler recalled the economic fallout of that decision. "We all had to exercise constraint in our normal activities in order to carry the additional burdens of the war without unduly damaging or wrecking the economy."[75]

Now the economy and dollar were increasingly at risk, as vast amounts of gold were flowing from the United States. America's share of world trade, which had approached 50 percent after World War II, dropped to 25 percent in 1964 and hit 10 percent in 1968.[76]

In tandem, bankers became more vocal with their concerns about the war as the economic crisis grew. Wriston told a group of European financial leaders in January that it would be possible to overcome the monetary crisis without changing the gold standard. But "the chances would be greater if the Vietnamese war ended."[77]

Public opinion soured rapidly on Johnson, while Robert Kennedy's standing in the Democratic Party rose. In the maelstrom of a pending economic crisis and a highly unpopular war, Johnson announced his withdrawal from the presidential race on March 31, 1968, leaving a wide-open space for Kennedy to fill. Aside from the war, the tax cut, and the civil rights acts he had pushed through after JFK's death, not to mention the sixty or so acts that defined the Great Society and his reduction of poverty, Johnson left a legacy of political acumen that incorporated a strong alliance of bankers and businessmen with the needs of the public good. By choosing not to focus on regulating industry and finance, he was able to push through progressive programs and keep the capitalists happy at the same time. His approach was sometimes brutish but often congenial. No other president since Johnson has been able to harness bipartisanship as effectively from a political power perspective.

Meanwhile, the bankers turned their attention to Congress to push domestic policy to their liking. On May 2, 1968, leading bankers from the United States and Europe gathered at the fifteenth annual monetary conference of the American Bankers Association in Dorado Beach, Puerto Rico. At the conference Wriston said that "now is the time for action": if serious problems were to be avoided, the tax package pending in Congress must become law within thirty days.

Alfred Schaefer, chairman of the Union Bank of Switzerland, echoed this sentiment. "Time is running out," he said. "Worried people" were looking to the United States to impose adequate restraint on its economy. Imports into the United States had risen 20 percent, a major factor, Wriston concluded, in undermining the nation's payments position.[78] Now bankers feared a new international finance crisis unless Congress increased taxes and cut government spending.

But it was a political and emotional crisis that shattered the nation, not a financial one. Two months after the assassination of Martin Luther King Jr. and four and a half years after the assassination of his brother, RFK was assassinated. He was shot shortly after midnight on June 5, 1968, in Los Angeles, after winning the California and South Dakota Democratic nomination primaries. Richard Nixon would benefit the most this time as he went on to finally capture the presidency he had sought against JFK.

Nixon's War

As soon as Nixon entered the White House, Vietnam became his war. He also assumed power at a moment when the market and broader economy were degrading quickly. From January to July 1969, the Dow dropped nearly 25 percent, from 985 to 800. This was only the beginning. Debt was transforming from a national crutch to a huge problem. Household credit— in the form of mortgages and consumer loans—had increased 78 percent during the 1960s, from $17.6 billion at the start of the decade to $31.4 billion by its close. Total household credit card debt had risen from $216 billion to $458.4 billion, a 112 percent rise.[79] Americans were suddenly worried about how they would pay their debt.

By the end of the 1960s, new home construction was sputtering, as were industrial expansion and jobs creation. The dollar was being crushed by international investors who held many more dollars than could be redeemed in available gold and wanted to dump them as fast as they could.[80]

There was a silver lining—for the big commercial bankers. On March 24, 1969, the *New York Times* reported that 1968 had been a "good year for banking," as profits "soared to record levels." The top execs did well, too. The fact that this was so prominently pointed out revealed a newfound media interest in showcasing the wealth of the powerful financiers, and ignoring the trials of the broader population.

Walter Wriston received what was dubbed a "whopping $53,000 increase" in 1968. When he was promoted to president, his salary was $128,139. David Rockefeller received $540,000 annually from Chase as its largest individual shareholder, plus a $23,000 raise to a salary of $253,000 when he became chairman—an increase equal to that given to George Champion, his predecessor as Chase chairman. Bank of America's Rudolph Peterson received the lowest salary among the major bankers: a base of $137,500 plus $37,500 in deferred compensation and some more from profit sharing, bringing him to $178,384. The Morgan Guaranty Trust Company paid the most: chairman Thomas Gates got $276,250 base and other "additional compensation" in 1968. Champion, who retired as Chase chairman on February 28, 1969, was due to get $119,000 in annual pension payments.[81] The Depression and postwar decades of humble behavior and pay were over, even as the economy was careening downward.

Rockefeller and the Middle East

As stakes in the world marketplace rose, competition between First National City Bank and Chase intensified. Newly elected Chase chairman Rockefeller was more interested in high-level diplomacy than in the details of CDs or bank capital controls that concerned his rival, Wriston (who cared equally about spreading his global power).

To enhance Chase's "global visibility worldwide," Rockefeller decided to create the International Advisory Committee, a group of prominent businessmen and politicians, many of whom were personal friends. Over the years, the IAC recruited C. Douglas Dillon, Henry Ford III, Cyrus Vance, and Henry Kissinger. And whether it helped business or merely the political openings for business, by 1969, deposits in Chase's overseas branches comprised nearly one-third of the firm's total deposits, and overseas foreign loans, one-fourth of its total loan portfolio. As Rockefeller wrote, "Earnings from the international side were expanding and would soon surpass domestic income."

Some banks chose to open new branches internationally for local access, while others chose to buy interest in local banks for similar expansion purposes. First National City and British banks tended to favor opening branches. Chase continued to prefer acquiring shares of banks in developing countries. But there were some hiccups on that accord.

But in 1969, bankers were nervous that the new Andean Pact, which sought to protect trade relationships in Latin America and limited the percentage acquisition by foreign banks of local banks to 20 percent, would curtail their expansion in that area. As a result, during the first few years that followed, US bankers refocused on building their presence in Europe.

Rockefeller increased his focus on the Middle East. In the fall of 1969, Egypt's UN ambassador visited Rockefeller at Chase's offices on President Nasser's request. It was a pivotal visit for Chase's Middle East relations, which would prove far more beneficial to Chase than to the American population.

Nasser told Rockefeller that US policy was "hostile to Arabs" and that the United States should modify support for Israel. A month later, Rockefeller was invited to discuss Middle East issues at the White House. There in the Oval Office sat his former boss, John McCloy, and the chairmen of Standard Oil, Mobil, and Amoco. They had not gathered to discuss diplomacy but a more critical matter—oil.

When the *New York Times* got wind of the meeting, it plastered the news across the front page with the words "Pro-Arab" next to "Pro Oil." Public opinion turned against Chase and its "anti-Israel stance." But the issue was just heating up. During the 1970s, the struggle for power among the political and financial elites would include the struggle for control of that most precious commodity: oil. The battle for the profits that oil brought and the international control that physical or financial access to it enabled would play out in the embassies of the Middle East, the boardrooms of Wall Street, and the Oval Office in Washington.

CHAPTER 13

THE EARLY TO MID-1970S: CORRUPTION, GOLD, OIL, AND BANKRUPTCIES

"I'm mad as hell and I'm not going to take this anymore."

—Howard Beale, *Network*

PRESIDENT RICHARD NIXON MAY HAVE BECOME THE NATION'S CEO IN 1969, but during the 1970s, the US financial throne, along with the unelected leadership it provided, belonged to the two most powerful banking titans: Walter Wriston, chairman of First National City Bank, and David Rockefeller, chairman of the Chase Manhattan Bank.

Their inevitable rise was more than the culmination of ladder climbing at their respective firms. The retirement of the two bankers they replaced—First National City Bank's George Moore and Chase's George Champion—severed all remnants of ties to post-Depression-era prudency and postwar unity in the eastern banking community. In the early 1970s, the banking industry continued the noticeable shift that had begun in the

1960s, back to the 1920s-style pursuit of private gain without even the pretense of public service or attention to public good.

An undertone of defiance on the part of the bankers that would have been unacceptable, even vulgar, in the postwar days festered alongside a dogmatic attachment to free-market ideals. They saw more opportunity in international pursuits—even if it meant diverging from US foreign policy initiatives—and pressed Nixon to abandon the Bretton Woods agreements, which had pegged the dollar to gold. For bankers, such restrictions were no longer palatable.

The oil crisis made this divergence all the more apparent. During the years when domestic inflation soared and oil prices quadrupled, the population suffered mightily. But the bankers were able to use price spikes to book massive petrodollar profits, off- and onshore. During the period, both Wriston and Rockefeller turned down cabinet posts, unwilling to leave the firms through which they were more globally powerful.

Whereas the 1960s encompassed a loss of youth and innocence, the 1970s evoked shattered trust, heightened cynicism, and economic fracture. It became increasingly clear that though the United States was a superpower, it couldn't control the oil prices upon which it was increasingly dependent, and so it wasn't omnipotent. In 1973, Rockefeller established the Trilateral Commission, an elite organization that gave the influential private-sector men of North America, Asia, and Europe opportunities to discuss ways to retain their global power. It was minted as a means to establish their "communication and cooperation." But it also served Rockefeller's aspirations to spread "democratic capitalism," as he put it—which in practice meant western financial control over international economies.

Its creation coincided with the growing fear among bankers that if US economic and political power became less dominant relative to Western Europe and Japan, then the unelected leaders of the private sector would lose their ability to dictate the path of global affairs. The organization was designed to ensure that if the goals of the bankers and the White House diverged on matters of importance, there would exist a body outside the elected political system to protect open trade and capital flows.

Nixon had a more distant relationship with Wall Street than his predecessor, one of the most probusiness Democrats in history. With his detached style and stiff persona, Nixon presided over an accelerated wave of multinational corporate expansions that drove bankers further away from the country's needs as they scrambled to service these giant customers in an increasingly international arena.

Wall Street's War

While the protests against the Vietnam War intensified in the first years of the Nixon administration, the financial elite was fighting its own war—over the future of banking and against Glass-Steagall regulations. Wriston was a steadfast warrior in related battles, as he fought with Rockefeller for supremacy over the US banker community and for dominance over global finance.

Rockefeller's sights were set on a grander prize, one with worldwide implications: ending the financial cold war. He made his mark in that regard by opening the first US bank in Moscow since the 1920s, and the first in Beijing since the 1949 revolution.

Augmenting their domestic and international expansion plans, both men and their banks prospered from the emerging and extremely lucrative business of recycling petrodollars from the Middle East into third world countries. By acting as the middlemen—capturing oil revenues and transforming them into high-interest-rate loans, to Latin America in particular—bankers accentuated disparities in global wealth. They dumped loans into developing countries and made huge amounts of money in the process. By funneling profits into debts, they caused extreme pain in the debtor nations, especially when the oil-producing nations began to raise their prices. This raised the cost of energy and provoked a wave of inflation that further oppressed these third world nations, the US population, and other economies throughout the world.

Bank Holding Company Battles

When Eisenhower signed the 1956 Bank Holding Company Act banning interstate banking, he left a large loophole as a conciliatory gambit: a gray area as to what big banks could consider "financially-related business," which fell under their jurisdiction. In practice, that meant that they could find ways to expand their breadth of services while they figured out ways to grow their domestic grab for depositors. On May 26, 1970, the "Big Three" bankers—Wriston and Rockefeller, along with Alden "Tom" Clausen, chairman of Bank America Corporation—appeared before the Senate Banking and Currency Committee to press their case for widening the loophole.

During the proceedings, Wriston led the charge on behalf of his brethren in the crusade. Tall, slim, elegantly dressed, and the most articulate of the three, he dramatically called on Congress to "throw off some of the shackles on banking which inhibit competition in the financial markets."[1]

The global financial landscape was evolving. Ever since World War II, US bankers hadn't worried too much about their supremacy being challenged by other international banks, which were still playing catch-up in terms of deposits, loans, and global customers. But by now the international banks had moved beyond postwar reconstructive pain and gained significant ground by trading with Cold War enemies of the United States. They were, in short, cutting into the global market that the US bankers had dominated by extending themselves into areas in which the US bankers were absent for US policy reasons. There was no such thing as "enough" of a market share in this game. As a result, US bankers had to take a longer, harder look at the "shackles" hampering their growth. To remain globally competitive, among other things, bankers sought to shatter post-Depression legislative barriers like Glass-Steagall.

They wielded fear coated in shades of nationalism as a weapon: if US bankers became less competitive, then by extension the United States would become less powerful. The competition argument would remain dominant on Wall Street and in Washington for nearly three decades, until the separation of speculative and commercial banking that had been invoked by the Glass-Steagall Act would be no more.

Wriston deftly equated the expansion of US banking with general US global progress and power. It wasn't so much that this connection hadn't occurred to presidents or bankers since World War II; indeed, that was how the political-financial alliances had been operating. But from that point on, the notion was formally and publicly verbalized, and placed on the congressional record. The idea that commercial banks served the country and perpetuated its global identity and strength, rather than the other way around, became a key argument for domestic deregulation—even if, in practice, it was the country that would serve the banks.

Penn Central Debacle

There was, however, a fly in the ointment. To increase their size, bankers wanted to be able to accumulate more services or branches beneath the holding company umbrella. But a crisis in another industry would give some legislators pause. The Penn Central meltdown, the first financial crisis of Nixon's presidency, temporarily dampened the ardency of deregulation enthusiasts. The collapse of the largest, most diverse railroad holding company in America was blamed on overzealous bank lending to a plethora of nonrailroad-oriented entities under one holding company umbrella. The debacle renewed debate about a stricter bank holding company bill.[2]

Under Wriston's guidance, National City had spearheaded a fifty-three-bank syndicate to lend $500 million in revolving credit to Penn Central, even when it showed obvious signs of imminent implosion.

Penn Central had been one of the leading US corporations in the 1960s. President Johnson had supported the merger that spawned the conglomerate on behalf of a friend, railroad merger specialist Stuart Saunders, who became chairman. He had done this over the warnings of the Justice Department and despite allegations of antitrust violations called by its competitors. With nary a regulator paying attention, Penn Central had morphed into more than a railroad holding company, encompassing real estate, hotels, pipelines, and theme parks. Meanwhile, highways, cars, and commercial airlines had chipped away at Penn Central's dominant market position. To try to compensate, Penn Central had delved into a host of speculative expansions and deals.[3] That strategy was failing fast. By May 1970, Penn Central was feverishly drawing on its credit lines just to scrounge up enough cash to keep going.

The conglomerate demonstrated that holding companies could be mere shell constructions under which other unrelated businesses could exist, much as the 1920s holding companies housed reckless financial ventures under utility firm banners.

Allegations circulated that Rockefeller had launched a five-day selling strategy of Penn Central stock, culminating with the dumping of 134,400 shares on the fifth day, based on insider information he received as one of the firm's key lenders.[4] He denied the charges.

In a joint effort with the bankers to hide the Penn Central debacle behind a shield of federal bailout loans, the Pentagon stepped in, claiming that assisting Penn Central was a matter of national defense.[5] Under the auspices of national security, Washington utilized the Defense Production Act of 1950, a convenient bill passed at the start of the Korean War that enabled the president to force businesses to prioritize national security–related endeavors.

On June 21, 1970, Penn Central filed for bankruptcy, becoming the first major US corporation to go bust since the Depression.[6] Its failure was not an isolated incident by any means. Instead, it was one of a number of major defaults that shook the commercial paper market to its core. ("Commercial paper" is a term for the short-term promissory notes sold by large corporations to raise quick money, backed only by their *promise* to pay the amount of the note at the end of its term, not by any collateral.) But the agile bankers knew how to capitalize on that turmoil. When companies stopped borrowing in the flailing commercial paper market, they had to turn to major banks like Chase for loans instead. As a result, the worldwide loans of Chase, First

National City Bank, and Bank of America surged to $27.7 billion by the end of 1971, more than double the 1969 total of $13 billion.[7]

A year later, the largest US defense company, Lockheed, was facing bankruptcy, as well. Again bankers found a way to come out ahead on the people's dime. Lockheed's bankers at Bank of America and Bankers Trust led a syndicate that petitioned the Defense Department for a bailout on similar national security grounds. The CEO, Daniel Haughton, even agreed to step down if an appropriate government loan was provided.

In response, the Nixon administration offered $250 million in emergency loans to Lockheed—in effect, bailing out the banks and the corporation. To explain the bailout at a time when the general economy was struggling, Nixon introduced the Lockheed Emergency Loan Act by stating, "It will have a major impact on the economy of California, and will contribute greatly to the economic strength of the country as a whole."[8] After the bill was passed, not a single Lockheed executive stepped down.[9]

It would take several years of political-financial debate and more bailouts to sustain Penn Central. One 1975 article labeled the entire episode "The Penn-C Fairy Tale" and condemned the subsequent federal bailout: "While the country is in the worst recession since the depression and unemployment lines grow longer every day, Congress is dumping another third of a billion dollars of your tax payer dollars down the railroad rat hole."[10] (The incident was prologue: Congress would lavish hundreds of billions of dollars to sustain the biggest banks after the 2008 financial crisis, topped up by trillions of dollars from the Fed and the Treasury Department in the form of loans, bond purchases, and other subsidies.)

More Bank Holding Company Politics

Despite the Penn Central crisis, the revised Bank Holding Company Act decisively passed the Senate on September 16, 1970, by a bipartisan vote of seventy-seven to one. The final version was far more lenient than the one that Texas Democrat John William Wright Patman, chair of the House Committee on Banking and Currency, or even the Nixon administration had originally envisioned. The revised act allowed big banks to retain nonbank units acquired before June 1968. It also gave the Fed greater regulatory authority over bank holding companies, including the power to determine what constituted one.[11] Language was added to enable banks to be considered one-bank holding companies if they, or any of their subsidiaries, held any deposits or extended any commercial loans, thus broadening their scope.[12]

President Nixon signed the bill into law without fanfare on New Year's Eve 1970. In fact, his inner circle decided against making a splash about it. They didn't think the public would understand or care. Plus, they realized that there was a prevailing attitude that the Nixon administration had favored the big banks, and though it had, this was not something they wanted to draw attention to.[13]

The End of the Gold Standard

The top six banks controlled 20 percent of the nation's deposits through one-bank holding companies, but second place in that group wasn't good enough for Wriston, who noted to the Nixon administration that his bank was really the "caretaker of the aspirations of millions of people" whose money it held.[14] Wriston flooded the New York Fed with proposals for expansion. His applications "were said to represent as many as half of the total of all of the banks." The Fed was so overwhelmed, it had to enlist First National City Bank to interpret the new law on its behalf.[15]

By mid-1971, the Fed had approved thirteen and rejected seven of Wriston's applications. His biggest disappointment was the insurance underwriting rejection. The possibility of converting depositors for insurance business had been tantalizing. It would continue to be a hard-fought, ultimately successful battle.

Around the same time, New York governor Nelson Rockefeller (David Rockefeller's brother) approved legislation permitting banks to set up subsidiaries in each of the state's nine banking districts. This was a gift for Wriston and David Rockefeller, because it meant their banks could expand within the state. Each subsidiary could open branches through June 1976, when the districts would be eliminated and banks could merge and branch freely.

Several months later, First National City Bank was paying generous prices to purchase the tiniest upstate banks, from which it began extending loans to the riskiest companies and getting hosed in the process; a minor David vs. Goliath revenge of local banks against Wall Street muscle.

By that time, the stock market had turned bearish, and foreign countries were increasingly demanding their paper dollars be converted into gold as they shifted funds out of dollar reserves. Bankers, meanwhile, postured for a dollar devaluation, which would make their cost of funds cheaper and enable them to expand their lending businesses.

They knew that the fastest way to further devalue the dollar was to sever it from gold, and they made their opinions clear to Nixon, taking care to blame the devaluation on external foreign speculation, not their own movement of capital and lending abroad.

The strategy worked. On August 15, 1971, Nixon bashed the "international money speculators" in a televised speech, stating, "Because they thrive on crises they help to create them."[16] He noted that "in recent weeks the speculators have been waging an all-out war on the American dollar."[17] His words were true in essence, yet they were chosen to exclude the actions of the major US banks, which were also selling the dollar. Foreign central banks had access to US gold through the Bretton Woods rules, and they exercised this access. Exchanging dollars for gold had the effect of decreasing the value of the US dollar relative to that gold. Between January and August 1971, European banks (aided by US banks with European branches) catalyzed a $20 billion gold outflow.

As John Butler wrote in *The Golden Revolution*, "By July 1971, the US gold reserves had fallen sharply, to under $10 billion, and at the rate things were going, would be exhausted in weeks. [Treasury Secretary John] Connally was tasked with organizing an emergency weekend meeting of Nixon's various economic and domestic policy advisers. At 2:30 P.M. on August 13, they gathered, in secret, at Camp David to decide how to respond to the incipient run on the dollar."[18]

Nixon's solution, pressed by the banking community, was to abandon the gold standard. In his speech the president informed Americans that he had directed Connally to "suspend *temporarily* the convertibility of the dollar into gold or other reserve assets." He promised this would "defend the dollar against the speculators." Because Bretton Woods didn't allow for dollar devaluation, Nixon effectively ended the accord that had set international currency parameters since World War II, signaling the beginning of the end of the gold standard.

Once the dollar was no longer backed by gold, questions surfaced as to what truly backed it (besides the US military). According to Butler, "The Bretton Woods regime was doomed to fail as it was not compatible with domestic US economic policy objectives which, from the mid-1960s onwards, were increasingly inflationary."[19]

It wasn't simply *policy* that was inflationary. The expansion of debt via the joint efforts of the Treasury Department and the Federal Reserve was greatly augmented by the bankers' drive to loan more funds against their capital base. That established a *debt inflation* policy, which took off after the dissolution of Bretton Woods. Without the constraint of keeping gold in reserve to back the dollar, bankers could increase their leverage and speculate more freely, while getting money more easily from the Federal Reserve's discount window. Abandoning the gold standard and "floating" the dollar was like navigating the waters of global finance without an anchor to slow down the dispersion of money and loans. For the bankers, this made expansion much easier.

Indeed, on September 24, 1971, Chase board director and former Treasury Secretary C. Douglas Dillon (chairman of the Brookings Institution and, from 1972 to 1975, the Rockefeller Foundation) told Connally that "under no circumstances should we ever go back to assuming limited convertibility into gold."[20] Chase Board chairman David Rockefeller wrote National Security Adviser (and later Secretary of State) Henry Kissinger to recommend "a reevaluation of foreign currencies, a devaluation of the dollar, removal of the U.S. import surcharge and 'buy America' credits, and a new international monetary system with greater flexibility . . . and less reliance on gold."[21]

With the dollar devalued, investors poured money into stocks, fueling a rally from November 1971 led by the "Nifty Fifty," a group of "respectable" big-cap growth stocks. These were being bought "like greyhounds chasing a mechanical rabbit" by pension funds, insurance companies, and trust funds.[22] The Chicago Board of Trade began trading options on individual stocks in 1973 to increase the avenues for betting; speculators could soon thereafter trade futures on currencies and bonds.

The National Association of Securities Dealers rendered all this trading easier on February 8, 1971, when it launched the NASDAQ. The first computerized quote system enabled market makers to post and transact over-the-counter prices quickly. With the stock market booming again, NASDAQ became a more convenient avenue for Wall Street firms to raise money. Many abandoned their former partnership models whereby the firm's partners risked their own capital for the firm, in favor of raising capital by selling the public shares. That way, the upside—and the growing risk—would also be diffused and transferred to shareholders. Merrill Lynch was one of the first major investment bank partnerships to go "public" in 1971. Other classic industry leaders quickly followed suit.

Meanwhile, corporations were finding prevailing lower interest rates more attractive. Instead of getting loans from banks, they could fund themselves more cheaply by issuing bonds in the capital markets. This took business away from commercial banks, which were restricted by domestic regulation from acting as issuing agents. But bankers had positioned themselves on both sides of the Atlantic to get around this problem, so they were covered by the shift in their major customers' financing preferences. While their ability to service corporate demand was dampened at home, overseas it roared.

Currency market turmoil also led many countries to the Eurodollar market for credit, where US banks were waiting. Thus, the credit extended through international branches of major US banks tripled to $4.5 billion from 1969 to 1972.

The market rally, cheered on by the media, was enough to bolster Nixon's fortunes. In the fall of 1972, Nixon was reelected in a landslide on promises to end the Vietnam War with "peace and honor." Wall Street reaped the benefits of a bull market, and more citizens and companies were sucked into new debt products.[23] The Dow hit a 1970s peak of 1,052 points in January 1973, as Nixon began his second term.[24]

Nixon's Personality and the Bankers

For the most part, Nixon resented the East Coast money establishment. Yet he maintained a warm relationship with Gabriel Hauge, president of Manufacturers Hanover, whom he had known since the Eisenhower era, when Hauge worked as Ike's economic adviser. Hauge began informing Nixon of his economic opinions, as he had with Eisenhower. But Nixon didn't respond by seeking them out, as Eisenhower had done, and soon the opinions stopped coming.[25]

The personal distance between Nixon and the Wall Street bankers cut both ways. For instance, Rockefeller had corresponded in some manner with Johnson every other week: through letters, meetings, notes, memos, invitations, and other event appearances. The two horse-traded their support for each other.

But when he tried similar tactics with Nixon, he found himself spurned more often than not. Still, he remained proactive about dropping by the White House, as he did on September 13, 1971, when he visited to discuss international economic developments and their policy implications.[26] Rockefeller had a tremendous stake in aligning his intentions with those of the president. But it was harder to get a direct audience with Nixon. Rather than being able to meet with Nixon, he was asked three weeks later to submit a formal proposal on the matter, including an outline of his recommendations.[27] The idea that he would be denied these types of personal meetings did not sit well with him. On October 18, Rockefeller requested a face-to-face meeting with Nixon. Again he was denied.

In general, comments to Nixon, including personal correspondence, were filtered through his aides. For instance, economic adviser Peter Flanigan sent Nixon a memo about Merrill Lynch chairman Don Regan for the dual purposes of policy discussion and providing money: "You will be interested to learn that Don Regan shares the concern for the lack of growth in the money supply and has taken action to make his concern forcefully known in the right places," Flanigan wrote. "You will also be happy to learn that the Merrill Foundation, of which Don Regan is President, has granted $100,000 to redo the reception area on the second floor of the White House."[28]

Rockefeller's Appointments and Wriston's Ambitions

Nixon's relative insularity may explain the frosty relationships between the White House and Wall Street in the early 1970s. This didn't imply there was no relationship, just a colder one.

Both Wriston and Rockefeller received requests to become Nixon's Treasury secretary, and both were insulted that the request didn't come directly from Nixon. Though they cited conflicts of interest for turning down the post, it might have been conflicts of ego. Rockefeller, in fact, declined the offer twice—first in the fall of 1968 and then in January 1974, when he learned from General Alexander Haig that George Shultz was stepping down.

Among other disagreements, Rockefeller opposed Nixon's price and wage controls. "My own inclination," he said, "was to allow the markets to have free rein."[29] Perhaps more to the point, a Washington post would have been constrictive for a power broker like Rockefeller. Besides, with economic problems mounting, he didn't want to become Nixon's scapegoat. It turned out to be a wise decision.

Meanwhile, Wriston was determined to convince Wall Street that First National City Bank was better than any other bank. He had to find investors to raise more capital, and investors had to be persuaded that the returns were worth it. So Wriston made the bold move of promising a 15 percent return on equity throughout the 1970s. Considered gutsy at the time, Wriston's promise held true. By 1972, First National City Bank shares had broken through a 20 percent return-on-equity barrier and were fast becoming one of the hottest plays on Wall Street. In the process, shorter-term stock market performance became more important than longer-term, more prudent behavior, and the rise of Wall Street analysts touting stocks to small investors soon followed.

Free-Market Float

As stocks prices rose, so did inflation. Democratic Congressman Wright Patman blamed the banks for inflaming this problem through rate manipulation. Wriston retorted that the federal government's efforts were making the banking industry "more volatile."[30] The Justice Department entered the fray when it launched an investigation into rate setting. When Wriston was interrogated, he explained that the practice of explicitly setting prime rates was obsolete anyway. Like many future bank leaders, he escaped unscathed from the allegations of rate manipulation.

On October 20, 1971, at the prestigious Fairmont Hotel in downtown Los Angeles, Wriston and Edward Palmer, his executive committee chairman, decided to unleash market forces that would dictate the level of the prime rates banks charged as interest on loans to their most "credit-worthy" customers. In a public statement, Palmer announced that he was responsible for the changes, but he was deliberately vague as to what they would be in practice.[31] The practice of floating rates was considered a bold move for banks at the time.

Wriston remained obsessed with the idea of a "free-market float" in all of its forms. He disdained price and wage controls as fiercely as he did fixed currencies. While in Manila, Philippines, on October 28, 1971, Wriston initiated a public attack against Nixon's wage and price controls that lasted until the controls were lifted in 1974.[32]

To more privately press his ideas, in late November 1971, Wriston met with Nixon and Treasury Secretary Connally. Over ham and cheese sandwiches, he told Connally, "At the end of the day, the dollar is going to be floating" before suggesting devaluing it further. Wriston's support for devaluation "meant a great deal to Connally."[33] On November 13, at an informal news conference following his seventeen-day trip to Asia, Connally told reporters that world monetary uncertainty could continue for "an almost indefinite period" given that most major currencies were "floating," but he noted that the United States was well positioned regardless.[34] Shortly thereafter, Connally announced another 10 percent devaluation of the dollar. Wriston had influenced the direction of the US currency to the benefit of its banks, for whom "cheaper" money meant a greater supply of it for their purposes.

Four months after Nixon's suspension of dollar convertibility into gold, the Group of Ten major countries agreed to appreciate their currencies relative to the US dollar. To facilitate the action, the Smithsonian Agreements (named for the Smithsonian Institution, where the group met) were passed on December 18, 1971. They allowed the IMF to adjust the relationships of currency rates.[35] As a result of the agreements, the price of gold rose from $35 per ounce to $38.

Nixon called it "the most significant monetary agreement in world history."[36] A year later, it became clear that it had failed. The banker-led movement toward an international, floating-rate multicurrency system proved too powerful a force against government or central bank desires to peg currencies. Within fifteen months, all the major currencies were floating against one another.

By May 1972, free-marketer George Shultz had replaced Connally as Treasury secretary. A product of the Chicago School of Economics and a "close friend" of Chicago School icon Milton Friedman, he and Wriston were kindred spirits.[37] Both believed the world financial system should be "free." Through their relationship Wriston could exercise even greater influence on Washington. As Wriston's biographer Phillip Zweig wrote, "When Wriston spoke, Shultz did more than listen; he acted."[38]

Wriston led bankers to embrace floating prime rates in the fall of 1972. First National City earned the distinction of being labeled a "floating bank" by the White House, a designation shared with Bankers Trust and Irving Trust. As such, Wriston also chose to raise rates without caring about the Fed's posture on the matter. His main rivals were the "nonfloating banks" Chase, Morgan Guaranty, Bank of America, and Manufacturers Hanover. These were considered more politically aligned with the administration because they operated within the confines of federally dictated monetary policy and hadn't yet pressed the floating rate boundary.

In an internal memo to Treasury Secretary Shultz, Peter Flanigan, who would later be a managing director at Dillon, Read, proposed contacting these nonfloaters and asking them not to raise their rates no matter what the floaters were doing.[39] This would maintain the illusion of Washington control over rates. But in reality, it was Wall Street that was king of domestic financial policy, and Wriston who wielded the control.

Wriston elevated his attacks on Nixon's policies at an April 1973 speech at the New York Bar Association titled "Freedom and Controls." He said, "The freedom to win or lose, to succeed or fail, is basic to our way of life. When the marketplace is hobbled by regulation, the distortions created are eventually reflected across the country."[40] Wriston's way would prevail.

By the time of Wriston's diatribe, First National City Bank had surpassed Bank of America as the nation's most profitable bank. "Walt's Bank," also known as "Fat Citi," was considered one of the best managed companies in America by the business press. The *International Herald Tribune* called Wriston the world's "most influential banker."[41] He was a major force propelling multinational companies to further expand beyond the United States. As he said in a September 1973 speech titled "The World Corporation: New Weight in an Old Balance," "The pressure to develop the economy of the world into a real community must come, in part, from an increasing number of multinational firms which see the world as a whole." If theoretically the White House had a say in US economic policy, practically, it was Wriston who controlled its financial trajectory.

Rockefeller, the Soviet Union, and the People's Republic of China

In March 1973, David Rockefeller infiltrated the Eastern Bloc with the skill of a *Mission Impossible* agent. Under his tutelage, Chase had become the first US bank since 1929 to open a fully operational office in the Soviet Union. Four months earlier, Chase had opened a representative branch at One Karl Marx Square, near the Kremlin.

Rockefeller pushed Chase to provide the first loan by a US bank in the Soviet Union by the summer of 1973: $86 million to finance a truck foundry on the Kama River.[42] Unlike Wriston, he was still partial to aligning himself more closely with Nixon. Linking his expansion desires to foreign military policy, he told the Joint Economic Committee that "the desire of the Soviets to use Western trade, credits, and technology to bolster their own economy hopefully could be accompanied by their giving lower priority to military programs."[43] Like his former boss, John McCloy, he believed international finance could replace competitive armament stockpiling. Later, instead of a Cold War lined with weapons, there would be bank wars based on economic competition.

Wriston was less enthusiastic about the area. He refused to grant loans to the Soviet Union except on a floating-rate basis. Though First National City Bank had opened a Moscow office in the spring of 1974 (after which eleven of its New York City branches had their windows smashed), it wound up closing after six years and made no money in the interim.

Rockefeller led Chase on another global expansion spree, adding forty foreign branches, representative offices, affiliates, subsidiaries, and joint ventures. In July 1973, after he returned from a business trip to Hong Kong, Rockefeller steered Chase to become the first US correspondent to the Bank of China since the 1949 Chinese Revolution.[44]

His actions preempted Washington to some extent, or were at least nearly parallel in timing. In early 1973 the Nixon administration had established the National Council on US-China Trade, a "public-private group" whose goal was to increase trading opportunities with China. (The council would later become known as the United States Business Council.) Rockefeller was appointed its vice chairman, and he attended its first conference in Washington in May of that year.[45]

With that political credential in the bag, he made his first visit to China, becoming the first American bank executive to enter since the 1949 revolution. Chase was subsequently invited to become the first US bank in China. Its branch office was established at the Peking Hotel, where many US corporations would be introduced to officials and business opportunities.

On one hot, muggy night in late June 1973, Rockefeller, his wife, Peggy, and his entourage waited at the Great Hall of the People in Beijing. "Zhou Enlai . . . stood at the top of the steps to greet us," he later wrote. This was an unusual gesture; "he did not extend such a welcome to Nixon or Kissinger."[46] When they met, Rockefeller told Zhou that the weak US dollar had been caused by faulty US policies (that had emanated from Johnson through Nixon) rather than "fundamental economic ills."

Rockefeller considered this meeting critical for all future US-China relations. "I felt our new connection was supporting of broader American interests as well," he wrote. "The diplomatic opening achieved by Nixon and Kissinger had enormous significance . . . [but] contact with the PRC at the private as well as at the government level would be necessary."[47] Soon after his visit, Chase made its first loan to China. Subsequently, the Chase World Information Corporation, a Chase subsidiary focused on Eastern Europe, the Soviet Union, the Middle East, and China, began introducing American businesses to investment opportunities in China. Rockefeller visited China five more times over the next fifteen years.[48]

Rockefeller, McCloy, and the Middle East

Even more significant to Chase, and to Wall Street as a whole, was the oil-rich Middle East. At the start of 1970, Chase had little representation there, except for an office branch in Beirut, a joint venture in Dubai, and a role as a major depository for the Saudi central bank, SAMA—which kept funds at its head office and in London. By 1971, Chase had established a branch in Bahrain. In the wake of this growing trend of US interest in the region, the US government and the newly formed government of Bahrain agreed to establish a permanent naval base on its shores.[49] In concert with Rockefeller's expansion, the entire Fifth Fleet of the US Navy found a new home.

Rockefeller had been involved in Middle Eastern affairs for the better part of two decades. He was one of a handful of Americans with access to all the Arab leaders in the region.[50] McCloy was equally keen about the area.

By the spring of 1973, the Watergate cover-up was unraveling, and Nixon became obsessed with saving his presidency. McCloy, who had operated for decades in elite policy circles, his power and influence growing in tandem with that of American presidents, was appalled by Nixon's shenanigans. Now he felt disillusioned.[51]

McCloy believed that Watergate distracted Nixon from Middle East initiatives, just as Vietnam had distracted him from his European ones. He was increasingly focused on his oil company clients, the "Seven Sisters," and their position in the mix of oil and money politics. It was on their behalf that McCloy would flex his muscle.

With respect to other Middle East political-economic ventures, on September 22, 1973, Rockefeller and his assistant, Chase Bank vice president Joseph Reed, arrived in Cairo to meet with President Anwar Sadat. The two men were flown by an Egyptian air force plane to Alexandria, then driven west along the Mediterranean coast to Sadat's summer retreat.

Rockefeller recalled Sadat as warm. During the meeting, Sadat asked, "Mr. Rockefeller, would you be interested in establishing an office of your bank in Egypt?"[52] He responded by reminding Sadat of Chase's long-standing relationship with Israeli banks (though at the time there was no Chase branch in Israel). "Mr. President," he said, "how would you feel if we opened a branch in Tel Aviv at the same time we open one in Cairo?"

Sadat replied, "It is all a matter of timing."[53]

A week earlier, Citibank executive vice president G. A. "Al" Costanzo had flown to Beirut and announced that Citibank would lend $1 billion in the Middle East. He then flew on to Nairobi for an IMF annual conference.[54] Bankers were circling the region like sharks. They smelled money, and they assumed that political problems would be resolved if and when they arose.

But first, there would be blood.

Blood, Then Money

On October 6, 1973, Egypt and Syria launched a war against Israel. The conflict would come to be called the Yom Kippur War because it coincided with the Jewish holiday.[55] In the wake of the attack, Arab nations halted oil shipments to the United States. As a result of that embargo, oil prices would quadruple by early 1974.[56]

Two days after the Yom Kippur War began, a delegation of oil company officers, operating under the authority of McCloy's London administrative group, began negotiations with OPEC about prices. McCloy cleared the oil companies' collective bargaining strategy with the Justice Department, specifically working with Attorney General John Mitchell to circumvent antitrust issues. A lawyer from McCloy's firm, Milbank, Tweed, monitored the London group meetings.[57]

McCloy, working with officials of the Arab American Oil Company, wrote a letter to Nixon urging him not to side with Israel. "The real stakes are both our economy and our security," he said. Three days after he sent the letter, Nixon and Kissinger sent military supplies to Israel.[58] Lines were clearly drawn between what the banker and the president considered beneficial.

As the battle raged in the Sinai, McCloy continued to represent the big oil interests.[59] He defended his clients before a Senate subcommittee on multinational corporations. His monthly retainer from each of the five major oil companies jumped from $1,500 to $2,250 per month.[60]

On October 16, 1973, when OPEC members met in Kuwait City and decided to increase oil prices by 70 percent, to $5.11 a barrel, McCloy's clients found themselves to be partners-in-profit with the Arab nations.[61] It was a win for them. The "chairman of the establishment" had struck black gold. And so it would continue.

While Nixon continued to navigate Watergate, Arab members of OPEC unleashed their "oil weapon" in response to his October 20, 1973, $2.2 billion US-Israeli military aid package. The resulting spike in oil prices triggered a bear market that sent the Dow to 578 in a year, shaving about half off from its 1973 high.

But Nixon's political scandals also served as a distraction from bankers' initiatives in the wake of the war: recycling petrodollars. Global oil price shock presented US bankers with the perfect opportunity to bolster their international business and augment revenues. During the first half of 1974, foreign assets of US commercial banks quadrupled from $8.5 billion to $34 billion, more than double the 1973 pace.[62]

Ramifications of the war proved economically devastating around the rest of the world, though. Oil and energy spikes jolted the financial markets and threw many national economies into recession. US unemployment soared to 7.1 percent by December 1974 and stagflation (inflation at a time of economic stagnation) set in.[63] Developing countries were hit worse, as the dollars they had been loaned by US banks flowed back to the Middle East to pay for oil and the interest rates on their debt soared.

For those on the right side of the oil equation, however, crisis meant profit. The high oil prices brought excellent revenues to the bankers. From 1973 to 1974, earnings from oil-exporting nations in the Middle East grew

600 percent, to $140 billion, led by Saudi Arabia and Kuwait. OPEC countries sought new places to stash their petrodollar windfalls.[64] Though they kept most of the money in their own local banks, a sizable surplus found its way to western banks, including through the open doors of the bustling Euro-dollar market.

Rockefeller returned to Egypt to secure a joint venture with the National Bank of Egypt, forming Chase National Bank of Egypt with a 49 percent share. (Later, Chase opened more branches in Cairo, Alexandria, and Port Said.) Elsewhere, Chase's relationships with SAMA and Iran's central bank gave it exceptional access to the region's funds. Chase also enjoyed a strong Eurocurrency market position where the "surplus" could be recycled and the bank could direct funds beyond the Fed's purview and restrictions.[65]

In January 1974, a few months after the first "oil shock," Rockefeller jaunted over to the Swiss luxury locale of Saint Moritz, where the Shah of Iran was skiing.[66] His motive was to discuss Chase's effort to buy an interest in an Iranian commercial bank; from that vantage point, the bank could take in more petrodollar deposits.

He succeeded in spades. Over the next eighteen months, Chase created a joint venture with Iran's state-owned Industrial Credit Bank to form the International Bank of Iran, which was established in 1975. Chase retained a 40 percent share in the bank worth about $10.5 million initially.[67] More important than the size, though, was the access it provided Chase to the area.

By the mid-1970s, Chase was the leading bank for the National Iranian Oil Company. As oil prices rose, Iranian deposits at Chase escalated, along with Chase's trade finance business in the country. A high proportion of Iran's oil export money flowed through Chase's finance department—as much as $60 million a day.

According to Treasury Secretary William Simon, who succeeded Shultz after Rockefeller declined the position in 1974, $11 billion in foreign oil money was directly invested in the United States in 1974 alone.[68] Saudi Arabia, the biggest oil producer in the region, stowed its new petro-billions with US banks as CDs or in US Treasury bonds. Less conservative investors, like the Kuwaitis, stuck revenues into US and European stock markets, buying up large chunks of shares in companies like Daimler-Benz. The Iranians bought portions of steel companies, but the most notable purchase was of US weaponry. The Pentagon's foreign sales of arms more than doubled in 1974, to $8.3 billion, with almost half accounted for by Iran.[69]

Though political relationships with the Saudis were somewhat strained during the 1973 oil embargo, Wriston remained optimistic about a long-term relationship with his bank. He was right. The billionaire Saudi prince al-Waleed bin Talal became one of Citigroup's largest shareholders, with 218 million shares by 2008.

As for Israel, though US foreign policy was supportive, this was an area in which financial and political intentions diverged. US bankers remained less engaged financially. The country held little interest for them from a profit or power perspective. During a January 17, 1975, meeting with Deputy Prime Minister Yigal Allon, Israeli ambassador Simcha Dinitz convened with Vice President Nelson Rockefeller and Henry Kissinger to discuss US banking in Israel. But they held little sway over David Rockefeller regarding the merits of banking there.

Allon suggested "it would be nice if he [David Rockefeller] could arrange $150 million when he visits Israel, because the other banks are waiting to see what Chase does." To this proposal, Nelson Rockefeller replied, "I can't really get into the family business."[70]

When David Rockefeller later visited Israel, Israeli finance minister Yehoshua Rabinowitz asked him to open a Chase branch there. But Rockefeller decided there wouldn't be enough local business to justify opening a branch. Other US banks followed his lead and also decided against opening branches in the country. They knew they stood to make far more money siding with the Middle Eastern countries that possessed oil reserves. With such potential, it didn't really make a difference to them what US foreign policy was regarding Isreal.

Recycling Oil into Loans

In London, US banks were able to perform investment bank activities outlawed within US borders by Glass-Steagall. These included loan syndication, private placements (the private sale of securities to a small number of select investors, such as other large banks, mutual funds, insurance companies, and pension funds, to raise capital), foreign currency trading, bond underwriting, corporate finance, and mergers and acquisition advice.

In the United States, commercial banks could offer clients financial advice, but they could not charge fees for it like the investment banks could. Merchant banks, which were designed to deal mostly with international loans and financings to large multinational corporations, provided another way to recoup some of that inequity. As such, Citibank had established its London merchant bank, Citicorp International Bank Limited, in January 1973.[71]

CIBL became the world's largest repackager of syndicated Eurocurrency loans. It was sort of like a major hub airport, but instead of being a focal point for flights it was a fulcrum for international loans. In terms of banking culture, CIBL spawned a new breed of "salesman bankers" who "spent more time in the first-class cabins of Boeing 747s than they did in New York and London."[72] With good reason: fees for syndication were collected up front. A $100 million loan could net bankers about $500,000 in fees.

More and more commercial banks opened offices in London to circumvent Glass-Steagall. Soon, the commercial banks were beating the investment banks at their own fee-driven game.

With petrodollars gushing through its doors during the oil embargo, Citibank aggressively pursued Latin America, particularly Brazil, as a target for loans. The response was enthusiastic. Brazil agreed to pay higher rates for the ability to have fifteen-year loans as opposed to the normal eight-year ones. As a result, Brazil's trade deficit surged from $1 billion in 1973 to $6.2 billion in 1974. Citibank's loans to Brazil shot from $2 billion to $5 billion in six years. The country provided 13 percent of the bank's earnings in 1976.[73] Other US bankers clambered to lend to Venezuela, an OPEC member located outside the tense Middle East region that had potential to become a cash cow. But Citibank was the only foreign bank permitted to operate relatively freely in Colombia and Venezuela.

US bankers were also lending liberally to Mexico, Argentina, Bolivia, and Peru, forgetting the 1930s Peruvian military junta and the problems associated with its struggle to aggregate power, and ignoring the violent dictatorial bent of US-trained Bolivian president Hugo Banzer, who had been placed into power after a Nixon-ordered coup.[74] Investors wanted more Peru bonds than were available in 1973 and 1974.

Leverage and Lending

The Arab nations restricted their own lending to neighbors in Sudan, Egypt, and Kenya. Otherwise, they used the western banks' recycling programs. Wriston focused on developing a "successful" strategy for recycling petrodollars. As a result, he came in "first place" in the profits sweepstakes. Rockefeller took second, and John McGillicuddy, president of Manufacturers Hanover, was third.

US regulators enabled the recycling process by allowing banks to extend more than half of their capital to Brazil without worrying about the consequences if petrodollar profit faucets stopped flowing or Brazil stopped being able to repay its loans. This ratio of capital to loans was already 10 percent lower than it had been during the post-Depression years.

As bank capital ratios plummeted (more money was being loaned out than taken in despite the excess petrodollar funds) and regulators equivocated, Wriston advocated further reductions in capital standards, asserting that "countries never go bankrupt."[75] The entire banking industry adopted his mantra in a strategy that would lead to a nearly decade-long debt crisis in the 1980s.

When Treasury Secretary George Shultz resigned in April 1974, Wriston was tapped for the position of Treasury secretary. But like Rockefeller, who had rejected the offer twice, Wriston also refused; there was much more money and power in banking. "I have a young wife. I need the capital," he said when he got the call from General Alexander Haig.[76]

Flipping the tables on the president, Wriston offered Shultz the post of vice chairman of Citicorp (the same position future Citigroup chairman Sandy Weill would offer Robert Rubin, President Clinton's Treasury secretary, after Rubin resigned from public office in May 1999).[77] However, Shultz decided to take an executive vice president position at Bechtel Company; he rose to the post of president and remained there until 1982.[78]

Treasury Secretary William Simon, who replaced Shultz (and who would later be chairman of the Nicaraguan Freedom Fund, which would be involved in the Iran/Contra scandal), took his cues from Wall Street. He responded to the oil crisis by backing the bankers' strategy; he tried to persuade oil-producing nations to place their petrodollar surpluses in US bank deposits while discouraging them from direct investment in US corporations.[79] Foreign policy had again overlapped with banker policy.

The abundance of petrodollar money flows caused the IMF and commercial banks to engage in their own version of a lending war. In September 1974, the IMF set up a special oil facility unit from which to help struggling oil-importing nations, although it was mostly used by Britain and Italy.[80]

The World Bank established a recycle unit as well. But Simon shared Wriston's view that the banks didn't need the extra competition, and repeatedly refused World Bank president Robert McNamara's requests for funding the unit.

Years later, Wriston, Simon (who also became a Bechtel consultant), and Shultz wrote a piece in the *Wall Street Journal* claiming that "the IMF is ineffective, unnecessary and obsolete" and called for its abolishment from the global system.[81]

Ford and the Bankers

Nixon finally resigned in August 1974. Governors, bankers, and close advisers accused him of being the key catalyst to the faltering economy.[82] Vice President Gerald Ford stepped in, declaring, "Our long national nightmare is over."[83]

Ford established some important connections to the banking community. On September 1974, Wriston joined his White House Labor Management Committee. The committee of seventeen was split between eight management members, eight labor members, and a neutral coordinator. The business side contained Bechtel chairman Stephen Bechtel, Mobil Oil Corporation CEO Rawleigh Warner, and General Electric chairman and CEO Reginald Jones. Big Labor's representatives included AFL-CIO head George Meany and United Steelworkers president I. W. Abel.

The group was assembled to advise the White House on domestic policy as it pertained to "free and responsible collective bargaining, [and] industrial peace . . . which could contribute to the longer-run economic well-being of the Nation."[84]

In the halls of Chase, the nation's well-being took a back seat to the bank's speculating. In the fall of 1974, Hilliard Farber, senior vice president in charge of the bond department, bought $800 million (the equivalent of $3.6 billion in today's terms) worth of government bonds, betting rates would drop and prices would rise. The opposite happened. He neglected to report the loss, causing Chase's third-quarter statement in 1974 to be overstated by $34 million.

Chase president Willard C. Butcher and Rockefeller were in Washington, DC, hosting Chase's annual dinner for the World Bank/IMF financial elite, when they heard the news. They immediately secured a flight back to New York, arriving at Rockefeller's five-story townhouse on Sixty-fifth Street just before midnight. His wife, Peggy, served hamburgers and mugs of hot chocolate while they mulled their course of action. This was, to them, far more a public relations crisis than a matter of criminal fraud.

They decided to face the issue head-on. Rockefeller released a statement about the "serious errors of judgment" that had been made, noting that Chase had asked Farber to resign. There was no mention of accountability at the top.[85] The incident was the precursor to another move by a future head of JP-Morgan Chase, Jamie Dimon, who blamed reporting errors for a $6.2 billion loss in 2012. The firm was ultimately instructed to pay a paltry $1.02 billion fine, less than 1 percent of its total asset base at the time, just more dust swept beneath the carpet of banker impunity.

As it turned out, several months later, interest rates did drop. Rockefeller announced that Chase would restate its financial statements once it had done a complete securities inventory.[86] (On September 21, 1976, Chase accepted the SEC's findings of "inadequate controls," and that was the end of the matter.)

The nation's nightmare was not over by a long shot. A steep recession had engulfed the country following the energy price hikes and related inflation in 1974.[87] Hundreds of thousands of autoworkers had been laid off by Christmas of that year. New York City hovered on the brink of bankruptcy. The "me decade" investors got hosed. Mutual funds would experience eight years of declines during which customers extracted their money rather than see it diminish to nothing. The "misery index" (the rate of unemployment plus inflation) was 17 percent, with inflation at 11 percent.

Wriston leveraged the economic malaise to strengthen his influence over domestic economic policy. In late December 1974, he inserted an extra $15 billion personal income tax cut into Ford's 1975 tax reduction package through the back door of the Labor Management Committee. President Ford decided this tax reduction should be expedited and asked Congress to streamline the process for the next two years.[88]

Global Shock and Opportunity

By early 1975, all that oil-related money in the hands of bankers began to concern Congress, particularly the multinationals subcommittee of the Senate Foreign Relations Committee, which had begun investigating the political implications of American investment abroad in 1971.[89] Chairman Frank Church began asking banks to reveal the details of their petrodollar deposits from each OPEC nation.

The senators were unconcerned that these money flows crisscrossing the globe were evading US banking laws. The committee's concern centered on the question of whether these Arab billions could be used to influence American foreign policy. Of course, the answer was yes. The committee sent a list of questions about the OPEC country funds to all the major banks. The biggest ones, Citibank, Chase, Morgan, and the Bank of America, refused to reply. In fact, they were outraged.

"Much of the information you requested would involve a break of our obligation to keep confidential the affairs of particular clients," wrote J. P. Morgan chairman Ellmore Patterson to the committee.

"We consider information of the type requested to be highly confidential," wrote Chase vice president Michael Esposito, "since its disclosure would be very useful to our competitors."

Church responded defiantly by holding another hearing in the Capitol. David Rockefeller flew to DC in his private plane to attend. When he arrived, he warned Congress that disclosing the banks' figures could bring down the whole western banking system.[90]

The banks that were later too big to fail were, in the 1970s, too big to tell. Though Rockefeller later wrote that throughout the 1960s and 1970s, whenever he traveled to the Middle East he checked to see if there had been any US policy changes since the last time, and debriefed Washington upon his return,[91] the idea of sharing the finances that stemmed from his liaison was too much to ask.

Chase's Ridiculous REIT

For David Rockefeller, the problems were multiplying. Congress had passed a bill that allowed investors to speculate in collections of real estate assets, as long as 90 percent of the profits were returned to them. This spawned a flimsy product called Real Estate Investment Trusts, which ignited the biggest domestic lending debacle since the 1930s. The REITs enabled banks and lenders to go into speculative overdrive, borrowing big from investors on the back of shady real estate deals (a reoccurrence with slightly different characteristics would spark the financial crisis of 2008). Ultimately, the REITs had to pay out far more than the underlying real estate contained in them was worth, and as a result many went bust.

Under Rockefeller's guidance, Chase Manhattan had been the first major bank to create its own REIT. The REIT was established in April 1970 within a subsidiary, CMART (pronounced "smart"), which collected approximately $1 billion in assets to back it. The First National City Bank and First Chicago Bank each made $750 million worth of loans to their own REITs.[92]

For four years, CMART netted big fees and paid juicy dividends to its shareholders. As speculative capital flooded in to take advantage of these trusts, though, pressure mounted to keep sourcing more real estate projects to line the trusts—in other words, for banks to lend more money to bad real estate deals. Just as in the 1920s, lenders lowered their standards and fraudulent real estate evaluations escalated, just to make the REITs appear profitable. From 1971 through 1974, Chase more than doubled its real estate lending from $2 to $5 billion. Four times the value of its equity capital was exposed to real estate including $827 million in loans to REITs.[93]

Thus when the bustling real estate market came to a screeching halt, CMART was hit hard. A chain reaction that tanked many REITs had begun

in December 1973. The dominos fell fast. Chase real estate loans got cruci-
fied. By mid-1975, its nonperforming loans totaled $1.87 billion, reaching a
July 1976 peak of $2.2 billion.[94]

From 1975 to 1979 Chase would charge-off $600 million in real estate
loans. That plus other nonperforming assets produced a total loss of $1 bil-
lion (nearly $4 billion today). Only the international loans and operations
saved Chase from greater failure.[95] Hence, it was more important than ever
to Rockefeller that all his high-powered friends in the Middle East remained
business partners. As domestic finances went south, the banker's international arms would save the day. That was a major reason global expansion
was crucial, not just to Rockefeller but to any big US bank chairman. There
would always be some geographical area or emerging market producing profits to offset losses from bad bets or risky practices.

The Big Apple Faces Bankruptcy

New York City was facing dire financial straits by early June 1975. The Big
Apple had nearly run out of funds to pay for its daily operations and had no
way of refinancing its short-term debt. Mayor Abraham Beame gathered a
group of Wall Street bankers to come up with solutions to his debt problem,
even though the city's biggest banks, notably Chase and Citibank, had happily
extended much of New York City's debt to begin with. But the bankers didn't
get very far.

Beame even turned to the bankers for a bridge loan to keep the city running. Chase rejected the request. J. P. Morgan CEO Ellmore Patterson demanded that the mayor balance the city's budget "immediately" in exchange
for financial assistance.[96] The mayor responded by releasing a public letter to
Patterson criticizing the bankers' efforts to pass laws restricting taxes as part
of the initial $641 million package, which included taxes on the financial in-
dustry to balance the budget. But that was the kind of tit-for-tat that could
only be won by the side with the money.

On June 14, the day before New York City would have defaulted, the state
deferred to the bankers' demands for effective austerity measures, and created the Municipal Assistance Corporation (MAC) to audit city operations
and issue long-term bonds, backed by sales-tax revenues, that would replace
short-term debt and give the city some breathing room.

But investors shunned MAC's $3 billion in bonds.[97] Bankers didn't really
try to sell them very hard either. As a result, the city flirted with defaulting
again. Finally, the bankers agreed to purchase more MAC bonds—for a price.

Wriston was largely heralded for saving New York City, but in actuality, he refused to buy MAC bonds unless New York City made austerity concessions. So to satisfy Wriston, Mayor Beame froze wages, cut twenty-seven thousand city jobs, hiked subway fares, and allowed the state to "nationalize" certain city programs. He also cut social programs to pay for banker and bondholder bailouts. In response, the banks agreed to buy $2 billion of the $3 billion MAC securities. However, investors still balked.

The MAC couldn't sell enough of the rest of the bonds to keep the city from tanking.[98] To get their money back, the bankers decided to try to persuade President Ford to aid the city. On September 23, 1975, Rockefeller, Wriston, and Patterson met with Ford, Treasury Secretary Simon, and Fed chairman Arthur Burns to talk about a government bailout for the loans they had extended to New York City. It would be a banker bailout, not a citizens' one.[99]

By early October, the Fed and other central banks intervened to prop up the dollar, which was being hurt by the New York City credit problem. They promised to lend more money to banks in case of a default. New York City owed $2 billion to the banks at this point, including $400 million to Chase and $340 million to Citicorp.

New York City desperately awaited Ford's decision. On October 20, 1975, Ford responded, "This nation will not be stampeded. . . . It will not panic when a few desperate politicians and bankers try to hold a gun to its head."[100]

Nine days later, Ford rejected New York City's request for federal aid, a slap in the face to the city and its bankers. The next day, the *New York Daily News* ran the infamous headline "Ford to City: Drop Dead."[101] Ford would later claim that headline cost him the 1976 presidential election, though it took some months before the bankers abandoned him.

Billy Joel memorialized the perils facing New York in his hit song "Miami 2017 (Seen the Lights Go Out on Broadway)." His lyrics evoked the stark class divide between the bankers on Wall Street and the politicians in Washington, and the citizens of all the boroughs of New York City—the difference between the haves and the have-nots.

On November 15, 1975, New York State passed the Emergency Moratorium Act, putting a three-year freeze of principal payments on $4.54 billion of short-term loans. The act increased taxes and cited the inability of New York City to "provide those basic services essential to the health, safety and welfare of its inhabitants." In practice, this was a default, but not in language.[102] The act wound up saving the city's finances and the bankers' loans, but it inflicted much hardship on its citizens through austerity measures. The entire episode revealed the extent to which the bankers would refuse to use their power to even help their own city.

Just before the 1976 election, with Jimmy Carter holding a decisive lead, the *New York Times* ran an article headlined "Anxious Wait of Business for Carter's Economic Lineup." Carter's choice for Treasury secretary was already "the favorite guessing game in business and economic circles." The best odds were given Bank of America chairman and "expert" in the international field A. W. Clausen.[103]

After Carter won the election, Ford returned to private life. He was noted primarily for pardoning Nixon, turning his back on New York City, and two assassination attempts during his presidency.

Perhaps it was the fact that Nixon wasn't inclined to fully embrace the bankers, or that Ford had rejected New York citizens and its bankers— whatever the case, the fracture between the president and the bankers in the early 1970s would open up to reveal the Frankenstein nature of the financiers by the end of the decade. In the past few decades, an alignment with US foreign policy had helped the financiers expand globally. But now they realized that whether their power and goals were aligned with, or divergent from, those of the Oval Office, they would be perfectly fine.

CHAPTER 14

THE LATE 1970S:
INFLATION,
HOSTAGES, AND BANKERS

"Our people are losing that faith, not only in government itself
but in the ability as citizens to serve as the ultimate rulers
and shapers of our democracy."

—Jimmy Carter, "Crisis of Confidence" speech, July 15, 1979

WHEN JIMMY CARTER TOOK OFFICE ON JANUARY 20, 1977, HE INHERITED AN agitated country on economic thin ice. In his inaugural speech, Carter was requisitely humble. He told the nation that "your strength can compensate for my weakness, and your wisdom can help to minimize my mistakes."[1]

The annals of history paint Carter as a caring, populist governor, a former peanut farmer, and a man whose heart was with the people, all of which was true. But he was also savvy enough to know that he had to turn to the Eastern Establishment to pick his cabinet. To retain the bankers' support, he embarked upon a domestic policy of widespread deregulation. With respect

---

301

to foreign policy, he attempted to reduce the cost of US military might for peace and economic reasons, a strategy that would have severe repercussions when it came to the Middle East.

Just as Carter entered the White House, Eugene Black sent Secretary of State Cyrus Vance a Morgan Guaranty report describing the status of the billowing Less Developed Countries (LDC) debt.[2] The report was very popular among the Wall Street crowd because it didn't consider this debt a warning of potential problems to come. Instead, Black noted that Morgan Guaranty's chief international economist, Rimmer de Vries, advocated even more lending to these nations. The major bankers continued to see tremendous opportunity in extending loans to the developing countries. They wanted to ensure the Carter administration would concur and back their strategy.

By 1977, the LDC were running a $100 billion deficit. (In contrast, the OPEC countries posted $128 billion in revenues.)[3] Approximately $75 billion in loans, accounting for 40 percent of their debt, had been originated by US commercial banks, with debt extension levels having increased by 20–25 percent each year since 1973. Brazil and Mexico were the largest debtors, owing nearly half of the total. The speed of debt accumulation continued to exceed the ability of LDC to pay it. The debt was simply growing faster than their economies could sustain it. Yet the Morgan report, widely cited throughout the banking industry, proclaimed a confidence that the "enormous buildup of external debt by deficit countries [was] manageable."[4]

Like his fellow bankers at Morgan Guaranty, Wriston believed that liberal lending to the third world remained a safe proposition. Ever since the worldwide recession and OPEC price spikes in 1973, and despite the debt overhang, Wriston argued, non-oil-producing LDCs had doubled their exports and their international reserves had risen by $23 billion. His bank continued to pile even more debt upon a region beginning to stagger economically.

But despite the enthusiasm with which the bankers portrayed the region, the bankers privately worried that the party might not last forever. For the US banks to continue lending and expanding their activities into the developing nations, they needed to ensure there would be enough capital on hand in case the LDC defaulted on their loan payments. Capital would also be necessary if speculators soured on the notion of purchasing the bonds banks were selling to augment their funding of the LDC debt. On that score, Wriston was constantly seeking new ways to push for banking deregulation within the United States and to promote his dual agenda of domestic and international expansion. His goal was to consolidate more power by aggregating more deposits and capital into his bank. This wasn't a matter of free-market philosophy alone; it was one of practicalities. If Citibank could gain access to more customer deposits, these could be translated into more loans to the current golden goose: the third world.

Wriston hit upon a new argument on behalf of his goal: technology. On May 19, 1977, he set out to persuade Carter that deregulating the banks and embracing their technological advances was critical to US financial growth and thus to US strength internationally. Cutting-edge financial technology would not only revolutionize banking. It also offered a compelling motive for deregulating the entire industry. If funds could travel between accounts at the speed of a keyboard tap, it stood to reason that past restrictions on banks that prohibited them from operating across state lines would be obsolete. By the same token, any geographical or other form of border inhibiting capital flow should logically be pushed aside.

Wriston arranged a meeting between his protégé, John Reed, and Carter's assistant director of domestic policy, Franklin Raines, regarding Citibank's new electronic funds transfer (EFT) systems. (Raines later served as chairman of Fannie Mae from 1999 to 2004, during which time it "misstated" billions of dollars of earnings.)

This meeting was one of Reed's first forays into the realm of political influence. Raines took warmly to Reed, confiding in him that his department was "continuing work on a financial institutions reform package." He added that he hoped "to be able to call on Reed" for advice and assistance on EFT policy.[5] This was exactly the result that Wriston and Reed wanted.

As it turned out, EFT did indeed become a pillar of the administration's policy to adopt a more "streamlined" regulatory framework. About a month after Reed's meeting, his advisory team—Stuart Eizenstat, Bert Lance, Charles Schultze, and Jack Watson—presented Carter with the first of many memos on banking deregulation that reflected the banker-promoted logic. Incorporating Wriston's technological argument, they concluded, "Current regulation impedes innovative changes such as the use of Electronic Fund Transfers and various banking services among institutions."[6]

Domestic deregulation and third world debt were two of three sides of a triangular expansionary agenda within the banking community. Domestic deregulation would corner more US depositors, and third world debt would push the boundaries of financial neoliberalism. The third side entailed maintaining a solid relationship with the oil-rich leaders of the OPEC nations whose petrodollars funded those LDC loans. On that accord, the Shah of Iran would be visiting the White House on November 15, 1977.

Rockefeller, the Shah, and Carter

On November 10, 1977, Secretary of State Vance outlined key objectives for Carter in anticipation of that meeting. The first goal, he said, was to "establish a close personal relationship" with the Shah and assure him of the US commitment to continue its "long-standing special relationship." The second was to discuss the future of the US-Iranian military supply arrangement.[7]

Over the decades since the British- and CIA-led Iranian coup of 1953 instated the regime of Prince Mohammad Reza Pahlavi, a serious quid pro quo between the US government and the Shah had developed. This was augmented by personal relationships between the Shah and Chase bankers David Rockefeller and John McCloy. The United States received foreign policy assistance from the Shah in the form of regional support for its Cold War operations, including intervention on behalf of the United States in Oman, providing jets on short notice to the United States for fighting in Vietnam, providing space for US military bases on the Iranian border from which the CIA could monitor Soviet missile installations, and many other military maneuvers. Plus, the Shah ensured a regular supply of oil to the United States. For his part, the Shah also had paid for and amassed an extensive stockpile of US weaponry.

According to the State Department, the Shah was committed to sustaining the "security of the vital Persian Gulf waterway" and to acting on behalf of the western powers "vis-à-vis the Soviet Union and radical regional forces."[8] The Shah's ongoing support was an essential component of US foreign policy. It was also a critical part of US banker policy for growth in the Middle East—not just in Iran but also across the region. On this score, Carter and the Chase bankers were in solid agreement in the fall of 1977 that they would stand behind the Shah—though the bankers would prove more steadfast in that support later.

Rockefeller remained committed to this policy, not only as a self-appointed ambassador to the world but also as chairman of a major private US bank that facilitated important international financial transactions. After he returned from a short Middle East trip on March 5, 1978, National Security Council head Zbigniew Brzezinski recommended Carter speak with Rockefeller for intel. "David has been helpful to us on a number of issues," Brzezinski said, "and this would seem to be a useful opportunity for a meeting."[9]

Chase continued to profit from its earlier ventures into the Middle East, including from Iranian monies. By late 1978, the bank's Iranian deposits exceeded $1 billion. In addition, Chase had led $1.7 billion of syndicated loans for Iran to fund large public sector projects.

Chase International Investment Corporation, which had been established by John McCloy in the 1950s, had maintained several long-standing
joint ventures in Iran. According to McCloy, the Shah kept $2.5 billion of his
personal wealth at an account with Chase, as did his private family trust.[10]
(Rockefeller denied the Shah was a Chase customer, and said he kept most of
his money in Switzerland.)[11] From a national standpoint, Iran kept $6 billion
on deposit with Chase.[12] The amount, as Rockefeller would often point out
later, was not much relative to Chase's overall deposit base. However, in the
game of global finance, it is not always size that matters but position and
the opportunities that come with the deposit.

By late 1978, Rockefeller's relationship with the Shah was so well known
within the Carter administration that the White House decided to contact him about a possible visit to Iran on which he could "talk to the Shah
about the political and financial situation" there.[13] Iran was undergoing a
severe economic crisis amid growing revolutionary tensions on the streets
and workplaces. From late 1978 through March 1979 oil production for oil
exports dropped from 5.5 million barrels a day to zero, and twenty-seven
thousand workers within the oil industry lost their jobs. The Carter administration, facing the "petro-pinch," as *Time* magazine called it, feared that
the situation could threaten Iran's alliance with the United States, as well as
with other countries in the region. With his close ties to the Shah, Rockefeller could be useful to them as a stabilizing force. He could gather intelligence
for the administration while reassuring the Shah about US backing for him.

But Rockefeller didn't stop by Iran or the Middle East during the tension-
lined days of late 1978. Instead, he spent the last five weeks of 1978 traveling
across Europe and Asia in his hybrid capacity as a representative of the Treasury and State Departments. Just before Christmas, he returned to the United
States and offered Carter his impressions of the international views on the US
dollar and Carter's anti-inflation policies.

"I have had an opportunity to visit five countries in Asia, including Japan
and Australia, and three countries in Europe, including the UK, the USSR
and West Germany," he told Carter. "In each case, I have met with high government officials, as well as bankers and businessmen, and I also held press
conferences."

He assured Carter, "I did my best at private, as well as public, meetings to
express my conviction that you and the members of your Administration are
deeply concerned about inflation and the weakness of the dollar . . . and to
indicate that, in my judgment, the measures which you announced . . . were
the right steps."[14]

Flirting with Bankruptcy

Part of the reason Rockefeller and other bankers were spending extra time abroad was to unearth profitable opportunities to offset the brewing economic instability in the United States. By early 1979, US inflation was rising, the dollar was falling, and gas prices and unemployment were escalating.

American corporations were flirting with bankruptcy due to increasingly expensive debt, lack of access to private loans, and lower demand for their products. The rest of the population was feeling the squeeze more acutely. On January 20, 1979, domestic policy adviser Stuart Eizenstat was worried about a full-scale corporate meltdown. He informed Carter that the nation's major corporations were bombarding the government with loan guarantee requests to ensure their survival.

The largest requests emanated from the auto industry, specifically American Motors Corporation and Chrysler Corporation. Chrysler needed $1.8 billion over the next four years to stay afloat. Despite the assistance that the government had provided to Penn Central and Lockheed (and their bankers) a few years earlier, Eizenstat wanted to restrict government bailouts. His task force recommended limiting loan guarantees to $50 million per firm.[15] But the companies and their bankers pressed for more. (In August 1979, Treasury Secretary G. William Miller proposed $1.5 billion in guaranteed loans. On December 20, 1979, Congress ratified the Chrysler Corporation Loan Guarantee Act, which Carter subsequently signed into law.)

As the broader hardships of tighter credit befell the population, Wriston's fight for deregulation remained on point. His suggested remedy was to provide citizens with higher interest rates for their savings accounts, which Citibank and other commercial banks were still prohibited from doing because of Regulation Q restrictions.

The administration decided to take the bankers' side. On May 23, an enthusiastic Wriston wrote Carter's secretary, Anne Wexler, "I was delighted to read in the paper about the President's program to raise the ceilings on interest rates. . . . This is a program, which has our wholehearted support." Wriston cemented his push by also meeting with Schultze on the topic.[16] Inflation served as a potent reason for deregulation.

The Shah Seeks Asylum

Over in the Middle East, other matters had reached a boiling point. Following months of agitated demands that he abdicate power and leave Iran, the Shah finally fled to Egypt on January 16, 1979.[17]

On January 31, Ayatollah Ruhollah Khomeini, who had been ejected by the Shah and exiled from Iraq since October 3, 1978, flew by a charter plane from France to Iran. He returned on February 1 to adoring crowds, ending Pahlavi's thirty-seven-year reign. Iran broke off diplomatic relations with Egypt on April 30 and canceled $9 billion in armament contracts with the United States.

Where would the Shah live now that he was deposed? McCloy approached Brzezinski regarding asylum. And the Shah's twin sister, Princess Ashraf, begged Rockefeller to persuade Carter to permit the Shah to enter the United States—or at least help him find a haven elsewhere. Rockefeller discussed the issue while dining with Henry Kissinger and Happy Rockefeller, his brother Nelson's widow. The Shah had been a friend of theirs too.[18]

McCloy was displeased with the Carter administration's reluctance to offer the Shah asylum. All the work and relationship building he had done in the region would be for naught if the administration refused to support the Shah in his hour of need. Like Rockefeller, McCloy considered the Pahlavi regime an ally of the United States, a force for stability in the region that should not be cold-shouldered—not to mention a piggy bank for profits linked to the Middle East.

McCloy, Rockefeller, Kissinger, and Rockefeller's personal assistant, Joseph Reed, decided to create a "special project team" that would be headed by Rockefeller to seek US asylum for the Shah.[19] The team addressed the Shah's travel arrangements while lobbying Carter to permit entry. On March 27, Carter received notice of the Shah's plans. The Shah was traveling to the Bahamas, which he regarded as a temporary stop on the way to Mexico.[20]

More critical to global economic conditions than the Shah's location, though, was the fact that OPEC had decided to raise the price of market crude by 9 percent, to $14.54 per barrel. The increase added a staggering $12 billion to world oil import bills.[21] It wreaked further havoc on the non-oil-producing countries, especially within the third world, where the costs of debt and commodities were rising perilously at the same time. It also weakened the US economy further—which put its banks at risk. But despite this tangle of events, US bankers guiltlessly and voraciously continued extending credit to the third world and baited the Middle East over the Shah.

Finally, Kissinger persuaded the foreign minister of the Bahamas to grant the Shah a temporary visa. Once the Shah was situated in a beachfront villa, Robert Armao, a PR man who had been hired by Princess Ashraf to improve the Shah's image in the United States (and who had worked for Vice President Nelson Rockefeller), met with him to make him comfortable.

Rockefeller organized Project Alpha to address the Shah's plight.[22] Frequent strategy meetings about his US entry were held at One Chase Plaza,

Chase Manhattan Bank's headquarters. For months, Project Alpha pressed the Carter administration to provide sanctuary for the Shah (code-named the Eagle). Rockefeller personally visited the White House on April 9, 1979, to persuade Carter to take the Shah in. As Carter wrote in his diary, "David Rockefeller . . . came in to spend time with me. . . . The main purpose of this visit, apparently, is to try and let the Shah come into our country. Rockefeller, Kissinger and Brzezinski seem to be adopting this as a joint project."[23]

Ten days later, Secretary of State Vance informed Carter, "A campaign remains in progress to change our position with respect to the Shah's admission to the U.S. John McCloy . . . is continuing to call influential people throughout the country. We understand that McCloy's effort continues to be stimulated by Henry Kissinger and by the efforts of [Iranian ambassador to the United States] Ardeshir Zahedi."[24]

Both Vance and Carter wanted the Shah to go anywhere but the United States. Their view was further strengthened by Khomeini's verbal attacks on American influence and the withdrawal of two-thirds of the Iranian guard force from the US embassy compound, as he declared April 1, 1979, "the first day of God's Government."[25]

In April, Vance confirmed that he had received a new evaluation from Tehran confirming the State Department's assessment that the safety of officials and unofficial Americans would be jeopardized if the Shah came to the US.[26]

And yet Rockefeller's team succeeded in obtaining the State Department's support for the Shah's family to enter the United States. On May 2, 1979, Vance informed Carter that "we have decided we can tell the Shah his children would be welcome to pursue their studies here."[27] Two weeks later, Rockefeller's office informed the State Department that the Shah's three younger children and mother-in-law would move to Connecticut within the next few weeks.[28]

The Shah and the rest of his family entered Cuernavaca, Mexico, on June 10, 1979. By that time, Princess Ashraf was having difficulty placing his three younger children in New York–area schools. Rockefeller informed David Newsom, undersecretary of state for political affairs, that he surmised this was because the schools were afraid of the security risk involved.[29]

Despite the Shah-related disagreements, Carter and Rockefeller maintained good relations. A month after the Shah arrived in Mexico, Carter interviewed Rockefeller for a job in his administration: Treasury secretary. Rockefeller rejected the potential offer, perhaps because he didn't welcome the idea of "an interview" or because the tense economic and foreign policy atmosphere made it unpalatable, or perhaps he simply felt that it had a narrower girth of power compared to his hybrid post as Chase chairman and US diplomat.

Rockefeller and October 1979

Three months after the Shah arrived in Mexico, his health took a sharp turn downward. On October 1, 1979, Rockefeller informed the State Department that the Shah was ill and that he had sent his personal physician to examine him.[30] Vance warned Carter, "If the Shah's condition is serious, we might be asked to admit him to the US for treatment." But that presented a major conundrum.

Local hostility in Iran toward the Shah was intense. In addition, said Vance, "the augmented influence of the clerics might mean an even worse reaction than would have been the case a few month ago if we were to admit the Shah, even for humanitarian purposes."[31]

The Carter team had no doubt that admitting the Shah was playing with fire. On the morning of October 18, Vance sent a secret report to Carter regarding the Shah's condition that said, "David Rockefeller's assistant, Joe Reed, informed Dave Newsom on October 17 that the Shah's . . . illness was initially thought to be infectious hepatitis, but a significant deterioration . . . with cancer not being excluded [had occurred]."

Rockefeller "clearly wanted" to bring the Shah to Memorial Sloan-Kettering Cancer Center in New York City for a medical examination and treatment. Vance added, "Rockefeller's medical adviser—an eminent Columbia Medical School professor who treated the Shah two weeks ago—is traveling to Mexico on October 18 to see the Shah and will make a joint recommendation with the State Department Medical Director." As a matter of more careful diplomacy, Vance concluded, "If we decide to permit the Shah to come to the United States for treatment, we would want to inform the Iranians that we were doing so for humanitarian purposes and to leave open any question of future residence."[32] That meant there was a possibility that the United States might decide to admit the Shah for other purposes.

The next day, in the margin of Vance's report, Carter scribbled a fateful "OK."[33]

Deputy Secretary of State Warren Christopher informed Carter that Dr. Benjamin Kean, a tropical disease specialist at Cornell Medical School, had seen the Shah and suggested examination in the United States. Rockefeller requested the United States admit the Shah to Sloan-Kettering for diagnosis and treatment. The State Department's physician concurred.[34]

Christopher informed Carter that the Shah, "through David Rockefeller," "has expressed his gratitude to you."[35]

Thus, Rockefeller and McCloy succeeded in gaining US entry for the Shah. The Shah arrived in New York by charter plane the morning of October 23. The Iranian government reacted with moderation when the news came that the Shah would be visiting the United States for medical reasons. In a secret October 24 memo, Vance informed Carter that he had received word from the US embassy in Tehran that "the past two days have been calm."[36]

Still, in response to the embassy's request, Vance agreed to augment security forces guarding the compound. A demonstration from Tehran University was scheduled to pass the embassy that Friday.[37] All was not exactly calm.

On October 26, Christopher informed Carter, "Rockefeller's staff has told us that the Shah's lymphoma is a Class III malignancy. This condition gives him a 50/50 chance to survive the next 18 months; if he does so, he could then live for several more years. Meanwhile, the Shah's recuperation from his operation will require another two to three weeks' hospitalization."[38]

Four days later, at Rockefeller's request, Brzezinski addressed Chase's international advisory committee on world affairs and the Iran situation.[39] The next day, one million people demonstrated through the streets of Tehran.

On November 4, Islamic students swarmed the US embassy in Tehran, seizing sixty-two Americans. They demanded the Shah's immediate extradition to Iran. More critical to the US bankers, ten days later, the new Iranian foreign and economics minister, Bani-Sadr, threatened to withdraw $9 billion in Iranians funds from US banks unless the Shah was extradited.

The bankers who had dealings with Iran were now at the center of a hostage crisis that had been unleashed by Rockefeller and his crew. The crisis metastasized because of a relationship between powerful men over money and position, and it would unfold along those exact same lines—though this element of the crisis would not be the one the public would see plastered across newspaper headlines or TV screens. And yet to the US government the issues concerning money and loans would turn out to be as important as the issue of freeing the hostages.

For Washington, freeing the hostages became the top priority. On November 9, the White House began formulating plans for the return of American personnel: "In addition to the 62 official American and at least 5 third-country nationals held on the compound, there are three at the Foreign Ministry and an additional six Americans at a separate location in Tehran," noted an internal report.

The US government, believing at first that the matter could be quickly resolved, carefully mapped out a return route for the hostages from Istanbul through Frankfurt, which was to be followed by an "appropriate reception on arrival" at Andrews Air Force Base with the president in attendance.[40]

But it was not to be.

The 2012 Oscar-winning film *Argo* illuminated the pressure surrounding the six US workers who found refuge in a Canadian safe house in Tehran for a few months until they escaped. But the bulk of the hostage crisis played out between Carter's White House and the banks involved with Iran's loans and deposits. There were no grand "savior spies," no Ben Affleck to the rescue—only bankers and politicians and a race against time.

The Chase Hostage Wrinkle

Chase provoked the already tense situation because of an interest payment, something that otherwise would have been just another financial transaction between a US bank and a foreign customer. The same day that the hostages were seized, the Iranian central bank (Bank Markazi) notified Chase, as was standard protocol, that a $4 million interest payment on its $500 million loan would be forthcoming, despite the unfolding hostage situation. A syndicate of eleven banks led by Chase had issued the loan in 1977. Chase's portion was $50 million, the largest of Iran's debts to the bank.

On November 9, Chase chose to ignore the interest payment notification. Five days later, Carter issued an executive order that froze all Iranian "assets and deposits in US banks and their overseas branches."[41] The events that followed nearly unleashed another major international crisis.

Rockefeller maintained that no one at Chase ever persuaded Carter to freeze Iranian assets, and that the amounts were not significant anyway. Chase held $366 million in Iranian loans and $509 million in deposits.

Carter didn't blame Rockefeller for his decision to seize Iranian assets. Yet the decision was instigated by the hostage situation, which had been catalyzed by the news that the Shah would stay in the United States longer than a few days. This event followed months of pressure from Rockefeller's network. It was the implications of Chase's actions rather than the size of its Iranian assets or loans that mattered.

Citing the freeze, Chase refused to accept the $4 million interest payment on the loan on November 15, the date it was due. As a result, Chase declared the Iranian government in default on the *entire* loan without consulting any of the other banks that had been involved in the syndicate. On November 23,

Chase informed Bank Markazi that it had seized its accounts and used the monies in them to offset its debts.[42] The action was akin to Chase taking over a mortgage borrower's home after one missed payment.

Tempers immediately flared. The Special Coordination Committee (SCC) rushed to convene in the White House Situation Room to address Chase's default decision (which had not been disclosed in advance to the White House).

Chase's declaration had potentially vast implications—not just regarding hostage negotiations but also on the entire realm of global financial relationships with allied countries. Foreign bankers and governments were livid over the bank's unilateral move.[43]

Tensions were rapidly escalating to the level of a full-blown crisis. Then things got worse. The State Department received word that Morgan Guaranty, under president (and ex-marine) Lewis Preston's directive, would copy Chase's lead and declare Iran in default of its loan obligations. The bank had filed a court order in Essen, Germany, that would "attach" Iran's shares in Friedrich Krupp, a German industrial giant, to their outstanding claims of $40 million. In other words, Morgan Guaranty was planning to take unrelated assets and use them to pay for the loans. In addition, the Export-Import Bank was contemplating declaring Iran in default, which would be the first such instance in Iran's history.[44] The United States didn't want to run the risk of antagonizing the captors any further during negotiations, yet these financial moves were doing just that.

Further, the SCC worried that "the declarations of default may spread and accelerate." The group decided to intervene to attempt to mitigate the fallout. Treasury Secretary Miller informed other German banks of the impending Morgan action and warned European bankers of the threat to their own positions if they spread Iranian default.[45] He was concerned about repercussion to the hostages if the bank situation got out of hand. German courts allowed the seizure of Iranian assets on November 29.

At that point, Bank Markazi sued Chase in England, alleging Chase owed it $320 million that had been on deposit at Chase's London branch at the time of the "off-set."[46] On December 6, Chase countersued Bank Markazi in New York, seeking damages of $366 million against the Iranians. (Judge Thomas Griesa rejected Chase's motion on February 15, 1980, to stop the Iranian suit.[47] After that, the case stalled.)

Rockefeller was the target of multiple public criticisms from Iran's central bank, which claimed that he had capitalized on his close connections with the Shah and benefited personally from oil money profits.[48] He later devoted a full chapter in his *Memoirs* to explain that his relationship with the Shah wasn't as tight as reporters claimed, concerns about the Shah's sister's kids in Connecticut schools notwithstanding. He stressed that he hadn't spent much time with the Shah. But it is noteworthy that the two men held a similar position in their societies: as princes of lineage, both men wielded tremendous unelected power.

Mark Hulbert, author of *Interlock: The Untold Story of American Banks, Oil Interests, the Shah's Money, Debts, and the Astounding Connections Between Them*, put the matter into sharper perspective, noting, "At the time there was a lot of discussion that a default of Third World debt could bankrupt the entire banking system, and yet, here was a country flush with oil money, going out of its way to make sure the money would be paid and Chase was trying to punish the country."[49] This made no economic sense.

Considering the timing of the interest payment notification came *before* Carter's asset freeze, it did seem that egos played a role in rejecting the payment. Plus, it was coming *into* an account; it was not deposit money that would have been frozen under Carter's decree.

By December 22, the SCC had made some headway in undoing the damage Chase had unleashed. "The French and British were now unanimously opposed to the default mechanism," it reported, "fearful that they would bear legal responsibility for any losses suffered by their banks in carrying out such action."[50]

Yet the situation in the Middle East remained far from resolved. On Christmas Eve, the Soviet Union invaded Afghanistan. As the decade drew to a close, Carter's foreign policy was unraveling at the seams.

Desperation Grows: The 1980s Began in the 1970s

On January 17, 1980, Chase's lawyers informed the White House that the bank had been served with a writ regarding the seized funds. At that point, Chase was the only American bank served with such a writ.[51]

Yet the bankers appeared to emerge from the crisis unscathed financially, as for them, the turmoil that had resulted from the block of Iranian assets largely diminished.[52] On March 10, 1980, an intelligence memo on the long-term implications of an Iranian asset freeze concluded, "The competitive position of US banks is unlikely to be significantly affected. . . . The surge in OPEC surpluses will provide most banks with huge new deposits. US bankers are reportedly flooded with requests to accept Arab deposits . . . other than Iran."[53] The bankers, in short, were secure, even if the hostages were not.

Amid the fallout of the Iran situation and general economic upheaval, Carter had an election to consider. He had to raise money for his campaign, and like many presidents before him, he turned to the banking community for help. His staff suggested he schedule a series of luncheons with Wall Street executives, such as Walter Wriston and the emerging Democratic power broker Robert Rubin, to rally their support for the fall.[54]

The banking community, in turn, saw a way to push its deregulation agenda as a quid pro quo. On March 31, seven months before the election, Carter signed what he characterized as a "landmark financial reform bill": the Depository Institutions Deregulation and Monetary Control Act of 1980. It was a gift to the banking community. The act began phasing out Regulation Q caps on interest rates that commercial banks could pay for deposits. It authorized savings and loan associations to issue credit cards; removed the geographic restrictions on S&Ls to make real estate loans; and expanded their ability to make acquisition, development, and construction loans. It also exempted mortgages and other types of loans from state usury laws that prohibited excessive or abusive interest rates charges, and it permitted banks to provide automatic transfers from savings to checking accounts. The act allowed national banks to circumvent individual state interest rate limits regarding what they could pay on deposit accounts, and ultimately led to the banks' ability to charge higher subprime lending rates in later decades. The bankers had been waging the battle against Regulation Q since the 1950s, and they had finally won. To commemorate the event, Carter sent each major banker a signing pen.[55]

Failed Rescue and the Election

The hostage negotiations were slowly creeping forward. At the initiative of the Iranian government, a group of people representing high government officials had made contact with US officials. Secret negotiations were conducted between the United States and Iran until it became apparent that "Iranian powers—particularly Khomeini—had neither the will [n]or desire to peacefully resolve the crisis," according to a summary report compiled by Carter's chief of staff, Hamilton Jordan.[56]

Carter authorized a rescue mission to extract the hostages.[57] But on April 24, 1980, Operation Eagle Claw was aborted. "Equipment failure in the rescue helicopters made it necessary to end the mission," he had to admit. "Two of our aircraft collided on the ground in a remote desert location in Iran . . . to my deep regret, 8 of the crewmen on the two aircraft were killed, and several other Americans were hurt in the accident."[58]

The mission was a disaster on many levels. Not only did it fail to rescue the hostages, and not only did it take the lives of eight American military professionals, it also provoked the resignation of Cyrus Vance. His loyalty had been vital to Carter. Deputy Secretary of State Warren Christopher assumed his role.

The Shah was eventually relocated to Panama and later to Egypt, where he died in June 1980. Official funeral arrangements were handled by the Carter administration. Former president Nixon was the only US dignitary in attendance.[59]

As Americans went to the polls in November, the hostages weighed heavily on the minds of the population. Months of negotiations had failed to reach a resolution in time. Carter lost the election to California governor Ronald Reagan, another Beltway outsider.

Progress had occurred, albeit too slowly, in the background. A few days after the election, Christopher happily confirmed his trip to Algeria, where he would oversee the release of the hostages and the simultaneous unfreezing of Iranian assets, the second piece of the negotiations. He had prepared ten Iran-related declarations and presidential orders that would become effective once the hostages had safely departed from Iran.[60]

The talks had come down to anger about money, specifically the freezing of Iranian assets and the use of the Iranian deposits to offset the loans that had been declared in default. The speaker of the Iranian Parliament stressed lingering difficulties over how to lift American claims against Iran and lift the freeze on Iranian assets in the United States. The sticking point was that US banks' overseas offices had held more than $4 billion of Iranian deposits at the time of the freeze, and had also made large unsecured loans to the Iranian government and Iranian government entities. However, US government officials, somewhat still headlocked by the bankers, were forced to inform Iran that full compliance regarding lifting private claims by American companies was beyond its power.[61]

By late 1980, the White House had adopted Rockefeller's line of defense, that "largely, because of the U.S. freeze, Iran was unable to pay installments of interest and principal due on the loans and the loans went into default. As a result, these banks exercised their right to require full payment of the loans and used Iranian bank deposits to pay off the loans in a process called 'set-offs,'" whereby banks would reduce the size of the loans by the amount they took from Iranian deposits.[62]

In mid-December the State Department proposed a solution amid ongoing lawsuits about the "propriety of these set-offs" in foreign courts. Iran would be given access to its current balances in the banks, and the banks and the Iranian government would collaborate to bring the loans up-to-date.[63] In other words, the White House left it up to the banks to act responsibly.

Closing the Deal

As Carter's presidency approached its end, hope remained that a resolution to the hostage crisis would occur during his administration. But the outcome would lie in the balance until issues related to the frozen Iranian funds and the bankers' whims were resolved. The beginning of the end of the hostage ordeal began when Warren Christopher arrived in Algeria on January 8, 1981. (The Algerian government was acting as intermediary between the United States and Iran.)

From the onset, the exchange of hostages for Iranian assets was plagued with delays, recalcitrance on the part of the Iranian central bank and private banks involved, and heated negotiations over the minute details of what was then the largest international funds transfer in history.[64]

First, about $8 billion of frozen assets would be placed in an escrow account encompassing the $5.5 billion of deposits in overseas branches of US banks and $2.5 billion of gold, securities, and other assets in the Federal Reserve. The remaining frozen assets (more than $3 billion) would be unfrozen.

Closing the "deal" was no simple matter. It involved three governments, four central banks, twelve US commercial banks, and hundreds of officials and lawyers in Washington, New York, London, Algiers, and Tehran.[65]

Throughout the closing period, which began on the evening of January 18, 1981, Carter and his advisers remained in tight communication with US team members in the Treasury, State, and Justice Departments, as well as with Christopher and his team in Algiers. A labyrinth of steps was designed to calm the distrust between the United States and Iran.

The Algerian government notified the United States and Iran that both were ready to proceed. In Washington, Carter signed the official US statement of adherence and nine executive orders. By phone, he authorized Christopher to sign the Declarations of Algiers, which would facilitate the transfer.[66]

Iran's minister of state, Behzad Nabavi, signed the documents on behalf of Prime Minister Mohammad-Ali Rajai of Iran. Algeria proclaimed the two Declarations of Algiers effective at 2:17 A.M. EST on January 19. It seemed as if Carter would see at least part of his negative legacy cleared.

That's when the trouble started. Iran refused to sign an annex with the text of Bank Markazi's instructions to US banks regarding the payment of

Iranian deposits to the Federal Reserve for transfer into an escrow fund on its behalf. Iran denounced the US bankers and their "underhanded" maneuver of altering the balance amounts on the Iranian accounts. After stern words from the White House, the US banks agreed to a corrective, but Bank Markazi rejected the overture.

Finally, after intense arguing, a telex with new directives was transmitted across the seas, forcing the twelve banks involved to transfer precise amounts of deposits, aggregating $5.5 billion, to the Federal Reserve.[67]

It was now early morning of the day that Reagan would become president. Politics, banking, and lives still hung in the balance.

Once the telex was received, Treasury Secretary Miller delivered an executive order to the US bank officials huddled in his office to pay the frozen deposits in their overseas branches over to the Federal Reserve Bank of New York.

But now another potentially agreement-killing crisis arose. The telex that the bankers had sent contained errors in the code numbers of Iranian accounts. At last, an amended telex was received at the London solicitor's office representing all twelve US banks. The ensemble of lawyers, bankers, and Fed and Treasury officials in Washington and at the US embassy in Algiers awaited an "all-clear" sign.[68]

Enough Was Enough

At 3:45 A.M. Miller broke another impasse over language that would satisfy the US bankers. He instructed the US banks to transfer the money. By 4:10 they had transferred most of the $5.5 billion to the Federal Reserve Bank of New York, which then transferred the funds to its account at the Bank of England. Once the stipulated $7.97 billion was sitting at the Fed's account in Britain, it was transferred to the escrow account of the Algerian Central Bank at the Bank of England.[69]

To everyone's great relief, the hostage release now seemed certain.

After another round of disputes, at 6:18 A.M., the escrow and depository agreements were finally signed in Algiers. The transfer of the New York Fed money to the escrow at the Algerian central bank at the Bank of England was completed at 6:45, and at 8:06, the Algerian central bank certified it had the money.[70]

Five hours later, Ronald Reagan took the oath of office. At precisely 12:33 P.M., the first aircraft of hostages was allowed to take off from Iran. The second aircraft followed ten minutes later. The planes departed Iranian airspace and flew over Turkey en route to Athens. After a brief stop for refueling, the planes arrived in Algiers at 7 P.M. In a ceremony of solemnity and emotional intensity, Algerian foreign minister Mohamed Ben Yahia turned over the fifty-two American hostages to Warren Christopher shortly after 8 P.M. Their 444 days of captivity were over.[71]

As Reagan began his presidency, the lawsuits between the US banks and the Iranian government were ongoing. Wriston and Rockefeller stood poised to extend their influence and profits into the 1980s. They had outlasted three presidents in the process of tipping the balance of political-financial power away from the collaborative, more aligned, and publicly spirited alliance between the president and the key bankers that had defined the postwar and early Cold War decades, and in favor of the bankers.

The importance of oil and energy policy as an adjunct of economic and financial policy had provided bankers the impetus to seek their own Middle Eastern alliances, whether or not they dovetailed with those of the president. This precedent would render the bankers less concerned with toeing the presidents' line from a foreign policy perspective, for they had become powerful enough in their own right over increasingly rapid movements of capital. They would still *want* US government protection and alliances with presidents, who would return the favor anyway, but they would not *need* federal support except in times of trouble.

Bankers' increasingly reckless behavior would lead to more global economic strife in the 1980s. The petrodollar-fueled loans that carried the bankers through an inflationary domestic economy that hurt the United States and other populations would push the third world into a global debt crisis in which the government would subsidize the bankers' losses and bail them out. Going forward, elite US financiers would face no real challenges on the road to further deregulation and open financial policy from presidents, whether they were Republicans or Democrats, and regardless of the state of the global or national economy. Bankers' rapaciousness would translate into riskier, more speculative practices. Their influence over monetary and economic policy would flourish. In that vein, US bankers would strive to enhance their power by remaining "competitive" with foreign banks, and presidents would support this stance as critical to maintaining the US status of international financial superpower.

CHAPTER 15

THE EARLY TO MID-1980S: FREE-MARKET RULES, BANKERS COMPETE

*"If you say you're a capitalist,
then the next thing you must say is, 'I compete.'"*

—Donald Regan, Treasury Secretary for Ronald Reagan[1]

THE BEGINNING OF THE NEW DECADE COULD NOT ESCAPE THE LINGERING HANGOVER of the previous one. The American hostages had been released from Iran and Ronald Reagan had won the White House, but other than that, not much had changed. Inflation hovered above 14 percent, Treasury bills yielded more than 15 percent, and the unemployment rate persisted at 7.5 percent. The Dow sat at 937, lower than its mid-1960s levels. US economic power was being compromised by the growing strength of Europe and, increasingly, Japan, which was competing for superpower status. Though Reagan would focus on the US economy and ideological dominance, the financial muscle of the US bankers would be integral to retaining international control in the face of that competition. Ensuring bankers' ability to compete on the global stage would become US foreign policy for presidents of both parties from that point onward.

According to Reagan's former assistant secretary of the Treasury for economic policy, Paul Craig Roberts, "The Reagan administration had no banking agenda." He said that "Reagan wanted to renew the economy so that pressure could be put on the Soviets to end the Cold War. Those were Reagan's two main goals."[2]

Wall Street commercial and investment banks and insurance companies were angling to obliterate the restrictions of Glass-Steagall and the Bank Holding Company Act so that they could acquire one another's business, while relying on Glass-Steagall borders as lines of defense around the services they already provided to keep their domestic competitors out. The S&Ls and smaller financial firms sprinkled across the United States were battling the big commercial banks for depositors and borrowers and the right to invest in riskier assets. These bit players would prove no match for the commercial banks, which would thrive as their little brethren hit a crisis.

Alliances between the powerful bankers and Presidents' Reagan and Bush would continue, but the relationships would be more perfunctory and less personal than in the past. They would also be less important, increasingly replaced by an implicit understanding that the perspective of free-market capitalism suited both Reagan's political doctrine and the bankers' expansionary agenda, and fortified by a growing group of well-paid lobbyists and lawyers working to deregulate policy to suit the bankers' ambitions. The notion of "free market," though, was code for freedom to dominate ever more "liberalized" countries from a financial perspective, to amass profits at the expense of the local populations. Global competition, cited as the reason to spread financial capitalism in ever riskier manners, was also a means to persuade Washington to back the bankers in preparing for whatever global atmosphere would follow the end of the Cold War. But just as in military wars, the country with the greatest financial arsenal (a nation of depositors and a government with parallel ideologies to the bankers) would dominate on the world scene.

As global recession loomed, additional clouds gathered on the economic horizon. On the international front, developing countries were treading water beneath waves of bank debt. Ultimately, US bankers would force a government- and multinational-entity-backed bailout of their third world loans. The deal, which brought harsh austerity measures in return for extra financial aid to the regions affected, would save the bankers billions of dollars.

Domestically, a burgeoning S&L bank crisis born of deregulation, fraud, and moves by Wall Street banks eager to "pump and dump" toxic securities into thrifts following Carter's 1980 "reforms" (along with the ones Reagan offered in 1982) threatened to crush the national economy—battering the real estate market and the population's confidence in banks, which had taken five decades to rebuild.

Once big banks stopped lending as much to developing countries, a new crop of chairmen reinvigorated their predecessors' efforts to exploit regulatory loopholes at the state level so they could acquire noncommercial banking businesses as well as deposits across state lines. Rather than stopping them, a group of men within the Reagan administration, led by Vice President George H. W. Bush and his deregulation task force, pressed to convert these loopholes into national policy. They were aided by former Wall Street executives in cabinet roles and in the private sector. Meanwhile, investment and commercial banks fought both against one another and against the New Deal regulations that kept their businesses separated.

Merrill Lynch Chairman Donald Regan Becomes Treasury Secretary

Reagan won the presidency on a tide of campaign promises: ending the hostage crisis, cutting the deficit, reducing the size of government and the amount of regulations, and cutting taxes.[3] Though his participation in the final hostage release negotiations was negligible, to the public it appeared that Reagan had facilitated the release of the hostages on his inauguration day. That provided a shot in the arm of the American body politic.

Reagan and his team wasted no time using the warm feelings of the public to usher through foreign and domestic policies—including the ones dealing with deregulation. Reagan's unofficial group of advisers, or "kitchen cabinet," was a cadre of about a dozen free-market-embracing businessmen.[4] They had already selected Merrill Lynch chairman Donald Regan to be Treasury secretary in the fall of 1980. Reagan himself hadn't proactively scouted the man who would run the world's most powerful treasury. As Reagan later wrote in his autobiography, *An American Life*, "I had appointed Don Sec. of the Treasury on the advice of some of the members of my old kitchen cabinet in California; they called him a wizard on economic matters. [Don did] an outstanding job at the Treasury Department, especially by helping get tax reform off the ground and winning Wall Street support of [my] economic recovery program." Like President Johnson, Reagan would cut taxes with the support of bankers.

The idea of running the Treasury had never crossed Regan's mind before Reagan offered him the post. But Regan's pedigree was unquestionable. A member of the elite Council on Foreign Relations, he graduated from Harvard University in 1940, entered the Marine Corps, and retired after World War II as a lieutenant colonel.

Regan had joined Merrill Lynch in 1946 and steadily rose through its ranks. In 1951 he was appointed to run the scandal-ridden trading department, which handled "10 [percent] of the total volume traded on the New York markets."[5] He replaced John Thompson as chairman when Thompson retired in January 1971.[6]

In the 1970s Regan's political activity had been "marginal," he later noted, consisting of personal donations to Republican candidates and voting in every election. In 1976, he backed Gerald Ford, whose primary opponent was Ronald Reagan. When Reagan campaigned in New York that fall, Regan was invited to meet him at "a small luncheon for Wall Streeters." Regan's memories of that first meeting consisted of a joke Reagan made about the pronunciations of their names.

Regan met him again in the spring of 1980, when Reagan was campaigning for the presidential nomination. Bill Rogers, whom Regan had put on the board of Merrill Lynch after Rogers resigned as Nixon's secretary of state, suggested Regan support Reagan. Shortly thereafter, Regan was invited to a fundraiser at the elite New York City Sky Club. There, Reagan had difficulty remembering Regan, name pronunciation notwithstanding.

In September, once Reagan's nomination was secured, he revisited New York. Bill Casey, Reagan's campaign manager, suggested Regan help raise money. Along with John Whitehead, a Goldman Sachs partner who later became deputy secretary of state, Regan organized a $1,000 per plate fundraiser.[7]

Just before the election, a Wall Streeter in Reagan's camp informed Regan that his name was on a shortlist of candidates for the Treasury secretary post. Another name was William Simon, who had served as Treasury secretary under Nixon and Ford. Once Simon withdrew, Regan's name floated to the top, courtesy of Casey. On December 3, 1980, Regan was at home in Colts Neck, New Jersey, when the phone rang.

"Let me tell you why I'm calling," Reagan said in his "whispery tenor": "I'd like you to be my secretary of the Treasury."

Regan said, "Thank you very much, I accept."[8]

On January 20, 1981, Reagan formally nominated Regan to the post. Unlike Wriston and Rockefeller, who had rejected similar offers from

Nixon and Carter because they were too engaged in conquering the postwar banking world, "The Wizard" accepted immediately. In the process, Reagan became the first president to hire a major Wall Street chairman to the post of Treasury secretary. Without having given the matter much thought, Reagan united the power of Wall Street and the presidency into 100 percent alignment.

At the time, the financial arena appeared unstable. The key bankers needed structural deregulation to come from Washington. It wasn't so much that Regan was too connected to Wall Street to help the broader economy, as critics pointed out; it was the fact that his ideologies were glued to the experiences of his work there. His views on open competition, which by default would mean a conquering of competition by the larger banks, would drive another stake into the heart of Glass-Steagall (even though he would be more known for his stance on tax and monetary policy during his term). Democrat Bill Clinton and Republican George W. Bush would repeat Reagan's precedent with their own Treasury secretary choices culled from Goldman Sachs. Wall Street was officially in the White House.

Mass Deregulation Begins

A little over a week after he took office, on January 29, Reagan terminated Nixon's wage and price regulatory program.[9] From the onset, Reagan made his deregulatory agenda clear. After his first week in office, Reagan issued an executive order removing all controls on price and allocation of crude oil and refined petroleum.[10]

Deregulating the banks would prove more time-intensive. The nature of the banking system was such that the commercial and investment banks both wanted to expand their services, but more specialized groups like insurance companies, real estate boutiques, and thrifts were clamoring to preserve their piece of the pie. The administration, through Vice President George H. W. Bush and Treasury Secretary Regan, sided with the big boys—the commercial banks, with their large FDIC-insured deposit bases, lending prowess, and international aspirations. But toward the later years, the administration would also support their investment bank rivals.

In general, Reagan tended to avoid direct dealing with the elite financiers. Whereas Reagan was focused on ending the Cold War from a political perspective, the bankers felt they had already moved in that direction from a financial perspective, so they had no need to be deeply involved in Reagan's plans for embracing glasnost, the Soviet policy that called for a more "open" political and financial atmosphere internally and externally. As for tax policies and the notion of "trickle-down economics" (also known as "Reaganomics"), those Reagan worked on through his Treasury secretaries. When prompted (as they were), the bankers supported Reagan's tax policies. They had similarly supported Johnson's tax cuts in the 1960s, but this was more of a self-serving decision than a public service one—it was a chip on the table for future favors. Besides, they were busy exploring innovative ways to dodge taxes through offshore entities anyway.

Reagan was barely involved in discussions with the bankers over deregulation. He was absent from negotiations and rarely copied on related correspondence. Instead he relegated these dealings to Bush and Regan. Regan later wrote that Reagan's policy came in his speeches, and it was up to the people in his cabinet to execute the details. Banker demands were handled in a similar fashion.

The only banker with whom Reagan had established a personal relationship before entering the White House was A. W. "Tom" Clausen, who had chaired the California-based Bank of America. Reagan and his wife, Nancy, also maintained a friendly relationship with Clausen's successor, Sam Armacost. Like Truman, Reagan had no prior need or opportunity to foster alliances with the East Coast, Wall Street banker sect beyond their fundraising prowess. He hadn't been an inside Washington player, so there was no real occasion to achieve such closeness. Yet many of the moves that were made during his time in office would contribute to a major overhaul of the US banking system and helped pave the way toward a full repeal of the Glass-Steagall Act in 1999. Most of Reagan's financial and banking policies would be defined in two ways: first, they would encompass the same tone of his deregulation policies for other industries; and second, they would push through the walls of Glass-Steagall. But Bush and Regan coordinated that aspect; accolades for financial deregulation initiatives and free-market dogma were only occasionally inserted into the president's speeches.

In February 1981, a couple of weeks after his term began, Reagan appointed Bush and Regan to head a new task force on "regulatory relief," code for "deregulation." The group was self-charged with finding ways "to relieve the public of excessive and costly regulations."[11]

This mission was positioned as consumer-friendly. The administration claimed, "Banking laws should be changed to enable the consumers of financial services, the banking industry, and the economy in general to enjoy the benefits of increased competition and greater efficiency in delivery of financial services."[12] In reality, the resultant wave of mergers served to consolidate power in the hands of the nation's largest banks and their chairmen, effectively *decreasing* competition everywhere else.

Wall Street and Washington became a battleground between investment and commercial banks. Each camp stood on opposite lines of the Glass-Steagall Act. Both aggressively coveted each other's territory.

Elizabeth Dole, Reagan's public liaison assistant (and former member of the Federal Trade Commission and Nixon's deputy assistant for consumer affairs), sought to prevent Reagan from getting caught in the financiers' cross fire. Though "the commercial banking element is most likely to contain supportive individuals," she wrote in a memo, "those responsible for inflicting the heaviest damage . . . are likely to remain hostile."[13]

Rather than risk a negative media frenzy over any disagreements among the bank factions, which could reflect badly on Reagan, Dole chose to shield Reagan. So she recommended Regan deal with the Wall Street crowd instead.[14] This "switch" would continue throughout Reagan's presidency. It fit both men's expertise perfectly. Reagan would hardly interact with the bankers over deregulation and had minimal social interaction.

Within three months of settling into the White House, Bush was decisively promoting the commercial bankers' position. At a media briefing held on Tax Day 1981, he stressed their views as a key element of Reagan's four-step economic recovery agenda. "The third ingredient of the economic program," Bush proclaimed, "and one with which I am rather intimately involved, is the question of reducing the excesses of regulation."[15]

Banker Policy Support

Reagan's team was tactical about enlisting bankers and corporate leaders to support his policies, though. When it was time to garner muscle behind his tax and budget bill, the team recommended enlisting Citibank chairman Walter Wriston to help.

When David Rockefeller retired from his post as Chase chairman, Wriston became the undisputed king of Wall Street and chairman of the Business Council, succeeding GE chairman Reginald Jones. In January 1981, Reagan selected Wriston to serve on his Economic Policy Advisory Board.[16]

Reagan made the necessary phone call. "As you are aware," he told Wriston, "the importance of this tax struggle transcends the bill itself, since it is only one element of our greater overall economic recovery program. The success of each element is crucial—spending cuts, tax rate cuts, regulatory relief and stable monetary growth. I hope I can count on your support." Wriston responded: "I'm on board."[17]

Reagan's staff also recommended soliciting the support of Wriston's friend George Shultz, president of Bechtel Group, for backup. He too rallied behind Reagan. It was not exactly a hardship for most corporate leaders to approve tax reductions. Bankers, however, expressed concerns about inflation ramifications.

Monetarist Wriston was particularly vocal on the matter of inflation. As he had pronounced in April 1980, "living with inflation is like living in a country where everybody lies."[18] He reiterated his anti-inflationary stance frequently and considered taming inflation far more important than cutting taxes. But in practice, he focused more of his time on abolishing New Deal constraints on commercial banking, which prohibited him from entering the insurance business and extending the bank's reach across state lines. With banking deregulation tantamount, he traded the favor of supporting Reagan's tax package.

Taking a page out of the Johnson handbook, the Reagan team peppered coalition building with friendly discourse. The strategy worked. At a press briefing on August 1, 1981, Chief of Staff James Baker III; Edwin Meese III, counselor to the president; and Treasury Secretary Regan announced, "We finally have a tax bill. . . . It's a good tax bill. It's about 95 percent of what the President wanted; a three-year across-the-board tax cut."[19]

Whereas debate would ensue for decades as to the meaning and effectiveness of Reagan's tax policies, the manner in which support was garnered underscored the financial-political alliances with the business elite that Reagan could draw upon when necessary.

Shifting Bankers, Brewing Problems

Outside the US borders, bankers' loans to developing countries had grown at an unprecedented rate and volume during the 1970s. The pace was almost certain to erupt in massive losses for banks and economic calamity for the indebted countries; it was just a matter of time. So it was fortuitous for Bank of America chairman Tom Clausen that just before noon on October 23, 1980, President Carter had summoned him to the White House to discuss the possibility of becoming president of the World Bank.[20]

By accepting the job, Clausen could execute a double save. First, he would leave his bank before its loan situation deteriorated further, as it inevitably would. Second, he could preside over an organization that could amass governments' aid to help back those loans, or at least keep funds funneling into developing countries until a better solution presented itself.

It would be Reagan who officially appointed him. In April 1981, Clausen handed Bank of America, with its festering debt problems, to his protégé, Sam Armacost, and headed off to run the World Bank. Under Clausen, the World Bank would pressure the third world to adopt structural adjustment programs that would destabilize the region for decades, causing widespread economic decay. Revolts and bloodshed would accompany private companies racing into developing countries to take over once-nationalized industries and install private sector replacements through which they could extract profits and wealth.

According to the *New York Times,* when Clausen departed after thirty-one years with Bank of America, he told his stockholders, "I'm happy that it is in such sound and vital condition."[21] The true nature of the bank's health would be revealed after he left.

Armacost, in turn, had exuded support for his fellow Californian Ronald Reagan, through the election and beyond. In return, Reagan appointed him to his Commission on Executive Exchange and the Private Sector Survey on Cost Control in 1982. When the president and first lady hosted Queen Elizabeth II's visit to San Francisco on March 3, 1983, Armacost and his wife were invited to the reception.[22]

That April marked the end of another era. When David Rockefeller retired from Chase in April 1981, he passed the stewardship of the nation's second largest bank to Willard Butcher, another international power broker with growing political ties.[23] But Rockefeller didn't relinquish his political inclinations or alliances just because he left the Chase chairman post.

In September 1981, Reagan appointed Rockefeller to be a member of his Commission on Executive Exchange.[24] Two months later, Rockefeller reciprocated by inviting Reagan to make a major foreign policy address on the Caribbean Basin Initiative before the Americas Society, which he chaired.[25]

"Your appearance," Rockefeller wrote Reagan, echoing his letters to Johnson two decades earlier regarding the Alliance for Progress, "would reinforce the mutual commitment of the public and private sectors in our nation to this hemisphere."[26] Six years later, at a White House briefing for the Council of the Americas, Reagan said, "The entire hemisphere owes its gratitude to the council, and in particular to your chairman, one of the great citizens of the Americas, David Rockefeller."[27]

All his global gallivanting aside, Rockefeller left Butcher a mess, just as Clausen had done for Armacost. Bad loans and faulty deals that had gathered under Rockefeller's leadership plagued Chase from everywhere. Major foreign and domestic positions were blowing up, including the marquee crisis he left behind: Drysdale Government Securities.[28] The firm held $4.5 billion of positions in government securities, a large portion of which was financed by Chase, along with various unclear amounts financed by other principal bank dealers. When Drysdale was unable to repay Chase, it faced going belly up. But the sheer size of its positions threatened the entire market, including all the other banks that had lent money to Drysdale.

Federal Reserve chairman Paul Volcker saw the problems for what they were: a dangerous cocktail of nontransparency and speculation. He described the cloak around the Drysdale incident as such:

> There is a firm . . . involved in highly speculative [transactions] that apparently has a large and highly leveraged position and can't meet its bills. . . . So, we have a potentially large amount of securities overhanging in the market in a distressed situation, and we're trying to figure out what to do about it. *Chase Manhattan is in the middle of this as the middleman in the shorted securities.* The people they borrowed the securities from claim that Chase is liable and Chase claims it is not, so we have a [mess] there. Losses are well in excess of $100 million just on that set of transactions, and we don't know what else is involved. . . . Chase and others held a meeting this morning; they tried to make a pro bono publico contribution [by providing] money to meet this payment yesterday. Nobody else volunteered because they all think it is Chase's liability.[29]

In short, no one knew what had transpired in the dark shadows of government securities trading. But Chase was central to the issue, and it could get worse.

After Drysdale went bankrupt, Chase wound up forking out the $117 million of the interest Drysdale owed on its loans, having acted as intermediary on $160 million of its deals, to contain the crisis and calm the markets. It remained somewhat of a mystery how the issue had snowballed so secretly and quickly out of control. But the incident evoked no extra regulations on the trading or shorting of government bonds.

A few months later, Chase wrote off $161 million for loans it had purchased from Penn Square Bank, which collapsed under a $2.5 billion mountain of unsecured oil and natural gas loans.[30] In a subsequent lawsuit regarding the $212.2 million of Penn Square loans it had bought, Chase claimed it was "unfair to make 'preferential distributions' by offsetting Penn Square deposits against Penn Square loans."[31] In the Penn Square situation, Chase took a tax writeoff, rather than dipping into its client's deposits. This was the opposite of the approach it had taken regarding Iran's monies, wherein it had no problem taking deposits to pay off loans.

Despite the financial chicanery, Butcher was as keen, if not as skilled, as Rockefeller at establishing a relationship with Reagan and his people. Butcher's relationship with the White House began, as many such relationships did, with a warm letter. A few days after the 1980 election, he wrote Reagan, "My personal congratulations on your stunning victory. Your campaign was thoroughly professional, as can be seen in the dimensions of your win, in the GOP capture of the Senate and in the deep inroads you made in the House."[32]

Such niceties—and many were exchanged—contained a hidden agenda. Like Wriston, Butcher desired a nationwide banking system, with Chase sitting at the top of a connected labyrinth of little Chases in every state. Current regulations did not accommodate such an endeavor, but Butcher and other big bank leaders would keep pushing until they did.

Wriston, Head of Reagan's Economic Advisory Board

On August 16, 1982, Reagan asked Walter Wriston to take George Shultz's place as chairman of his Economic Advisory Board. Shultz was moving over to become secretary of state. In his new position, Shultz chose retired Goldman Sachs partner John Whitehead as his deputy secretary of state.[33] Wriston replied, "I'd be honored to accept."[34] Wriston was officially appointed on September 3.

Thus, Wriston now balanced running Citibank and chairing Reagan's Economic Advisory Board, all the while continuing to espouse free-market doctrine. In a November 1982 speech for the Tufts University Fletcher School of Law and Diplomacy at the Ritz Carlton Hotel, Wriston conflated a libertarian view of individual freedoms with what he characterized as a *broader* need for liberal banking policies.[35]

"Can we really impose fewer and fewer restrictions on our own conduct as individuals, assuring everyone's right to a personal life style," he demanded of his audience, "while simultaneously imposing harsher, and increasingly irrational, restriction on all of our institutions?"[36] The answer from Washington to Wall Street was—of course we can't.

Monetary Policy and Merger Fights

Meanwhile, a battle was being waged between the Federal Reserve and the White House over monetary policy. In the summer of 1981 Volcker had resisted Regan's urging to grow the money supply (the amount of currency and liquid instruments in the country's economy, including cash, coins, and balances in checking and savings accounts) by reducing interest rates.

Regan believed Volcker's tight monetary policy had aggravated the early 1980s recession.[37] Most bankers concurred; they wanted access to cheaper money while they awaited the deregulation that would provide greater access to customer deposits. Volcker believed that reducing rates would feed inflation, whereas Regan believed that tight policy was strangling the economy, or at least the financial system. In either case, the level of debt that the private bankers had injected into the United States and third world economies with which the United States traded was a major, and uninspected, contributor to the slowing of the US economy and high inflation. The fight between Regan and Volcker would last for years.

Reagan embodied what the *New York Times* dubbed a "hands-off policy regarding mergers unless they significantly reduced competition."[38] In practice that meant a hands-off policy toward all mergers.

Yet the way in which mergers were being approved so quickly worried North Dakota Democratic congressman Byron Dorgan, among others. William Baxter, attorney general of the antitrust division, responded to Dorgan's letter to Reagan regarding merger activity by assuring Dorgan that he was fully committed to "vigorous enforcement of the antitrust laws."[39]

Dorgan wasn't the only one questioning the antitrust division's liberal merger policy. Consumer advocate Ralph Nader wrote Reagan a lengthy letter on April 26, 1982, criticizing the administration for displaying "an unprecedented disregard for the most fundamental safety and economic rights of American buyers."[40]

In his detailed list of the "Administration's actions and inactions," Nader noted, "William Baxter, your assistant attorney general for antitrust . . . has indicated such carte blanche support for mergers of almost any kind that many analysts believe him to be the chief 'go-signaler' for the current merger wave."[41]

Anticompetition wasn't the only problem that the mergers brought to light. Bigger companies contained more places on the books to commit or hide fraud or losses. Yet the administration turned a blind eye to such possibilities.

For his part, Anthony Solomon, president of the Federal Reserve Bank of New York, rejected the very thought of tighter regulation of the securities market, noting that dealers were already scrutinizing credit risks and revising practices related to Drysdale's activities.[42] The idea was that firms were self-policing. The concept of protecting the public from securities violations hadn't gained much traction in the face of such fraud. About a decade later, investment bank Salomon Brothers would commit another round of government bond manipulation. By 2012, JPMorgan Chase was mismarking billions of dollars of derivatives trades that future chairman Jamie Dimon would deem a mere "mistake" and for which the bank would pay an inconsequential fine.

The World Bank vs. the World's Bankers

From an international perspective, private bankers remained reluctant to clean up their mess in the third world. They had adopted an isolationist view of responsibility that left no room for what they perceived as throwing good money after bad. Even though they had overburdened these countries with loans to begin with, they wanted other entities to deal with the fallout while they sought to mitigate their own losses. Despite his external optimism when he took the World Bank president post, Clausen knew his organization didn't have unlimited funds to help the third world, nor would the private bankers forgive debt to make repayment viable. If anything, they would opt for "rescheduling" the debt. Worse than that, the funds that the World Bank would provide would come with austerity measures.

In a clear sign of desperation, Clausen announced his new strategy in January 1983. Despite the "shakiness of many borrowers," he now encouraged "more commercial bank lending to Third World countries."[43] Up to that point, the World Bank had maintained a solid line between its lending and that of the commercial bankers, just as John McCloy had designed it to be back in 1947. If anything, access to World Bank loans bolstered the viability of countries to get private ones by rendering them more attractive to investors—a condition that continues to this day. Knowing the extent of the financial woes that could befall the debtor nations, though, the World Bank needed to enlist the private banks' capital and power.

No one understood that better than Clausen, who had wanted the World Bank to help the private banks when he was a private bank chairman. Now sitting in the opposite seat, he persuaded the Reagan administration to back loan syndicates made up of the World Bank and commercial banks for the first time. He believed this combination would provide commercial banks greater security and encouragement to lend more to developing countries, or at least enough to cover interest payments on outstanding debts.[44]

The situation was dire. According to FDIC reports, "By October 1983, 27 countries owing $239 billion had rescheduled their debts to banks or were in the process of doing so. . . . Sixteen of the nations were from Latin America."[45]

The US government reluctantly agreed to a loose partnership, but the commercial bankers didn't. They had no desire for an alliance on the matter. By May 29, 1984, the US government, caught in a vise-grip of Clausen's instigation and the private bankers' recalcitrance, announced it would provide a loan guarantee to Argentina indefinitely.[46]

To mitigate the appearance of a backhanded bank bailout, Regan explained, "The loans to Argentina have no time limit. The United States comes into play only when the Argentines get their International Monetary Fund agreement."[47] He had shrewdly placed the government behind the multinationals in terms of risk, though both fell behind the banks. The loan guarantee was part of a $500 million aid package extended on March 30, when Argentina's first-quarter interest payment came due.[48] That was the end of Clausen's good graces with the Reagan administration.

This move put commercial banks in the driver's seat, for the IMF controlled less of the world's money than they did, but would subsume a disproportionate amount of the risk they had created. Third world leaders had preferred to deal with the bankers, who didn't ask many questions and just gave them money during the 1970s. But now they saw the devil in those details. Private bankers and their speculator clients opportunistically entered and exited financing deals quickly, leaving the political and economic fallout to governments and multinationals—and the general populations.

Third World Debt Crisis

From the summer of 1982 through mid-1983, many of the Least Developed Countries—particularly in Latin America—grew less solvent. The major US banks pressed the Reagan administration to ask Congress for a sizable increase of US support for the IMF, which would, in turn, support them.

In May 1983, the world's main finance ministers gathered at the colonial town of Williamsburg, Virginia, for an economic summit to discuss the global debt crisis. President Reagan read their seven-point concluding statement, which advocated low inflation and interest rates globally. He expressed the group's "concern [over] the international financial situation and especially the debt burdens of many developing countries."

Reagan said, "We view with concern the international financial situation and especially the debt burdens of many developing countries. . . . We will seek . . . increases in resources for the International Monetary Fund and the general arrangements to borrow. We encourage close cooperation and timely sharing of information among countries and the international institutions in particular, between the International Monetary Fund, IMF, the International Bank for Reconstruction and Development, known as IBRD, and the GATT."[49]

The bankers had won. They had garnered the financial help they needed from nonprivate sources to sustain their flailing lending activities. A reckless precedent had been approved, whether wittingly or not, to use the power of the presidency to feed the power of the private bankers as they left financial landmines around the world. Two weeks later, Reagan met with members of the National Security Council, who remained concerned on a foreign policy level about the dangers of the rising debt in the developing countries.[50]

The Fed and Treasury vs. the Banks

On the domestic front, Volcker remained concerned about developments in banking. As bankers turned to lure depositors and more business from inside US borders, Volcker sent Congress a proposal to "slow the blending of banks and other types of business."[51] He was becoming a thorn in Wall Street's and Washington's sides.

The issue of financial institutions deregulation legislation appeared on the staff meeting schedule regularly throughout 1983.[52] By July 1983, Bush's task force had drawn opposition from various industry groups, notably the smaller players in the financial spectrum, who were increasingly worried about losing their piece of the financial services industry pie.[53] Notwithstanding, on July 8, 1983, Bush sent Reagan a draft of the bill that would provide commercial banks far more latitude.[54]

The Treasury Department also went to bat for the bankers. On July 18, 1983, Regan provided testimony before the Senate Banking Committee regarding the proposed Financial Institutions Deregulation Act (FIDA).[55] It was the second of the administration's two-part proposal for bank holding company deregulation, following the Garn–St. Germain Depository Institutions Act of 1982, which layered on Carter's 1980 Depository Act, removing the interest rate ceiling that banks and S&Ls had to abide by for customer accounts. In addition, the act raised the limit of investment that S&Ls could make in nonresidential real estate from 20 percent to 40 percent of their assets, and raised the consumer lending limit from 20 percent to 30 percent of assets.

The previous act had allowed S&Ls to offer new products like interest-bearing checking accounts and commercial loans, in addition to savings accounts. Deregulation of those lending standards was a major contributing factor to the brewing S&L crisis. The S&Ls' new ability to invest in riskier ventures opened them up to sales of dubious-quality assets by rapacious banks anxious to sell them junk wrapped as valuable investments.

Regan further informed the committee that "developments in the financial service industry have all but eliminated most traditional distinctions between banking and nonbanking services" anyway.[56] He argued that legislation should follow the practice. Besides, diversified nonbanking firms like Sears, Roebuck; Merrill Lynch; Shearson/American Express; and Prudential-Bache were rapidly approaching the point of being able to offer "one-stop financial shopping."[57] Commercial banks should be allowed to expand their role in order to compete.

In November 1983, after convening more than forty meetings with industry groups to get their reactions to the bill, Bush's Working Group on Financial Institutions Reform submitted its report to the Council of Economic Advisers.[58]

The package included various industry reactions to FIDA. Not surprisingly, non–bank holding companies wanted bank holding companies to stay out of their turf, whereas commercial and investment banks wanted more deregulation. Insurance companies wanted a "prohibition on states authorizing banks to enter other businesses" and "opposed any insurance authority for banks."[59]

Investment banks advocated broadening the deregulation proposals "to include full securities powers for banks and bank power for securities firms." They also wanted to be permitted to expand across state lines so they could be subject to national rather than state laws—it was easier to lobby the federal government on deregulation than deal with each state individually. And they wanted the "expanded rights" that the commercial banks wanted, including easier paths to becoming bank holding companies and the right to create mutual funds within their firm, in order to keep customers from taking such business elsewhere.[60] In short, they wanted full reversion to pre-Glass-Steagall times.

All the other financial service factions wanted to preserve their corner of the market and have more deregulation. For their part, thrifts, or S&Ls—which tended to be smaller, more localized institutions—believed FIDA put them at a competitive disadvantage. Mortgage bankers supported FIDA as it applied to banks but thought the entire idea of the holding company approach "limits flexibility."[61] The housing industry objected to subsidiaries of bank holding companies and S&L holding companies participating in direct real estate investment, development, and brokerage, because it would infringe on their business. They also generally opposed FIDA because it would "tend to create fewer, larger financial institutions."[62] That was exactly what the commercial banks counted on.

Commercial banks, with their powerful and politically connected leaders, were angling for broader powers, including authority for corporate underwriting in their securities affiliates.[63] Their demands would be honored to the extent the administration could get them through Congress.

Taking all this into account, on November 19, 1983, Bush's task force crafted a list of bills that largely ignored noncommercial bank concerns. Title I, the Financial Institution Competitive Equity clause, for instance, deregulated a wide range of financial services that could be offered by depository institution holding companies.[64]

But it took time to wriggle these concepts through Congress. So on March 28, 1984, Regan had to testify again before the Senate Banking Committee regarding Senator Jake Garn's Financial Services Competitive Equity Act, which was based on the group's proposals. His logic remained that banks were already moving past their boundaries, so their initiative might as well be made legal. For instance, BankAmerica had moved into the insurance business by allowing Capital Holding Company, a Louisville-based firm, to sell insurance in its branches. Citicorp was operating S&Ls in California, Florida, and Illinois. And national banks were already permitted to offer investment advice.[65]

"You can continue to do nothing, and allow the marketplace, the states, and the federal regulators to mold the financial services industry as they see fit," he told the committee, "or you can enact legislations, which will respond to the realities of today."[66]

Wriston Retires

The New York Fed was fully supportive of expanding the powers of commercial bankers, too, such that they could acquire the depositors and business of other banks. In addition to authorizing commercial banks to purchase flailing thrifts, New York Fed president Anthony Solomon also promoted "a practical, federal plan for phasing in nationwide banking."[67]

Citicorp particularly benefited from this expansionary stance and interstate banking loophole. On January 20, 1984, the Federal Reserve Board permitted it to purchase two flailing thrifts, First Federal Savings & Loan Association of Chicago and New Biscayne Savings & Loan Association of Miami.[68] The acquisitions placed Citicorp, the biggest US commercial bank holding company, and now one of the nation's biggest S&L association operators, a step closer to full-service interstate banking. Citicorp flexed its muscle by bending laws that still prohibited banks from taking deposits across state lines.

American Banker observed that Citicorp's takeovers had been pushing legal boundaries for years: "Citicorp . . . has used a weakening in the regulatory fabric to gain a foothold in California, Florida, and Illinois . . . [which] emerged in cases of failing S&Ls when regulators have taken merger bids from out-of-state institutions rather than let a thrift fail. The acquisition of Fidelity, now with $3.3 billion in assets and the new name of Citicorp Savings, was the first merger over state lines to be approved by federal regulators."[69]

On September 1, 1984, John Reed succeeded Wriston as chairman and CEO of Citicorp.[70] Initially, he kept a relatively low profile that matched his more subdued personality relative to the broad media Wriston had coveted to express his views.

Wriston's seventeen-year reign had catapulted Citibank past Chase to become America's largest commercial bank, with $130 billion in assets. When he retired, a few years after his old rival David Rockefeller retired from Chase, he similarly bequeathed a company saddled with unstable Latin American debt and other crises. The *Wall Street Journal*'s Charles Stabler described the situation by declaring that the risk-free world of banking in 1967 had transformed into a risky, aggressive, innovative, and exciting enterprise, adding that "the adaptation of banks to this revolution, and even the encouragement of it, is Walt Wriston's doing."[71] Stabler neglected to mention the downside of that excitement.

Reagan praised Wriston and a group of other businessmen at a White House dinner on May 21, 1986. "We've raised $7 million this year. That's almost enough to buy a small oil company," said Reagan.[72] Wriston continued his post-Citicorp influence through op-eds, speeches, and fundraising.

"Sweeping Revisions" for Bankers

Following a brief one-month review period, Reagan approved Bush's task force recommendations for submission to Congress. (Reagan vetoed only thirty-nine acts in his first four years in office, compared to Ford's total of sixty-six in less than two years.) On February 2, 1984, Bush announced that "the task group's regulatory proposals, together with the administration's pending legislation concerning product deregulation [are] the most comprehensive revision of federal law affecting financial institutions in the last 50 years."[73]

The focal point of Bush's recommendations was the Group's Blueprint for Reform. Bush considered the proposal a "sweeping revision of the federal regulatory system for commercial banks." With an obligatory nod to the public, he promised the plan would put "the overall regulatory structure in a position to protect the integrity and stability of financial markets over the coming decades."[74]

In July 1984, Butcher pressed Chase to acquire the Lincoln First Corporation. The acquisition marked a radical shift in federal regulatory sentiment. During the mid-1960s, Chase failed to gain the regulatory approval to become a holding company a fraction of the size of Lincoln First.[75] Now size was no longer an obstacle.

Emboldened by the situation, Butcher beat the drum harder for full interstate banking. "We want to be an interstate bank," he said during a press conference at the annual American Bankers Association convention on October 26, 1984. "We can put a branch in Bangkok, Thailand, which I can tell you is exactly half-way around the world, but not in New Jersey, which I can see over the river."[76]

By 1985, Chase had facilities in twenty-three states and Washington, DC, and spanned seventy-one nations. It was assiduously buying international banks to access fresh networks of clients. Piggy-backing on Rockefeller's legacy, twenty-two offices for private banking of high-net-worth individuals spanned the globe, concentrating in Latin America, the Middle East, and, increasingly, Asia.[77]

Reagan's Reelection

During the summer of 1984, Volcker met with Reagan and his chief of staff, James Baker, in the East Wing of the White House to discuss interest rates in the lead-up to the 1984 presidential campaign.

"For Baker, it was more a routine discussion," wrote Bob Woodward in his biography of Alan Greenspan, *Maestro*. "He didn't want to be seen as pressuring Volcker. Of course the administration wanted lower rates. The White House always did."[78] So did the bankers. Lower rates would enable banks to fund themselves more cheaply so as to plug holes from potential losses arising from third world debt defaults or payment delinquencies.

Volcker ultimately did lower rates.[79] The Fed obtained greater influence over banking, too. On October 9, 1984, Bush's task force sent its final report to Reagan. It contained fifty legislative recommendations. The report called for extending the power of the Federal Reserve by requesting the nearly nine thousand nonmember state banks supervised by the FDIC to fall under Federal Reserve supervisory jurisdiction. The Fed would maintain control over the fifty largest US bank holding companies.[80]

A month later, Reagan was reelected in a landslide. After his victory, on January 9, 1985, Reagan announced that Treasury Secretary Regan and Chief of Staff Baker would switch roles.[81]

The Independent Bankers Association of America, among others, believed that Baker understood "the value of strong regional banks," whereas former Wall Street leader Regan "maintained close ties to the giant New York money center banks" and was thus perceived as being more sympathetic to their demands.[82]

Yet the distinction was meaningless in the scheme of deregulation and the commercial bank support it had in Washington. It was true that Regan had gone to bat for Wriston and the rest of the commercial bankers repeatedly, and that he was philosophically aligned with them. But Baker would turn out to be equally helpful to their power plays.

Baker, Bankers, and the Developing World

Baker unveiled the rough version of his plan for dealing with the third world debt crisis at a joint meeting of the World Bank and IMF in Seoul, South Korea, on October 6, 1985, and provided more details two days later. He called for a "new global compact among commercial bankers, debtor countries, and the international development institutions."[83] The plan urged private banks to increase their lending. It also called for $9 billion in IMF and World Bank loans in exchange for austerity measures.

Tom Clausen, president of the World Bank and the International Finance Corporation, also delivered a speech there. He stated, "Developing countries must undertake policy reforms, and they must receive adequate capital flows to support their reform efforts."[84]

Clausen believed the third world needed funds to avoid defaults, but he also thought that it would have to give up resources and control to private companies in return for the financial aid. He criticized commercial banks for slowing their lending at this critical juncture and blamed them for taking "a narrow view of their own interests."

Clausen knew well that private bankers would only help in ways that suited them. They did not want defaults, nor did they want to forgive debt or put more of their money at risk if there were other avenues through which to deal with the situation.

During his speech, Baker also urged banks "to boost their lending to the fifteen major debtor nations by $20 billion over the next three years." He demanded debtor countries "adopt policies favoring economic growth, modeled on the tax-slashing and private-sector-oriented ideas of the Reagan administration" as well as for "continued tough scrutiny by the IMF." In practice, Baker was calling for struggling countries to sink further into debt, plus give up more of their economic sovereignty and resources to external financial forces.

Though in essence the plan differed little from Clausen's, Clausen was not consulted regarding Baker's speech.[85] He informed Baker that he would not be seeking a second term.[86] The feeling of the administration was mutual.

CHAPTER 16

THE LATE 1980S: THIRD WORLD STAGGERS, S&Ls IMPLODE

"Greed is good."

—Gordon Gekko, Oliver Stone's leveraged buyout king in *Wall Street*

AS THE BIG BANKERS WORRIED ABOUT THE THIRD WORLD, THEY CONTINUED TO press the Reagan administration to back their related bets. Domestically they worried about the attempts of the S&Ls to encroach upon their depositor territory. On the one hand, deregulated S&Ls meant the larger banks could use the smaller firms as dumping grounds for questionable real estate deals. On the other, big banks had their own deregulation agenda to push in Washington.

Meanwhile, flailing S&Ls were angling for more deregulation, too. John Rousselot, president of the National Council of Savings Institutions, complained directly to Reagan that "efforts to regulate the savings industry in the name of protecting the deposit insurance funds are misguided. The key to helping the industry regain its financial health is to free it up to compete."[1] The competition argument was everywhere.

To back his argument, Rousselot presented a twenty-one-page analysis of all 202 S&L failures between January 1981 and September 1985. The report was created by George Bentson, a University of Rochester professor who had found "no connection between those failures and the sector's use of the new powers that had been granted by Congress and the states."[2] The Cato Institute and similar entities undertook their own studies with equivalent results.[3]

That conclusion ignored the codependent and carnivorous nature of banking, and the increasing intermingling of security creators and distributors and traders who needed to be regulated properly to protect the public from reckless practices within that chain. The Garn–St. Germain Depository Institutions Act of 1982 had removed the last restrictions on the level of interest rates that S&Ls could pay for deposits. That meant they could entice hoards of new consumers to open money market accounts with checking privileges at rates that matched inflation. The floodgates of depositors seeking higher returns were opened, and the S&Ls eagerly invited them into their firms.

As Martin Mayer wrote in *The Greatest-Ever Bank Robbery,* "The owners of what had just become decapitalized S&L's could raise endless money and take it to whatever gambling table was most convenient. If they won, they kept it . . . if they lost, the government would pay."[4]

It was no coincidence that securities backed by packages of risky mortgages simultaneously became vogue at Wall Street investment banks that converted questionable loans into more questionable securities and sold these for a hefty price. The business was so profitable that Wall Street took to sourcing deposits for the S&Ls, just so the S&Ls had more assets as collateral to buy more lucrative (to the investment banks) but risky securities from them.

The thrifts did, in turn, use those deposits (through arrangements called repurchase agreements) as collateral to buy additional securities (like faulty mortgage-backed securities).[5] Those securities were also subsequently repurposed as collateral against additional loans with which to buy even more of them. The entire process resembled a casino wherein the house enabled even the most deadbeat players to keep making bets in a winner-take-all situation for the house. Wall Street houses used the S&Ls as a commission-producing dumping ground on all of the above-mentioned fronts. And they often traded against the positions they sold the S&Ls, hastening their demise.

Wall Street bankers were occupied with other forms of shady deals in the mid-1980s as well. In 1986, $50 billion of fresh junk bonds hit the market (compared to $3 billion in 1976).[6] In an elaborate web of fraudulent corporate deals to augment the real estate deals plaguing the S&L industry, Drexel Burnham Lambert's "Master of the Universe" banker Michael Milken fused together a network of junk bonds and investors, earning billions of dollars in the process. His boss, Ivan Boesky, complemented his efforts by breaking insider-trading rules.[7] (Milken later pled guilty to six counts of securities fraud and served twenty-two months of a ten-year prison sentence.[8])

Clausen after the World Bank, Armacost in Trouble

As the casino mentality minted millionaires on Wall Street, the tone in Washington turned more nationalist with respect to protecting US bankers against the world. In February 1986, the Senate Banking Committee heard another round of testimony from major bankers regarding the need for "competitive" deregulation.

"In order to assure continued leadership of our capital markets and of American financial institutions our laws must be updated," Dennis Weatherstone, chairman of Morgan Guaranty Trust's executive committee (later JP-Morgan Chase), declared before the committee. "American banks must be freed to compete with foreign banks in the US securities markets."[9] The matter to him was of fundamental liberty and national power.

Part of the fervent push for deregulation was a reaction to the epic failure of banking decisions regarding international lending, especially to the developing Latin American countries. These failures had to be supplanted by other means. The industry as a whole was buckling under the failure of the late-1970s loans it had extended, but BankAmerica was showing the worst record of the top five US banks. Clausen's former exploits and Armacost's subsequent leadership at the bank were suddenly under media scrutiny.

According to a *Fortune* magazine article, under Clausen's leadership, "From 1976 to 1980, the bank's rating had been sliding at an alarming pace."[10] During his five-year tenure as the president and CEO, Armacost regularly had to dodge bullets about the bank's problems.[11] For years, the board continued to believe Armacost when he promised that the sour loans, made so liberally under Clausen, were in fact solid.[12]

In the ongoing flare-up of Latin American debt problems, Armacost was forced to resign. In a bizarre déjà vu, this made room for Clausen's return to the helm of BankAmerica on October 12, 1986.[13] BankAmerica's board reinstated the man who had so zealously pushed for those loan extensions to begin with rather than choose someone, anyone, with a more restrained notion of risk taking. The move even surprised an industry predicated on revolving public-private doors. The *LA Times* noted, "Clausen's expected return to the bank . . . is a shock."[14]

As the World Bank described Clausen, "He felt more comfortable with the private sector than with government bureaucracies and [took] his cues from the financial markets rather than the demands of the developing countries."[15] Shortly after he rejoined BankAmerica, the firm posted a $1 billion first-quarter loss.[16] But that was nothing.

BankAmerica stood to lose more than $7 billion if the larger Latin American countries (including Mexico, Brazil, and Venezuela) defaulted.[17] Once back on the private side, Clausen needed the multinational cavalry to save his bank. So he proposed that the IMF and other agencies provide guarantees to the banks to enable them to lend more.

On the surface this seemed like a way to subsidize bank lending and provide support for existing loans while staving off a larger crisis. But the idea didn't sit well with all the other bankers. Citicorp chairman John Reed adopted his predecessor's philosophy that banks, not bureaucratic political institutions like the IMF, should make decisions about loans. His feeling on the matter would soon translate into bold action.

At a financial meeting in Washington in May 1987, Paul Volcker told a group of New York bankers that keeping Mexico afloat would be cheaper than rescuing BankAmerica.[18] But either strategy amounted to rescuing the bank.

Reed's Gambit and the Rise of Greenspan

In May 1987, J. P. Morgan became the first commercial bank to receive Fed approval to underwrite commercial paper for its own account.[19] In June 1989, the Fed would grant Morgan another key perk—authorization to underwrite corporate debt, making it the first commercial bank to be able to do so since 1933.[20] Reed later described the move as "the beginning of the crack in the door."[21]

But in mid-1987, Reed was more focused on his mammoth exposure to third world debt. While other bankers prevaricated, Reed played a crafty game to instigate more government aid for the situation.[22] On May 21, 1987, having decided the government wasn't moving fast enough to help private banks contain the growing crisis, Reed announced that Citicorp would add $3 billion to its loan-loss reserves against third world loans, racking up a $2.5 billion quarterly loss.[23]

Treasury Secretary Baker hadn't even formally acknowledged that there was a problem at that point. By setting aside $3 billion in reserves, Reed knew he would cause a reaction in Washington.[24]

Morgan chairman Lewis Preston was caught off guard by the aggressiveness and noncollaborative nature of Reed's move, not to mention the positive acclaim Reed was receiving for "admitting the obvious about Third World Debt." Hence, he promptly followed Reed's lead by presenting Mexico with his own plan "to recapture the initiative."[25]

With the potential for serious foreign loan losses mounting while the White House considered the details and nature of government bailouts, bankers still needed cheap money to cover the holes in their income. They decided that Volcker wasn't lowering rates quickly enough or pushing for the kind of deregulation that would enable them to grow by buying banks or financial services companies. According to Bob Woodward, before Volcker's second term was due to expire, Baker advised Reagan, "It's time to have your own Fed chairman . . . in my mind, there is only one person to turn to."[26] The person he was referring to was Alan Greenspan.

In addition to having been called upon to educate Reagan on the economy during his campaign, and laughing at his jokes on the road, Greenspan had served for ten years on J. P. Morgan's board of directors as the firm waged its fight to repeal Glass-Steagall.[27] He later wrote that as a board member in 1977, he "would sit in the same conference room at 23 Wall Street where much of the financial chaos of 1907 had been resolved."[28] He marveled at J. P. Morgan's character and personal influence during that panic.

Charles Geisst, a historian and professor of finance at Manhattan College, recounted Greenspan's attempts to dismantle the Glass-Steagall Act from within the J. P. Morgan fold in a PBS *Frontline* interview: "Morgan produced a pamphlet called 'Rethinking Glass-Steagall' in 1984, which he [Greenspan] obviously . . . had contributed to. . . . The pamphlet was advocating getting rid of the Glass-Steagall Act so that commercial bankers particularly could begin to underwrite corporate securities again, as they hadn't done since before 1933."[29]

On August 3, 1987, the Senate confirmed Greenspan as chairman of the Federal Reserve by a vote of ninety-one to two.[30] A week later, at his swearing-in ceremony, Reagan declared, "Alan is making perhaps the most dramatic personal sacrifice of his career, taking his name down from the door of Townsend-Greenspan, the firm he guided as president and chairman for nearly thirty years."[31]

But more important for US bankers' power over international finance was what Reagan said after that. Merging the topics of the world marketplace,

Greenspan, and the two most important initiatives for bankers into one sentence, he stated, "With the entire globe becoming a single—[and highly competitive]—marketplace, Chairman Greenspan will play an important role in seeking solutions to the problems of developing countries . . . [and] he will be deeply involved in the restructuring and modernization of the American Banking System."[32]

In his first testimony before Congress as Fed chair on October 6, 1987, Greenspan proclaimed the banking system "frozen within a regulatory structure fashioned some fifty years ago" and urged legislators "to come to grips with the difficult decisions that must be made to update our laws to the new circumstances of technology and competition."[33] And so he exemplified his full support for the nation's largest bankers in Washington.

Market Crash

Despite structural fault lines emerging in the global financial system, the US stock market was unperturbed. The Dow hit 2,000 for the first time in January 1987 and reached 2,700 in August. Computer technology contributed to the buzz and the speed of the rise. Corporate takeovers that took stock out of circulation, rendering what was left or new more enticing (if not objectively more valuable) helped further buoy the market.

Adding to the party, on October 15, Reagan's Council of Economic Advisers prepared a briefing titled "Record-Breaking Peacetime Expansion."[34] It noted that October 1987 marked the fifty-ninth month of the current expansion, setting the record for the longest peacetime expansion in US economic history. Real GNP had risen more than 20 percent, and real per capita disposable income was up 11 percent. Inflation stood at a third of its 1979–1980 rate, and the unemployment rate had declined by almost 5 percent since November 1982.[35]

Between mid-1982 and the fall of 1987, the stock market experienced its longest and sharpest bull market in fifty years. Daily shares traded on the New York Stock Exchange more than doubled, from 82 million in 1982 to 180 million in 1987. But the party was about to end with a sudden crash.

On "Black Monday," October 19, 1987, the Dow plunged almost 23 percent.

Greenspan issued a career-defining statement before the markets opened the following morning. "The Federal Reserve, consistent with its responsibility as the nation's central bank, affirmed today its readiness to serve as a source of liquidity to support the economic and financial system."[36] In other words, the Fed stood ready to bail out banks of tremendous size. Whereas once the markets needed to know the private bankers would buy up shares to keep them afloat, now the Fed chief's promise of cheap liquidity did the trick.

Only with that promise did Federal Reserve of New York president Gerald Corrigan urge certain banks to keep money flowing so that the system would appear stable. Banks and other companies began buying their own stock at the lower prices to bolster them up. At 1 P.M. the Major Market Index futures market staged the largest rally in history.[37] The extreme volatility of the move overshadowed anything that the bankers had done in past crash periods. Their Federal Reserve cavalry was firmly in place.

Greenspan looked golden for opening the Fed floodgates to the bankers. Five weeks after Black Monday, the *Wall Street Journal* headlined an article "Passing a Test: Fed's New Chairman Wins a Lot of Praise on Handling the Crash."[38]

Officially, the drop was blamed on "program trading" computers dumping blocks of stock at certain "sell" levels. Some publications attributed the crash to nonreasons like "the market needed a correction." The whole event was an exercise in hiding the fact that a lot of fraud and debt had gone into building up those stock prices.

On October 23, 1987, Reagan appointed Bush's friend Nicholas Brady, chairman of the politically connected Wall Street firm Dillon, Read & Company, to chair a three-member task force to investigate the crash and recommend future safeguards.[39]

Three months later, the task force released its 340-page report. Brady criticized Wall Street's computer-driven trading practices that automatically dump large blocks of stock when prices drop significantly, amplifying declines.[40]

"The financial systems came close to gridlock," the report stated, adding that "the experience illustrates how a relatively few, aggressive, professional market participants can produce dramatic swings in market prices."[41]

Separately, President Reagan created another working group on financial markets (colloquially described as the Plunge Protection Team) on March 18, 1988.[42] Its purpose was to further examine causes of the Black Monday crash while "enhancing the integrity, efficiency, orderliness, and competitiveness of [United States] financial markets and maintaining investor confidence."[43]

In its interim May 1988 report, the working group, which included Greenspan and Commodity Futures Trading Commission chair Wendy Gramm, sent Reagan their recommendations. They suggested coordinating "circuit breakers" during times of high market volatilities, higher margins for stocks than for stock index futures, and continuing the working group.[44] They did not address the high debt levels that crushed the market.

Black Monday proved nothing more than a pothole on the deregulation highway. It created an opportunity for Greenspan to appear brilliant for holding the banking sector together by opening the Fed faucets, which provided him with an even stronger reputational platform to help commercial banks gain reentry into more speculative businesses.

That summer, when Reagan announced the resignation of James Baker, who was moving over to become chairman of George Bush's presidential campaign, and the nomination of Nicholas Brady as Treasury secretary, Reagan told Baker, "You've been a secret of our success. Now, Jim, go do it for George."[45]

Like Regan, Brady was of prime Wall Street stock. His father, Clarence, and former Treasury Secretary C. Douglas Dillon were close friends. Clarence had fashioned Dillon, Read & Company into a Wall Street powerhouse in the 1920s. Like his buddy George Bush, Nicholas Brady was an avid athlete and Yale University graduate.[46] Also, he was a proponent of deregulation.[47]

Bush Wins

By the time George H. W. Bush became president on January 20, 1989, the economy was limping again. Federal debt stood at $2.8 trillion. The S&L crisis had escalated. Still, his financial policies remained in sync with those of the period's most powerful bankers, notably Citicorp chairman John Reed, Chase chairman Willard Butcher, JPMorgan chief Dennis Weatherstone, and BankAmerica chairman Tom Clausen.[48]

These bankers, in turn, continued to find in Bush and his core cabinet kindred deregulatory spirits. Though like Reagan, Bush rarely interacted directly with the Wall Street bankers, they did correspond liberally with Bush's "people" before and during his presidency. By that point, the third world debt crisis had been simmering beneath various ineffective band-aids since 1982. Plus, the S&L industry was collapsing, the result of abject deregulation, an abundance of fraudulent real estate assets, and criminality. Into that cauldron of S&L and third world debt crises came the most critical demands for landscape changes in banking since the Great Depression.

With economic odds stacked against him, Bush remained surrounded by his most loyal, business-friendly companions, who had tight relationships with Wall Street or came directly from there. On January 27, 1989, Bush swore in Baker as his secretary of state. At the ceremony, he remarked, "Jim and I have been friends for a long time, going back perhaps more years than either of us would care to admit—long, really, before our public lives began."[49]

In a preordained arrangement with Reagan, Bush retained Brady as Treasury secretary.[50] Their ties, first established on a tennis court, extended to Wall Street and back again. In 1977, Brady had even offered Bush a position at Dillon, Read after Bush left the CIA. Though he didn't accept Brady's offer, Bush enlisted him to run his 1980 presidential campaign and suggested Brady as interim senator for New Jersey in 1982.[51] The press dubbed Brady Bush's "Official Confidant."[52]

Bush appointed one of his right-hand men, Richard Breeden, who had drafted his task group's Blueprint for Reform, as assistant for issues analysis and later as head of the Securities and Exchange Commission. Breeden proceeded to advocate deregulation from the entity established to protect the public from an overly reckless banking industry.[53]

Bush's choice for Federal Reserve chairman was clear. He received a deluge of mail on the topic of reappointing Alan Greenspan—from average citizens and businessmen alike, with about 75 percent urging him to oppose the reappointment and 25 percent in favor of it.[54] Undaunted, Bush reappointed Greenspan.[55]

Bush unveiled his plan to rescue the ailing S&L banks on February 6, 1989.[56] Initial bailout estimates were put at $40 billion to rescue 223 firms. Two weeks later, the Bush administration raised the estimate to $157 billion. With public wrath decidedly against any kind of bailout, Brady adopted a more aggressive tack. On February 22, 1989, he issued an emotional press release themed "Never again": "Never again should the nation's savings and loan system . . . be put in jeopardy." He promised that "the Administration's plan meets these standards."[57]

Brady, on the offensive, stressed that this proposal wasn't a bailout. Instead, as he wordsmithed before a group of businessmen at the Dallas Chamber of Commerce, it represented "the fulfillment of the Federal Government's commitment to depositors," which "relies on a combination of industry and taxpayer funds."[58]

Under Greenspan's Fed, a few months later, J. P. Morgan Securities, the investment banking subsidiary of J. P. Morgan & Company, became the first bank subsidiary to lead a corporate bond underwriting since the Great Depression.[59] On October 10, 1989, it won a bid to issue a $30 million bond for the Savannah Electric and Power Company.[60]

Over the next decade, commercial banks would issue billions of dollars of corporate debt on behalf of energy and public utility companies as a result of Greenspan's decision to open that door.[61] A chunk of it would implode in fraud and default when Bush's son, George W. Bush, became president in 2001.

Third World Debt Crisis Redux

It was fitting for US bankers to turn toward the pursuit of domestic corporate debt issuance, given that developing countries now faced plummeting economies because of the financiers' overzealous lending practices.

The world's largest banks had dumped about $1 trillion in aggressively extended "recycled" loans into the least developed (mostly Latin American) countries. They now faced a tipping point: either these nations would default on all debt or work out some kind of agreement whereby a portion could be forgiven or subsidized while they figured out how to repay the rest. The bankers wanted to take as few hits as possible by enlisting the support of sovereign governments and multinational entities.

Since 1982, Latin American countries had transferred $184 billion to creditor countries and private banks, severely crippling them economically. By 1989, the region's GDP per capita was 8 percent lower than it had been in 1980.

Financial conditions bore a striking resemblance to the period between World War I and World War II, when US bankers stressed the need for some forgiveness, or at least restructuring, of Germany's debt at the hands of the US government. Doing that had allowed Germany and the European countries to which it owed reparations money to remain strong enough to accept more debt at the hands of the private banks (which, as discussed earlier, had devastating consequences). Now the same banks were repeating the demands, though with less finesse than their 1920s predecessors, pressing the White House to forgive their loans to the third world so that private loans could remain.

At an internal March 7, 1989, White House policy meeting on international debt, Brady stated that the Treasury would "attempt to create new incentives for commercial banks and debtor countries to negotiate voluntary debt reduction." The incentives included "changes in bank regulations" and "using IMF and World Bank resources to support debt securitization proposals."[62] The stipulations favored the private bankers.

In his March 10 speech to the Bretton Woods Committee's conference on third world debt, sponsored by the Brookings Institution, Brady publicly unveiled his plan.[63] He called it "a cooperative global program which places special emphasis on debt reduction and stronger efforts to attract private capital" to resolve the crisis.[64] Days before his speech, three hundred people had been killed in Venezuela amid violent protests over IMF austerity measures.[65]

Brady needed private banker support so that the government wouldn't be caught subsidizing all the potential damage. The debt overhang was so

nefarious that the banks were in grave danger themselves, but they were waiting out the government rather than collaborating with it.

Brady tailored a plan he thought would be sure to make them happy. On
its surface, the Brady plan would induce banks to voluntarily forgive a portion of the principal and the interest for third world loans.[66] Banks would
have the "obligation" to exchange their outstanding developing-country
debt with bonds at a discount, or to lend new money, or both. In return,
banks would receive less risky bonds secured by US Treasury bonds. The action would increase national debt in the process.

Funds required to purchase those Treasury bonds would come from international organizations. Thus, the plan would effectively subsidize private
banks using the IMF and the World Bank channels that, in turn, were supplied by an increase in federal debt on the backs of US taxpayers. Like many
bank bailouts, it was a way for Wall Street to cook its books rather than allow
for debt forgiveness or bankruptcies that would have been less costly to the
developing countries. It "rescheduled," for example, $20 billion of Mexico's
$84 billion of debt, adding an extra $1.5 billion in new debt. Because of the
Brady plan, local banks ceased providing loans, delaying Mexican recovery in
jobs and wages and growth. Mexico, meanwhile, opened its banking system
to more privatization for foreign speculators to raise extra cash.

Technically, the banks should write off some of the debt, and they could
also lend new money to the struggling countries. But that didn't happen. The
banks still didn't lend and wouldn't lend for another nine months or so, and
then only after additional incentives were added.[67]

Bank of America, Clausen, and Third World Debt

Three years after Clausen returned to the top slot at Bank of America, the
firm with the largest US bank exposure to Mexico was still reeling. Thus,
Clausen was particularly keen on the Brady plan.[68] In July 1989, he helped
bang out its details alongside Alan Greenspan; Gerald Corrigan; Pedro Aspe,
Mexico's finance minister; and Citibank chairman John Reed, who led the
fifteen-bank advisory committee on behalf of no less than three hundred
creditor banks.[69]

As leader of the negotiations and head of the bank with the second biggest
exposure to Mexico, Reed had already officially lent Brady his support after
a visit to the White House in late March.[70] Unofficially, US banks were mired
in private negotiations. They refused to fully embrace the proposed Brady

plan or comply with the US government's request that they forgive a portion of loans, despite Brady's incentives or "additional financial support" from the IMF and World Bank that was designed to get the banks on board.[71] Former Citibank chairman George Moore had strong thoughts of his own regarding the crisis, which he had penned in his 1987 book, *The Banker's Life*, and augmented in a March 1989 paper that circulated around the White House.[72]

Moore admitted that the banking system had gone "too far" in recycling oil profits when OPEC quadrupled the price of oil. But rather than blame banks for overzealous lending (that far exceeded the reasonable country limits set in the 1930s), he put the onus on the IMF and the Bank for International Settlements, who, he said, had "to know of the extreme heights to which these debts had rapidly risen."[73] It was not unlike bankers and politicians blaming the Fed for the late 1920s speculation that led to the Crash of 1929, as opposed to the banker culprits who had stood to gain more personally from their speculative practices.

As Moore summarized the situation: "It was a wonderful party—before the check came. It was a trillion dollar binge. The banks thought they were making a lot of money, the borrowers never had it so good. All ordered more drinks, as long as the bar was open. Meanwhile, responsible international institutions like the IMF and World Bank were looking out the window when they should have stopped the party!"[74]

On June 2, 1989, the World Bank unveiled its three-year program for Least Developed Countries (LDC) debt relief, as per Brady's proposals.[75] Three months later, J. P. Morgan added $2 billion in loss reserves anyway, to indicate the program was insufficient. Chairman Lewis Preston stated, "The action we've taken should give us greater flexibility to work with these countries advising government and private sector clients."[76] It was a version of Reed's what's-in-it-for-us doctrine, which entailed banks soliciting the government to buoy their positions but not helping in return to alleviate the problems—and as such, placing the burden of their actions on the taxpaying population. It also opened avenues for bankers to further extend themselves into the region for merger and acquisition business.

Reed Slams Regulation

Meanwhile, Reed still had national policies to change. He was called before the Senate Banking Committee on July 13, 1989, to provide testimony on domestic financial policy.[77] This time, he stressed his opposition to deposit insurance premiums.

Reed proposed that the level of deposit insurance be gradually cut back.[78] He wanted depositors to judge for themselves whether banks and savings institutions were taking undue risks. His logic was similar to that of Chase chairman Winthrop Aldrich during the Depression; the big banks that were better at managing their risk should not have to pay the same premium for insurance as the banks that weren't, or any if possible. Customers could decide if their deposits were safe or not.

Reed also united with Corrigan before the Senate Banking Committee to argue that the US banking system was falling behind that of other countries.[79] Reed demanded no less than a "major restructuring of our financial system" to keep up with a rapidly changing "competitive environment."[80]

As the latest torch carrier for that global competitiveness argument, Reed paved the path for Robert Rubin, Larry Summers, and the man who would be his partner in finally breaking Glass-Steagall, Sandy Weill. Now deregulation was presented as even more critical in the fight against potential European banking supremacy, and thus to America's position as a global financial power.

The S&L Blowout and Greenspan's Game

The deregulation of the S&L industry between 1980 and 1982 had enabled thrifts to compete with commercial banks for depositors, and to invest that money (and money borrowed against it) in more speculative real estate ventures and junk bond securities. When those bets soured, the industry tanked. Between 1986 and 1989, 296 thrifts failed. An additional 747 would shut down between 1989 and 1995.[81]

Among those, Silverado Banking, Savings and Loan Association went bankrupt in December 1988, costing taxpayers $1.3 billion.[82] Neil Bush, George H. W. Bush's son, was on the board of directors of Silverado at the time. He was accused of giving himself a loan from Silverado, but denied all wrongdoing. Records in the Bush archives show seven pages of redacted communication related to Neil Bush in early 1990.[83] Another son, Jeb Bush, had already been dragged through headlines in late 1988 for his real estate relationship with Miguel Recarey Jr., a Cuban American mogul who had been indicted on one charge of fraud and suspected of up to $100 million of Medicare fraud charges.[84]

But the most expensive S&L failure was Lincoln Savings, a debacle that cost taxpayers $3 billion.[85] The flameout also led to the Keating Five political scandal, in which five US senators were implicated in accepting campaign contribution bribes from Charles Keating.[86] Keating had secured a study from Alan Greenspan, then a private sector economist, concluding that direct speculative investments were not harmful.[87]

It took several months of internal political battles before the Bush S&L plan headed to the House floor for consideration, but finally, on June 14, 1989, it was ready.[88] On the same day that the Bush team was presenting its S&L package, Greenspan was swiping at Glass-Steagall, retreading the well-worn theme of global competition before the Senate banking subcommittee. He claimed that current regulation put US banks at a competitive disadvantage and thus inhibited the US financial system's growth globally, and by extension the very stability of the country (using the angle Reagan had mentioned at his swearing-in ceremony).

"There is no question we are being significantly suppressed by the Glass-Steagall restriction," said Greenspan. "My concern is that as we continue to internationalize . . . we are in effect inhibiting our institutions from fully participating in that."[89]

With Greenspan on deck advocating the repeal of Glass-Steagall, New York bankers reinvigorated their drive to expand across state lines and to circumvent New Deal limitations on the financial services they could hold under one roof, such as the inability to purchase insurance companies. Their argument was that insurance restrictions should not apply to subsidiaries of bank holding companies. In other words, just because banks couldn't own insurance companies, why couldn't their subsidiaries?

In practice, this was a minor but important distinction. As Philip Corwin, senior legislative counsel for the American Bankers Association, put it, the issue had gone from a "turf fight (between insurance and banks) to a consumer issue." In a rather odd alliance, the Consumer Federation of America supported the big banks' campaign for insurance powers.[90] The CFA subscribed to the notion that the more firms were involved in insurance, the more it would increase competition and thus decrease rates for individual consumers, an argument disproven time and time again. For when big firms expand their reach, consolidation, and power, the actual result is higher prices.

Bush's S&L bailout plan became the Financial Institution Reform, Recovery and Enforcement Act, signed on August 9, 1989.[91] The FIRREA abolished the Federal Savings and Loan Insurance Corporation (FSLIC) and allowed the Federal Deposit Insurance Corporation (FDIC) to insure S&L deposits.[92]

The centerpiece of the act was the establishment of the Resolution Trust Corporation (RTC) to handle savings and loan failures.[93] The first president of its oversight board was Daniel Kearney, a banker who had spent a decade in Salomon's real estate financing department creating the very securities that had combusted on the books of the S&Ls.[94] The RTC would be funded via a new privately owned corporation, the Resolution Funding Corporation (REFCORP), which would issue $30 billion in long-term bonds to raise the needed capital beginning in 1990.[95]

This proved another boon for the big commercial banks. They could profit by virtue of their intermediary position selling those bonds into the market, while the government was subsidizing the entire project.[96]

Within six years, the RTC and the FSLIC sold $519 billion worth of assets for 1,043 thrifts that had gone belly up. Key Wall Street banks were involved in distributing those assets, making money on financial destruction once again. Washington left the public on the hook for $124 billion in losses; the thrift industry lost another $29 billion.[97]

Bankers vs. Senators: Venezuela

Willard Butcher, CEO of the Chase Manhattan Bank, succeeded Dennis Weatherstone in 1989 on the Fed's advisory council.[98] He, too, had a wide range of concerns about the restrictive nature of current regulation and the LDC debt problem for US banks. While his compatriots wrestled with the Treasury Department and Congress on the issue of LDC debt, he took up the issue with the media.

On July 25, 1989, Butcher wrote a letter excoriating a *New York Times* editor over his assumption that banks rejected a proposal for Venezuela's debt reduction because "it did not offer them the option of lending Venezuela new money to use for repaying its existing debt." Butcher claimed, "The banks rejected the proposal because that country's request for debt reduction was excessive and not based on needs."[99]

But his harshest criticism centered on the piece's suggestion that the United States "announce that there will be no international guarantees on Third World debt for any bank unless all the banks jointly approve sizable debt reduction."[100]

He declared the idea "naive and illogical" on the basis that US banks accounted for only 31 percent of Venezuela's bank debt versus that extended by foreign institutions, and thus, it was unlikely anyway that "all the banks will ever jointly agree."[101] Butcher warned, "The progress of these negotiations cannot be helped by editorials that are illogical and wrong."[102]

More broadly, he was using the globalization of excessive debt as an argument against US banks doing their part to alleviate a situation they had created, while his brethren in Washington were arguing that US banks had to be deregulated in order to compete with these international firms for more such opportunities.

Two months later, a team of five senators sent letters to eight top bankers including Preston, Clausen, Butcher, and Reed.[103] They implored the bankers to support the government's plan for Venezuela debt restructuring. They even played hardball, promising to support funding to the IMF and World Bank for "market-oriented economic reforms" *only* if banks reduced debt or began lending again.[104]

The bankers battened down their hatches and refused to respond to federal threats or promises of rewards for "good behavior." As the World Bank said in its annual report, "the hard reality is that less debt has been forgiven in 1989 than in 1988, and that the amount of resources marshaled to finance debt relief is pitifully small."[105]

Economic Suffering

As the 1980s drew to a close, unemployment soared and the economy limped, just as they had when the decade began. The Brady plan turned out to be a bust; the bankers ignored the senators' pleas, as Reed, Preston, and Weatherstone effectively forced the government to back them. The glut of debt that the banking sector had spewed into the world absent full repayment left them in the position of needing to find another "game." While pundits and economists debated the impact of deficits and tax policy on the general economy, it remained the bankers' actions that had driven an immense bubble of bad debt domestically and internationally, with sizes that far overshadowed the US deficit.

As former undersecretary of the Treasury Paul Craig Roberts had warned Don Regan in August 1986, and later wrote in a *Wall Street Journal* piece on October 28, 1986, "A stronger force than tax cuts was operating on U.S. Capital outflows."[106]

Roberts noted that "a fundamental change in the lending practices of U.S. banks" was the critical factor. "Money-center banks were heavy lenders to the Third World, expecting rising commodity prices such as oil and copper to service and repay loans. When [price] inflation collapsed, the bankers realized that they had overexposed their capital and stopped lending."[107]

The deluge of bank debt combined with recessionary economies inevitably accelerated economic suffering throughout the world. In the United States, 614 out of 3,200 thrifts had collapsed by the end of the 1980s (the most since the Great Depression), costing the US government more than $85 billion, as larger banks swept in to pick up their remains and enhance their own customer base in the process. Another 429 would fail during the first half of the 1990s, bringing the total to 1,043 failures.[108]

Moreover, the federal government and Fed response to the third world debt crisis, S&L bailout, and 1987 stock market crash was to subsidize the banking system with federal and multinational money. The bankers had succeeded in pushing the presidency to back losses domestically and from a foreign lending perspective in ways that would have been embarrassing to the bankers of an earlier era. They had succeeded in privatizing their profits and socializing the costs of failure. This financial policy had officially become US domestic and foreign policy.

Bank leverage ratios and risk-taking decisions, already growing, increased exponentially as a result, only to be later compounded by derivatives and other complex financial instruments. Bankers now wielded enormous power to alter the economic and financial nature of the world in more extreme ways, and with more money at stake, than ever before. No longer was there even a pretense of alignment with domestic concerns or collaboration with the White House, except as fodder for arguments about why the biggest banks should be allowed to increase in size. If anything, it was the other way around. Financial voracity and the bankers' quest for power, enabled by an increasingly subordinated Washington, had trumped reason and would continue to do so in the 1990s.

CHAPTER 17

THE EARLY TO MID-1990S: KILLER INSTINCT, BANK WARS, AND THE RISE OF GOLDMAN SACHS

"Some men know the price of everything and the value of nothing."
—Oscar Wilde

THE 1990S WERE A DECADE THAT RAN ON TECHNOLOGICAL STEROIDS, FROM THE sheer speed at which financial transactions took place to the dot-com mania that Federal Reserve Board chairman Alan Greenspan dubbed "irrational exuberance."[1]

With the Cold War over, America lacked a great external enemy. There was no major national distraction to divert the tide of the global dispersion of US financial power, no public interest to protect against outside enemies in reality or in rhetoric. There were no restraints on the drive for self-interested accumulation or the final dismantling of banking rules in the name of

American competitiveness. The moneyed elites were now full-fledged gladiators with no business need for a social compass but every need for a warrior spirit. The men running Wall Street didn't come from families with famous names on the high-society circuit; they were men who fought for power in their firms and around the world without such attachment to lineage.

The conundrum for these bankers was that Europe's banks had reemerged as true challengers thanks to the global expansion of firms like UBS in Switzerland, Deutsche Bank in Germany, and Barclays in Britain. Fearful of losing their position in the hierarchy of financial influence, US bankers demanded domestic deregulation with increasing intensity—while embracing far riskier practices.

It was America versus the world, only now financial products and more substantive mergers and derivatives trading augmented the spread of political doctrines. The assumption was that "democratic capitalism," the ideology that merged US political goals with financial ones, had successfully defeated more "socialistic" international commerce, trade, and business doctrines. The proof was increasingly evident in the extreme divergence of US CEO pay versus that of average American workers and their global counterparts. Big balance sheets bolstering the most powerful US banks were as important as large weapons arsenals. In this war of international opportunism, the American government remained keen to aid and invest. As President Bush's policies gave way to Clinton's, the White House yielded to more bankers' demands—just as they had in the 1980s but with a much greater degree of completion and higher global stakes.

The Continuing S&L Crisis

In May 1990, Chase chairman and CEO Willard Butcher met with President Bush to discuss his views about America's global competitive position. Butcher and his international advisory committee saw real opportunity to finance reconstruction efforts in post-Communist Eastern Europe, which would augment their other international business. Butcher wanted to ensure that Bush was on board with the foreign policy initiatives that would be necessary to complement his plan, which entailed supplementing standard lending with more complex deals across borders, including the use of derivatives markets.

Bush was receptive. As Butcher later wrote him, "You are just as we think of you: warm, articulate, committed and concerned not only about the American people but about the state of the world."[2]

President Bush didn't respond personally. With lobbyists and lawyers inserting themselves into the political-financial complex, the personal connections characterized by gestures like Johnson's thank-you phone calls and Eisenhower's carefully crafted letters had become relics of another time.

Instead, Roger Porter, assistant to the president for economic and domestic policy, replied that Bush "enjoyed the session very much."[3] But that was all that the Chase bankers needed to push forward; it had become enough that agendas were "understood" among all parties.

On the domestic front, by mid-1990 Bush's S&L bailout plans were hitting severe legal speed bumps. Wall Street firms eyed the legal circus like vultures before swooping in for a kill. In a May 7 letter to C. Boyden Gray, counsel to the president, John Aldridge, a prestigious attorney who advised the Bush administration on failed S&L asset liquidations—and represented an array of big bank clients on the private side—remarked, "We are going to have to enlist the aid of the commercial banking industry in order to spread this problem across a base sufficiently broad to deal with the problem."[4]

Aldridge submitted a bid to the Resolution Trust Corporation on behalf of his clients, who sought to act as financial advisers on the nonperforming assets. "If our bid is accepted," he wrote Gray, "We hope to be of assistance to the RTC in engineering the 'early victory.'"[5] There was no altruism in the bankers' intentions. The assistance was in fact a play for buying cheap assets that could be repackaged and sold to investors at substantial profits. "Victory" meant optimum wealth extraction in the process.

Both investment and commercial banks viewed the episode as a means to purchase bargain-basement S&L assets and restructure them into new securities imbued with profit. The backing of the RTC, which carried with it the implicit guarantee of the US government, rendered the prospect less risky and more lucrative.

Meanwhile, lawsuits and indictments were piling up, including against President Bush's son.[6] The Justice Department flexed its judiciary muscle against banks run by less powerful men than those at the helm of the major Wall Street firms. From October 1988 to August 1990, the department filed 274 indictments involving 403 defendants. Of those, 316 were convicted for S&L frauds or losses involving sums of more than $100,000.[7] The massive cleanup operation of the S&Ls, however, neglected to serve as a warning bell for looming precarious practices.

The New Game in Town

The S&L trouble sparked a broader credit crisis and recession. On September 21, 1990, Chase Manhattan took a $1 billion hit and fired 5,000 employees because of real estate and emerging market fallout.[8] Manufacturers Hanover cut 1,400 workers. Citibank reported a $457 million loss for 1991.[9] Citibank chairman Reed admitted later that "a horrible real estate portfolio and inappropriate capital and reserves" caused the situation.[10] But he maintained his opposition to any corrective regulations.

Like other banks, Chase was also reeling from property-related losses, including on a massive set of loans to Donald Trump for which Chase, Citibank, and others had considered concocting a bailout to provide temporary forgiveness of Trump's interest payments.[11] Troubled LDC loans rounded out Chase's problems from overzealous debt extensions, though these did not receive the same potential support as Trump.[12]

Thomas Labrecque, the newly selected chairman and CEO of Chase—who had leapfrogged over a bunch of men when he replaced Butcher—also came out gunning against other regulations.[13] He wanted banks to be permitted to engage in more nonbanking activities. This, despite the crushing blows the industry was taking for various maneuvers that had already pushed such boundaries.[14]

Labrecque added his own flourish to the global competition arguments that influential bankers were using to promote deregulation. On April 3, 1990, he testified before the Senate Banking, Housing, and Urban Affairs Committee that "US banks have lost market share in the core businesses of banking, are less efficient, more risky, and less capable of serving the needs of our customers and the nation's economy."[15] Something had to be done regarding the breadth of banking services offered under one roof—for the sake of America!

The congressional committee was debating the so-called modernization of the financial services industry, which in practice would mean breaking down remaining barriers separating deposits and loans from securities creation and trading activities within the same institution. This also meant allowing commercial banks to expand into nontraditional banking activities, such as insurance provision and fund management. Key testimony came from Robert Downey of Goldman Sachs, also representing the Securities Industry Association, and Labrecque, also representing the American Bankers Association and the Association of Bank Holding Companies.[16]

These hearings became showcases for the competition arguments of the biggest bankers, but they were not the only means by which the bankers sought to capture power over the political system. Their forays before various committees, supported as they were by presidential leanings, were more aggressive and demanding than they had been in the past, when they had to play defense in response to concerns about the industry. Another piece of the deregulatory puzzle was critical to their ambitions: reentering the stock market business so that commercial bankers could issue and trade shares for their corporate clients, as they had in the 1920s. Later that fall, on September 20, 1990, the Federal Reserve Board approved J. P. Morgan & Company's application to trade corporate stocks. In doing so, the Fed dismantled the element of the Glass-Steagall rule that separated banking and securities businesses.[17]

Bankers knew that issuing initial public (stock) offerings (or IPOs), creating more complicated bonds customized with bells and whistles to suit clients' needs, and transacting more derivatives business offered much greater rewards than traditional lending did. In banking, the more complicated the deal, the more profit a banker could extract from it. Complexity was the new game in town.

The bankers' goals still overlapped with those of the White House, which believed in financial deregulation as a means to maintain global supremacy. Treasury Secretary Nicholas Brady was keen to put the bankers' desires ahead of the public interest. In a press release he warned that "our banks are falling behind international competitors," as if removing restrictions on their practices would somehow ameliorate the greater economy.[18]

The reason commercial banks were falling behind, though, was mostly because US bankers had taken larger risks than their European counterparts had in real estate markets. Buildings and complexes along the East Coast erected on the back of liberal bank loans stood nearly 95 percent vacant. Tenants couldn't meet the massive rents and developers were going bankrupt.[19] Meanwhile, the sales of new homes had fallen 17.5 percent in 1990, reaching their lowest levels since 1982.

During the first quarter of 1991, Citicorp's profits fell 81 percent. And though Chase's earnings rose slightly in comparison, Labrecque waxed pessimistic about the future. "None of us wants a lowering in the quality of real estate accounting standards," Labrecque said. "Rather what is needed is a sounder, more balanced approach for evaluating real estate."[20] His intent amounted to effectively massaging the numbers.

The Bush administration aided the bankers by advocating the repeal of key elements of Glass-Steagall. Related bills to dismantle the Depression-era act won support of the House and Senate banking committees in the fall of

1991, though they were defeated in the House in a full vote.[21] But for many important regulations, the writing was on the wall.

Preston's Pledge

While the deregulation dance was going on domestically, a shift in the supranational arena threatened to shake the private bankers' confidence in the World Bank as a partner for their international aspirations. On March 6, 1991, Bush's old buddy World Bank president Barber Conable Jr. unexpectedly announced his retirement. Conable had played a critical role in that capacity of integrating private and supranational bank activities. The Bush administration did not want to risk installing someone who would be less sympathetic to the private bankers' requirements when the general economic atmosphere remained shaky.

Bush's solution was to appoint another old friend: Lewis Preston, who had just retired from his $2 million a year position as chairman of the executive board of J. P. Morgan & Company.[22] Preston was a Harvard graduate, former marine, captain of the 1948 Olympic hockey team, and a lifelong Republican.

Under Preston's tutelage, Morgan's global presence and investment banking division had grown considerably. Described as "reticent" and "taciturn," Preston had been heavily involved in crafting Wall Street's solutions to the third world debt crisis and shielding Morgan from as much fallout as possible.[23]

For the first time since their inception, the World Bank, IMF, and other international lenders held more than half of third world debt.[24] They were thus exposed to more risk than the private banks were.

Preston pledged to reinstitute a more "market-friendly" balance between public and private investment in underdeveloped countries.[25] In practice, this meant more World Bank collaboration with private banks in areas where investors had already extracted profits and left behind weak economies throughout Latin America. It also united economic development and private banking policy under one roof. The reinvigorated alliance would soon lead to another major debt crisis—this time, in Asia.

Breeden Fights for Investment Bankers' Rights

As commercial bankers pushed to enter nonbanking businesses, Bush's SEC chairman, Richard Breeden, championed the *other* side of the Glass-Steagall divide: that of the investment banks and securities houses.

Breeden fought for the rights of investment banks to own commercial banks. To him, the balance had been tipping too much in favor of the commercial bankers and their demands.[26] Their government-backed deposits could be parlayed into the growing, risky, and highly profitable derivatives business, giving them an advantage over other types of financial institutions. Investment bankers hungered to even the score.

The Fed had already given commercial banks approval to underwrite and sell certain previously "ineligible" securities in December 1986, due to its liberal interpretation of Section 20 of the Glass-Steagall Act.[27] Now the Bush administration's plan to deregulate the financial system presented an opportunity for Breeden to expand his power. It would allow the SEC to monitor the growing number of businesses that banks could enter. As Breeden put it, "I don't know any parts of the package on financial reform that are not S.E.C. related."[28] With Breeden representing investment banks and Brady representing commercial banks, all bases were covered by Bush's probanking deregulation team. A return to pre–1929 Crash banking conditions had all the political backing it needed.

Wendy Gramm, head of the Commodity Futures Trading Commission established in 1974, helped the bankers' goal of unconstrained derivatives trading. Gramm had first been appointed chair of the CFTC by Reagan (who called her his "favorite economist") in 1988, and then reappointed by Bush.[29] She was determined to push for unregulated commodity futures and swaps, in response to lobbying from Texas-based energy trading company Enron and various commodity-trading bankers.

After several behind-the-scenes moves designed to garner appropriate political support around Washington, in June 1990 Gramm had sent a six-page fax to President Bush amalgamating the widespread approval for futures deregulation she had gathered throughout his cabinet. Her package included a letter from Treasury Secretary Brady to influential Senator Charles Robb, a Virginia Democrat, advocating he "join the Administration in supporting the Gorton-Wirth-Heinz proposal." Championed by Republicans Slade Gorton (Washington) and John Heinz (Pennsylvania) and Democrat Timothy Wirth (Colorado), the proposal modified the "exclusivity clause" of the Commodity Exchange Act of 1936, and removed "barriers to innovation in the financial markets." Their proposal would allow hybrid securities free regulatory rein. Gramm contended it would add "stability and competition to the markets," and urged the Senate to consider this when reviewing the broader bill.[30]

At the time, the SEC regulated both stocks and stock option trading, but stock index futures were regulated by the CFTC. The Gorton-Wirth-Heinz proposal would put authority for both under the SEC.[31] This sounded like tighter regulatory policy on the surface. But the fine print removed regulatory oversight from a host of new "hybrid" derivatives products spewing from the banks—multiheaded, esoteric transactions that, for instance, linked the price of oil with levels of interest rates, or linked the stock prices of energy companies with foreign exchange rates, all within one security whose attributes were difficult to gauge.

Brady also claimed the proposal would "end pointless litigation and remove barriers to innovation in the financial markets." Like Gramm and the bankers, he argued these financial hybrids were "simply not amenable to trading on a futures exchange."[32] So why bother even trying?

The proposal had been floating around Washington since October 1989 and would continue to do so for another two years. But with the backing of the investment bank trading community and the Bush administration, Gramm kept pushing (Greenspan also lent his support).

The related Bond-Wirth bill was introduced on April 11, 1991. It would essentially leave hybrids outside standard regulatory boundaries. A letter from Goldman Sachs circulated around the White House, praising "the reduction in regulation of hybrid instruments" (though it complained that the law still left too many hybrids subject to regulation.[33])

While awaiting official legislative approval, bankers got the ball rolling, sending their trading exemption requests to Gramm. She began granting exemptions to companies to circumvent various trading limitations.[34] In October 1991, she granted J. Aron, a Goldman Sachs subsidiary that specialized in commodity trading, a key exemption. The firm would no longer have to operate under prevailing trading position limits of five thousand futures at a time; they could technically trade volumes of commodity futures without limits. The exemption was granted on the grounds that "their speculative positions were really 'hedges.'"[35]

The obfuscation of what constituted a "hedge" versus a "bet" would provide bankers wiggle room for decades and gave Congress and regulators an excuse to avoid doing their jobs properly. If an investment bank wanted to trade a large position in the derivatives market, there was no way for a regulator, much less a senator, to know whether this was necessary to facilitate a client's business strategy (say a cereal producer buying wheat futures at a certain price that guaranteed him a lower price in the future) or the bank's desire to make money trading in the markets, period.

Regardless, the Bond-Wirth bill was finally reintroduced in 1991 as part of the Futures Trading Practices Act of 1992, and thus the bill exempting hybrid instruments was signed into law on October 28, 1992.[36] The act also gave the CFTC wider authority to decide whether energy futures contracts should be regulated at all.

Mega-Mergers

In the midst of deregulation talks, mega bank mergers were escalating in a manner not seen since the mid-1950s.[37] On July 15, 1991, Chemical Banking Corporation and Manufacturers Hanover announced a $2 billion merger.[38] The instigator, Manufacturers chairman and CEO John McGillicuddy, had served as a board director for the New York Fed since 1988, and had been a policy adviser to Bush and Reagan.[39]

The *New York Times*, like the bankers, seemed to believe that the appropriate reaction to major losses from atrocious LDC bets was bankers' finding new fertile ground and growing in size. According to the *Times*, "The books of most major New York banks are carrying millions in dud loans to bankrupt Third World countries and on half-empty office buildings. They need to raise more capital and grow to compete worldwide."[40]

McGillicuddy added an obligatory public-service justification for the deal: "The result will be a much stronger entity that can serve our customers with distinction and compete effectively with any financial institution in the world. That's good for New York and good for the United States."[41] Under the Chemical moniker, the new corporation would become the second largest US bank in terms of assets ($135 billion), behind struggling Citicorp. A larger financial marriage would soon eclipse that merger as the biggest in US history: the $5 billion BankAmerica/Security Pacific merger in April 1992.

Since the S&L debacle, federal regulators had been actively promoting such mergers. McGillicuddy and Chemical Banking CEO Walter Shipley had consulted with Gerald Corrigan, president of the Federal Reserve Bank of New York, who publicly urged them to merge.[42] Senator Charles Schumer considered the merger critical for the country, as it formed "a large, efficient institution that can compete with the likes of Deutsche Bank and Sumitomo Bank."[43] After the merger, 6,200 people lost their jobs, mostly in the New York area.[44]

The 1992 Election and the Rise of Clinton

Challenging Bush for his second term, Arkansas governor Bill Clinton announced he would seek the 1992 Democratic nomination for the presidency on October 2, 1991. The upcoming presidential election would not alter the path of mergers or White House support for deregulation.

Already a consummate fundraiser, Clinton cleverly amassed backing and established early alliances with Wall Street. One of his key supporters would later alter American banking forever. As Clinton put it, he received "invaluable early support" from Ken Brody, a Goldman Sachs executive seeking to delve into Democratic politics. Brody took Clinton "to a dinner with high-powered New York businesspeople, including Bob Rubin, whose tightly reasoned arguments for a new economic policy," Clinton later wrote, "made a lasting impression on me."[45]

The battle for the White House kicked into high gear the following fall. William Schreyer, chairman and CEO of Merrill Lynch (Donald Regan's old firm), showed his support for Bush by giving the maximum personal contribution to Bush's campaign committee permitted by law: $1,000. But he wanted to do more. So when one of Bush's fundraisers solicited him to contribute to the Republican National Committee's nonfederal, or "soft money," account, Schreyer made a $100,000 donation.[46]

The bankers' alliances remained divided among the candidates, as they considered which man would be best for their own power trajectories, but their donations were plentiful: mortgage and broker company contributions were $1.2 million; 46 percent to the GOP and 54 percent to the Democrats.[47] Commercial banks poured in $14.8 million to the 1992 campaigns at a near fifty-fifty split.[48]

Clinton, like every good Democrat, campaigned publicly against the bankers: "It's time to end the greed that consumed Wall Street and ruined our S&Ls in the last decade," he said. But equally, he had no qualms about taking money from the financial sector. In the early months of his campaign, *BusinessWeek* estimated that he received $2 million of his initial $8.5 million in contributions from New York, under the care of Ken Brody.

"If I had a Ken Brody working for me in every state, I'd be like the Maytag man with nothing to do," said Rahm Emanuel, who ran Clinton's nationwide fundraising committee and later became Obama's chief of staff. Wealthy donors and prospective fundraisers were invited to a select series of small meetings with Clinton at the plush Manhattan office of the prestigious private equity firm Blackstone.[49]

Pounding the Pound

That fall, while the US election season kicked into high gear, European markets fell in disarray. Europe was trying to combine its currencies into one exchange rate mechanism, and the countries that met the criteria into one trade economy. As the date for integration neared, speculators rushed to make money off any uncertainty or national economic discrepancies. One casualty was Britain.

Smelling blood and profit, George Soros had heavily borrowed sterling (around 6.5 billion pounds) and converted it into deutsche marks and francs (the "stronger" currencies), a trade that would profit if the pound fell. By midmorning on September 16, 1992, pound selling was so intense that Bank of England officials were buying two billion pounds of sterling an hour to keep it stable. News programs "used words such as 'slaughter' and 'disaster' to describe the situation."[50]

Soros reaped about $1.5 billion on the trade. Britain raised interest rates twice to defend the pound. But the international trading community slammed the currency anyway. The Bank of England took a $40 billion hit between August and September.[51]

As Soros wrote in his book *Soros on Soros,* he went for the "jugular" on the British currency.[52] He decided raising rates to defend the currency was an "untenable move" because otherwise "ganging up on it" wouldn't have pushed the pound out of the exchange rate mechanism.[53] Such is the way that traders justified their attacks on policies and populations, though the "Black Wednesday" crash and pound devaluation caused loan shocks, housing price crashes, and small business closures.

Major banks, including Citicorp, J. P. Morgan, Chemical Bank, Chase Manhattan, and Bank of America, made an extra $1 billion from currency trading that quarter, in various "copycat" trades.[54] It would not be the last time the big banks profited from the economic inequalities and the wrath of speculators seeking profits from currency trades among the European countries. But it would be a signature turning point, indicating the power that bankers and financiers had over national governments when they wanted to take out an economic "hit."

The turmoil provided a minor but inconsequential diversion from the US election. On November 3, 1992, Clinton beat Bush and businessman H. Ross Perot of the Reform Party. Though Clinton received only 43 percent of the popular vote, he amassed 370 of 538 electoral votes.[55] His presidency would prove manna for the big bankers.

Sandy Weill's Killer Instinct

After Bush lost the election, Wendy Gramm brought the matter of deregulated commodities trading to a quick vote. On January 14, 1993, with two of the five CFTC seats vacant, she voted with the majority in a two-to-one decision to exclude commodity contracts from relevant oversight.

As a result, companies like Enron and various Wall Street commodity-trading desks were waived from important disclosure requirements. Six days later, as Clinton took the presidential oath, Gramm resigned from her CFTC post. Five weeks later, Enron appointed her to its board of directors and audit committee.[56]

Times had truly changed. No longer were family ties and inbred relationships the key to internal ascension at the nation's biggest banks; a tough predatory, more sociopathic nature was required and rewarded. Mental combat, voracious killer instincts, and acquisitions of other banks (with their share of citizens' deposits) propelled the banking elite to the top of their field. Huge compensations followed.

Sandy Weill mastered the art of accumulation by acquisition. Weill had the rags-to-riches American Dream story down pat. He played stickball as a kid, supported the New York Yankees, and joined Bear Stearns as a clerk in 1955.[57] Five years later, he and three of his friends formed a boutique firm called Carter, Berlind, Potoma & Weill.

While serving as chairman of this firm, subsequently renamed Cogan, Berlind, Weill & Levitt (after Arthur Levitt, who was appointed by Clinton as head of the SEC in 1993), from 1965 to 1984, Weill conducted fifteen key acquisitions. In 1979, the firm became known as Shearson Loeb Rhoades, and was the second largest US securities brokerage firm, after Merrill Lynch. In 1981, Weill sold Shearson Loeb Rhoades to American Express for $930 million in stock, and in 1984, he became chairman and CEO of American Express's insurance subsidiary, Fireman's Fund Insurance Company. While at American Express, Weill also began mentoring his protégé, Jamie Dimon. Weill resigned in August 1985 because of internal battles.[58]

In 1986, Weill assumed the helm of Commercial Credit, and then purchased Travelers Insurance and his old brokerage, Shearson. In 1988, he paid $1.5 billion for Primerica, the parent company of Smith Barney.

The following year, benefiting from the fallout of the Milken-Boesky junk bond scandal, Weill acquired sixteen of Drexel Burnham Lambert's retail brokerage outlets.[59] In 1993, Weill reacquired his old Shearson brokerage from American Express for $1.2 billion, and took over Travelers Corporation in a $4.2 billion stock deal.[60]

Weill wasn't the only banker growing his powerful empire through acquisitions, but during the 1980s and 1990s, he was the best. Under Clinton, he'd find more influence, and a superior ally.

Robert Rubin Comes to Washington

Clinton had met President Kennedy while on a Washington field trip as part of a Boys Nation delegation when he was seventeen years old. He even got to shake Kennedy's hand.[61] Though he would follow in Kennedy's distant footsteps, he would learn from Kennedy's banker-alliance mistakes, and choose his friends wisely.

Clinton knew that embracing the bankers would help him get things done in Washington, and what he wanted to get done dovetailed nicely with their desires anyway. To facilitate his policies and maintain ties to Wall Street, he selected a man who had been instrumental to his campaign, Robert Rubin, as his economic adviser.

In 1980, Rubin had landed on Goldman's management committee alongside fellow Democrat Jon Corzine.[62] A decade later, Rubin and Stephen Friedman were appointed cochairmen of Goldman Sachs.[63] Rubin's political aspirations met an appropriate opportunity when Clinton captured the White House. On January 25, 1993, Clinton appointed him as assistant to the president for economic policy. Shortly thereafter, he created a unique role for his comrade, head of the newly created National Economic Council.

"I asked Bob Rubin to take on a new job," Clinton later wrote, "coordinating economic policy in the White House as Chairman of the National Economic Council, which would operate in much the same way the National Security Council did, bringing all the relevant agencies together to formulate and implement policy. . . . [I]f he could balance all of [Goldman Sachs'] egos and interests, he had a good chance to succeed with the job."[64] (Ten years later, President George W. Bush gave the same position to Rubin's old partner, Friedman.[65])

Back at Goldman, Jon Corzine, co-head of fixed income, and Henry Paulson, co-head of investment banking, were ascending through the ranks. They became co-CEOs when Friedman retired at the end of 1994.[66]

Those two men were the perfect bipartisan duo. Corzine was a staunch Democrat serving on the International Capital Markets Advisory Committee of the Federal Reserve Bank of New York (from 1989 to 1999). He would cochair a presidential commission for Clinton on capital budgeting between 1997 and 1999, while serving in a key role on the BorrowingAdvisory Committee of the Treasury Department.[67] Paulson was a well-connected Republican and Harvard graduate who had served on the White House Domestic Council as staff assistant to the president in the Nixon administration.[68]

Despite the problems of late 1992, 1993 was a banner year for banks. The St. Louis Fed reported, "U.S. commercial banks had their best year since World War II" and "balance sheets of commercial banks expanded at the briskest pace since 1986."[69] Clinton's presidency would provide further firepower.

Throughout the 1990s, building power was essential to American financiers, not just domestically. US bankers feared their control over global finance could be upended by the euro and, even more than that, by European moves toward banking deregulation. Europe's Maastricht Treaty had been signed on February 7, 1992. Under the treaty, European Union members agreed to adopt the euro as their common currency, drop trade barriers, and create a common defense and foreign policy.

Separately, Europe adopted its own version of Glass-Steagall repeal. A Commission of the European Communities "Second Banking Directive" had taken effect in early 1993. The EU decided that allowing banks and securities companies to merge would strengthen their global position, exacting what it believed to be a first-mover's advantage in financial warfare. American bankers would not be sideswiped in the global financial stakes, nor would Clinton's government.

In order to compete, American banks had to grow domestically and internationally, in every manner—in terms of people's deposits, their total assets, different kinds of services (from loans to complex derivatives deals), and more global expansion buoyed by financial liberalization stemming from US trade policy.

NAFTA and Statewide Deregulation

Clinton had championed the North American Free Trade Agreement—which would create a free-trade zone between Canada, the United States, and Mexico—from the moment he arrived in Washington. The administration felt it was critical not only for the US economy but for its strategic interests, especially in light of the economic consolidation in Europe. On January 1, 1994, NAFTA took effect.

For bankers, one element of NAFTA—that of lending—was of minor importance. First, they had already plowed the region with respect to lending, and that had resulted in a debt crisis. Second, as John Donnelly, Chemical's country manager in Mexico, summed it up on behalf of the industry, "Our top priorities are trading, foreign exchange, and advisory work. Lending is probably our bottom priority."

Bankers were more interested in structuring complicated cross-border derivatives deals that had more "margin" (or money) in them than straight loans.[70] They prepared to rush into the area, readying applications to set up a bevy of local and regional banks to act as local financial "command stations" within months of NAFTA's passage.[71]

Inside US borders, the Clinton administration concentrated on breaking barriers to bank acquisitions across state lines. Such deregulation would benefit the nation's largest banks and most powerful bankers, who could then accumulate more capital (from people's deposits in more states) to eat up their smaller competitors.

On September 13, 1994, by a vote of ninety-four to four, the Senate joined the House in passing the Riegle-Neal Interstate Banking and Branching Efficiency Act, which permitted full interstate banking, though it also limited the amount of deposits any one bank could have to 10 percent of the total deposits of the United States.[72] It was the first major pillar of Clinton's deregulation policy. White House documents oozed a self-congratulatory tone, noting that the act broke "fifteen years of legislative gridlock on the issue." The Clinton administration "has accomplished what had eluded the Carter, Reagan and Bush administrations," enthused an internal memo.[73]

All that was missing was a posh event to cap off this victory. On September 29, 1994, at an afternoon ceremony in the Cash Room of the Treasury Department, about 170 guests gathered to do just that. Treasury Secretary Lloyd Bentsen opened the festivities by introducing two key American bankers: Richard Kovacevich, president and CEO of Norwest Corporation (now Wells Fargo), and Thomas Labrecque, chairman and CEO of Chase Manhattan Bank.

Labrecque spoke of the broad economic benefits of interstate legislation—including, of course, the enhancement of international competitiveness. Kovacevich, whose bank enjoyed a large presence in the Midwest, considered the bill essential to weathering economic downturns.[74] Deregulation was again equated with US strength.

Seated in the audience were two other bankers whose "leadership," Clinton remarked, helped make the act "a reality": Mike Halloran, general counsel of Bank of America, and Hugh McColl, chairman of NationsBank. McColl was an old friend of Clinton's, whom Clinton considered "one of the most enlightened bankers in America."[75] Kenneth Cline, a reporter for *American Banker*, wrote, "The chairman and CEO of NationsBank Corp. put more effort into lobbying for the [Interstate Banking Act] than any other banker in the country."[76]

Clinton credited McColl in his signing speech, saying he "stayed with me half the night once. You may think you can't stay up half a night talking about interstate banking. [Laughter] You may think it would put you to sleep even though—but you have never heard Hugh McColl talk about it."[77]

"We know this bill is good for consumers for reasons that have already been stated," Clinton continued. "I wish I had thought of Tom's line myself—it's easier for a New York bank to expand into Kuala Lumpur than Jersey City."[78]

That would no longer be the case. From now on, banks could do both.

When Clinton thanked Labrecque and Kovacevich for participating in the ceremony, he told them, "Since the beginning of my administration I have looked for ways to tear down outdated and unnecessary regulatory barriers to economic activity. . . . I intend to continue pursuing similar opportunities to streamline and modernize government regulation."[79]

Mexico Falters, Bankers Quiver

Outside US borders, the post-NAFTA world wasn't the nirvana Clinton had promised. An international financial crisis had been simmering for months, most acutely in Mexico, where the Brady plan enabled US banks to "reschedule" $20 billon of Mexico's $84 billion of debt, thereby adding more debt and causing local banks to shun the needs of citizens and small businesses in preservation mode. US banks took advantage of this weakness by buying Mexican banks. In 1990, the only foreign bank operating in Mexico was Citibank, with assets amounting to about 0.5 percent of banks' total assets. Under NAFTA, market share limits rose to a 30 percent cap on the equity interest of foreign banks in Mexico's banking system. By 1994, twenty-four of the thirty major Mexican banks were foreign-owned or -operated, including by Citigroup, Santander, J. P. Morgan, and Chase Manhattan. NAFTA took away Mexico's control over its financial system and shifted it to the United States and Europe.

As Clinton talked up the benefits of NAFTA, Mexico was buckling under oppressive debt and a declining currency in a potential redux of the LDC debt crisis of the previous decade. After liberalization and NAFTA, the Mexican peso dove nearly 50 percent within six months, causing a vicious recession.[80] Real income levels for many Mexican citizens and the newly emerging Mexican middle class got slammed as a result.

On December 2, 1994, Mexico's finance minister, Jaime Serra Puche, met with US bankers at the New York Fed to assure them that his government would support the faltering peso. He promised that Mexico would restrict domestic credit and adopt austerity measures to protect the currency.[81] But promises weren't enough to spark a rise in the peso or economic stability in the country. Stanford-educated economist Guillermo Ortiz Martínez replaced him in a matter of days.

That same week, on December 7, 1994, after Bentsen resigned from his Treasury secretary post, Clinton announced that Rubin would replace him.[82] A few weeks after the announcement, Mexican president Ernesto Zedillo devalued the peso.[83] The devaluation unleashed a currency meltdown that rippled through Latin America. Worse for the bankers, the possibility of a default and a chain reaction of large potential bank losses loomed. They needed a bailout.

Clinton considered the Mexican financial crisis that struck between late 1994 and early 1995 "one of the biggest crises" of his first term. On the evening of January 10, 1995, after Rubin was sworn in, he met with Treasury official Larry Summers, Clinton, and his advisers to discuss it.

According to Rubin's account of the evening, "Sitting on a sofa in the Oval Office during my first hour on the job, I was answering questions from the President that I had been asking others only a couple of weeks before. Larry had phoned me in December, while I was on vacation in the Virgin Islands, to bring me up to speed on the unfolding Mexican situation. I didn't know much about Mexico's economic problems, and I didn't understand why a peso devaluation was urgent enough to interfere with fishing."[84]

Rubin must have come up to speed fairly quickly because Clinton recalled that Rubin was very concerned about a crisis. "If Mexico defaulted," wrote Clinton in his memoirs, "the economic 'meltdown,' as Bob Rubin tried to avoid calling it, would accelerate . . . [and it] could have severe consequences for the United States . . . [and] a damaging impact on other countries, by shaking investors' confidence in emerging markets in the rest of Latin America, Central Europe, Russia, South Africa, and other countries we were trying to help modernize and prosper."[85]

Rubin and Summers recommended asking Congress to approve $25 billion in loans to help Mexico pay its debts and bolster investors' confidence in return for Mexico's "commitment to financial reforms."[86] The figure was the largest US government–offered foreign aid since the Marshall Plan.

The Mexican Bailout

By January 30, 1995, Mexico's reserves had shriveled to $2 billion, from $24.4 billion a year earlier.[87] Rubin proclaimed, "Mexico has about forty-eight hours to live."[88] The next day, President Clinton invoked his emergency powers to extend a $20 billion loan to Mexico from the Treasury Department's Exchange Stabilization Fund. It was just one part of the full bailout, but it was the part that Rubin could push and Clinton could approve immediately without going through Congress.

Heavy hitters like BankAmerica, Chase Manhattan, Chemical Banking, Citicorp, Goldman Sachs, and J. P. Morgan, who learned nothing from the first LDC debt crisis—except that the government would help them contain losses—accounted for nearly 74 percent of Latin American exposure, or $40.4 billion.[89] The bailout saved them, and later enabled them to buy Mexican banks that were weakened as a result. A decade later, foreign banks, led by Citigroup in the United States, owned 74 percent of Mexican financial assets, more external ownership than in any other country.

The backlash against Rubin was immediate. Accusations that he would personally benefit from what became a $51 billion bailout package traversed Congress. Before a congressional panel on February 23, 1995, Rubin, who had made $26 million in his last year at Goldman Sachs, retorted, "What Goldman Sachs has to do with Mexico is of no interest to me."[90]

But that wasn't quite the truth. Rubin's command of Goldman had coincided with its bulking up on Mexican deals. In his February 28, 1995, address to the House on the matter, Indiana Republican Dan Burton pointed out, "Goldman Sachs was the largest United States underwriter of Mexican bonds . . . [with] $5.17 billion in investments made in the Mexican markets, more than double . . . the next two highest companies."

On March 9–10, 1995, the Senate Banking Committee held hearings on the administration's use of funds to bail out Mexico and whether it caused the crisis or exacerbated it.[91] Those investigations went nowhere. The committee acknowledged connections between the Treasury and Mexico, but it all floated away as hot air from a leadership claiming to have taken appropriate action. Rubin had a clear conflict of interest—but was never held accountable.

The Mexican bailout stabilized the bankers' positions. Rather than the losses they would have booked without it, Citicorp posted a $3.5 billion profit for 1995, the most in history by a US bank. In November of that year, it negotiated a new headquarters building in Mexico City, with 85,000 square feet of office space.[92] (Chase Manhattan recorded a $2.46 billion in net profit for 1995.)

In October, President Zedillo visited the White House to discuss the success of NAFTA and the bailout. In a joint press conference, Clinton addressed the bailout: "I did it because I wanted to stop bad things from happening. I did it because I have a vision of what our partnership will be in the future. But I seek no special advantage for the United States and certainly no influence over the internal affairs of Mexico."[93] As a result of the US bank bailout, Mexico was forced to undergo a $135 billion bailout of its own banks in the late 1990s. Furthermore, the bailout did nothing to help Mexican citizens. Instead, it extended the cause of financial liberalism and saved US banks with Mexican exposure from potential losses.

In February 2010 Zedillo became a member of Citigroup's board of directors.[94]

Bankers Forge Ahead

Rubin and the bankers resumed their focus on domestic deregulation as if nothing had happened—indeed, as if deregulation was needed to combat such international economic strife. In May 1995, Rubin resumed warning that the Glass-Steagall Act could "conceivably impede safety and soundness by limiting revenue diversification."[95]

Banking deregulation was still inching through Congress despite the Mexican crisis. As they had during the Bush administration, both the House and Senate Banking Committees had approved separate versions of legislation to repeal Glass-Steagall. Conference negotiations had fallen apart, though, and the effort was stalled.[96]

By 1996 other industries, representing core clients of the banking sector, were being deregulated. On February 8, 1996, Clinton signed the Telecom Act, which killed many independent and smaller broadcasting companies by opening a national market for "cross-ownership."

Deregulation of energy companies that could transport energy across state lines led to blackouts in California and a slew of energy derivatives trades that further crushed the economy. Before deregulation, state commissions regulated companies that owned power plants and transmission lines, which worked together to distribute power. Afterward, these could be divided and effectively traded without uniform regulation or responsibility to regional customers.

The number of mergers and stock and debt issuances ballooned. As industries consolidated and ramped up their derivatives transactions and special purpose vehicles (off-balance-sheet, offshore constructions tailored by the banking community to hide the true nature of their debts and shield their profits from taxes), bankers kicked into hyperdrive to generate fees and create related securities and deals. Many of these later blew up in the early 2000s in a spate of scandals and bankruptcies.

Meanwhile, bankers ploughed ahead with their advisory services, speculative enterprises, and deregulation pursuits. President Clinton and his team would soon provide them an epic gift, all in the name of US global power and competitiveness.

CHAPTER 18

THE LATE 1990S: CURRENCY CRISES AND GLASS-STEAGALL DEMISE

"Today I am pleased to sign into law S. 900, the Gramm-Leach-Bliley Act. This historic legislation will modernize our financial services laws, stimulating greater innovation and competition in the financial services industry. America's consumers, our communities, and the economy will reap the benefits of this act."

—President Bill Clinton, November 12, 1999[1]

DURING THE SECOND HALF OF THE 1990S, THE FINANCIAL, TELECOM, AND ENERGY industries accumulated $4 trillion in bond and loan debt, eight times the amount of the first half of the decade. Debt issuance from 1998 to 2000, the height of the stock bubble, was four times what it had been from 1990 to 1998, and six times more for the energy and telecom sectors.[2] The financial sector issued $1.7 trillion in loans to itself.[3]

The frenzy of consolidating and speculation pushed the stock market to greater heights. On October 14, 1996, the Dow Jones closed above 6,000 for the first time in history.[4] The economy appeared to be buzzing along as well. And no one was looking beneath the surface of all this newfound market-connected, banker-incited, policy-enabled wealth to inspect the debt being accumulated to subsidize it all.

Against the backdrop of the soaring stock market and bubbling economy, on November 5, 1996, President Clinton dispatched Republican presidential candidate Bob Dole to recapture the White House. Clinton gained just 49.2 percent of the popular vote, but increased his Electoral College total to 379.[5]

The markets were euphoric, in particular within the telecom and energy sectors, and "dot-com" mania escalated another notch. On December 5, 1996, Federal Reserve chairman Alan Greenspan gave his infamous speech suggesting that "irrational exuberance" could be causing the extraordinary boom in stock prices.[6] He did not suggest that inflated merger deals and derivatives trading had anything to do with it.

Public Responsibility Goes Down, Wall Street Bonuses Go Up

The American public lost $6 billion through stock fraud in 1996 alone.[7] In addition, commercial banks funneled money into expanding private equity and hedge funds that invested in dot-coms and other stocks. The emergence of these funding relationships was far more significant than the herd psychology of individual investors looking for a deal. Money was plentiful— and as with railroads a century earlier, speculators had to find ways to spend it. The stock market was one place to find startups and "deals"; the other avenues would be in Asia and Eastern Europe.

Before Christmas 1996 (effective March 1997), the Federal Reserve Board issued another precedent-shattering decision. The Fed would permit non-bank subsidiaries of bank holding companies to own investment bank affiliates with up to 25 percent of their business in securities underwriting (an increase from the prevailing 10 percent).[8]

This was an expansion of the Fed's prior relaxing of Section 20 of Glass-Steagall in the spring of 1987 (which occurred by overriding opposition from then-chairman Paul Volcker).[9] The latest Fed decision effectively rendered one major cornerstone of Glass-Steagall obsolete. Virtually any bank holding company could issue securities and appear to stay under the 25 percent limit on revenue. It was game on.

In September 1997, the Fed announced it would eliminate more restrictions "to the prudential limits or firewalls" that applied to bank holding companies engaged in securities underwriting and dealing activities, effective October 27, 1997.[10] Now, banks could not only issue corporate bond securities; they could also buy entire securities firms.[11] Because many target institutions also owned asset management businesses, parent banks could sell stocks and bonds they issued right into those investment portfolios (including pension and retail investor funds). This would ensure that more demand for bubbling shares of stocks stemmed from the new merged entities. The phenomenon that stoked the market was not unlike the one that prevailed during the "money trusts" era at the turn of the twentieth century, when the Morgan group of financiers, by virtue of their joint position atop various firms, could buy securities from one of their firms concocted by another, providing the illusion of heightened demand, which, in turn enticed more external investors.

On that tide of enthusiasm, Sandy Weill acquired Salomon Brothers for $9 billion and merged it with Smith Barney. Travelers president and chief operating officer James "Jamie" Dimon noted, "Merging Smith Barney and Salomon Brothers accomplishes in a short time what it would have taken either of us a considerable time to build."[12] Dimon, who had become CEO of Smith Barney in January 1996, became cochairman and co-CEO of the combined brokerage after the merger.[13]

As the stock market soared in 1997, so did Wall Street bonuses. On March 13, 1998, the *New York Post* reported that Weill had banked "a whopping $220.2 million" in 1997 by exercising stock options in "one of the largest paydays in corporate history." He also received $49.9 million in salary, bonus, restricted stock, and options, almost double his 1996 compensation of $26.8 million. Likewise, Dimon banked $36.8 million by exercising his options.[14]

These astronomical sums were not even on the same planet as those achieved by bankers in the middle of the twentieth century. The level of public responsibility that bankers felt or exuded—which was already nearly nonexistent by the late 1990s—declined in inverse proportion to the rise in their compensations.

The amount of money that bank CEOs could amass with the advent of stock option growth substantially increased their risk appetite. More simply wasn't enough. Power had to be infinite. The new game was winner-take-all. One enticing spot in which to make currency and derivatives bets was Asia. Things were going so well in the United States that even the crisis that would result in the region would not curb the bankers' appetite.

The Asian "Contagion"

As the US markets soared, a major global upheaval occurred when speculators began slamming the Asian markets' stocks and currencies. In July 1997, a 20 percent devaluation of the Thai baht (to a record low) ignited a pan-Asian economic crisis. The action caused the Thai government to request "technical assistance" from the IMF.[15] Bankers stood poised to take related losses on the chin without such subsidization.

J. P. Morgan & Company, an emerging credit derivatives player entangled in the region, took a major hit, posting a 35 percent reduction in earnings in the fourth quarter of 1997 compared to the same period the previous year. But it could have been much worse without the supranational cavalry to bail out the firm's speculative positions.

The Asian disaster was a byproduct of the moral hazard that the 1994 Mexican peso crisis had produced in the banking community. The $51 billion bailout—upon which Robert Rubin and IMF head Michel Camdessus collaborated ($20 billion from the United States, $18 billion of IMF loans, and $13 billion from the Bank for International Settlements) in return for austerity measures—showed Wall Street that bankers would be protected by the US government from losses at the eleventh hour.[16]

"Thus bailed out," observed right-wing commentator Pat Buchanan, "Wall Street's hot money took off to chase the higher rates of return in Asia, confident that if losses loomed, they had reliable friends at Treasury and the IMF."[17]

Asia represented a fresh place to pillage, just as Latin American had during and immediately after the Cold War. As Klaus Friedrich, chief economist at Germany's Dresdner Bank, put it, "We were all standing in line trying to help these countries borrow money. We would all see each other at the same places. We all knew each other."[18] Derivatives upped the ante.

As rampant speculation and the thirst for expansion again triggered widespread devastation, bankers were getting worried about how the crisis would affect their books.[19] Camdessus traveled to Seoul in early December 1997 to negotiate a bailout of Korea. From 1997 to 1998 the IMF gave $36 billion in support to Indonesia, Korea, and Thailand.[20] These monies propped up private bankers' positions.

Several weeks later the *New York Times* reported that commercial bankers from Chase, BankAmerica, Citicorp, and J. P. Morgan, along with investment bankers from Goldman Sachs and Salomon Smith Barney, were meeting at the Federal Reserve Bank of New York to discuss ways to prevent further defaults in South Korea and Asia. A separate, more private meeting would be held at J. P. Morgan without regulators.[21] There was no reason for banks to take the losses for their practices if they could be subsumed otherwise.

Impeachment and Citicorp

The Asian turmoil barely registered with most Americans. More lascivious problems were unfolding. In January 1998, President Clinton was embroiled in a scandal concerning his relationship with young intern Monica Lewinsky. His denial of a sexual relationship with her led to calls for his impeachment.[22] On December 19, 1998, the House of Representatives voted 228 to 206 on the first article of impeachment, accusing Clinton of perjury for misleading a federal grand jury about the nature of his relationship. A second article of impeachment, charging him with obstruction of justice, passed by 221 to 212.

Throughout the year, bankers welcomed the media and political frenzy as a distraction while they focused on their own houses. In late February 1998, Sandy Weill and John Reed embarked upon a transformative financial alliance. After a dinner in Washington, Weill invited Reed back to his Park Hyatt hotel room and proposed corporate matrimony.[23] The results of their courtship would irrevocably alter the structure of American banking.

On April 6, 1998, Weill and Reed announced a $70 billion stock swap merger of Travelers and Citicorp to create Citigroup, the world's largest financial services company. It was the biggest corporate merger in history.[24]

As Reed put it casually at the press conference, "You know, Sandy had this idea about four and a half weeks ago. He approached me and said, 'Hey, John, it might make some sense to put our two companies together.' . . . Sandy and I have known each other about thirty years. . . . And so when Sandy said to me it might be something that we should do, I knew it was worth taking a look at."[25]

The proposed merger extended well beyond existing laws. It required Weill and Reed to privately obtain temporary approval from Alan Greenspan.[26] Ultimate approval for bank mergers came from the Federal Reserve, but the men used a loophole under the Bank Holding Company Act to get a two-year reprieve before the merger could be disallowed. That gave them ample time to lobby for Glass-Steagall repeal.

Weill and Reed weren't the only bankers hankering for a union to increase the size and global position of their financial services. They were just the ones who forced the legality of the issue. This was another precedent: in the past there was more discourse between presidents and bankers before such bold moves. Now, mergers between European securities houses and banks were rapidly occurring. Global bank mergers were moving at breakneck pace.

Between 1960 and 1979, there had been 3,404 bank mergers. From 1980 to 1994, that number swelled to 6,345. But that was nothing compared to the rest of the 1990s. From 1995 to 2000 the number of bank mergers topped 11,100.

The day of the duo's press conference, CNBC invited the CEOs to talk about "the biggest corporate merger ever." Their segment foreshadowed their future split before they were even fully together. Host Allan Chernoff asked Weill, "Do you see any potential conflict in actually sharing the top position of the new company?"

Weill replied, "Well, I don't see any problem in sharing it."

Reed injected, "Look, I—let's be straight here. Two people sharing a job is inherently difficult, so I would start out by saying you acknowledge that I'm gonna learn a lot from Sandy and I'm gonna have to change because of that. My suspicion is, he's gonna find he'll have to change a little bit, too."[27]

That afternoon, the press buzzed about Washington for quotes. Sarah Rosen, deputy assistant for economic policy and deputy director for national economic policy, circulated deregulation talking points for the chairman of the White House Economic Council, Gene Sperling, in preparation for his *Washington Post* interview. There was no concern that these firms were breaking existing laws. Instead, the talking points read: "The companies . . . say that they 'expect that current laws restricting bank holding companies from participating in insurance underwriting activities will change in the foreseeable future to make the U.S. more openly competitive in global markets.' . . . The Administration believes that financial services integration is happening regardless of the statutory barriers, because it makes market sense."[28]

Three days later, Rosen circulated an email to the National Economic Council team—deputy director Lael Brainard, who later served as undersecretary of the Treasury for international affairs in the Obama administration; deputy chief of staff Brian A. Barreto; and economic policy and deputy director Sally Katzen—on the impact that the merger announcement might have on "financial modernization" discussions in Washington.

The Clinton administration supported what it dubbed "true" financial modernization, which would allow the new firm to retain a span of activities. The inner cabinet confidently expected Citigroup to be a "powerful force pressing for some legislation soon."[29] But there was a wrinkle.

The Community Reinvestment Act

Two weeks later, the National Community Reinvestment Coalition (NCRC) sent a letter to congressional leaders requesting an immediate halt on mega-mergers until the General Accounting Office could study their impact on reinvestment and consumer protection.

The NCRC was concerned that the mergers in the pipeline, if approved without careful consideration, would harm the "dramatic progress of the last several years in community reinvestment." Of particular concern were the pending Citicorp-Travelers merger and Bank of America–NationsBank merger, whose combined deposits would near the 10 percent limit in the Riegle-Neal Interstate Banking and Branching Efficiency Act of 1994.[30]

This was not of great concern in the White House. Bank mergers had already resulted in massive industry concentration for the larger banks. In his April 29, 1998, testimony before the House Committee on Banking Services, Andrew C. Howe Jr., acting chairman of the FDIC, noted that "while 41 banking companies held 25 percent of domestic deposits in 1984," only "11 companies accounted for that same 25 percent share by the end of 1997." Adjusted to reflect the large pending mergers, "just 7 banking companies would hold 25 percent of domestic deposits."[31]

The administration tried to make it seem that all this was natural. A few weeks after the Citigroup announcement, Clinton stated that "the wave of mergers was probably inevitable," and that "the government must make sure consumers are protected."[32]

On May 13, 1998, Reuters reported that the White House was fashioning a high-level group to examine the phenomenon. It was headed by merger supporter Gene Sperling and included Treasury Secretary Robert Rubin and his deputy Treasury Secretary Lawrence Summers (who was appointed as director of the National Economic Council and chief economic adviser for Obama in 2009). "Over $114 billion mergers involving U.S. companies had been announced in May alone, coming after a record $260 billion in mergers in April," cited Reuters.[33]

That list included several record-breaking marriages. In addition to the union of Travelers and Citicorp, SBC Communications and Ameritech had announced a $61 billion stock deal that would create the country's largest telephone company. And Daimler-Benz was planning to buy Chrysler in a $50 billion deal, the largest cross-border transaction ever. By May 1998, "$614 billion worth of corporate mergers and acquisitions had been announced vs. a record $908 billion for all of 1997."[34]

In May 1998, the House had passed HR 10, the Financial Services Act of 1998 by a vote of 214 to 213.[35] In September 1998, the Senate Banking Committee voted sixteen to two to approve related legislation. But that bill didn't pass the broader Senate vote despite the push of Senate Banking Committee chairman, Alfonse D'Amato, a Republican from New York who was up for reelection.[36]

D'Amato's interests aligned with his Wall Street constituents. In return, Wall Street was his primary source of contributions. As the top Senate fundraiser from 1993 to 1998, D'Amato got $19 million—more than any other senator for his six-year cycle.[37]

Dimon Gets the Axe

In a September 1, 1998, letter to employees and customers, Reed was so sure that his merger would be approved that he announced "plans for our merger are absolutely on track." Weill was so confident that he "established an office in Citicorp Tower complete with a working fireplace."[38] The combined firm would cut up to eight thousand staff by Christmas "in a first round of cost-cutting," with more "likely" to come.[39]

Three weeks later, Gene Sperling and Sarah Rosen were notified that the Citicorp-Travelers merger would be approved within the week and completed by October 8. In theory, the new Citigroup would divest its insurance underwriting business within five years. At the time of its announcement, the merger was worth $70 billion, but its value had since fallen to $43.8 billion.[40] That drop did not appear to raise any alarm bells at the White House or the Fed.

On September 22, Sperling received a memo from the Office of Public Liaison regarding his pending meeting with Weill and Reed, who were coming to Washington to express their concerns regarding the passage of HR 10.[41]

"[They] are likely to raise three major points," read the memo. The first: this was "the first time (in a long legislative history) all major financial associations agree on a reform bill." Second, combinations like Travelers and Citicorp "will continue with or without HR 10." Lastly, this was an excellent "opportunity to get a major laudatory public policy accomplishment under the nation's belt."[42]

The meeting was unnecessary, as the administration was firmly on the duo's side. As Lisa Andrews, deputy assistant secretary of public liaison, wrote Rubin, "Despite several near death encounters, HR 10 managed to survive thanks in large part to the extraordinary efforts of its core advocates: Merrill Lynch, Citicorp/Travelers and Nations' Bank/Bank of America."[43]

In the opposition camp remained several community groups opposed to HR 10 on the grounds that it would weaken the Community Reinvestment Act.[44] On September 23, eight hundred community groups and fifty national groups sent a signed letter to each senator requesting opposition to HR 10 because it "promotes concentration of economic power [and] undermines [the] CRA."[45]

The bankers were doing more than sending letters. They were sending funds. The prospect of full Glass-Steagall repeal, coupled with high stock prices, translated into gobs of lobbying money. Citigroup donated $13 million in political contributions from 1990 to 1998. In 1998, Bank of America forked over the most money in its history to the deregulation cause; 63 percent of it to the Republicans, the party that controlled the Senate Banking Committee. Bank of America chairman Hugh McColl directed $4.6 million in lobbying efforts in 1998 to repeal Glass-Steagall.[46]

Yet Congress failed to pass final legislation before the end of its 1998 session primarily because legislators were focused on the midterm elections. Despite his Wall Street backing, D'Amato lost his seat to Democrat Chuck Schumer (who also had Wall Street's support). Republican senator Phil Gramm of Texas became chairman of the Senate Banking Committee in 1999.[47]

The banking sector suffered another internal political defeat. On November 6, 1998, Weill fired Jamie Dimon.[48] Wall Street lore suggests the final contributing factor to Dimon's ouster was an argument about the firm's direction at a Citicorp and Travelers bonding boondoggle, which took place over four days of golf at a West Virginia resort.

Shortly afterward, Weill summoned Dimon to their Armonk office and gave him the axe.[49] There were lots of reasons given and surmised, from personal to political, but in the end Weill's 2010 statement in the *New York Times* said all that needed to be said: "The problem was in 1999 he wanted to be C.E.O. and I didn't want to retire."[50]

It was a classic case of ambition without sufficient outlet. But in the long battle for power and supremacy, Jamie Dimon would emerge the victor. He eventually wound up running what became the world's most powerful bank, JPMorgan Chase. While Citigroup's power faded after Weill's departure, Dimon would eventually rule the financial world.

The Euro and Bank Beasts

After years of debates as to the merits of a consolidated currency amid so many disparate national economies, on January 1, 1999, the euro was officially born. A driving force behind the euro was the idea that Europe could regain financial superpower status and compete with the dollar by combining its national economies in the form of a united currency.

Bankers in Europe, particularly at American company subsidiaries, were at first exuberant because their compensation would be tied to more European growth and deals than their New York brethren. Peter Sutherland, chairman of Goldman Sachs International, said that the monetary union is "the single most important political project" in more than forty years.[51]

But in the months before the euro's birth, derivatives bets ballooned as banks and hedge funds gambled on which countries would succeed in joining the union, and how quickly they would do so. As a result, these foreign markets were experiencing another wave of hell. The Asian crisis had morphed into a speculative attack on the Russian ruble, for similar reasons. Speculators knew that Russia would try to maintain its currency peg, and it would have to borrow to the hilt in foreign currency to do so.

Speculators shorted the currency to near-death. With the ruble devalued, the country defaulted on its international loans on August 17, 1998. Citigroup's third-quarter earnings fell $200 million, or 67 percent, due to Russian exposure and other world market turmoil. This time, George Soros lost $2 billion.[52]

Hedge funds, capitalized by banks and massively leveraged (as they borrowed heavily to make their bets), took a big stake, too. But the bigger they were, the more protected from losses. The Fed, spurred by a set of personally invested CEOs, considered bailing out the hedge fund Long Term Capital Management to the tune of $3.65 billion as a result of leveraged bets that soured when the Russian crisis hit. LTCM's gaggle of Nobel Prize–winning economists and exalted traders, including its head, Salomon Brothers bond trader John Meriwether, failed to recognize that highly leveraged trades can make tons of money if they work but can lose even more money, more quickly, if they don't. New York Fed president William McDonough selected thirteen banks to participate in helping LTCM survive. (Lehman Brothers and Bear Stearns declined to be involved.) In September 1998, eleven banks put up $300 million each to keep LTCM from bankruptcy in return for 90 percent of the partners' shares.[53] They weren't just saving LTCM; they were also protecting their own versions of LTCM's trade. The last thing they wanted was to experience an unraveling in the markets that would hurt their own books. Within three weeks of the LTCM bailout, Greenspan cut rates by fifty basis points to make sure there was enough liquidity in the system to pave over the crisis.

Big banks had made similar bets. But they held a government shield. As long as they had depositors' funds, they would enjoy protection from losses from governments and supranational banks. They used this cushion to get further involved in derivatives transactions that were designed to make bets on the same types of European convergence trades that LTCM had done, and to seek profit from positioning these bets on peripheral countries joining the euro. Some banks, like Goldman Sachs, would even help countries like Greece by creating derivatives deals that shielded Greece's true debt status, thereby helping it meet the criteria to join the currency union.

The Fight Against the Euro Intensifies

On February 12, 1999, Rubin addressed the House Committee on Banking and Financial Services, claiming that "the problem US financial services firms face abroad is more one of access than lack of competitiveness."[54]

This time, he was referring to the European banks' increasing control of distribution channels into the European institutional and retail client base. Unlike US commercial banks, European banks had no restrictions keeping them from buying and teaming up with US or other securities firms and investment banks to create or distribute their products. He did not appear concerned about destruction caused by sizeable bets throughout Europe.

Rubin stressed that HR 665 (the most recent version of HR 10), now called the Financial Services Modernization Act of 1999 and officially introduced on February 10, 1999, took "fundamental actions to modernize our financial system by repealing the Glass-Steagall Act prohibitions on banks affiliating with securities firms and repealing the Bank Holding Company Act prohibitions on insurance underwriting."[55]

Three days later, Rubin, Greenspan, and Summers landed on the cover of *Time* magazine as the "Committee to Save the World," effusively lauded for their efforts to prevent a global economic collapse.[56] The piece painted a violins-strumming picture of the trio of "marketeers" as financial saviors and cozy operators:

> When the three talk about their special relationship, they are hinting at how fortunate it is that they can work together instead of apart. Says Robert Hormats, vice chairman of Goldman Sachs International: There have been moments in the past year when it has been, as Churchill said, a very near thing. These guys kept a near thing from becoming a disaster. That has happened because the men feel that being at the right place at the right time also means doing the right thing, putting their egos aside and, in an almost antique sense of civic duty, answering the phone when it rings.

Several European counterparts scoffed at the piece. As a high German financial official who played an active role in advising the Thai, South Korean, and Indonesian governments put it, "All those who experienced the Asian turbulence—from Thailand letting the baht float freely in early July 1997 to the turmoil spreading to South Korea and Indonesia—tell a very different story."[57]

The Gramm-Leach-Bliley Act
Marches Forward

On February 24, 1999, in more testimony before the Senate Banking Committee, Rubin pushed for fewer prohibitions on bank affiliates that wanted to perform the same functions as their larger bank holding company, once the different types of financial firms could legally merge. That minor distinction would enable subsidiaries to place all sorts of bets and house all sorts of junk under the false premise that they had the same capital beneath them as their parent. The idea that a subsidiary's problems can't taint or destroy the host, or bank holding company, or create "catastrophic" risk, is a myth perpetuated by bankers and political enablers that continues to this day.

Rubin had no qualms with mega-consolidations across multiple service lines. His real problems were those of his banker friends, which lay with the financial modernization bill's "prohibition on the use of subsidiaries by larger banks." This technicality was "unacceptable to the administration," he said, not least because "foreign banks underwrite and deal in securities through subsidiaries in the United States, and US banks [already] conduct securities and merchant banking activities abroad through so-called Edge subsidiaries."[58]

In a letter to Senate Banking Committee chairman Phil Gramm, Clinton briefly considered the ramifications of multipurpose financial mergers: "The bill could expand the ability of depository institutions and nonfinancial firms to affiliate, at a time when experience around the world suggests the need for caution in this area."[59] But that notion was subsequently dropped.

Instead, he ended his letter with a plea for the Community Reinvestment Act: "I agree with you that reform of the laws governing our nation's financial services industry would promote the public interest. However, I will veto the bill if it is presented to me in its current form."[60] It was as if providing loans to small communities, which should have been a given, made the idea of big banks running roughshod over the global financial sphere copacetic.

The CRA was not an obstacle in bankers' greater fight for banking deregulation. They knew that if banks could become bigger, they could lend to smaller communities and capture their business anyway. If they had to promise to do so, so be it; they would find a way to make money off that promise.

On March 1, 1999, Gramm released a final draft of the Financial Services Modernization Act of 1999, or the Gramm-Leach-Bliley Act, and scheduled committee consideration for March 4.[61] A bevy of excited financial titans including Sandy Weill, Hugh McColl, and American Express CEO Harvey Golub called for "swift congressional action."[62]

The Quintessential Revolving-Door Man

The stock market continued its rise in anticipation of a banker-friendly conclusion to the legislation that would deregulate their industry. Rising consumer confidence reflected the nation's fondness for the markets and lack of empathy with the rest of the world's economic plight. On March 29, 1999, the Dow closed above 10,000 for the first time.[63] Six weeks later, on May 6, 1999, the Financial Services Modernization Act passed the Senate.[64]

It was not until that point that one of Glass-Steagall's main assassins decided to leave Washington. Six days after the bill passed the Senate, on May 12, 1999, Robert Rubin abruptly announced his resignation. As Clinton wrote, "I believed he had been the best and most important Treasury Secretary since Alexander Hamilton. . . . He had played a decisive role in our efforts to restore economic growth and spread its benefits to more Americans."[65] Clinton named Larry Summers to succeed Rubin.

Two weeks later, *BusinessWeek* reported signs of trouble in merger paradise—in the form of a growing rift between Reed and Weill at Citigroup. As Reed said, "Co-CEOs are hard." Perhaps to patch their rift, or simply to take advantage of a political opportunity, the two men enlisted a third person to join their relationship: none other than Robert Rubin.

Rubin's resignation from Treasury became effective on July 2. At that time, he announced, "This almost six and a half years has been all-consuming, and I think it is time for me to go home to New York and to do whatever I'm going to do next."[66] Rubin became chairman of Citigroup's executive committee and a member of the newly created "office of the chairman." His initial annual compensation package was worth around $40 million.[67] It was more than worth the "hit" he took when he left Goldman for the Treasury post.

Three days after the conference committee endorsed the Gramm-Leach-Bliley Bill, Rubin assumed his Citigroup position, joining the institution destined to dominate the financial industry. That *very same* day, Reed and Weil issued a joint statement praising Washington for "liberating our financial companies from an antiquated regulatory structure," stating that "this legislation will unleash the creativity of our industry and ensure our global competitiveness."[68]

On November 4, the Senate approved the Gramm-Leach-Bliley Act by a vote of ninety to eight.[69] (The House voted 362–57 in favor.[70]) Critics famously referred to it as the Citigroup Authorization Act.

Mirth abounded in Clinton's White House. "Today Congress voted to update the rules that have governed financial services since the Great Depression and replace them with a system for the twenty-first century," Summers said. "This historic legislation will better enable American companies to compete in the new economy."[71]

There were some who expressed concern about this giant step backward in banking legislation and what it could mean going forward. "I think we will look back in ten years' time and say we should not have done this but we did because we forgot the lessons of the past," said Senator Byron Dorgan, Democrat of North Dakota. Senator Paul Wellstone, Democrat of Minnesota, said that Congress had "seemed determined to unlearn the lessons from our past mistakes."[72] But these warnings were ignored in the truly irrational exuberance of the moment.

Several days later, a broad coalition of consumer and community groups called for an investigation into the fact that Rubin was simultaneously job hunting and lobbying for legislation that would benefit his eventual employer.[73] Retired government officials were prohibited from lobbying their former agencies on behalf of an employer for at least one year after leaving public service. Yet only four months had elapsed between Rubin's resignation and his appointment to Citigroup's board.

Rubin claimed that his decision to take a job at Citigroup had nothing to do with any work he had done in the government. "During the time I was Treasury secretary, my sole concern was to produce the best possible public policy," he said. "I could not have cared less how anyone in the industry reacted to my position or my views."[74]

Regardless of whatever his internal thinking was, history shows that Rubin was the quintessential revolving-door man, cultivating the appearance of working for the people while angling for private gain. He was instrumental in destroying the last vestige of the Glass-Steagall Act, which had prevented big banks from gambling with other people's money and government guarantees. His ideology would be at the epicenter of mega-meltdowns and bailouts to come.

Beneath the surface of a massive deregulation victory, Reed and Weill continued having a tough time dealing with each other. Reed resigned in February 2000, though he didn't do too shabbily in the process. According to *Bloomberg*, "From 1997 to 1999, Reed received salary and bonuses totaling $23.4 million, and a retirement bonus of $5 million."[75]

Inequality and Heady Stock Prices

Clinton epitomized the vast difference between appearance and reality, spin and actuality. As the decade drew to a close, he basked in the glow of a lofty stock market, budget surplus, and the passage of this key banking "modernization." It would be revealed in the 2000s that many corporate profits of the 1990s were based on inflated evaluations, manipulation, and fraud. When Clinton left office, the gap between rich and poor was greater than it was in 1992, and yet the Democrats heralded him as some sort of prosperity hero.

When he had resigned in 1997, Robert Reich, Clinton's labor secretary, said, "America is prospering, but the prosperity is not being widely shared, certainly not as widely shared as it once was. . . . We have made progress in growing the economy. But growing together again must be our central goal in the future."[76] Instead, the growth of wealth inequality in the United States accelerated, as the men yielding the most financial power wielded it with increasingly less culpability or restriction.

By 2003, the number of households living on less than $2 a day would skyrocket.[77] In addition, as economists Emmanuel Saez and Thomas Piketty reported, during the Clinton administration, the incomes of the wealthiest 1 percent of Americans increased by 98.7 percent, while the bottom 99 percent increased by only 20.3 percent.[78]

The power of the bankers increased dramatically in the wake of the repeal of Glass-Steagall. The Clinton administration had rendered twenty-first-century banking practices similar to those of the pre-1929 Crash. But worse. "Modernizing" meant utilizing government-backed depositors' funds as collateral for the creation and distribution of all types of complex securities and derivatives whose proliferation would be increasingly quick and dangerous.

Eviscerating Glass-Steagall allowed big banks to compete against Europe and also enabled them to go on a rampage: more acquisitions, greater speculation, more risky products. The big banks used their bloated balance sheets to engage in more complex activity, while counting on customer deposits and loans as capital chips on the global betting table. Bankers used hefty trading profits and wealth to increase lobbying funds and campaign donations, creating an endless circle of influence and mutual reinforcement of boundary-less speculation, endorsed by the White House.

Deposits could be used to garner larger windfalls, just as cheap labor and commodities in developing countries were used to formulate more expensive goods for profit in the upper echelons of global financial hierarchy. Energy and telecoms proved especially fertile ground for investment banking fee business (and later for fraud, extensive lawsuits, and bankruptcies). Deregulation greased the wheels of complex financial instruments such as collateralized debt obligations (CDOs), junk bonds, toxic assets, and unregulated derivatives.

Glass-Steagall repeal led to unfettered derivatives growth and unstable balance sheets at commercial banks that merged with investment banks and at investment banks that preferred to remain solo but engaged in dodgier practices to remain "competitive." In conjunction with the tight political-financial alignment and associated collaboration that began with Bush and increased under Clinton, bankers channeled the 1920s, only with more power over an immense and growing pile of global financial assets and increasingly "open" markets. In the process, accountability would evaporate.

Every bank accelerated its hunt for acquisitions and deposits to amass global influence while creating, trading, and distributing increasingly convoluted securities and derivatives. As the size of their books grew, banks increasingly provided loans or credit in exchange for higher-fee business, thereby increasing global debt and leverage. These practices would foster the kind of shaky, interconnected, and nontransparent financial environment that provided the backdrop and conditions leading up to the financial meltdown of 2008.

CHAPTER 19

The 2000s:
Multiple Crises,
the New Big Six, and
Global Catastrophe

"That's why I'm richer than you."

—Jamie Dimon, JPMorgan Chase chairman and CEO, February 26, 2013[1]

AT THE DAWN OF THE TWENTIETH CENTURY, THE POWERFUL "BIG SIX" BANKERS used a major bank panic to help make the case for the establishment of the Federal Reserve, which could back them in future panics. Subsequently, during World War I, their alignment with Woodrow Wilson unleashed the current era of American financial and military dominance. This superpower position was solidified not just through America's prowess in two world wars, but also through the intricate synergies between White House policies and Wall Street voracity, the nature of which remains tighter than in any other country.

Over the decades, the faces at the helm of America's two poles of power changed (though certain bank leaders remained in their seats far longer than presidents), but the aspirations of the unelected financial leaders coalesced with the goals of the elected leaders—occasionally to the benefit of the US population, often to its detriment, but always to drive America's particular breed of accumulation and expansionary capitalism.

In the new millennium, the most powerful banks were for the most part permutations of the original Big Six. Chase, J. P. Morgan, and Morgan Guaranty became JPMorgan Chase and Morgan Stanley; the National City Bank of New York and First National Bank became Citigroup. Goldman Sachs's entry into the New Big Six stemmed from the close relationship between FDR and former Goldman senior partner Sidney Weinberg. Rounding out the New Big Six were Bank of America and Wells Fargo, which had broken into the East Coast clan over the years. But the chief bankers of the twenty-first century were more powerful than their ancestors by virtue of the sheer volume of global capital and derivatives they controlled (which could exceed a quadrillion dollars globally by 2022). In addition, as the power of the president receded relative to that of the bankers during the post-Nixon period, the financial sphere had become more complex and the potential risk to the global economy of banker practices had become limitless. These mercenary bankers operated in a manner lacking public orientation or humility, whereas in the past this might have at least been an after- or adjacent thought.

The Bush and Obama presidencies represented a climax in the development of relationships and codependent actions that began with Teddy Roosevelt. But whereas Roosevelt, Wilson, FDR, Eisenhower, and Johnson had nursed synergies that enabled useful public-oriented legislation, Bush and Obama had become followers and reactors to bankers' whims. By the 2000s, bankers no longer debated economic policy in thoughtful correspondences with presidents or Treasury secretaries, as they once had. Alliances abounded, but their character was more perfunctory. Top bankers visited the White House and attended government functions (more frequently under Obama than Bush), but their efforts were recklessly self-serving and one-sided. It would be unimaginable for JPMorgan Chase chairman Jamie Dimon to spend months running a food drive for people in war-torn countries, as his Chase chairman ancestor Winthrop Aldrich had, or to negotiate disarmament plans, as another ancestor, John McCloy, had. These millennial masters of capital reigned over worldwide economies from atop a mountain of customer deposits, debt, intricate securities, and opaque derivatives. Their power dwarfed central banks and presidents. Banks were not just too big to fail; certain bankers were too influential to restrain.

By 2012, the Big Six held $9.5 trillion of assets, an amount equivalent to about 65 percent of US GDP.[2] Their combined trading revenues amounted to nearly 93 percent of the total trading revenues for all the other banks combined.[3] Systemic risk, even after the onset of the 2008 financial crisis and subsequent bailouts, had intensified. A rush of tepid reforms, from the Sarbanes-Oxley Act under Bush to the Dodd-Frank Act under Obama, were glorified for political purposes, but they were inconsequential considering the concentration of economic influence in the hands of a few megalomaniacs.

US bank chairmen's rise through the ranks of international dominance had become akin to military strategy, whereas they had once operated in the realm of familial inheritance and lineage. To modern bankers, anything economically negative was a byproduct of chance or the business cycle, and anything positive was a byproduct of inherent genius—not the genius of collaboration, of which Louis Brandeis had spoken a century earlier, but of a more distinct sociopathic detachment from ordinary people. Bankers were ruthless in their egocentric competitiveness by the 2000s, and the effects were worse than decades earlier because they had witnessed the level at which they could rely on government subsidies and borrowed capital. The very threat of "catastrophic" consequences was enough to bring Treasury secretaries to their knees—literally. The Oval Office, no matter the party in charge, had become simultaneously fearful and blindly reverent of their power.

Bankers of the 2000s didn't care who was president. They only needed the White House support in action, if not rhetoric. Into the 2000s, from Clinton to Bush to Obama, political parties and certain bank leaders changed. But the reckless greed animating the bankers' mission did not, nor did their thirst for global supremacy. The crises of the 2000s were manifestations of the power bankers had captured by design, enabled by presidents unwilling to thwart or challenge it.

Bank Wars and Bank Leverage Intensify

Since the global competition argument had proved so successful for the Glass-Steagall abolitionists, Goldman Sachs chairman and CEO Henry Paulson adopted it on behalf of the investment bank community in one of the decade's first financial hearings. Before Clinton left the White House, Paulson addressed Congress on the need for investment banks to increase their leverage. As former Treasury Secretary Robert Rubin had argued on behalf of the commercial bankers, Paulson stressed the need for investment banks to borrow more, and reserve less capital for emergencies, in order to "compete" with the world.

At a Senate hearing on February 29, 2000, Paulson urged the SEC to "reform its net capital rule" to allow the more "efficient use of capital." He warned that existing capital constraints were the "most important factor in driving significant parts of our business offshore." Reducing the limit of capital required to be reserved against risky trades, he reasoned, would enable American banks to "remain competitive with our foreign competitors' risk-based capital standards."[4] Implicitly, he was saying that US banks could "handle" the risk of their decisions, and thus should be allowed to take on more risk. It was a more complex version of the pre-Rubin competition argument. With structural deregulation complete, altering the very manner in which capital could be used was the next step toward national and international financial control.

The real problem Paulson and other investment bank titans faced was that they couldn't rely on deposits and loans to back their bets, or so-called growth strategies. After the Glass-Steagall repeal, commercial banks augmented by investment banking and insurance arms could do just that. But stand-alone investment banks had three options: merge with a commercial bank and risk an internal political battle for control, find a way to make their capital stretch further, or do both. Investment banks like Goldman Sachs, Morgan Stanley, and Merrill Lynch fancied themselves more "innovative" and superior to commercial banks. Yet they faced a "competitive disadvantage" in the bank wars. Paulson wasn't trying to empower the United States; he was trying to empower his firm.

Commercial bankers were increasingly entering investment bankers' turf, engaging in trading, securities creation, and other investment banking activity, plus expanding. As a sign of this warrior state, by late 2000, Chase CEO William Harrison and J. P. Morgan CEO Douglas Warner had obtained Fed permission to merge their banks. The $28.6 billion stock deal closed on December 31, 2000.[5] This kind of acquisitive combat was characterized by terms like "clear winner" and "losers." "There will be less than a handful of end-game winners," proclaimed Harrison. "[JPMorgan Chase] will be an end-game winner."[6]

The value of JPMorgan Chase stock dove from $207 per share when the merger was announced to $157 per share when it closed. Four thousand people lost their jobs.[7] But this was not a concern of the Fed. A decade later, the value of JPMorgan Chase stock hovered around $40 a share. Value had not been created through a succession of highly compensated CEOs and chairmen or complicated deals—it had been destroyed.

This merger was particularly significant, for it represented not just a marriage of two major banks but the conclusion of the century-old House of

Morgan and Chase rivalry that shaped the nation's financial landscape. Now, four of the oldest Eastern Establishment banks (Chase, J. P. Morgan, Chemical, and Manufacturers Hanover) were joined under one roof.

Winthrop Aldrich, who led Chase during the Depression and promoted the Glass-Steagall Act beside FDR, had chosen to retain the commercial bank side while spinning off the investment bank. He was posthumously awarded the whole shebang; commercial banking, investing banking, and the House of Morgan. His decision, which also had the effect of fostering US economic stability for decades, had paid off—but his prudence would not prevail.

9/11 Attacks Overshadow Enron Scandal

In late 2001, amid the fading light of Clinton's rosy economy and an election result validated by the Supreme Court, President George W. Bush entered the White House. The true state of the economy remained hidden, teetering on a flimsy base of fraud, inflated stocks, and bank-created debt. The corporate and banking world appeared glorious amid so many mergers. But the bankers' efforts to support these transactions would soon give way to a spate of corporate bankruptcies, the domestic complement to the havoc caused by the foreign debt crises of the 1980s and the currency crises of the 1990s.

As bankers bulked up their balance sheets with customer deposits in the post-Glass-Steagall merger period, they were able to secure more investment banking business, particularly from the energy and telecom sectors, in return for extending more credit, regardless of the integrity of the underlying collateral for those loans or their construction. Wall Street bankers helped clients mask their true debt levels through various means of profitable financial subterfuge. Some tricks were administered domestically and others internationally, such as the transactions Goldman Sachs created to hide debt for Greece so it could meet the EU's criteria for accession.[8]

But it was Texas-based energy-turned-trading company Enron that would emerge as the poster child for financial fraud in the early 2000s. Enron used the unregulated derivatives markets—and colluded with bankers—to create a slew of colorfully named offshore entities (or "special purpose vehicles," in Wall Street jargon) where the company piled up debt, shirked taxes, and hid losses.

The true status of Enron's fabricated books, and those of other corporate fraudsters, remained initially unexamined because of a more acute danger. The 9/11 attacks at the World Trade Center, blocks away from many of Enron's trading partners, provided a temporary reprieve from probes.[9] Instead,

Bush called on bankers to uphold national stability in the face of terrorism. In an internal voicemail to Goldman employees the night of the attacks, CEO Henry Paulson urged the "people of Goldman Sachs" to stay strong.[10]

On September 16, 2001, Bush took his opportunity to equate financial and foreign policy. "The markets open tomorrow, people go back to work, and we'll show the world," he said.[11] To assist the bankers in this mission, Bush-appointed SEC chairman Harvey Pitt waived certain regulations to allow corporate executives to prop up their share prices as part of the plan to demonstrate national strength through market levels.[12] A month later, the spirit of unity was stifled. On October 16, 2001, Enron posted a $681 million third-quarter loss and announced a $1.2 billion hit to shareholders equity, due to an imploding pyramid of fraudulent transactions.[13]

Bankers were potentially on the hook for billions of dollars at the hands of a client that had bulked up through bipartisan support. Aside from ties to Vice President Dick Cheney, Enron chairman Ken Lay had persuaded the Clinton administration to subsidize nearly $1 billion of its overseas projects. He had also persuaded big bankers to lend Enron big money. On October 25, 2001, Enron announced it had eaten through its $3.3 billion credit facility.[14]

This prompted a group of JPMorgan Chase and Citigroup bankers to travel to Houston, where they attempted to fashion a last-minute merger deal with Dynegy, a Texas-based electric utility company. Dynegy agreed to buy Enron for $8 billion and provide it with $1.5 billion cash up front until the deal closed. That meant it would be supporting bank creditors.[15]

But on November 8, 2001, the credit rating agency Moody's informed Enron it would drop its rating below investment grade.[16] The move could hurt the merger and Enron's credit-paying ability. Neither possibility appealed to the bankers. Moody's received numerous calls from the financial elite, including Robert Rubin of Citigroup (who had once been offered an Enron board position by Lay), Michael Carpenter of Salomon Smith Barney, and William Harrison of JPMorgan Chase.[17] They assured Moody's that they wouldn't back out of the merger. They needed it more than Enron.[18]

Citigroup was particularly exposed to possible losses. That day, Rubin called Peter Fisher, then undersecretary of the Treasury for domestic financial markets. He suggested Fisher intervene to keep Enron's rating up. With measured words, Rubin later explained that he said that it was "probably" a "bad idea" for Fisher to pressure the rating agencies to delay downgrading Enron, and said he had only asked what Fisher "thought of the idea."[19] In January 2003, a Senate committee deemed Rubin's role in proposing the "idea" both legal and insubstantial.[20]

Rubin's call didn't change the outcome anyway. On November 28, 2001, Dynegy backed out of the merger.[21] Enron filed for bankruptcy on December 2, 2001, becoming the country's largest bankruptcy at the time.[22] Its original Chapter 11 filing documents listed the twenty largest creditors, including Citigroup's banking unit, Citibank, at $3 billion and Chase at about $2 billion.[23]

Corporate Corruption Unleashed

Amid this financial turmoil, Bush was narrowly focused on retaliation for 9/11. On January 10, 2002, he signed a $317.2 billion defense bill.[24] In his State of the Union address, he spoke of the Axis of Evil, fighting the growing recession, and creating jobs, not of Enron or the dangers of Wall Street's chicanery.[25]

Corporate bankruptcies hit new records in 2001 and again in 2002, with fraud playing a central role.[26] Public opinion on the matter was so bad that in June 2002, Paulson endorsed the SEC's demands for more funds, and said publicly, "I cannot think of a time when business overall has been in such low repute." He went on to criticize US accounting standards for being so complex and "rule-based" that they were "leaving room for manipulation by unscrupulous management."[27] Rather than blame lax accounting standards for *enabling* manipulation by nefarious bankers, he blamed *too many* rules for allowing inappropriate conditions to exist. Thus, for Paulson, noninvestment bankers were the problem, not investment bankers.

About a month later, telecom giant WorldCom was found to have embellished its books by $3.7 billion (a figure that escalated to $11 billion worth of puffed-up statements.[28]) It supplanted Enron as America's biggest fraud— the firm's subsequent bankruptcy kicked up a scandal surrounding its main banker, Citigroup's Sandy Weill, and Jack Grubman, Weill's highly compensated analyst, who touted WorldCom's stock while it was crashing. WorldCom's stock dove from $64.5 to $.09 per share.[29] Workers' pensions took a $4.4 billion hit.[30] The firm ultimately paid a $750 million federal fine and a $2.25 billion civil penalty, and CEO Bernie Ebbers was slapped with a twenty-five-year prison sentence.[31] The frauds were so obvious that Bush didn't consider bailouts, inadvertently forcing banks to deal with their own losses as they regrouped for fresh opportunities.

Bush Takes Action

Due to public wrath about corporate crime and the possibility that it would become an election issue—as well as the cozy relationship between the White

House and Ken Lay—Bush took another tack. At a March 2002 conference he called for regulations to be "clearer" (though not increased) and penalties for wrongdoing be "tougher."[32]

Then, on July 9, he unveiled his plan to "curb" corporate crime in a speech given in the heart of New York's financial district. Barely a swipe at his Wall Street friends, he urged bankers to provide honest information to investors. With that kind of tepidity, bankers knew they had nothing to fear from their commander in chief. The fact that Merrill Lynch was embroiled with the Enron scandal was not something Bush would confront. Merrill's alliances with the Bush family stretched back many years.[33]

Three weeks later, Bush signed the Sarbanes-Oxley Act of 2002.[34] It purportedly ensured that CFOs and CEOs would confirm that the information in their SEC filings was presented truthfully, kept accounting and auditing firms from servicing the same client (as Arthur Andersen had done for Enron), and required analysts (such as Jack Grubman) to disclose any conflicts of interest their employers might have with the companies whose stocks they touted. Republicans complained that the act created unnecessary paperwork—as they still do today. And Democrats refused to understand that the act was essentially useless as a fraud deterrent—as it remains today.

To do his part, Alan Greenspan cut interest rates, ultimately down to 1.5 percent, to help banks remain liquid during the scandal-induced credit crunch. Still, by September 2002, half a million telecom jobs had been eliminated as the result of fraud-induced bankruptcies, and $2 trillion of $7 trillion in stock market value had been erased. Twenty-three telecoms went bust, including WorldCom on July 21, 2002.[35] The combination of corporate crime and bankers' coyness dragged down the market, the overall economy, and citizens' pension accounts, as Washington continued to waffle on the notion of corporate reform amid a series of after-the-fact hearings.[36]

Tepid Reform amid the March to War

Bush's primary concerns transcended issues of corporate honesty and banker collusion. On March 19, 2003, he launched the Iraq War with a shower of cruise missiles into the Iraqi night sky.[37] Two days later, by a vote of 215 to 212, the House approved Bush's $2.2 trillion budget, including $726 billion of tax cuts. Shortly afterward, Bush appointed former Goldman Sachs co-CEO Stephen Friedman director of the National Economic Council, the same role Robert Rubin had played for Clinton.[38]

Amid the "shock and awe" that launched the Iraqi invasion, notions of banker culpability and reform took a back seat in the media and for the population at large. But a month later, a $1.4 billion Wall Street settlement spearheaded by New York attorney general Eliot Spitzer, with input from the SEC, was finalized. For his efforts, Spitzer was dubbed "the Enforcer" on a September 2002 *Fortune* cover.[39] On April 28, 2003, ten major banks agreed to pay $875 million in various penalties, in addition to $432.5 million to fund independent research and $80 million to promote investor education, a paltry sum compared to their pre-scandal profits.[40]

According to Spitzer's official statement, the settlement implemented "far-reaching reforms that will radically change behavior on Wall Street."[41] But it did nothing of the kind. Not a single item in the settlement was a serious threat to bankers' status quo.[42] Off-balance-sheet vehicles and unregulated derivatives would resurface a few years later, causing far greater damage—this time to the global population.

On October 15, 2003, Democrat Timothy Geithner was chosen to succeed William McDonough as president and CEO of the Federal Reserve Bank of New York. Geithner was serving as director of policy development at the IMF, following a stint at the Council on Foreign Relations.[43] Prior to that, he had served as undersecretary of the Treasury for international affairs from 1998 to 2001, during the Asian currency and Russian debt crises. Geithner had powerful friends, having served under both Rubin and Summers.[44] The two former Treasury secretaries advised the search committee that supported Geithner.[45] It was their deregulatory ideas that led to the economic crumbling of the early 2000s (and to the later crisis beginning in 2007, after which Summers became Obama's economic adviser). But now they ensured another like-minded compatriot would take the helm of the New York Fed and fortify the big bankers.

Bush's Reelection Campaign and Capital Limits

By the end of 2003, in the wake of the Wall Street settlement and Sarbanes-Oxley Act—over which bankers grumbled publicly but weren't particularly concerned about privately—bankers began amassing funds for Bush's 2004 reelection campaign.[46] A bevy of Wall Street Republicans, including Hank Paulson, Bear Stearns CEO James Cayne, and Goldman Sachs executive George Herbert Walker (the president's second cousin) fell under the category of Bush's "Pioneers," raising at least $100,000 each.[47]

The top seven financial firms raised nearly $3 million for his campaign. Merrill Lynch emerged as his second biggest corporate contributor (after Morgan Stanley), providing more than $586,254.[48] The firm's enthusiasm wasn't surprising. Reagan's Treasury secretary, Donald Regan, had been its chairman. Way before that, in 1900, George Herbert Walker had founded the investment bank G. H. Walker and Company, which employed various members of the Bush family over the following decades, until becoming part of Merrill in 1978.[49] Merrill Lynch CEO Earnest "Stanley" O'Neal received the distinguished moniker of "Ranger," having raised more than $200,000 for Bush's campaign.[50] O'Neal and Cayne had hosted Bush's first New York City reelection fundraiser in July 2003.[51]

Campaign support from bankers appeared to have its benefits. Paulson, for one, was still beating the drum for more leverage for investment banks. On April 28, 2004, five SEC commissioners convened to consider the issue.[52] Four years had lapsed since Paulson had first made his request to raise leverage parameters before Congress.[53] This time, under the leadership of William Donaldson (who began his career at G. H. Walker and Company), the SEC approved the request.[54]

Whether leverage parameters were officially raised or not remains a matter of debate, but official language provided bigger banks (with more than $5 billion in assets) more latitude with capital requirements.[55] The largest investment banks, all of which were part of Bush's top ten fundraisers, were permitted to use their own systems to determine leverage, which amounted to the same thing as parameters being raised. Goldman Sachs, Morgan Stanley, Merrill Lynch, Lehman Brothers, and Bear Stearns applied for "consolidated supervised entities" status, which enabled them to use in-house models to determine how much capital they should set aside to back risky bets.[56]

At the time, SEC commissioner Harvey Goldschmid warned, "If anything goes wrong, it's going to be an awfully big mess."[57] Within a few years, leverage had risen from 12 percent to 30–40 percent, depending on the firm, and that figure didn't even begin to account for the leverage that could be embedded in any one security or the risk associated with codependent securities.[58] Whereas in the 1980s Wall Street created corporate junk bonds and in the 1990s enabled companies like Enron to hide off-book losses and gains, now Wall Street began minting toxic securities lined with subprime loans and wrapped up in derivatives. And the more loans a bank could get, the more toxic securities and derivatives linked to those securities could be spawned and sold.

Meanwhile, another merger that would alter the trajectory of Wall Street was brewing. In July 2004, William Harrison announced that JPMorgan

Chase would acquire Chicago-based Bank One for $59 billion.[59] By December 31, 2005, Bank One CEO Jamie Dimon assumed the helm of the conglomerate. From there, he eventually rose to take his former boss's mantle of King of Wall Street.

Government by the Goldman, for the Goldman

The bankers' help might have tipped the scales in Bush's favor. On November 3, 2004, Bush won his second term in a tight election, capturing 51 percent of the popular vote and 274 electoral votes against Democrat John Kerry's 252.[60]

From an alignment perspective, Goldman Sachs bankers now saturated Washington. New Jersey Democrat Jon Corzine, a former Goldman CEO, was on the Senate Banking Committee. Joshua Bolten, a former executive director at the Goldman Sachs office in London, was director of the Office of Management and Budget. And Stephen Friedman was Bush's economic adviser.[61] None of them expressed concern about the housing market or the growing leverage at the nation's investment banks. Under Geithner, the New York Fed issued a report examining the risks of a potential housing bubble. It concluded there was no such thing on the horizon.[62]

Yet from 2002 to 2007, the biggest US banks created nearly 80 percent of the approximately $14 trillion worth of global mortgage-backed securities (MBS), asset-backed securities (ABS), collateralized debt obligations (CDOs), and other concoctions of packaged assets fashioned during those years. International banks created the other 20 percent.[63] Subprime loan packages were the fastest-growing segment of the MBS market. This meant that the financial products exhibiting the most growth were the ones containing the most risk.

In that interim, Bush picked Ben Bernanke to replace Alan Greenspan as chairman of the Federal Reserve. The bankers needed to keep their party going. Bernanke made it immediately clear where his loyalties lay, stating, "My first priority will be to maintain continuity with the policies and policy strategies during the Greenspan years."[64]

On February 1, 2006, after telling his nomination hearing committee he thought "derivatives, for the most part, are traded among very sophisticated financial institutions and individuals who have considerable incentive to understand them and to use them properly,"[65] Bernanke was appointed Fed chair.[66] Bankers could keep manufacturing derivatives with their new chief regulator's approval. Commercial and investment banks entered overdrive, packaging and repackaging the subprime and commercial real estate loans they had extended when rates were so low, pumping money into subprime lenders and developers building in "growth" areas throughout the United States, and selling the related securities and derivatives within the United States and around the world.

Two years after persuading the SEC to adopt rules that enabled many of those assets to be undercapitalized and underscrutinized, President Bush selected Paulson to be his third Treasury secretary. Josh Bolton had arranged the pivotal White House visit between the two men that sealed the deal. As Bush wrote in his memoir, *Decision Points*, "Hank was slow to warm to the idea of joining my cabinet. Josh eventually persuaded Hank to visit with me in the White House. Hank radiated energy and confidence. Hank understood the globalization of finance, and his name commanded respect at home and abroad."[67]

On May 30, 2006, when Bush officially announced Paulson's nomination, he, like Clinton had with Rubin, equated Paulson to Alexander Hamilton. Robert Rubin remarked that the choice was "well done."[68]

When Paulson assumed the Treasury post on July 10, 2006, Lloyd Blankfein took the reins of Goldman. Paulson's free-market ideas aligned with those of Bush. In response to a question from Idaho Republican Mike Crapo at his Senate confirmation hearing, Paulson echoed Bernanke's stance regarding derivatives regulation. He said he was "wary" of proposals to strengthen regulation of derivatives because of their importance in managing risk.

Under Bush, Paulson, and Bernanke, the banking sector would buckle and take the global economy down with it. Its nearly $14 trillion pyramid of superleveraged toxic assets was built on the back of $1.4 trillion of US subprime loans, and dispersed throughout the world.[69] European buyers, in particular, as well as pension funds, small municipalities, and local banks became fertile dumping ground for toxic assets, precipitating years of widespread economic collapse.[70]

Housing Problems Brewing

On March 9, 2007, Paulson cohosted a conference on US capital market competitiveness along with his undersecretary of domestic finance, Bob Steel, another Goldman veteran.[71] The conference was announced the day after China's stock market plunged more than 9 percent and the Dow fell 3.3 percent. Its central report warned "a regulatory race to the bottom will serve no useful competitive purpose."[72] It implied that tighter regulations will restrain competition, not enforce stability.

Six weeks later, Paulson delivered an upbeat assessment of the economy to a business group gathering in New York. Despite evidence that 2006 foreclosures had topped 1.2 million, rising 42 percent from 2005, he declared that the US economy was "very healthy" and "robust."[73]

The following month, in a speech before the Federal Reserve Bank of Atlanta, Geithner said innovations like derivatives had "improved the capacity to measure and manage risk" and declared that "the larger global financial institutions are generally stronger in terms of capital relative to risk."[74]

None of what Paulson or Geithner said was accurate. By mid-2007, bank liquidity was drying up. Bankers were scrambling to dump whatever complex securities they could into a market where the savvy players were reluctant to buy them. Others were not so shielded from the salesmanship of the bankers.

Behind the scenes, Geithner met with key Citigroup execs, including Chairman and CEO Charles Prince; Vice Chairman Lewis Kaden; and Thomas Maheras, who ran various trading operations. Geithner wanted to discuss certain off-book Citigroup units that were imperiled by deteriorating CDOs. He also met with Rubin, though he later denied discussing anything material with him.[75] He lunched separately with Jamie Dimon and Lloyd Blankfein to ascertain the strength of their operations in the face of a mounting credit crunch and defaulting securities.

There were massive problems plaguing Wall Street. Yet in a July 9, 2007, *Financial Times* interview, Prince talked up Citigroup's strength. Reminiscent of Charles Mitchell nearly eighty years earlier, he said, "When the music stops, in terms of liquidity, things will get complicated. But as long as the music is playing, you've got to get up and dance. We're still dancing."[76]

Bear Stearns Hedge Funds Collapse and Goldman Reaches the Top

The problem with rating as triple-A trillions of dollars of flimsy assets was that when some faltered, others followed. The whole industry was concocting and leveraging securities, passing them around like hot potatoes. It was only a matter of time before some insider got scalded. The first major burn was at Bear Stearns.

Two Bear Stearns funds had been created in 2003 and 2006 to buy and leverage triple-A and double-A assets, mostly CDO securities ranked as high credit quality by the rating agencies (to which banks paid fees for such evaluations). To raise money to buy these securities, they, like *many* other such funds, borrowed from eager big-bank suppliers. Thus, banks created junk and subsequently lent money to buyers to purchase it, creating a modern version of the Ponzi scheme.

By early 2007, the Bear funds were imploding, their demise hastened by participants extracting money as quickly as they could and by banks pressing them with margin calls—requiring more cash as collateral for loans they had originally provided to buy the securities in the funds. By the time the funds collapsed in June 2007, investors had lost around $1.8 billion.[77]

The chain reaction unleashed by the collapse of Bear's funds echoed that of the interconnected trust collapses in the late 1920s and during the Panic of 1907. But it was worse on two accounts: first, the advent of derivatives added layers of darkness; and second, Bear had bought components of the same deals that other investors bought, so when it had to sell them to raise money for the margin calls, it forced the price of related securities downward. Many of these were already being downgraded or defaulting, but Bear's move caused their values to plummet even faster. All the bank players got hit, some worse than others.

As a result of Citigroup's hemorrhaging positions, on November 4, 2007, at an emergency board meeting, Prince wasn't dancing—he was resigning. He said, "Given the size and nature of the recent losses in our mortgage-backed securities business, the only honorable course for me to take as chief executive officer is to step down." He had bagged $53.1 million in salary and bonuses in the previous four years, and left with a $99 million golden parachute.[78]

Robert Rubin was named acting chairman.[79] Earlier that week, Merrill Lynch CEO Stan O'Neal had also been booted out for similar reasons.[80] He was replaced by former Goldman Sachs copresident John Thain.[81] Thus, former Goldman leaders briefly sat atop three of the largest US financial firms, as well as the Treasury Department, the National Economic Council, and the Office of Management and Budget.

As the crisis was building, Geithner continued to cultivate relationships with key bankers. From mid-2007 through late 2008, he attended multiple lunches and meetings with senior execs from Goldman Sachs and Morgan Stanley at swanky Manhattan locales and private corporate dining rooms. He even dined at the home of Jamie Dimon.[82]

Geithner's relationships with Citigroup's elite were particularly tight and long-standing. Aside from having worked in the Treasury Department for Rubin, he was also close to former chairman Sandy Weill and had even joined the board of one of Weill's nonprofit organizations in January 2007.[83] At one point, Weill had approached Geithner about taking over Prince's CEO spot.

But at the New York Fed, Geithner had the capacity to do far more good for Citigroup.[84] Citigroup would need him by late 2008.

Dimon Conquers the Bear

The markets and much of the media remained oblivious to the chaos churning within the banks. On October 9, 2007, the Dow closed at 14,164, an all-time high. All the signs the bankers worried about—rising defaults, the combustion of Bear Stearns hedge funds, the insane levels of leverage within and around securities, the "shitty" deals, and the "game of thrones" among bank CEOs—hadn't broken the broader population's concept of economic security.[85] Yet.

Then, on December 21, 2007, Bear Stearns posted a loss of $1.9 billion, its first quarterly loss in its eighty-four-year history.[86] The breaking point had arrived.

As the inevitable storm approached, Dimon—as many bankers before him did when they sensed domestic conditions in jeopardy—shifted to the international arena to beef up alliances. In January 2008, he hired former British prime minister Tony Blair as a senior adviser. Blair declared JPMorgan Chase "at the cutting edge of the global economy."[87] This was shortly after Northern Rock, a British bank, collapsed, causing scores of depositors to circle the bank waiting to extract their money, in shades of past panics.[88]

Three months later, Bear Stearns was facing its demise.[89] Dimon sensed a lucrative domestic opportunity and decided that JPMorgan Chase would buy it, but only if it didn't have to take on the risk of Bear's toxic asset portfolio. Paulson and Geithner fashioned a solution. The Fed would lend about $29 billion against Bear's crippled mortgage holdings, effectively shielding JPMorgan Chase from the related risk.[90]

Thus, on April 3, 2008, with the Fed now acting in an investment banking capacity as both a financing agent and facilitator of a private bank merger, Dimon acquired Bear Stearns, with its $360 billion in assets, under a quasi-government guarantee. He later told a congressional committee, "We viewed that as an obligation of JPMorgan as a responsible corporate citizen."[91] An obligation, to be sure, that the government backed and that enabled Dimon to extend his bank's prime brokerage business, catapulting JPMorgan Chase to third place, behind competitors Goldman Sachs and Morgan Stanley, in the lucrative business of servicing hedge funds.[92]

While Dimon's "benevolence" did nothing to contain the bloodletting, Paulson attempted to reassure the public: "It's a safe banking system, a sound banking system." He said, "Our regulators are on top of it."[93]

Lehman Brothers Goes Bankrupt

By the summer of 2008, 158-year-old Lehman Brothers was staggering. Though many Wall Street firms were highly leveraged and exposed to junky subprime assets, Lehman was another extreme case. On September 10, it announced a $3.9 billion loss for the third quarter, the worst result in its history. The end was near.

As Bush later wrote, "There was no way the firm could survive the weekend. The question was what role, if any, the government would play in keeping Lehman afloat. The best possible solution was to find a buyer for Lehman, as we had for Bear Stearns. We had two days."[94]

Bush got most of his information about the unfolding crisis from Paulson, who informed him of two possible buyers: Bank of America and the British bank Barclays. London regulators rejected the idea of a Barclays purchase of the whole firm, though Barclays did buy one of Lehman's units, its New York headquarters, and two data centers for $1.75 billion. Bank of America bought Merrill Lynch instead. Lehman was out of options.

Richard Fuld Jr., Lehman's CEO, begged regulators to convert his investment bank into a bank holding company in order to provide access to federal funding. But as the *New York Times* reported, "Geithner told him no."[95] Fuld's alliances weren't as tight as those of his surviving compatriots. He filed for bankruptcy on September 15, 2008.[96]

Nearly a week later, the Fed granted Goldman and Morgan Stanley approval to be designated bank holding companies.[97] It didn't hurt that Blankfein had been a member of the New York Fed's advisory panel since 2004.[98] Or that he had worked for Paulson.

"We believe that Goldman Sachs, under Federal Reserve supervision, will be regarded as an even more secure institution," Blankfein stated.[99] But in reality, this was a highly self-serving way to retain power, with Fed and government backing.

Ken Lewis's Big Mistake

Ken Lewis rose through the ranks of Bank of America after joining North Carolina National Bank—the predecessor to NationsBank and Bank of America—in 1969. By April 2001, he was chairman, CEO, and president of Bank of America.[100] Lewis acquired Fleet Boston in April 2004, MBNA in January 2006, and ABN Amro North America in October 2007. He had accumulated $110 million in compensation.[101]

That wasn't enough, though, so he decided to buy Countrywide Financial, a comparatively small acquisition announced at $4 billion in January 2008. This was a huge mistake, as Countrywide CEO Angelo Mozilo left Bank of America with a fraud- and lawsuit-infested cesspool of a firm.[102] Even the Fed questioned its massive thousand-basis-point credit spreads at the time, which followed an 85 percent drop in Countrywide's value over the preceding year. But that didn't stop the Fed from approving the merger on June 5, 2008.[103] The "go big or go home" mentality prevailed at the chief regulator.

Three months later, on September 15, 2008, the day Lehman went bust, Lewis made an even bigger mistake—buying Merrill Lynch in a $50 billion all-stock deal.[104] Bank of America stock was trading at $33.74; three months later, when the deal closed, it had fallen to $5.10.

Paulson later admitted to pressuring Lewis to acquire Merrill, at one point threatening that if he backed out, it could result in "government-imposed changes" in the bank's management—in effect, Lewis's removal. He used the power of his public office to press a private company into a deal that would bring years of chaos. The move represented a new kind of alliance between Washington and Wall Street, a full-fledged investment banking advisory role from the Treasury that was more about financial than political expedience, more about saving certain banks than stabilizing the country.

The merger proved fortuitous for Paulson's old number-two, Merrill Lynch head John Thain, who was spared the bankruptcy proceedings that befell Lehman. From September through December 2008, many conversations took place among the interested parties. Thain and Paulson spoke twenty-one times. Lewis got through thirty-five times.[105] But Lewis couldn't stop the merger.

After the merger, Bank of America received $230 billion in bailout subsidies—and $150 million in SEC fines.[106] It would also fork out a record $42 billion in various legal settlements for the pain it caused people over the next five years, with more pending.[107]

Lewis's decision to pay bonuses to Merrill execs, including Thain's former Goldman Sachs recruits and others, while Bank of America was getting government bailouts fell under intense scrutiny. The matter festered for two years. A March 17, 2009, House Committee even requested Merrill Lynch's records regarding the $3.62 billion in bonuses agreed to before the merger.[108]

The incident lingered, and on December 31, 2009, Lewis announced his resignation.[109] Brian Thomas Moynihan took his place.[110] Moynihan proved adept at political alliances and had visited the White House thirteen times by February 2012.[111]

Goldman Trumps AIG

Insurance goliath AIG stood at the epicenter of an increasingly interconnected financial world deluged with junky subprime assets wrapped up with derivatives. Its financial products department had insured nearly half a *trillion* dollars of them for the big banks. When Fitch, S&P, and Moody's downgraded AIG's rating on September 15, 2008, it catalyzed $85 billion worth of margin calls.[112]

The firm would not only fail, Paulson warned Bush, but "it would bring down major financial institutions and international investors with it." Paulson's fearmongering convinced President Bush: "There was only one way to keep the firm alive: the federal government would have to step in."[113]

Blankfein and Dimon were the only CEOs Geithner called to discuss AIG's condition on the morning of September 15.[114] Paulson also appeared to have had Blankfein on speed-dial. Between March 2008 and January 2009, the men spoke thirty-four times, mostly during the AIG incident.[115]

The next day, the New York Fed authorized a loan of up to $85 billion to AIG (the size of its margin calls by the big banks) in return for a 79.9 percent equity interest. On October 8, it provided an additional $37.8 billion in liquidity against securities. Total AIG subsidies reached $182 billion.[116]

The main US recipients of AIG's bailout were strongly allied firms: Goldman Sachs with $12.9 billion, Merrill Lynch with $6.8 billion, Bank of America with $5.2 billion, and Citigroup with $2.3 billion. Some foreign banks that had trading relationships with them, including Société Générale and Deustche Bank, got about $12 billion each. Barclays got $8.5 billion, and UBS got $5 billion.[117]

Lehman crashed. Merrill and AIG were saved in two different ways. The selective bailout behavior echoed that of the Panic of 1907, when the big New York bankers let the Knickerbocker Trust Company—with which they had fewer personal and financial ties—tank but got the government involved to help save the American Trust Company. The bankers with the strongest political alliances needed AIG to survive. And it did.

Bankers' Bailouts and Citizens' Pain

On September 18, 2008, Bush told Paulson, "Let's figure out the right thing to do and do it." He later wrote, "I had made up my mind: the US government was going all in."[118]

The Big Six firms (and marginally other institutions) were subsidized by a program designed by Bernanke, Paulson, and Geithner. The trio deemed the bailout and bank subsidization as a matter of public interest, essential steps to divert a Great Depression. But the main recipients were the big bankers, not everyday Americans, who were unable to renegotiate their mortgage loans as easily as the bankers received backing.

An initial rejection of the bailout package provoked a 778-point drop in the Dow on September 29, 2008. Paulson had dramatically gotten down on one knee three days earlier to beg Democratic house speaker Nancy Pelosi to get her party to pass the bailout. Congress bowed to this chief banker on behalf of all his former colleagues and compatriots, and approved a $700 billion congressional bank bailout package. The Troubled Asset Relief Program, also known as TARP, was part of the Emergency Economic Stability Act of 2008, signed by Bush on October 3.[119] Considered by much of the media and Congress as the total bailout, it comprised just 3 percent of the full bank bailout and subsidization program. According to Bush, "TARP sent an unmistakable signal that we would not let the American financial system fail."[120]

The market rose after the intervention was announced, as it had temporarily done in October 1929. But this time, intervention came from the government—not from the bankers. The Dow shot up 936 points, the largest one-day rise in stock market history. The euphoria would be equally illusory and temporary.

As it had during the days of the original Big Six, the bankers' unruliness had crippled the real economy. By October 30, 2008, US real GDP fell at a 0.3 percent annual rate, the second negative quarter in a row.[121] Housing prices plummeted. Foreclosures and unemployment escalated.

Over the next few months, Bank of America, Citigroup, and AIG needed more assistance. And over the year, the Dow lost nearly half its value. At the height of the bailout period, $19.3 trillion of subsidies were made available to keep (mostly) US bankers going, as well as government-sponsored enterprises like Fannie Mae and Freddie Mac. The Big Six received a combined $870 billion in bailouts, not including multitrillion-dollar subsidies from various Federal Reserve lending facilities and other guarantees.[122]

But first, an election loomed.

Obama: The Preferred Choice for Bankers

Bankers believed Democratic candidate Barack Obama would help them more than his opponent, John McCain—particularly at Goldman Sachs, Obama's largest corporate contributor for the 2008 election.[123] Contributors Goldman Sachs and JPMorgan Chase ranked sixth and seventh, respectively, throughout Obama's political career.[124] Plus, Obama had Robert Rubin in his corner. According to investigative journalist Greg Palast, billionaire Penny Pritzker had introduced then-Senator Obama to Rubin at a Chicago "ladies who lunch" event. Later, Rubin opened the "doors to finance industry vaults" for Obama.[125] Obama raised more than three times as much from the banking and finance industries during the 2008 campaign as McCain.

In classic Democratic Party fashion, Obama promised to "rein in Wall Street forces and their risky practices" while taking their contribution money. (Republicans tend to take the money without such promises.) Obama won in a decisive victory. Bankers would visit the White House more frequently than they did when his predecessor was in office, and his administration, in partnership with the Federal Reserve, would continue subsidizing bankers while talking up the importance of jobs creation.[126]

At the end of 2008, liquidity remained tight and bankers still couldn't move their worst assets. So on December 16, 2008, the Federal Reserve cut rates to an all-time low of 0 percent, down from 1 percent and 0.25 percent earlier in the year, thereby initiating Bernanke's zero-interest rate policy. No American catastrophe since the Fed was created had evoked such a policy. Even during World War II, rates didn't remain as low for as long; this was a true reaction and capitulation to financial warfare.

On January 9, 2009, shortly before Obama took office, Rubin announced his retirement from Citigroup. In a letter to Citigroup CEO Vikram Pandit, Rubin wrote, "My great regret is that I and so many of us who have been involved in this industry for so long did not recognize the serious possibility of the extreme circumstances that the financial system faces today."[127] At the time, Citigroup was existing on $346 billion in various federal subsidies, including a $301 billion asset guarantee and $45 billion of TARP.[128] Rubin remained cochair of the Council on Foreign Relations.[129]

Upon taking office, Obama called Wall Street bankers' $18.4 billion in 2008 bonuses "shameful." "There will be time for them to make profits, and there will be time for them to get bonuses," he said at an Oval Office appearance. "Now's not that time. And that's a message that I intend to send directly to them."[130] The message might have gotten lost in translation. For 2009, cash bonuses rose 17 percent over 2008, to $20.3 billion, on the back of Washington-created, taxpayer-provided subsidies, despite a crippled economy.

Obama's Favorite Banker

Obama's economic policy appointments could have been made by Bill Clinton. (Maybe they were; as I explained in the Preface, Obama's records will not be fully revealed for decades.) Clinton's selections had all promoted banking deregulation during his presidency.

For Treasury secretary, Obama chose New York Fed chief and bailout architect Tim Geithner. Larry Summers would be chief economic adviser. William Dudley, former Goldman Sachs CEO and chairman of the New York Fed's board of directors, assumed Geithner's slot.[131] Rahm Emanuel, having served time as an investment banker after his years working in the Clinton administration, was selected Obama's chief of staff.

Geithner's contact with bankers intensified in his early months as Treasury secretary, as bankers remained scared. Between January 2009 and March 2010, he spoke with Lloyd Blankfein at least thirty-eight times, more than with any congressperson. (Blankfein visited the White House fourteen times in 2011.) During his first five months in office, Geithner communicated with elite financial CEOs at least seventy-six times.[132]

As for the new king of Wall Street, Dimon had established ties with the new president years earlier. According to the *New York Times*, Dimon first met Obama during his 2004 Senate run "at a living room discussion with about 10 pro-business Democrats," and donated the maximum of $2,000 to his campaign.[133] Dimon had spent several years in Obama's hometown of Chicago while running Bank One (Obama was a state senator at the time). Dimon had also contributed to the campaigns of Obama's first chief of staff, Rahm Emanuel. In addition, both were Harvard grads: Dimon obtained an MBA in 1982, and Obama graduated with a JD in 1991 (Obama became the eighth president to have graduated from Harvard).[134]

In July 2009 the media dubbed Dimon Obama's "favorite banker." Dimon made at least sixteen trips to the White House and met at least six times with Obama between February 2009 and March 2012, including thirteen trips in 2011.[135] Obama also kept about $1 million of his own money parked at JPMorgan Chase Private Client Asset Management.[136]

During the fall of 2009, with the economy still a shambles, Obama levied harsh words on the bankers' role in the financial crisis at Federal Hall on Wall Street.[137] Up to that point, top bankers had visited the Obama White House twelve times. By 2012, the figure had risen to fifty-nine. Obama's words didn't change alliances; instead, the frequency of interactions appeared to have increased.

Crisis and Popular Anger

As Obama entered his second year, the economy remained a mess. Absent the bankers' desire to renegotiate mortgages for their hurting customers, nearly five million home foreclosures had been initiated since the beginning of 2008. Standing at 7.9 percent when he took office, the official unemployment rate shot as high as 10 percent, though the figure rose to around 17 percent when actual unemployment and underemployment were considered.[138] Meanwhile, the new Big Six consumed cheap capital, parlaying it into stocks and derivatives as opposed to deploying it to restructure the population's debt or issue small business loans to stimulate the economy.[139]

In August 2009, Obama renominated Bernanke, whom he called the "architect of the recovery," as Fed chair. In January 2010, the Senate reconfirmed him by a vote of 70 to 30, the lowest vote for a Fed chair since the Fed was created. The bankers knew that with Bernanke's reconfirmation, their support would continue.[140]

The $700 billion TARP package accounted for about 3 percent of the government's and Federal Reserve's creative largesse during the Bush-Obama presidencies. More than $19 trillion in bailouts and subsidies had been deployed at the height of the crisis to bolster the industry and its toxic assets before various aid avenues were eventually closed. Of that figure, the New York Fed and Federal Reserve made available $8.2 trillion in loans and asset guarantees; the Treasury Department provided $6.8 trillion in subsidies and bailouts; and the FDIC initiated a $2.3 trillion liquidity guarantee program to keep the wheels of bank capital greased. Jointly, the Fed and Treasury agreed to buy $1.3 trillion of assets, a figure that grew as the Fed expanded its "money-printing," bond-buying program. The most powerful bankers left the repercussions of their irresponsible and fraudulent practices behind them, save for some fines.[141]

In February 2010, Obama told *Bloomberg Businessweek* that he didn't begrudge Blankfein and Dimon their $17 million and $9 million bonuses (respectively), saying, "I know both those guys, they are very savvy businessmen." Indeed, they were savvy and politically aligned enough to beat their competitors to recovery. Wall Street posted its second best year in its history in 2010.[142]

Globally, economic conditions were abysmal. Throughout the Middle East and parts of Europe, youth unemployment topped 25 percent; in some places, it was double that figure.[143] Country after country, from Greece to Spain to Ireland, struggled under immense debt and crippled economies. Governments pushed through austerity measures in conjunction with the supranational banks to make up for the debt incurred by losses from toxic securities, in the wake of a fraudulently stimulated global housing market. The general rage pushed people to the streets, from demonstrations in the Middle East and Europe to the US-launched Occupy movements, where anger was aimed at the bankers and the politicians who favored them.[144]

Dodd-Frank and the
Changing Nature of Power

The Obama administration's response to the crisis was the Dodd-Frank bill, an 848-page colossus also known as the Wall Street Reform and Consumer Protection Act.[145] Despite its girth and public-oriented title, it did not alter the banking landscape. It did not separate banks' speculative and derivatives-churning abilities from their federally backed deposit side. And it did not remove a single financial conglomerate "service" or practice, as Glass-Steagall had in 1933. A litany of correspondence between lawmakers and lobbyists did nothing to ensure that another meltdown would be avoided.

The bill was riddled with holes punched out by bank lobbyists with Washington connections: forty-seven of fifty Goldman Sachs lobbyists had previously held government jobs (or were "revolvers"). In addition, forty-two of forty-six JPMorgan Chase lobbyists in 2010 were revolvers, as were thirty-five of Citigroup's forty-six.[146]

President Obama signed the bill into law on July 21, 2010.

Beneath the surface, a critical presidential power shift underscored the political theater and the partisan vote on the Dodd-Frank Act. In the 1930s, the Glass-Steagall Act had been "swiftly approved by both houses of Congress" with a resounding bipartisan vote.[147] Sixty-six years later, the act that repealed it passed the Senate by another overwhelmingly bipartisan vote. In other words, FDR passed regulation across party lines that stabilized the banking sector with the support of certain major bankers and the population, and Clinton passed deregulation across party lines that destabilized the global financial arena with the support of (effectively) the same bankers.

In contrast, Dodd-Frank passed along party lines. Perhaps the 60 to 40 Senate vote showed that Obama was incompetent as a politician. Or maybe it showed that the power of the presidency to pass such legislation, even in the wake of a historic crisis, had waned considerably—or a combination of the two. Obama had no power to force a restructuring of Wall Street, nor did he appear to try. His speeches promoting sweeping reform were empty words uttered with practiced elocution, absent any of the details that FDR had explained so carefully to the nation. Not only that, Obama couldn't persuade any politician across the aisle to support the act he promoted, even though it was toothless. He aligned with Wall Street in a haze of denial but did not, or refused to, consider the potential impact of promoting its desires. Worse, his spin on reform was accepted by most of his party and the press, though it paled in comparison to the real reform of the 1930s, which had kept extreme financial crises at bay for the better part of the century.

According to Geithner, the Dodd-Frank Act represented the "most sweeping set of financial reforms since those that followed the Great Depression."[148] But that meant nothing either. The act left the Big Six bankers in a more influential position than before the Crash of 1929. It did nothing to alter their power and control; they held a record 60 percent of US deposits, consolidated during the fall of 2008 at the bequest of their Washington allies, the largest concentration of capital in US history.

The opportunity for real Glass-Steagall-type reform—the kind that revises the entire financial landscape and diffuses at least some of the power of private bankers to hurt the population—was blown again. But the entire exercise was as wrongly viewed as an unmitigated, world-saving success by Obama and his team as it was castigated by the Republicans, the party that had initiated the Pecora hearings, which revealed the extent of the damage unconstrained bankers could bring on the overall population. Meanwhile, after Lehman Brothers went bankrupt and Bear Stearns and Merrill Lynch were acquired by JPMorgan Chase and Bank of America, the largest banks had become bigger, and their leaders more powerful than ever before.

On the Campaign Trail

In the absence of true reform, an abundance of national debt was issued to bolster the banking system. From the beginning of 2009 through the end of 2011, Geithner added $2.4 trillion of US debt, but there was more to come.[149] The US debt-to-GDP ratio rose to nearly 100 percent and would surpass 104 percent by 2012.[150] The United States lost its triple-A debt rating in August 2011 amid painful equivocation on Capitol Hill, none of which addressed how much of that debt was created by the Treasury, punted through the banks, and landed on the Fed's books as requested by its member banks. The country's economic future and borrowing power had been compromised by the bankers' actions with the advocacy of the White House, and no one said a word about it. Blame fell on the "weak economy," not the explicit role of bankers in depleting it.

By 2011, JPMorgan Chase had surpassed Bank of America as the largest US bank, with nearly $4 trillion in assets.[151] Somewhere, the ghosts of the men who had traveled to Jekyll Island a century earlier were chuckling. Jamie Dimon had secured the financial crown that had belonged to J. P. Morgan without any of the family pedigree or style. He was placed on *Time*'s list of the hundred most influential people in 2006, 2008, 2009, and 2011.[152]

In the wake of the crash, Dimon remained the most vocal advocate of status quo. At a March 30, 2011, US Chamber of Commerce address, he warned that the "best system in the world" should not be destroyed by too many regulations. Imposing higher capital requirements on US banks, he said, would be "putting the nail in the coffin."[153] Global competition remained useful as an argument for less regulation.

By early 2012, Obama had reentered heavy campaign mode. Goldman Sachs had uncharacteristically miscalculated Obama's chances and flipped to backing GOP challenger Mitt Romney.[154] But knowing the stakes were high, Obama made sure to praise his old favorite banker on *The View*—that beacon of high-quality political discussion—calling Dimon "one of the greatest bankers we have." In a sign of his own rising power in the political-financial game, and the shift away from having to maintain tight alliances with the president, Dimon did not contribute to Obama's 2012 campaign.

On the campaign trail, Obama avoided addressing the first major post-Dodd-Frank blow-up, known as the "London Whale." On April 6, 2012, JPMorgan Chase's London office reported that its bad bet on corporate spreads through the derivatives market could cost the firm at least $5.8 billion.[155] (Tony Blair was still on the firm's payroll at the time; he received a $6.3 million mortgage loan from JPMorgan Chase in September 2012.[156])

Two months later, at a Senate hearing on the transaction, Dimon testified with the bored and sullen face of a teenager who crashed the family car and didn't want to deal with his parents' wrath. The senators treated him with kid gloves—they even asked Dimon for advice on running the economy.[157] Yet when Dimon gave a speech at the Council on Foreign Relations in October 2012, he complained about his ordeal, saying, "When people do commit, you know, not fraud, but, you know, they make mistakes, you're attacked by seventeen different agencies as opposed to, you know, in the old days, it would be the one who's responsible for it."[158] He added, "[We] went through '06, '07, '08, '09, 2010, 2011, 2012, never lost money in a quarter. So we made a stupid error. I mean, if an airplane crashes, should we stop flying all airplanes? . . . [O]nly when I come to Washington do people act like, you know, making a mistake . . . should never happen."[159]

A month later, Obama won his second term as president. The perils of the financial crisis were tidily swept under the rug as the president and his staff issued overly optimistic recovery claims. The Fed inhaled Wall Street's assets and paid banks interest on their excess reserves, while keeping rates at zero. Several months later, the London Whale incident was repurposed and blamed on a decimal-point error in JPMorgan Chase's evaluation reports, a mistake for which Dimon emerged inculpable. His shareholders ensured he retained both his chairman and CEO roles. Obama and Dimon would continue their reigns and mutually beneficial alliance.

The Justice Department
Goes Soft on Bankers

Many congressional hearings and investigations have probed the bankers' practices since the crisis that began in 2007. Similar to the Pujo hearings after the Panic of 1907, though, they have resulted in nothing material against the bankers with the strongest political alliances. And unlike the impact of the 1932–1933 Pecora Commission hearings, no substantive regulatory act has passed to significantly alter their behavior. Though banks would end up paying various fines and legal settlements, that amounted to fractions of pennies on the dollar relative to their immense asset bases. Their structure and influence remained unaltered.

As of September 1, 2013, the SEC reported it had levied just $1.53 billion in fines and $1.2 billion in penalties, disgorgement, and other money relief against the big banks for their multitrillion-dollar global Ponzi scheme—or as the SEC put it, "addressing misconduct that led to or arose from the financial crisis."[160] Goldman paid a $550 million fine from the SEC for a similar allegation. The firm admitted no guilt for the related activities. Bank of America paid a $150 million fine without admitting any guilt for misleading shareholders regarding its payment of Merrill Lynch's bonuses when it took over the firm. JPMorgan Chase eventually settled the London Whale probe with a $1.02 billion fine, greater than the fines it paid the government for all of its housing-related infractions. Though the firm admitted that it had violated banking rules by not properly monitoring trading operations, that kind of admission was akin to copping a misdemeanor plea while facing a major felony.

On August 1, 2013, a federal judge approved a $590 million settlement by Citigroup in a shareholder lawsuit accusing the bank of hiding billions of dollars of toxic mortgage assets.[161] On that same day, a jury found former Goldman Sachs banker Fabrice Tourre liable for his role in the Abacus deal, which lost some investors $1 billion. The ruling was dubbed a major victory for the SEC. "We are obviously gratified by the jury's verdict and appreciate their hard work," lead SEC lawyer Matthew Martens said.[162]

The Justice Department chose not to criminally prosecute the chairmen from Goldman or JPMorgan Chase (both of whom ranked in the top twenty for Obama's career campaign contributors) or from anywhere else for creating faulty CDOs, trading against them, dumping them on less knowledgeable investors, or otherwise speculating with capital supposedly siphoned off for more productive and less risky purposes.

Similarly, the Justice Department punted on prosecuting Jon Corzine, the former governor of New Jersey and a top-tier bundler for Obama. Steering his firm MF Global into an abyss, Corzine had bet more than $6 billion on European sovereign debt.[163] The $1 billion MF Global "mistake," the multi-billion-dollar losses on bets made by Chase, the CDOs chosen by the firm's biggest hedge fund clients that had been set up to fail—these were apparently just minor events in the scheme of making money and maintaining alliances. On October 31, 2011, MF Global filed Chapter 11, with $41 billion in assets and $39.7 billion in debt, the eighth largest bankruptcy in US history. Four days before the collapse, Corzine sent an email to an employee "to strategize how they could use customer segregated funds [and get JPMorgan Chase] to clear MF Global's trades more quickly." He avoided criminal fraud charges.

The general response of Obama and his cabinet toward Wall Street criminality and the sheer unsavoriness of its leaders showed the degree to which nothing had changed and the lack of commitment to reform. If nothing changes fundamentally in the banking landscape, more and larger crises are a given. The most powerful banks are bigger, more interconnected, and more reliant on cheap money and federal largesse than ever. Their leaders are unrepentant and unaccountable. Their political alliances require nothing of them anymore except some fines that can be easily re-earned.

Lucky 2013

By 2013, the major global banks were sitting on nearly $3.3 trillion of excess reserves (about $2 trillion for the US banks at the Fed and the rest at the European Central Bank), refusing to share their government aid with the citizens of the world.

By October 2013, the government was careening toward a debt cap of $16.49 trillion, and the weakness of the US political system relative to the financial one was demonstrated by a government shutdown over budget and ego squabbles. The Fed's balance sheet had ballooned to a historic record of just over $3.7 trillion, comprised in part by $2.1 trillion of Treasuries, or nearly $2 trillion in *excess* bank reserves.[164] These government debt securities were issued by the US Treasury, purchased by the banks, and then reverted as excess (nonrequired) reserves to the Fed—in other words, a nonproductive circle of extra national debt issued for no real reason. In addition, the Fed books

contained $1.34 trillion of mortgage-backed securities (following the estab-
lishment of an $85 billion per month mortgage-backed and Treasury securities
purchase program, totaling more than $1 trillion per year).[165] The size of the
Fed's books had increased by 25 percent since July 2011 and 50 percent since
July 2009, and it stood at ten times the amount it had been in July 2008. All of
this debt was held as means to prop up bond prices so the bankers could maintain higher values on their books of associated securities, and to keep rates low
so that money remained cheap, under the guise of aiding the broad economy.

In numerous speeches, Bernanke condoned his zero-interest rate policy and "quantitative easing" bond-buying policies, which kept the rates at
which banks borrowed money at zero. The bankers were certainly happy.
They could use their money on other speculative ventures, and their remaining faulty mortgage-backed securities would be bought by the Fed.[166] Their
2012 bonuses rose $20 billion, up 8 percent from 2011.[167]

The cycle of banker–White House alliances persisted. The Senate confirmed Obama's choice of Jack Lew to succeed Tim Geithner as Treasury secretary on February 27, 2013.[168] Lew was no stranger to big bankers either. In
his prior role as Obama's director of the Office of Management and Budget,
he met often with Wall Street's elite. Before that, he had served in the Clinton White House with Rubin, and with Summers during the Glass-Steagall
repeal days.[169]

Like his mentor, Rubin, Lew had worked at Citigroup, where he served
as chief operating officer of the alternative investments unit.[170] He got paid
$940,000 in early 2009, while Citigroup was inhaling bailout funds. He
had served in the division that the SEC charged with hiding $39 billion of
subprime debts in off-balance-sheet structured investment vehicles.[171] In
Washington, he just might help Citigroup regain some of its old glory.

Banks Wrapping Up

By November 2013, four years after the Federal Crisis Inquiry Commission
first convened (it went on to hold nineteen days of public hearings and review
millions of pages of bank documents on the causes of the financial crisis), the
total amount of SEC fines levied along with various, mostly mortgage-related,
legal settlements for the six major US banks reached about $80 billion, or
about 0.8 percent of their assets.[172] Of that, only the $1 billion levied for
JPMorgan Chase's London Whale trade involved admission of a crime. The
total figure was equivalent to one month of the Fed's mortgage and Treasury
securities purchase program, which entailed buying many similar potentially

questionable securities from the banks, thereupon aiding the funding of their "punishments."

The media reported the multibillion-dollar bank settlements as if they had far more meaning to the population than they actually did, especially considering only approximately $20 billion of them involved cash fines.

Relative to the Big Six banks' assets of approximately $9.6 trillion and their profits over the years preceding the financial crisis, the figure was a drop in the bucket, and revealed a "let them shoot first, get questioned later" attitude on the part of the federal justice and regulatory system.

The Obama administration remained silent on what constituted, if even unofficially, mass organized crime, or at least gross incompetency and fraud (though not admitted) on the part of the banking system and its leaders. Moreover, even though most of these repercussions were related to the banks' ability to issue, source, repackage, trade, and distribute complex mortgage and related securities from under one roof, there came no bold statements from the White House on resurrecting a Glass-Steagall act that would once again prohibit these joint activities within one bank. Neither the details nor the occurrence of the settlements and ongoing investigations served to shake the support, and thus the unofficial endorsement, of the Oval Office for the bankers' power in the form of their overall structure or their Federal Reserve–backed status.

Though WorldCom CEO Bernie Ebbers and Enron CFO Andrew Fastow went to jail for their corporate misdeeds, no major bank CEO was found to have done anything criminally wrong while presiding over practices that caused great global harm, though some of their more junior staff took the heat. That too had historical precedent: bankers with tighter ties to the president or Treasury secretary tend to get passes. They control the money flow. If the "money trusts" back in the 1910s were powerful, after a century of Fed backing and tightening political-financial alliances, the millennial money masters of today are even more so.

The moral hazard of supporting their movements has become far greater. One major difference between now and then is that the control of finances by private bankers is far broader, the complexity of financial instruments greater, and the danger of a total systemic collapse more likely.

We Must Break the Alliances

In a November 2009 interview with London's *Sunday Times,* Lloyd Blankfein, was asked about the size of his firm's staff bonuses. He claimed that he was just a banker doing "God's work." As for the economic disparities that "work" engendered, he said, "We have to tolerate the inequality as a way to achieve greater prosperity and opportunity for all." After all, he explained, Goldman Sachs is helping "companies to grow by helping them to raise capital. We have a social purpose."[173] His words, which he noted as tongue-in-cheek later, echoed so false against the backdrop of a deflated public economy that all manners of media slammed them.

But there was a kind of truth to what he said.

There have been times when the biggest bankers shattered public trust and times when the public believed that bankers' interests somewhat aligned with their own. In those periods, bankers took public service roles that weren't just related to the economy, and they didn't flaunt their wealth. The Great Depression provoked a climate of social responsibility. Related bank regulation lasted for decades. During World War II, many Americans even equated bankers with patriotism.

Today, no such attitude prevails. Never before have the government and the Federal Reserve collaborated so extensively by propping up the banking system to the detriment of the population. Never has the world been so quick to push austerity on countries whose only crime was standing in the way of banker speculation. Never have bankers thought this was copacetic. Never have their political alliances been so widespread yet so impersonal. Never have their rewards been so high.

When money has no cost, the consequences of using it irresponsibly have no cost either. The bankers' bets and actions crushed the global economy before, and they will again. The most powerful ones emerged unscathed. They had proven to be as influential, if not more so, than their alliances. But they cannot be allowed to continue. For absent a true shakeup in the structure of the financial industry and realignment of the power bankers wield over the general economy, we will surely face more financial crises in the years to come.

The nature of twenty-first-century political-financial alliances will reinforce and fortify the bankers' power, even as bankers continue to behave in ways that will lead to more widespread economic pain. The reality is that financial crises will worsen and may spread to Latin America, the Middle East, and Asia, for the mechanisms of global finance are more destructive.

US hegemony and the strength of Wall Street have been closely aligned for more than a century, during which certain private bankers have achieved a position of greater power than the presidency (or central banks). The crises of the past decade were a manifestation of what happens when US bankers operate beyond the control of government, often enabled by the highest political office in the world. Whereas the mid-twentieth-century ushered in a sense of humility and unity between private finance and public service, by the 1970s that ship had sailed.

There's a reason that the Fed bailed out the biggest banks, that Dodd-Frank was toothless, and that Obama dared even to consider Larry Summers, a tried-and-true Clintonian Rubinite, to head the Fed after Bernanke. After Summers's withdrawal, on October 9, 2013, Obama similarly opted for Janet Yellen—a former chair of Clinton's economic council while Glass-Steagall was being dismantled and Fed vice chair beside Bernanke, who advocated massive subsidy programs to buoy the banking system.

It no longer matters who sits in the White House. Presidents no longer even try to garner banker support for population-friendly policies, and bankers operate oblivious to the needs of national economies. There is no counterbalance to their power. And since America's latest elected leader pressed the pretense of financial reform instead of actually pushing for real reform, bankers can do greater damage than ever before. Bankers dominate the globe using other people's money, and presidents gain command through other people's votes, but in the ongoing game of influence and control, these are mere chips that grant players a seat at the table of power.

America operates on the belief that if its biggest banks are strong, the nation will be too. It is not US military might alone that evokes global trepidation; it is also US financial might, in the form of the alliance between the presidency and the major bankers.

No other country on the planet is driven by such a critical symbiotic and costly relationship. This is why US hegemony, from a financial superpower perspective, is not in decline. The most elite US bankers and government officials understand that their positions are mutually reinforcing, with the Fed serving as a support vessel in the middle. The US bank heads retain more influence over global capital than any government, and their unique alignment with the presidency is a force that will fortify America's power, often at the expense of populations the world over.

Our choice is simple: either we break the alliances, or they will break us.

GLOSSARY OF
FINANCIAL TERMS

All definitions include information obtained from Federal Reserve or FDIC reports, www.investopedia.com, and the author's fifteen years of experience as an analyst, strategist, and senior managing director in the financial field.

Asset-Backed Security: A financial security collateralized, or backed, by a pool of underlying assets that could be auto loans, leases, credit card debt, a company's receivables, etc.

Balance of Payments: The relationship between the payments and receipts of the residents of one country versus those of other countries. A surplus means one country has acquired more assets than another. A deficit means it has acquired fewer.

Bankers' Acceptance: A short-term debt instrument issued by a firm and guaranteed by a commercial bank, often used in international trade.

Bond: A debt security through which a corporation or government borrows money from an investor for a fixed period of time at a fixed or floating interest rate.

Capital Market: An open national or global market in which individuals and institutions trade financial securities generally underwritten, distributed, or sold by banks, companies, governments, or supranational entities to raise funds.

Central Bank: An entity that oversees the monetary system of a nation (or, in the case of the European Central Bank, a group of nations). Its role could include overseeing monetary policy, issuing currency and maintaining currency stability, taming inflation and attempting to maintain full employment, regulating commercial banks and the credit system, and acting as a lender of last resort. (Recently, the Federal Reserve and ECB acted in unprecedented ways to bail out the world's largest private banks.)

Certificate of Deposit (CD): A type of deposit account that usually provides a higher interest rate than regular savings accounts in return for keeping the funds "parked" for a specified period of time, which enables banks to use the funds for other purposes.

Collateralized Debt Obligation (CDO): A financial product that pools together (or combines) various debt assets on which interest is paid (like subprime loans or corporate bonds) and repackages them into discrete slices called tranches—each of which has different risk attributes and can be individually sold to investors depending on their risk preference, as quantified by a credit rating (AAA is supposed to mean low risk; CCC is junk, or very risky).

Commercial Bank: A financial institution that provides deposit and loan services, such as accepting deposits, extending loans and mortgages, and offering customers basic products like checking, savings accounts, and certificates of deposit.

Commercial Paper: A short-term promissory note (with a maturity of 270 days or less) sold by large corporations to raise quick money, backed by their *promise* to pay the amount of the note at the end of its term, but not by hard assets or collateral.

Corner a Market: To acquire enough of the available portion of a particular security, commodity, or other asset to enable price manipulation.

Corporate Trust: See "Trust."

Credit Default Swap (CDS): A contract designed to transfer credit exposure or speculation over a default (on a country, corporation, group of subprime loans, etc.) between parties; the swap buyer makes payments to the seller until the maturity date of the contract. The seller agrees to pay off the debt underlying the swap in the event of a default. A CDS buyer believes, or bets, that the third party will default on the debt.

Credit Derivative: A privately held and negotiated contract designed to mitigate exposure to credit default risk, or otherwise bet on the direction of credit spreads (the wider the spread of a corporate credit relative to a government security, the riskier it is).

Debt: A sum of money borrowed by one party from another, generally with the stipulation that it will be repaid at some future date, with a certain amount of interest.

Derivative: A security whose price is dependent upon, or derived from, the behavior of one or more underlying assets, depicted by a contract between two or more parties. Common underlying assets include stocks, bonds, commodities, currencies, interest rates, and market indexes.

Discount Rate: The interest rate charged to commercial banks and other deposit-taking institutions on loans they receive from their regional Federal Reserve Bank's lending facility (or "discount window").

Equity: An ownership stake in any asset or firm. Stocks are considered equity because they represent ownership in a company.

Excess Reserves: The amount of capital reserves in excess of regulatory requirements, in the form of cash or other acceptable liquid securities, that banks choose to keep at a central bank for financial stability purposes.

Federal Reserve Bank Note: A note issued and redeemable by each individual Federal Reserve member bank. These were phased out in the mid-1930s.

Federal Reserve Note: Paper currency (dollar bills) circulated in the United States, printed by the US Treasury at the instruction of the Federal Reserve member banks.

Fixed Interest Rate: An interest rate that does not move.

Floating Interest Rate: An interest rate that moves up and down with the market or some other index or reference.

Future: A financial contract obligating the buyer to purchase (or the seller to sell) an asset, such as a commodity or security, at a predetermined future date and price. Contains more leverage than simple stocks and bonds.

Hedge Fund: Privately owned investment schemes that invest capital on behalf of so-called qualified investors (firms or people with a lot of money) speculatively to maximize returns in a variety of markets, deploying a variety of less regulated (sometimes unregulated) strategies.

Hybrid Security: A security that combines two or more types of financial instruments or asset classes (debt, equity, foreign exchange, commodity, derivatives) into one security, whose price or behavior has links to each type. Hybrids can get so complicated that pricing them is difficult and information on them is nontransparent.

Interstate Banking: The expansion of a bank or bank holding company across state lines, due to legislation enabling bank holding companies to acquire out-of-state banks.

Investment Bank: A financial institution focused on raising capital and creating and trading securities. Investment banks underwrite, distribute, and trade new debt and equity and derivatives securities.

Issuer: An entity that develops, registers, and sells financial securities to raise money. Issuers may be domestic or foreign governments, corporations, or investment trusts.

Lease Financing: A financial service that entails financing the purchase of an item, which will be leased or rented out rather than retained by a borrower.

Leverage: Generally, any technique in which the capital involved in the investment exceeds the value of the investment, achieved by borrowing money or deploying various derivatives in transactions, with the result of a multiplier effect on gains and losses.

Loan: The act of giving money, property, or other material goods to another party in exchange for future repayment of the principal amount or value, plus interest.

Loan Syndicate (Syndicated Loan): A large loan provided by a group of lenders that is generally structured, arranged, and administered by several "arranger" banks.

Merchant Bank: A bank that deals mostly in (but is not limited to) international finance and long-term loans for companies and underwriting. Merchant banks do not generally provide regular banking services to the general public.

Money Supply: The entire stock of currency and other liquid instruments in a country's economy at a given time. It can include cash, coins, and other bank balances.

Money Trust: A term used by various people at the turn of the twentieth century (from Teddy Roosevelt to Louis Brandeis to Samuel Untermyer, who led the 1912 Pujo hearings) to refer to a select group of powerful financiers who exercised control over the concentration of money and capital through stockholding, interlocking directorates, and other forms of relationships across financial and industrial firms.

Monopoly Trust: A company or select group of companies or individuals that has obtained exclusive or predominant control of a service or product and has become powerful enough to drive competitors out of business and control prices.

Mortgage-Backed Security (MBS): A type of security whose payments to investors come from the payments of a group of mortgages that are contained in the security, or "pooled together," and act as collateral.

Option: A financial contract sold by one party (option writer or seller) to another party (option holder or buyer) that offers the buyer the right, but not the obligation, to buy (call) or sell (put) a security or other financial asset at an agreed-upon price (the strike price) during a certain period of time or on a specific date (exercise date).

Prime Rate: The interest rate that commercial banks charge their most creditworthy customers, such as large corporations, used as a base rate from which to set other forms of retail lending rates like mortgages and small business and personal loans.

Private Placement: The sale of securities to a small number of select investors, in a form that doesn't need to be registered with the SEC. Investors include large banks, mutual funds, insurance companies, and pension funds.

Public Issue: The sale of securities that are registered and available for sale to anyone (the opposite of private placement).

Quantitative Easing (QE): A means by which a central bank maintains a low level of interest rates through the purchase of government debt or other securities, thereby increasing money supply by flooding banks with capital. A byproduct of QE is keeping those securities' prices artificially high, and theoretically increasing lending and liquidity.

Rediscounting: Lowering the interest rate on short-term debt instruments or loans in order to move them in a tight market and add market liquidity.

Savings and Loan (S&L) Bank: See "Thrift."

Security: A tradable asset (or financial instrument) of any kind, broadly categorized into equity, debt, or derivative classifications.

Setoff: The ability of a debtor to reduce the amount of debt by an amount the creditor owes to the debtor from another avenue of funds.

Short Sale: A sale in which an investor sells borrowed securities in anticipation of a price decline.

Stock: A security signifying an ownership percentage in a company, also referred to as "shares" or "equity."

Subprime Loan: A loan offered at an interest rate above prime to individuals whose credit scores are low, or who otherwise present a greater risk than those receiving prime rate loans.

Thrift: A financial institution mostly focused on taking deposits and originating mortgages, originally designed to take the business of making mortgage loans away from insurance companies. Trusts tend to be smaller and more community-focused than commercial or investment banks. In the years leading up to the S&L crisis, many thrifts were allowed to expand their services to include more speculative investments, with disastrous results.

Trust: A legal construct in which a business entity consolidates power over a particular commodity or product, such as steel, copper, or oil.

Underwriter: A company or other entity that administers the public issuance and distribution of securities, collaborates with the issuer to determine the offering price of the securities, and buys the securities from the issuer and sells them to investors, receiving underwriting fees from issuers and profits from selling the issue to investors.

Wash Sale: A sale in which an investor sells a security that has lost value to claim a capital loss for tax purposes, and repurchases it for a bargain. Also done to fabricate the appearance of demand, to entice other investors to buy or sell the security.

ACKNOWLEDGMENTS

THIS BOOK WOULD NOT HAVE BEEN POSSIBLE WITHOUT THE ASSISTANCE AND support of many people, from my friends and family to researchers to archivists to fellow authors, journalists, and historians who generously shared their energy and knowledge. To thank everyone who participated in *All the Presidents' Bankers* would be to invite the internal sounds of award-ceremony music signaling a conclusion to the list. However, there are people without whom this book simply wouldn't have come into being, and certainly not within the time frame it did.

I'm grateful to my chief editor and "coach," Carl Bromley, Dan LoPreto for his editorial eye, Mark Sorkin for his meticulous copyediting, Melissa Raymond for moving things along, Jaime Leifer and her marketing staff, and the rest of the wonderful Nation Books team for their energy and support—they "got" the concept immediately and more clearly than even I did. Thank you to Katrina vanden Heuvel for her support for my work through various *Nation* channels over the years.

I'm deeply thankful to my agent, Andrew Stuart, who pressed me to do this book even when its scope was so daunting to me. My heartfelt appreciation to my publicist, Celeste Balducci, whose support over the years has been a delight and necessity.

I'd like to especially thank my interns and researchers, who passionately devoted so many hours, weekends, and holidays to exploring the motivations and actions of former presidents and bankers. I'm grateful for the heroic efforts of Alex Amend, Craig Wilson, Krisztina Ugrin, Johnnie Kallas, Laura Huley, Clark Merrefield, and Elaine Yu.

The preservation of historical archives requires general praise. It is astonishing to consider the volume of material that has been preserved. Perusing century-old hand-written letters and emails of recent times, as well as spending time in the various presidential libraries across America—from Hyde Park, New York; to Atlanta, Georgia; to Yorba Linda and Simi Valley, California; to Abilene, Kansas; to Independence, Missouri; to Little Rock, Arkansas; and to College Station and Austin, Texas—was a tremendous experience.

I'd like to thank all the archivists who helped me with this project, including at the libraries and collections of Franklin Delano Roosevelt, Winthrop Aldrich, John McCloy, Harry S. Truman, Dwight D. Eisenhower, John F. Kennedy, Lyndon Baines Johnson, Richard Nixon, Jimmy Carter, Ronald Reagan, George H. W. Bush, and William J. Clinton, as well as the Jekyll Island Museum. Special thanks to Allen Fisher at the LBJ library for teaching me the "archive ropes," to Marta Brunner at the UCLA library, who helped me access ample Woodrow Wilson records and shared all sorts of tricks to find information, and to the entire staff at the Carter Library, whose warmth was truly special. I'm grateful for the West Hollywood library, where I spent hundreds of hours while working on this book. Thanks also to Miles Rapoport, Rich Benjamin, and everyone at Demos. My gratitude to Morris Berman for his guidance though the creation of this book.

Lastly, I thank my partner, Lukas, and furry partner, Homer, for just being there with patience and love.

This book has not just been an exploration of relationships and people, but of the very character of the American political-financial system. A vast amount of material wound up on the "cutting-room floor" in the process. Any mistakes in this book are solely my own.

NOTES

Epigraph

1. Herbert Hoover, *The Cabinet and the Presidency 1920–1933* (New York, NY: Macmillan, 1952), 327–328.

Introduction: When the President Needed the Bankers

1. Thomas Kessner, *Capital City: New York City and the Men Behind America's Rise to Economic Dominance, 1860–1900* (New York, NY: Simon & Schuster, 2003), 208.

2. Matthew Josephson, *The Robber Barons* (New York, NY: Harcourt, 1962), 394.

3. James Stillman was president of National City Bank until 1906, whereupon he shifted to the post of chairman and Frank Vanderlip took his slot as president.

4. Josephson, *Robber Barons*, 397.

5. John Moody, *The Masters of Capital* (New Haven, CT: Yale University Press, 1919), 63–65. According to Moody, Stillman's first "plaything" was a toy bank.

6. Josephson, *Robber Barons*, 399.

7. James Stillman Rockefeller became chair of National City Bank in 1959.

8. Brandeis was appointed to the Supreme Court by President Woodrow Wilson in 1916 and served until 1939.

9. Louis D. Brandeis, *Other People's Money and How the Bankers Use It* (Chevy Chase, MD: National Home Library Foundation, 1933), 15.

10. Josephson, *Robber Barons*, 409.

11. Ibid., 402.

12. Ibid., 409.

13. Frank A. Vanderlip and Boyden Sparkes, "From Farm Boy to Financier: Stories of Railroad Moguls," *Saturday Evening Post,* February 9, 1935.

14. "Men of Means" plaque outside the Sans Souci dwelling on Jekyll Island, Georgia.

15. Charles R. Morris, *The Tycoons* (New York, NY: Henry Holt, 2006), 235.

16. Josephon, *Robber Barons,* 297.

17. Ibid., 414.

18. George E. Mowry, *Theodore Roosevelt and the Progressive Movement* (Madison, WI: University of Wisconsin Press, 1946).

19. David Graham Phillips, *The Treason of the Senate* (New York, NY: Monthly Review Press, 1953), 10.

20. Theodore Roosevelt, "Man with the Muck Rake" speech, April 15, 1906, at www.pbs.org /wgbh/americanexperience/features/primary-resources/tr-muckrake/.

21. Phillips, *Treason of the Senate*, 24.

22. Louis Glackens, "He loves me!," April 17, 1907. Library of Congress Prints and Photographs division, at Theodore Roosevelt Digital Library, Dickinson State University, at www .theodorerooseveltcenter.org/Research/Digital-Library/Record.aspx?libID=o285736.

23. Theodore Roosevelt, *An Autobiography by Theodore Roosevelt,* prepared by The Project Gutenberg, based on an edition first published by Charles Scribner's Sons in 1920. The original was published in 1913.

24. "Panic of 1907," Federal Reserve Bank of Boston, 4.

25. Ibid., 5–6.

26. Ibid., 7–10.

27. Ellis W. Tallman and Jon R. Moen, "Lessons from the Panic of 1907," Federal Reserve Bank of Atlanta, *Economic Review*, May/June 1990, 5–6.

28. "Developments in Bank Situation," *New York Evening Telegram*, October 22, 1907.

29. Ibid.

30. Ibid.

31. Roosevelt, *An Autobiography*.

32. "Frank Vanderlip, Banker, Dies at 72," *New York Times*, June 30, 1937.

33. "Cortelyou Puts in $25,000,000," *New York Times*, October 24, 1907.

34. Ibid.

35. "Bankers Calm, Sky Clearing," *New York Times*, October 26, 1907.

36. "All Day Siege at Doors of Eight Banks," *New York Evening Telegram,* October 24, 1907.

37. During the Pujo hearings, Cortelyou testified that he met with Morgan and other big bankers in the evenings and was stationed at the subtreasury during the day, where he met with a "great many people of prominence in the banking business." In response to questioning about which national banks received the bulk of the $25 million, Cortelyou replied, "The national banks which could most quickly put up the collateral" and added that Morgan was the "leading spirit" of the conferences.

38. "Bankers Calm, Sky Clearing."

39. Ibid.

40. Tallman and Moen, "Lessons from the Panic of 1907," 11.

41. Ibid., 10.

42. Morris, *The Tycoons,* 250.

43. Edward M. Lamont, *The Ambassador from Wall Street* (Madison Books, 1994), 37.

44. Lamont, *Ambassador,* 39.

45. Ron Chernow, *The House of Morgan: An American Banking Dynasty and the Rise of Modern Finance* (New York, NY: Grove Press, 1990), 127–128.

46. Roosevelt, *An Autobiography*.

47. Letter from Samuel Untermyer, July 3, 1912, Woodrow Wilson Papers, Vol. 24. Arthur S. Link, ed., *The Papers of Woodrow Wilson* (Princeton, NJ: Princeton University Press, 1966).

48. Ibid.

49. M.A. Frank Moore Colby, ed., *The New International Year Book: A Compendium of the World's Progress for the Year 1907* (New York, NY: Dodd, Mead and Company, 1908), 262.

50. "John Pierpont Morgan: A Bank in Human Form," *New York Times,* November 10, 1907.

51. William Greider, *Secrets of the Temple: How the Federal Reserve Runs the Country* (New York, NY: Simon & Schuster, 1987), 273.

52. "Federal Aid Up to $150,000,000," *New York Times*, November 18, 1907.

53. Woodrow Wilson, Addresses at Three Schools, Some Ideals of Public Life, November 7, 1907, Wilson Papers, Vol. 17, 474.

54. Ibid.

55. Letter from Junius Spencer Morgan, January 10, 1909, Wilson Papers, Vol. 18.

56. Letter to Mary Allen Hulbert Peck, October 25, 1908, Wilson Papers, Vol. 18.

57. Letter to Frank Arthur Vanderlip, April 1, 1908, Wilson Papers, Vol. 18.

58. Letter to Melancthon Williams Jacobus, November 11, 1908, Wilson Papers, Vol. 18.

59. Letter from Frank Arthur Vanderlip, December 11, 1909, Wilson Papers, Vol. 19.

60. Franklin MacVeagh, formerly a wealthy wholesale grocer of Chicago, served as Secretary of the Treasury in the Taft administration.

61. Letter to Frank Arthur Vanderlip, December 11, 1909, Wilson Papers, Vol. 19.

62. Letter from Frank Arthur Vanderlip, December 17, 1909, Wilson Papers, Vol. 19.

63. Letter to Frank Arthur Vanderlip, December 20, 1909, Wilson Papers, Vol. 19. See also four news reports of Wilson's address, January 18, 1910, Wilson Papers, Vol. 20.

Chapter 1. The Early 1910s: Post-Panic Creature and Party Posturing

1. Nelson W. Aldrich Jr., *Old Money: The Mythology of Wealth in America* (New York, NY: Alfred A. Knopf, 1988). Senator Aldrich's grandson Nelson Aldrich Rockefeller became a four-term governor of New York and vice president under Gerald Ford.

2. "Monetary Inquirers Set Sail," *New York Times*, August 5, 1908.

3. Julie Miller, "Frieda Schiff Warburg," *Jewish Women: A Comprehensive Historical Encyclopedia,* Jewish Women's Archive website, at http://jwa.org/encyclopedia/article/warburg -frieda-schiff.

4. "World's Money Centre Here," *New York Times,* March 5, 1910.

5. Ibid.

6. "President Stillman Sails," *New York Times,* August 29, 1910.

7. Frank Vanderlip, *From Farm Boy to Financier* (New York, NY: D. Appleton-Century, 1935), 210.

8. Charles F. Speare, "Frank A. Vanderlip, Banker-Journalist," *The American Review of Reviews,* January–June 1908.

9. Vanderlip and Sparkes, "From Farm Boy to Financier."

10. Ibid.

11. Author interview with Jekyll Island Museum historical director John Hunter, February 7, 2013.

12. "Aldrich Not Badly Hurt," *New York Times,* October 22, 1910.

13. Author interview with John Hunter.

14. Ibid.

15. G. Edward Griffin, *The Creature from Jekyll Island,* 5th ed. (New York, NY: American Media, 2010), 5.

16. Vanderlip and Sparkes, "From Farm Boy to Financier."

17. Author interview with John Hunter. In the hotel where the Clubhouse once stood, there are two meeting rooms by the dining room hallway: one is marked "Aldrich," and the other is marked "Federal Reserve Room."

18. Vanderlip and Sparkes, "From Farm Boy to Financier."

19. "A Brief History of the Bureau of Engraving and Printing," paper prepared by the Historical Research Center, Washington, DC, 2004.

20. Federal Reserve Act, Section 16. "1. Issuance of Federal Reserve notes; nature of obligation; where redeemable: Federal Reserve notes, to be issued at the discretion of the Board of Governors of the Federal Reserve System for the purpose of making advances to Federal reserve banks through the Federal Reserve agents as hereinafter set forth and for no other purpose, are hereby authorized. The said notes shall be obligations of the United States and shall be receivable by all national and member banks and Federal Reserve banks and for all taxes, customs, and other public dues. They shall be redeemed in lawful money on demand at the Treasury Department of the United States, in the city of Washington, District of Columbia, or at any Federal Reserve bank."

21. Vanderlip and Sparkes, "From Farm Boy to Financier." In Vanderlip's account of the men at the Jekyll Island meetings, he omits Charles Norton, president of the First National Bank of New York, as do later versions of Griffin's *The Creature from Jekyll Island*. The Jekyll Island Museum includes Norton as one of the team members, but it admits that it has not come to a "conclusive" decision as to his presence.

22. Ibid.

23. "The Central Bank Question," *New York Times*, January 17, 1911.

24. "Partner of Morgan Bank Praises Bank Plan," *New York Times*, January 20, 1911.

25. "Aldrich Money Plan Praised in Speech," *New York Times*, February 5, 1911.

26. "Vanderlip on Bank Defects," *New York Times*, February 25, 1911.

27. Richard T. McCulley, *Banks and Politics During the Progressive Era* (New York, NY: Routledge, 2012), 228.

28. "Taft Advocates Currency Reform: State Bankers Pleased When He Endorses Aldrich's Reserve Bank Plan," *New York Times*, June 23, 1911.

29. "The Titanic Launched," *New York Times*, June 1, 1911.

30. "Money Trust Begins with Coffee," *New York Times*, May 16, 1912.

31. Charles A. Lindbergh Sr., *Banking and Currency and the Money Trust* (National Capital Press, 1913).

32. "The Money Trust at Work," *New York Times*, May 25, 1912.

33. "Questions Annoy Banks," *New York Times*, June 7, 1912.

34. "Untermyer Sees Taft," *New York Times*, September 26, 1912.

35. "Money Trust Inquiry Halts," *New York Times*, July 5, 1912.

36. John Wells Davidson, *A Crossroads of Freedom: The 1912 Campaign Speeches of Woodrow Wilson* (New Haven, CT: Yale University Press, 1956). In his "Speech of Acceptance, Delivered at Sea Girt, New Jersey," on August 7, 1912, Wilson said, "No mere bankers' plan will meet the requirements, no matter how honestly conceived. It should be a merchants' and farmers' plan as well, elastic in the hands of those who use it as an indispensable part of their daily business. I do not know enough about this subject to be dogmatic about it; I know only enough to be sure what the partnerships in it should be and that the control exercised over any system we may set up should be, as far as possible, a control emanating not from a single special class but from the general body and authority of the Nation itself."

37. Ferdinand Lundberg, *America's Sixty Families* (New York, NY: Vanguard Press, 1937), 114.

38. Vanderlip and Sparkes, "From Farm Boy to Financier."

39. Ibid.

40. "Wilson Departs with Labor Speech," *New York Times*, September 2, 1912.

41. Davidson, *A Crossroads of Freedom*, 433. Speech delivered at Georgetown, Delaware, October 17, 1912.

42. Ibid., 23. Speech of Acceptance, delivered at Sea Girt, New Jersey, August 7, 1912.

43. October 11, 1912, campaign speech, Wilson Papers, Vol. 24, 1912.

44. According to the November 6, 1912, edition of the *New York World,* the popular vote was Wilson 6,293,019, Roosevelt 4,119,507, Taft 3,484,956, and Debs 901,873. The vote in the Electoral College was Wilson 435, Roosevelt 88, and Taft 8.

45. "Thinks Only Wilson Will Curb Trusts," *New York Times,* November 4, 1912.

46. Letter from Samuel Untermyer, November 6, 1912, Wilson Papers, Vol. 12.

47. Letter to Untermyer, November 12, 1912, Wilson Papers, Vol. 12.

48. Henry Park Willis (1874–1937) was an adjunct professor and professor at Washington and Lee University from 1898 to 1905 and a professor of finance at George Washington University from 1905 to 1906 and 1907 to 1912. At various times after 1901, he was a financial writer and correspondent for the *New York Evening Post, Springfield Republican,* and *New York Journal of Commerce.* He was a consultant to the House Ways and Means Committee in 1911 and to the House Banking and Currency Committee in 1912. Fifteen years earlier, Willis had served on a private banker-sponsored commission to promote an earlier version of monetary reform.

49. Letter from Carter Glass, November 7, 1912, Wilson Papers, Vol. 12.

50. Glass and Willis conferred for two hours with Wilson in his home in Princeton on December 26. Wilson was in bed with a severe cold. The discussion centered around a draft of a banking and currency reform bill, which Willis had drawn up for Glass's subcommittee. It called for a decentralized, privately controlled reserve system with an unspecified number of local reserve banks, each having the full reserve banking system's power. Wilson agreed with most of the provisions of the draft but doubted that Willis's plan to give the comptroller of the currency general supervisory authority over the reserve system would provide sufficient coordination and control. Willis felt that the conversation indicated clearly that Wilson "was desirous of effecting a substantial degree of centralization, although heartily maintaining the concept of local self-control. . . . It appeared probable that he would favor an organization designed to control and supervise and that he felt no partiality to the idea of a central bank. He recognized that such an organization was politically impossible even if economically desirable, and that what was to be sought was the provision of those central banking powers which were unmistakably desirable and the elimination of those central banking powers which had caused danger in the past." Henry Parker Willis, *The Federal Reserve System: Legislation, Organization and Operation* (New York, 1912).

51. Letter from Carter Glass, December 29, 1912, Wilson Papers, Vol. 12.

52. "Taft Won't Aid Hunt for Bank Secrets: Declines to Order Controller Murray to Aid the Pujo Money Inquiry," *New York Times,* December 29, 1912.

53. "Investigation of Financial and Monetary Conditions in the United States under House Resolutions Nos. 429 and 504, Part 28," (Washington: Government Printing Office, 1913). Also referred to as the "Final Report of the Pujo Committee," February 28, 1913, at http://fraser.stlouisfed.org/docs/historical/house/money_trust/montru_pt28.pdf. Wash sales would be

employed in spades during the pre-Enron and WorldCom frauds of the early 2000s. Short sales would be used liberally in the same period and during the 2008 financial crisis.

54. "Final Report of the Pujo Committee," 89.

55. Brandeis, *Other People's Money,* 21.

56. Ibid., 91.

57. "Praise for Morgan at Finance Forum," *New York Times,* December 19, 1912.

58. "Mr. Morgan's Sermon," *New York Times,* December 22, 1912. See also "Preaching to the Preachers," *New York Times,* February 28, 1913.

59. Ron Chernow, *The House of Morgan* (New York, NY: Grove Press, 1990), 158.

60. Letter from Carter Glass, January 27, 1913, Wilson Papers, Vol. 27.

61. McAdoo married President Wilson's daughter, Eleanor Randolph Wilson, on May 7, 1914, at the White House.

62. Diary entry of Colonel House, April 11, 1913, Wilson Papers, Vol. 27.

63. Letter from Louis Dembitz Brandeis, June 14, 1913, Wilson Papers, Vol. 27.

64. Wilson had conferred with Glass, McAdoo, and Senator Owen at the White House during the evening of June 17. About this meeting, see *The New Freedom,* 120–121; Glass, *An Adventure in Constructive Finance,* 112–113; and Willis, *The Federal Reserve System,* 250–251.

65. Letter from Carter Glass, June 18, 1913, Wilson Papers, Vol. 27.

66. Thomas Edward Powell, *The Democratic Party of the State of Ohio: A Comprehensive History, Vol. 2* (The Ohio Publishing Company, 1913), 23.

67. Letter from Carter Glass, June 18, 1913, Wilson Papers, Vol. 27.

68. Address on Banking and Currency Reform to a Joint Session of Congress, June 23, 1913, Wilson Papers, Vol. 27.

69. Wilson signed the measure at 6:02 P.M. in the Oval Office before an audience including members of his family and the cabinet, Democratic leaders, and newspapermen.

70. The establishment and naming of *The Nation* magazine in July 1865 reflected this nationalist tide. See Eric Foner, *A Short History of Reconstruction* (New York, NY: Harper Perennial 1990), 10.

71. Remarks upon Signing the Federal Reserve Bill, December 23, 1913, Wilson Papers, Vol. 29, with minor corrections from the complete text in the *New York Times,* December 24, 1913.

72. Letter to Carter Glass, December 23, 1913, Wilson Papers, Vol. 29.

73. "Strong Is Chosen by Reserve Bank," *New York Times,* October 6, 1914. Strong served from October 5, 1914, until he died on October 16, 1928.

74. Chernow, *The House of Morgan,* 182.

75. "State Banks Seek Changes in the Law," *New York Times,* December 31, 1913.

76. William Greider, *Secrets of the Temple: How the Federal Reserve Runs the Country* (New York, NY: Simon & Schuster, 1989), 270.

77. Telegram to Joseph Patrick Tumulty, January 6, 1914, Wilson Papers, Vol. 29. On January 2, J. P. Morgan & Company announced that John Pierpont Morgan Jr. and four other members of the firm were resigning from their directorships in banks, railroads, and industrial companies. The announcement said further that there would be numerous other resignations from directorships by members of the firm in coming months. For detailed reports on the action and a complete list of the directorships, see the January 3 and January 4, 1914, editions of the *New York Times.*

78. Telegram from Joseph Patrick Tumulty, January 6, 1914, Wilson Papers, Vol. 29.

79. Letter to Paul Moritz Warburg, April 30, 1914, Wilson Papers, Vol. 29.

Chapter 2. The Mid-1910s: Bankers Go to War

1. "Wilson and Morgan Have Friendly Chat," *New York Times*, July 3, 1914.

2. Remarks at a press conference, July 2, 1914, Wilson Papers, Vol. 30.

3. "Austria Formally Declares War on Serbia," *New York Times,* July 28, 1914.

4. Introduction, Wilson Papers, Vol. 30.

5. Letter from William Jennings Bryan, August 10, 1914, Wilson Papers, Vol. 30.

6. Ibid.

7. Woodrow Wilson, "Message to Congress," 63rd Congress, Second Session, Senate Document No. 566 (Washington, 1914), 3–4.

8. Edward M. Lamont, *The Ambassador from Wall Street: The Story of Thomas W. Lamont, J.P. Morgan's Chief Executive* (Madison Books, 1994), 68.

9. Personal letter from John Pierpont Morgan Jr., September 4, 1914, Wilson Papers, Vol. 30.

10. Ibid.

11. Ibid.

12. Introduction, Wilson Papers, Vol. 31.

13. Wilson Papers, Vol. 31. Printed in the *New York World,* October 16, 1914.

14. Priscilla Roberts, "Frank A. Vanderlip and the National City Bank During the First World War," *Essays in Economic and Business History* (2002), 145.

15. Letter from Vanderlip to Stillman, December 31, 1915, Vanderlip papers, box 6, series B-1.

16. Introduction, Wilson Papers, Vol. 33.

17. Letter from John Pierpont Morgan Jr., May 14, 1915, Wilson Papers, Vol. 33.

18. Lamont, *The Ambassador from Wall Street,* 62.

19. Chernow, *House of Morgan,* 194.

20. Lamont, *The Ambassador from Wall Street,* 74.

21. Introduction, Wilson Papers, Vol. 35.

22. Introduction, Wilson Papers, Vol. 36.

23. Wilson Reappoints Warburg to Federal Reserve Board, Wilson Papers, Vol. 39. See also Letter from Warburg, August 10, 1916, Wilson Papers, Vol. 39.

24. The men had come from New York in two special trains. They brought a band with them, and their march onto the lawn, stepped in time to a refrain of "Four more years for Wilson," made the event a rousing political rally. Time and again the crowd interrupted Wilson with shouts of "We want peace!" See "Wilson Thrills Crowds, Bitterly Flays Opponents," *New York Times,* October 1, 1916. See also *New York World,* October 1, 1916.

25. Wilson Papers, Vol. 39, with additions from the text in the *New York Times,* September 30, 1916.

26. Introduction, Wilson Papers, Vol. 38.

27. Letter from John Skelton Williams, December 6, 1916, including press release, December 4, 1916, Wilson Papers, Vol. 40.

28. President Woodrow Wilson, Thirty-third Inaugural Address, March 5, 1917.

29. Letter from Edward Mandell House, March 25, 1917, Wilson Papers, Vol. 41.

30. Rodney Carlisle, "The Attacks on U.S. Shipping that Precipitated American Entry into World War I," *The Northern Mariner* XVII, no. 3 (July 2007): 41–66.

31. Introduction, Wilson Papers, Vol. 41.

32. From the Diary of Thomas W. Brahany, April 5, 1917, Wilson Papers, Vol. 41.

33. Letter from J. P. Morgan Jr., April 4, 1917, Wilson Papers, Vol. 41.

34. Brahany Diary, April 5, 1917.

35. Letter to John Pierpont Morgan Jr., April 7, 1917, Wilson Papers, Vol. 42.

36. Letter from William Gibbs McAdoo, April 10, 1917, Wilson Papers, Vol. 42.

37. Enclosure to letter from William Gibbs McAdoo, April, 10, 1917, Wilson Papers, Vol. 42.

38. Sun Wong Kang and Hugh Rocknoff, "Capitalising Patriotism: The Liberty Bonds of World War I," National Bureau of Economic Research, January 2006, at http://www.nber.org /papers/w11919.

39. Chernow, *House of Morgan,* 203.

40. Letter from Edward House with enclosure, July 17, 1917, Wilson Papers, Vol. 43. Other top lenders included US Steel Corporation with $30 million and the National Bank of Commerce with $17 million.

41. "C.E. Mitchell, 78, Banker, Is Dead," *New York Times,* December 15, 1955.

42. Introduction, Wilson Papers, Vol. 45.

43. Letter from Lamont, January 9, 1918, Wilson Papers, Vol. 45.

44. Lamont, *The Ambassador from Wall Street,* 94.

45. Confidential letter from William Gibbs McAdoo with enclosure, December 14, 1917, Wilson Papers, Vol. 45.

46. "Frank A. Vanderlip Is Back: National City President Called Here by James Stillman's Death," *New York Times,* March 22, 1918.

47. Priscilla Roberts, "Frank A. Vanderlip and the National City Bank During the First World War," *Essays in Economic and Business History* (2002): 157–159.

48. "Vanderlip Quit Bank to Get Time to Think," *New York Times,* June 21, 1919.

49. "Germans on the Run, Time to Hit Hard, March Declares," *New York Times,* August 11, 1918.

50. Memorandum of a conversation between Lamont and Wilson, October 4, 1918, Wilson Papers, Vol. 51. The memo was based on notes Lamont wrote during or immediately after the interview.

51. Lamont appointed Sedgwick, editor of *The Atlantic Monthly* and president of the Atlantic Monthly Company, as one of the three trustees of the *Evening Post.*

52. Memorandum of a conversation, October 4, 1918.

53. Letter from Herbert Clark Hoover, November 2, 1918, Wilson Papers, Vol. 51.

54. Introduction, Wilson Papers, Vol. 53.

Chapter 3. The Late 1910s: Peace Treaties and Domestic Politics

1. Woodrow Wilson, William Bayard Hale, ed., *The New Freedom* (New York and Garden City: Doubleday, Page and Company, 1913).

2. Office of the Historian, State Department, Travels of President Woodrow Wilson, at http://history.state.gov/departmenthistory/travels/president/wilson-woodrow.

3. Woodrow Wilson, Address on the League of Nations, September 25, 1919, in J. Michael Hogan, ed., "Voices of Democracy: The U.S. Oratory Project," 2006, at http://voicesofdemocracy .umd.edu/wilson-the-pueblo-speech-speech-text/.

4. Letter from Thomas Lamont, March 19, 1919, Wilson Papers, Vol. 56.

5. From the Diary of Colonel House, March 24, 1919, Wilson Papers, Vol. 56.

6. From the Diary of Vance Criswell McCormick, March 31, 1919, Wilson Papers, Vol. 56.

7. Dulles believed it was dangerous to hold Germany responsible for high war reparations. Later, given Wilson's failure to gain US support for the League of Nations, he realized the necessity of obtaining strong domestic support for foreign policy.

8. Introduction, Wilson Papers, Vol. 59.

9. Letter from Thomas William Lamont, with enclosure, Financial Conditions in Europe, Paris, May 15, 1919, Wilson Papers, Vol. 59.

10. Ibid.

11. From the Diary of Dr. Grayson, May 24, 1919, Wilson Papers, Vol. 59.

12. The subject of Vanderlip's address was the economic problems Western Europe faced in the aftermath of the war. He declared that only the United States could provide the financial credits necessary to enable the European nations to restart their industries and transportation systems. The full text of his speech was printed in the *New York Times* on May 27, 1919.

13. Joseph Patrick, Tumulty memo, June 4, 1919, Wilson Papers, Vol. 60.

14. Ibid.

15. "Trade World Issue," *New York Times,* January 16, 1921.

16. Letter from Thomas William Lamont, June 5, 1919, Wilson Papers, Vol. 60. Lamont's letter included an enclosure, based on information he requested from Morrow, marked "For Auchincloss only from Polk: Please deliver the following to Lamont from Morrow." The publication of the official summary of the terms of the preliminary peace treaty with Germany came as a great shock to Herbert David Croly, the editor of *The New Republic,* and to his editorial associate Walter Lippmann. They both believed that it represented a betrayal of the principles of the Fourteen Points and that its harsh terms could only add to future conflict. At a conference held sometime between May 10 and May 13, they and the other members of the editorial staff decided that the magazine had to oppose the treaty, regardless of the cost in terms of influence and circulation.

17. "Davison Takes Charge," *New York Times*, May 16, 1917.

18. From the Diary of Dr. Grayson, June 11, 1919, Wilson Papers, Vol. 60.

19. From the Diary of Vance Criswell McCormick, June 11, 1919, Wilson Papers, Vol. 60.

20. Telegram from Frank Lyon Polk to the American Mission, Washington, June 11, 1919, Wilson Papers, Vol. 60.

21. Ibid.

22. Enclosed copy of cable to Tumulty with treaty suggestions from Lamont, Wilson Papers, Vol. 60.

23. Letter from Thomas William Lamont, June 13, 1919, Wilson Papers, Vol. 60.

24. "Export Bank Bill Passed by Senate," *New York Times,* September 10, 1919.

25. Memorandum by Robert Lansing, Signing of the Treaty of Peace with Germany at Versailles, June 28, 1919, Wilson Papers, Vol. 61.

26. From Herbert Clark Hoover, July 5, 1919, Wilson Papers, Vol. 61.

27. Ibid.

28. Ibid.

29. Personal Letter from Thomas William Lamont, July 11, 1919, Wilson Papers, Vol. 61.

30. Henry Cabot Lodge to James Grover McDonald, July 10, 1919, Wilson Papers, Vol. 61.

31. Introduction, Wilson Papers, Vol. 62.

32. News report: "Wilson Continues Firm: Tells Senators Smaller Nations Would Oppose Treaty Modification," July 23, 1919, Wilson Papers, Vol. 61.

33. Letter from Thomas William Lamont, July 25, 1919, Wilson Papers, Vol. 61.

34. "Food Problems at the Fore," Wilson Papers, Vol. 62. The memo also said, "Walter [Walker] D. Hines, Director of Railroads, F.B. [William B.] Colver of the Federal Trade Commission, and Assistant Sec Leffingwell of the Treasury Department were appointed members of the Committee" to explore the domestic problem.

35. Letter to Thomas William Lamont, August 1, 1919, Wilson Papers, Vol. 62.

36. Letter from Robert Lansing, with enclosure from Breckinridge Long to Robert Lansing, August 14, 1919, Wilson Papers, Vol. 62.

37. Letter to Robert Lansing, August 14, 1919, Wilson Papers, Vol. 62.

38. Letter from Thomas William Lamont, August 25, 1919, Wilson Papers, Vol. 62.

39. Introduction, Wilson Papers, Vol. 63.

40. Letter from Thomas William Lamont, September 10, 1919, Wilson Papers, Vol. 62.

41. Arthur S. Link, "A Disabled President," *Constitution,* Spring/Summer 1992, 8.

42. Introduction, Wilson Papers, Vol. 66.

43. The Treaty of Versailles, official Senate history records.

44. "President Bids Good-bye to his Cabinet," Wilson Papers, Vol. 67. Printed in the *New York Times,* March 2, 1921.

45. Wilson died of a stroke on February 4, 1924.

Chapter 4. The 1920s: Political Isolationism, Financial Internationalism

1. President Calvin Coolidge, Fourth Annual Message, December 7, 1926, at www .presidency.ucsb.edu/ws/index.php?pid=29567.

2. Barry Eichengreen and Marc Flandreau, "The Rise and Fall of the Dollar, or When Did the Dollar Replace Sterling as the Leading Reserve Currency?," draft paper prepared for the conference in honor of Peter Temin, Cambridge, May 9, 2008, 13, at http://emlab .berkeley.edu/~eichengr/rise_fall_dollar_temin.pdf.

3. Letters to Harding: Box 97–99 via Lamont, *Ambassador.*

4. Lamont, *Ambassador,* 171.

5. "Is Assured No Cancellation Was Promised," *Telegraph,* February 16, 1921.

6. Ibid.

7. Lamont, *Ambassador,* 173.

8. "Thomas W. Lamont to Tour Europe," *New York Times,* April 5, 1921.

9. Lamont, *Ambassador,* 174.

10. Ibid.

11. "Nye Calls Oil Deal a 'Slush Fund' Only," *New York Times*, May 30, 1928.

12. "Hoover Accepts Place in Cabinet; Keeps Relief Post," *New York Times,* February 25, 1921.

13. David Cannadine, *Mellon: An American Life,* 3rd ed. (New York, NY: Knopf, 2006).

14. "The Millionaire Yield of Pittsburgh," *Munsey's Magazine,* October 1911, 785.

15. University of Virginia Miller Center, "American President: Warren Gamaliel Harding: Domestic Affairs," at http://millercenter.org/president/harding/essays/biography/4.

16. "Mellon for Budget Bill," *New York Times,* April 9, 1921.

17. Allen Schick and Felix LoStracco, *The Federal Budget: Politics, Policy, Process* (Washington, DC: Brookings Institution Press, 2000), 14. See also US Government Accountability Office, "GAO: Working for Good Government Since 1921," at www.gao.gov/about/history/articles/working-for-good-government/01-introduction.html.

18. The White House, "Presidents: Warren G. Harding," at www.whitehouse.gov/about/presidents/warrenharding.

19. Miller Center, "Harding: Foreign Affairs."

20. Herbert Hoover, *The Memoirs of Herbert Hoover: The Cabinet and the Presidency, 1920–1933* (New York, NY: Macmillan, 1952), 47.

21. Ibid., 185.

22. US State Department, Office of the Historian, "Milestones 1921–1936: The Dawes Plan," at http://history.state.gov/milestones/1921–1936/Dawes.

23. Lamont, *Ambassador,* 186.

24. Ibid., 188.

25. "Germany Admits Default in Payment on Jan. 15," Associated Press, January 6, 1923.

26. "Italy's Progress Lauded by Lamont," *New York Times,* April 15, 1925.

27. "Lamont and Kahn Defend Mussolini," *New York Times*, January 24, 1926.

28. "Coolidge Takes Oath of Office," *New York Times,* August 3, 1923.

29. David Greenberg, "Keeping It Cool with Silent Cal," *New York Sun*, December 20, 2006.

30. Lundberg, *America's Sixty Families*, 150.

31. "Coolidge Tries a New Method," *New York Times*, September 16, 1923.

32. Lundberg, *America's Sixty Families,* 139.

33. Harold Nicolson, *Wall Street and the Security Markets* (New York, NY: Harcourt, Brace, 1935), 125–128.

34. Calvin Coolidge, *The Autobiography of Calvin Coolidge* (New York, NY: Cosmopolitan Book Corporation, 1929), 174.

35. Ibid., 28.

36. Ibid., 181.

37. Lamont, *Ambassador,* 201–203.

38. "Bankers Blaze Way for a German Loan," *New York Times,* July 28, 1924.

39. "Paris Cool to German Loan," *New York Times,* September 5, 1924.

40. Lamont, *Ambassador,* 207.

41. Ibid.

42. B. J. C. McKercher, ed., *Anglo-American Relations in the 1920s* (University of Alberta Press, 1990), 156. Letter from J. P. Morgan & Company to J. P. Morgan, October 14, 1924, no. 24/2707.

43. Miller Center, "Harding: Foreign Affairs."

44. Hoover, *Memoirs,* 89.

45. Andrew W. Mellon, *Taxation: The People's Business* (New York, NY: Macmillan, 1924), 17.

46. "Coolidge Declares Press Must Foster America's Idealism," *New York Times,* January 18, 1925.

47. "Andrew W. Mellon's Ignorance," *The Nation,* May 28, 1924.

48. Donald Barlett, *America: Who Really Pays the Taxes* (New York, NY: Touchstone, 1994), 65.

49. Lundberg, *America's Sixty Families,* 167.

50. David Cannadine, *Mellon: An American Life* (New York, NY: Random House, 2006), 318.

51. David Greenberg, *Calvin Coolidge* (New York, NY: Times Books, 2006), 78.

52. Earnest Elmo Calkins, *Business, the Civilizer* (Boston, MA: Little, Brown and Company, 1928), 13.

53. "Mitchell Expects Loan's Success," *New York Times,* September 12, 1924.

54. "The Week Reviewed," *Barron's,* September 28, 1925, 4.

55. Ibid.

56. Greenberg, *Calvin Coolidge,* 90.

57. "Mitchell Expresses Confidence in Cuba," *New York Times,* January 27, 1922.

58. "Sees Remarkable Recovery in Cuba," *New York Times,* January 31, 1922.

59. "1924 a Banner Year for New York Banks," *New York Times,* January 31, 1925.

60. "Optimism in Trade Justified, He Says," *New York Times,* July 24, 1925.

61. Donald L. Barlett and James B. Steele, *America: Who Really Pays the Taxes?* (New York, NY: Touchstone, 1994), 66.

62. President Calvin Coolidge, Fourth Annual Message, December 7, 1926, at www .presidency.ucsb.edu/ws/index.php?pid=29567.

63. Hoover, *Memoirs,* 89.

64. "Predicts Prosperity Brought by New Ford," *New York Times,* December 10, 1927.

65. Ibid.

66. Benjamin M. Anderson Jr., "Cheap Money, Gold, and Federal Reserve Bank Policy," *Chase Economic Bulletin,* 4, no. 3 (August 4, 1924).

67. "Hungry Reporter Complains About Money Wizards Delaying Dinner," Associated Press/United Press International, January 13, 1925.

68. C. W., "The National City Fiasco," *The Nation,* January 1, 1930.

69. "Washington Sees 1928 Field Open; Some Talk of Drafting Coolidge," *New York Times,* August 2, 1927.

70. Leo Grebler, David M. Blank, and Louis Winnick, *Capital Formation in Residential Real Estate: Trends and Prospects* (Princeton, NJ: NBER and Princeton University Press, 1956), 350. See also www.library.hbs.edu/hc/crises/forgotten.html#fn23.

71. The White House website, "Herbert Hoover 1929–1933," at www.whitehouse.gov/about /presidents/herberthoover.

72. Laurence Todd, "Government by Millionaires," *The Nation,* March 27, 1929.

73. Ibid.

74. Lamont, *Ambassador,* 248.

75. Anna J. Schwartz, "The Misuse of the Fed's Discount Window," Review, St. Louis Fed, September/October 1992, 58.

76. *Federal Reserve Bulletin,* vol. 15 (November 1929), at http://fraser.stlouisfed.org/docs /publications/FRB/1920s/frb_111929.pdf.

77. "Stocks on the Bargain Counter!" *Forbes*, November 15, 1929.

78. "Governor," *Time*, March 31, 1930.

79. "Wiggin Now Head of Chase National," *New York Times*, January 12, 1911.

80. "Nothing Resounding," *Time*, August 2, 1931.

81. Ibid.

82. Ibid.

83. "Billion Dollar Bank Formed by Merger with Chase National," *New York Times*, February 12, 1926.

84. "Banker Upholds Debt Reduction," *New York Times*, January 10, 1927.

85. Ibid.

86. Advertisement for the National City Bank, *The American Magazine*, July–December 1921.

87. "Troubles of Mitchell," *Time*, November 18, 1929.

88. Ibid.

89. Drexel Burnham Lambert's Ivan Boesky and Michael Milken shared that late 1980s distinction of selling bonds for far more than they were really worth. They later went to jail, and landed Drexel the largest fine in banking history as of that date.

90. Stock Exchange Practices: Hearings Before a Subcommittee of the Committee on Banking and Currency, US Senate, Seventy-second Congress, Second Session, on S. Res. 84 and S. Res. 239, Resolutions to Thoroughly Investigate Practices of Stock Exchanges with Respect to the Buying and Selling and the Borrowing and Lending of Listed Securities, the Values of Such Securities and the Effects of Such Practices, February 21, 1933. (National City: Continuation of Richard Whitney Testimony). At http://fraser.stlouisfed.org/publications /sensep/issue/3912/download/64693/19330221_sensep_pt06.pdf.

91. Paul Gomme and Peter Rupert, "Per Capita Income Growth and Disparity in the United States, 1929–2003," *Economic Commentary: Federal Reserve Bank of Cleveland*, August 15, 2004.

92. "Damnation of Mitchell," *Time*, March 6, 1933.

93. "Bankers Break Money Squeeze," *United Press*, March 28, 1929.

94. W. F. Wamsley, "The Ruler of the World's Largest Bank," *New York Times*, September 29, 1929.

95. "Norris Urges Mitchell to Quit Reserve Bank," *United Press*, March 31, 1929.

96. No senator demanded a Fed–private banker resignation again until Vermont Independent Bernie Sanders did of JPMorgan Chase chairman Jamie Dimon, in June 2012. Mitchell remained through his term. Then, as now, no president demanded any such thing.

97. "Stock Slump Revives Talk of Investigation," *American Banker*, October 28, 1929.

98. "Mitchell Warns of Undue Speculation," *Universal Press*, March 29, 1929.

99. Wamsley, "The Ruler."

100. John Kenneth Galbraith, *The Great Crash, 1929* (New York, NY: Houghton Mifflin Harcourt, 2009), 151–154.

101. Chernow, *House of Morgan*.

102. "Mitchell Regards Our Business Is Sound," *New York Times*, October 9, 1929.

103. Letter from Thomas W. Lamont to President Herbert Hoover, National Archives and Records Administration, PPF 1072, October 19, 1929.

Chapter 5. 1929: The Room at 23 Wall, Crash, and Big-Six Take

1. "Radicals: A Jaunty Young Man," *Time*, May 19, 1923.

2. "Frequently Asked Questions," Herbert Hoover Presidential Library and Museum, at http://hoover.archives.gov/info/faq.html#chicken.

3. "Financiers Ease Tension: Five Wall Street Bankers Hold Two Meetings at Morgan Office," *New York Times*, October 25, 1929.

4. John Kenneth Galbraith, *The Great Crash, 1929* (New York, NY: Houghton Mifflin Harcourt, 2009), 74.

5. B. C. Forbes, "Stocks on the Bargain Counter!," *Forbes*, November 15, 1929.

6. "Bankers Halt Stock Debacle," *Wall Street Journal*, October 25, 1929.

7. "Business Is Sound, Bankers Declare," *Daily Boston Globe*, October 25, 1929.

8. "Banks Restore Stability to Raging Stocks," *Chicago Tribune*, October 26, 1929.

9. "Financiers Ease Tension."

10. "Banking Buoys Up Stricken Stocks," *New York Times*, October 27, 1929.

11. "Financiers Ease Tension."

12. Richard Hiltzik, *The New Deal: A Modern History* (New York, NY: Free Press, 2011), 178.

13. "Richard Whitney, 86, Dies; Headed Stock Exchange," *New York Times*, December 6, 1974.

14. Evan W. Thomas, "The Clubs: Pale but Still Breathing," *Harvard Crimson*, September 20, 1971, at www.thecrimson.com/article/1971/9/20/the-clubs-pale-but-still-breathing/.

15. "End of a World," *Time*, November 7, 1949.

16. Ibid.

17. "Financiers Ease Tension."

18. "Shortage of Bankers Bills Expected to Lift Bond Prices," *New York Times*, October 26, 1929.

19. Forbes, "Stocks on the Bargain Counter!"

20. "Record Christmas Bonuses Are Expected as Rewards in Brokerage Houses This Year," *New York Times*, November 3, 1929.

21. Eighty years later, headlines would be similar. In early January 2010, a year after the biggest bank bailout in US history began, the *New York Times* reported, "Bank Bonuses, Bigger than Ever."

22. "Stock Slump Revives Talk of Investigation," *American Banker*, October 28, 1929.

23. "Federal Reserve Bulletin," Board of Governors of the Federal Reserve System, November 1929, 703.

24. Ibid.

25. "TW Lamont Sees Market as Normal, Morgan Partner Speaks for Banking Group After an Informal Meeting," *New York Times*, November 16, 1929.

26. "Bankers to Cooperate, Four of American Association Chosen for Capital Conference," *New York Times*, November 27, 1929.

27. Galbraith, *The Great Crash*, 139.

28. *The Pecora Investigation: Stock Exchange Practices and the Causes of the 1929 Wall Street Crash* (New York, NY: Cosimo, 2010), 325.

29. Ibid., 325.

30. Ibid.

31. Charles D. Ellis and James R. Vertin, *Wall Street People: True Stories of the Great Barons of Finance* (Hoboken, NJ: Wiley, 2003), 188.

32. Jerry Markham, *A Financial History of the United States: Volume II* (Armonk, NY: M. E. Sharpe, 2002), 146.

33. "History," The Roosevelt Hotel, at www.theroosevelthotel.com/defaultaspx?pg=history.

34. Herbert Hoover, "Remarks to a Chamber of Commerce Conference on the Mobilization of Business and Industry for Economic Stabilization," December 5, 1929, posted by Gerhard Peters and John T. Woolley, American Presidency Project, at www.presidency.ucsb.edu/ws/?pid=22023. The president spoke at 10:15 A.M. in the assembly room of the Chamber of Commerce in Washington, DC. The address was also broadcast over a chain of National Broadcasting Company stations.

Chapter 6. The Early 1930s: Tenuous Times, Tax-Evading Titans

1. "National City Head Sees Bright Future," *Atlanta Constitution*, January 16, 1930.

2. "Dow Jones Industrial Average Index Chart," Yahoo Finance, at http://finance.yahoo.com/echarts?s=^dji+interactive.

3. Herbert Hoover, "Address to the Chamber of Commerce of the United States," American Presidency Project, at www.presidency.ucsb.edu/ws/?pid=22185.

4. "Federal Reserve Bulletin," Federal Reserve Board 16 (Washington, DC: Government Printing Office, October 1930), 613.

5. Ibid., 615.

6. Paul B. Trescott, "The Failure of the Bank of United States, 1930," *Journal of Money, Credit and Banking* 24 (August 1992): 384.

7. Liaquat Ahamed, *Lords of Finance: The Bankers Who Broke the World* (New York, NY: Penguin Group, 2009), 388.

8. "Bank's Depositors Get Loan Aid Today," *New York Times,* December 16, 1930.

9. Jonathan Alter, *The Defining Moment: FDR's Hundred Days and the Triumph of Hope* (New York, NY: Simon & Schuster Paperbacks, 2007), 77.

10. "Constituent Charter of the Bank for International Settlements," *BIS Basic Texts*, Bank for International Settlements, January 20, 1930.

11. "Business: Bankers' Outlook," *Time*, January 19, 1931.

12. Donald R. Wells, *The Federal Reserve System: A History* (Jefferson, NC: McFarland & Company, 2004), 45.

13. Federal Reserve Archive, "The Discount Rate Controversy Between the Federal Reserve Board and the Federal Reserve Bank of New York," Document X-6737, November 1930, at http://fraser.stlouisfed.org/docs/meltzer/bogsub110130.pdf.

14. "National Affairs: Reserve Review," *Time*, February 16, 1931.

15. "International: Nothing Resounding," *Time*, August 24, 1931.

16. Ibid.

17. For more on dollar-to-marks currency conversion, see www.history.ucsb.edu/faculty/marcuse/projects/currency.htm. See also Gianni Toniolo, *Central Bank Cooperation at the Bank for International Settlements, 1930–1973* (Cambridge, UK: Cambridge University Press, 2005), 100.

18. Ibid.

19. Aurel Schubert, *The Credit-Anstalt Crisis of 1931* (Cambridge, England: Cambridge University Press, 1991), 99.

20. Drew Pearson, "The Washington Merry-Go-Round," *Spokane Daily Chronicle*, May 2, 1941.

21. "Bankers Sending Dulles to Berlin," *New York Times*, May 19, 1931.

22. Drew Pearson, "Dulles' Early Defense of Germany Laid to Clients' Investments," *United Feature Syndicate*, September 28, 1944, at http://tinyurl.com/c498bvu.

23. "International: Nothing Resounding," *Time*.

24. "100 Largest Banks Show Deposit Gain," *New York Times*, January 20, 1931. See also Thomas Ferguson and Peter Temin, *Made in Germany: The German Currency Crisis of 1931* (Cambridge, MA: Massachusetts Institute of Technology, 2001), 51–52.

25. Jerry W. Markham, *A Financial History of the United States* (New York, NY: M. E. Sharpe, 2002), 71–72.

26. Herbert Hoover, "The President's News Conference," June 20, 1931, posted online by Gerhard Peters and John T. Woolley, American Presidency Project, at www.presidency.ucsb.edu/ws/?pid=22719#axzz2gP1iPE3o.

27. Ibid.

28. "Mr. Hoover, Call Congress!" *The Nation*, August 12, 1931.

29. "Federal Reserve Bulletin," Federal Reserve Board 16 (March 1930), 100.

30. Irving Bernstein, *The Lean Years* (Chicago, IL: Haymarket Books, 2010), 313.

31. Hoover, *Memoirs*, vi.

32. "The Administration: The Sky Room's the Limit," *Time*, July 7, 1950.

33. "Increase in Federal Reserve Bank Credit; More Money in Circulation, Report Shows," *New York Times*, May 6, 1932.

34. S. Palmer Harman, "Finance: The Bond-Purchase Plan," *The Nation*, May 4, 1932.

35. Patman Address to the House of Representatives regarding Mellon's impeachment: Congressional Record—House of Representatives, January 6, 1932, 1399–1401.

36. "Patman Cites High Crime by Head of Treasury," *The Milwaukee Sentinel*, January 7, 1932.

37. Leslie Geary Haggin, "Tax Troubles of the Rich and Famous," *CNN Money*, February 20, 2003.

38. "Mellon Drafted Envoy to London," *The Spokesman-Review*, February 4, 1932.

39. "Taxation: U.S. v. Mellon, Lamont et al.," *Time*, March 19, 1934.

40. Noah Feldman, *Scorpions: The Battles and Triumphs of FDR's Great Supreme Court Justices* (New York, NY: Hachette Book Group, 2010).

41. Ibid.

42. "Revised Glass Bill Curbs Speculation, Helps Failed Banks," *New York Times*, March 18, 1932.

43. Federal Reserve Archive, Text of Glass-Steagall Act of 1932, Federal Reserve Bank of St. Louis, at http://fraser.stlouisfed.org/docs/historical/brookings/17620_04_0006.pdf.

44. 5443 Folder: Weinberg, Sidney J., FDR Library.

45. Charles D. Ellis, *The Partnership: The Making of Goldman Sachs* (New York, NY: Penguin Press, 2008).

46. Ibid.

47. Joseph Persico, "First Chapter: Roosevelt's Secret War," *New York Times*, October 21, 2001. See also "Story of Man Beside Roosevelt," *New York Times*, February 16, 1933.

48. "Newest Morgan Partner Won Fame in War Loans," *New York Times*, July 8, 1923.

49. PPF 866 Folder: Leffingwell, Russell C., 1935–1944 and cross-references, FDR Library.

50. Program transcript, *American Experience: FDR* (PBS), at www.pbs.org/wgbh/american experience/features/transcript/fdr-transcript/.

51. ASN Files, Box 52, Folder: Lamont, Thomas W., FDR Library.

52. Letter from Lamont, February 27, 1933, PPF File 70, Folder: Lamont, Thomas W., FDR Library.

53. Ibid.

54. "Morgan's Proffer of Stock to Woodin," *New York Times*, May 25, 1933.

55. William Silber, "Why Did FDR's Bank Holiday Succeed?," Federal Reserve Bank of New York, *Economic Policy Review*, July 2009.

56. United States Senate Committee on Banking and Currency, *Stock Exchange Practices: Report of the Committee on Banking and Currency* (Washington, DC: Government Printing Office, 1934), 102.

57. Ibid., 62.

58. Letter to James Perkins, March 9, 1933, PPF 54, Perkins, James H., FDR Library.

59. "J.D. Rockefeller, Jr., Weds Miss Aldrich," *New York Times*, October 10, 1901.

60. "Largest Bank in the World Formed in New York Merger," Associated Press, March 19, 1930.

61. "Wiggin Retires as Chase Executive," Associated Press, January 11, 1933.

62. A. Tabarrok, "The Separation of Commercial and Investment Banking: Morgans vs. Rockefellers," *Quarterly Journal of Austrian Economics* 1, no. 1 (1998): 1–18.

63. Research Correspondence I: Box 8, Aldrich Archives.

64. Thomas Ferguson, "From Normalcy to the New Deal: Industrial Structure, Party Competition, and American Public Policy in the Great Depression," *International Organization* 38, no. 1 (Winter 1984): 41–94.

65. "Chase Dropping Affiliate," *New York Times*, March 9, 1933.

66. Ibid.

67. Ferguson, "From Normalcy to the New Deal."

68. Chernow, *House of Morgan*, 362.

69. Letter to James H. Perkins, Letter to Winthrop W. Aldrich, March 9, 1933, PPF 54, Perkins, James H., FDR Library.

70. Letter from Winthrop W. Aldrich, March 12, 1933, PPF 54, Perkins, James H., FDR Library.

71. Franklin D. Roosevelt, Fireside Chat on Banking, March 12, 1933, American Presidency Project, at www.presidency.ucsb.edu/ws/?pid=14540#axzz2gP1iPE3o.

72. Ibid.

73. Letter to Mr. McIntyre from A. P. Giannini, March 16, 1933, PPF File 1135, Folder Giannini, A. P. 1933–1936, FDR Library.

74. *The Pecora Investigation: Stock Exchange Practices and the Causes of the 1929 Wall Street Crash* (New York, NY: Cosimo, 2010), 181–182.

75. "Mitchell Cleared, Weeps at Verdict, Ovation in Court," *New York Times*, June 23, 1933.

76. Galbraith, *The Great Crash, 1929*, 154.

77. Letter to E. S. Greenbaum, March 9, 1938, OF 3169, Folder: Mitchell, Charles E., 1933–1938, FDR Library.

78. Letter to Aldrich from M. A. Le Hand, March 27, 1933, FDR Library.

79. "Aldrich Hits at Private Bankers in Sweeping Plan for Reforms," *New York Times,* March 9, 1933.

80. Internal White House Memo from Daniel C. Roper, March 28, 1933, PPF 7591, Folder: Aldrich, Winthrop W., FDR Library.

81. Internal White House Memo from Huston Thompson, March 29, 1933, PPF 7591, Folder: Aldrich, Winthrop W., FDR Library.

82. Memo for the President. April 11, 1933, PPF File 70, Folder: Lamont, Thomas W., FDR Library.

83. United States Senate Committee on Banking and Currency, "Stock Exchange Practices: Report of the Committee on Banking and Currency," 321–322.

84. Statement of J. P. Morgan & Company submitted to Senate Committee on Banking and Currency at Its Hearings in Washington, May 23 to June 9, 1933, PPF, File/Folder 143: Morgan, Junius P. [J. P.], FDR Library.

85. Senate Committee on Banking and Currency, "Stock Exchange Practices: Hearings Before the Committee on Banking and Currency United States Senate, Part I: May 23, 24, and 25, 1933" (Washington, DC: Government Printing Office, 1934), 3.

86. Senate Committee on Banking and Currency, "Stock Exchange Practices: Hearings Before the Committee on Banking and Currency United States Senate, Part II: May 26, 31, June 1, 2, 5, 6, 7, 8, and 9, 1933" (Washington, DC: Government Printing Office, 1934), 558.

87. Chernow, *House of Morgan*, 373–374.

88. "Let the Banking Inquiry Go On!" *The Nation,* June 14, 1933.

89. "Glorifying the House of Morgan," *The Nation,* June 21, 1933.

90. Final Statement of J. P. Morgan & Company submitted to Senate Committee on Banking and Currency.

91. Galbraith, *The Great Crash, 1929*, 150.

92. "Aldrich Criticizes Bank Act 'Fallacy,'" *New York Times,* December 7, 1933.

93. May 22, 1933, PPF 7591, Folder: Aldrich, Winthrop W., FDR Library.

94. "Bank Deposit Bill Approved by House," *New York Times*, May 24, 1933.

95. PPF File 866, Leffingwell, Russell C. 1933–1934, FDR Library.

96. Telegram to Aldrich: M. H. McIntyre, Assistant Sec to the President, December 26, 1933, OF 1599, Folder: Chase National Bank, 1933–1943, FDR Library.

Chapter 7. The Mid- to Late 1930s: Policing Wall Street, World War II

1. Franklin D. Roosevelt: "Acceptance Speech for the Renomination for the Presidency, Philadelphia, Pa.," June 27, 1936. Posted online by Gerhard Peters and John T. Woolley, American Presidency Project, at www.presidency.ucsb.edu/ws/?pid=15314 #axzz2gP1iPE3o.

2. Economic History Association, "US Banking History: Civil War to World War II," Compiled by Richard S. Grossman, Wesleyan University, at http://eh.net/encyclopedia/article /grossman.banking.history.us.civil.war.wwii.

3. "Public Control," *The Nation,* February 21, 1934.

4. "House Members Invited to Floor of Exchange," *New York Times,* February 24, 1934.

5. "Fletcher's Statement on Stock 'Propaganda,'" *New York Times,* February 22, 1934.

6. "Roosevelt Wants 'Teeth' in Stock Exchange Bill; Seeks Speculation Limit," *New York Times,* March 26, 1934.

7. "New Leeway Put in Exchange Bill," *New York Times,* April 11, 1934.

8. Letter from Leffingwell, January 4, 1934, PPF File 866, Leffingwell, Russell C., 1933–1934, FDR Library.

9. Letter from Leffingwell, February 20, 1934, PPF File 866, Leffingwell, Russell C., 1933–1934, FDR Library.

10. Ibid.

11. Telegram to Winthrop Aldrich from McIntyre, February 14, 1934, OF 1599, Folder: Chase National Bank, 1933–1943, FDR Library.

12. Letter to Leffingwell from McIntyre, March 1, 1934, PPF File 866, Leffingwell, Russell C., 1933–1934, FDR Library.

13. Letter from Leffingwell, March 4, 1934, PPF File 866, Leffingwell, Russell C., 1933–1934, FDR Library.

14. Telegram to Aldrich from McIntyre, April 16, 1934, OF 1599, Folder: Chase National Bank, 1933–1943, FDR Library.

15. Memo for FDR f/McIntyre, April 30, 1934, OF 1599, Folder: Chase National Bank, 1933–1943, FDR Library.

16. "Chase Bank to Cut Ties with 2 Units," *New York Times,* May 11, 1934.

17. "City Bank Drops Its Security Unit," *New York Times,* June 5, 1934.

18. "J. M. Landis Slated for Stock Market Chief by Recess Appointment to Avoid Battle," *New York Times,* May 26, 1934.

19. Letter from Jack Morgan, June 8, 1934, FDR Library.

20. Letter to Jack Morgan, June 13, 1934, FDR Library.

21. "Kennedy Is Reported Chosen by President," *New York Times,* June 30, 1934.

22. Stock Exchange Practices: Hearings Before a Subcommittee of the Committee on Banking and Currency, US Senate, Seventy-third Congress, Second Session, on S. Res. 84 (72nd Congress) Resolutions to Thoroughly Investigate Practices of Stock Exchanges with Respect to the Buying and Selling and the Borrowing and Lending of Listed Securities and S.Res. 56 and S.Res. 97 (73rd Congress) Resolutions to Investigate the Matter of Banking Operations and Practices, February 21 to February 26, 73rd Cong. 6222 (1934) (Part 14 Alcohol Pools).

23. "J.P. Kennedy Has Excelled in Various Endeavors," *New York Times,* July 4, 1934.

24. "Kennedy Started as a Candy Vendor," *New York Times,* July 3, 1934.

25. "Four Men & One," *Time,* July 9, 1934.

26. Letter to Joe Kennedy, May 11, 1933, PPF File 207, Folder: Kennedy, Joseph P., 1933–1938, FDR Library.

27. "No Venom," *Time,* August 6, 1934.

28. "Whitney, Exchange Head, Approves Stand of Kennedy of Securities Commission," *New York Times,* July 27, 1934.

29. Letter from Giannini to McIntyre, September 2, 1934, PPF File 1135, Folder: Giannini, A.P., 1933–1936, FDR Library.

30. Notes from a New York dinner with bankers from Tom Lamont to FDR, October 1, 1934, PSF Box 141 Lamont, FDR Library.

31. "Reform & Realism," *Time,* July 22, 1935.

32. Richard Whalen, *The Founding Father: The Story of Joseph P. Kennedy* (Washington, DC: Regnery, 1993), 138–144.

33. October 10, 1936, PPF File 207, Folder: Kennedy, Joseph P., 1933–1938, FDR Library.

34. Address at the dinner of the Democrat Business Men's League of Massachusetts at the Hotel Copley-Plaza, Boston, October 24, 1936, PPF File 207, Folder: Kennedy, Joseph P., 1933–1938, FDR Library.

35. Sasoon G. Ward, "Giannini Fights Morgan," *The Nation*, June 26, 1935.

36. Ibid.

37. Frederick A. Bradford, "The Banking Act of 1935," *The American Economic Review* 25, no. 4 (December 1935): 661–672.

38. "Bank Bill Assailed by Guaranty Trust," *New York Times*, May 13, 1935.

39. "Menace to Nation Is Seen by Aldrich in Banking Bill," *New York Times*, May 15, 1935.

40. "Congress Extends Deposit Insurance," *New York Times*, June 28, 1935.

41. "New Bill Will Let Banks Underwrite Securities Again," *New York Times*, June 29, 1935.

42. "Glass Is Incensed by Bank Bill News," *New York Times*, June 30, 1935.

43. "Wall Street Bankers Split on Glass Bill," *New York Times*, July 6, 1935.

44. "Bank Bill Revision Out," *New York Times*, July 2, 1935.

45. July 11, 1935, OF 1599, Folder: Chase National Bank, 1933–1943, FDR Library.

46. President's Personal File, July 1935, Folder 1358, Roosevelt Papers, FDR Library.

47. "Cup & Lip," *Time*, September 2, 1935.

48. "House Divided," *Time*, September 16, 1935.

49. "Morgan Stanley & Co. Launched at 2 Wall Street, Taking over Underwriting of Morgan & Co.," *New York Times*, September 17, 1935.

50. Bureau of Labor Statistics, "The Economy 1934–1936," at www.bls.gov/opub/uscs/1934–36.pdf.

51. "Son's Scheme," *Time*, October 19, 1936.

52. "Fadeout," *Time*, February 10, 1936.

53. US Senate, "An Era of Investigations: 1921–1940: Merchants of Death," at www.senate.gov/artandhistory/history/minute/merchants_of_death.htm.

54. Franklin Delano Roosevelt to William E. Dodd, March 16, 1936, FDR Library, at http://docs.fdrlibrary.marist.edu/PSF/BOX32/t300d01.html.

55. Letter to Giannini, May 7, 1936, PPF File 1135, Folder: Giannini, A. P., 1933–1936, FDR Library.

56. Assortment of newspaper clippings from mid-1936 to the beginning of 1937, PPF File 1135, Folder: Giannini, A. P., 1933–1936, FDR Library.

57. Letter from Leffingwell, September 8, 1936, PPF 866, Folder: Leffingwell, Russell C., 1935–1944 and cross-references, FDR Library.

58. "Franklin Roosevelt's Address Announcing the Second New Deal," October 31, 1936, at http://docs.fdrlibrary.marist.edu/od2ndst.html.

59. William E. Leuchtenburg, "When Franklin Roosevelt Clashed with the Supreme Court and Lost," *Smithsonian*, May 2005, at www.smithsonianmag.com/history-archaeology/showdown.html.

60. Ibid.

61. "Mussolini Will Receive Lamont," *New York Times*, April 18, 1937.

62. "1937 Erratic Year on Stock Exchange," *New York Times*, January 3, 1938.

63. James H. Perkins, "The Economic Situation: Extract from the Report to Shareholders," January 11, 1938, PPF 54, Perkins, James H., FDR Library.

64. "National Economic Accounts: Gross Domestic Product," US Department of Commerce Bureau of Economic Analysis, at www.bea.gov/national/index.htm#gdp.

65. Robert M. Coen, "Labor Force and Unemployment in the 1920's and 1930's: A Re-Examination Based on Postwar Experience," *The Review of Economics and Statistics* 55, no. 1 (February 1973): 46–55.

66. "T. W. Lamont Sees a 'Capital Lockout,'" *New York Times,* January 18, 1938.

67. Letter from Lamont, February 25, 1938, FDR Library.

68. Ibid.

69. Note from Lamont, September 28, 1938, PPF File 70, Folder: Lamont, Thomas W., FDR Library.

70. "F.D.R. Says His Policies Not Changed," *Evening Independent*, December 6, 1938.

71. FDR Message to Adolph Hitler and Benito Mussolini, April 14, 1939, at www.presidency.ucsb.edu/ws/index.php?pid=15741.

72. "FDR," *American Experience* (PBS), 1994.

73. Hitler Speech to the Reichstag, April 28, 1939, WWII Archives, at www.wwiiarchives.net/servlet/action/doc/bbb_21.

74. Letter from Lamont, April 28, 1939, PPF File 70, Folder: Lamont, Thomas W., FDR Library.

75. Lamont, *Ambassador,* 458.

76. Ibid., 457.

77. "Aldrich Analyzes New Deal Policies," *New York Times,* May 24, 1939.

78. Barton Biggs, *Wealth, War, Wisdom* (Hoboken, NJ: Wiley, 2008).

79. Chernow, *House of Morgan,* 441.

80. Letter from Leffingwell, September 2, 1939; Response to Leffingwell, September 5, 1939, FDR Library.

81. Lamont, *Ambassador,* 444.

82. Arthur M. Johnson, *Winthrop W. Aldrich: Lawyer, Banker, Diplomat* (Cambridge, MA: Harvard University Press, 1968), 257–259.

83. "War and Peace: Businessmen," *Time,* November 27, 1939.

84. Letter from Lamont, December 27, 1939, PPF File 70, Folder: Lamont, Thomas W., FDR Library.

Chapter 8. The Early to Mid-1940s: World War II, Bankers, and War Bucks

1. Letter from W. Randolph Burgess to Fed Reserve chairman Marriner Eccles, February 18, 1943, Marriner S. Eccles Document Collection, Federal Reserve Archives (FRASER). In response to request to report on the banks' role with respect to Treasury financing related to the war effort.

2. "Simplified Message of Redemption of War Bonds Effective October 2," *New York Times,* August 30, 1944.

3. "James H. Perkins, Banker, Is Dead," *New York Times,* July 13, 1940.

4. "Gordon S. Rentschler," American Business Leaders of the Twentieth Century, Harvard Business School website, at www.hbs.edu/leadership/database/leaders/gordon_s_rentschler.html.

5. Burgess later became undersecretary of the Treasury for the Eisenhower administration and a lead figure in NATO negotiations.

6. In 1946, Burgess helped secure a job for his friend Henry Wriston's son, Walter, who became Citibank chairman in 1970. Henry Wriston served as president of Brown University from 1937 to 1955, as president of the Council on Foreign Relations from 1951 to 1964, and in various advisory roles for Eisenhower.

7. Morgenthau Box 41, Folder: Burgess, W. Randolph, 1940–1944, FDR Library.

8. PPF 866, Folder: Leffingwell, Russell C., 1935–1944 and cross-references, FDR Library.

9. December 18, 1940, PPF File 70, Folder: Lamont, Thomas W., FDR Library.

10. Letter from Lamont, December 24, 1940, PSF Box 141, Lamont, FDR Library.

11. "National City Bank Financing Defense," *New York Times,* January 15, 1941.

12. Ibid.

13. Ibid.

14. Rentschler remained in charge of National City Bank until 1948. His prominence earned him a spot on President Truman's 1946 twelve-member committee of business leaders charged with restoring foreign trade in the postwar era. He died of a heart attack while vacationing with his wife in one of his key growth areas, Cuba. William Gage Brady Jr., who was in charge of domestic operations for the bank in 1938 and became president in 1940, succeeded him. Brady grew up in New York City, received his BA from Columbia University, and worked at Bankers Trust before joining National City Bank. He also served on the Council on Foreign Relations.

15. "Beale Makes Plea to Retain Funds," *New York Times,* January 21, 1941.

16. John Donald Wilson, *The Chase* (Cambridge, MA: Harvard Business School, 1986), 18.

17. October 2, 1941, PPF 7591, Folder: Aldrich, Winthrop W., FDR Library.

18. Letter from Lamont, October 27, 1941, PSF Box 141 Lamont, FDR Library.

19. Anthony Sampson, *The Money Lenders* (New York, NY: Penguin, 1983), 85.

20. Joseph J. Thorndike, "Wartime Tax Legislation and the Politics of Policymaking," Tax Analysts, October 15, 2001, at http://www.taxhistory.org/thp/readings.nsf/0/f9cb12c7ca3ccf9185256e22007840e7.

21. Letter from Davies, Hon. Joseph E., November 14, 1942, OF 1599, Folder: Chase National Bank, 1933–1943, FDR Library.

22. "Federal Sales Tax Urged by Aldrich," *New York Times,* January 22, 1943.

23. Letter from Aldrich, February 27, 1943, OF 1599, Folder: Chase National Bank, 1933–1943, FDR Library.

24. Letter from Aldrich, June 2, 1943, OF 1559, Folder: Chase National Bank, 1933–1943, FDR Library.

25. Various places in the White House to which checks had come in, were deferred to Rentschler, beginning October 15, 1943, OF 1559, Folder: Chase National Bank, 1933–1943, FDR Library.

26. Letter from W. Randolph Burgess to Marriner Eccles, February 18, 1943, The Marriner S. Eccles Document Collection, Federal Reserve Archives, at http://fraser.stlouisfed.org/docs/historical/eccles/042_03_0001.pdf.

27. Ronald F. King, *Money, Time and Politics: Investment Tax Subsidies and American Democracy* (New Haven, CT: Yale University Press, 1993), 121–122. Cited in Joseph J.

Thorndike, "Soak the Rich Republicans?," Tax History Projects, at Tax Analysts. Thorndike has used the term "class tax" in many articles.

28. Letter from Burgess to Morgenthau, September 27, 1943, Morgenthau Box 41, Folder: Burgess, W. Randolph, 1940–1944, FDR Library.

29. PPF File 70, Folder: Lamont, Thomas, FDR Library.

30. John H. Williams, "Currency Stabilization: The Keynes and White Plans," *Foreign Affairs*, July 1943.

31. John H. Williams, "Currency Stabilization: American and British Attitudes," *Foreign Affairs*, January 1944.

32. Luke Fletcher, "A More Perfect Adjustment: The Bretton Woods Agreement and the Beautiful World of Harry Dexter White," draft chapter of PhD thesis (unpublished), Cambridge University, September 2013, Chapter 2, 2–11.

33. Ibid., 9–21.

34. Orin Kirshner and Edward M. Bernstein, *The Bretton Woods–GATT System: Retrospect and Prospect After Fifty Years* (Armonk, NY: M. E. Sharpe, 1996), 16.

35. "Aldrich's Proposed Currency Plan," *New York Times*, September 16, 1944.

36. Allan H. Meltzer, *A History of the Federal Reserve, Volume 2, Book 1, 1951–1969* (Chicago, IL: University of Chicago Press, 2010), 55.

37. Sampson, *Money Lenders*, 88.

38. US Department of State Office of the Historian, "The Yalta Conference," Milestones 1937–1945, at http://history.state.gov/milestones/1937–1945/YaltaConf.

39. Author conversation with Truman archivist Randy Sowell at the archives in Independence, Missouri, August 22, 2012.

40. Robert H. Ferrell, *Harry S. Truman: A Life* (Columbia, MO: University of Missouri Press, 1996), 87.

41. This point was underscored by returning to his modest Victorian home in small-town Independence, Missouri, after his presidency.

42. Letters between Frank K. Houston and Truman, April 13, 1945, and May 18, 1945, PPF: Box 502, Folder 1275, Harry S. Truman Library and Museum.

43. PPF: Box 502, Folder 1275, Truman Library.

44. Michael J. Sniffen, "Truman Is Remembered for Courage, Decisiveness," *Free-Lance Star* (Fredericksburg, Virginia), December 26, 1972.

45. Letter from Aldrich, June 29, 1945, Papers of Harry S. Truman, General Files, Box 24, Folder: Aldrich, Winthrop W., Truman Library.

46. Ibid.

47. Letter from Aldrich, October 30, 1945, Papers of Harry S. Truman, General Files, Box 24, Folder: Aldrich, Winthrop W., Truman Library.

48. "Winston Churchill's Iron Curtain Speech," The History Guide: Lectures on Twentieth Century Europe, at www.historyguide.org/europe/churchill.html.

49. September 14, 1951, Papers of John W. Snyder, 1946–1952, Congress, Box 8, Folder 2, Truman Library.

50. Martin Mayer, *The Bankers* (New York, NY: Ballantine, 1976), 503.

51. Hanson W. Baldwin, "America at War: Victory in Europe," *Foreign Affairs*, July 1945.

52. William G. Hyland, "John J. McCloy, 1895–1989," *Foreign Affairs*, Spring 1989.

53. Letter from Alan G. Weiner, American history major at Long Island University taking a course on World War II, February 12, 1965, PPGF: Box 444, Folder: General, Weinc–Weiq, Truman Library.

54. "War Rate Ended by Reserve Banks," *New York Times*, April 24, 1946.

55. Aldrich address on "The Control of Inflation," May 2, 1946, Papers of Harry S. Truman General Files, Box 24, Folder: Aldrich, Winthrop W., Truman Library.

56. Report C. 67, "Rating National Problems," October 30, 1946, Confidential File, Box 6, Folder: Bureau of the Budget, Immigration, World Food Dist., Foreign Trade Relations, 1946, Truman Library.

Chapter 9. The Late 1940s: World Reconstruction and Private Bankers

1. Winthrop W. Aldrich, "American Interest in European Reconstruction," address before the seventy-third annual convention of the American Bankers Association, September 30, 1947.

2. Letter to Aldrich, July 2, 1946, Papers of Harry S. Truman General Files, Box 24, Folder: Aldrich, Winthrop W., Truman Library.

3. June 17, 1946, General File, Box 886, Folder: Giannini, Truman Library.

4. Ibid., Internal White House correspondence, September 26, 1946.

5. Wilson, *The Chase*, 32.

6. Oral history interview with John W. Snyder, August, 13, 1969, by Jerry N. Hess, Truman Library, at www.trumanlibrary.org/oralhist/snyder.htm.

7. "John Wesley Snyder (1895–1985)," *The Encyclopedia of Arkansas History and Culture*, at www.encyclopediaofarkansas.net/encyclopedia/entry-detail.aspx?entryID=5095.

8. "The 50th Anniversary of the Treasury–Federal Reserve Accord 1951–2001: Biographies: John Wesley Snyder," Federal Reserve Bank of Richmond.

9. Oral history interview with John W. Snyder, June 18, 1969.

10. Ibid.

11. Ibid.

12. Barry Eichengreen and Peter M. Garber, "Before the Accord: US Monetary-Financial Policy, 1945–1951," *Financial Markets and Financial Crises* (January 1991), at www.nber.org/chapters/c11485.pdf.

13. Paper from the Bank for International Settlements, Monetary and Economic Department, Basel, July 10, 1947, Papers of John W. Snyder, Truman Library.

14. Marquis James and Bessie R. James, *The Story of Bank of America: Biography of a Bank* (Washington, DC: Beard Books, 2002), 478–479.

15. "Aldrich Hopeful of Marshall Plan, Financier Back from Europe Says Proposal Is Vitally Important to World," *New York Times*, July 1, 1947.

16. Sampson, *The Money Lenders*, 92.

17. "Europe Submits Its Marshall Plan," *Life*, October 6, 1947.

18. Oral history interview with John W. Snyder, August 13, 1969.

19. Kai Bird, *The Chairman: John J. McCloy and the Making of the American Establishment* (New York, NY: Simon & Schuster, 1992), 272.

20. "Meyer Quits World Bank Helm, Saying He Was Only to Launch It," *New York Times*, December 5, 1946.

21. Charles Hurd, "McCloy Is Elected World Bank Head," *New York Times*, March 1, 1947.

22. Bird, *The Chairman,* 285.

23. Ibid.

24. Ibid.

25. Letter from Snyder to Nelson Rockefeller, March 7, 1947, Papers of John W. Snyder, IBRD-IMF and IBRD (legislation), Box 54, Folder: International Monetary Funds and Bank, publications and correspondence, 1947, Truman Library.

26. Bird, *The Chairman,* 289.

27. Sampson, *The Money Lenders,* 90.

28. Letter from Snyder to McCloy, January 10, 1949, Papers of John W. Snyder, Truman Library.

29. David Cushman Coyle, *Survey of United States Foreign Economic Cooperation Since 1945* (New York, NY: The Church Peace Union, 1957), 12.

30. Papers of John W. Snyder, 1946–1952, Box 14, Folder: Fiscal, banks 1946–1952, Truman Library.

31. "World Bank Chary on Backward Lands," *New York Times,* February 1, 1949.

32. Wilson, *The Chase,* 31.

33. Harry S. Truman, "The President's News Conference," January 12, 1950, posted online by Gerhard Peters and John T. Woolley, American Presidency Project, at www.presidency .ucsb.edu/ws/?pid=13468.

34. "Thomas W. Lamont, Banker, Dies at 77 in Florida Home," *New York Times,* February 3, 1948.

35. "Russell C. Leffingwell Is Dead; Ex-Chairman of Morgan Bank," *New York Times,* October 3, 1960.

36. Papers of John W. Snyder, 1946–1952, Box 14, Folder: Federal Reserve Bank (Interest, 1948–1950), Fiscal (banks), October 9, 1948 (sent to Secretary of Treasury by Thomas B. McCabe on October 13, 1948), "U.S. Bond Peg Still Necessary, Says F.A. Potts," *Philadelphia Evening Bulletin,* Truman Library.

37. Ibid.

38. "Russell C. Leffingwell Is Dead."

39. PFF Box 584, Folder 4316, Russell Leffingwell, Truman Library.

40. Letter from Leffingwell, November 26, 1948, PFF Box 584, Folder 4316, Russell Leffingwell, Truman Library.

41. Ibid., cross-reference sheet. Correspondence between Morris L. Ernst and President Truman between December 2, 1948, and December 9, 1948.

42. Wilson, *The Chase,* 37.

43. PSF Box 160, Foreign Affairs File, Folder: McCloy, John J., Truman Library.

44. Bird, *The Chairman,* 305.

45. Ibid., 305–306.

46. Letter from Snyder to Eugene Black, June 24, 1949, Papers of John W. Snyder, Folder: General, 1947–1952, Truman Library.

47. Bird, *The Chairman,* 363.

48. Wilson, *The Chase,* 26.

49. "A Report to the National Security Council: NSC 68," April 12, 1950, President's Secretary's File, Truman Papers, Truman Library. The report was declassified by Henry Kissinger on February 27, 1975.

50. Ibid., 60.

51. Ibid.

52. Ibid., 62.

53. Ibid., 63.

54. Ibid., 65.

55. Ibid., 4.

56. December 28, 1950, White House Central Files: Confidential Files, Box 63, Folder: Foreign Trade, Truman Library.

Chapter 10. The 1950s: Eisenhower's Buds, Cold War, Hot Money

1. Jordan Weissmann, "60 Years of Economic History, Told in One Graph," *The Atlantic,* August 23, 2012, at www.theatlantic.com/business/archive/2012/08/60-years-of-american-economic-history-told-in-1-graph/261503/.

2. Wilson, *The Chase,* 41.

3. Press Release, June 30, 1950, Harry S. Truman Administration File, Elsey Papers, Truman Library.

4. "Tax Legislation, 1950–1959," Tax Policy Center, at www.taxpolicycenter.org/legislation/1950.cfm.

5. "Investing Abroad Hit," *New York Times,* July 7, 1950.

6. Statement by the President, May 15, 1951, Truman Library.

7. Dwight D. Eisenhower, *At Ease: Stories I Tell to Friends* (Cape Cod, MA: Eastern Acorn Press, 1981), 373.

8. White House Central Files, Alpha Files: Weinberg Sidney J. (1), Dwight D. Eisenhower Presidential Library and Museum.

9. Author interview with William Cohan, August 25, 2012.

10. Files: John Macy, Box 629, Weinberg, Sidney, LBJ Library.

11. White House Central Files, Alpha Files: Weinberg Sidney J. (1), Eisenhower Library.

12. "Eisenhower Picks 3 Aides," *New York Times,* December 15, 1952.

13. Ibid.

14. Oral history interview with Gabriel Hauge (1 of 4), March 10, 1967, OH-190, Columbia University Oral History Project, Eisenhower Library.

15. White House Central Files, PPF, Hauge, Gabriel, Records, 1952–1958, Box 1, Eisenhower Library.

16. Gabriel Hauge, Memorandum for the President, June 22, 1953, Re: Proposed bill H.R. 1437 as modified by the Department of Defense.

17. Oral history interview with John J. McCloy, December 18, 1970, OH 221 (1 of 2), Eisenhower Library.

18. Alexander's file at the Eisenhower Library in Abilene, Kansas, is slimmer than that of many other bankers who appear in this chapter. There is nothing in it to substantiate the term "Ike's Boss" used by the popular press at the time.

19. January 19, 1954, PPF, Folder: George Whitney, Eisenhower Library.

20. "Two Way Trade Urged by Aldrich," *New York Times,* June 13, 1953.

21. Document 597, December 10, 1953, Presidential Papers, Diaries, Eisenhower Library.

22. Ibid.

23. Ibid.

24. Oral history interview with John J. McCloy.

25. Ibid.

26. Letter regarding appointments to John Foster Dulles, January 15, 1953, White House Central Files, Hauge, Gabriel: Records, 1952–1958, Box 1, Eisenhower Library.

27. May 18, 1953, PPF 275, White House Central Files, Eisenhower Archives.

28. Diary entry by James C. Hagerty, February 25, 1954, White House Press Secretary Papers, Box 1, January 1–April 6, 1954, Eisenhower Library.

29. John J. McCloy Papers, 1897–1989, Historical (Biographical) Note, Amherst University, at www.amherst.edu/media/view/393545/original/McCloy%20Papers.pdf.

30. Dwight D. Eisenhower, "Special Message to the Congress on the Mutual Security Program," June 23, 1954, posted online by Gerhard Peters and John T. Woolley, American Presidency Project, at www.presidency.ucsb.edu/ws/?pid=9931#axzz2gWAhNEeE.

31. Folder: McCloy, White House Central Files, Eisenhower Library.

32. Ralph Hendershot, "Ike's Policies Brake Forces of Depression," *New York World Telegram,* July 6, 1954.

33. Wilson, *The Chase,* 397.

34. Dwight D. Eisenhower, "Statement by the President on the Mutual Security Program," April 11, 1955, American Presidency Project, at www.presidency.ucsb.edu/ws/?pid=10448#axzz2gWAhNEeE.

35. Edward G. Miller Jr., "A Fresh Look at the Inter-American Community," *Foreign Affairs,* July 1955.

36. Statement by Senator Milton R. Young, July 30, 1955, OF-115, A Banking (1), Eisenhower Library.

37. August 13, 1955, Folder: McCloy, White House Central Files, Eisenhower Library.

38. John J. McCloy Papers, Box SP2, Folder 7, McCloy Archives.

39. Ibid., "A Statement on Bank Mergers," July 5, 1955.

40. William T. Lifland, "The Supreme Court, Congress and Bank Mergers," *Law and Contemporary Problems* (Winter 1967): 15–39, at http://scholarship.law.duke.edu/lcp/vol32/iss1/3.

41. Wilson, *The Chase,* 88.

42. "Every Man a Capitalist," *Time,* November 21, 1955.

43. April 30, 1956, WHCF, Folder: McCloy, Eisenhower Library.

44. OF 115, A Banking (4), Eisenhower Library.

45. "The History of Chemical Bank," Chase Alumni Association, Courtesy of JPMorgan Chase archives, at www.chasealum.org/article.html?aid=197.

46. Citigroup website, history, at www.citigroup.com/citi/about/history/index.htm.

47. Kai Bird, *The Chairman: John J. McCloy and the Making of the American Establishment* (New York, NY: Simon & Schuster, 1992), 445.

48. Ibid., 452–53.

49. Irene L. Gendzier, *Notes from the Minefield: United States Intervention in Lebanon, 1945–1959* (New York, NY: Columbia University Press, 2006), 211.

50. Anthony Sampson, *The Money Lenders* (New York, NY: Penguin, 1983), 112.

51. Oral history interview with Winthrop Aldrich, October 16, 1972, OH 250, Columbia University Oral History Project, Eisenhower Library.

52. Bird, *The Chairman,* 453.

53. Oral history, Aldrich.

54. Bird, *The Chairman,* 450.

55. Oral history, Aldrich.

56. Ibid.

57. October 8, 1956, PPF 1270, Alpha Files (2), Weinberg, Eisenhower Library. Weinberg's role in financing and developing many industries was equally tactical. The Ford family, with whom he became very close, hired him for his legal prowess. He directed the reorganization of Ford and its listing on the Stock Exchange. McCloy, a Ford Foundation trustee, also played a large role in Ford's decision to go public in late 1955.

58. May 31, 1956, PPF 1270, Box 972, Weinberg, Eisenhower Library.

59. July 15, 1956, Alpha Files (2), Weinberg, Eisenhower Library.

60. May 31, 1956, PPF 1270, Box 972, Folder 1300, Weinberg, Eisenhower Library.

61. White House Central Files, Official File, 1953–1961, OF 115 Finances and Monetary Matters (1), Box 483, Eisenhower Library.

62. Gabriel Hauge, "Prosperity Has Its Problems Too, What Are They?" Economic Club of Detroit, March 11, 1957, Administration File, Ann Whitman File, Hauge, Gabriel, 1956–1957 (2), Eisenhower Library.

63. "President Upholds Tight Monetary Policy," *New York Herald*, May 8, 1957.

64. Phillip L. Zweig, *Wriston: Walter Wriston, Citibank, and the Rise and Fall of American Financial Supremacy* (Crown Business, 1996), 88.

65. "Bank Names Senior Vice Presidents," *New York Times*, March 20, 1957.

66. "Project for Cuba Gets $100,250,000," *New York Times*, August 23, 1957.

67. "The Recession of 1958," *Time*, October 15, 1958.

68. "Henry C. Alexander," *New York Times*, December 15, 1969.

69. Unlike other prominent bankers who influenced Eisenhower at the time, Alexander has no oral history in the Eisenhower archives.

70. Letter to Henry Clay Alexander, January 23, 1959, White House Central File, Official File 2-B-1, Eisenhower Library.

71. Oral history interview with W. Randolph Burgess, September 13, 1974, by Eisenhower Library Staff member Dr. Maclyn Burg.

72. Ralph A. Young, "In Memoriam: Warren Randolph Burgess, 1889–1978," *The American Statistician* 33, no. 3 (1979): 136.

73. Wilson, *The Chase*, 111.

74. Sampson, *The Money Lenders*, 98–102.

Chapter 11. The Early 1960s: "Go-Go" Youth, Murders, and Global Finance

1. "Stocks Reel Downward—Wall Street Shaken over Kennedy's Death," Associated Press, November 25, 1963.

2. "Debt Growth by Sector," Federal Reserve Board, at www.federalreserve.gov/releases /z1/19960912/z1r-2.pdf.

3. "Stock Offered in Johnson Chain," *New York Times*, May 19, 1961.

4. "Donald J. Tyson, Food Tycoon, Is Dead at 80," *New York Times*, January 8, 2011.

5. Kingsford Capital Management, *Kingsford Capital: The First 100 Years* (San Francisco, CA: Bentrovato Books, 2011), 54–64.

6. February 10, 1966, White House Confidential File, Box 152, Folder: Wall, LBJ Library.

7. "John F. Kennedy: January 3, 1960," *Meet the President with Tim Russert* (NBC News).

8. Ibid.

9. "Gross Domestic Product," US Department of Commerce Bureau of Economic Analysis, at www.bea.gov/index.htm.

10. Donald Gibson, *Battling Wall Street: The Kennedy Presidency* (New York, NY: Sheridan Square Publications, 1994), 5.

11. David Rockefeller, *Memoirs* (New York, NY: Random House, 2002), 230. According to Rockefeller, after McCloy worked his way through college (Amherst) and law school (Harvard) by tutoring, he traveled to Maine in 1912 in the hopes of securing a job on Mount Desert Island by contacting the wealthiest families, including the Rockefellers. "Jack always imparted the story at great length," wrote Rockefeller, "walking the quarter-mile from the main road up to the Eyrie, knocking on the massive door, and explaining to the butler why he was there, only to be turned away with the explanation that a tutor had already been hired for the Rockefeller children."

12. Rockefeller, *Memoirs*, 179.

13. Author's note: My first job on Wall Street was as a programmer analyst at One Chase Plaza, in a cubicle on the twenty-fifth floor.

14. "John J. McCloy Papers, 1897–1989," Amherst College Archives and Special Collections, at www.amherst.edu/media/view/393545/original/McCloy%20Papers.pdf.

15. Bird, *The Chairman*, 491.

16. Ibid., 498.

17. McCloy Papers. Later, McCloy was appointed chairman of the Coordinating Committee of the United States on the Cuban Missile Crisis.

18. "McCloy Cool to Soviet Disarm Plan," Associated Press, February 26, 1961.

19. Copy of letter to JFK, including the attached "Disarmament Document Series. No. 35: United States Arms Control and Disarmament Agency," October 6, 1961, Post Presidential Files, Box 97, Folder: McCloy, John J., Truman Library.

20. Jack Raymond, "President Meets His Top Advisors on Berlin Crisis," *New York Times*, June 30, 1961.

21. Ascension Image KN-C18923, President John F. Kennedy Meets with Disarmament Advisors, September 24, 1961, John F. Kennedy Presidential Library and Museum, at www.jfk library.org/Asset-Viewer/Archives/JFKWHP-KN-C18923.aspx.

22. HR 9118: Public Law 87-297. See also John F. Kennedy, "Remarks in New York City upon Signing Bill Establishing the U.S. Arms Control and Disarmament Agency," September 26, 1961, American Presidency Project, at www.presidency.ucsb.edu/ws/?pid =8353.

23. John McCloy, "Balance Sheet on Disarmament," *Foreign Affairs*, April 1962.

24. Ibid.

25. "President John F. Kennedy: On the Alliance for Progress, 1961," Modern History Sourcebook (Fordham University), at www.fordham.edu/halsall/mod/1961kennedy-afp1 .html.

26. "David Rockefeller," The Rockefeller Archive Center, at www.rockarch.org/bio/david .php.

27. "Kennedy: On the Alliance for Progress, 1961."

28. Sampson, *The Money Lenders*, 115.

29. "David Rockefeller," The Rockefeller Archive Center.

30. Rockefeller, *Memoirs*, 199.

31. Ibid., 198.

32. Roger Lane, "U.S. Steel's Roger Blough No Stranger to 'Trouble,'" *Schenectady Gazette*, April 13, 1962.

33. James Hoopes, "When a Leader Overreaches: JFK's Pyrrhic Victory over U.S. Steel," Babson College, at www.babson.edu/executive-education/thought-leadership/babson-insight/Articles/Pages/When-a-Leader-Overreaches.aspx.

34. "Businessmen," 2, April 25, 1962, JFK Library, at www.jfklibrary.org/Asset-Viewer/Archives/JFKPOF-096–008.aspx.

35. Gibson, *Battling Wall Street*.

36. The other members of the council were Roger Blough and Leonard McCollum.

37. Arthur M. Schlesinger Jr., *Robert Kennedy and His Times* (New York, NY: Houghton Mifflin, First Mariner Books edition, 2002), 225.

38. Burton Crane, "Record Decline in Dollar Value," *New York Times*, June 3, 1962.

39. "The Day of the Bear," *Time*, June 8, 1962.

40. "Council of Economic Advisers (CEA), May 1962: 1–5," JFK Library, at www.jfklibrary.org/Asset-Viewer/Archives/JFKPOF-074–005.aspx.

41. Ibid.

42. Ibid., 16–31.

43. "Dow Jones Industrial Average (1960–1980 Daily)," stock charts, at http://stockcharts.com/freecharts/historical/djia19601980.html.

44. Richard E. Mooney, "Kennedy Studies Economic Policy," *New York Times*, June 30, 1961.

45. "A Businessman's Letter," *Life*, July 6, 1962.

46. John F. Kennedy, "Letter to David Rockefeller on the Balance of Payments Question," July 6, 1962, posted online by Gerhard Peters and John T. Woolley, American Presidency Project, at www.presidency.ucsb.edu/ws/?pid=8759.

47. Financial Policy Meeting, JFK Appointment Index, July 13, 1962, JFK Library.

48. "Businessmen," 4–5, JFK Library, at http://www.jfklibrary.org/Asset-Viewer/Archives/JFKPOF-096–008.aspx.

49. "Thomas Lamont, Banker, 68, Dead," *New York Times*, April 11, 1967.

50. "The Man at the Top," *Time*, September 7, 1962.

51. National Security Archive, "The Cuban Missile Crisis, 1962: The 40th Anniversary," George Washington University, at www.gwu.edu/~nsarchiv/nsa/cuba_mis_cri/photos.htm.

52. Telephone Recordings: Dictation Belt 30, October 22, 1962, JFK Library, at www.jfklibrary.org/Asset-Viewer/Archives/JFKPOF-TPH-30.aspx.

53. Letter from Chairman Khrushchev, October 28, 1962, JFK Library, at http://microsites.jfklibrary.org/cmc/oct28/doc1.html.

54. Ibid.

55. Walter Isaacson and Evan Thomas, *The Wise Men: Six Friends and the World They Made* (New York, NY: Simon & Schuster, 1986), 730.

56. RFK had congratulated McCloy on February 17, 1961, for joining his brother's administration and promised "to extend [McCloy] the services of the Department of Justice, especially the Office of Legal Counsel, should the need for such services arise."

57. Bird, *The Chairman*, 541.

58. Several months later, McCloy was informed he would receive a Medal of Freedom from JFK at a ceremony scheduled for December 6, 1963. But on November 22, 1963, shortly after McCloy finished having breakfast with Eisenhower, JFK was shot. McCloy immediately sent his condolences to LBJ, who ultimately presented him with the medal.

59. John F. Kennedy, "Annual Message to the Congress on the State of the Union," January 14, 1963, posted online by Gerhard Peters and John T. Woolley, American Presidency Project, at www.presidency.ucsb.edu/ws/index.php?pid=9138.

60. "Question and Answer Period at the American Bankers Association Symposium on Economic Growth, February 25, 1963," JFK Library, at http://www.jfklibrary.org/Asset-Viewer /Archives/JFKWHA-165–006.aspx.

61. "David Rockefeller Offers a Plan of Business Advice on Latin America," *New York Times,* April 24, 1963.

62. Sampson, *The Money Lenders,* 139.

63. Recorded Conversation 25A.1: Kennedy and C. Douglas Dillon, July 31, 1963, JFK Library, at www.jfklibrary.org/Asset-Viewer/Archives/JFKPOF-TPH-25A.aspx.

64. Zweig, *Wriston,* 157.

65. Ibid., 57.

66. Ibid., 87.

67. Office of the White House Press Secretary, President Johnson's Archives, John Macy Files, Folder: Wriston, Walter B., October 2, 1963, LBJ Library.

68. When the interest equalization tax finally took effect on September 2, 1964, President Johnson had watered it down considerably as per the bankers' demands.

69. "David Rockefeller Joins Protest on Cut by House in Latin Aid," *New York Times,* October 12, 1963.

70. "Remarks at Amherst College upon Receiving an Honorary Degree," October 26, 1963, JFK Library.

71. "Statement of the Honorable Douglas Dillon, Secretary of the Treasury, Before the Joint Economic Committee," July 8, 1963, in US National Economy, 1916–1981: Unpublished Documentary Collections from the Treasury Department, Part 4: Kennedy-Johnson Administration (1961–1969), microfilm (Frederick, MD: University Publications of America), Item 0525.

72. Zweig, *Wriston,* 159.

73. Walter Wriston, "No Turning Back," *The Twilight of Sovereignty and the Information Standard*, Tufts Digital Library, at http://dl.tufts.edu/view_text.jsp?urn=tufts:central:dca :UA069:UA069.005.DO.00243&chapter=c1s2.

74. Sam Dawson, "Experts Confident Drastic Action Unlikely in Threat to Reserves," Associated Press, October 3, 1963.

75. November 22, 1963, Treasury Department Folder, LBJ Library.

76. December 20, 1963, White House Confidential Files, Thomas S. Gates File, LBJ Library.

77. John M. Lee, "National and Commodities Markets Shaken; Federal Reserve Acts to Avert Panic," *New York Times,* November 23, 1963.

78. "Congressional Probe Asked in Presidential Assassination," Associated Press, November 25, 1963.

79. "Joseph Kennedy Watches Son's Funeral at Home, Hyannisport, Massachusetts," UPI, November 26, 1963.

80. Drew Pearson, "Kennedy . . . Man of Destiny," *Sarasota Journal*, November 26, 1963.

81. Edward Cowan, "Young Banker in Foreign-Service: Wriston Is at Helm of National City Units Abroad," *New York Times*, November 24, 1963.

82. Ibid.

83. Daily Diary Collection, C. Douglas Dillon, LBJ Library.

84. Letter from David Rockefeller, November 29, 1963, White House Confidential Files, Name File: David Rockefeller, LBJ Library.

85. Letter to David Rockefeller, December 11, 1963, LBJ Library.

86. David Rockefeller memo to President Johnson, December 11, 1963, White House Confidential Files, Name File: David Rockefeller, LBJ Library.

Chapter 12. The Mid- to Late 1960s: Progressive Policies and Bankers' Economy

1. "Blue Chips Lead Dow Average to All-Time High," Associated Press, December 5, 1963.

2. "Market Makes Big Comeback," Associated Press, November 27, 1963.

3. "State of Business: Banish Your Fears," *Time*, December 13, 1963.

4. First National City Bank, Monthly Economic Letter, January 1964, White House Central Files (WHCF), Box 104: First National City Bank, LBJ Library.

5. "Business: A Surprisingly Good Year," *Time*, December 27, 1963.

6. "The 1920s Economy: A Statistical Portrait," San Francisco State University College of Behavioral and Social Sciences.

7. "Debt Growth by Sector," Federal Reserve Board, at www.federalreserve.gov/releases /z1/19960912/z1r-2.pdf.

8. "President Johnson's Address Before Congress," November 27, 1963, LBJ Presidential Library, at www.lbjlib.utexas.edu/johnson/kennedy/Joint%20Congress%20Speech/speech .htm.

9. "A Surprisingly Good Year," *Time*.

10. Dillon had also served in government for nearly a decade even before Kennedy appointed him, including in the Eisenhower administration as ambassador to France, undersecretary of state for economic affairs, and undersecretary of state.

11. Transcript, C. Douglas Dillon Oral History Interview (I) with Paige Mulholland, June 29, 1969, LBJ Library.

12. Ibid.

13. Ibid.

14. Memorandum for the President from Robert E. Kintner, August 11, 1966, LBJ Library.

15. Letter from John McCone, January 9, 1964, White House Confidential Files, Name File: John J. McCloy, LBJ Library.

16. Bird, *The Chairman*, 550.

17. Warren Report, Summary, 18, at www.aarclibrary.org/publib/jfk/wc/wr/html/WC Report_0021b.htm.

18. Resignation letter from John J. McCloy, January 20, 1965, John Macy Files, Box 374, Folder: McCloy, John J., LBJ Library. All ties were not erased following McCloy's resignation. Johnson eventually engaged him once more for what he was best at—dealing with Germany. On October 11, 1966, Johnson appointed McCloy as the US representa-

tive to the trilateral conversations of the United States, the Federal German Republic, and Britain. His purpose would be "to undertake a searching reappraisal of the threat to security and . . . of the forces required to maintain adequate deterrence and defense in Central Europe. Statement by the President on Tripartite Talks, October 11, 1966, Office of the White House Press Secretary, John Macy Files, Box 374, Folder: McCloy, John J., LBJ Library.

19. "Debate Widens on Trade with Communists," *New York Times,* March 12, 1964.

20. Rockefeller, *Memoirs,* 226.

21. Ibid., 230.

22. Letter to David Rockefeller, August 24, 1964, White House Confidential Files, Names File: David Rockefeller, LBJ Library.

23. President Johnson's Message to Congress, August 5, 1964, Senate Committee on Foreign Relations, 90th Congress, 1st Session, Background Information Relating to Southeast Asia and Vietnam (3rd revised ed.) (Washington, DC: US Government Printing Office, July 1967), 120–122.

24. Vietnam Summary, JFK Library, at www.jfklibrary.org/JFK/JFK-in-History/Vietnam .aspx.

25. Gulf of Tonkin, 1964: Perspectives from the Lyndon Johnson and National Military Command Center Tapes, Miller Center, Presidential Recordings Program, by Marc Selverstone and David Coleman, at http://whitehousetapes.net/exhibit/gulf-tonkin-1964 -perspectives-lyndon-johnson-and-national-military-command-center-tapes.

26. May 19, 1965; May 24, 1965; June 10, 1965, Alpha Files, Folder: Weinberg, Sidney, LBJ Library.

27. Ibid. The folder has White House event invitations to Weinberg spanning Johnson's presidency, about as many as David Rockefeller among the bankers, beginning on July 16, 1964.

28. Files: John Macy, Box 629, Weinberg, Sidney, LBJ Library.

29. Letter to Sidney Weinberg, September 18, 1964, Alpha Files, Folder: Weinberg, Sidney, LBJ Library.

30. Letter from Weinberg to Jack Valenti, October 9, 1964, Alpha Files, Folder: Weinberg, Sidney, LBJ Library.

31. Edward T. Folliard, "LBJ's Vision of the 'Great Society,'" *St. Petersburg Times,* November 10, 1964.

32. On August 23, 1968, Johnson appointed Weinberg to a public advisory committee on US trade policy with David Rockefeller, Rudolph Peterson, and thirty-eight others. In July 1969, Johnson thanked Weinberg for his "consistent efforts in helping to move the tax surcharge and expense reduction legislation through the Congress. The Revenue and Expenditure Control Act of 1968 will work to extend the unprecedented prosperity, which Americans have been enjoying for the past seven years." Alpha files, Folder: Weinberg, Sidney, LBJ Library Archives.

33. *Public Papers of the Presidents of the United States: Lyndon B. Johnson, 1965* (Washington, DC: Government Printing Office, 1965), vol. I, entry 27, 71–74.

34. US Census Bureau, "Historical Poverty Tables—People," Table 3, at www.census.gov /hhes/www/poverty/data/historical/people.html.

35. Invitation, February 16, 1965, White House Confidential Files, Subject File: Chase Manhattan Bank, LBJ Library.

36. Memo for the President from John Macy, Re: Advisory Committee on Balance of Payments, February 23, 1965, John Macy files, Box 629, Folder: Weinberg, Sidney, LBJ Library.

37. Letter to Rockefeller, February 18, 1954, White House Confidential Files, Folder: David Rockefeller, LBJ Library.

38. Ibid., March 30, 1965.

39. Ibid., November 30, 1965.

40. Letter to Thomas S. Gates, March 3, 1965, White House Confidential Files, Name File: Thomas S. Gates, LBJ Library. Gates's file is fairly thin, but all evidence is of a warm, respectful relationship. Gates served on the National Advisory for Selective Service in 1966, and Johnson wrote of his August 1966 address on Business and Government before the Edison Electric Institution as a great speech and one of rare perception.

41. Thomas S. Gates, note to Johnson, August, 3, 1967, White House Confidential Files, Name File: Thomas S. Gates, LBJ Library.

42. Mike Manatos, memorandum for Johnson, March 18, 1963, White House Confidential Files, Name File: David Rockefeller, LBJ Library.

43. Memo to President Johnson from Douglas Dillon, December 29, 1964, John Macy Files, Box 494, Folder: David Rockefeller, LBJ Library.

44. Document WH6503.10, LBJ Library.

45. Phone call with Henry Fowler, March 18, 1965, 7120 tape conversation, LBJ Library.

46. Phone call with George Moore, March 18, 1965, 7122 tape conversation, LBJ Library.

47. March 22, 1965, White House Confidential Files, EX FI 2 Box 13 (Banks and Banking), LBJ Library.

48. Letter to George Champion, March 26, 1965, White House Confidential File, Name File: Champion D-G, Box 168, LBJ Library.

49. March 26, 1965, Alpha Files: Folder: Weinberg, Sidney, LBJ Library.

50. Letter to George Champion, June 16, 1965, White House Confidential File, Name File: Champion D-G, Box 168, LBJ Library.

51. "This Day in Truman History: July 30, 1965, President Lyndon B. Johnson Signs Medicare Bill," Truman Library Website, at www.trumanlibrary.org/anniversaries/medicarebill .htm.

52. Letter to Jack Valenti, May 19, 1964, Business–Economics 2–4, Folder: Monopoly-Antimonopoly, November 22, 1963, to July 8, 1965, LBJ Library.

53. Robert Caro, *The Years of Lyndon B. Johnson: The Passage of Power* (New York, NY: Vintage, 2013), 523–24.

54. Ibid., 525.

55. For Marvin Watson, July 2, 1965, White House Confidential Files, Folder: Hauge, LBJ Library.

56. July 9, 1965, to November 12, 1966, Folder: Business-Economics 2–4, Monopoly-Antimonopoly, LBJ Library.

57. Ibid., November 13, 1966, to March 15, 1967.

58. Ibid., March 16, 1967, to June 30, 1968.

59. Letter to Rockefeller, September 18, 1965, White House Confidential Files, Alpha Files: David Rockefeller, LBJ Library.

60. Gibson, *Battling Wall Street*, 77.

61. Memo for Walt Rostow, Subject: Latin America: Progress over the Past Two Years, June 24, 1966, National Security Files, Box 1, Folder: Bowdler Memos [2 of 2], LBJ Library.

62. October 31, 1966, Papers of Lyndon Baines Johnson, National Security Files, Name File, Box 1, Folder: Bowdler Memos [1 of 2], LBJ Library. See also Leroy F. Aarons, "RFK Would Cut Latin Aid," *Washington Post*, October 31, 1966.

63. Letter from George Moore, August 25, 1965, White House Confidential Files, Name File: George Moore S., Box 538 (First National City), LBJ Library.

64. "Statement by the President upon Signing the Tax Adjustment Act of 1966," American Presidency Project, at www.presidency.ucsb.edu/ws/index.php?pid=27496.

65. Memo to Johnson, January 25, 1966, WHCF, Name File: David Rockefeller, LBJ Library.

66. James Carter, *Inventing Vietnam: The United States and State Building, 1954–1968* (Cambridge University Press, 2008).

67. Robert Buzzanco, "Ruling Class Anti-Imperialism? The Military and Wall Street Confront the Vietnam War," University of Houston Conference, Oxford University, April 2011 (revised October 2011).

68. Lyndon B. Johnson, "Letter to the President of the Senate and to the Speaker of the House Transmitting Bill Encouraging the Substitution of Private for Public Credit," April 20, 1966, American Presidency Project, at www.presidency.ucsb.edu/ws/index.php?pid =27551&st=participation&st1=sales#axzz1p7nEd8na.

69. Memo from Robert E. Kintner, Subject: Business Support for the President, July 6, 1966, WHCF, LBJ Library.

70. Internal Memo to Johnson, September 16, 1967, WHCF, Name File: Sidney Weinberg, LBJ Library.

71. February 8, 1965; June 3, 1966; July 5, 1967, John Macy Files, Folder: Wriston, Walter B., LBJ Library.

72. Zweig, *Wriston*, 266

73. "Banking Timeline," Walter B. Wriston Archives, at http://dca.lib.tufts.edu/features /wriston/about/bankingtimeline.html#footnote52.

74. "Interview: Walter Wriston," *Frontline* (PBS), November 23, 2004, at www.pbs.org/wgbh /pages/frontline/shows/credit/interviews/wriston.html.

75. Transcript, Henry H. Fowler Oral History Interview III, July 31, 1969, by David G. McComb, LBJ Library.

76. Buzzanco, "Ruling Class Anti-Imperialism?"

77. Address by Walter B. Wriston, January 17, 1968, Fowler Papers, Box 82, Folder: Domestic Economy: Gold, 1968 [1 of 2], LBJ Library.

78. H. Erich Heinemann, "Bankers Fear a Crisis," *New York Times*, May 24, 1968.

79. Board of Governors of the Federal Reserve System, *Flow of Funds Accounts of the United States: Annual Flows and Outstandings, 1955–1964* (Washington, DC: 2012), at www.federal reserve.gov/releases/z1/Current/annuals/a1955–1964.pdf. See also *1965–1974*, at www .federalreserve.gov/releases/z1/Current/annuals/a1965–1974.pdf.

80. John Brooks, *The Go-Go Years: The Drama and Crashing Finale of Wall Street's Bullish 1960s* (Hoboken, NJ: Wiley, 1998), 3–4.

81. H. Erich Heinemann, "Peak Profits Raising Salaries of Bank Chiefs, Survey Finds," *New York Times*, March 24, 1969.

Chapter 13. The Early to Mid-1970s: Corruption, Gold, Oil, and Bankruptcies

1. Walter Wriston, testimony given at the US Senate Banking and Currency Committee, Washington, DC, May 26, 1970, at http://hdl.handle.net/10427/36018.

2. *The Penn Central Failure and the Role of Financial Institutions; Staff Report, Ninety-second Congress, First Session* (Washington, DC: US Government Printing Office, 1972), 289.

3. Rush Loving, *The Men Who Loved Trains: The Story of Men Who Battled Greed to Save an Ailing Industry* (Bloomington, IN: Indiana University Press, 2006), 96.

4. Ibid., 348.

5. "Penn Central Gets Pentagon Loan Guaranty," *St. Petersburg Times*, June 11, 1970, at http://tinyurl.com/73h6vdh.

6. Brian Laverty, "Book Review: *When Giants Stumble: Classic Blunders and How to Avoid Them* by Robert Sobel," *American Journal of Business* 15, no. 1 (Spring 2000), at www.bsu.edu/mcobwin/ajb/?p=296.

7. Alfred Broaddus, "Financial Innovation in the United States—Background, Current Status and Prospects," Federal Reserve Bank of Richmond, *Economic Review,* January/February 1985, at www.richmondfed.org/publications/research/economic_review/1985/er710101.cfm.

8. Richard Nixon, "Richard Nixon: Statement About Senate Approval of the Emergency Loan Guarantee Act," American Presidency Project, at www.presidency.ucsb.edu/ws/index.php?pid=3095.

9. William D. Hartung, *Prophets of War: Lockheed Martin and the Making of the Military-Industrial Complex* (New York, NY: Nation Books, 2011), 107.

10. Luis Kohlmeier, "The Penn-C Fairy Tale," *Chronicle Telegram* (Elyria, Ohio), February 27, 1975.

11. "Historical Framework for Regulation of Activities of Unitary Savings and Loan Holding Companies," Office of Thrift Supervision, at www.ots.treas.gov/_files/48035.html.

12. Alfred Hayes, "The 1970 Amendments to the Bank Holding Company Act," Federal Reserve Bank of New York, at http://data.newyorkfed.org/research/monthly_review/1971_pdf/02_1_71.pdf.

13. Memo to Kenneth Cole from Peter Flanigan, December 16, 1970, WHCF, subject files Finance (FI), EX FI 2, banks and banking (5 of 8), Box 8, Nixon Presidential Library and Museum.

14. Internal White House memo, citing letter from Wriston accompanying his speech "Anatomy of an Investment," May 6, 1971, WHCF, Finance FI 2, banks and banking, Box 10, Nixon Library.

15. Zweig, *Wriston,* 324.

16. Richard Nixon, "Address to the Nation Outlining a New Economic Policy," August 15, 1971, American Presidency Project, at www.presidency.ucsb.edu/ws/index.php?pid=3115#axzz1xglSWGWB.

17. Lewis E. Lehrman, "The Nixon Shock Heard 'Round the World," *Wall Street Journal,* August 15, 2011.

18. John Butler, *The Golden Revolution: How to Prepare for the Coming Global Gold Standard* (Hoboken, NJ: Wiley, 2012), 13.

19. Ibid., 19.

20. Memo for Secretary Connally from Peter Flannigan, September 24, 1971, WHCF, Subject: Finance FI-9, monetary system, Box 55, Nixon Library.

21. Memo for Henry Kissinger from David Rockefeller on International Monetary Arrangements, October 5, 1971, WHCF, Subject: finance FI 9, monetary system, Box 55, Nixon Library.

22. Burton Gordon Malkiel, *A Random Walk Down Wall Street: The Time-Tested Strategy for Successful Investing* (New York, NY: W.W. Norton, 2007), 69–70.

23. The Learning Network, "Jan. 23, 1973: Nixon Announces End of U.S. Involvement in Vietnam," *New York Times*, January 23, 2012.

24. Sam Zuckerman, "Way the World Was When Dow Broke 1,000," *San Francisco Chronicle*, March 30, 1999.

25. Note from Gabriel Hauge, May 2, 1969, WHCF, Subject: Finance (FI), Box 54, Nixon Library.

26. Memo for the President, September 13, 1971, WHCF, Subject: Finance (FI), Box 55, Nixon Library.

27. Memo for Henry Kissinger from Robert Hormats, October 5, 1971,WHCF, Subject: Finance (FI), Box 55, Nixon Library.

28. Memo from Peter Flanigan, November 29, 1971, WHCF, Subject: Finance (F1), Box 55, Nixon Library.

29. Rockefeller, *Memoirs,* 486.

30. Erich H. Heinemann, "Patman Says Loan Board Makes 'Ambitious Grabs': House Committee Head Has Reservations on Conversion Ideas," *New York Times*, November 14, 1972.

31. Erich H. Heinemann, "Float Weighed for Prime Rate: National City Is Considering Letting Loan Charge Move with Yields in Market," *New York Times*, October 19, 1971.

32. Walter Wriston, "Currency of Change," October 18, 1971, Walter B. Wriston Papers 1918–2006, Tufts Digital Library, at http://hdl.handle.net/10427/36021.

33. Zweig, *Wriston,* 350.

34. Edwin L. Dale Jr., "Connally Doubts Accord on Monetary System Soon," *New York Times,* November 14, 1971.

35. International Monetary Fund, IMF Chronology, at www.imf.org/external/np/exr/chron/chron.asp.

36. Barry Eichengreen, "Managing a Multiple Reserve Currency World" (paper), University of California, Berkeley, 2010, at http://aric.adb.org/grs/papers/Eichengreen.pdf.

37. Oral history interview with George Shultz, December 18, 2002, University of Virginia Miller Center.

38. Zweig, *Wriston,* 369.

39. Memo for Secretary Shultz, October 11, 1972, WHCF, Subject: Finance FI 1, Box 9, Nixon Library.

40. Walter Wriston, "Freedom and Controls," *New York State Bar Journal,* April 1973, at http://dl.tufts.edu/catalog/tei/tufts:UA069.005.DO.00231/chapter/title.

41. Martin Douglas, "Walter Wriston, 85, Citicorp Innovator Who Redefined Banking," *International Herald Tribune* (New York), January 22, 2005.

42. "The Chase Manhattan Corporation Annual Report, 1973," America's Corporate Foundation, 1973, 6–7.

43. "David Rockefeller Backs Soviet Trade," *New York Times*, July 17, 1973.

44. "Chase and Bank of China to Establish Ties," *Wall Street Journal*, July 5, 1973.

45. Gene Theroux, "The Founding of the US-China Business Council," *China Business Review*, December 22, 2002, 2.

46. Rockefeller, *Memoirs,* 257.

47. Ibid.

48. Ibid.

49. Buzz Theberge, "U.S. Base in Bahrain: Guarding the Gulf," *MERIP Reports*, March/April 1972.

50. Rockefeller, *Memoirs,* 280.

51. Bird, *The Chairman,* 637.

52. The abruptness of this conversation, as Rockefeller depicts the encounter, strains credibility.

53. Rockefeller, *Memoirs,* 282.

54. "Citibank Offers Arabs $1 Billion Assistance," *New York Times*, September 15, 1973.

55. "1973: Arab States Attack Israeli Forces," BBC News, June 10, 1973, at http://news.bbc.co.uk/onthisday/hi/dates/stories/october/6/newsid_2514000/2514317.stm.

56. Sampson, *The Money Lenders,* 151.

57. Bird, *The Chairman,* 635.

58. Jacob Heilbrunn, "The Real McCloy," *New Republic,* May 11, 1992.

59. Bird, *The Chairman,* 635.

60. Ibid., 639.

61. Daniel Yergin, *The Prize: The Epic Quest for Oil, Money, and Power* (New York, NY: Simon & Schuster, 1991), 587.

62. Andrew F. Brimmer, "Capital Flows, Bank Lending Abroad, and the U.S. Balance of Payments" (lecture), July 17, 1974, at https://fraser.stlouisfed.org/docs/historical/federal%20reserve%20history/bog_members_statements/brimmer_19740717.pdf.

63. Paul O. Flaim and Gilroy F. Thomas, "Employment and Unemployment in 1974," *Monthly Labor Review*, February 1975.

64. Rockefeller, *Memoirs,* 285.

65. Ibid., 286.

66. Ibid., 360.

67. "Chase Manhattan Says Iran, Egypt Ventures Are Approved by Fed," *Wall Street Journal*, November 27, 1974.

68. "Oil Nations Cash Surging into U.S.," *New York Times*, February 13, 1975.

69. Sampson, *The Money Lenders,* 153.

70. Memorandum of Conversation, January 17, 1975, Box 8, Document #NODIS/XGD-3, Gerald R. Ford Presidential Library, at www.geraldrfordfoundation.org/memorandums-of-conversation/#Box8.

71. "Citicorp Merchant Bank Being Established in London," *Wall Street Journal*, January 19, 1973.

72. Sampson, *The Money Lenders,* 402.

73. John H. Makin, *The Global Debt Crisis* (New York, NY: Basic Books, 1984), 133–134.

74. In 1999–2000, Banzer was in power during the Cochabamba protests, or Water Wars, a civil uprising in response to the privatization of the municipal water supply by

Bechtel, Suez Lyonnaise, and the World Bank requiring the privatization in return for renewing a $25 million loan.

75. Jeffrey Sachs, ed., *Developing Country Debt and the World Economy* (Chicago, IL: University of Chicago Press, 1989).

76. Zweig, *Wriston,* 448. See also Nicholas Lemann, "The Man Who Freed the Banks," *New York Times,* May 12, 1996.

77. John M. Broder and David E. Sanger, "Rubin Resigning as Treasury Secretary," *New York Times,* May 13, 1999. "Robert E. Rubin," Robert Rubin News, Times Topics, *New York Times,* at http://topics.nytimes.com/top/reference/timestopics/people/r/robert_e_rubin/index.html.

78. "Milestones," Bechtel Corporation website, at www.bechtel.com/milestones.html.

79. "William E. Simon (1974–1977)," US Department of the Treasury, at www.treasury.gov /about/history/pages/wesimon.aspx.

80. Sampson, *The Money Lenders,* 392.

81. Walter Wriston, William Simon, and George Schultz, "Who Needs the IMF?" *Wall Street Journal,* February 3, 1998.

82. A note on tapes and presidents: after Watergate, there were no more tapes. The difference between Nixon's memoir and the words on the tape should make one think carefully about what people say when they are candid versus when they want to self-aggrandize—as with David Rockefeller's *Memoirs.*

83. Howard Zinn, "The Seventies: Under Control?" *A People's History of the United States: 1492–Present* (New York, NY: HarperCollins, 2003), 545.

84. "Appointment of Seventeen Persons to Serve on the President's Labor-Management Committee," Office of the White House Press Secretary, September 28, 1974, at www.ford librarymuseum.gov/library/document/0248/whpr19740928–009.pdf.

85. "Chase Overvalued Bonds," *Lowell Sun,* October 3, 1974.

86. John H. Allan, "Chase Overvalued Bonds by $34 Million," *New York Times,* October 3, 1974.

87. Thayer Watkins, "The 1974–1975 Recession in the U.S.," San Jose State University Economics Department, at www.sjsu.edu/faculty/watkins/rec1975.htm.

88. Peter Milius, "$10 Billion Reduction Considered," *Washington Post,* January 11, 1975.

89. Multinational Oil Corporations and U.S. Foreign Policy, Report to the Committee on Foreign Relations, United States Senate, by the Subcommittee on Multinational Corporations, US Government Printing Office, January 2, 1975.

90. Sampson, *The Money Lenders,* 157.

91. Rockefeller, *Memoirs,* 272.

92. Jerry W. Markham, "1 Financial Turmoil," in *A Financial History of the United States Vol. 2* (Armonk, NY: M. E. Sharpe, 2002).

93. Wilson, *The Chase,* 314.

94. Ibid., 240.

95. CMART filed for bankruptcy in 1979.

96. Steven Weisman, "Mayor Seeking New Delay for Submitting of Budget," *New York Times,* May 24, 1975.

97. "State Oversight: The New York Approach," Citizens Research Council of Michigan, March 2012.

98. Rockefeller, *Memoirs,* 502.

99. Martin Tolchin, "Buckley Opposes U.S. Intervention in City's Crisis: Says He Fears an Erosion of the Federal System," *New York Times,* September 23, 1975.

100. Summary document of New York City situation, October 20, 1975, WHCF, Box 5, Folder: New York City, October 1975, Unit Files, Gerald R. Ford Presidential Library, at www.fordlibrarymuseum.gov/library/document/0010/1554451.pdf.

101. "Ford to City: Drop Dead," *New York Daily News,* October, 30, 1975.

102. Donna E. Shalala and Carol Bellamy, "A State Saves a City: The New York Case," *Duke Law Journal* 1976, no. 1119 (1977): 1,129–1,130.

103. Thomas E. Mullaney, "Anxious Wait of Business for Carter's Economic Lineup," *New York Times,* November 5, 1976.

Chapter 14. The Late 1970s: Inflation, Hostages, and Bankers

1. Jimmy Carter, Inaugural Address, January 20, 1977, American Presidency Project, at http://www.presidency.ucsb.edu/ws/?pid=6575#axzz2h4CdjPzZ.

2. Memo from Eugene R. Black to Cyrus Vance, January 1977, Council of Economic Advisers, Box 180, Folder: General Correspondence [B][3], Jimmy Carter Presidential Library and Museum.

3. FDIC, *An Examination of the Banking Crises of the 1980s and Early 1990s,* 192, at www.fdic.gov/bank/historical/history/191_210.pdf.

4. Message to Cyrus Vance from Eugene R. Black, January 1977, Council of Economic Advisers, Box 180, Folder: General Correspondence [B][3], World Financial Markets Report, Morgan Guaranty Trust Company of New York, Carter Library.

5. Dialogue between Walter Wriston and John Reed with Franklin D. Raines regarding EFT, May 19, 1977, WHCF, Name File: Reed, John S., Carter Library.

6. Internal Memo on Regulatory Reform Program to Carter, June 29, 1977, Council of Economic Advisers, Charles L. Schultze Subject Files, Box 75, Folder: Regulatory Reform [1], Carter Library.

7. Memo from Cyrus Vance, November 10, 1977, RAC Project Number: NLC-5–5–7–9–5, Brzezinski Matl: VIP Visit File, Carter Library.

8. Ibid.

9. Memo between Rockefeller and White House (Fran Voorde and Zbigniew Brzezinski), March 23 and March 31, 1978, Carter Presidential Papers, WHCF, Carter Library.

10. Bird, *The Chairman,* 640.

11. Rockefeller, *Memoirs,* 360.

12. Bird, *The Chairman,* 640.

13. Summary Conclusions of White House Situation Room Meeting regarding Iran, November 21, 1978, RAC System, NLC-15–20–4–11–7, Carter Library.

14. Rockefeller memo regarding international sentiment over US currency, December 22, 1978, Carter Presidential Papers, WHCF, Carter Library.

15. Memo from Stuart Eizenstat regarding loan to US corporations, January 20, 1979, Office of Chief of Staff Secretary, President Handwriting Files, Box 116, Folder: January 22, 1979 [1], Carter Library.

16. Dialogue between Walter Wriston and Anne Wexler, May 23, 1979, May 31, 1979, Carter Presidential Papers, WHCF, Name File: Regan, Donald T., Carter Library.

17. Lyn Boyd, "A King's Exile: The Shah of Iran and Moral Consideration in U.S. Foreign Policy," University of Southern California, Case 234, 2000.

18. Rockefeller, *Memoirs,* 366.

19. Scope and Content Description Page, Series 28, Shah of Iran, 1979–1981, Series 28, Shah of Iran, McCloy Papers, Amherst Library.

20. Office of Staff Secretary Files, Handwriting Files, Box 182, folder 4/25/80, NLC-128-14-5-18-0, March 27, 1979, Carter Library.

21. Ibid.

22. Heilbrunn, "The Real McCloy."

23. Jimmy Carter, *Keeping Faith: Memoirs of a President* (Fayetteville, AR: University of Arkansas Press, 1995), 461.

24. Memo to Secretary of State, April 19, 1979, Office of Staff Secretary Files, Handwriting Files, Box 182, Folder: April 25, 80, NLC-7-29-3-4-6, Carter Library.

25. Iran Chamber Society website, "Historic Personalities of Iran: Ayatollah Khomeini," at www.iranchamber.com/history/rkhomeini/ayatollah_khomeini.php.

26. Memo to Secretary of State, April 19, 1979.

27. Plains File Box 25, Folder: Iran Update 11/79, NLC-128-14-7-2-5, May 2, 1979, Carter Library.

28. Plains File Box 25, Folder: Iran Update 11/79, NLC-128-14-7-10-6, May 15, 1979, Carter Library.

29. Ibid., NLC-128-14-8-18-7, June 27, 1979.

30. Ibid., NLC-128-14-12-1-0, October 1, 1979.

31. Ibid.

32. Ibid.; Vance memo to President Carter, NLC-128-14-12-12-8, October 18, 1979.

33. Carter, *Keeping Faith,* 463.

34. Ibid., 464.

35. Plains File Box 25, Folder: Iran Update 11/79, NLC-128-14-12-13-7, October 22, 1979, Carter Library.

36. Secret memo from Cyrus Vance, October 24, 1979, NLC-128-14-12-15-5, Carter Library.

37. Ibid. See also RAC System, NLC-128-14-12-15-5, October 24, 1979, Carter Library.

38. Plains File Box 25, Folder: Iran Update 11/79, NCL-128-14-12-17-3, October 26, 1979, Carter Library.

39. Rockefeller letter to Secretary of State, October 30, 1979, Carter Presidential Papers, WHCF, Name File: Rockefeller, David, Carter Library.

40. Contingency Plans for Iran Embassy Personnel, Plains File Box 25, Folder: Iran, Update 11/79, November 9, 1979, Carter Library.

41. Treasury Department website, Executive Order 12170 of the International Emergency Economic Powers Act of 1977, at www.treasury.gov/resource-center/sanctions/Programs/Documents/Executive%20Order%2012170.pdf.

42. Plains File Box 25, Folder: Iran, Update 11/79, Carter Library.

43. Ibid.

44. Ibid., NLC-17-17-24-2-7, November 22, 1979.

45. Ibid.

46. Jeff Gerth, "Chase's Lawsuit Against Iran," *New York Times,* November 11, 1980.

47. THE CHASE MANHATTAN BANK, N.A., Plaintiff, *v.* THE STATE OF IRAN, also known as ISLAMIC REPUBLIC OF IRAN, BANK MARKAZI IRAN, et al., Defendants, February 15, 1980, at http://ny.findacase.com/research/wfrmDocViewer.aspx/xq/fac.19800215_0000080.SNY.htm/qx. Case, 79 Civ. 6644.

48. Gerth, "Chase's Lawsuit Against Iran."

49. Author conversation with Mark Hulbert, April 16, 2012.

50. Office of Staff Secretary Files, Handwriting Files, Box 182, Folder: 4/25/80, RAC System, NLC-33–13–49–5, Special Coordination Committee, December 22, 1979, Carter Library.

51. Office of Chief of Staff Secretary, President Handwriting Files, Box 122, Folder: 3/7/79 [1], NLC-16–123–1–22–3, January 17, 1980, Carter Library.

52. Office of Staff Secretary Files, Handwriting Files, Box 182, Folder: 4/25/80, NLC 12–27–5–7–7, March 10, 1980, Carter Library.

53. Ibid.

54. Memo from Anne Wexler regarding luncheon, March 25, 1980, Carter Presidential Papers, WHCF, Name File: Regan, Donald T., Carter Library. See also Luncheon with Wall Street Executives via Anne Wexler, June 16, 1980.

55. Memo from President Carter, April 29, 1980, WHCF, File: A. W. Clausen, Carter Library.

56. Presidential Papers, Plains File, Subject File: Iran 10/80 through 1/21/81, Box 24, Folder: Iran, 10/80; Eyes Only/Private; To: President Carter; From: Hamilton Jordan, Carter Library.

57. Ibid., Cyrus Vance letter to President Carter.

58. Speech Text, April 25, 1980, Office of Staff Secretary Files, Handwriting Files, Box 182, Folder: 4/25/80, Carter Library.

59. Boyd, "A King's Exile."

60. Presidential Papers, Plains File, Subject File: Iran, Folder: 11/1–23/80, November 8, 1980, Carter Library. The documents included presidential declarations and orders unlocking all Iranian assets, directing payment by the Federal Reserve Bank, revoking attachments on Iranian assets held by the Federal Reserve Bank, authorizing placement of Federal Reserve funds in third-country financial institutions, unblocking Iranians' deposits in US banks overseas, settling claims, and freezing the Shah's assets.

61. Presidential Papers, Plains File, Subject File: Iran, Folder: 10/80 through 1/21/81, Box 24, Reuters News Story, November 19, 1980, Carter Library.

62. Ibid., December 3, 1980.

63. Ibid., December 13, 1980.

64. Ibid., Declarations of Algiers.

65. Ibid.

66. Ibid.

67. Ibid.

68. Ibid.

69. Ibid.

70. Ibid.

71. Presidential Papers, Plains File, Subject File: Iran 10/80 through 1/21/81, Box 2, Folder 1/21/1981, Declarations of Algiers, Carter Library.

Chapter 15. The Early to Mid-1980s: Free-Market Rules, Bankers Compete

1. Donald Regan, *For the Record: From Wall Street to Washington* (New York, NY: Harcourt, Brace, Jovanovich, 1988), 123.

2. Author conversation with Paul Craig Roberts, via email, July 23, 2013. Roberts had been opposed to the national banking initiatives that came in after he left his post, which deregulated the banking industry and caused the larger, more powerful banks to become more so.

3. "The 1982 Recession, Reagan, WGBH," *American Experience* (PBS) website, at www.pbs .org/wgbh/americanexperience/features/general-article/reagan-recession/.

4. The kitchen cabinet included Bloomingdale's heir Alfred Bloomingdale; Earl Brian, combat surgeon for the CIA's Vietnam War–period Phoenix Program (in 1995 he was convicted on ten counts of fraud and sentenced to four years in prison); Justin Whitlock Dart, son of prominent industrialist Justin Dart, "godfather" of the Americans with Disabilities Act of 1990; William French Smith, US attorney general from 1981 to 1985; Charles Wick, head of the United States Information Agency from 1981 to 1989; Los Angeles businessman William A. Wilson; auto dealer Holmes Tuttle; steel magnate Earle Jorgensen; and beer mogul Joseph Coors, who funded several think tanks at the time, including the Heritage Foundation.

5. Regan, *For the Record*, 123.

6. Ronald Reagan, nomination speech for Donald T. Regan to be Secretary of the Treasury, January 20, 1981, Press Secretary, Press Releases and Briefings, Box 1, Series 1: Press Releases, Item 10, Ronald Reagan Presidential Library. "In 1946, Mr. Regan joined Merrill Lynch. . . . [He was] named Chairman and Chief Executive Officer of Merrill Lynch, Pierce, Fenner & Smith in January 1971. He relinquished those titles in January 1980 and continues as a Director and member of the Executive Committee of the Company . . . is a member of the Policy Committee of the Business Roundtable . . . a trustee of the Committee for Economic Development, [and] a member of the Council on Foreign Relations."

7. Regan, *For the Record*, 139.

8. Ibid., 140.

9. Executive Order No. 12288, January 29, 1981, Termination of the Wage and Price regulatory program, WHORM, BE: Business-Economics BE002 R0008655, Reagan Library.

10. Ronald Reagan, Inaugural Address, January 20, 1981, Public Papers of the President, Reagan Library, at www.reagan.utexas.edu/archives/speeches/1981/12881b.htm.

11. Regulatory Reform Initiative, Fact Sheet, WHORM, Files: Cribb, Kenneth, Box 28, Folder: Deregulation, The White House, Office of the Press Secretary, Reagan Library.

12. Ibid.

13. Memo from Elizabeth Dole to Richard Darman regarding Wall Street meeting, September 11, 1981, WHORM, Business Economics, BE 003 (026000-041399), 041197SS, Reagan Library.

14. Ibid.

15. Remarks of the Vice President at the Economy Recovery Program Media Briefing, April 15, 1981, Press Releases and Briefings, Box 7, 515, Series 1, Reagan Library.

16. Zweig, *Wriston*, 721.

17. Call to Wriston, June 10, 1981, WHORM, PSF: Calls Box 001, Folder 003, 027931 PR007-02, Reagan Library. Reagan's cabinet provided him with the contacts, background, and even language to insert in various personal calls.

18. Phillip H. Wiggins, "Inflation's Impact on Companies," *New York Times,* April 16, 1980.

19. Press Briefing by James Baker III, Edwin Meese III, Donald Regan, August 1, 1981, WHORM, Press Releases, Box 12, 1045, Reagan Library.

20. Diary, October 23, 1980, Carter Library, at www.jimmycarterlibrary.gov/documents /diary/1980/d102380t.pdf.

21. Martin Meyer, "The Humbling of BankAmerica," *New York Times Magazine,* May 3, 1987, at www.nytimes.com/1987/05/03/magazine/the-humbling-of-bankamerica.html ?pagewanted=all&src=pm.

22. Letter from Samuel Armacost, March 25, 1983, WHORM, Alpha File, Folder: Armacost, Samuel, Reagan Library.

23. Author's Note: I began my career in international banking in the late 1980s, joining Chase as a junior programmer-analyst, when Butcher was the CEO. On Black Monday, October 19, 1987, the department in which I worked was frantically trying to hedge the bank's short position, a bet taken through a new product that linked CDs with the stock market index. Years later, I realized this product circumvented Glass-Steagall.

24. Ronald Reagan, "Appointment of the Chairman, Executive Director, and Membership of the President's Commission on Executive Exchange," September 14, 1981, American Presidency Project, at www.presidency.ucsb.edu/ws/?pid=44250.

25. In a July 10, 1986, letter sent to Rockefeller, following a weekend spent at the Rockefeller estate, Reagan wrote, "The Reagans, the Davises and all our staff people want you to know how grateful we are for the warm hospitality and many kindnesses bestowed on us by the Rockefellers. . . . Nancy joins me in heartfelt thanks to all of you for a weekend we shall always remember."

26. Letter from David Rockefeller, December 18, 1981, Canzeri, Joseph Files, Series III, Subject File, Box 010, Caribbean Project, Reagan Library. Several months later, in remarks on the Caribbean Basin Initiative at a White House briefing for American CEOs, Reagan said, "I conceived the idea of doing something for Jamaica when Seaga won the election and took that country back from Communist rule. . . . And I turned to the private sector and asked—and asked David Rockefeller to be chairman of a group—[and] go and see how we could use private enterprise to help restore the economy." As Rockefeller wrote in his *Memoirs,* "I rallied the American business community to support the newly elected conservative government of Edward Seaga in Jamaica."

27. Ronald Reagan, "Remarks at a White House Briefing for Members of the Council of the Americas," May 12, 1987, American Presidency Project, at www.presidency.ucsb.edu /ws/?pid=34270.

28. "Chase Lowers Drysdale Write-off," *New York Times,* June 15, 1982, at www.nytimes.com /1982/06/15/business/chase-lowers-drysdale-write-off.html?n=Top%2FReference% 2FTimes%20Topics%2FSubjects%2FT%2FTaxes

29. Minutes, Meeting of the Federal Reserve FOMC, May 18, 1982, 1–2.

30. "The Chase Manhattan Corporation," International Directory of Company Histories.

31. Douglas Martin, "Chase Is Suing F.D.I.C. on Penn Square Moves," *New York Times,* July 20, 1982.

32. Telegram to President Elect Reagan from Willard Butcher, November 8, 1980, WHORM, Alpha File, Folder: Butcher, Willard C., Reagan Library.

33. "About John C. Whitehead '43," Haverford College, at www.haverford.edu/campuscenter /about.php.

34. Telephone call to Walter Wriston, August 16, 1982, WHORM, PHF: Calls, Box 003, Folder 039, 081348 PR007-02, Reagan Library. The press release stated, "He is a director of six corporations, and a member of several business and civic organizations. He is Chairman of the Business Council, Director of the Economic Council of New York, a member of the Advisory Committee on Reform of the International Monetary Systems, and a trustee of the American Enterprise Institution."

35. Letter to Walter Wriston from Edwin Meese, November 8, 1982, WHORM, Alpha File, Folder: Wriston, Walter, Reagan Library.

36. Ibid.

37. Jonathan Fuerbringer, "The Fed vs. the White House: A Collision Is Brewing over the Course of Recovery," *New York Times*, January 10, 1982.

38. "U.S. Merger Policy Stated," Reuters (*New York Times*), October 27, 1981.

39. Letter to Byron Dorgan, March 23, 1982, WHORM, BE 001 (047000–047699), Case No. 047101, Reagan Library.

40. Letter from Ralph Nader, April 26, 1982, WHORM, BE 001, Box 5 (075000–078899), Reagan Library.

41. Ibid. Ominously, Nader also pointed out that Richard Pratt, chairman of the Federal Home Loan Bank Board, had stripped away virtually all consumer safeguards on the adjustable rate mortgage and authorized the use of balloon mortgages, which were one of the principal causes of widespread foreclosures in the Depression. Elizabeth Dole was worried about the message this might send the public on the back of "Consumer Awareness Week." She believed "we would be safer taking the 'high road' in this response. [Because] we must assume that this letter will end up in the newspapers." In Dole's response, she recounted Reagan's earlier words: "By preserving the rights and responsibilities of consumers, we can assure the vitality of the marketplace and obtain a more desirable balance of competitive and regulatory forces in our society," Reagan Library.

42. Ibid.

43. "World Bank Loan Plan," *New York Times*, January 13, 1983.

44. Ibid. See also FDIC, *History of the Eighties—Lessons for the Future, Volume I: An Examination of the Banking Crises of the 1980s and Early 1990s,* Chapter 5, at www.fdic.gov/bank/historical/history/191_210.pdf.

45. Ibid.

46. Andrew Albert, "Regan Aims to Calm Fears on Argentina," *American Banker,* May 29, 1984.

47. Ibid.

48. Ibid.

49. Joint statement by the participants at the Williamsburg Economic Summit, May 30, 1983, WHORM, Press Releases, Box 058, 4465, Reagan Library.

50. Ronald Reagan, *The Reagan Diaries* (New York, NY: HarperCollins, 2007), 160.

51. "Volcker Plan to Curb Bank Mergers," AP (*New York Times*), June 24, 1983, at www.nytimes.com/1983/06/24/business/volcker-plan-to-curb-bank-mergers.html.

52. Senior Staff Meeting Action Items, July 6, 1983, WHORM, FG 006–01, Subject File, Box 49, Case No. 152218 (4 of 9), Financial Institutions Deregulation Bill, Reagan Library.

53. Ibid., July 7, 1983, Case No. 3152220 (9 of 9).

54. Ibid., July 8, 1983, Box 50, Case No. 154077 (8 of 10).

55. Memorandum for Edwin L. Harper from Thomas J. Healey, July 18, 1983, WHORM, FG 012, Box 2, Case No. 157912; enclosed, a copy of the testimony of Honorable Donald T. Regan, Secretary of the Treasury before the Senate Committee on Banking, Housing, and Urban Affairs, Reagan Library.

56. "Volcker Plan to Curb Bank Mergers," *New York Times*, June 24, 1983, at www.nytimes.com /1983/06/24/business/volcker-plan-to-curb-bank-mergers.html. Memorandum for Edwin L. Harper from Thomas J. Healey, July 18, 1983.

57. Ibid.

58. Cabinet Council on Economic Affairs Agenda, 1. Report of the Working Group on Financial Institution Reform (CM#149), 2. Report of the Working Group on Financial Institutions Deregulation Act (FIDA) (CM #385), November 23, 1983, WHORM, Federal Government Organizations, 010-02, Box 43, Case No. 168834CS, Reagan Library.

59. Memo from Thomas J. Healey, November 18, 1983, WHORM, Federal Government Organizations, 010-02, Box 43, Case No. 168834CS, Reagan Library.

60. Memo for R. T. McNamara, November 8, 1983, WHORM, Federal Government Organizations, 010-02 Box 43, Case No. 168834CS, Reagan Library.

61. Ibid.

62. Ibid.

63. Ibid.

64. Cabinet Council on Economic Affairs, November 29, 1983, WHORM, FG010-02, Box 44, Case No. 168838, Reagan Library.

65. Fraust, "NY Fed Chief: Merit in View of Agency Lag; Solomon Concedes Delays on New Powers," *American Banker*, January 27, 1984.

66. Testimony of the Honorable Donald T. Regan, Secretary of the Treasury, before the Senate Committee on Banking, Housing and Urban Affairs, March 28, 1984, WHORM, FG 012, Box 2, Case No. 219399, Reagan Library.

67. Fraust, "NY Fed Chief." Solomon was a director of S.G. Warburg in London from 1985 until 1991 and Chairman of S.G. Warburg USA from 1985 until 1989.

68. Ibid.

69. "Is a Texas Thrift the Next Course for Hungry Citicorp? Analysts Say State's Economy, Thriving Institutions Could Lure New York Holding Company," *American Banker*, January 9, 1984.

70. Laura Gross and John Forde, "Reed Wins Banking's Big One—The 'CitiSweeps'; Appointment of Retail Banker as Wriston's Successor Is Seen as Setting Precedent for Other Institutions," *American Banker*, June 21, 1984.

71. Zweig, *Wriston*, 827.

72. Ronald Reagan, "Remarks at the Annual Republican Senate/House Fund-raising Dinner," May 21, 1986, American Presidency Project, at www.presidency.ucsb.edu/ws /?pid=37320.

73. "Bush Task Group Statement," *American Banker*, February 2, 1984.

74. Ibid.

75. Wilson, *The Chase*, 342.

76. Robert M. Garsson, "Digesting the Convention's Issues—and Shrimp; Executives Head Home from ABA Gathering, End 5-Day Immersion in Industry Topics," *American Banker*, October 26, 1984.

77. Wilson, *The Chase*, 343.

78. Bob Woodward, *Maestro* (New York, NY: Simon & Schuster, 2000), 17.

79. David Warsh, "How Volcker Acted When Chips Were Down," *Boston Globe*, January 31, 1988.

80. Memo for the Cabinet Council of Economic Advisers from Roger B. Porter, October 5, 1984, WHORM, FG 010-02, Box 54, Case No. 169082, Reagan Library. See also Andrew Albert, "Bush Group Urges Reallocation of Powers; Fed Wins Expanded State Supervisory Role," *American Banker*, February 1, 1984.

81. Andrew Albert and Jay Rosenstein, "Baker Appointment Seen as Plus for Regional Banks, Though Not as Harbinger of Any Change in Philosophy," *American Banker*, January 9, 1985. See also Ronald Reagan, "Remarks Announcing the Nomination of James A. Baker III to Be Secretary of the Treasury and the Appointment of Donald T. Regan as Assistant to the President and Chief of Staff," January 8, 1985, American Presidency Project, at www.presidency.ucsb.edu/ws/?pid=38244.

82. Albert and Rosenstein, "Baker Appointment Seen as Plus."

83. Jonathan Friedland, "Baker Urges $20 Billion Boost in Bank Lending to 3d World: Treasury Secretary Proposes Global Compact on Debt Crisis," *American Banker*, October 9, 1985.

84. A. W. Clausen, Address to the Board of Governors, October 8, 1985, WHORM, Bledsoe, Ralph C. Files (DPC), Box 157, Reagan Library.

85. Peter T. Kilbom, "Washington Watch; Administration and Clausen," *New York Times*, October 21, 1985, at www.nytimes.com/1985/10/21/business/washington-watch-administration-and-clausen.html.

86. Ibid.

Chapter 16. The Late 1980s: Third World Staggers, S&Ls Implode

1. George Bentson study presented to Congress, October 12, 1985, WHORM, FG (federal government): Organizations, Box 21, Case File 341076, Reagan Library. The study found that "Deregulation is responsible for the failures of the 1980s only in allowing risk-prone managers to obtain funds. Direct investments, however, do not appear to be among the risks taken."

2. Ibid.

3. Elizabeth E. Bailey, "Airline Deregulation: Confronting the Paradoxes," *Regulation Magazine* (Cato Institute), Summer 1992, at http://www.cato.org/sites/cato.org/files/serials/files/regulation/1992/7/v15n3–6.pdf, 1.

4. Martin Mayer, *The Greatest-Ever Bank Robbery: The Collapse of the Savings and Loan Industry* (New York, NY: C. Scribner's Sons, 1990).

5. Repurchase (or repo) agreements are a way to borrow money short-term, where deposits or government securities are sold or lent to another party in exchange for cash and returned (usually) the following day.

6. Kingsford Capital Management, *Kingsford Capital: The First 100 Years* (San Francisco, CA: Bentrovato Books, 2011), 76.

7. James Sterngold, "Boesky Sentenced to 3 Years in Jail in Insider Scandal," *New York Times*, December 19, 1987.

8. Scot J. Paltrow, "Sobbing Milken Pleads Guilty to Six Felonies," *Los Angeles Times*, April 25, 1990. See also Myles Meserve, "Here's How You Make a Comeback on Wall Street—The Michael Milken Story," *Business Insider*, August 16, 2012.

9. Bartlett Naylor, "Executives Call US Securities Laws a Hindrance in World Capital Markets," *American Banker*, February 28, 1986.

10. Gary Hector, "Botching up a Great Bank Under Tom Clausen," *Fortune*, June 6, 1988. Excerpted from *Breaking the Bank: The Decline of BankAmerica* (New York, NY: Little, Brown & Co., 1988).

11. Mike Carroll, "Will Armacost's Luck Hold at Bank of America?," *American Banker*, February 28, 1986.

12. Hector, "Botching Up a Great Bank."

13. "BankAmerica Picks Clausen to Replace Armacost as Chair, CEO," *Chicago Sun-Times*, October 12, 1986.

14. John M. Broder, "Armacost Quits at BofA; Clausen May Get Post," *Los Angeles Times*, October 11, 1986, at http://articles.latimes.com/1986-10-11/news/mn -2772_1_world-bank.

15. "Alden Winship ('Tom') Clausen," World Bank Archives, at http://web.world bank.org/WBSITE/EXTERNAL/EXTABOUTUS/EXTARCHIVES/0,,contentMD K:20487071~pagePK:36726~piPK:437378~theSitePK:29506,00.html.

16. John M. Broder, "Hike in Bad-Loan Reserve Nets $1 Billion B of A Loss," *Los Angeles Times*, June 9, 1987, at http://articles.latimes.com/1987-06-09/news/mn-6019_1 _net-loss.

17. "Mexico, Venezuela Falling Behind on Loans," Associated Press via *Chicago Sun-Times*, March 28, 1986.

18. Meyer, "The Humbling of Bank America."

19. "The History of JPMorgan Chase & Co.: 200 Years of Leadership in Banking," JPMorgan Chase, 2008, at www.jpmorganchase.com/corporate/About-JPMC/document/shorthistory .pdf.

20. Ibid. See also "J. P. Morgan to Underwrite Corporate Debt," *Los Angeles Times*, June 20, 1989, at http://articles.latimes.com/1989–06–20/business/fi-2479_1_chase-manhattan -corp-fed-s-decision-debt-securities.

21. Eric Dash, "Dennis Weatherstone, Banking Sage, Dies at 77," *New York Times*, June 18, 2008, at www.nytimes.com/2008/06/18/business/18weatherstone.html.

22. "Citicorp Bad-Loan Action Lauded Firm Sets Up $3b Fund as Shield on Losses," *Albany Times Union* (Albany, NY), May 21, 1987.

23. Robert A. Bennett, "Citicorp's Defiant Leader: John Shepard Reed," *New York Times*, May 21, 1987, at www.nytimes.com/1987/05/21/business/man-in-the-news-citicorp-s-defiant -leader-john-shepard-reed.html?pagewanted=all&src=pm.

24. Tom Redburn, "Banks Led Way in Easing Crisis on Mexico Debt," *Los Angeles Times*, January 10, 1988, at http://articles.latimes.com/1988-01-10/business/fi-34708_1 _commercial-bank.

25. "2-Bank Rivalry Key to Mexico Breakthrough," *Chicago Sun-Times*, February 16, 1988.

26. Woodward, *The Maestro*, 20.

27. Alan Greenspan, *The Age of Turbulence* (New York, NY: Penguin, 2008), 28.

28. Ibid.

29. "Interview with Charles Geisst," *Frontline* (PBS), February 5, 2003, at www.pbs.org/wgbh /pages/frontline/shows/wallstreet/interviews/geisst.html.

30. Woodward, *The Maestro*, 25.

31. Swearing-in Ceremony for Alan Greenspan as Chairman of the Federal Reserve Board, August 11, 1987, WHORM, PHF: Box 28, Presidential Speeches, Folder 572, No. 5187295C, Reagan Library.

32. Ibid.

33. "Fed Boss Urges Bank Changes," Associated Press (*Boston Globe*), October 6, 1987.

34. Economic Briefing for the President, "Record-Breaking Peacetime Expansion: A Summary of Economic Accomplishments," October 15, 1987, BE Business-Economics (50000–533999), Case No. 527983SS, Reagan Library.

35. Ibid.

36. Adam M. Zaretsky, "Learning the Lessons of History: The Federal Reserve and the Payments System," *The Regional Economist*, July 1996, at www.stlouisfed.org/publications/re/articles/?id=1805.

37. Woodward, *The Maestro*, 45.

38. Alan Murray, "Fed's New Chairman Wins a Lot of Praise Handling the Crash," *Wall Street Journal*, November 5, 1987, at http://online.wsj.com/article/SB112404015636012610.html.

39. Susan F. Rasky, "Blue-Chip Leader for Task Force: Nicholas Brady," *New York Times*, October 23, 1987, at www.nytimes.com/1987/10/23/business/man-in-the-news-blue-chip-leader-for-task-force-nicholas-frederick-brady.html?pagewanted=all&src=pm.

40. "Report of the Presidential Task Force on Market Mechanisms," January 1988, Internet Archives, at http://archive.org/stream/reportofpresiden01unit/reportofpresiden01unit_djvu.txt.

41. Woodward, *The Maestro*, 48.

42. Executive Order 12631: Working Group on Financial Markets, March 8, 1988, at Reagan Library, at www.reagan.utexas.edu/archives/speeches/1988/031888d.htm.

43. Ibid.

44. Report from the Working Group on Financial Markets, May 1988, Sprinkel, Beryl Box 6, OA17742, Folder: Working Group on Financial Markets (2 of 2), Reagan Library.

45. Ronald Reagan, "Remarks Announcing the Resignation of James A. Baker III as Secretary of the Treasury and the Nomination of Nicholas F. Brady," August 5, 1988, American Presidency Project, at www.presidency.ucsb.edu/ws/?pid=36215.

46. Michael Quint, "The Financier 'Who Knows What Is Going On,'" *New York Times*, August 6, 1988, at www.nytimes.com/1988/08/06/us/the-financier-who-knows-what-is-going-on.html.

47. Tom Redburn, "Overhaul of Bank System Indicated: Deregulation," *Los Angeles Times*, July 26, 1990, at http://articles.latimes.com/1990-07-26/news/mn-944_1_federal-deposit-insurance.

48. According to the Bush archives in College Station, Texas, the banker relationships within archival material had been unexplored until I visited them. Many files will remain unopened until my FOIA requests are processed.

49. George Bush, "Remarks at the Swearing-in Ceremony for James A. Baker III as Secretary of State," January 27, 1989, American Presidency Project, at www.presidency.ucsb.edu/ws/?pid=16630.

50. David E. Rosenbaum, "The Treasury's 'Mr. Diffident,'" *New York Times,* November 19, 1989, at www.nytimes.com/1989/11/19/business/the-treasury-s-mr-diffident.html?page wanted=all&src=pm.

51. "The Official Confidant," *Washington Post,* April 22, 1986, WHORM, Files, Alpha File, B: Folder: Brady, Nicholas, F., Reagan Library. Brady was a member of the Armed Services Committee and the Banking, Housing and Urban Affairs Committee.

52. White House Office of Media Affairs, Subject File: Nicholas Brady, September 21, 1988, Treasury News Press Release, Reagan Library.

53. Bush Presidential Records: Staff and Office Files, Category FG134, Richard Breeden Files, Issues and Analysis, Folder: Notebook: United States Chamber of Commerce Meeting—Economic Policy Committee and Task Force on the Thrift Industry, March 10, 1989, at http://archive.org/stream/blueprintforrefo01unit#page/n1/mode/2up.

54. WHORM, Alpha File, Folder: Greenspan, Alan (1), Reagan Library.

55. John M. Berry, "Fed's Greenspan Disagrees with Bush Economic Forecast; Strong Growth Is Called Not 'Probable,'" *Washington Post,* February 1, 1989.

56. FDIC, "The S&L Crisis: A Chrono-Biography," at www.fdic.gov/bank/historical/s&l/.

57. US Chamber of Commerce meeting, Economic Policy Committee and Task Force on the Thrift Industry, March 10, 1989, Staff and Office Files, Category FG134, Richard Breeden Files: Issues and Analysis, George H. W. Bush Presidential Library and Museum.

58. Remarks by Nicholas F. Brady, Dallas Chamber of Commerce, Sheraton Park Central Hotel, Dallas, Texas, March 28, 1989, Staff and Office Files, Category FG134, Richard Breeden Files, Folder: S&L Rescue, Brady's Statement, Bush Library.

59. "Fed Gives Moran Subsidiary Permission to Underwrite Corporate Debt," Associated Press, June 20, 1989, Associated Press News Archives at www.apnewsarchive .com/1989/Fed-Gives-Morgan-Subsidiary-Permission-to-Underwrite-Corporate-Debt /id-7070c63aa99efb3c913d7dc66e897ecd, http://www.riskglossary.com/link/united _states_financial_regulation.htm.

60. "J. P. Morgan Unit Wins Lead in Savannah Electric Offer," *New York Times,* October 11, 1989.

61. Nomi Prins, *Other People's Money,* paperback ed. (New York, NY: New Press, 2006), 35.

62. Stephen P. Farrar files, Folder: Debt, Files: Brady Plan, White House Office of Policy Development.

63. Remarks by Treasury Secretary Nicholas F. Brady to the Brookings Institution and the Bretton Woods Committee conference on third world debt, *Treasury News,* US Treasury Department, March, 10 1989.

64. Redraft of Bretton Woods Committee speech, sent from Brady to Sununu, March 9, 1989, WHORM, Subject File: C.F., FO 0004-02, Folder: Loans—Funds, Bush Library.

65. Robert Devlin, "From Baker to Brady: Can the New Plan Work?," *Revista de Economia Politica* 10, no. 2 (38): April–June, 1990.

66. Haluk Unal, Asli Demirguc-Kunt, and Kwok-Wai Leung, "The Brady Plan, the 1989 Mexican Debt Reduction Agreement, and Bank Stock Returns in the United States and Japan," Policy Research Working Papers, Debt and International Finance, World Bank, November 1992, WPS 1012, at www-wds.worldbank.org/servlet/WDSContentServer /WDSP/IB/1992/11/01/000009265_3961003160143/Rendered/PDF/multi_page.pdf.

67. Hobart Rowen, "Is It Time for a 'Debt Czar'?" *Washington Post,* December 28, 1989.

68. Peter T. Kilborn, "Mexico and Banks Reach Accord to Lower Debt; Pact Includes Big Cut in Amount Owed—New Loans Are Set," *New York Times,* July 24, 1989, at www.nytimes.com/1989/07/24/world/mexico-banks-reach-accord-lower-debt-pact-includes-big-cut-amount-owed-new-loans.html?pagewanted=all&src=pm.

69. Ibid. See also "Participants in the Marathon Talks," *New York Times,* July 31, 1989, at www.nytimes.com/1989/07/31/business/international-report-participants-in-the-marathon-talks.html.

70. Letter to John S. Reed from John H. Sununu, March 31, 1989, WHORM, FI 009, Box 49, Document 021813, Bush Library.

71. Paul Blustein and Hobart Rowen, "Brady Urges New Debt Policy; Some Forgiveness Sought on 3rd World Loans," *Washington Post,* March 11, 1989.

72. Letter from William F. Gorog, of Arbor International in Virginia, forwarding Moore's thoughts to Roger Porter, assistant to the president for economic and domestic affairs, April 1, 1989, WHORM, Bush Library.

73. The LDC Debt Problem and the Banks, a supplement to the "Banker Initiative" by George S. Moore sent to Roger Porter, April 14, 1989, WHORM, Box FI 002, Folder: 021324-032804, Document 029414, Bush Library.

74. Ibid.

75. Richard Lawrence, "World Bank Unveils Three-Year Program for LDC Debt Relief," *Journal of Commerce,* June 2, 1989, White House Office of Policy Development, Stephen P. Farrar Files, Folder: Debt Files: Brady Plan, Bush Library.

76. Steven Mufson, "Morgan Adds $2 Billion to Loss Reserves; Largest Set-Aside of 3 Banks in Week," *Washington Post,* September 22, 1989.

77. Testimony by Alan Greenspan Before the Subcommittee on Securities of the Committee on Banking, Housing, and Urban Affairs, US Senate, June 14, 1989, at http://fraser.stlouisfed.org/docs/historical/greenspan/Greenspan_19890614.pdf.

78. "Citicorp Chairman Recommends Cut in Deposit Insurance," *Albany Times Union,* July 14, 1989.

79. "Banking Officials Call for Restructuring of U.S. Financial System," *Deseret News,* July 17, 1989.

80. Statement of Citicorp Chairman John S. Reed Before the Committee on Banking, Housing, and Urban Affairs, US Senate, July 13, 1989. Summary of Testimony, Reed, WHORM, FI 002, Document 58025, Bush Library.

81. Timothy Curry and Lynn Shibut, "The Cost of the Savings and Loan Crisis: Truth and Consequences," *FDIC Banking Review,* December 2000, at www.fdic.gov/bank/analytical/banking/2000dec/brv13n2_2.pdf.

82. Ibid.

83. Withdrawal/Redaction Sheet, WHORM, FI 002 112877-119799, Bush Library.

84. Michael K. Frisby, "Bush Sons' Ventures Expose Him to Scrutiny," *Austin American-Statesman,* May 17, 1992.

85. "Keating Five" (Times Topics), *New York Times,* at http://topics.nytimes.com/topics/reference/timestopics/subjects/k/keating_five/index.html.

86. FDIC, "The S&L Crisis: A Chrono-Bibliography."

87. Nathaniel C. Nash, "Showdown Time for Danny Wall," *New York Times,* July 9, 1989, at www.nytimes.com/1989/07/09/business/showdown-time-for-danny-wall.html.

88. Brady to Republican Leader Robert H. Michel, US House of Representatives, June 14, 1989, Staff and Office Files, Category FG134, Richard Breeden Files, Folder: S&L Rescue, Bush Library.

89. Internationalization of Securities Markets, June 14, 1989, Senate Committee on Banking, Housing, Urban Affairs, Subcommittee Hearings, C-SPAN Video Library, at www.c-spanvideo .org/program/Securiti (beginning at 47.30). See also "Greenspan Says Bank Law Dated Urges Wider Securities Business to Help U.S. Compete," *Albany Times Union,* June 15, 1989.

90. "Banks in Insurance Reports," January 1989, Staff and Office Files, Banking and Insurance 1989, Category FG134, Files: Richard Breeden, Folder: S&L Rescue, Bush Library.

91. Ibid., Economic Policy Committee and Task Force. The plan entailed merging the New Deal–created FSLIC into the FDIC, increasing S&L capital requirements, and increasing commercial bank and thrift insurance premiums to the FDIC insurance fund for the first time since 1935.

92. Bill Summary and Status, 101st Congress (1989–1990), H. R. 1278, Financial Institutions Reform, Recovery, and Enforcement Act of 1989, Library of Congress, at http://thomas.loc .gov/cgi-bin/bdquery/z?d101:h.r.01278.

93. The act also abolished the Federal Home Loan Bank Board (FHLBB) and created both the Federal Housing Finance Board (FHFB) and the Office of Thrift Supervision (OTS) to take its place.

94. Mayer, *Greatest-Ever Bank Robbery,* 276.

95. Curry and Shibut, "The Cost of the Savings and Loan Crisis."

96. Ibid.

97. Ibid.

98. Federal Open Market Committee, Federal Reserve Bulletin A96, June 1989, at http:// fraser.stlouisfed.org/download-page/page.pdf?pid=62&id=308766.

99. "Venezuela's Creditors Are Unlikely to Agree," *New York Times,* July 29, 1989, at www .nytimes.com/1989/07/29/opinion/l-venezuela-s-creditors-are-unlikely-to-agree-329689 .html. See also "Brady to the Banks: Stop Stonewalling," *New York Times,* July 21, 1989, at www .nytimes.com/1989/07/21/opinion/brady-to-the-banks-stop-stonewalling.html.

100. Willard C. Butcher, "Venezuela's Creditors Are Unlikely to Agree" (letter), *New York Times,* July 25, 1989.

101. "Venezuelan Debt Payment," *New York Times,* October 7, 1989, at www.nytimes .com/1989/10/07/business/venezuelan-debt-payment.html.

102. Butcher, "Venezuela's Creditors Are Unlikely to Agree."

103. The senators were Christopher Bond, Orrin Hatch, Larry Pressler, Bob Dole, and Trent Lott.

104. Letter from five senators to major American banks urging their cooperation with Venezuela debt restructuring, December 18, 1989, WHORM, General FO-004-02, Folder: Loans–Funds, Bush Library. The other bankers were Walter Shipley, chairman of Chemical Bank; Charles Sanford Jr. of Bankers Trust; John McGillicuddy, chairman and CEO of Manufacturers Hanover Trust; and Barry Sullivan, chairman of First Chicago.

105. Rowen, "Is it Time for a Debt Czar?"

106. Paul Craig Roberts, "Beneath the 'Twin Towers of Debt,'" *Wall Street Journal,* October 28, 1986, Folder: Paul Craig Roberts [2 of 2], Reagan Library.

107. Ibid.

108. Curry and Shibut, "The Cost of the Savings and Loan Crisis."

Chapter 17. The Early to Mid-1990s: Killer Instinct, Bank Wars, and the Rise of Goldman Sachs

1. Alan Greenspan, "The Challenge of Central Banking in a Democratic Society," *Federal Reserve Board*, December 5, 1996, at www.federalreserve.gov/boarddocs/speeches/1996/19961205.htm.

2. Document 142712, May 26, 1990, Presidential Files, WHORM FG 001-07, Bush Library.

3. Document 201298, June 9, 1990, WHORM, FI 002, Bush Library. See also www.hks.harvard.edu/about/faculty-staff-directory/roger-porter.

4. Document 140558CU, Letter to C. Boyden Gray from John G. Aldridge, May 7, 1990, WHORM, BE Box 4, Folder 302736 [2], Bush Library.

5. Ibid.

6. Mark D. Fefer, Wilton Woods, and John Labate, "Favorite S&L Felonies," *CNN Money*, November 5, 1990, at money.cnn.com/magazines/fortune/fortune_archive/1990/11/05/74309/index.htm.

7. Justice Department Release, "How Prosecutions Have Fared in S&L Area During Past Two Years," White-Collar Crime Reporter 17, September 6, 1990.

8. Barnaby J. Feder, "Chase Manhattan to Cut 5,000 Jobs and Trim Dividend," *New York Times*, September 22, 1990.

9. Michael Quint, "Citicorp Sees Payout Likely Again by 1994," *New York Times*, October 9, 1992.

10. John Authers, "Engineer Behind the Bank's Global Quest," *Financial Times*, April 14, 1998.

11. Robert Lenzner, "N.Y. Banks' Bailout Proposal Would Buy Time for Trump," *Boston Globe*, June 12, 1990.

12. "Forgive and Forget (Brazil's Debt)," *The Economist*, September 1, 1990.

13. Robert Guenther and Douglas R. Sease, "Chase Manhattan's Labrecque, Ryan Face Investors' 'Show-Me Attitude,'" *Wall Street Journal*, June 29, 1990.

14. Michael Quint, "Chase to Consider Ties to Non-Bank Partners," *New York Times*, October 23, 1990.

15. Louise Glass, "Taking Stock (and Other Securities)," *ABA Banking Journal*, 1990.

16. US Senate, Daily Digest, April 3, 1990, Topic: Financial Service Industry, Congressional Record, 101st Congress, at http://thomas.loc.gov/cgi-bin/query/B?r101:@FIELD(FLD003+d)+@FIELD(DDATE+19900403).

17. Michael Quint, "Regulatory Shift Allows U.S. Banks to Trade Stocks," *New York Times*, September 21, 1990, at www.nytimes.com/1990/09/21/business/regulatory-shift-allows-us-banks-to-trade-stocks.html?pagewanted=all&src=pm. In March 1991, J. P. Morgan underwrote a $56 million equity issue by AMSCO International, the first common stock underwriting by a commercial bank since the Glass-Steagall Act.

18. Document 213358, February 5, 1991, WHORM, FI 002, Bush Library.

19. Steve Lohr, "Banking's Real Estate Miseries," *New York Times*, January 13, 1991.

20. Robert J. McCartney. "Citicorp's Earnings Fall 81%; Profits Also Decline at 4 Other Big Banks," *Washington Post*, April 17, 1991.

21. "White House Threat on Banking Bill," *New York Times*, September 18, 1991.

22. "Federal Reserve Bulletin," *St. Louis Federal Reserve* 75, no. 5 (1987), at http://fraser.stlouisfed.org/docs/publications/FRB/1980s/frb_051987.pdf and http://fraser.stlouis

fed.org/docs/publications/FRB/1980s/frb_111984.pdf. See also Hobart Rowen, "Conable Says He'll Retire as World Bank President; Bush to Name Lewis T. Preston as Successor," *Washington Post*, March 7, 1991.

23. Lewis Thomas Preston, "World Bank Archives," at http://web.worldbank.org/WBSITE /EXTERNAL/EXTABOUTUS/EXTARCHIVES/0,,contentMDK:20505265~page PK:36726~piPK:437378~theSitePK:29506,00.html. See also "Banks Led Way in Easing Crisis on Mexican Debt," *Los Angeles Times*, January 10, 1998, at http://articles.latimes .com/1988-01-10/business/fi-34708_1_commercial-bank.

24. Hobart Rowen, "Preston Facing Big Job As Head of World Bank," *Washington Post*, March 17, 1991.

25. Preston, "World Bank Archives."

26. Stephen Labaton, "Wall Street's Ambitious Top Cop," *New York Times*, March 24, 1991.

27. Ivan C. Roten and Donald J. Mullineaux, "Debt Underwriting by Commercial Bank-Affiliated Firms and Investment Banks: More Evidence," *Journal of Banking and Finance*, November 27, 2000, at http://pages.stern.nyu.edu/~eofek/InvBank/papers/DebtUnder _JBF.pdf. Section 20 of the Glass-Steagall Act prohibited banks from affiliating with companies "engaged principally" in the underwriting or dealing with securities.

28. Labaton, "Wall Street's Ambitious Top Cop."

29. Ronald Reagan, "Remarks at a Republican Party Fundraising Dinner in Houston, Texas," September 22, 1998, American Presidency Project, at www.presidency.ucsb.edu/ws/index .php?pid=34876.

30. Document 15164001-159070, WHORM, BE Box 2, Folder BE 000, Bush Library.

31. Ibid.

32. Ibid.

33. Document 241932, From Robert T. Swanson, April 12, 1991, WHORM, FI 002, Box 12, Bush Library.

34. US Commodity Futures Trading Commission, "E9-6187," Law & Regulation: Proposed Rules, March 24, 2009, at www.cftc.gov/LawRegulation/FederalRegister/ProposedRules /e9-6187.

35. Robert Barone, "Commodity Bubble Redux in Full Effect," *Forbes*, April 25, 2011.

36. George W. Bush, "Statement on Signing the Futures Trading Practices Act of 1992," October 28, 1992, American Presidency Project, at www.presidency.ucsb.edu/ws/index.php?pid =21696.

37. Stephen A. Rhoades, "Bank Mergers and Industry Wide Structure," *Board of Governors of the Federal Reserve System*, January 1996, 6, at www.federalreserve.gov/pubs/staff studies/1990–99/ss169.pdf.

38. "Manufacturers Hanover, Chemical Banks to Merge Transaction, Biggest Ever in Industry, Worth $2 Billion," *Post-Tribune* (Indiana), July 16, 1991.

39. Eric Dash, "John F. McGillicuddy, 78, Banking Leader," *New York Times*, January 6, 2009. See also "Executive Changes," *New York Times*, February 18, 1988.

40. Lawrence Malkin, "Hanover Swaps Stock with Chemical: Banks Join to Form 2d Biggest in U.S. Manufacturers," *New York Times*, July 16, 1991.

41. Transcript of the announcement, "Special Report: The Engagement of Chemical and Manufacturers Hanover," *American Banker*, July 16, 1991.

42. Malkin, "Hanover Swaps Stock with Chemical." See also "Manufacturers Hanover, Chemical Banks to Merge."

43. Malkin, "Hanover Swaps Stock with Chemical."

44. Ibid.

45. Bill Clinton, *My Life* (New York, NY: Alfred A. Knopf, 2004), 377.

46. Charles R. Babcock, "Both Parties Raise Millions in 'Soft Money'; Campaign Laws Let CEOs, Companies, Unions Donate Big Checks," *Washington Post*, July 26, 1992.

47. Open Secrets, Center for Responsive Politics, "Mortgage Bankers & Brokers: Long-Term Contribution Trends," February 18, 2013, at www.opensecrets.org/industries/totals .php?ind=F4600.

48. Ibid.

49. "Bill Clinton: The Terror and Toast of Wall Street," *BusinessWeek*, April 5, 1992, at www .businessweek.com/stories/1992-04-05/bill-clinton-the-terror-and-toast-of-wall-street. Attendees included Kohlberg Kravis Roberts & Company partner Theodore Ammon, Bloomberg Financial Markets president Michael Bloomberg, and Lazard Freres & Company partner Peter Tufo.

50. Phillip Inman, "Black Wednesday 20 Years On: How the Day Unfolded," *Guardian*, September 13, 2012.

51. "2005 Freedom of Information Requests—The Cost of Black Wednesday Reconsidered," *HM Treasury*, August 6, 1997, at www.hm-treasury.gov.uk/foi_erm4_2005.htm.

52. George Soros, Byron Wien, and Krisztina Koenen, *Soros on Soros: Staying Ahead of the Curve* (New York, NY: J. Wiley, 1995).

53. Ibid., 81.

54. Thomas Jaffe and Dyan Machan, "How the Market Overwhelmed the Central Banks," *Forbes*, November 9, 1992.

55. "1992 Presidential Election," American Presidency Project, at www.presidency.ucsb.edu /showelection.php?year=1992.

56. Tyson Slocum, "Blind Faith: How Deregulation and Enron's Influence Over Government Looted Billions from Americans," *Public Citizen*, December 2001.

57. Sandy Weill entry on "Forbes List," *Forbes*, at www.forbes.com/lists/2006/10/HRFZ .html.

58. Chris Jones, "Wall Street Legends: Sandy Weill," *Here Is the City*, at http://hereisthe city.com/2011/05/11/wall-street-legends-no-14-sandy-weill/.

59. Pat Widder, "Drexel Sells Half of Its Retail Units," *Chicago Tribune*, April 26, 1989, at http://articles.chicagotribune.com/1989-04-26/business/8904070433_1_drexel -burnham-lambert-smith-barney-retail-units.

60. Leah Nathans Spiro, "Smith Barney's Whiz Kid," *BusinessWeek*, October 21, 1996, at www.businessweek.com/1996/43/b3498153.htm.

61. "Bill Clinton: Life Before the Presidency," University of Virginia Miller Center, at http://millercenter.org/president/clinton/essays/biography/2.

62. Lisa Du, "The Rise and Spectacular Fall of Jon Corzine," *Business Insider*, November 2011, at www.businessinsider.com/the-rise-and-fall-of-jon-corzine-2011-10?op=1.

63. Robert J. McCartney, "Goldman Places Duo at Helm; No Major Change in Strategy Planned," *Washington Post*, August 15, 1990.

64. Clinton, *My Life*, 452.

65. "President Names Stephen Friedman as Director of the National Economic Council," White House Archives, George W. Bush, December 12, 2002, at http://georgewbush-whitehouse.archives.gov/news/releases/2002/12/20021212-8.html. See also "President Thanks Steve Friedman," The White House Archives, George W. Bush, November 29, 2004, at http://georgewbush-whitehouse.archives.gov/news/releases/2004/11/20041129-9.html.

66. William D. Cohan, "Goldman's Alpha War," *Vanity Fair*, May 2011.

67. "Jon Corzine Biography," Project Vote Smart, at http://votesmart.org/candidate/biography/43268/jon-corzine.

68. The White House, Henry M. Paulson Jr. Biography, US Treasury Government Archives, at http://georgewbush-whitehouse.archives.gov/government/paulson-bio.html.

69. William B. English and Brian K. Reid, "Profits and Balance Sheet Developments at U.S. Commercial Banks in 1993," *St. Louis Federal Reserve*, June 1994, at http://fraser.stlouisfed.org/docs/publications/FRB/pages/1990-1994/33467_1990-1994.pdf.

70. G. Bruce Knecht, "Major U.S. Banks Plan Units in Mexico—Move Could Help Modernize Financial Infrastructure," *Wall Street Journal*, May 31, 1994.

71. Ibid.

72. H.R. 3841, 103rd Congress: Riegle-Neal Interstate Banking and Branching Efficiency Act of 1994, at www.govtrack.us/congress/bills/103/hr3841.

73. Clinton Presidential Records, WHORM, Subject File: General, FG001–07, Folder 28562055, September 29, 1994, William J. Clinton Presidential Library.

74. Clinton Presidential Records, WHORM, Subject File: General, FG001–07, Folder 28562055, FI002, 082208SS [OA/ID 21860], September 29, 1994, Schedule for the President, Clinton Library.

75. William J. Clinton, "Public Papers of the Presidents of the United States: William J. Clinton (1993, Book II)—Remarks to the National Urban League," US Government Printing Office, August 4, 1993, at www.gpo.gov/fdsys/pkg/PPP-1993-book2/html/PPP-1993-book2-doc-pg1328.htm.

76. Kenneth Cline, "McColl Plays Down Starring Role in Long Campaign for Branching," *American Banker*, September 15, 1994.

77. Clinton Presidential Records, September 29, 1994. In July 1992, Clinton and McColl met over southern comfort food at a Holiday Inn in Valdosta, Georgia—"Rice and butter beans and tomato and okra," McColl later recalled—and discussed banking deregulation and horse-trading. In exchange for McColl's promise to support inner-city banks, Clinton agreed to support interstate banking. Sure enough, two years later he signed the Interstate Banking Act. Two years after the Chemical and Chase merger in 1995, McColl's NationsBank acquired Barnett for four times its book value. The last of McColl's conquests was the $62 billion merger between Bank of America and NationsBank in late September 1998, which put him at the helm of Bank of America.

78. Clinton Presidential Records, September 29, 1994, Clinton Library.

79. Clinton Presidential Records, 082208SS and 088313 [OA/ID 21860], November 19, 1994. The turnaround time for this thank-you was longer than that of other presidents to supporters in similar instances.

80. EIU, "Mexico Finance: The Peso Crisis, Ten Years On," January 3, 2005.

81. Louis Uchitelle, "US Losses in Mexico Assessed," *New York Times*, December 26, 1994.

82. James Gerstenzang, "Bentsen Resigns; Clinton Drafts Wall Street Veteran," *Chicago Sun-Times,* December 7, 1994.

83. Joseph A. Whitt Jr., "The Mexican Peso Crisis," Federal Reserve Bank of Atlanta, *Economic Review,* January/February 1996, at www.frbatlanta.org/filelegacydocs /J_whi811.pdf. Zedillo took office following the March 23 assassination of Luis Colosio. He later joined the board of Citicorp and became a professor at Yale. He was also given immunity for a massacre in the Zapatista/Chiapas region, where forty-five indigenous Mexicans were murdered. See Daniel Sisgoreo and Tapley Stephenson, "State Department Seeks Immunity for Zedillo," *Yale Daily News,* September 10, 2012, at http://yaledailynews.com/blog/2012/09/10/state-dept-suggests -immunity-for-zedillo/.

84. Robert Rubin, *In an Uncertain World: Tough Choices from Wall Street to Washington* (New York, NY: Random House, 2004), 5.

85. Clinton, *My Life,* 641.

86. Ibid.

87. "Mexico's Financial Crisis—Origins, Awareness, Assistance, and Initial Efforts to Recover," US General Accounting Office, Report to the Chairman, Committee on Banking and Financial Services House of Representatives, February 1996, at www.gao.gov/archive/1996 /gg96056.pdf.

88. Clinton, *My Life,* 643. Clinton wrote, "Rubin and Summers came to the White House to see Leon Panetta and Sandy Berger, who was handling the issue for the National Security Council."

89. James R. Kraus, "Clinton's Executive Order to Back Peso Raises New Worries on Bank Exposure," *American Banker,* February 1, 1995.

90. James H. Rubin, "Rubin Denies Any Personal Financial Interest in Mexico Deal," Associated Press, February 23, 1995, at www.apnewsarchive.com/1995/Rubin-Denies-Any-Personal-Financial-Interest-in-Mexico-Deal/id-200a13019d2f48ddaf88bc 414145182d.

91. "Mexican Peso Crisis and Bailout," *Congressional Record* 141, no. 43 (March 8, 1995), Government Printing Office, at www.gpo.gov/fdsys/pkg/CREC-1995-03-08/html/CREC -1995-03-08-pt1-PgS3664-4.htm.

92. Anthony DePalma, "In Land of the Peso, the Dollar Is Common Coin," *New York Times,* November 21, 1995.

93. William J. Clinton, "The President's News Conference with President Ernesto Zedillo of Mexico," October 10, 1995, American Presidency Project, at www.presidency.ucsb.edu /ws/?pid=50633.

94. "Citi Board Nominates Ernesto Zedillo to Board of Directors," Citibank press release, February 26, 2010, at www.citigroup.com/citi/press/2010/100226a.htm.

95. Nomi Prins, *It Takes a Pillage* (Hoboken, NJ: Wiley, 2009), 147.

96. Keith Bradsher, "No New Deal for Banking; Efforts to Drop Depression-Era Barriers Stall, Again," *New York Times,* November 2, 1995.

Chapter 18. The Late 1990s: Currency Crises and Glass-Steagall Demise

1. William J. Clinton, "Statement on Signing the Gramm-Leach-Bliley Act," November 12, 1999, American Presidency Project, at www.presidency.ucsb.edu/ws/?pid=56922#ixz z2hOCPkNPf.

2. Nomi Prins, *Other People's Money: The Corporate Mugging of America* (New York, NY: New Press, 2004). Based on information compiled from Thomson Financial databases for the book.

3. Ibid.

4. Suzanne McGee, "Monday's Markets: Dow Breaks 6,000, but for How Long?" *Wall Street Journal,* October 15, 1996.

5. Dole won 40.7 percent of the popular vote and 159 votes in the Electoral College. Perot received only 8.4 percent of the popular vote.

6. Alan Greenspan, "The Challenge of Central Banking in a Democratic Society," Federal Reserve, December 5, 1996, at www.federalreserve.gov/boarddocs/speeches /1996/19961205.htm.

7. Leslie Eaton, "Investment Fraud Is Soaring Along with the Stock Market," *New York Times*, November 30, 1997.

8. "Holding Companies Engaged in Underwriting and Dealing in Securities," Board of Governors of the Federal Reserve System, March 6, 1997, at www.federalreserve .gov/boarddocs/press/boardacts/1996/19961220/R-0841.pdf. See also www.newyork fed.org/banking/circulars/10922.html.

9. Rolfe Winkler, "Bring Back Glass-Steagall," Reuters, January 21, 2008.

10. "Section 20 Subsidiaries of Bank Holding Companies," Federal Reserve Bank of New York, Supervision and Regulation, September 4, 1997, at www.newyorkfed.org/banking/circulars /10979.html.

11. Ibid.

12. Rachel Beck, "Travelers Group Buys Salomon for Over $9 Billion," Associated Press, September 24, 1997.

13. Dimon Biography, J. P. Morgan & Company website, at www.jpmorgan.com/cm/Blob Server/hy_bio_dimon.pdf?blobkey=id&blobwhere=1320592119839&blobheader =application%2Fpdf&blobcol=urldata&blobtable=MungoBlobs.

14. "Traveler's Sandy Weill Breaks Bank," *New York Post,* March 13, 1998.

15. "IMF Welcomes Thailand's Exchange Rate Action," International Monetary Fund news brief, July 2, 1997, at www.imf.org/external/np/sec/nb/1997/nb9712.htm.

16. Joseph A. Whitt Jr., "The Mexican Peso Crisis, Federal Reserve Bank of Atlanta, *Economic Review*, January/February 1996, at www.frbatlanta.org/filelegacydocs/J_whi811. pdf.

17. Patrick Buchanan, "Bagmen Rubin, Camdessus Bear the Blame for Asian Crisis," *Insight on the News*, February 16, 1998.

18. Timothy O'Brien, Edmund Andrews, and Sheryl WuDunn, "Covering Asia with Cash: Banks Poured Money into Region Despite Warning Signs," *New York Times,* January 28, 1998.

19. "Korea Letter of Intent," International Monetary Fund, December 3, 1997, at www.imf .org/external/np/loi/120397.HTM.

20. "The Asian Crisis: Causes and Cures," International Monetary Fund, *Finance and Development* 35, no. 2 (June 1998), at www.imf.org/external/pubs/ft/fandd/1998/06/imf staff.htm.

21. Timothy O'Brien, "Jockeying for Position in South Korea—U.S. Bankers Prepare for Talks with the Fed," *New York Times*, December 27, 1997.

22. William J. Clinton, "Response to the Lewinsky Allegations," January 26, 1998, University of Virginia Miller Center, at http://millercenter.org/scripps/archive/speeches /detail/3930.

23. "The Long Demise of Glass-Steagall," *Frontline* (PBS), at www.pbs.org/wgbh/pages/front line/shows/wallstreet/weill/demise.html.

24. "Watch Out for the Egos," *The Economist*, April 11, 1998.

25. Lauren Thierry, "Travelers/Citicorp Press Conference," *Trading Places* (CNNfn), April 6, 1998.

26. "Worldcom: The Players: The Wall Street Fix," *Frontline* (PBS), May 8, 2003 at www.pbs .org/wgbh/pages/frontline/shows/wallstreet/wcom/players.html.

27. CNBC News Transcripts, Show: Dow 9000, April 6, 1998, National Economic Council, Files of Sally Katzen [OA/box Number [OD] 17444], Folder: Citicorp/Travelers[1], Clinton Library.

28. Email from Sarah Rosen, Subject: Travelers-Citicorp Merger, April 6, 1998, Automated Records Management System (ARMS) (email), OPD [Citicorp and Travelers Group Merge] [April 6, 1998, to April 9, 1998] [OA/ID 250000], Clinton Library.

29. Email from Sarah Rosen to Lael Brainard, Brian A. Barreto, cc: Sally Katzen, April 9, 1998, ARMS (email), folder CEA (Citicorp and Travelers Group Merge) [April 9, 1998, to May 13, 1998] [OA/ID 950000], Clinton Library.

30. Email from John Taylor and Josh Silver to Friends of Community Reinvestment, re: Moratorium on megamergers, April 23, 1998, ARMS (email), folder CEA (Citicorp and Travelers Group Merge) [April 9, 1998, to May 13, 1998] [OA/ID 950000], Clinton Library.

31. Email: Text of Testimony by Andrew C. Hove Jr. on Mergers in the Financial Service Industry before the House Committee on Banking and Financial Services, April 29, 1998, ARMS (email), Folder: Interstate Banking and Branch Efficiency Act, January 3, 1995, to April 23, 2000, Clinton Library.

32. Email to Dorothy Robyn, Subject: Mergers, May 13, 1998, ARMS (email), Folder: CEA (Citicorp and Travelers Group Merge) [April 9, 1998, to May 13, 1998] [OA/ID 950000], Clinton Library. See also Steve Holland, "Clinton Authorizes Group to Monitor Merger Mania," Reuters, May 13, 1998.

33. Ibid.

34. Ibid.

35. "The Long Demise of Glass-Steagall."

36. "H.R. 10 (105th): Financial Services Act of 1998," GovTrack.us, May 13, 1998, at www.govtrack.us/congress/votes/105–1998/h151.

37. Prins, *Other People's Money*, 40.

38. Memorandum from Eric Heilman to Gene Sperling and Sarah Rosen, Subject: Citicorp/ Travelers, Reed/Weill Briefing, September 22, 1998, National Economic Council, Files of Sally Katzen [OA, box no. OD 17444], Folder: Citicorp/Travelers[1], Clinton Library. This folder contains seventeen pages of withdrawals or redactions, including a memo from Rubin to Bowles and Sperling (re: Meeting on Financial Modernization with Citicorp and Travelers Group, Talking Points for meeting with Sandy Weil and John Reed).

39. Ibid.

40. Ibid.

41. Ibid., Memo from Jay Dunn, Business Outreach, Office of Public Liaison, to Gene Sperling, September 22,1998.

42. Ibid., Memo for Gene Sperling.

43. Ibid., Memo from Lisa S. Andrews to Secretary Rubin, Subject: Industry positions on HR 10, September 22, 1998.

44. Ibid.

45. Ibid., email to Melissa G. Green, Shannon Mason, and Sally Katzen, Subject: FYI re HR 10, September 23, 1998.

46. Prins, *It Takes a Pillage*, 182.

47. "Senate Banking Shake-Up Could Hinder Reform Bill," *American Banker*, February 9, 2013.

48. Duff McDonald, "When a Banking Feud Got Physical," *CNN Money*, September 18, 2009.

49. Timothy L. O'Brien and Peter Truell, "Heir Apparent's Departure May Signal Strain at Citigroup," *New York Times*, November 3, 1998.

50. Katrina Brooker, "Citi's Creator, Alone with His Regrets," *New York Times*, January 3, 2010.

51. Fleming Stewart, "The Euro's Big Bang," *Institutional Investor* (international ed.), January 1, 1999.

52. Joshua Ramo, "The Three Marketeers," *Time*, February 15, 1999.

53. George A. Akerlof and Robert J. Shiller, "Why Do Central Bankers Have Power?" in *Animal Spirits: How Human Psychology Drives the Economy, and Why It Matters for Global Capitalism* (Princeton, NJ: Princeton University Press, 2009), 84–85.

54. Robert E. Rubin, "Text as Prepared for Delivery," Committee on Financial Services press release," February 12, 1999, at http://democrats.financialservices.house.gov/banking /21299rub.shtml.

55. Ibid.

56. Ramo, "The Three Marketeers."

57. Klaus C. Engelen, "American Arrogance," *The International Economy* 13, no. 5 (September/ October 1999): 10–13.

58. Copy of Robert Rubin's testimony before the Senate Banking Committee, Policy Development, Lisa Green OA/ID 20587, Box 3 of 19, CRA (Folder 1), February 24, 1999, Clinton Library. Rubin added that "foreign bank subsidiaries hold $450 billion in assets and Edge Act subsidiaries hold about $250 billion in assets."

59. Letter to Phil Gramm, March 2, 1999, Policy Development, Lisa Green, OA/ID 20587, Box 4 of 19, CRA (Folder 2), Clinton Library.

60. Ibid.

61. "Chairman Gramm Releases Draft of Financial Services Legislation, Committee Mark-Up Set for March 4," Capitol Hill Press Releases, March 1, 1999.

62. Dean Anason, "Clinton to Gramm: Change Reform Bill or Face a Veto," *American Banker*, March 4, 1999.

63. "Sampled History," Dow Jones Industrial Average, at www.fedprimerate.com/dow-jones -industrial-average-history-djia.htm.

64. "S. 900 (106th): Gramm-Leach-Bliley Act," GovTrack.us, April 28, 1999, at www.govtrack .us/congress/bills/106/s900.

65. Clinton, *My Life*, 857.

66. "Treasury Secretary Rubin Resigns: Clinton Losing Trusted Friend, Adviser," CNN, May 12, 1999.

67. Joseph Kahn and Alessandra Stanley, "Enron's Many Strands: Dual Role: Rubin Relishes Role of Banker as Public Man," *New York Times,* February 11, 2002.

68. John Schmid and Philip Segal, "Deregulation to Unleash New Competition: Giant Banks Prepare for a U.S. Onslaught," *New York Times*, October 5, 1999, at www.nytimes.com /1999/10/25/news/25iht-banks.2.t_1.html.

69. Stephen Labaton, "Congress Passes Wide-Ranging Bill Easing Bank Laws," *New York Times*, November 5, 1999.

70. Ibid.

71. Ibid.

72. Ibid.

73. Joseph Kahn, "Consumer Groups Seek Ethics Inquiry on Rubin's New Job," *New York Times*, November 18, 1999.

74. Ibid.

75. Bob Ivry, "Reed Says 'I'm Sorry' for Role in Creating Citigroup," *Bloomberg*, November 6, 2009.

76. Secretary of Labor Robert Reich resignation remarks, Council on Excellence in Government, US Department of Labor, January 9, 1997, at www.dol.gov/oasam/programs/history /reich/speeches/sp970109.htm.

77. Luke Schaefer and Kathryn Edin, "Extreme Poverty in the United States, 1996 to 2001," Policy Brief 28, February 2012, National Poverty Center, University of Michigan.

78. Emmanuel Saez with Thomas Piketty, "Income Inequality in the United States, 1913–1998," *Quarterly Journal of Economics* 118, no. 1 (2003): 1–39.

Chapter 19. The 2000s: Multiple Crises, the New Big Six, and Global Catastrophe

1. JPMorgan Chase 2013 Investor Day, JPMorgan Chase & Co., February 26, 2013. Dimon was responding to a question from Credit Lyonnais Securities Asia bank analyst Michael Mayo.

2. Louis Jacobson, "Bernie Sanders Says Six Bank Companies Have Assets Equaling 60 Percent of U.S. GDP," PolitiFact 2012, at www.politifact.com/truth-o-meter /statements/2011/oct/06/bernie-s/bernie-sanders-says-six-bank-companies-have -assets/.

3. Robert Lenzner, "Banking Concentration Still a Systemic Risk," *Forbes,* April 7, 2011, at www.forbes.com/sites/robertlenzner/2011/04/07/banking-concentration-still-a-systemic -risk/.

4. "Prepared Testimony of Mr. Henry M. Paulson," hearing on the Financial Marketplace of the Future, Senate Banking Committee, February 29, 2000, at www.banking .senate.gov/00_02hrg/022900/paulson.htm.

5. "Approval of Application and Notice of Chase Manhattan," Board of Governors of the Federal Reserve press release, December 11, 2000. See also "Chase and J. P. Morgan Shareholders Approve Merger," J. P. Morgan press release, December 22, 2000.

6. Patrick McGeehan and Saul Hansell, "Chase Hopes Deal for Morgan Will Bring It Prestige," *New York Times*, September 14, 2000.

7. Liz Moyer, "JPM-Chase, Fleet Feel Pain of Slow Markets," *American Banker*, July 19, 2001.

8. David Smith, "Into the Belly of the Beast, Part II (Goldman Sachs and the European Crisis)," *Economy Watch,* February 2, 2012, at www.economywatch.com/economy-business -and-finance-news/into-the-belly-of-the-beast-part-two.02–02.html. In 2002, Greece was advised by Goldman Sachs on how to legally hide its debt using complex derivatives deals that optically reduced the size of government debt below the limit of 60 percent of the economy. Greek debt was issued in dollars and yen, then swapped for euro debt for a period and swapped back later, for a "secret" credit of about $1 billion.

9. Author's note: In September 2001, I was working at Goldman Sachs and ran the credit derivatives strategies group. Some of our research had been posted on Enron's website for informational purposes. Enron and Goldman were trading partners, as well as competitors for credit derivatives business.

10. Author's experience as a staff member at Goldman Sachs.

11. "Remarks by the President Upon Arrival," White House press release, September 16, 2001, at georgewbush-whitehouse.archives.gov/news/releases/2001/09/20010916–2.html.

12. "SEC Biography: Chairman Harvey L. Pitt," US Securities and Exchange Commission, at www.sec.gov/about/commissioner/pitt.htm. See also "Bush Expected to Nominate Harvey Pitt as SEC Chief," *CFO*, May 7, 2001, at www.cfo.com/article.cfm/2994814. Prior to being appointed SEC chairman on August 3, 2001, Pitt had defended several clients in fraud cases, most notably Ivan Boesky, who paid a record $100 million to settle his civil fraud case in 1986.

13. "Timeline of Enron's Collapse," *Washington Post*, September 30, 2004.

14. Alex Berenson and Richard A. Oppel Jr., "Once-Mighty Enron Strains Under Scrutiny," *New York Times*, October 28, 2001.

15. Robin Sidel and Rebecca Smith, "Dynegy Holds Talks to Buy Enron, Inject $1.5 Billion to Shore Up Firm," *Wall Street Journal*, November 8, 2001.

16. "Rating the Raters: Enron and the Credit Rating Agencies," hearing before the Senate Governmental Affairs Committee, 107th Congress, S. Hrg. 107-471, March 20, 2002.

17. "Lay Offered Rubin Job on Enron Board," CNN.com, February 21, 2002.

18. "Rating the Raters."

19. US Congress Senate Committee, "Enron's Credit Rating: Enron's Bankers' Contacts with Moody's and Government Officials," Staff Report, January 3, 2003.

20. Ibid.

21. "Dynegy Scraps Enron Deal," CNNMoney, November 28, 2001.

22. Enron Creditors Recovery Corporation, "The Springfield Case Fact Sheet," at www.enron .com/index_option_com_content_task_view_id_96_Itemid_35.htm. See also Bob Lyke and Mark Jickling, *WorldCom: The Accounting Scandal*, CRS Report for Congress, August 29, 2002.

23. Dan Ackman, "Enron Files Chap. 11," *Forbes*, December 3, 2001.

24. George W. Bush, "Statement on Signing the Department of Defense and Emergency Supplemental Appropriations for Recovery from and Response to Terrorist Attacks on the United States Act, 2002," American Presidency Project, January 10, 2002 at www .presidency.ucsb.edu/ws/?pid=73224#axzz2hO8LW54t.

25. George W. Bush, "Address Before a Joint Session of the Congress on the State of the Union," American Presidency Project, January 29, 2002.

26. American Bankruptcy Institute, Annual Business and Non-business Filings by Year (1980–2012), at www.abiworld.org/AM/AMTemplate.cfm?Section=Home&CONTENTID =66471&TEMPLATE=/CM/ContentDisplay.cfm.

27. "Paulson Backs SEC's Demand for More Cash," *Financial News,* June 6, 2002.

28. US District Court, "Judge's Opinion and Order," Securities and Exchange Commission, July 7, 2003.

29. US District Court, "Complaint: SEC v. Bernard J. Ebbers," Securities and Exchange Commission. See also "WorldCom Bankruptcy Plan Wins Judge's Approval (Update 2)," *Bloomberg,* October 31, 2003; and Dan Arnall, "Worldcom at a Glance," ABC News, March 15, 2005.

30. "On 1st Anniversary of WorldCom Fraud Scandal: Web-Based Countdown Clock Shows U.S. Taxpayer Dollars Being Used to 'Bailout' Scandal-Ridden Company," PR Newswire, June 25, 2003.

31. "The Honorable Jed Rakoff Approves Settlement of SEC's Claim for a Civil Penalty Against WorldCom," Securities and Exchange Commission press release, July 7, 2003.

32. George W. Bush, "Fact Sheet: Corporate Responsibility," American Presidency Project, July 9, 2002, at www.presidency.ucsb.edu/ws/?pid=79680.

33. US Senate, "Oversight of Investment Banks' Response to the Lessons of Enron," Hearing before the Permanent Subcommittee on Investigations of the Committee on Governmental Affairs, December 11, 2002, Second Session, vols. 1 and 2.

34. Kellogg Insight, "Lobbyists Speak in Numbers—Based on the Research of Yael Hochberg, Paola Sapienza, and Annette Vissing-Jørgensen," Northwestern University, May 1, 2008.

35. Paul Starr, "The Great Telecom Implosion," *The American Prospect,* September 8, 2002.

36. "Clambering Back Up: Corporate Reform," *The Economist,* July 23, 2002.

37. "U.S. Launches Cruise Missiles at Saddam," CNN World, March 20, 2003.

38. "Goldman Faces Battle at Shareholders' Meeting," *Financial News,* March 30, 2003.

39. Mark Gimein, "Eliot Spitzer: The Enforcer," *Fortune,* September 16, 2002.

40. "Ten of Nation's Top Investment Firms Settle Enforcement Actions Involving Conflicts of Interest Between Research and Investment Banking," Securities and Exchange Commission press release, April 28, 2003. See also "SEC Charges Merrill Lynch, Four Merrill Lynch Executives with Aiding and Abetting Enron Accounting Fraud," Securities and Exchange Commission press release, March 17, 2003. Separately, in July 2003, JPMorgan Chase agreed to pay $135 million and Citigroup agreed to pay $120 million to settle SEC allegations that it helped Enron (and Dynegy) commit fraud. Merrill Lynch had already agreed to pay $80 million to settle investigations into its Enron relationship.

41. Wolters Kluwer, "Global Settlement with Investment Banks Announced," at http:// business.cch.com/securitieslaw/news/4-30-03.asp.

42. In my 2004 book, *Other People's Money,* I specifically called this settlement out as not altering Wall Street's behavior and warned that without more rigorous, real reforms, a worse crisis would occur. In 2008, it did.

43. Board of Governors of the Federal Reserve, "Appointment of Timothy F. Geithner as President," press release, October 15, 2003.

44. Martin Crutsinger, "Former Clinton Administration Official Tapped to Head New York Fed," AP Worldstream, October 15, 2003. Geithner first joined George H. W. Bush's Treasury Department in 1988, following three years at Kissinger Associates.

45. Testimony Before the House Committee on the Budget, "Fannie Mae, Freddie Mac, and FHA: Taxpayer Exposure in the Housing Market," hearing, June 2, 2011.

46. Michelle Heller, "Investment Banks Top Bush Donor List," *American Banker*, October 24, 2003.

47. Ben White, "Wall Street Bankers, Reelection Backers; New York's Financial Titans Support Bush in a Big Way," *Washington Post*, January 24, 2004.

48. Center for Responsive Politics, "George W. Bush: Top Contributors," at www.opensecrets .org/pres04/contrib.php?cycle=2004&cid=N00008072.

49. Lucas Kawa, "Why the Bush Dynasty Is America's First Family of Finance," *Business Insider*, November 27, 2012.

50. Caren Chesler, "The Bush Juggernaut," *Investment Dealers' Digest*, February 4, 2004.

51. Texans for Public Justice, Bush Donor Profile, December 11, 2004, at http://info.tpj.org /docs/pioneers/pioneers_view.jsp?id=832.

52. Securities and Exchange Commission, "SEC Open Meeting Agenda," April 28, 2004, at www.sec.gov/news/speech/spch042804whd.htm.

53. Stephen Labaton, "Agency's '04 Rule Let Banks Pile Up New Debt," *New York Times*, October 2, 2008.

54. Sam Zuckerman and Zachary Coile, "Wall Street Figure Tapped to Head SEC/ Donaldson's 'Mission' to Police Corporations," *San Francisco Chronicle*, December 11, 2002.

55. The rule published in the Federal Register as a final rule on June 21, 2004 (Fed. Reg. 34428). The final rule establishes a voluntary alternative method for computing net capital for certain broker-dealers. Under the rule, a broker-dealer that maintains certain minimum levels for tentative net capital and net capital may apply for a conditional exemption from the application of the standard net capital calculation. As a condition to granting the exemption, the broker-dealer's ultimate holding company must consent to group-wide commission supervision related to the financial stability of the broker-dealer. US General Accounting Office, B-294184, June 25, 2004.

56. US Securities and Exchange Commission, "Final Rule: Alternative Net Capital Requirements for Broker-Dealers That Are Part of Consolidated Supervised Entities," Release No. 34-49830, File No. S7–21–03, June 9, 2004.

57. Kevin Drawbaugh, "US SEC Clears New Net-Capital Rules for Brokerages," Reuters, April 28, 2004.

58. Sebnem Kalemli-Ozcan, Bent E. Sorensen, and Sevcan Yesiltas, "Leverage Across Firms, Banks, and Countries," presentation at the Dallas Fed Conference on Financial Frictions and Monetary Policy in an Open Economy, March 2012.

59. "$58B Bank Deal Set," CNN Money, January 15, 2004. See also JPMorgan Chase, "Bank One Complete Merger," press release, July 1, 2004.

60. Congressional Record, Senate, S 6969, June 17, 2004.

61. "Government by Goldman," *US Banker*, May 1, 2004. See also US Commodity Futures Trading Commission, Former Commissioners, Chairman Reuben Jeffery III, at www.cftc .gov/About/Commissioners/FormerCommissioners/rjefferyiii; Center for Strategic and International Studies (CSIS), "Reuben Jeffery III, Former Under Secretary of State for Economic, Energy, and Agricultural Affairs Joins CSIS as Senior Adviser," press release, April 27, 2009.

62. Federal Reserve Bank of New York, "Are Home Prices the Next 'Bubble'?" *Economic Policy Review* 10, no. 3 (December 2004).

63. Prins, *It Takes a Pillage*, 44–45.

64. Edmund L. Andrews, "Bush Nominates Bernanke to Succeed Greenspan as Fed Chief," *New York Times*, October 24, 2005.

65. US Senate, "Nomination of Ben S. Bernanke," Hearing before the Committee on Banking, Housing, and Urban Affairs, First Session, November 15, 2005, vols. 22–23.

66. Board of Governors of the Federal Reserve System, "Board Members: Ben S. Bernanke," April 4, 2013 (last update).

67. George W. Bush, *Decision Points* (New York, NY: Crown Publishers, 2010), 449.

68. Edmund L. Andrews and Jim Rutenberg, "Bush Nominates Wall Street Chief for Treasury Job," *New York Times*, May 31, 2006.

69. Prins, *It Takes a Pillage*, 44–45.

70. Nomi Prins, "As the World Crumbles: The ECB spins, FED smirks, and US Banks Pillage," www.nomiprins.com (blog), November 21, 2011.

71. US Department of the Treasury, "Schedule for Treasury Conference on US Capital Markets Competitiveness," press release, March 9, 2007.

72. Nomi Prins, "Paulson's Deregulation Mission," *The American Prospect*, April 1, 2007.

73. RealtyTrac, "More Than 1.2 Million Foreclosure Filings Reported in 2006," press release, January 25, 2007. See also US Department of the Treasury, "Secretary Paulson Speaks at Committee of 100 16th Annual Conference in New York," press release, April 20, 2007; Greg Robb, "Paulson Says U.S. Housing Sector 'At or Near Bottom,'" Market-Watch, April 20, 2007.

74. Timothy Geithner, "Liquidity Risk and the Global Economy," Federal Reserve Bank of New York, May 15, 2007.

75. "Geithner's Calendar at the New York Fed: January 2007 to January 2009," *New York Times*, at http://documents.nytimes.com/geithner-schedule-new-york-fed.

76. Michiyo Nakamoto and David Wighton, "Citigroup Chief Stays Bullish on Buy-outs," *Financial Times*, July 9, 2007.

77. Securities and Exchange Commission, "SEC Charges Two Former Bear Stearns Hedge Fund Managers with Fraud," press release, June 19, 2008, at www.sec.gov/litigation/litre leases/2008/lr20625.htm. A year after the funds failed, the SEC charged the managers with fraud for misleading investors by not informing them of the downward spiral. They were indicted by the Department of Justice but were eventually acquitted.

78. Claire Suddath, "Biggest Golden Parachutes," *Time*, October 8, 2008.

79. "Statement from Citigroup on the Resignation of C.E.O. Charles O. Prince III," *New York Times*, November 5, 2007.

80. Robin Sidel, Monica Langley, and Gregory Zuckerman, "Citigroup CEO Plans to Resign as Losses Grow," *Wall Street Journal*, November 3, 2007.

81. Maria Bartiromo, "John Thain on His New Job as CEO of Merrill Lynch," *Bloomberg Businessweek*, November 25, 2007.

82. "Geithner's Calendar at the New York Fed: January 2007 to January 2009," *New York Times*, at http://documents.nytimes.com/geithner-schedule-new-york-fed.

83. Jo Becker and Gretchen Morgenson, "Geithner, Member and Overseer of Finance Club," *New York Times*, April 26, 2009.

84. Ibid.

85. Permanent Subcommittee on Investigations, "Exhibits: PSI Hearing on Wall Street and the Financial Crisis: The Role of Investment Banks," April 27, 2010.

86. David Ellis, "Bad News at Bear Stearns," CNNMoney, December 20, 2007.

87. Matt Ackermann and Matthias Rieker, "People: Across the Pond," *American Banker*, January 11, 2008. See also *"*Tony Blair Appointed Senior Advisor to JPMorgan Chase,*"* PR Newswire, January 10, 2008.

88. "Northern Rock to be Nationalised," BBC News, February 17, 2008. See also Bank of England, "Liquidity Support Facility for Northern Rock plc," news release, September 14, 2007.

89. Bush, *Decision Points*, 453.

90. Federal Reserve Bank of New York, "Statement on Financing Arrangement of JPMorgan Chase's Acquisition of Bear Stearns," March 24, 2008, at www.newyorkfed.org/newsevents /news/markets/2008/rp080324.html.

91. US Senate, "Turmoil in U.S. Credit Markets: Examining the Recent Actions of Federal Financial Regulators," Hearing before the Committee on Banking, Housing, and Urban Affairs, April 3, 2008, Second Session, at www.banking.senate.gov/public/_files /OpgStmtDimonJPMorganChase040308.pdf.

92. Katherine Burton and Edgar Ortega, "Bear Acquisition Brings JPMorgan a Prime Broker for Hedge Funds," *Bloomberg*, March 18, 2008.

93. "Treasury Chief: Banking System Safe," Associated Press via San Francisco Gate, July 21, 2008.

94. Bush, *Decision Points*, 456.

95. Julie Creswell and Ben White, "The Guys from 'Government Sachs,'" *New York Times*, October 17, 2008.

96. Lehman Brothers, "Lehman Brothers Holdings Inc. Announces It Intends to File Chapter 11 Bankruptcy Petition," press release, September 15, 2008.

97. Board of Governors of the Federal Reserve System, "Order Approving Formation of Bank Holding Companies," September 21, 2008. See also Board of Governors of the Federal Reserve System, "Order Approving Formation of Bank Holding Companies and Notice to Engage in Certain Nonbanking Activities," September 21, 2008.

98. Federal Reserve Bank of New York, "Advisory Groups," Annual Report 2010.

99. "Goldman, Morgan Stanley Enter New Era," *The Bond Buyer*, September 23, 2008.

100. "Executive Profile: Kenneth D. Lewis," *Bloomberg Businessweek*, at http://investing .businessweek.com/research/stocks/people/person.asp?personId=592192&ticker=BAC.

101. Prins, *It Takes a Pillage*.

102. Ibid.

103. Board of Governors of the Federal Reserve System, "Approval of Proposal by Bank of America," press release, June 5, 2008.

104. Bank of America, "Bank of America Buys Merrill Lynch, Creating Unique Financial Services Firm," press release, September 15, 2008.

105. Author analysis of Paulson's calendar, at www.treasury.gov/FOIA/Pages/docs_Paulson Calendar_index2.aspx.

106. Nomi Prins and Krisztina Ugrin, "Bailout Tally Report," October 1, 2010, at www .nomiprins.com/reports. See also Securities and Exchange Commission, "SEC Enforce-

ment Actions—Addressing Misconduct that Led to or Arose from the Financial Crisis," Key Statistics (through February 1, 2013).

107. Sam Carr, "Largest US Banks Have Built a $60B Settlement Tab, So Far," SNL Financial, March 5, 2013.

108. Wallace Witkowski, "House Wants B. of A. Info on $3.62 Bln Merrill Bonuses: WSJ," MarketWatch, March 17, 2009.

109. Bank of America, "Ken Lewis Announces His Retirement," press release, September 30, 2009.

110. "Brian T. Moynihan, Chief Executive Officer," Bank of America executive biography. He had joined Bank of America in 2004 following its merger with FleetBoston Financial.

111. Data.gov, White House Visitor Records Requests, at https://explore.data.gov/dataset /White-House-Visitor-Records-Requests/644b-gaut.

112. Mark Pittman, "Goldman, Merrill Collect Billions After Fed's AIG Bailout Loans," *Bloomberg*, September 29, 2008,

113. Bush, *Decision Points*, 457.

114. Tim Geithner's calendar at the New York Fed obtained through FOIA by the *New York Times*, Entry Date: September 15, 2008, 10 AM call, at http://documents.nytimes.com /geithner-schedule-new-york-fed.

115. Author analysis of Paulson's calendar.

116. Federal Reserve Bank of New York, "Actions Related to AIG," Timeline, at www.new yorkfed.org/aboutthefed/aig/timeline.html.

117. Mary Williams Walsh, "A.I.G. Lists Banks It Paid with U.S. Bailout Funds," *New York Times*, March 15, 2009.

118. Bush, *Decision Points*, 459.

119. "H.R. 1424—110th Congress: Emergency Economic Stabilization Act of 2008," GovTrack.us, at www.govtrack.us/congress/bills/110/hr1424.

120. Bush, *Decision Points*, 465.

121. "Real GDP Fell Slightly in 2008: Q3," Econbrowser, October 30, 2008.

122. Prins and Ugrin, "Bailout Tally Report."

123. Center for Responsive Politics, "Goldman Sachs: All Recipients—Among Federal Candidates, 2008 Cycle," at www.opensecrets.org/orgs/recips.php?id=D000000085& type=P&state=&sort=A&cycle=2008. See also Center for Responsive Politics, "Barack Obama—Top Contributors, 2008 Election Cycle," at www.opensecrets.org/pres08/contrib .php?cycle=2008&cid=N00009638.

124. Center for Responsive Politics, "Top Contributors, Senator Barack Obama," at www.opensecrets.org/politicians/contrib.php?cycle=Career&type=I&cid=N000096 38&newMem=N&recs=20.

125. Greg Palast and Ted Rall, *Billionaires and Ballot Bandits: How to Steal an Election in 9 Easy Steps* (New York, NY: Seven Stories Press, 2012), 62.

126. "Factbox: Has Obama Delivered on his 2008 Campaign Promises?" Reuters, October 28, 2011.

127. Mara Der Hovanesian, "Citigroup's Rubin Resigns," *Bloomberg Businessweek*, January 9, 2009.

128. Prins and Ugrin, "Bailout Tally Report."

129. Council on Foreign Relations, "Robert E. Rubin," at www.cfr.org/experts/world/robert-e-rubin/b292.

130. Sheryl Gay Stolberg and Stephen Labaton, "Obama Calls Wall Street Bonuses 'Shameful,'" *New York Times*, January 29, 2009.

131. Federal Reserve Bank of New York, "New York Fed Names William C. Dudley President," at www.newyorkfed.org/newsevents/news/aboutthefed/2009/oa090127.html.

132. Shahien Nasiripour, "Geithner Calendar: Met with Goldman's Blankfein More Than Pelosi, Reid, McConnell, Boehner," Huffington Post, September 14, 2010, at http://www.huffingtonpost.com/2010/09/14/geithner-blankfein-pelosi_n_715334.html.

133. Jackie Calmes and Louise Story, "In Washington, One Bank Chief Still Holds Sway," *New York Times*, July 18, 2009.

134. The others were John Adams, John Quincy Adams, George W. Bush, Rutherford B. Hayes, John F. Kennedy, Franklin Roosevelt, and Teddy Roosevelt.

135. Data.gov, White House Visitor Records Requests, at https://explore.data.gov/dataset/White-House-Visitor-Records-Requests/644b-gaut.

136. Executive Branch Personal Public Financial Disclosure Reports 2011 / 2012 at www.whitehouse.gov/sites/default/files/president_obama_2011_oge_form_278_certified.pdf.

137. The White House, "Remarks by the President on Financial Rescue and Reform," press release, September 14, 2009.

138. US Department of Labor, "Data Retrieval: Labor Force Statistics (CPS)," Table A-15, alternative measures of labor underutilization, February 4, 2011.

139. Board of Governors of the Federal Reserve System, "Aggregate Reserves of Depository Institutions and the Monetary Base," statistical release H.3, February 4, 2010.

140. As of September 2013, there was talk that Obama would replace Bernanke upon the end of his term with Larry Summers, further underscoring the alignment of policies and interests with Wall Street and its free-market, deregulatory, influential doctrine. But once Summers withdrew from contention on September 15, 2013, Fed vice chairman Janet Yellen became Obama's choice for the post.

141. Prins and Ugrin, "Bailout Tally Report."

142. Thomas P. Di Napoli, New York State Comptroller, "DiNapoli: Wall Street Bonuses Declined in 2010: Earnings Down from Record High, but Wall Street Has Second Best Year Ever," press release, February 23, 2011.

143. OECD, "Employment and Labour Markets: Key Tables from OECD," January 3, 2011, at www.oecd-ilibrary.org/employment/youth-unemployment-rate-2010_20752342-2010-table2.

144. Nomi Prins, "The Greek Tragedy and Great Depression Lessons Not Learned," Thoughts Blog, February 21, 2012, at www.nomiprins.com/thoughts/2012/2/21/the-greek-tragedy-and-great-depression-lessons-not-learned.html.

145. Library of Congress, H.R. 4173, The Wall Street Reform and Consumer Protection Act of 2009, Bill Text Versions, 111th Congress (2009–10).

146. Open Secrets, Center for Responsive Politics, Lobbying Database, at www.opensecrets.org/lobby/index.php.

147. "Banking Reform Bill Swiftly Approved," *New York Times*, June 13, 1933.

148. US Department of the Treasury, "Statement from Secretary Geithner on the Financial Reform Conference," press release, June 25, 2010.

149. Standard & Poor's Financial Services LLC, "United States of America Long-Term Rating Lowered to 'AA+' Due to Political Risks, Rising Debt Burden; Outlook Negative," press release, August 5, 2011. See also Prins and Ugrin, "Bailout Tally Report."

150. Christopher Chantrill, Government Debt Chart, usgovernmentspending.com, at www.usgovernmentspending.com/spending_chart_2008_2017USp_XXs1li111mcn_H0f.

151. Hugh Son, "BofA Loses No. 1 Ranking by Assets to JPMorgan as Chief Moynihan Retreats," *Bloomberg*, October 18, 2011. See also Nelson D. Schwartz, "Bank of America Loses Title as Biggest in U.S.," *New York Times*, October 18, 2011.

152. Charles Ferguson, "Jamie Dimon, Colossus of Wall Street," *Time*, April 21, 2011.

153. David Benoit, "Jamie Dimon Bashes Financial Regulation," *Wall Street Journal*, March 30, 2011.

154. Julianna Goldman, "Goldman CEO Blankfein Said to Meet with Obama Adviser Lew," *Bloomberg Businessweek*, July 18, 2012.

155. Gregory Zuckerman, "'London Whale' Rattles Debt Market," *Wall Street Journal*, April 6, 2012. See also Gregory Zuckerman, "J.P. Morgan 'Whale' Report Signals Deeper Problem," *Wall Street Journal*, July 14, 2012; JPMorgan Chase, CEO Taskforce Update, July 13, 2012.

156. Colin Fernandez, "Feeling the Pinch, Tony? Blair Takes Out £4.2 Million Loan Against His Central London Des Res from U.S. Bank He Advises," Mail Online, September 16, 2012. See also PR Newswire, "Tony Blair Appointed Senior Advisor to JPMorgan Chase," press release, January 10, 2008.

157. US Senate Committee on Banking, Housing, and Urban Affairs, "A Breakdown in Risk Management: What Went Wrong at JPMorgan Chase?" Hearings, June 13, 2012.

158. Council on Foreign Relations, "The State of the Global Economy," Transcript, October 10, 2012, at www.cfr.org/economics/state-global-economy/p29251.

159. Ibid.

160. Revised Statistics, "SEC Enforcement Actions Addressing Misconduct That Led to or Arose from the Financial Crisis," as of September 1, 2013, at www.sec.gov/spotlight/enf-actions-fc.shtml.

161. Nate Raymond and Bernard Vaughan, "Judge Approves Citigroup $590 Million Settlement," Reuters, August 1, 2013, at www.reuters.com/article/2013/08/01/us-citigroup-settlement-idUSBRE9700T420130801.

162. Nick Summers, "Ex-Goldman Banker Found Liable in $1 Billion Fraud Case," *Bloomberg Businessweek*, August 1, 2013.

163. Jonah Goldberg, "Obama's Tainted Bundler," *Los Angeles Times*, April 24, 2012.

164. Federal Reserve Board, "Factor Affecting Reserve Balances," H.4.1. Release, October 10, 2013, at http://www.federalreserve.gov/releases/h41/Current/.

165. Federal Reserve Board, "Statement Regarding Transactions in Agency Mortgage-Backed Securities and Treasury Securities," press release, September, 13, 2012, at www.newyorkfed.org/markets/opolicy/operating_policy_120913.html.

166. Pedro da Costa and Alister Bull, "Bernanke Says Fed Stimulus Benefits Clear, Downplays Risks," Reuters, February 26, 2013.

167. Office of the State Comptroller, "Wall Street Bonuses Rose in 2012," February 26, 2013.

168. The White House, "Statement from the President on the Confirmation of Jack Lew as Secretary of Treasury," press release, February 27, 2013.

169. The White House, "Former Chief of Staff Jack Lew," at www.whitehouse.gov /administration/staff/jack-lew.

170. Siddhartha Mahanta, "Flashback: Lew's Time at Citi and Other Disappointments," *Mother Jones*, January 9, 2012.

171. Pam Martens, "Democrats Disgrace Themselves with Jack Lew Confirmation for Treasury Secretary," *Wall Street on Parade*, February 28, 2013.

172. National Mortgage Settlement Fact Sheet: Settlement, October 19, 2013, filed as a consent judgment in US District Court for the District of Columbia, at https://d9klfgi bkcquc.cloudfront.net/Mortgage_Servicing_Settlement_Fact_Sheet.pdf. See also "$25 Billion Mortgage Servicing Agreement Filed in Federal Court," March 12, 2012, joint press release from the Department of Justice, the Department of Housing and Urban Housing Development, and forty-nine state attorneys general, at https://d9klfgibkcquc .cloudfront.net/Settlement-USDOJ-FILING-news-release.pdf. "SEC Enforcement Actions Addressing Misconduct That Led to or Arose from the Financial Crisis," as of October 27, 2013, at www.sec.gov/spotlight/enf-actions-fc.shtml. "Independent Foreclosure Review to Provide $3.3 Billion in Payments, $5.2 Billion in Mortgage Assistance," January 7, 2013, joint press release from the governors of the Federal Reserve System and the Office of the Comptroller of the Currency, at www.federalreserve.gov/newsevents/press /bcreg/20130107a.htm.

173. Victoria Bryan, "Goldman Sachs Boss Says Banks Do 'God's Work,'" Reuters, November 8, 2009.

INDEX

A. Steinam Company, 168
Abacus deal, 418
Abel, I. W., 295
Acheson, Dean, 195
Adams, Charles Francis III, 88
Adams, Sherman, 203, 216
Afghanistan, 313
Agricultural Adjustment Act of 1933,
    132, 149
Ahamed, Liaquat, 108
AIG, bailout of, 410, 411
Aldrich, Nelson, 7, 15, 20–21, 23–24
Aldrich, Winthrop
    Aldrich plan, 24–26
    as ambassador to Britain, 206
    Banking Act of 1933, against
        amendment to, 142–143
    banking strategies of, 164, 200–201,
        397
    as chairman and president of Chase,
        123
    Committee for Financing Foreign
        Trade, chairman of, 179, 180, 181
    Eisenhower, relationship with, 202,
        219
    Europe, organization of financial
        relief for, 181
    FDIC, opposition to, 130–131
    FDR, relationship with, 125–128,
        133–134
    free trade, support for, 207–208
    Glass-Steagall Act, support for,
        124–125, 139

inflation, ideas for curbing, 177–178
International Chamber of Commerce,
    president of, 174, 181
Marshall Plan, support of, 183–184
Middle East, visit to, 199–200
multinational banks, opposition to,
    171–172
national debt, stabilization of,
    166–167
National War Fund, chairman of,
    167–168
Truman, relationship with, 174, 179,
    181
war, varying opinions on, 154–155,
    156
war financing, role of in, 166
Aldrich Bill, 31–32
Aldrich plan, 25–26
Aldrich-Vreeland Act of 1908, 19
Aldridge, John, 359
Alexander, Henry, 206, 225–226
Allegheny Corporation, 89, 129
Alliance for Progress, 236, 245, 247, 250,
    264, 265
Allon, Yigal, 292
Aluminum Company of America
    (Alcoa), 74, 88
American Bankers Association, 172
Amherst College, alumni in politics and
    banking, 79, 186, 247
Andean Pact, 273
Anderson, Benjamin, 86
Anderson, Robert, 224

Andrew, Abraham Piatt, 23
Andrews, Lisa, 384
Antitrust laws, 263
Argentina, 332
Argo (film), 311
Armacost, Samuel, 324, 327, 342
Armao, Robert, 307
Arthur Anderson, 400
Ashraf, Princess, 307, 308
Asian crisis, 380, 386
Aspe, Pedro, 350
Asset-backed securities (ABS), 403
Aswan Dam, Egypt, 212, 218

Bahrain, 288
Bailouts. *See* Government bailout
    programs
Baker, George Jr., 98
Baker, George Sr., 3, 11, 27, 86
Baker, J. Stewart, 215
Baker, James III, 326, 337, 338–339, 344,
    347
Balance of payments deficit, 240, 245,
    259, 262, 265–266, 269
Banco Chase Manhattan, 237
Bani-Sadr, Abolhassan, 310
Bank for International Settlements
    (BIS), 108–109, 351, 380
Bank Holding Company Act of 1956,
    216, 276
Bank Holding Company Act of 1970,
    279, 320, 381, 387
Bank Markazi, 311, 312, 316–317
Bank Merger Act of 1960, 263
Bank Merger Act of 1966, 263
Bank of America
    bailout subsidies for, 409, 410, 411
    Bank Holding Company bill, effect
        on, 217
    credit cards, 270
    debt problems, 326–327, 342–343,
        350
    expansion of, 185, 225
    Glass-Steagall Act, support for repeal
        of, 385
    insurance business, 335
    legal settlements, 409

    Marshall Plan, role in, 185
    mergers, 365, 383, 409
    Merrill Lynch, purchase of, 408
    SEC fine of, 418
Bank of England, 5, 70, 80, 367
Bank of Manhattan, 215
Bank of United States, 107–108
Bank One, 403
BankAmerica. *See* Bank of America
Bankers
    collaboration with politicians, 29–32,
        34–39, 158–159, 180–183, 204–
        205, 211, 321, 333, 335, 338, 342
    oil crisis, profits from, 275
    OPEC leaders and, 303
    presidents, evolution of relationship
        with, 300, 318, 320, 333, 394–395,
        409, 417
    private gain, pursuit of, 50, 275–276,
        293
    public perception of, 18, 27, 30, 48,
        49, 179, 414
    salaries, 272, 379, 412
    settlements and fines, 401, 418–419
    social responsibility, lack of, 229–230,
        379, 422
    See also Government bailout
        programs
Banking
    activities outlawed in US, 247, 292
    commercial *vs.* investment banks,
        136, 321, 325, 362–363, 395–396
    financial fraud, 111, 119, 297, 321,
        352–354, 378, 397–399
    international expansion of, 64, 164,
        197–199, 201, 207, 221, 245, 249,
        275, 298
    See also Deregulation
Banking Act of 1935, 142–145
Banking Act of 1933 (Glass-Steagall
    Act), 130–131, 137, 142, 390, 392
Bankruptcies, corporate, 399, 400, 408
Banzer, Hugo, 293
Barings banking house, 5
Barney, Charles, 9
Barreto, Brian A., 382
Baruch, Bernard, 60, 63

Batista, Fulgencio, 222
Baxter, William, 330
Bay of Pigs invasion, 235
Beal, Louis, 163
Beame, Abraham, 298–299
Bear Stearns, 405–407
Bechtel, Stephen, 295
Beirut, Lebanon, 218, 224–225
Ben Yahia, Mohamed, 318
Bentsen, Lloyd, 371
Bentson, George, 341
Berlin Wall, 236
Bernanke, Benjamin, 101, 403, 410, 412, 414
Bernstein, Irving, 113
Bernstorff, Johann von, 45
Big Six, 98–99, 100, 105, 228, 394, 395, 410, 411, 414
Big Three, 108, 119, 134
Bin Abdul-Rahman, Abdullah, 244
Bird, Kai, 218
Black, Eugene, 193, 212, 217, 218, 302
Black Monday (1987), 345–347
Black Thursday (1929), 96–100
Blair, Tony, 407, 417
Blankfein, Lloyd, 404, 405, 408, 410, 413, 421–422
Bliss, Tasker H., 58
Blough, Roger, 238
Blue Monday (1962), 240
Blueprint for Reform, 337, 348
Boesky, Ivan, 342
Bolling, Richard, 263
Bolten, Joshua, 403, 404
Borah, William, 59
Boyce-Thomson, William, 51
Brady, Nicholas, 346, 347, 348, 349–350, 353, 355, 361, 363
Brahany, Thomas, 48
Brainard, Lael, 382
Brandeis, Louis, 3–4, 33, 35, 395
Brazil, 293, 302
Breeden, Richard, 348, 362–363
Bretton Woods Agreement, 171, 175, 281, 349
Britain, 59, 113, 155, 199, 206, 208, 212, 219, 227, 231, 294, 317, 358, 367

British War Relief Society of America, 164
Broderick, Joseph, 108
Brody, Kenneth, 366
Bryan, William Jennings, 19, 41
Brzezinski, Zbigniew, 304, 307, 308, 310
Buchanan, Pat, 380
Budget and Accounting Act of 1921, 74–75
Bulkley, Robert, 35
"Bull Moose" party, 30
Bullis, Harris, 210
Burgess, Warren Randolph, 160–161, 163, 168, 169, 172, 187, 194, 204–205, 227, 246
Burton, Daniel, 374
Bush, George H. W.
    bankers, relationship with, 347, 394
    Blueprint for Reform, 337
    Brady plan for third world debt reduction, 349–351, 353, 355
    Butcher, meeting with, 358–359
    deregulation, promotion of, 321, 323–325, 334–335, 337–338, 361, 363–364
    election of 1988, 347
    savings and loan crisis, 348, 352–354, 353, 359
    as vice president, 321, 323–325, 333–338
Bush, George W.
    bank bailout plan (TARP), 411
    bankers, relationship with, 402
    campaign funding, 401–402
    corporate crime, curb for, 400
    election of 2000, 397
    Iraq, invasion of, 400
    on Lehman Brothers crisis, 408
    quantitative easing, approval of, 101
    reelection in 2004, 403
    retaliation for 911, 399
Bush, Neil, 352, 359
Bush, Jeb, 352
Business Advisory Council, Department of Commerce, 118
Business Group for Latin America, 250, 259

Butcher, Willard C., 295, 327–329, 337, 347, 354, 355, 358, 360
Butler, John, 281
Buzzanco, Robert, 267

Califano, Joseph "Joe" Jr., 264
Calkins, Earnest Elmo, 83
Camdessus, Michael, 380
Cannon, Joseph G., 15
Capital limits, 395–396, 402, 417
Capital "lockout," 151–152
Caribbean Basin Initiative, 327
Carpenter, Michael, 398
Carter, Jimmy
   bankers, relationship with, 301
   deregulation, 301, 303, 314
   election of 1976, 301
   foreign policy, 302
   Iran hostage crisis, 310–318
   Shah of Iran, admittance of to US, 308–309
Carter, John Franklin, 169
Casey, William, 322
Castro, Fidel, 222, 223, 242
Cayne, James, 401–402
Celler, Emanuel, 214
Center for Inter-American Relations, 237
Cermak, Anton, 118
Certificates of deposit (CDs), 233
Chamberlain, Austen, 83
Chamberlain, Neville, 155
Chamoun, Camille, 224
Champion, George, 232, 233, 261, 266, 272, 274
Chase Harris Forbes Corporation, 139
Chase International Investment Corporation, 305
Chase Manhattan Bank
   creation of, 215
   credit crisisrecession of 1990, 360
   Eurodollar market, use of, 234
   financial problems, 328–329
   financial statement error, 295–296
   global expansion, 225, 287, 288, 291, 304–305
   Iranian government, declarations of default against, 311–313

Lincoln First Corporation, acquisition of, 337
   net profit in 1995, 374
   One Chase Plaza, 232–233
   Vietnam War and, 266
   See also Chase National Bank; JPMorgan Chase
Chase National Bank
   Chase Securities Corporation, establishment of, 125
   global expansion, 181, 184–185, 201, 211, 213, 222
   mergers, 4, 91–92, 123, 215
   See also Chase Manhattan Bank; JPMorgan Chase
Chase National Bank of Egypt, 291
Chase Securities Corporation, 125
Chase World Information Corporation, 288
Chemical Bank New York Trust, 217
Chemical Banking Corporation, 365
Cheney, Dick, 398
Chernoff, Allan, 382
Chernow, Ron, 34, 37
China, 287–288
Christopher, Warren, 309, 310, 315, 316, 318
Chrysler Corporation Loan Guarantee Act of 1979, 306
Church, Frank, 296–297
Churchill, Winston, 173, 175, 208
Citibank, 270, 293, 360
Citicorp, 335, 336, 343, 361, 374, 384
Citicorp International Bank Limited (CIBL), 292–293
Citigroup, 3, 375, 381, 389, 398, 411, 418
City Company of New York, 139
Civil Rights Act of 1964, 253
Clausen, Alden W. "Tom," 276, 300, 324, 326–327, 331–332, 338–339, 342–343, 350
Clay, Lucius, 204
Clayton Antitrust Act of 1914, 43, 214, 263
Clearing House Association, 108
Clemenceau, Georges, 58–60
Clémentel, Étienne, 81
Cline, Kenneth, 371

Clinton, Bill
  bankers, alliances with, 366, 369
  deregulation policies, 371, 375, 390, 392
  impeachment, calls for, 381
  Mexican crisis bailout, 372–375
  North American Free Trade Agreement (NAFTA), 370
  reelection in 1996, 378
CMART, 297–298
Cohan, William D., 203
Cold War, 194, 197, 198, 202, 216, 233, 243, 256, 323, 357
Collado, Emilio, 187
Collateralized debt obligations (CDOs), 403, 405, 419
Colombia, 293
Commercial banks
  ban on dealing in securities, 128
  Cold War-related loans, 202
  corporate bonds, underwriting of, 343, 348
  deregulation of, 314, 326, 333, 337
  Federal Deposit Insurance and, 335
  foreign assets of, 290
  Glass-Steagall Act, repeal of, 381, 385, 392, 396
  global expansion of, 292–293
  Less Developed Countries, debt burden of, 302
  London, offices in, 293
  separation from investment banking, 125
  S&L bailout, profit from, 354, 359
  World Bank, cooperation with, 331
  World War II debt burden of, 167, 182
Commercial paper market, 278
Commodity Exchange Act of 1936, 363
Commodity Futures Trading Commission (CFTC), 363
Communism, perceived threat of, 183, 194–195, 197, 218
Community Reinvestment Act of 1977, 384, 388
Comptroller of the Currency, 28, 33, 36, 47, 263
Conable, Barber Jr., 362

Congress of Industrial Organizations, 145
Connally, John, 281, 285
Consumer Federation of America, 353
Cook, Don, 260
Coolidge, Calvin, 67, 78–79, 82–85
Corn Exchange Bank Trust Company, 94–95, 217
Corrigan, Gerald, 346, 350, 352, 365
Cortelyou, George, 8, 10, 11
Corwin, Philip, 353
Corzine, Jon, 369, 403, 419
Costanzo G. A. "Al," 289
Council of Economic Advisors, 334, 346
Council of the Americas, 237
Council on Foreign Relations, 219, 244
Countrywide Financial, 409
Cox, James A., 67
Crapo, Michael, 404
Credit-Anstalt, 111
Credit cards, 252, 269–270
Crissinger, Daniel Richard, 80
Cuba, 84, 257
Cuban missile crisis, 242–243
Cummings, Homer, 116
Current Tax Payment Act of 1943, 169

D'Amato, Alfonse, 384, 385
Davis, James, 88
Davis, John W., 59–60, 63, 128
Davis, Norman, 129
Davison, Henry, 21, 23, 25, 62–63
Dawes, Charles, 79, 83
Dawes plan, 79–81
Day, Henry Mason, 139
De Vries, Rimmer, 302
Dean, Arthur, 235
Debt inflation policy, 281–282
Declarations of Algiers, 316
Defense Production Act of 1950, 278
Depew, Chauncey, 6
Deposit insurance premiums, 351–352
Depository Institutions Deregulation and Monetary Control Act of 1980, 314, 333
Depression. *See* Great Depression
Deregulation, banking, 301, 303, 306, 314, 320, 333–334, 337–338, 342, 360, 391–392

Derivatives
  Asian market, 379, 380
  Bear Stearns collapse and, 406
  cross-border, 371
  deregulation and, 392, 402
  Dodd-Frank bill and, 415
  energy, 375
  Enron, use by, 397
  Goldman Sachs, use of, 410
  government shield for, 386, 387, 391
  hybrid, 364
  increased profit from, 361, 363
  JPMorgan Chase, investment in, 417
  mismarking by JPMorgan Chase, 331
  objections to regulation of, 404–405
Dewey, Thomas, 192
Di Stefani (or De Stefani), Alberto, 78
Dillon, C. Douglas, 234, 246, 248, 254,
  260, 272, 282, 347
Dimon, James "Jamie," 331, 368, 379,
  385, 403, 405–407, 410, 413,
  416–417
Dinitz, Simcha, 292
Disarmament, negotiations on, 234–235
Dodd, William, 148
Dodge, Cleveland, 14
Dole, Elizabeth, 325
Dollar, as global reserve currency, 72,
  170
Dollar, devaluation of, 280–282, 285
Dollar Saving Bank, 11
Donaldson, William, 402
Donnelly, John, 370
Dorgan, Byron, 330, 390
Downey, Robert, 360
Drexel Burnham Lambert, 342
Drysdale Government Securities, 328
Du Pont, Pierre, 147
Dudley, William, 413
Dulles, John Foster, 60, 112, 208, 209,
  218, 219
Dunn, Harry, 203
Dynegy, 398–399

Ebbers, Bernard, 399, 421
Eccles, Marriner, 142, 152
Economic Cooperation Act of 1948, 189

Economic Policy Advisory Board, 325,
  334, 346
Economy, global
  in 2010, 414
  risky banker practices and, 394, 404,
  422
  US dominance of, 177
Economy, US
  Panic of 1907, 7–13
  Great Depression, 113–115
  in 1930s, 105–108, 135, 145–147,
  150–151
  post–World War II, 177, 180
  in 1950s, 196–198, 220–221
  1958 recession, 223–224
  in 1960s, 231, 252, 270, 271–272
  1962 Blue Monday, 239–240
  in 1970s, 296, 306, 307
  in 1980s, 319–320, 355–356
  1987 market crash, 345
  1990 credit crisis/recession, 360
  in 1990s, 377–378
  in 2000s, 397, 413–414, 416
Edge, Walter Evans, 64
Edge Act of 1919, 64
Egypt, 212, 217–219, 221, 224, 273,
  289–291, 315
Eisenhower, Dwight D.
  banker friends of, 202–204, 206
  domestic policy of, 197, 204, 211
  Eisenhower Doctrine, 221
  election of 1952, 203
  foreign policy of, 204
  international trade policy, 208
  Joseph McCarthy and, 210
  Korean War, termination of, 208
  Lebanon, deployment of troops to,
  225
  military isolationism, opposition to,
  207
  Mutual Security Program, 210–211,
  212, 230
  North Atlantic Treaty Organization,
  commander of, 202
  Suez crisis, 219
Eisenhower Doctrine, 221
Eizenstat, Stuart, 303, 306

Electronic funds transfer (EFT), 303
Elliott, William, 78
Emanuel, Rahm, 366, 413
Emergency Economic Stability Act of 2008, 411
Emergency Loan Guarantee Act of 1971, 279
Emergency Moratorium Act (New York, 1975), 299
Energy companies, deregulation of, 375
Enron, 363, 368, 397–399
Equitable Life Assurance Society, 4
Equitable Trust Company, 123–124, 232
Esposito, Michael, 296
Euro, 385–386
Eurodollar market, 233, 245, 250, 269, 283
European banks, global expansion of, 358
Everything Card, 269
Excess Profits Act of 1950, 200
Export-Import Bank, 312

Fall, Albert, 74
Fannie Mae, 303, 411
Farber, Hilliard, 295
Fastow, Andrew, 421
FDIC. *See* Federal Deposit Insurance Corporation
FDR. *See* Roosevelt, Franklin Delano
Federal Crisis Inquiry Commission, 420–421
Federal Deposit Insurance Corporation (FDIC), 130–132, 332, 353, 414
Federal Emergency Relief Administration, 132
Federal Reserve
    Bank Holding Company Act and, 216–217
    bank mergers and, 263
    bank trading of corporate stocks, approval of, 361
    Crash of 1929, reaction to, 100, 101
    Crash of 1987, reaction to, 345–346
    Great Depression, policies during, 107
    inception of at Jekyll Island, SC, 23–25

    interest rates, 178, 183, 330, 337–338, 400, 412, 417, 420
    Kennedy assassination, reaction to, 249
    monetary policy, conflict with Regan about, 330
    purpose of, 37, 90
    quantitative easing, 85
    securities underwriting, changes in rules on, 378–379
    wartime financing, 163
    Wriston's proposals for bank expansion, 280
Federal Reserve Act of 1913, 34–39
Federal Trade Commission, 136
Ferguson, Thomas, 124
Financial Institution Reform, Recovery and Enforcement Act of 1989, 353
Financial Institutions Deregulation Act (FIDA), 333–335
Financial Services Act of 1998 (HR10), 383–385
Financial Services Competitive Equity Act, 335
Financial Services Modernization Act of 1999 (Gramm-Leach-Bliley Act), 387, 389, 390
First National Bank, 4, 33, 217
First National City Bank of New York, 223, 233, 266, 269, 284
    See also Citibank; Citigroup
First of Boston Corporation, 139
Fisher, Peter, 398
Flanagan, H. C., 224
Flanigan, Peter, 283–284, 286
Fleishhacker, Herbert, 102
Fletcher, Duncan, 137, 138
Fletcher-Rayburn bill, 136
Floating prime rates, 286
Folsom, Marion, 205
Forbes, Bertie Charles, 50, 91, 98, 100
Ford, Gerald, 295, 299, 300
Ford, Henry, 113
Ford, Henry III, 272
Foreign Assistance Act of 1948, 189
Fowler, Henry "Joe," 203, 261, 266
Fox, Grace, 168

France, 59, 112
Freddie Mac, 411
Free-market float, 284–285
Free trade, 207–208
Frick, Henry Clay, 12
Friedman, Stephen, 369, 400, 403
Friedrich, Klaus, 380
Fulbright, J. William, 247
Fuld, Richard Jr., 408
Funston, George Keith, 215, 252
Futures, trading, 282, 363, 364–365
Futures Trading Practices Act of 1992,
    364

Gage, Lyman, 5
Galbraith, John Kenneth, 97, 102–103
Garfield, James A., 171
Garn, Jake, 335
Garn–St. Germain Depository
    Institutions Act of 1982, 333, 341
Garner, Robert, 187
Gary, Elbert, 12
Gates, Thomas, 206, 260, 272
Gay, Charles, 151
Geisst, Charles, 344
Geithner, Timothy, 401, 405, 406, 410,
    413
Geneva Conference (1961), 235
Germany, 45, 58–60, 63, 79–81, 109,
    111–113, 173
Giannini, A. P., 126, 135–136, 140, 142,
    148, 181, 182, 184
Giannini, Mario, 182
Gibson, Donald, 231
Glackens, Louis, 7
Glass, Carter, 31–32, 37, 51, 58, 94, 116,
    118, 128, 137, 143
Glass-Owen bill, 34–36
Glass-Steagall Act of 1932, 116–117
Glass-Steagall Act of 1933, 132, 325,
    344, 353, 385, 390, 392
  repeal of, 381, 385, 392, 396
Glass-Willis draft bill, 31
Gold standard, 72, 246, 280–282
Goldman Sachs
  as designated holding company, 408
  Greece, shield of debt status of, 387

hybrid instruments, support for
    deregulation of, 364
  Mexican bailout and, 374
  Obama, campaign contributions to,
    411, 417
  politicians, alliances with, 202–203,
    322–323, 329, 366, 369, 403, 406
  SEC fine of, 418
  Weinberg's relationship with FDR,
    117–118
Goldschmid, Harvey, 402
Goldwater, Barry, 257, 258
Golub, Harvey, 389
Good, James, 88
Gorton, Slade, 363
Government bailout programs
  AIG bailout, 410, 414
  Argentina, loan guarantee for, 332
  Bank of America bailout, 409, 410,
    411
  Brady plan, 350–352
  Chrysler Corporation Loan
    Guarantee Act, 306
  Lockheed Emergency Loan Act, 279
  Long Term Capital Management
    bailout, 386
  Mexican bailout, 373–375
  Penn Central debacle, 278
  Reconstruction Finance Corporation,
    114
  savings and loan banks, 348, 353–354
  third world loans, 320
  Troubled Asset Relief Program
    (TARP), 411, 414
Gramm, Phil, 385, 388
Gramm, Wendy, 346, 363, 364, 367–368
Gramm-Leach-Bliley Act (Financial
    Services Modernization Act of
    1999), 387, 389, 390
  see also Glass-Steagall repeal
Gratz, Earl Jay, 203
Gray, C. Boyden, 359
Grayson, Cary T., 60, 65, 67
Great Depression, 107, 109–110, 111,
    114, 118–120, 146–147, 151
Great Society initiatives, 253
Greenberg, David, 83

Greenspan, Alan, 343–348, 350, 353, 381, 386, 387, 400

Greider, William, 13, 38

Grey, Edward, 45

Griesa, Thomas, 312

Grobe, Edward, 23

Grossman, Max, 168

Grubman, Jack, 399, 400

Guaranty Trust, 215, 217

Gulf Oil Company, 74

Gutt, Camille, 175

Hagerty, James, 210

Haig, Alexander, 284, 294

Halloran, Mike, 371

Hammarskjold, Dag, 219

Hanover Bank, 4

Harding, Warren G., 67, 70, 71, 73, 74, 78

Harriman, Edward Henry (E. H.), 3, 6

Harrison, William, 396, 398, 402

Hauge, Gabriel, 205–206, 207, 221, 224, 263, 283

Haughton, Daniel, 279

Hayes, Alfred, 249

Hearst, William Randolph, 6, 140

Hedge funds, 378, 386, 407

Heinz, John, 363

Heinze, F. Augustus, 8–9

Heller, Walter, 239–240

Hill, James, 3, 6

Hitler, Adolf, 148, 153–154, 176

Holding companies, 216, 277–280, 333–335, 338, 353, 378–379, 382, 388

Hollins, Harry, 9

Hoover, Herbert
bankers, post-Crash conference with, 102
Belgium, report on economic situation of, 55–56
Depression, blame for, 114
economy, denial of true state of, 106
election of 1928, 88
on European economic crisis, 64
excessive private loans, concern about, 82, 85
German debt moratorium, 112

Reconstruction Finance Corporation, establishment of, 114
as secretary of commerce, 74
World War Foreign Debt Commission, 75

Hoover, J. Edgar, 255

Hormats, Robert, 387

Hotel Manhattan, meeting at, 10–12

House, Edward, 35, 45, 48, 51, 58

House Banking and Currency Committee, 27–28

House Un-American Activities Committee, 189, 210

Houston, Frank, 174

Howe, Andrew C. Jr., 383

Hughes, Charles Evans, 46, 75, 76, 79

Hulbert, Mark, 313

Humphrey, George, 204

Hybrid derivatives products, 363–364

Hyde, Henry, 4

Hyland, William, 176

Ibn Saud, 200

IMF. *See* International Monetary Fund

Income tax, imposition of, 34

Inflation, 169, 177, 284, 290, 305, 306, 319, 326, 330

Interest equalization tax, 269

Internal Security Act of 1950, 210

International Advisory Committee, 272

International Bank for Reconstruction and Development. *See* World Bank

International Bank of Iran, 291

International Development Advisory Board, 190

International Monetary Fund (IMF), 165, 171, 285, 294, 332–333, 349, 351, 380

Interstate Commerce Commission, 42

Interstate Highway Act of 1956, 216

Interstate Trust Company, 123

Investment banks
deregulation, 323, 334, 362–365, 378, 392
London, offices in, 293
perceived need to increase leverage, 395, 402

Investment banks *(continued)*
  risky practices of, 402–403
  shares, sales of, 282
Iran, 291, 306–307
Iran hostage crisis, 310–318
Iron Curtain, 175
Isolationism
  during Coolidge's presidency, 78–79
  during Harding's presidency, 69–75
  post-World War I, 58, 62, 63, 67
  pre-World War II, 147, 148, 154–155,
    156, 178
  in 1950s, 197

J. Aron, 364
J. P. Morgan & Company. *See* Morgan
  Bank
J. P. Morgan Securities, 348
Japan, 66, 176
Jekyll Island, Georgia, 4, 22–25
Jekyll Island Club, 22–23
Joel, Billy, 299
Johnson, Baxter, 187
Johnson, Lyndon B.
  accomplishments of, 270–271
  Alliance for Progress, use of by
    bankers, 264
  balance of payments deficit, concern
    about, 259, 269
  bank mergers, facilitation of,
    263–264, 278
  bankers, relationship with, 250,
    251–252, 254–255, 259–263, 267,
    269
  as conservative Democrat, 253
  election as president in 1964, 258
  Great Society initiatives, 253
  international capital flows, control
    of, 269
  John Jones, deal with, 263
  Kennedy, contrast to, 254–255
  tax cut bill, 253
  Vietnam War, 255, 257, 258, 260, 266,
    268
  War on Poverty, 259
  war surtax bill, 268
Jones, John Jr., 263

Jones, Reginald, 295, 325
Jordan, Hamilton, 314
Josephson, Matthew, 3
JPMorgan Chase, 331, 396–397,
    402–403, 407, 411, 416, 418
  See also Morgan Bank
Junk bonds, 341–342, 392

Kaden, Lewis, 405
Katzen, Sally, 382
Kean, Benjamin, 309
Kearney, Daniel, 353
Keating, Charles, 353
Keating Five scandal, 352–353
Kellogg, Frank B., 78
Kennedy, John F.
  Alliance for Progress, 236, 247
  Amherst College speech, 247
  assassination of, 248
  balance of payments deficit, 240, 245
  bankers, relationship with, 231–232,
    239, 241
  capital-restraining proposals, 241
  Cuban missile crisis, 242–243
  domestic agenda of, 244–245
  election to Congress in 1946, 193
  Eurodollar accounts, concern about,
    245
  monetary flow, 248
  Rockefeller-Kennedy letters in *Life*
    magazine, 240–241
  steel industry, confrontation with, 238
  tax proposals, 239
  trade initiative, 241, 256
Kennedy, Joseph Patrick, 139–141, 231,
    249
Kennedy, Kathleen, 231
Kennedy, Robert, 244, 264–265,
    270–271
Keynes, John Maynard, 165, 170–171
Khomeini, Ayatollah Ruhollah, 307
Khrushchev, Nikita, 235, 243, 256–257
King, Martin Luther Jr., 271
King, William Henry, 101
Kintner, Robert, 268
Kissinger, Henry, 272, 290, 292, 307, 308
Knickerbocker Trust Company, 9

Korean War, 195, 197, 200–201, 208
Kovacevich, Richard, 371, 372
Kuhn, Loeb & Company, 3

Labrecque, Thomas, 360, 361, 371, 372
Lamont, Robert Patterson, 88
Lamont, Thomas
  on capital "lockout," 151–152
  Crash of 1929, reaction to, 99
  death of, 191
  European war debt repayment,
    70–71, 76–77
  FDR, relationship with, 121–122, 141,
    157, 161–162, 164
  Foreign Relations Committee,
    subpoena by, 62
  on Hitler, 153
  as international banker/diplomat,
    73–74, 77–78, 150, 152–154
  investigations of, 128, 147
  League of Nations, support of, 65–67,
    72
  letter to Hoover on stock market, 95
  Morgan Stanley and Company,
    creation of, 144
  Mussolini, ties to, 77–78, 150, 154
  at Paris Peace Conference, 58–60
  as partner and head of Morgan Bank,
    11
  Republican Party, break with, 72
  Vanderlip, disagreement with, 44
  warning of excessive foreign loans, 87
  Wilson, friendship with, 18, 54–55, 60
  World War I, role in, 51
Lamont, Thomas S., 116
Lance, Bert, 303
Lansing, Robert, 58, 64, 66
Larragoiti, Antonio, 237
Latin America, 188–189, 198, 201, 208,
    212–213, 221–223, 265
Lay, James Jr., 194
Lay, Kenneth, 398
League of Free Nations Association, 65
League of Nations, 52, 58–62, 64–65,
    67, 68
Least Developed Countries, debt burden
    of, 332–333, 351

Lebanon, 197, 225
  See also Beirut
Leffingwell, Russell, 49, 89, 118, 133,
    137–138, 148–149, 161, 191–192
Lehman Brothers, 408
Less Developed Countries (LDC), debt
    accumulation of, 302
Leverage ratios, 356, 407
Lew, Jack, 420
Lewinsky, Monica, 381
Lewis, Kenneth, 408–409
Liberty Bank and Trust, 4
Liberty bonds, 49
Lincoln First Corporation, 337
Lincoln Savings, 352
Lindbergh, Charles, 156
Lindbergh, Charles A. Sr., 27
Lloyd George, David, 58–60
Locarno agreements (1925), 83
Lockheed, bailout of, 279
Lodge, Henry Cabot, 57, 62–63, 65
Loeb, Nina, 20
Loeb, Solomon, 20
London, 227–228, 233, 292–293
London Whale incident, 417, 418, 420
Lundberg, Ferdinand, 29, 78

Maastricht Treaty (1992), 370
MacVeagh, Franklin, 15
Maheras, Thomas, 405
Malraux, André, 240
Manufacturers Hanover Trust Company,
    205, 217, 224, 263, 293, 360, 365
Marshall, George C., 185
Marshall Plan, 181, 183–185, 189–190,
    226
Martínez, Guillermo Ortiz, 373
MasterCard, 270
Mayer, Martin, 176, 341
McAdoo, William Gibbs, 29, 35, 37, 48,
    49, 51, 52, 118, 129, 132
McCarthy, Joseph, 210
McClellan, George Jr., 11
McCloy, John
  as Amherst alumnus, 79
  antitrust laws, victory over, 214
  Aswan Dam deal, 217–219

McCloy, John *(continued)*
  asylum for Shah of Iran, role in,
    307–308, 310
  Bank Holding Company Bill, warning
    about, 216
  banking strategies of, 211–212
  Chase, head of, 186
  Eisenhower, relationship with, 206,
    209, 210–211
  General Advisory Committee on
    Arms Control and Disarmament,
    chairman of, 234
  investigation of, 210
  Japan, opinion on invasion of, 176
  Kennedy, relationship with, 244
  oil companies and, 244, 290
  public office, offer of appointment
    to, 209
  return to private sector, 243–244
  as US high commissioner of
    Occupied Germany, 192–193
  Warren Commission, member of,
    255
  World Bank, head of, 186–188
McColl, Hugh, 371, 372, 385, 389
McCone, John, 255
McCormick, Vance Criswell, 58, 59, 63
McDonough, William, 386
McGarrah, Gates, 92, 109–111
McGillicuddy, John, 293, 365
McIntyre, M. H., 138, 143–144
McNamara, Robert, 294
Meany, George, 295
Mechanics and Metals National Bank,
  91
Medicare program (1965), 262
Meese, Edwin III, 326
Mellon, Andrew, 70, 74, 77, 80, 82–83,
  87, 88, 113–114
Mellon Bill (1926), 84
Mercantile National Bank, 8
Meriwether, John, 386
Merrill Lynch, 282, 283, 322, 334, 366,
  368, 384, 396, 400, 402, 409
Mexico, 302, 373–375
Meyer, Eugene, 63, 186
MF Global, 419

Middle East, 75, 153, 193, 197, 198, 199,
  201, 213, 217, 218, 221, 224, 244,
  272, 288–289
Milken, Michael, 342
Miller, Edward Jr., 212
Miller, G. William, 306, 312, 317
Mills, Ogden, 116
Mitchell, Charles
  Crash of 1929, reaction to, 100–101
  Cuba, investment in, 222
  as debt-structuring ambassador,
    83–84
  Federal Reserve rates, influence on,
    110
  financial strategies of, 18, 51, 54, 70,
    86, 93–95
  Forbes Magazine article on, 50
  global expansion, 70, 91
  investigation of, 119, 127
  resignation from National City Bank,
    119
Mitchell, John, 290
Moore, George, 223, 247, 248, 251, 261,
  265–266, 351
Moore & Schley, 12
Morgan, Henry, 145
Morgan, J. S., 42
Morgan, John Pierpont (J. P.)
  congressional investigation of, 18
  death of, 34
  financial holdings, 2
  international influence of, 4–5
  investigation of, 27, 32–34
  loss of investment in *Titanic,* 27
  New York Times and, 12
  organization of 1907 bank bailout,
    8–12
  side deals with Theodore Roosevelt,
    8, 12
  US Treasury, loan to, 5
Morgan, John Pierpont "Jack" Jr.
  attempted assassination of, 45
  code of ethics speech, 86
  Depression, blame of Federal Reserve
    for, 131
  FDR, friendship with, 139
  Germany, loan to, 80

as head of J. P. Morgan & Company, 34

investigation of, 128–129, 131, 147

subpoena of by Foreign Relations Committee, 62, 63

World War I, role of during, 18, 41–43, 47–48

Morgan, Junius Spencer, 14

Morgan Bank (J. P. Morgan & Company)

in 1958 recession, 224

in Asian crisis, 380

financial strategies of, 72, 73, 89

foreign bond issues by, 87

international lending policy of, 184

mergers, 217, 225–226

Morgan Stanley and Company, creation of, 144

ties to Italy, 78

See also JP Morgan Chase; Morgan Stanley

Morgan Guaranty Trust, 224, 226

See also JPMorgan Chase; Morgan Stanley

Morgan Stanley and Company, 144, 396, 402, 407, 408

Morgenthau, Henry, 133, 150, 160–161, 165, 168–170, 172

Morrow, Dwight, 59, 79, 81

Morse, Charles, 8–9

Mortgage-backed securities, 403, 406, 420

Moynihan, Brian Thomas, 409

Mozilo, Angelo, 409

Muckrakers, 6–7

Multicurrency loan agreement, 269

Munich Agreement, 153

Municipal Assistance Corporation (MAC), 298–299

Mussolini, Benito, 77, 148, 154

Mutual funds, consequences for banks, 230

Mutual Security Program, 210–211, 212, 230

Nabavi, Behzad, 316, 318

Nader, Ralph, 330

NAFTA (North American Free Trade Agreement), 370, 372

NASDAQ, 282

Nasser, Gamal Abdel, 218, 221, 273

National Advisory Council, 181, 185–186

National Banking Act of 1863 (with revisions in 1864 and 1865), 36

National City Bank

in 1958 recession, 224

financial strategies of, 91

as financial supermarket, 50–51

global expansion of, 43–44, 53, 168, 185, 213, 222, 225, 246

history of, 3, 18

as largest bank in US, 84

multicurrency loan agreement, 269

national defense program, financing of, 162

purchase of First National Bank of New York, 217

war, beneficial effect of, 163

See also Citigroup

National City Company, 29

National Council on US-China Trade (later US Business Council), 287–288

National Economic Council, 369, 382, 400

National Industrial Recovery Act of 1933, 132, 149

National Monetary Commission, 19

National Reserve Association, 24, 26

National War Fund, 167–168

NATO. *See* North Atlantic Treaty Organization

Neutrality Act of 1939, 156, 164

Neutrality laws, 148

New Deal, 132–133, 145–146

New York Banking Department, 108

New York City, threatened bankruptcy of, 298–300

New York Trust, 217

Newsom, David, 308, 309

Nicaraguan Freedom Fund, 294

Nixon, Richard M.

bankers, relationship with, 275, 279–280, 283–284

Nixon, Richard M. *(continued)*
  election of 1968, 271
  gold standard, end of, 281
  House Un-American Activities
    Committee, member of, 189
  Israel, support for, 290
  Lockheed, bailout of, 279
  McCloy's opinion of, 234
  National Council on US-China Trade,
    establishment of, 287–288
  reelection in 1972, 283
  resignation of, 295
Norbeck, Peter, 119
Norman, Montagu, 80
Norris, George, 94
North American Free Trade Agreement
    (NAFTA), 370, 372
North Atlantic Security plan, 190
North Atlantic Treaty Organization
    (NATO), 202, 227
Northern Securities Company, 6
NSC 68 (national security report), 194
Nuclear bomb testing, 236
Nye, Gerald Prentice, 74, 147

Obama, Barack
  bankers, relationship with, 394,
    411–412, 415–416
  on bankers' bonuses, 412, 414
  campaign contributors of, 411, 417
  economic policy appointments,
    412–413
  Goldman Sachs, 411–413
  Jamie Dimon, friendship with, 413
  quantitative easing, approval of, 101
  Wall Street dishonesty, reaction to,
    419, 421
Ochs, Adolph, 129
Oil, recycling into loans, 292–294
O'Neal, Earnest "Stanley," 402, 406
OPEC (Organization of the Petroleum
    Exporting Countries), 244,
    289–290, 302, 307
Organization for European Economic
    Cooperation (later Organization
    for Economic Cooperation and
    Development), 227

Orlando, Vittorio, 58, 60
Owen, Robert Latham, 35, 37

Pact of Steel, 154
Pahlavi, Mohammad Reza Shah, 304,
    306–309, 310, 315
Palast, Greg, 412
Palmer, Edward, 285
Pandit, Vikram, 412
Panic of 1893, 3
Panic of 1907, 7–13
Paris Peace Conference, 58–60
Participation Sales Act of 1966, 267
Patman, Wright, 115, 279, 284
Patterson, Ellmore, 296, 298
Paulson, Henry "Hank," 203, 369, 395,
    398, 399, 401, 404, 407, 409–411
Payne-Aldrich Tariff Act of 1909, 25, 30
Pearson, Drew, 249
Peck, Mary Allen Hulbert, 15
Pecora, Ferdinand, 119, 139–140
Pecora Commission hearings, 118–120,
    127–131
Pelosi, Nancy, 411
Penn Central, 264, 277–279
Penn Square Bank, 328–329
Perkins, George W., 4, 10, 15
Perkins, James, 119, 122–124, 139, 140,
    151, 160
Perón, Juan, 222
Peterson, Rudolph, 272
Petrodollars, 276, 290, 293–294, 303
Phillips, David Graham, 6
Piketty, Thomas, 391
Pitt, Harvey, 398
Porter, Roger, 359
Potter, William, 97, 125, 142
Pound, devaluation of, 367
Prado, Manuel, 222
Preston, Lewis, 312, 344, 351, 362
Prime rates, floating, 286
Prince, Charles, 405, 406
Pritzker, Penny, 412
Progressive "Bull Moose" party, 30
Progressive Era, 2, 68
Prosser, Seward, 97
Puche, Jaime Serra, 372

Pujo, Arsène, 27
Pujo Committee, 13, 30, 32, 33
 hearings, 27, 49, 119, 127, 418

Quantitative easing, 85, 101, 420

Rabinowitz, Yehoshua, 292
Railroads, regulation of during World
 War I, 42–43, 52
Raines, Franklin, 303
Rajai, Mohammad-Ali, 316
Reagan, Nancy, 324
Reagan, Ronald
 1987 market crash, investigation of,
  346
 Argentina, loan guarantee for, 332
 bankers, relationship with, 323–324,
  326
 campaign promises, 321
 deregulation policy, 320, 321,
  337–338
 economic recovery program, 325–326
 election of 1980, 315
 Greenspan, appointment of, 344–345
 mergers, policy regarding, 330
 reelection in 1984, 338
 tax policies, 324, 326
 third world debt crisis, solutions for,
  332–333, 338–339
Real Estate Investment Trusts (REITs),
 297–298
Recarey, Miguel Jr., 352
Reciprocal Tariff Act of 1934, 169
Reciprocal Trade Agreements Act of
 1943, 169
Reconstruction Finance Corporation,
 114
Reed, John, 270, 303, 336, 343–344, 350,
 351–352, 381, 384, 389, 390
Reed, Joseph, 289, 307, 309
Regan, Donald, 283–284, 321–323, 326,
 333, 334, 335, 338, 402
Regulation Q, 133, 136, 233, 306, 314
Reich, Robert, 391
Reichsbank, 79, 92
Rentschler, Frederick, 160
Rentschler, Gordon, 160, 168, 181

Resolution Funding Corporation, 254,
 354
Resolution Trust Corporation, 359
Revenue Act of 1932, 145
Revenue Act of 1935, 145–146
Revenue Act of 1942, 146, 165
Revenue Act of 1943, 169
Revenue Act of 1944, 146, 169
Revenue Acts of 1924, 1926, 1928, 82
Revenue Acts of 1950 and 1951, 200
Riegle-Neal Interstate Banking and
 Branching Efficiency Act of 1994,
 371, 383
Robb, Charles, 363
Roberts, Owen, 149
Roberts, Paul Craig, 320, 355
Rockefeller, David
 Alliance for Progress, use of, 250
 appointments to public office, offers
  of, 210, 284, 308
 on business-government synergies,
  245
 as co-CEO of Chase Bank, 232
 global expansion, 201, 237, 256–257,
  273, 287, 288–289, 291–292
 International Advisory Committee,
  creation of, 272
 as international power broker, 238
 Kennedy, relationship with, 231–232
 retirement from Chase, 327
 Rockefeller-Kennedy letters in *Life*
  magazine, 240–241
 Rostow's theories, belief in, 237, 238
 salary in 1968, 272
 Shah of Iran, relationship with,
  304–305, 307–310
 start of Chase career, 193–194
 Time magazine article about, 242
 Trilateral Commission, creation of,
  275
Rockefeller, Happy, 307
Rockefeller, James Stillman, 3, 223
Rockefeller, John D., 2, 3
Rockefeller, Margaret "Peggy," 288, 295
Rockefeller, Margaretta "Happy," 307
Rockefeller, Nelson, 186, 188, 190, 249,
 280, 292

Rockefeller, Neva, 256–257
Rockefeller, Percy, 84
Rockefeller, William, 3, 27
Rockefeller, William Goodsell, 3
Rogers, William P., 322
Roosevelt, Eleanor, 121
Roosevelt, Franklin Delano
    Aldrich, alliance with, 123–125
    assassination attempt on, 118
    bankers, alliance with, 126
    banking reforms, 122–123, 133,
        136–137
    death of, 173
    election of 1920, 67
    election of 1932, 117
    FDIC, concern about, 130
    fireside chat about banking, 126
    Glass-Steagall Act and, 122–125
    New Deal, 132–133, 145–146
    Perkins, secret meeting with, 122–123
    reelection in 1936, 149
    reelection in 1940, 161
    reelection in 1944, 173
    Weinberg, alliance with, 117–118
    Yalta Conference, 173
Roosevelt, James, 121
Roosevelt, Theodore, 5–6, 7, 8, 12, 31,
    46
Root, Elihu, 59, 63
Rose, H. Chapman, 205
Rosen, Sarah, 382, 384
Rostow, Walt "W. W.," 236, 238, 264
Rousselot, John, 340–341
Royall, Kenneth, 189
Rubin, Robert
    Citigroup, acting chairman of, 406
    conflict of interest, accusation of, 390
    deregulation, pursuit of, 375, 387, 388
    Enron, deal involving, 398
    Goldman Sachs, co-chairman of, 369
    mergers, investigation of, 383
    Mexican bailout, 374, 380
    National Economic Council,
        chairman of, 369
    Obama, support for, 411–412
    as Treasury Secretary, 373–374, 380,
        383, 387, 388, 389

Rusk, Dean, 231, 235, 257
Russian crisis, 386

Sadat, Anwar, 221, 289
Saez, Emmanuel, 391
Salomon Brothers, 331, 379
Sampson, Anthony, 218, 228
Sarbanes-Oxley Act of 2002, 400
Saudi Arabia, 244, 291
Saunders, Stuart T., 259, 264, 278
Savings and loan associations (S&Ls),
        314, 321, 333–335, 336, 340–341,
        347, 359
    See also Thrifts
Schaefer, Alfred, 271
Schiff, Jacob, 3, 20, 27, 28
Schreyer, William, 366
Schultze, Charles, 303, 306
Schumer, Charles "Chuck," 365, 385
Scott, John, 102
SEATO (Southeast Asia Treaty
        Organization), 1954, 257
Securities and Exchange Commission
        (SEC), 139, 141, 240, 348, 363, 396,
        418–419, 420
Securities Exchange Act of 1934,
        136–138
Sedgwick, Ellery, 54
Senate Foreign Relations Committee, 256
Seventeenth Amendment (1913), 34
Shadow banking, 234
Shaw, Leo, 222
Shelton, Arthur, 23
Sheperd, Howard, 222–223
Sherman Antitrust Act of 1890, 6, 263
Shipley, Walter, 365
Short-term profit-seeking, 18
Shultz, George, 284, 286, 294, 326, 329
Silverado Banking, Savings and Loan
        Association, 352
Simon, William, 291, 294, 322
Sinclair, Upton, 7
Sixteenth Amendment (1913), 34
Skidmore, Owings and Merrill, 233
Smith Barney, 379
Smithsonian Agreements (1971),
        285–286

Snyder, John, 175, 182, 184, 191, 192
Social Security Act of 1935, 145
Social Security Administration, 132
Solomon, Anthony, 331, 335
Soros, George, 367, 386
Soviet Union, 194–195, 233, 235–236, 242–243, 256–257, 287, 313
Special Committee on Investigation of the Munitions Industry, 147
Special Coordination Committee (SCC), 312, 313
Sperling, Gene, 382, 383, 384
Spitzer, Eliot, 401
Sproul, Allan, 163
Stabler, Charles, 336
Stagflation, 290
Stalin, Joseph, 173
Standard Brands, 129
Standard Oil Company, 2, 3, 6–7, 75
Stanley, Harold, 144–145, 187
Steagall, Henry, 116
Steel, Robert, 404
Sterling, John, 53
Stillman, Elsie, 3
Stillman, James, 3, 5, 10, 21, 27, 44, 53
Stimson, Henry, 88, 176
Stock market crash of 1929, 85–87, 96–100
Stock options, 363
Strauss, Albert, 58
Strong, Benjamin, 11, 23, 25, 27, 37
Subprime loans, 402, 403, 404, 420
Suez Canal, Egypt, 218
Summers, Lawrence "Larry," 352, 373, 383, 387, 389, 390, 413
Supreme Court, rulings of, 127, 149
Sutherland, Peter, 386
Swift and Company, 141
Syndicated loans, 247–248, 278, 293, 304, 311, 331
Syria, 221, 224

Taft, William Howard, 18, 19, 25–26, 28, 31, 33
Tarbell, Ida, 7
TARP (Troubled Asset Relief Program), 411, 414

Teapot Dome scandal, 74
Telecom Act of 1996, 375
Tennessee Coal and Iron Company, 12
Thain, John, 406, 409
Third world
    debt crisis, 332–333, 338–339, 349–350, 356
    exploitation of, 211–212, 226–227, 265, 276, 293, 327
Thomas, E. R., 8
Thrifts, 323, 334, 335–336, 341, 352, 355–356
    See also Savings and Loans (S&Ls)
Title II (of Banking Act of 1935), 142
Title III (of Banking Act of 1935), 142–143
Tonkin Resolution (1964), 257
Tourre, Fabrice, 418
Townsend, John, 142
Trade Expansion Act of 1962, 241, 256
Travelers, 381, 384
Trilateral Commission, 275
Troubled Asset Relief Program (TARP), 411, 414
Truman, Bess, 262
Truman, Harry S.
    background, 173–174
    defense contracts, financing of, 201–202
    Four Points Plan, 190
    Japan, invasion of, 176–177
    Korean War, funding for, 200
    Medicare card for, 262
    relationship with Aldrich, 174, 179, 181
    Truman Doctrine, 183
Trump, Donald, 360
Trust Company of America, 9–12
Trustbusting, 5–6
Truth in Securities Act of 1933, 132
Tumulty, Joseph Patrick, 38
Turner, Donald, 263

Union Pacific, 3
Union Steel Company, 74
Unitas, 171
United Corporation, 129

United Nations, 190
United States, post-World War II
    dominance of, 177
Untermyer, Samuel, 27–28, 31
US Arms Control and Disarmament
    Agency, 235
US Steel, 2, 12, 238
U.S.S.R. *See* Soviet Union

Valenti, Jack, 265
Van Sweringen brothers, 88, 89, 129
Vance, Cyrus, 272, 302, 304, 308,
    309–310, 315
Vanderlip, Frank, 10, 14–15, 23–25,
    29–32, 44, 53, 54, 61–62
Venezuela, 293, 354–355
Versailles, Treaty of (1919), 58, 62, 64,
    66, 68, 77
Victory Bond Drive, 166, 168, 169
Vietnam War, 255, 257–260, 265–268,
    270
Volcker, Paul, 328, 330, 333, 338, 343

Al-Waleed bin Talal, Prince, 292
Walker, George Herbert, 401, 402
Wall Street Reform and Consumer
    Protection Act of 2010 (Dodd-
    Frank Act), 415–416
Wall Street Seventeen, 190
War bonds, 159–160, 163, 166, 168, 169
Warburg, Paul Felix, 20, 23, 27, 39, 45,
    203
Warner, Douglas, 396
Warner, Rawleigh Jr., 295
Warren Commission, 255
Watergate, 289
Watson, Jack, 303
Weatherstone, Dennis, 342
Weill, Sanford "Sandy," 294, 352, 368,
    379, 381, 384, 389, 399
Weinberg, Sidney, 117–118, 202–203,
    204, 206, 220, 252, 258–259, 261,
    268
Weiner, Alan, 176
Wellstone, Paul, 390
Wertenbaker, Charles, 185
Wexler, Anne, 306

White, Harry Dexter, 165, 170–171, 175,
    189
White, Henry, 58
White House Economic Council, 382
Whitehead, John, 322, 329
Whitman, Ann, 220
Whitney, George, 89, 99, 144, 147, 187,
    206–207, 217
Whitney, John Hay, 258
Whitney, Richard, 99, 136–137, 140
Wiggin, Albert "Al," 82, 91–92, 97, 102,
    103, 109–114, 122, 123, 125, 130
Wiggin Committee, 111
William, John, 279
Williams, John H., 170
Willis, H. Parker, 31
Wilson, John, 163–164
Wilson, Woodrow
    Aldrich plan, view of, 28
    attempts to force peace negotiations,
        47
    election of 1912, 30–31
    election of 1916, 46
    election of 1920, 67
    failing health of, 65, 67
    Federal Reserve Act of 1913, signing,
        36–37
    Fourteen Points address, 52
    Germany, pre-war relationship with,
        45
    global popularity of, 54
    as governor of New Jersey, 27
    Jack Morgan, alliance with, 40–43, 48
    at Paris Peace Conference, 57–61
    on Payne-Aldrich Tariff Act, 30
    on role of government in shaping
        economy, 14
    support of by *Evening Post,* 54–55
    Vanderlip, relationship with, 14–15,
        29–32
    war financing *vs.* neutrality, 41–42
Wirth, Timothy, 363
Wolfe, Tom, 93
Woodin, William, 122, 129
Woodward, Bob, 337, 344
Working Group on Financial
    Institutions Reform, 334

Works Progress Administration, 132
World Bank, 165, 171, 187–188, 214, 218, 294, 326–327, 331–332, 349, 351, 362
World Trade Center, 9/11 attacks on, 397
World War Foreign Debt Commission, 77
World War I
    debt repayment, 75–77
    entry of US into the war, 48
    financing, war-related, 43–44, 47, 49
    Liberty bonds, 49
    outbreak of, 40–41
    postwar economic crises, 64, 66
    railroads, regulation of, 42–43, 52
    war reparations, 58–60, 63, 79–81, 109
World War II
    Axis powers, creation of, 154
    beginning of, 148, 152–153
    inflation during, 165–166, 169
    merchant ships, arming of, 164
    multinational finance entities, creation of, 170–172
    Munich Agreement, 153
    one-world reconstruction and development, plans for, 165
    Pearl Harbor, bombing of, 164
    US declaration of war on Japan, Germany, and Italy, 164–165
    Victory Bond Drive, 166, 168, 169
    war bonds, 159–160, 163, 166, 169
WorldCom, 399
Wriston, Henry, 194, 246

Wriston, Walter
    banking strategies, 293–294, 302–303
    deregulation, fight for, 246, 248, 277, 306
    Economic Policy Advisory Board, 325, 329
    expansion, proposals for, 280
    global influence of, 286–287
    Kennedy task force, 246–247
    Labor Management Committee, 295
    public office, offers of appointments to, 284, 294
    rate setting, allegations of, 285
    retirement from Citibank, 336
    Rockefeller, rivalry with, 276
    salary in 1968, 272
    start of career at National City Bank, 194, 302–303
    war surtax bill, support for, 268

Yalta Conference, 173
Yellen, Janet, 423
Yom Kippur War, 289–290
Young, Milton, 213, 216
Young, Owen, 109
Young, Roy, 110, 111
Young plan, 109

Zahedi, Ardeshir, 308
Zangara, Giuseppe, 118
Zedillo, Ernesto, 373–375
Zhou Enlai, 288
Zorin, Valerian, 235–236
Zweig, Phillip, 286

Matthew Dean Photography

NOMI PRINS is a journalist, speaker, respected TV and radio commentator, and former Wall Street executive. Author of five other books, including *Other People's Money* and *It Takes a Pillage*, her writing has also been featured in the *New York Times, Fortune, Mother Jones,* the *Guardian,* the *Nation,* and other publications. She is a senior fellow at Demos.

NATION BOOKS

The Nation Institute
Nation.

Founded in 2000, **Nation Books** has become a leading voice in American independent publishing. The inspiration for the imprint came from the *Nation* magazine, the oldest independent and continuously published weekly magazine of politics and culture in the United States.

The imprint's mission is to produce authoritative books that break new ground and shed light on current social and political issues. We publish established authors who are leaders in their area of expertise, and endeavor to cultivate a new generation of emerging and talented writers. With each of our books we aim to positively affect cultural and political discourse.

Nation Books is a project of The Nation Institute, a nonprofit media center established to extend the reach of democratic ideals and strengthen the independent press. The Nation Institute is home to a dynamic range of programs: our award-winning Investigative Fund, which supports ground-breaking investigative journalism; the widely read and syndicated website TomDispatch; our internship program in conjunction with the *Nation* magazine; and Journalism Fellowships that fund up to 20 high-profile reporters every year.

For more information on Nation Books, the *Nation* magazine, and The Nation Institute, please visit:

www.nationbooks.org
www.nationinstitute.org
www.thenation.com
www.facebook.com/nationbooks.ny
Twitter: @nationbooks

u/14